Corinth in Context

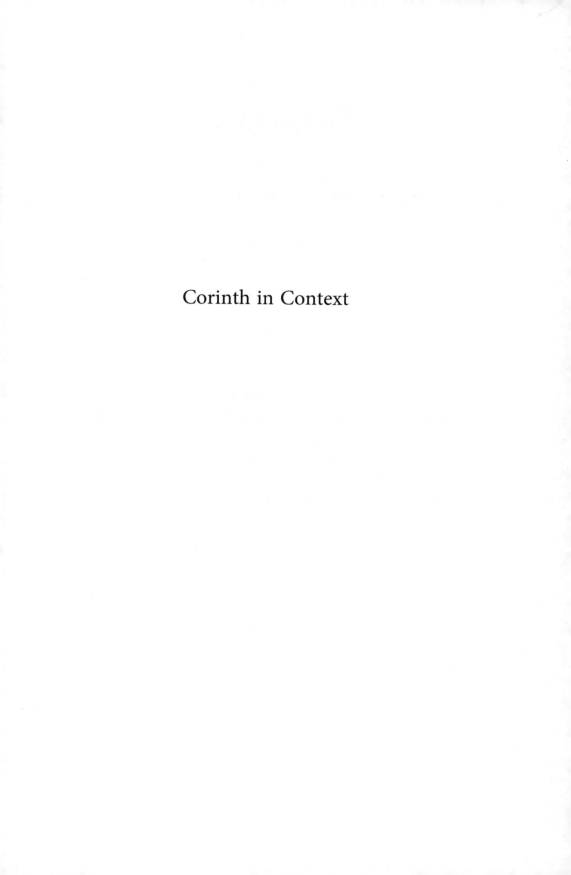

Supplements
to
Novum Testamentum

VOLUME 134

Corinth in Context

Comparative Studies on Religion and Society

Edited by

Steven J. Friesen, Daniel N. Schowalter, and James C. Walters

BRILL

LEIDEN • BOSTON
2010

This book is printed on acid-free paper.

Library of Congress Cataloging-in-Publication Data

Corinth in context : comparative studies on religion and society / edited by Steven Friesen, Dan Schowalter, and James Walters.
    p. cm. — (Supplements to Novum Testamentum, ISSN 0167-9732 ; v. 134)
    Includes bibliographical references and index.
    ISBN 978-90-04-18197-7 (hardback : alk. paper) 1. Corinth (Greece)—Religion—Congresses. 2. Religion and sociology—Greece—Corinth—History—Congresses. 3. Corinth (Greece)—Church history—Congresses. 4. Christian sociology—Greece—Corinth—History—Early church, ca. 30-600—Congresses. 5. Corinth (Greece)—Antiquities—Congresses. 6. Christian antiquities—Greece—Corinth—Congresses. I. Friesen, Steven J. II. Schowalter, Daniel N., 1957– III. Walters, James C. (James Christopher) IV. Title. V. Series.

BL793.C6C67 2010
200.938'7–dc22

                                                                          2009053423

ISSN 0167-9732
ISBN 978 90 04 18197 7

Copyright 2010 by Koninklijke Brill NV, Leiden, The Netherlands.
Koninklijke Brill NV incorporates the imprints Brill, Hotei Publishing, IDC Publishers, Martinus Nijhoff Publishers and VSP.

Mixed Sources
Productgroep uit goed beheerde bossen en andere gecontroleerde bronnen.
www.fsc.org Cert no. CU-COC-803902
FSC © 1996 Forest Stewardship Council

PRINTED BY DRUKKERIJ WILCO B.V. - AMERSFOORT, THE NETHERLANDS

CONTENTS

IMPERIALS: GREEK & ROMAN

SOCIAL STRATA

LOCAL RELIGION

LIST OF ILLUSTRATIONS

All images and plans of Corinth are reproduced courtesy of the Trustees of the American School of Classical Studies at Athens.

Chapter Three

Chapter Four

CHAPTER SIX

CHAPTER SEVEN

CHAPTER EIGHT

CHAPTER FOURTEEN

ACKNOWLEDGMENTS

The chapters in this volume are products of a conference held on the campus of the University of Texas at Austin, January 10–14, 2007. The conference was sponsored by three units on campus: the Institute for the Study of Antiquity and Christian Origins, the Department of Religious Studies,[1] and the Department of Classics. Funding for the conference was also provided by the Foundation for Biblical Studies and the Shive Foundation of Austin, Texas, without whose support this collaborative research could not have been undertaken.

The editors would also like to express their deep gratitude to Charles Williams, Nancy Bookidis, Guy Sanders, Ioulia Tzonou-Herbst, James Herbst, and L. Michael White for their advice and guidance. The conference and the volume are a direct result of their generous and collegial spirits. We also thank the Trustees of the American School of Classical Studies at Athens for permission to publish the images of Corinth contained in this volume.

The logistics of the conference posed problems that are best left to the imagination, and special thanks are due in this regard to Sarah James and Johanna Staples. The challenges of editing more than a dozen papers from several disciplinary perspectives and massaging them into a cohesive unit was only possible because of the work of Douglas Boin, without whose diligent care the editors would still be languishing over style questions, punctuation policy, and lacunose bibliographic entries.

Finally, we thank the Novum Testamentum Supplement Series for its support in the publication of this volume. The study of Christian origins has often been isolated from other developments in the study of the Roman Empire and Late Antiquity. The editors of that series, however, are committed to a fundamental axiom which also informs this volume; namely, that the early churches were a small but integral part of their socio-historical contexts in the ancient Mediterranean world. We trust that the quality and diversity of the contributions in this book will reward their faith in the project.

---

[1] At that time it was still the Program on Religious Studies and not yet a department.

LIST OF ABBREVIATIONS

ABSA	*Annual of the British School at Athens.*
AE	L'Année épigraphique; revue des publications épigraphiques relatives a l'antiquité romaine.
Agora	*The Athenian Agora: Results of Excavations Conducted by the American School of Classical Studies at Athens.*
	XXIV = A. Frantz, *The Athenian Agora: Late Antiquity, A.D. 267–700.* Princeton, 1988.
AHB	*Ancient History Bulletin.*
AJA	*American Journal of Archaeology.*
AJN	*American Journal of Numismatics.*
AJP	*American Journal of Philology.*
AncSoc	*Ancient Society.*
ANRW	*Aufstieg und Niedergang der Römischen Welt.*
AR	*Archaeological Reports.*
ArchCl	*Archeologia Classica.*
ArchDelt	*Archaiologikon Deltion.*
ArchEph	*Ephemeris Archaiologike. Athens.*
ArtB	*Art Bulletin.*
AW	*Antike Welt.*
BA	*Biblical Archaeologist.*
BCH	*Bulletin de correspondance hellénique.*
BJb	*Bonner Jahrbücher.*
BMC	B. V. Head, *Catalogue of the Greek Coins: Corinth, Colonies of Corinth (A Catalogue of the Greek Coins in the British Museum 12).* London, 1889.
BMCR	*Bryn Mawr Classical Review.*
BSA	*British School at Athens.*
BTB	*Biblical Theology Bulletin.*
ByzSt	*Byzantine Studies.*
CAH	*Cambridge Ancient History.*
CetM	*Classica et Mediaevalia.*
CIL	*Corpus Inscriptionum Latinarum.* Berlin. 1863–.
CJ	*The Classical Journal.*
Corinth	*Corinth: Results of Excavations Conducted by the American School of Classical Studies at Athens.*

I.1. = H. N. Fowler and R. Stillwell, *Introduction, Topography, Architecture*. Cambridge, 1932.

I.3 = R. Scranton, *Monuments in the Lower Agora and North of the Archaic Temple*. Princeton, 1951.

I.4 = O. Broneer, *The South Stoa and its Successors*. Princeton, 1954.

I.6 = B. H. Hill, *The Springs: Peirene, Sacred Spring, Glauke*. Princeton, 1964.

IV.1 = I. Thallon-Hill and L. S. King, *Decorated Architectural Terracottas*. Cambridge, 1929.

IV.2 = O. Broneer, *Terracotta Lamps*. Cambridge, 1930.

VI = K. M. Edwards, *Coins 1896–1929*. Cambridge, 1933.

VIII.1 = B. D. Meritt, *Greek Inscriptions, 1896–1927*. Cambridge, 1931.

VIII.2 = A. B. West, *Latin Inscriptions, 1896–1926*. Cambridge, 1931.

VIII.3 = J. H. Kent, *The Inscriptions, 1926–1950*. Princeton, 1966.

IX.1 = F. P. Johnson, *Sculpture, 1896–1923*. Cambridge, 1931.

IX.3 = M. C. Sturgeon, *Sculpture: The Assemblage from the Theater*. Princeton, 2004.

X = O. Broneer, *The Odeum*. Cambridge, 1932.

XII = G. Davidson, *The Minor Objects*. Princeton, 1952.

XIV = C. Roebuck and F. J. de Waele, *The Asklepieion and Lerna*. Princeton, 1951.

XVI = R. L. Scranton, *Mediaeval Architecture in the Central Area of Corinth*. Princeton, 1957.

XVIII.1 = E. Pemberton with K. Slane, *The Sanctuary of Demeter and Kore: Greek pottery*. Princeton, 1989.

XVIII.2. = K. W. Slane, *The Sanctuary of Demeter and Kore: The Roman Pottery and Lamps*. Princeton, 1990.

XVIII.3 = N. Bookidis and R. S. Stroud, *The Sanctuary of Demeter and Kore: Topography and Architecture*. Princeton, 1997.

XVIII.4 = G. S. Merker, *The Sanctuary of Demeter and Kore: Terracotta Figurines of the Classical, Hellenistic, and Roman Periods*. Princeton, 2000.

XX = C. K. Williams II and Nancy Bookidis (eds.), *Corinth: The Centenary, 1986–1996*. Princeton, 2003.

XXI = M. E. H. Walbank and G. Sanders. Forthcoming.

CP	*Classical Philology.*
CQ	*Classical Quarterly.*
CronErc	*Cronache ercolanesi.*
CTh	*The Theodosian Code and Novels and the Sirmondian Constitutions*, translated by Clyde Pharr. Princeton, 1952.
DOP	*Dumbarton Oaks Papers.*
EEBS	*Epeteris Etaireias Byzantinon Spoudon.*
EKAS	Eastern Korinthia Archaeological Survey.
FGrHist	F. Jacoby, *Fragmente der griechischen Historiker.* Berlin, 1923.
GazArch	*Gazette archéologique.*
GGA	*Göttingische gelehrte Anzeigen.*
GRBS	*Greek, Roman and Byzantine Studies.*
HSCP	*Harvard Studies in Classical Philology.*
HTR	*Harvard Theological Review.*
HTS	*Harvard Theological Studies.*
IG	*Inscriptiones Graecae.* Berlin, 1873–1927.
IJO	D. Noy, A. Panayotov and H. Bloedhorn, *Inscriptiones Judaicae Orientis: Eastern Europe.* Tübingen, 2004.
ILS	H. Dessau, *Inscriptiones Latinae Selectae.* Berlin, 1892–1916.
Isthmia	*Isthmia: Excavations by the University of Chicago under the Auspices of the American School of Classical Studies at Athens.* I = O. Broneer, *Temple of Poseidon.* Princeton, 1971. II = O. Broneer, *Topography and Architecture.* Princeton, 1973. III = O. Broneer, *Terracotta Lamps.* Princeton, 1977. IV = M. Sturgeon, *Sculpture I: 1952–1967.* Princeton, 1987. V = T. E. Gregory, *The Hexamilion and the Fortress.* Princeton, 1993. VI = S. Lattimore, *Sculpture II: Marble Sculpture, 1967–1980.* Princeton, 1996. VIII = C. Morgan, *The Late Bronze Age Settlement and Early Iron Age Sanctuary.* Princeton, 1999. IX = J. L. Rife, *The Roman and Byzantine Graves and Human Remains.* Princeton, forthcoming.
Isthmia Lamps	B. Lindros Wohl, *Lamps from the UCLA/Ohio State University Excavations, 1967–2002.* Forthcoming.

IstMitt   *Istanbuler Mitteilungen.*
JBL   *Journal of Biblical Literature.*
JDAI   *Jahrbuch des Deutschen Archäologischen Instituts.*
JEA   *Journal of Egyptian Archaeology.*
JFA   *Journal of Field Archaeology.*
JHS   *Journal of Hellenic Studies.*
JIAN   *Journal international d'archéologie numismatique.*
JMA   *Journal of Mediterranean Archaeology.*
JOAI   *Jahreshefte des Österreichischen Archäologischen Instituts.*
JR   *Journal of Religion.*
JRA   *Journal of Roman Archaeology.*
JRS   *Journal of Roman Studies.*
JSNT   *Journal for the Study of the New Testament.*
Kenchreai   *Kenchreai, Eastern Port of Corinth: Results of Investigations*
             by the University of Chicago and Indiana University.
             I = R. L. Scranton, J. W. Shaw, and L. Ibrahim, *Topography*
             and Architecture. Leiden, 1979.
             II = L. Ibrahim, R. Scranton, and R. Brill, *The Panels of*
             Opus Sectile in Glass. Leiden, 1976.
             III = R. L. Hohlfelder, *The Coins.* Leiden, 1978.
             IV = B. Adamsheck, *The Pottery.* Leiden, 1979.
             V = H. Williams, *The Lamps.* Leiden, 1981.
             VI = W. Stern, *The Wooden and Ivory Furniture.* Leiden,
             2007.
LGPN   3.A = P. Fraser and E. Matthews, *The Peloponnese (3.A):*
             Western Greece, Sicily, and Magna Graecia. Oxford, 1997.
LRBC   P. V. Hill, H. Kent, and R. Carson, *Late Roman Bronze*
             Coinage, A.D. 324–498. Two volumes. London, 1965.
MAAR   *Memoirs of the American Academy in Rome.*
MDAI(A)   *Mitteilungen des Deutschen Archäologischen Instituts,*
             Athenische Abteilung.
MDAI(R)   *Mitteilungen des Deutschen Archäologischen Instituts.*
             Römische Abteilung.
MEFRA   *Mélanges de l'École française de Rome: Antiquité.*
NC   *Numismatic Chronicle.*
NEEC   *Notitiae episcopatuum ecclesiae Constantinopolitanae,*
             edited by J. Darrouzès. Paris, 1981.
New Pauly   H. Cancik, H. Schneider, and C. Salazar, *Brill's New Pauly:*
             Encyclopaedia of the Ancient World: New Pauly. Leiden,
             2008.

NovT	*Novum Testamentum.*
NTS	*New Testament Studies.*
OChr	*Oriens Christianus.*
P&P	*Past and Present.*
PCPhS	*Proceedings of the Cambridge Philological Society.*
PMG	M. Davies, *Poetarum melicorum Graecorum fragmenta.* Oxford, 1991.
Prakt.	*Praktika tes en Athenais Archaiologikes Hetaireias.*
R&T	*Religion and Theology.*
RAC	*Rivista di archeologia cristiana.*
REA	*Revue des études anciennes.*
REG	*Revue des études grecques.*
RP	1 = A. D. Rizakis, S. Zoumbaki, and M. Kantirea, *Roman Peloponnese* I: *Roman Personal Names in their Social Context (Achaia, Arcadia, Argolis, Corinthia and Eleia).* Athens, 2001.
	2 = A. D. Rizakis, S. Zoumbaki, Cl. Lepenioti with G. Steinhauer and A. Makres, *Roman Peloponnese II: Roman Personal Names in their Social Context (Laconia and Messenia).* Athens, 2004.
RPC	I = A. Burnett, M. Amandry, and P. P. Ripollès, *Roman Provincial Coinage I: From the Death of Caesar to the Death of Vitellius (44 BC–AD 69).* London, 1992.
	II = A. Burnett, M Amandry, and I. Carradice, *Roman Provincial Coinage II: From Vespasian to Domitian.* London, 1999.
RPh	*Revue de philologie, de littérature et d'histoire anciennes.*
RSR	*Religious Studies Review.*
SEG	*Supplementum Epigraphicum Graecum.* Amsterdam. 1923–.
SIRIS	*Sarapiacae,* Berlin, 1969.
TAPA	*Transactions of the American Philological Association.*
ThesCRA	*Thesaurus cultus et rituum antiquorum,* five volumes, Los Angeles, 2004–06.
TMByz	*Travaux et mémoires. Centre de recherche d'histoire et de civilisation byzantines.*
TynBul	*Tyndale Bulletin.*
URRC	*Urban Religion in Roman Corinth: Interdisciplinary Approaches,* edited by D. N. Schowalter and S. J. Friesen. Cambridge, 2005.
VC	*Vigiliae christianae.*
ZPE	*Zeitschrift für Papyrologie und Epigrafik.*

LIST OF CONTRIBUTORS

STEVEN J. FRIESEN, Department of Religious Studies, University of Texas at Austin

TIMOTHY E. GREGORY, Department of History, Ohio State University; Director of The Ohio State University Excavations at Isthmia; Co-Director of the Eastern Korinthia Archaeological Survey

MARGARET L. LAIRD, Division of Art History, University of Washington, Seattle

BENJAMIN W. MILLIS, Blegen Library, American School of Classical Studies at Athens

JORUNN ØKLAND, Centre for Gender Research, University of Oslo

JOSEPH L. RIFE, Department of Classical Studies, Vanderbilt University; Co-Director, The Greek-American Excavations at Kenchreai

GUY D. R. SANDERS, Director of the Corinth Excavations, American School of Classical Studies at Athens

DANIEL N. SCHOWALTER, Departments of Religion and Classics, Carthage College

CHRISTINE M. THOMAS, Department of Religious Studies, University of California, Santa Barbara

MARY E. HOSKINS WALBANK, British School at Athens

MICHAEL B. WALBANK, University of Calgary

JAMES C. WALTERS, School of Theology, Boston University

BRONWEN L. WICKKISER, Department of Classical Studies, Vanderbilt University

CHAPTER ONE

INTRODUCTION: CONTEXT, COMPARISON

Steven J. Friesen

Context and comparison are fundamental for the studies in this volume. In one sense Corinth is the context for our work, for each chapter focuses on an aspect of life in that urban center. Every contributor has selected a Corinthian monument like the Sanctuary of Demeter and Kore or the Sacred Spring; a collection of artifacts like the colony's coinage or its early Byzantine epitaphs; a group of people like the early colonists or the churches there related to the apostle Paul; or affiliated communities like the port of Kenchreai or the Isthmian Sanctuary.

In another sense, the contextualization of these materials goes far beyond the Corinthia, for every chapter also makes comparisons with phenomena from other cities and regions in the Mediterranean basin. We cannot understand the Base of the *Augustales* of Corinth without surveying *Augustales* elsewhere; we cannot chart the changing significance of Corinth's Asklepios precincts without examining other healing sanctuaries; we cannot describe Corinth's municipal *oikonomos* without reference to *oikonomoi* of other cities; nor can we estimate the influence of Roman imperialism without knowledge of its effects in other cities and regions. The importance of comparison is driven home by a crucial document like Corinth's colonial charter, for the charter is lost and we would have no knowledge of the colony's constitution without parallels from the fragmentary remains of other colonial charters.

So our knowledge of the ancient world is necessarily contextual and comparative, charting relationships near and far. In this volume our method reflects this situation: each article combines an intensive analysis of minute details from particular Corinthian artifacts with a wide-ranging search for appropriate comparisons. The goal of this approach is to elucidate what Corinth had in common with its contemporaries and to identify distinctive features that set Corinth apart. The temporal limits of the investigations run from the Classical to the early Byzantine periods, but there is a special concentration on the Roman imperial era when the Greek city was reestablished as a Roman colony.

Our approach is also interdisciplinary. The fragmentary resources for contextualization and comparison are varied, which means they require many specializations. Thus, the contributors use their training in the study of inscriptions, architecture, sculpture, coins, burial customs, pottery, stone, soil, texts, society, and religion in order to develop a picture of Corinth that is as comprehensive as possible in light of the data at our disposal.

This interdisciplinary, comparative, contextual approach results in contributions that cover a range of materials and topics. Throughout the discussions, however, three interlocking themes emerge: the negotiation of Greek and Roman heritage in an imperial setting; the need to locate our subjects within their socially stratified settings; and the articulation of local religious identities.

IMPERIALS: GREEK AND ROMAN

A number of studies in this volume deal with the ways in which Corinthians contextualized themselves in relation to the multiple sources of their heritage. The chapters in this section of the volume focus particularly on the negotiation of Greek and Roman traditions in Corinth during the Roman imperial period.

There is a good deal of controversy about the population of Corinth after it was established as a Roman colony. Was the early colony composed primarily of Roman freedpersons, Greek freedpersons, impoverished Italians, and/or army veterans? By way of response, Benjamin Millis draws on a wealth of new resources. After a reconsideration of the handful of known literary sources, Millis introduces more precision into the analysis of the relevant inscriptions, showing where Latin and Greek usages would have been appropriate in a colony. He then expands the discussion to include masons' marks and graffiti, thereby giving us access to other strata of Corinthian society that have been neglected in the secondary literature. He concludes that veterans were not a significant presence in the colony because it was founded for its strategic commercial position in a relatively stable area. Rather, the early colony was dominated by freedmen from the Greek east who displayed a clear commitment to Roman culture as well as a significant attachment to their Hellenistic heritage. The full range of literary and material evidence, then, suggests an elite class of early Corinthian colonists whose layered identities were expressed in different ways in different social contexts, sometimes more Greek and sometimes more Roman.

Bronwen Wickkiser provides an overview of the cult of Asklepios in Corinth during the Greek and Roman periods, showing the way in which the appeal of religious institutions may change dramatically over the course of time in a particular location. Through comparison with other Asklepieia, she is able to suggest a reason for its early appeal during the Greek period. Moreover, the temple and its related institutions were reestablished in the Roman period, and Wickkiser shows how these new meanings generated Corinthian connections to Augustus and to Rome. But this new significance of the Asklepieion for politically active Corinthians did not replace its broad popularity with the general population. As patron and healer, Asklepios functioned as a savior for a wide spectrum of people. Although his sanctuary was on the edge of the city, it was in many ways central to the life of the Greek city and the Roman colony.

In the middle of the Corinthian Forum stand the oddly-shaped remains of a statue base erected by the Augustales. Margaret Laird reexamines this monument and, in the process, recasts our understanding of this crucial space at the center of the Roman colony. Laird dates the monument in the early to middle 1st century CE. She then goes on to provide a new reconstruction of the base's inscription, a new analysis of its design, a hypothesis that it held a statue of *divus* Augustus, and observations about the monument's role in the everyday life of the colony. Through design, materials, and placement, Laird argues that the Base of the *Augustales* situated its viewers in relation to the colony's Greek past and to its Roman imperial present. It claimed a deep connection to Corinth's heritage even as it focused attention on the Roman temples, altars, and basilicas of the Forum.

The invocation of Greek traditions within a Roman imperial framework was not uniquely Corinthian, however, for local elite groups engaged in this process throughout the cities of the Empire. The final chapter in this section by Christine Thomas provides comparative material for the phenomenon from the city of Ephesos. She argues that similar dynamics are evident in the two urban centers: local religious traditions took on new forms and meanings in the era of Roman imperial rule. In both locations we see the emergence of hybrid elite identities, with an emphasis on Roman citizenship and a taste for monumental public display. In Corinth, this is expressed by a tendency to revive old institutions like the Sanctuary of Demeter or the Asklepieion in their traditional locations but with new rituals and architecture. The reorganized space and the reformed rituals allowed the newer Corinthian elites to legitimize their dominance in the colony using the symbolic resources of local religion. In Ephesos, on the other hand, more of the local ruling elites came from established families as the city adjusted to life under Roman imperial control. Having less need to establish their continuity with the past, the Ephesians could relocate traditional religious institutions such as the association of the Kouretes to new areas of the Roman city. These local variations on hybridity, however, were more than efforts to appease the Roman rulers. The relocations, the monumentality, and the reformulations of local traditions can be read as an index of contested authority in which local interests competed with one other as they articulated their own sense of autonomy and their own ambivalence toward Roman rule.

Social Strata

A second theme woven into the volume is the importance of contextualizing our analyses of religion and society in terms of the stratification of society. The chapters in this section emphasize the need to distinguish at least three categories of people in our research: the elite fraction which dominates the evidence left to us from antiquity; the majority of the population whose lives remain mostly invisible to us; and the 'middling' groups who appear sporadically in the known texts and artifacts. Yet even these three categories are not homogenous, and so our reconstructions must account for a range of overlapping factors, including at least economy, political office, gender, legal status, enslavement, and occupation.

Mary Walbank provides an overview of the Roman colony's numismatic history and applies this information to our understanding of stratification in Corinthian religion. The coins of Roman Corinth have played an important role in the analysis of the archaeological remains, but there are remarkably few synthetic treatments of the coinage from this urban center. Walbank addresses the history of the colony's minting practices, some principles for interpreting them, and several important numismatic series and images. Her thesis is that the coins, understood within their historical contexts and within the conventions of die-making, supply a wealth of information about the public cults of Roman Corinth. This evidence does not reveal much about private religion in the colony, but it illuminates local expressions of public piety in the context of Corinth's civic religious identity. This public piety was a carefully calibrated phenomenon, guided by members of the colonial elite but informed by their relationships with the rest of the populace.

In her chapter on the Sanctuary of Demeter and Kore, Jorunn Økland takes this insight further, arguing that scholars have settled too often for an analysis that posits a unified population and then charts the changes of this supposed homogenous group through a Greek period and a Roman period. This 'continuity and change' approach results in a religious profile for the city that ignores the social stratification and difference that characterize any urban context. In order to develop an approach with more nuanced results, Økland works with the concept of 'divine personality definitions.' This methodology—which privileges local evidence above regional or imperial patterns—allows her both to discuss changing names and characterizations of the goddesses in Corinth and to connect these shifting definitions to the needs and perceptions of people according to gender, cultural heritage, economic status, and language abilities. By placing the institutions related to Demeter and Kore into the context of social stratification, Økland provides a reconstruction that accounts for the layered complexity of the urban center.

My chapter also argues that we need more attention to social stratification in contemporary research by reevaluating Paul's reference to a Corinthian named Erastus in Romans 16:23. Since the discovery in 1929 of a Corinthian inscription that mentions an elite official named Erastus, an academic tradition has developed that equates Paul's Erastus with this official and describes him as a newly-wealthy freedman. This tradition has contributed to a reconstruction of Paul's churches as havens for upwardly mobile imperial subjects whose social status was still lower than their financial status. I argue instead that specialists in early Christian literature have been overly eager to find signs of wealth in the early churches and that archaeologists have misinterpreted the inscription because of the alleged New Testament parallel. Careful attention to the material remains indicates that the inscription could not have referred to the Erastus mentioned by Paul, for the two Erasti were different men living decades apart from each other and inhabiting different levels of the socio-economic hierarchy. Moreover, careful attention to Romans 16 suggests that the Erastus mentioned by

Paul was not even a participant in the churches. Paul's Erastus was, rather, an example of a category of people Paul rarely names in his letters—individuals who knew Paul and had ongoing contact with him, but who rejected his message.

The section concludes with a chapter and substantial appendix by Michael Walbank. Working with published and unpublished materials from excavations and accidental finds, Walbank populates our picture of Corinth for the late 4th to early 7th centuries CE by reexamining the late Roman and early Byzantine grave inscriptions found on 662 stone fragments. This process allows him to identify 390 names, 107 occupations or offices, and even some nicknames. These tomb inscriptions served many purposes, providing identification of individuals, honor for the deceased and their families, and legal claim to the burial plots. Thus, Walbank's assembled data give us a good deal of information about one subgroup from Christian Corinth. The people commemorated on these stones represent a segment of the population that was relatively prosperous. They seem to have raised themselves up above the status of their parents, and there is little evidence that they were able to pass their enhanced economic standing on to their children. For at least their lifetimes, however, they were able to advance to the middling social strata between the elite fraction of society and the majority of Corinthians who could not afford marked gravesites.

LOCAL RELIGION

A third theme that permeates this volume is the locality of religion. In the midst of conflicting imperial, regional, and social forces, religious institutions flourish and wither in particular places. They articulate and promote verities for specific audiences, and so the volume concludes with chapters that focus on the situated character of religious groups and institutions. The first two chapters in this final section focus on the private religion of a small subgroup of Corinthians known to us now as 'Christians.' The remaining chapters examine the relationships of local public religion to regional trends.

The chapter by Daniel Schowalter deals with the question of where the Pauline churches in Corinth would have held their meetings. There are at least two major challenges in this topic. One challenge is that it touches on the thorny issue of integrating archaeological and textual materials into a single coherent interpretation. This challenge is made more difficult because the subject of the research—Pauline congregations—operated below the well-documented level of elite society. The second challenge is a problem specific to the discipline of New Testament studies: because we have more information about 1st century Corinthian house-churches (from 1 and 2 Corinthians) than about churches in other cities, many New Testament scholars have attempted to connect the textual information with specific archaeological remains from Roman Corinth. The results have been mixed. Schowalter cites some careless examples where superficial knowledge of the material remains has led scholars to completely unwarranted conclusions about the Pauline assemblies. He argues instead for a guarded approach, one that does not try to connect texts to specific monuments but works rather with the typical patterns for Roman cities that are attested in the urban areas under examination. Moreover, in the case of texts like the letters of Paul, which were written to religious groups who used everyday domestic spaces for their gatherings, he suggests that we need to pay special attention to the way physical spaces are transformed through ritual. Such rituals manipulate space through words and actions, giving new meanings to their surroundings even in the midst of everyday life.

James Walters extends this analysis by looking at the way in which a specific church ritual like the common meal provided an opportunity for the negotiation of authority. Walters focuses on the instructions to Christ-believers in Corinth from their Jewish apostle regarding how they should observe their community meal (1 Cor 11:17–31) in order to explore the ways in which hosting a meal can enhance a host's aspirations to leadership. He compares Paul's instructions to colonial laws about electioneering banquets, to Cicero's rhetoric about the differences between gifts and bribery, and to other literature on the proper and improper ways to gain positions of political leadership across a variety of social strata. Walters concludes that Paul's meal instructions can and should be understood in the context of such urban political competition. Paul was trying to establish the community's meal as the 'Lord's Supper' rather than as a household banquet. It was to be a meal with its own protocol that did not follow the normal codes of gift and obligation. As such, the ritual was to be understood as hosted by Jesus, and was to be an expression of unity—albeit unity on Paul's terms—rather than an opportunity for his competitors to gain authority at the apostle's expense.

The next chapter turns from local private groups to local public institutions with an examination of the enigmatic evidence for the Sacred Spring at Corinth. Guy Sanders works through the fragmentary architectural and epigraphic remains, and places them within their specific topographic and urban settings. Broader comparisons with other shrines and with related mythologies leads to the heightened awareness of the Sacred Spring's Peloponnesian connections that appear to have been overlaid by Attic interpretation. Several lines of evidence suggest that Artemis was probably the main deity of the shrine before its destruction, and that secondary figures may have included other characters associated with the Peloponnesos, such as Helen, her family, and her relatives through marriage. The resulting portrait is that of a local sacred site with regional associations that, in its early phases, connected with traditions to the south rather than those to the east.

Moving away from Corinth's city center, Joseph Rife's chapter provides the first systematic overview of religion and society in Corinth's eastern port of Kenchreai, where ongoing research is producing both interpretations of newly found artifacts for analysis and reevaluations of older material remains. Rife surveys cultic activity for Aphrodite, Isis, Poseidon, Asklepios, Dionysos, and Pan documented in literary, epigraphic, and archaeological sources. He then provides a preliminary description of lead tablets found in a funerary setting, and concludes with a description of the evidence for early Christianity. The emerging portrait gives us a greater awareness of Kenchreai as a typical small port in the Roman imperial period, a community with a full complement of public and private religious institutions expressed in a local idiom. But we also begin to see the importance of Kenchreai as one crucial feature in the Corinthian landscape, where society and religion developed in conversation with—and in distinction from—the other inhabitants of greater Corinth.

Timothy Gregory's chapter concludes the section and the book with a diachronic analysis of one locality over several centuries. His study takes us deeper into a consideration of 'other Corinthians' with a survey of Isthmia and the eastern Corinthia. He begins the discussion with a consideration of the pottery finds from Isthmia's rural environs during the early Roman period. The results, although preliminary, are nevertheless surprising. Contrary to Alcock's general findings for Achaia,[1] the early Roman period appears to have been not a time of

---

[1] Alcock 1993.

economic stagnation in the eastern Corinthia but rather a time of increased economic activity, surpassing even the Classical period. For the Middle and Late Roman periods the evidence is more ambiguous. The Temple of Poseidon at Isthmia ceased functioning rather early—in the mid 3rd century—but the presence of lamps indicates that there was activity of some sort at the temenos at least through the 4th century, and a range of data suggests ongoing use of nearby complexes through the 6th century. The absence of known churches in the area during the 5th and 6th centuries is perhaps due to the accident of discovery. By the 7th and 8th centuries, however, there is clear evidence for a small Christian settlement living at a basic level at Isthmia, and mixed conditions in the surrounding areas. In the countryside there is evidence for indigenous and immigrant communities, most of whom were engaged in subsistence agriculture while others lived in large villas and supported large churches.

The chapters that follow this introduction are, of course, much richer in content and in methodology than this brief summary can convey. The contributions result in part from the fact that the work in this volume builds on broader interdisciplinary research that has now spanned decades, involved dozens of scholars from several countries, and led to many other publications.[2] Nancy Bookidis has played an influential role in these ongoing conversations, both as advisor and collaborator. Her encouragement during the development of this conference and volume in particular made a crucial contribution to our work. In recognition of her intellectual leadership and personal engagement, we are pleased to dedicate this volume to her.

---

[2] For example, Koester 1995, Koester 1998, Schowalter and Friesen 2005, and Nasrallah *et al.* 2010.

IMPERIALS: GREEK & ROMAN

CHAPTER TWO

THE SOCIAL AND ETHNIC ORIGINS OF THE COLONISTS IN EARLY ROMAN CORINTH

Benjamin W. Millis*

INTERPRETATIONS OF THE EARLY COLONISTS

After the Roman consul L. Mummius sacked Corinth in 146 BCE, the Romans founded a colony at the same location almost a century later (ca. 44 BCE).[1] The population which inhabited the colony in the first century or two of its existence has seldom been studied in its own right; far more often, scholars have treated the population as an appendage to studies of other aspects of Corinth. What follows is an attempt instead to focus on the population itself by bringing to bear a variety of evidence, both literary and epigraphic, much of which has previously been neglected, and to examine what conclusions concerning the population can reveal about the culture and society of early Roman Corinth.

Understanding of the colony's population has varied over time, often depending upon what scholars have wished to find. Early excavators, for example, saw a clear division between the Greek and Roman phases of the city, thus simplifying the potentially overwhelming task of classifying and dating all of the site's architecture and material remains. This distinction rendered the use of the terms 'Greek' and 'Roman' unproblematic in relation to the excavated finds and historical periods.[2] While occasional comments make clear that the early excavators

---

* In addition to those present in Austin, I am grateful to the following, who also offered comments or other help which improved my paper: N. Bookidis, L. Moschou, S. Strack, R. Stroud. Many thanks to all of the above.

[1] The precise date of the colony's foundation is a matter of minor dispute. For a review of the evidence and opinions: Amandry 1988, 13.

[2] In this context, note that the relatively recent proliferation of studies on identity and, in particular, the study of Greek identity in Greece under Roman rule, has largely bypassed Corinth despite its wealth of evidence and its position as a focus of Greek-Roman interaction; Swain 1996, Goldhill 2001, and Ostenfeld 2002, although a notable exception is König 2001.

conceived of the original colonists as thoroughly Roman,[3] in practice the two terms were used primarily as chronological indicators, and little thought was given to the people who actually inhabited the city. Perhaps tellingly, a distinction between the populations of pre-Roman and Roman Corinth tended to be most emphasized in apologies for and explanations of the scantiness of pre-Roman remains; in other words, little attention was given to the people who actually inhabited Corinth, except on those occasions when positing a change in population served as a convenient means for understanding the archaeological record.

As the phases of the ancient city became better understood, however, the study of its population continued to lag behind that of its material remains. The few ancient references that provided evidence for the makeup of the city's population in the Roman period, for example, were duly noted but never exploited to their full extent; and as the study of Corinth broadened both spatially and temporally, the founding of the Roman colony became one more phase in the lengthy history of the city. Viewing this history as a succession of phases led to a strong sense of continuity over time, an interpretative point which was eventually applied without serious investigation to the character of its population as well. Corinth, after all, was located in Greece and, therefore, ought to have been inhabited by Greeks.[4] This view appears most clearly in references to Corinth's 'refounding,' which contains the implication that the Roman colony was simply another phase of the earlier Greek city.

In fairness, this elision of two quite distinct cities is not solely a feature of modern scholarship, since the Roman colonists themselves seem to have encouraged it as well. Their colony was not founded on a blank slate but on the site of a venerable city, and it incorporated, at least at first, both old and new side by side. Some ancient buildings

---

[3] Fowler (*Corinth* I.1, 16) contrasts the freedmen from Italy, who in his opinion formed the bulk of the colonists, with Greeks who soon immigrated to Roman Corinth. While Fowler presumably believed that the freedmen were ethnically Greek, his contrast leaves little doubt that he also believed them to have been thoroughly Romanized, perhaps over generations.

[4] A strong early statement of this trend appears in *Corinth* VI: "Probably many of these [freedmen colonists] were Greeks. With the remnant of the old inhabitants who remained in the ruined city or returned to it after its destruction by Mummius and with other Greeks who were enfranchised by Roman emperors or their representatives and given citizenship in Corinth, they helped to maintain the old Greek spirit under Roman rule" (6).

remained standing. Others were remodeled or renovated. All became an integral part of the fabric of the Roman city.[5] Without question the Forum itself was laid out in reference to pre-existing buildings of the Greek city.[6] A number of old cults, too, primarily those of the Olympian deities, were revived, if, that is, they had ever completely fallen into abeyance.[7] The colonists, as well, adopted symbols and images closely connected with the Greek city as their own.[8] The Isthmian Games returned to Corinthian control and from the start were administered in Greek, as befitted one of the preeminent festivals of Greece.[9]

In short, the early colonists of Roman Corinth, whatever their origins, were at pains to emphasize and promote their status not as interlopers but as legitimate successors and inheritors of the Greek city. Despite the occasional hiccup, such as Pausanias's careful and perhaps not

---

[5] The question of what exactly remained standing during the interim has never been systematically studied. Views concerning the extent of the destruction of the city, often formerly assumed to have been catastrophic and to have entailed the annihilation of the population, have been revised and softened, especially over the course of the last 30 years. For discussion and bibliography of the level and extent of inhabitation during the interim: Wiseman 1979, 491–96; Gebhard and Dickie 2003; Millis 2006. I will discuss elsewhere the Corinthians attested after the sack of the city.

[6] This holds true in spite of how one interprets the function of the forum area in the pre-Roman period. For the first 70 years of excavation, for example, scholars assumed without question that the Agora of the pre-Roman period lay beneath the Roman Forum. This assumption was sharply contested by Williams (1970, 32–39; and 1978a, 18–19 and 38–39). Although Williams's views have not won universal acceptance, they have yet to be challenged cogently in print. For the use of pre-Roman buildings in laying out the Forum, see *Corinth* I.3, 150; Robinson 1965b, 23–24; Williams and Russell 1981, 1–2; Walbank 1997a, 117–24; Romano 2005a, 32–36.

[7] For cultic continuity between the Hellenistic and Roman periods or lack thereof: Williams 1987a; Bookidis 2003, 257; Bookidis 2005.

[8] Most famous are perhaps the images of Bellerophon and Pegasus, which proliferate throughout the coinage of Roman Corinth. Imhoof-Blumer and Gardner (1885, 59), while somewhat over-enthusiastic in expression, are not far off the mark in their conviction that the Roman colonists readily adopted and adapted symbols of the pre-Roman city.

[9] Kajava (2002) discusses when the games returned to the Isthmus and to Corinthian control. For the 'Greekness' of the Isthmian games, see Geagan 1968, 71 n. 10: "Even at the time when Corinthian civic documents were written in Latin, Greek remained the official language at Isthmia." See also *Corinth* VIII.3, 19 n. 6. Biers and Geagan (1970, 90, n. 31) provide a convenient list of the known victors' lists, all of which are inscribed in Greek. For the join of *Corinth* VIII.1, no. 15 and 18, made subsequent to Biers and Geagan, see Spawforth 1974, 297–99. In contrast, inscriptions honoring an individual *agonthetes* tend to be written in Latin since they are public honorific monuments concerned with the individual person, not the games. For an important document (I.1970.39), which remains unpublished but contains much new information: Wiseman 1972, 20.

wholly laudatory distinction between the old and new populations,[10] they had been largely successful in achieving their goal of acceptance by the 2nd century CE, when, for example, the city was received into the Panhellenion[11] and claims could be made without irony about the inhabitants of the ancient city as their ancestors.[12] A mark of their success, and the success of the historical model of continuity in influencing modern as well as ancient perception, is Bowersock's influential characterization of these colonists as "Greeks returning home."[13]

During the final quarter of the 20th century, however, new trends in scholarship arose which emphasized a study of Roman Corinth in its own right, distinct from the Greek city. Studying Roman Corinth as such has greatly deepened and enriched our understanding of the city, its form, its social, civic and religious structures, and its status in the Greek world. This view has fit well with increasing interest in Roman Greece and with Roman involvement in the eastern Mediterranean. Further advances have been made by comparing Corinth not with other cities in Roman Greece but with other Roman colonies throughout the larger Mediterranean region. A necessary corollary of understanding Corinth in this way—as a purely Roman foundation with purely Roman culture and institutions—is that its population must also be purely Roman. This view, too, although often left unexpressed, is not without supporting evidence.[14]

---

[10] Paus. 2.1.2 and 5.25.1. At the same time, however, the author clearly regards the inhabitants of Roman Corinth as legitimate Peloponnesians (5.1.2). For a recent account of Pausanias at Corinth and his attitude toward the Roman city: Hutton 2005b, 147–49 and 166–73.

[11] Oliver 1978, 191.

[12] See Favorinus (= Dio Chr. 37.1–8) for a conflation of the populations. The same population that received Favorinus is referred to as having received other distinguished guests in the remote past. Favorinus subsequently (37.25) acknowledges the Roman origins of the current population but stresses the extent to which it has been Hellenized; White 2005; König 2001.

[13] Bowersock 1965, 67–71. Spawforth (1996, 175) offers a rare attempt to modify Bowersock's assertion. Kent's claim (Corinth VIII.3, 18), published a year after the appearance of Bowersock's book, that Latin was the language of the early colony, in part, "because the earliest settlers seem to have been for the most part of Italian stock," reflects older scholarship. At the same time, however, his statement underscores that the historiography on the topic of Corinth's population is not as linear as the sketch here implies. There has been no real consensus on the issue.

[14] It is difficult to overestimate the cumulative effect that 30 years of excavation reports and other work by C. K. Williams have had on shaping our understanding of Roman Corinth. Perhaps the single most influential statement, however, is Kent's brief sketch (Corinth VIII.3, 18–19), contrasting the use of Greek and Latin in inscriptions of the Roman period at Corinth. Given the enormous impact that these and other

Thus, it is clear that modern characterizations about Corinth's population have often depended more upon a scholar's personal opinions than upon any rigorous population study of the city *per se*. Interpretations of architecture, religion, and language, for example, have all been sources for scholars' arguments about the nature of the colony and its putative population. What follows here, however, is an attempt to reverse this process—first, by investigating what evidence, both literary and epigraphic, exists for the makeup of the population; and then, by discussing how these conclusions play out in terms of other evidence for the culture and society of Roman Corinth.

Veterans

Examination of the relatively scant literary testimony, although somewhat contradictory regarding the exact nature of the early colonists, shows a complete agreement that the founders were 'Roman.' There is no literary evidence at all for non-Roman colonists.[15] Some of this testimony is unspecific and unhelpful—recording, for instance, that "Corinth [was] no longer inhabited by any of the old Corinthians, but by colonists sent out by the Romans;"[16] or that "Corinth was destroyed and rebuilt again by the Romans."[17] What exactly 'Roman' means in

---

studies have had on our understanding of Corinth as a *Roman* city, Torelli's comments (2001, 162) seem wide of the mark; see also *SEG* 51.343. For recent affirmations of Corinth's essential Romanness, see the publications of Mary Walbank: "[I]n layout, organization and religious practice, Corinth was a Roman colony and not simply a restoration of the Greek city" (1989a, 394); "Today most scholars accept that Corinth was a traditional Roman colony" (1997a, 95); and, "[I]n Roman eyes *Colonia Laus Iulia Corinthiensis* was an entirely new foundation.... [T]he Romans were founding a new city, not rehabilitating an old one" (1997a, 107). See also Alcock 1993, 166–69 (this is the passage meant by the erroneous reference at Spawforth [1996, 167, n. 2]).

[15] The unanimity of the evidence regarding the Roman origin of the colonists does not imply anything about their ethnicity or self-identification, merely that they were Roman citizens—something expected in a Roman colony. A growing amount of archaeological evidence (n. 5, above), together with an oft-quoted passage from Cicero (*Tusc.* 3.53), strongly suggests there were some inhabitants in Corinth prior to the formation of the colony. The newly founded city presumably afforded great opportunity for work in a variety of trades, and so an influx of workers and tradesmen might be expected to have followed directly on its foundation, as well. Whatever the extent to which these people might have been absorbed into the population, ancient sources refer only to those who were Roman citizens.

[16] Paus. 2.1.2 (translated by Jones).

[17] Strab. 8.4.8 (translated by Jones).

these contexts is, perhaps, not as straightforward as appears, but this question is best dealt with after a presentation of the evidence.

The entirety of the specific evidence consists of the following four passages.[18]

1. πολὺν δὲ χρόνον ἐρήμη μείνασα ἡ Κόρινθος, ἀνελήφθη πάλιν ὑπὸ Καίσαρος τοῦ θεοῦ διὰ τὴν εὐφυΐαν, ἐποίκους πέμψαντος τοῦ ἀπελευθερικοῦ γένους πλείστους (Strabo 8.6.23).

Now after Corinth had remained deserted for a long time, it was restored again because of its favorable position by the deified Caesar, who colonized it with people that belonged, for the most part, to the freedmen class (translated by Jones).

2. ἠρημωμένης δ᾽ οὖν ἐπὶ πολὺν χρόνον τῆς Καρχηδόνος, καὶ σχεδόν τι τὸν αὐτὸν χρόνον, ὅνπερ καὶ Κόρινθος, ἀνελήφθη πάλιν περὶ τοὺς αὐτούς πως χρόνους ὑπὸ Καίσαρος τοῦ θεοῦ, πέμψαντος ἐποίκους Ῥωμαίων τοὺς προαιρουμένους καὶ τῶν στρατιωτῶν τινας (Strabo 17.3.15).

Carthage for a long time remained desolate, about the same length of time as Corinth; but it was restored again at about the same time as Corinth by the deified Caesar, who sent thither as colonists such Romans as preferred to go there and some soldiers (translated by Jones).

3. καὶ μετ᾽οὐ πολὺ τῶν ἀπόρων αὐτὸν ἐς Ῥώμην ἐπανελθόντα περὶ γῆς παρακαλούντων, συνέτασσεν ὡς πέμψων τοὺς μὲν ἐς τὴν Καρχηδόνα τοὺς δ᾽ ἐς Κόρινθον. ἀλλ᾽ ὅδε μὲν θᾶσσον ἀνηρέθη πρὸς τῶν ἐχθρῶν ἐν τῷ Ῥωμαίων βουλευτηρίῳ, ὁ δ᾽ ἐκείνου παῖς Ἰούλιος Καῖσαρ, ὁ Σεβαστὸς ἐπίκλησιν, ἐντυχὼν ἄρα ταῖς ὑπογραφαῖς τοῦ πατρὸς συνῴκισε τὴν νῦν Καρχηδόνα....οἰκήτοράς τε Ῥωμαίους μὲν αὐτὸν τρισχιλίους μάλιστα πυνθάνομαι, τοὺς δὲ λοιποὺς ἐκ τῶν περιοίκων συναγαγεῖν (Appian Pun. 136).

Returning to Rome not long after, and the poor asking him for land, [Julius Caesar] arranged to send some of them to Carthage and some to Corinth. But he was assassinated shortly afterward by his enemies in the Roman Senate; and his son Julius Caesar, surnamed Augustus, finding this memorandum, built the present Carthage....I have ascertained that he sent some 3000 colonists from Rome and collected the rest from the neighboring country (translated by White).

4. τὴν δ᾽ εὔνοιαν ὡς κάλλιστον ἅμα καὶ βεβαιότατον ἑαυτῷ περιβαλλόμενος φυλακτήριον ἀναλάμβανε τὸν δῆμον ἑστιάσεσι καὶ σιτηρεσίοις, τὸ δὲ στρατιωτικὸν ἀποικίαις, ὧν ἐπιφανέσταται Καρχηδὼν καὶ Κόρινθος ἦσαν, αἷς καὶ πρότερον τὴν ἅλωσιν καὶ τότε

---

[18] I have excluded from this discussion sources that lack any specific information. The epigram of Crinagoras (AP 9.284) is a special case and will be briefly discussed in n. 31 below.

τὴν ἀνάληψιν ἅμα καὶ κατὰ τὸν αὐτὸν χρόνον ἀμφοτέραις γενέσθαι συνέτυχε (Plut. *Caes.* 57.8).

And in the effort to surround himself with men's good will as the fairest and at the same time the securest protection, [Caesar] again courted the people with banquets and distributions of grain, and his soldiers with newly planted colonies, the most conspicuous of which were Carthage and Corinth. The earlier capture of both these cities, as well as their present restoration, chanced to fall at one and the same time (translated by Perrin).

Noteworthy first of all is that two of these passages—the second (Strabo) and the third (Appian)—say nothing at all, strictly speaking, about Corinth although both have been cited in the past as evidence for the character of the early colonists. Even if they are included, however, they add little to the other sources except for the assertion that the colonists included Rome's poor. Although the claim that Caesar transported Rome's poor to Corinth may seem dubious on its face, it has been taken seriously by some modern scholars. This latter segment of the population is notoriously difficult to document and is largely invisible in the evidence that survives, although what evidence there is for the non-elite in early Roman Corinth will be noted below.

Second, in these passages as in others that do not specifically discuss the nature of the colonists, Corinth and Carthage are closely linked and are portrayed as very similar operations with apparently similar objectives.[19] Precisely because Corinth and Carthage are superficially similar, not least because of the contemporaneous dates of the two cities' destructions and the colonies' foundations, we must be cautious in accepting these statements at face value. The ancient historians themselves were concerned to note, first, that it was Caesar who simultaneously 'refounded' the two venerable cities which had been destroyed by the Romans; and second, that he was a responsive leader who took care to secure the goodwill of those who formed the basis of his power. Discussion of any differences between these colonies or the complex processes of forming a colony itself would have weakened the authors' rhetorical points, and so we find these two different events collapsed

---

[19] Wiseman (1979, 492–3, n. 196) offers a selection of ancient sources that link the fates of Corinth and Carthage. See also Zonaras 9.31.9 (from Dio Cassius 21) and *Oracula Sibyllina* 4.105–06. The only study of this rhetorical connection seems to be Purcell (1995). A thorough examination of the extent to which the rhetorically joining of the two cities has led to a conflation of their histories would be particularly useful.

into a single episode. This analysis is particularly relevant in the case of Plutarch, who is the only witness to state unequivocally that Corinth was a veterans' colony. Plutarch's overriding concern at this point in the narrative, however, is to highlight the extent to which Caesar provided for his men, not to examine objectively the composition of Late Republican colonies. Armed with the knowledge that Caesar founded these two colonies at approximately the same time and perhaps with the fact that Carthage may have been a veterans' colony, Plutarch is happy to amplify his point and Caesar's largess by adding Corinth to the mix.[20]

In short, the literary evidence characterizing Corinth as a veterans' colony appears to be the result either of conflating Carthage and Corinth in an unwarranted manner, or of an attempt to make a rhetorical point about Caesar, or both. Therefore, one ought to be wary about accepting these statements without corroborating evidence. This suspicion seems particularly justified when we compare Corinth with Patras, a colony situated close to Corinth. Nearly contemporary in its foundation, the town was indisputably a veterans' colony.[21] Extant inscriptions from these two sites offer a sharp contrast: although generally the epigraphic evidence from Patras is even more scanty than at Corinth, tombstones set up for veterans are not uncommon at Patras[22] while in Corinth—where even though much more of the city and its surrounding cemeteries have been excavated and explored—evidence for veterans is practically non-existent.[23] The conclusion seems ines-

---

[20] For a brief synopsis of Plutarch's characterization of Caesar: T. Duff 1999, 98 and 303.

[21] For a brief history of the founding of Patras (16/15 BCE) and its population, based on epigraphic and numismatic evidence: Rizakis 1998, 24–28 and 49–52. For a collection and discussion of the literary evidence: Rizakis 1995, 110 no. 135, 165–67, 252, 308–09 and 531.10.

[22] For discussion of veterans at Patras: Rizakis 1998, 25–28. Literary evidence for veterans at Patras is as equally slim as for Corinth but is of greater weight (Strabo 8.7.5).

[23] An inscription from Kenchreai (Šašel Kos 1979, 56–57 no. 125) is the sole example of a veteran's tombstone from Corinthian territory. Two former military officers are also attested at Corinth: a military tribune of *Legio X Gemina* (*Corinth* VIII.3 no. 132) and a military tribune of *Legio VI Hispanensis* (*Corinth* VIII.2 no. 86–90; and VIII.3, no. 158–63). Spawforth (1996, 170–71) suggests several other possible colonists of veteran origin on the basis of onomastics; see also Spawforth 2002, 103. Not included here are a handful of former military officers whose service post-dates the Julio-Claudian period.

capable, then, that Corinth was not in any meaningful sense a veterans' colony.[24]

FREEDMEN

The one testimonium not yet discussed is Strabo's assertion (passage one, above) that Caesar sent people of the freedman class to Corinth as colonists. Strabo's remark deserves close attention because, unlike the others, he was interested in discussing Corinth, not Caesar. He visited Corinth some decades after its founding at a time when at least some of the original colonists may still have been alive and when their families were continuing to dominate local politics. Moreover, he was an intimate of the Roman elite of the early Empire. In this respect, he may even have been cognizant of the colony's planning and early development.[25] Perhaps most importantly of all, his statement seems to be corroborated by onomastic evidence.

Through epigraphic and numismatic material, coupled with a small amount of literary evidence, we know the names of a fair number of the members of early Roman Corinth's elite.[26] In one of the very few studies focusing on the population itself, Anthony Spawforth has analyzed the names of these elite members.[27] Spawforth reached two important conclusions. First, he showed the extent to which families and individuals of freedman origin dominated the upper echelons of Corinthian society in the early years of the colony; and second, he demonstrated that a large number of these individuals have names

---

[24] The notion that Corinth was a veterans' colony appears frequently in earlier scholarship but needs to be abandoned once and for all. Spawforth (1996, 170–71) acknowledges the scantiness of the evidence but justifies it by suggesting most veterans would not have had enough property to qualify for inclusion in the colonial elite and so would be absent from the epigraphic and numismatic evidence. Thus, his position hypothesizes the existence of a larger veteran presence than the evidence attests. Walbank (1997a, 97), on the other hand, is one of few scholars to have noted that any idea that Corinth was a veterans' colony ought to be dismissed. The lack of evidence is, indeed, so overwhelming that the silence ought to be interpreted not as the result of an insufficient or incomplete archaeological record but rather as an accurate representation of the minor, incidental role which veterans played in the colony's formation.

[25] Walbank (1997a, 97) has discussed the importance of Strabo's eyewitness account. For comments on the ancient author's visit: Wallace 1969.

[26] For a list of Romans known from Corinth, or for persons with Roman names, see *RP* 1.247–411. R. S. Stroud and I are currently compiling a prosopography of Corinth and the Corinthians in all periods.

[27] Spawforth 1996.

which strongly suggest a connection with Romans known to have been active in the east as either *negotiatores* or otherwise. Spawforth's first conclusion is uncontroversial. Despite the occurrence of relatively few persons who explicitly identify themselves as freedmen, the presence of large numbers of citizens with Roman *praenomina* and *nomina* but with Greek *cognomina* strongly indicates that these were freedmen or at least the descendants of freedmen.[28] The former hypothesis is more likely, especially if there was a prejudice in the second generation against names of Greek and, therefore, implicitly servile origin, as Spawforth himself argues.[29] His second conclusion results from the practice of freedmen taking their *nomina* from their former masters and from Spawforth's demonstration of the high degree of correlation between the *nomina* of early Corinth's elite and those of the *negotiatores* and other Romans active in the east.[30] Almost certainly, therefore, Spawforth's work has shown Strabo's assessment to be quite correct. Freedmen did indeed form the bulk of the colonists or at least the bulk of those who would have come to assume positions of prominence within the colony.[31]

The literary and onomastic evidence has thus come together to indicate the domination, whether by design or chance, of freedmen within the early colony. An important issue then becomes the origin of these freedmen. Clearly, on the basis of their nomenclature, they were demonstrably Greek. The question remains, however, whether they were Greeks from the east; Greeks who had become thoroughly Romanized, perhaps over several generations, presumably in Italy or elsewhere in the west; or Romanized Greeks who through activity in the east had to some extent become re-Hellenized. Answers to this question have often varied depending upon an individual scholar's view of the colony and the degree to which he or she has believed it exemplified Greek or Roman attitudes and *mores*. A more concrete

---

[28] Spawforth (1996, 169) also notes a lack of filiation as an additional indicator; see, perhaps most notably, the case of Cn. Babbius Philinus.

[29] Spawforth 1996, 175; Treggiari 1969, 231–32. Even if Spawforth is correct in identifying such a prejudice in the colony's early years, this bias seems to have died out during the 1st century CE as Greek *cognomina* grow more common—perhaps due to the colony's location in Greece.

[30] For compilation and discussion: Spawforth 1996, 175–82.

[31] An epigram by Crinagoras (*AP* 9.284), lamenting Corinth's fate at being handed over to the rule of repeatedly sold slaves, may offer additional support. The epigram suggests Corinth was perceived, at least in some circles, as a freedmen colony although we should probably not infer too much from this source for the population as a whole.

means of answering it, however, can be found in epigraphic evidence from Corinth itself.

Languages and Corinthian Society

That Latin was the dominant public language of Roman Corinth for more than the first 150 years of its existence has long been obvious.[32] According to Kent's calculations, prior to the reign of Hadrian reasonably well-dated inscriptions in Latin outnumber those in Greek by a factor just over 25:1. Latin was used for honorary inscriptions, dedications, funerary monuments, building inscriptions, records of benefactions—in short, in virtually all classes of inscriptions from this date with the notable exception of inscriptions concerning the Isthmian Games, which are exclusively in Greek.[33] The enormous preponderance of Latin has often been used to argue that the language of the early colony was Latin and that the colonists themselves were therefore Romans or at least thoroughly Romanized Greeks.[34]

This evidence, however, may not be quite as overwhelming as it appears. The inscriptions included in this tally are almost entirely public ones and are predominantly from the forum and theater areas, that is, the center of the city and its most overtly Roman area. Regardless of their precise nature, they were most frequently erected in prominent locations to emphasize the close relationship between an individual and the city; and the vast majority highlight individual benefactions and service—religious, secular or both, no matter whether it was personally erected or was erected to honor someone else. In a recently founded Roman colony, using a language other than Latin in this way would have been unthinkable, for the public face and the public identity of the colony were thoroughly Roman. In this regard, the inscriptions concerning the Isthmian Games are of crucial importance. These

---

[32] The clearest demonstration is Kent (*Corinth* VIII.3, 18–19). Although Latin was the dominant public language of the colony, referring to it as the 'official language' seems anachronistic. Nevertheless, it was used for all official purposes: on inscriptions emanating from the municipality, on coinage, and apparently on items manufactured for the municipality (see a discussion of roof tiles, below) as well as for public business, one presumes.

[33] See n. 9, above.

[34] This was Kent's own conclusion: "It might be assumed *a priori* that in the early days of the colony the language would be Latin...because the earliest settlers seem to have been for the most part of Italic stock" (*Corinth* VIII.3, 18).

Greek texts indicate quite clearly that the choice of language used in an inscription of the early colony had little to do with the ethnic or social origins of the colonists and everything to do with the context of the inscription itself. Public inscriptions were one way of expressing one's role and position in the community, but they also reflected the values of the community as a whole. The choice of language contributed to these statements. One would no more erect an inscription in Latin detailing the officials or victors of the Isthmian games than one would dedicate a building or monument in the Forum using an inscription in Greek.[35]

Funerary inscriptions, notoriously difficult to date, were largely excluded for that reason from Kent's calculations regarding the ratio of Latin to Greek inscriptions. Although perhaps seeming to reinforce the notion of a bias toward Latin in the early colony, funerary inscriptions must be used with great caution since they are part of a circular argument in which the Latin ones tend to be dated early and the Greek ones late. Nevertheless, they do offer partial support for some of the conclusions reached above. Only a single example of a veteran's gravestone has been found whereas those for freedmen are numerous.[36] Comparison with Patras is instructive since gravestones for veterans in that city occur regularly and are on a par numerically with those of freedmen and others.[37] While fully acknowledging the chronological difficulties in working with this material, dating primarily on the basis of language should probably be abandoned.

This opens up the possibility of comparing Latin and Greek funerary inscriptions rather than treating them as separate phenomena. In those funerary inscriptions which might plausibly be dated to the first two centuries of the colony, Latin outnumbers Greek by a ratio of nearly 5:1, which offers a somewhat different picture from that found by examining the public monuments of the Forum. Among the most interesting is an inscription written in Greek but using a Roman

---

[35] Contrast *Corinth* VIII.1 no. 70. It is an honorific inscription written in Greek shortly after the middle of the 1st century CE, most likely erected in or near the forum, but seems to be a special case, as Kent noted (*Corinth* VIII.3, 19). In addition to this inscription, whose fragmentary condition makes any conclusions about its length or content difficult, the honored man, C. Iulius Spartiaticus, a Greek provincial notable also received an inscription in Latin (*Corinth* VIII.2 no. 68), which fits the expected pattern. The relation, if any, between these two inscriptions remains uncertain. For the career of Spartiaticus: *RP* 2 'LAC 509' and *RP* 1 'COR 353.'

[36] Šašel Kos 1979, 56–57, no. 125.

[37] See n. 22, above.

formula.[38] Worth noting also in this context is a bilingual grave monument in which the names of the deceased (?) are written in Latin and are followed by an epigram written in Greek,[39] as well as an apparent example of a Latin inscription (which may or may not be a funerary inscription) written in Greek.[40] This overlap and conflation of traditions in funerary monuments suggests a significant percentage of the population was capable of drawing upon both Greek and Roman traditions and of effecting a combination of the two. Funerary inscriptions could be among the most personal of documents, yet still were vehicles for public display.[41] Possibly, the choice of Latin in many of them can be seen as an indicator of success achieved within the context of the Roman system; that is, the use of Latin was a mark of status and could be used to denote one's social level within the community or the group with which one wished to be identified.[42]

The Corinthian correspondence of the apostle Paul forms an additional set of evidence for the language used by one subset of the Corinthian population. These letters were written in Greek, thus implying that

---

[38] "Gaius Julius Marcianus, while still living, [acquired this burial place] for himself; Terentia Julia, his wife; and his daughter, who was still living, Julia Rectina" (*Corinth* VIII.3 no. 294, translated by Kent). M. Mitsos dated it to the 1st century BCE or CE while Kent preferred a date in the mid 2nd century CE. Kent's date is probably closer to the truth, although the inscription may be somewhat earlier than he allowed. Nevertheless, since letter forms are the only available criteria, the question remains open. Exactly parallel is the gravestone of P. Eg[natius?] Apoll[onius?] and his descendants (*Corinth* VIII.3 no. 303). Eg[natius] was an Ephesian who apparently resided in Corinth.

[39] *Corinth* VIII.1 no. 130. Meritt dated it to the later part of the 2nd century CE but it is probably much earlier. Also relevant, especially if it is a funerary inscription, is *Corinth* VIII.3 no. 342, which contains a fragmentary line of Latin above a fragmentary line of Greek. The inscription may be a Roman funerary formula followed by a Greek translation (?) beneath it although the translation contains at least one transliterated word, that is, if [φα]μιλίαι is restored correctly.

[40] *Corinth* VIII.2 no. 152 ([---]ΛΙΒΕΡΤ[---]). West assumed that a Greek mason was carving a Latin inscription and inadvertently substituted 'Λ' for 'L' and 'P' for 'R.' A more natural conclusion is that the inscription was written in Greek or at least in Greek letters and that it included Latin terms in transliteration. For example, see *Corinth* VIII.2 no. 65. Something similar went wrong in *Corinth* VIII.2 no. 66. West assumed this last example was the result of "an ignorant Greek workman."

[41] See Oliver 2000.

[42] Petersen 2006, 84–120 and 184–226 (on the importance to freedmen of funerary monuments as status markers). Although few funerary inscriptions from Corinth explicitly label the interred as freedmen (for example, *Corinth* VIII.1 no. 130; and VIII.3 no. 280), the combination of Greek *cognomina* and lack of filiation suggests that many, if not most, of these came from graves of freedmen. See also Rife *et al.* 2007, 156–58.

the use of this language was deemed appropriate, or at least acceptable, when addressing the local Christian community as a whole. The precise reasons for the suitability of Greek in this context are not entirely clear. Certainly, Greek was the *lingua franca* of the Greek East, and, in any case, a fair number of Paul's associates were from the Greek-speaking world. On the other hand, Paul's letters were not necessarily aimed solely at his intimates, and so his use of Greek may reflect a desire to reach the widest possible audience, at least within that segment of the Corinthian population to which he was speaking.

The best evidence for one's language of choice and, thus, for one's self-identification is the language used in writing of a strictly personal, nonpublic character. Our evidence for writing of this nature in early Roman Corinth comes primarily from certain types of graffiti. Graffiti in the sense of informal writing on buildings, walls, seats, or indeed any exposed bit of surface, often in a public location, unfortunately survives in Corinth in relatively small numbers. Moreover, such writing seldom has any discernable context and is extremely difficult to date since it may have occurred at almost any point in the life of the surface on which it is written. Finally, graffiti themselves are often cursorily published, if at all. Nevertheless, it is noteworthy that in such graffiti at Corinth Greek examples outnumber Latin ones, so far.[43] Indeed, there seems to be only a single certain Latin example, the letters 'NER' cut into a corner of a large tripod base set above the triglyph wall of the sacred spring.[44]

Far better for the purpose at hand, however, are graffiti on pottery. This material has the enormous advantage of being fairly closely dateable and occurs at Corinth in sufficient quantity to offer a representative sample. Irrelevant here is writing of a commercial nature, such as indications of content or origin although these do occur at Corinth in quite large numbers, both in Greek and Latin. While the language used in these cases is largely dictated by the point of origin and thus has little to do with the character of the local population, it may be of

---

[43] For Greek examples: *Corinth* I.4, 101 n. 1; VIII.3 no. 361; X, 135 no. 3–4; and Williams 2005, 227–29.

[44] *Corinth* I.6, 197–98. For a possible Latin example on a drain tile, see *Corinth* I.4, 65 n. 31. Also worth noting are three Roman numerals (III, IIII, and XXIIII) inscribed on a piece of concrete vaulting from the Odeon; *Corinth* X, 136 no. 6. It is unclear whether these numbers are graffiti or masons' marks (for discussion of the latter, see below).

interest that Greek graffiti and *dipinti* of this nature clearly appear to outnumber those in Latin.[45]

In any case, the graffiti most relevant here are personal marks made after acquisition of the vessel, usually indicating ownership.[46] This is not the occasion to discuss the material in detail, not least because it has barely been studied and is still awaiting publication. But for the purpose at hand, the general character of this material is what matters.[47] There are at least two dozen examples dated to the Early Roman period on the basis of the pottery on which they occur, and they have been found in a variety of areas across the excavation. The important point here is that Greek overwhelmingly outnumbers Latin in the graffiti indicating personal ownership by a factor approaching the reverse of that found in the public inscriptions.[48] In these graffiti, unlike the public monuments in the Forum or even the funerary monuments, there can be no question of public display. They are examples of private communication meant solely for internal consumption within a closed group. Thus, the graffiti strongly suggest that there existed at Corinth in the Early Roman period a significant portion of the population which, regardless of the language they may have used in public life, used Greek as the language of choice when communicating privately and amongst themselves.[49]

An additional set of evidence may shed light on the lower echelons of society. The truly poor are largely, if not entirely, invisible to modern scholars in the surviving evidence. Nevertheless, it is perhaps possible through masons' marks and other manufacturers' marks to

---

[45] Commercial graffiti and *dipinti* from Corinth have never been studied systematically. Many have been published incidentally with the pottery on which they were written. A study of this material might shed valuable light on Corinth's role as a mediator between eastern and western trade networks, for example.

[46] For an overview of this variety of graffiti: Guarducci 1974, 329–57.

[47] A small number of non-commercial graffiti has also been published incidentally with the pottery on which it was written.

[48] The Greek to Latin ratio of graffiti on pottery is similar to the ratio of Greek to Latin on curse tablets from the Demeter sanctuary. Of the 18 tablets found, all but one is written Greek. These objects will be published by Stroud.

[49] The social level of those who may have written ownership marks or the like on pottery remains an open question. To my knowledge, there has never been an investigation of the matter; nor is it clear that the evidence for such an investigation even exists. The act of writing might imply a certain level of education, which, in turn, would imply a certain social level; but this is far from certain. Perhaps the safest conclusion is that this pottery belonged to members of a broad group who represent neither the highest nor lowest levels of the social spectrum.

identify the cultural affiliation of the substantial portion of the population composed of builders, tradesmen, workmen and the like, who kept the city going. The study of masons' marks comes with a whole raft of problems. The term itself is rather unfortunate in that it can encompass quarry marks, builders' or contractors' marks, marks to facilitate the reconstruction of a disassembled building or monument, the products of idle workmen, and a variety of other things. In addition, masons' marks are seldom studied or published except incidentally. They are rarely dealt with systematically and are difficult to date unless they can be connected with a specific phase of a building.[50] They do, however, have something of value to offer to the present inquiry in so far as they are non-public writings of an informal character which must have been intelligible to their intended audience.

Examination of all mason's marks, in the broadest sense of the term, which could be located from the first two centuries of the colony's existence, has resulted in a picture entirely consistent with the evidence previously discussed.[51] Although there are perhaps several dozen occurrences of masons' marks from Roman Corinth, including those of all types mentioned above, there appears to be only a single certain example of masons' marks in Latin characters: the Roman numerals cut on the back of the blocks of the Timoleon monument, presumably for disassembling it and reassembling it elsewhere.[52] All others, whatever their nature, are in Greek. Some of these may be the result of workmen or specialized craftsmen who were brought in from elsewhere in the Greek world, as frequently happens with building projects and as was certainly the case with Theodotos the Athenian, whose signature, although inscribed in Greek, appears on a large Latin dedicatory inscription from the theater.[53] It seems highly unlikely, however, that all masons' marks can be accounted for in this fashion, and so a substantial number can most plausibly be attributed to the work of Corinthians.

---

[50] For an overview of types of masons' marks: Guarducci 1974, 377–93. McLean 2002, 204–05 is cursory but provides recent bibliography.

[51] As with most incidental inscriptions, masons' marks are seldom published except in conjunction with a building or monument and are very rarely treated systematically. The majority of those from Corinth remains unpublished and often undocumented.

[52] For the Timoleon monument itself: *Corinth* VIII.3 no. 23. For the masons' marks: Kent 1952, 9–10 and pl. 2b. For a second possible example, also depicting Roman numerals, see n. 44, above.

[53] *Corinth* VIII.1 no. 71 + VIII.3 no. 41. For the join, see IX.3, 49 (*SEG* LV 383).

Manufacturers' marks can help to round out this picture and seem to support the general trends suggested by the other evidence. Although somewhat later in date than much of the material discussed here, the signatures on lamps are noteworthy in that the use of Greek overwhelmingly dominates from their first appearance.[54] Particularly interesting is that most of the names from these signatures are Latinate and appear in Latin form on Italian lamps, thus suggesting a conscious adaptation to the prevailing market at Corinth.[55] Somewhat less clear is the situation with stamps on roof tiles. The majority of stamped roof tiles are written in Latin, yet the majority of these include the name of the colony with or without the addition of the manufacturer's name. The logical conclusion seems to be that such tiles were manufactured for the city, whether for a specific project or not, under some sort of municipal contract. For these items of public ownership, expressly manufactured for the city, the use of Latin is not surprising.[56] The number of stamped roof tiles which do not bear the name of the colony is fairly small and spilt between Greek and Latin, with the former perhaps predominating.[57] Other objects from Corinth which have makers' marks include simas, antefixes, water pipes and local pottery. Although many of these are poorly dated, Greek is used almost exclusively.[58]

---

[54] *Corinth* IV.2, 96–98. These lamps are all Broneer Type XXVII; signatures do not appear on early Corinthian lamps.

[55] This suggestion is not meant to imply a connection between the makers of the Corinthian lamps and those of the Italian lamps or even, as Broneer seems to suggest (*Corinth* IV.2, 98), that the Corinthian makers may have been freedmen of Roman lamp manufacturers.

[56] Stamped roof tiles tend to be published cursorily, as well. For a collection with references to other examples, published and unpublished: *Corinth* XVIII.3, 448–49 no. 13; 451 no. 22; and 471–72 no. 86–89. Although these are difficult to date, Bookidis and Stroud (*Corinth* XVIII.3, 472) offer some guidance on the basis of the abbreviation of the colony's name. Possibly by the 2nd century, Greek may have been acceptable for items manufactured for the colony if Broneer's understanding of the Greek abbreviation on a number of roof tiles from the Odeon is correct; *Corinth* X, 137–38 no. 100.

[57] For Greek examples: *Corinth* X, 137–38 d–h; and XVIII.3, 472–73 no. 90. For Latin examples: *Corinth* X, 137–38 b; and XVIII.3, 450–51 no. 21. See also *Corinth* XVIII.3, 456 no. 41, and 473 no. 91.

[58] For simas: *Corinth* IV.1, 81 no. S145, and 86 no. S212; and XVIII.3, 456 no. 40 (with further references). For antefixes: *Corinth* IV.1, 52 no. A46; and XVIII.3, 456 no. 40 (with further references). For water pipes: *Corinth* I.1,183; Scranton and Ramage 1964, 141 (from Kenchreai). For pottery: Hayes 1973, 464 no. 209.

Itinerant workers, such as Prisca and Aquila, must have been common in Corinth but are poorly represented in the surviving record and have left little trace outside Christian scripture. As an international port and a rapidly growing city, Corinth must have attracted fairly large numbers of such people who stayed for varying amounts of time, many perhaps settling there permanently but who often remained on the margins of the governing society and who had little involvement in the political life of the city. One might plausibly imagine, however, that the majority of these people originated in the Greek East, as indeed Aquila, his wife, and other associates of Paul seem to have done.[59]

A final group of people, also poorly represented in the surviving record, is the Jewish community. Two literary sources, aside from passages of Christian scripture, attest to a Jewish presence in Corinth in the 1st century CE. Philo includes Corinth in a list of places with Jewish colonies,[60] and Josephus reports that Vespasian sent 6,000 Jews to Corinth in 67 CE to work on Nero's canal across the Isthmus.[61] In addition, there are a few inscriptions although most are relatively late.[62] Apart from this evidence, we have few identifiable remains of the early Jewish community at Corinth.[63]

CORINTH, GREEK AND ROMAN

Examination of the literary evidence indicates a strong, if not dominant, freedman element in the population of the early colony. From a study of their names, as represented in the literary, numismatic, and epigraphic record, these freedmen were entirely Greek in origin. Once their dominance in the record is established, the question then becomes the extent to which these Greek freedmen were or were not influenced

---

[59] Foreigners at Corinth: *IG* 4.206 (a boy wrestler from Sardis), 4.207 (a group of Phoceans), and *Corinth* VIII.3 no. 303 (an Ephesian). Many of those represented in the epigraphic record, however, may have been relatively well-to-do. For further discussion of Corinth's hybrid population: Rife *et al.* 2007, 157–58.

[60] *Legat.* 281.

[61] *BJ* 3.540.

[62] *IJO* 1.182–89 (Ach 47–50), with a list of unpublished inscriptions (182), and rejected inscriptions (339–340 and appendix 18–18bis).

[63] Foerster (1981) summarizes the exiguousness of the remains. For an overview of the evidence: Wiseman 1979, 503–05; Avramea 1997, 131, 149–54; and *IJO* 1.181–82. For earlier scholarship: Bees 1941, 16–19.

by Roman culture. Analysis of the epigraphic evidence from Corinth suggests that simply counting the number of Latin inscriptions versus Greek inscriptions is not a reliable indicator of the colony's dominant cultural affiliation. Instead, the context of the inscription must be taken into account. Thus, the more an inscription was meant for public display and public consumption in a Roman context, the more likely it was to have been written in Latin. The more an inscription was used for private communication, the more likely it was to have been written in Greek. The quasi-public, quasi-private world of funerary monuments is one area in which these two languages meet and overlap.

The most plausible conclusion to be drawn from this material as a whole seems to be that the population of Corinth was composed of a group which was able to maneuver effectively in both the Greek and Roman worlds. This was a group which could navigate these overlapping worlds, adjusting to the context and to what was most appropriate or expedient in any given circumstance. Moreover, the extent to which both the Latin language and Roman culture, more broadly, were adopted at the same time that Greek was retained (presumably alongside Greek cultural affiliation) indicates that this was a very special group of people. It was not one which had so thoroughly identified itself with Roman culture as to lose its facility for Greek language and culture, but neither was it an immigrant group in the process of assimilation which had acquired merely a veneer of Romanness while remaining essentially Greek. Instead, it was a hybrid of both cultures— a group in which one language became the mode of expression within the public sphere and another within the private. This group was formed primarily of Greek freedmen. Having achieved success and status within the Roman world, they were very much a part of that world even though, in the end, they did not lose their Greek identity. At the same time, there is some evidence suggesting that a segment of the elite may have been composed of Roman families who had long been active in the east; that these families were Hellenized, to a certain extent; and that they had, perhaps, intermarried with prominent local families of the Greek East. The most notable example of this phenomenon is T. Claudius Dinippus.[64] While coming from the other end

---

[64] Spawforth 1996, 173 and 177–78; *RP* 1 'COR 170.'

of the spectrum, these Hellenized Romans shared many of the same characteristics of the Greek freedmen.

The existence of this hybrid society and its resulting dynamic between Greek and Roman culture make a precise characterization of Roman Corinth elusive. This elusiveness is further compounded by differing levels of participation in both Greek and Roman culture across the different strata of society. While undoubtedly the reality was rather more nuanced, the current evidence suggests that the elite seem the most capable, or willing, to straddle the cultural divide, while the lower strata seem more solidly Greek in outlook. One conclusion from this apparent divide is that the colony's social strata may have had different origins. The elite, composed primarily of freedmen, evince a familiarity and ease with Roman culture and language that indicates a long term involvement in the Roman world. In contrast, what evidence there is for society's lower strata perhaps suggests a more local or at least non-Roman origin.

In many ways, Corinth was a thoroughly Roman city like any other colony, and it presented a Roman face to the world, especially in its city center. At the same time, however, it was a city which from its founding was trying to lay claim to a Greek heritage, stressing an element of continuity between the Greek city of the past and the Roman colony of the present. This tension did not exist solely in the abstract or in the outward trappings of the city but was inherent in its population, particularly its elite members. These were people who had achieved a certain level of success in the Roman world and who saw this success and their participation in Roman culture and citizenship both as a mark of status and as part of their identity. At the same time, however, they continued to identify with Greeks and the Greek world to a greater extent than what might be expected from ethnic Greeks who had significantly invested in Roman culture. Similarly, although it was Roman colony and thus an enclave of Rome in Greece, Corinth in many ways maintained a very eastern, Greek outlook.

This attitude can be seen, for example, in the town's support of figures traditionally popular in the east such as Marc Antony[65] and, later,

---

[65] Support for Antony is perhaps not surprising in that a number of his freedmen seem to have been living there in prominent positions (Plut. *Ant.* 67.9–10) although this support seems to have evaporated after Actium (67.10). Nevertheless, M. Antonii continued to enjoy positions of leadership in the colony for generations. For the most convenient compilation of these people, see *RP* 1. For discussion: Spawforth 1996,

Nero.[66] It can be seen possibly in the working of the imperial cult[67] or certainly in the city's continued and direct involvement with the Sanctuary of Poseidon and the Isthmian Games. The dynamic relationships between cultures in Roman Corinth were manifested not only in mixed nomenclature and a certain level of bilingualism (or, more properly, 'diglossia') but appeared in virtually all aspects of everyday life. It was precisely this ability to bridge both Greek and Roman cultures which led to Corinth's early and continued importance and which made it a magnet for people throughout the Greek East. Because of its population, Corinth was able from the beginning to form a meeting ground between east and west and to form a route from one to the other in culture and society, as it did in trade.

Spawforth has called the notion that the Roman colony at Corinth was founded for commercial reasons "a confusing of aims with consequences."[68] His view is, I think, mistaken. Roman colonies were not founded haphazardly or for no other reason than the availability of land. Veterans' colonies in particular were not placed randomly but were often situated in strategic locations. There is no reason why a colony with economic aims should not similarly be founded in a commercially strategic area in order to capitalize on precisely that advantage. In the same way that colonies in militarily strategic areas were populated with veterans in order that Rome could have the population it wanted where it wanted, one should imagine that Corinth, too, was made attractive to a group of colonists who could make it a viable and successful commercial enterprise. Corinth's location obviously is highly strategic, both from a military and commercial vantage. Following the destruction of Corinth in 146 BCE, the trade routes, and particularly east-west routes, which crossed the Isthmus were severely

176. For discussion of the evidence attesting to Antony's relationship with Corinth: Wiseman 1979, 502.

[66] Nero's popularity at Corinth is hardly surprising given local circumstances. Although later authors may have viewed his attempt at digging a canal as hubristic, to the community at the time it would have potentially meant an economic windfall. Similarly, whatever the extent to which Nero's speech at the Isthmus, proclaiming the freedom of the Greeks, was intended to evoke historical precedents, to the Corinthians it gave prominence to their city and highlighted its importance; Wiseman 1979, 505–06.

[67] For imperial cult and other cults: Mary Walbank 1996.

[68] Spawforth 1996, 175 and n. 36.

disrupted.[69] As Roman domination extended farther in both direc-
tions, the control of and access to these routes became vitally important, as was the control of trade and commerce which passed through
these same points.

Spawforth has equated the freedmen who formed the bulk of early
Roman Corinth's population with Appian's "landless" class at Rome.[70]
Aside from the fact that Appian does not actually state that these
people went to Corinth, this identification suggests that the colony
was founded with the view of providing land to those who clamored
for it. Yet the people who became colonists turned out to be exactly
those who were best suited to its success as a commercial vehicle. The
colony was situated at a site where a commercial vacuum existed yet
which had the potential for being extremely lucrative. There was no
impediment, legal, social, or otherwise, to freedmen participating in
and even dominating the political structure of the early colony.[71] The
freedmen who from the outset formed the ranks of the colony's elite
were precisely those who had one foot in Rome and one in the east.
They were able to negotiate between these two worlds and perhaps
most importantly had eastern business contacts with which to restore
Corinth almost immediately to the role of a major player in east-west
trade.

The picture I have tried to present is one of a society that was neither
completely Roman nor completely Greek, but rather one that navigated
both cultures. Corinth was a Roman colony: its political structure, its
position within the province of Achaia, the architectural form of the
city center, the layout of the colony, and not least its strong political
allegiance were all wholly Roman. This very Roman city, however, had
strong, even dominant, Greek roots, some of which were manifest in
the mediating role Corinth played between east and west. This was a
city and a population which was capable, whether consciously or not,
of presenting different faces in different circumstances and contexts.
The Roman face appears most obviously in public display in Roman
contexts in the city center, where anything else would have been inap-

---

[69] For the disruption of trade networks across the east after 146 BCE, see Lawall
2005, 213–14; and Reger 1994, 267 n. 43.

[70] Spawforth 1996, 169; Appian *Pun.* 136.

[71] Aside from the overwhelming epigraphic evidence, which points to the involvement of freedmen at all levels of the colony's government, see Spawforth 1996, 16;
and Treggiari 1969, 63–64.

propriate and out of place. In sharp contrast, private contexts present a very different and notably Greek face. This conclusion is not meant to imply that the *romanitas* of the colonists was a veneer or a facade to be shed at will but that this group of people had found a way to navigate effectively between both worlds. Monuments throughout the city proclaimed the servile origins of their erectors, whether implicitly or explicitly. But such origins seem to have imposed no impediments, social or otherwise, to advancement to the highest levels within the community. This was a city which presented itself as a new foundation while simultaneously laying claim to the past, providing a focal point for the mixing of Greek and Roman cultures at a major crossroads in the eastern Mediterranean. It was, in short, a nexus of old and new, conquered and conquerors, Greek and Roman.

CHAPTER THREE

ASKLEPIOS IN GREEK AND ROMAN CORINTH

Bronwen L. Wickkiser

O Asklepios, who brings form great joy for all mortals... (Paus. 2.26. 7)

The cult of the doctor-god Asklepios enjoyed immense popularity across the Greco-Roman world. The earliest evidence for worship of Asklepios comes from Epidauros, some 60 km southwest of Corinth, where cult activity can be documented by the late 6th century BCE. The cult spread quickly and prospered for about a millennium. Throughout the cult's history, individuals flocked to Asklepieia in search of cures for maladies ranging from blindness, deafness, and paralysis to headaches, baldness, and insomnia. Here the sick would sleep, hoping to meet Asklepios in a dream whereby he would treat them with a medical procedure or prescribe a regimen for cure. As a healing god, Asklepios shares important points of contact with other divine healers, like Apollo and Jesus, and with his less divine counterparts—namely, the Greek doctors who venerated Asklepios as their patron deity.[1]

Within the context of Corinth in particular, the cult has special significance for several reasons. First, the sanctuary of Asklepios is one of a growing number outside the forum area that has now been excavated and provides valuable evidence for Corinthian cult activity.[2] Second, his sanctuary at Corinth is one of the earliest known Asklepieia anywhere and was apparently quite popular. Asklepios arrived in Corinth by the late 5th century and his cult quickly prospered, as indicated by

[1] The standard work on Asklepios remains Edelstein and Edelstein (1945), whose two volumes catalogue literary and epigraphic testimonia for Asklepios and provide detailed discussion of the cult (without, it must be noted, much attention to local or temporal variation). Recent studies of the material remains of Asklepieia supplement both the nature and extent of evidence included in Edelstein. See especially Riethmüller 2005, which includes extensive bibliography for all Asklepieia. For Greece: Semeria 1986, Stavropoulos 1996, Melfi 2007b. For the Roman world: Degrassi 1986; Musial 1992; Tiussi 1999; Renberg 2006–07.

[2] For an overview of cult activity and locations in Corinth, see Bookidis 2003; and *Urban Religion*, especially the contributions by Bookidis, Gebhard, Lanci, and Williams for recent discoveries and further references.

a wealth of votive dedications and a large-scale building project in the 4th century BCE. Third, his sanctuary is one of the first at Corinth to demonstrate cult activity after the Romans refounded the city, and it remained in use probably until the early 5th century CE when it suffered extensive damage.[3] Because of the cult's long existence spanning both the Greek and Roman periods of the city, it offers unique opportunities for diachronic as well as synchronic comparison.

This paper has two primary goals. First, it gives a general overview of the Greek and Roman phases of the cult in Corinth and discusses how these relate more broadly to the development of Asklepios cult elsewhere. While much of this evidence has been discussed in other publications, I summarize it here and supplement it with recent discoveries for those unfamiliar with Asklepios in Corinth. Second, the paper then focuses on the early Roman period of the cult to investigate why the early inhabitants of this Roman colony had a strong interest in Asklepios. In this regard, I will explore why his sanctuary was one of the first renovated after the founding of the colony, and why Asklepios was apparently more immediately appealing than other gods.

At first glance, the answer to these questions seems obvious and straightforward: the Corinthians wanted a talented healing god in their midst. Sickness and the maintenance of health are constants of the human condition, so it only makes sense to welcome the healing god par excellence into the community. This is a compelling explanation up to a point, and one that scholarship readily embraces. Although no distinct category of "religion" existed in the ancient world ("religion" as an analytical category is a product of the Enlightenment), Asklepios tends to be cast in the pages of books and articles as a sort of post-Enlightenment Jesus figure who inhabits the world of "religion" separate from all other aspects of culture.[4] Therefore scholars typically attribute the appeal of Asklepios to his ability to cure worshippers of plague or gout or lice or whatever other physical ailment they may happen to suffer, and leave it at that.

---

[3] Roebuck (1951, 160–64), dates the Asklepieion's destruction to the late 4th century based largely on coins (from the reigns of Constantine I through Theodosius II) and lamps associated with the destruction levels. However, Guy Sanders has recently proposed that these lamps date later than Roebuck thought; Sanders 2005, 430–37.

[4] For discussion and recent bibliography on the development of the category 'religion,' see Nongbri 2008, 444–47.

Such explanations undoubtedly are correct but underestimate the broader appeal of the cult. If it is true, as the historian of religion Jonathan Z. Smith has remarked, that "the historian's task is to complicate, not to clarify," then it seems time to explore the ties of Asklepios to other facets of Greco-Roman culture.[5] Roman Corinth, a major crossroads of the ancient Mediterranean, offers a most fruitful context for this type of exploration.

BACKGROUND ON THE CULT

Other than the remains of the Asklepieion in Corinth, there is very little evidence, material or literary, for the presence of Asklepios in the city. As we shall see, several statuettes and coins of the Roman period depicting Asklepios have been found outside the Asklepieion, but the Asklepieion itself remains the primary material evidence for the god and his cult.

Pausanias is the only literary source to mention Asklepios at Corinth, and it is due to him that we know there were two sanctuaries of Asklepios in the area: one within the walls of the city, and one at Kenchreai, Corinth's southern port. Pausanias describes the temple of Asklepios at Kenchreai as standing next to a temple of Isis and across from that of Aphrodite (Paus. 2.2.3); it was thus probably situated near the south mole of the harbor, but little else is known about it and the best that can be said for its date is that it was standing by the 2nd century CE when Pausanias records it. Nevertheless, its mere existence points to the popularity of Asklepios in the Corinthia in the Roman period.[6]

---

[5] J. Z. Smith 1993 [= 1978], 290. In his paper, Smith is in fact disparaging in his remarks about the ability of the historian to clarify her subject matter but seems to contradict himself in his claims about the nature of history. Is history an imagined terrain on which the historian will never find purchase (289), and thus the historian is justified in her halting and provisional speech (290)? Or is history an entity that one could touch if one were only brave enough (290, this of course being a much more positivist view of history than the former)? Although I have here called Smith a "historian of religion," this label may be inadequate given the far-reaching scope of his work. Tomoko Masuzawa, in a less-charitable reference to this same paper by Smith, has described Smith as a "necromancer of *Religionsgeschichte*" (Masuzawa 2000, 123). My thanks to Brent Nongbri for these reference and for discussing their significance with me.

[6] On Kenchreai and its cults, see the contribution to this volume by Joseph Rife. On the Asklepieion: *Kenchreai* I.53–90; Riethmüller 2005, vol. 2, no. 19.

About the sanctuary within the walls of Corinth, Pausanias is suc-
cinct: it stands, we are told, on the road to Sikyon, near a spring called
Lerna, a temple of Zeus, and a gymnasium (Paus. 2.4.5). He adds that
its statues of Asklepios and Hygieia are of white marble. That is all.

Fortunately, the Asklepios sanctuary has been identified and its
remains excavated. The site was excavated from 1929–34 by F. J. De
Waele, with supplementary study in 1947. The results of these investigations were published in 1951 by Carl Roebuck as Volume XIV in
the Corinth series. Roebuck's observations and conclusions about the
sanctuary and the nature of the cult in Corinth remain standard, but it
is important to note that they have not gone unchallenged. While the
overview of the Asklepieion offered here relies heavily on Roebuck's
analysis of the remains, I will endeavor to point out where scholars
have suggested new interpretations.[7]

Early Phases of the Asklepieion

As Pausanias describes, the sanctuary lies north of the Forum and Theater, just inside the city wall at the edge of Corinth's middle plateau
overlooking the coastal plain (see map 2). Its position at the edge of
the city is consistent with many other Asklepieia, such as those at Epidauros, Kos, Pergamon, and Rome, and makes sense for a cult that
relies upon incubation, or sleep, for its cures.[8]

The sanctuary was established sometime before the mid 6th century and belonged originally to Asklepios's father Apollo, as indicated by inscribed pottery.[9] Still more inscribed pottery indicates that
Asklepios joined Apollo here by the late 5th century.[10] The dynamic
of Asklepios joining a preexisting cult of Apollo is typical of many
Asklepieia, including neighboring Epidauros, as well as Delphi, Kos,

---

[7] Roebuck (1951, 1–7) summarizes investigation in the area of the Asklepieion
prior to Corinth XIV. For subsequent discussion and bibliography: Riethmüller 2005,
vol. 2, no. 21; Melfi 2007b, 289–312. For an engaging overview of Asklepios in Corinth,
see Lang 1977.

[8] See Graf (1992) on the topographical liminality of many Asklepieia. Those at Epidauros and Pergamon lay well beyond the city walls (in the case of Epidauros perhaps
as many as 9 km from the city, whose full extent is not yet known).

[9] A krater rim, found in a deposit dating ca. 600–540 BCE, inscribed Ἀπέ[λ]λονος
ἰμί; Roebuck 1951, 14–15, 152, no. 1. and fig. 4.

[10] Roebuck 1951, 135, no. 65–67 (mortar rims and a cup inscribed with the name
of Asklepios), no. 68 (a kantharos rim inscribed with the name Podalirios, who was a
son of Asklepios); and 152–53. All were found in closed deposits dating from the late
5th to late 4th centuries BCE.

and Pergamon, to name but a few. At all of these sanctuaries Apollo may well have remained in residence, but his own role gradually faded from prominence as his son's healing attracted increasing fame.

The architecture of the archaic and classical phases is seemingly modest and enigmatic: a small building of uncertain function (the so-called *oikos*), a cella-like structure containing four intriguing post-holes and a drainage channel, and a couple of wells to provide water (fig. 3.1).[11] None of these buildings has survived beyond their fleeting foundations in the bedrock. Moreover, given that the construction date of each building is uncertain, any temptation to associate the arrival of Asklepios with a change(s) in architecture is mere guesswork. The best that can be said is that these were the main structures of the sanctuary until the late 4th century when they were razed to make way for a more elaborate building program.[12]

Although the relative chronology of these buildings remains uncertain, all is not hopelessly obscure. New evidence from other early sanctuaries of Asklepios may dispel some of the darkness. Buildings of the 5th century similar in dimension to the small structure indicated by the four post-holes here in Corinth have been identified recently at the Asklepieia both in Epidauros and on the south slope of the acropolis in Athens. All measure roughly 2 × 3 m, and the one at Epidauros also has provisions for drainage. Although we do not yet know the function(s) of this structure, the presence of similar buildings at other Asklepieia suggests common cultic activity.[13]

The apparent modesty of the architecture at Corinth, moreover, is consistent with other early Asklepieia. At Epidauros, for instance, simple architecture in the 5th century masks bustling cult activity. An

---

[11] Roebuck (1951, 8) describes this early sanctuary as "a very unpretentious establishment." Its perceived lack of pretension almost certainly derives in part from our poor understanding of the architecture.

[12] The early architecture and finds of the Asklepieion are discussed by Roebuck (1951, 8–22); Riethmüller (2005, 1.123–30), who proposes a more detailed, but to my mind still tentative, reconstruction of the architectural history of this period; (Melfi 2007b, 290–94). On the various reconstructions of the 'cella' and problems associated with each, see Pfaff 2003, 125–27.

[13] For Epidauros: Lambrinoudakis 2002, 214–19, fig. 2 and 3. Because of cuttings possibly for couches and a table, and a water channel running around the perimeter of the room, Lambrinoudakis interprets the building as a place for ritual dining. For Athens, see Hallager (2006, 40), reporting the work of Michaelis Lefantzis and Jesper Jensen; also Lefantzis and Jensen 2009. Lefantzis and Jensen interpret these foundations as belonging to the first temple of Asklepios.

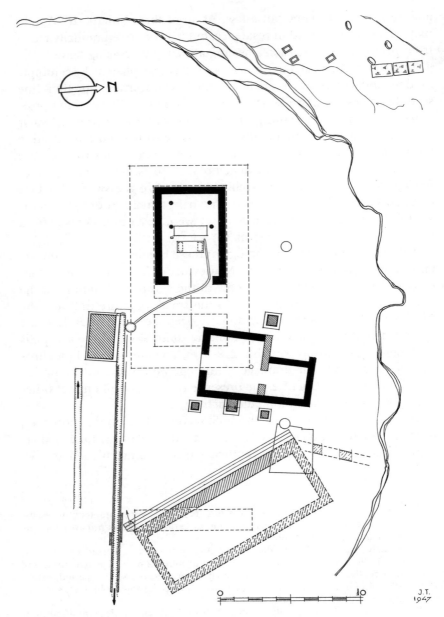

Fig. 3.1. Restored plan of the early sanctuary of Asklepios.
(Roebuck 1951, fig. 2)

L-shaped building created by two perpendicular stoas (Building E) with an ash altar in its courtyard, and a nearby well next to another small stoa, comprise the major architectural features of the early sanctuary.[14] But by this point Epidauros was receiving visitors from around the Greek world, as indicated both by its famous healing inscriptions that record the towns from which the sick traveled for cures,[15] and by Pindar's odes that allude to panhellenic festivals held here in honor of Asklepios.[16] And it is important to note that you do not need much in the way of architecture to worship Asklepios: water for purification and drinking, an altar for sacrifices, and a place for the sick to incubate, although incubation could well take place outside in the open air.

As at Epidauros, it would be a mistake to assume that the modest architecture of Corinth's Asklepieion signals a struggling cult. Quite the opposite is true, as indicated by this sanctuary's most famous remains: over 100 terracotta anatomical votives, most of them life-size, recovered from closed deposits in the bedrock. These votives date from the period between the last quarter of the 5th and the late 4th century.[17] They are marvelous: arms, legs, ears, eyes, heads, feet, hands, breasts, penises, and more (fig. 3.2).[18] We know from literary and epigraphic sources that Asklepios typically treated conditions like blindness, deafness, paralysis, infertility, gout, headaches, even baldness and insomnia. Such ailments can be mapped easily onto these anatomical votives—an eye perhaps indicating blindness, a breast or penis infertility, an arm or leg paralysis, a foot gout, and so on. The sick would

---

[14] Lambrinoudakis 2002, 216–19. The Asklepieion on the Athenian acropolis, too, has rather simple architecture in the 5th century; Riethmüller 2005, 1.241–73, with references; Lefantzis and Jensen 2009.

[15] The healing inscriptions, IG IV² 1.121–24, are translated and discussed by LiDonnici 1995. LiDonnici (76–82) argues convincingly that although the earliest healing accounts were inscribed in the 4th century BCE, some reflect events that took place in the 5th. The earliest inscriptions record visitors from Pellene, Athens, and Thessaly.

[16] Pind. Nem. 3.84, 5.52 and 5.95–97, Isth. 8.68; also schol. ad Nem. 5.95–96, Nem. 3.84. Not all scholars agree that these games had ties to the cult of Asklepios. For discussion: Edelstein and Edelstein 1945, 2.208–09. However, given that Nem. 3 mentions contests at Epidauros as well as Asklepios himself (lines 53–55), it is likely that Asklepios was linked with the Epidaureia just as Herakles (appearing in lines 20–26) was linked with the Nemean games (which are mentioned along with the Epidaureia at line 84).

[17] Roebuck 1951, 111–51, 154.

[18] My thanks to Guy Sanders, Director of the Corinth Excavations, and Ioulia Tzonou-Herbst, Curator, for allowing me to examine the anatomical votives as they were being prepared for a new exhibition in the Corinth museum.

Fig. 3.2. Anatomical votives from the Asklepieion. Photo by Brent Nongbri.

have dedicated these to Asklepios either in request of or thanks for healing. Most are pierced by holes for suspension from a ceiling, or, more often, from walls, perhaps the walls of the so-called cella.[19]

Anatomical votives are a very common dedication in Asklepieia but appear also in the sanctuaries of other Greek and Roman gods. This is an important reminder that just about every god in antiquity had the ability to heal and was worshipped as a healer.[20] I imagine most members of the Corinthian pantheon at one time or another were petitioned for healing. In this regard, the Asklepieion of the 5th and 4th centuries at Corinth is fascinating because it corresponds to the formative period of Asklepios cult generally—that is, the period when Asklepios began to edge out other divine healers in the Greek world. But why did Asklepios cult in particular experience this success now?

Asklepios had been known as a healer since Homer; he appears as a mortal doctor in the *Iliad*.[21] But it is not until about 500 BCE, at Epidauros, that we find any evidence for a cult of Asklepios. During the 5th century, the cult spread to places like Corinth, Aegina, and Athens, and in the 4th, spread rapidly across the Greek world.[22] According to one estimate, as many as 200 Asklepieia were founded at this time.[23]

What was going on in the 5th century that made Asklepios, of all healing gods, so attractive? I have argued elsewhere that his appeal derives in large part from his close association with doctors.[24] Asklepios

---

[19] Pfaff (2003, 125–27) argues convincingly, contra Roebuck, that this building was roofed. Pfaff notes, however, that its wide entrance remains difficult to explain. It occurs to me that if the building were one of the primary loci for displaying anatomical votives, a wide doorway would maximize light without interrupting wall space for windows.

[20] For anatomical votives in the ancient Greek world: van Straten 1981, 100–01; Forsén 1996. In Italic cults, too, there was a strong tradition of dedicating anatomical votives; Glinister 2006, with references; Turfa 2006, 72–75; also the contributions by Edlund-Berry, Glinister, and Turfa to *Archiv für Religionsgeschichte* 8 (2006).

[21] Hom. *Il.* 2.729–733, 4.193–94, 4.218–19, 11.517–18. There is no mention in Homer that Apollo is the father of Asklepios. On the mythological tradition of Asklepios: Edelstein and Edelstein 1945, 1.1–122 and 2.1–76; Riethmüller 2005, 1.32–54, with references.

[22] Asklepios arrived in Athens in 420/19 BCE, as documented by the inscription of the Telemachos monument celebrating the god's arrival (*SEG* 25.226). His cult on Aegina is mentioned in Aristophanes's *Wasps* of 422 BCE.

[23] 'Epidauros,' *Princeton Encyclopedia of Classical Sites*, 311–14. The problem with estimates like this is determining exactly which cults of Asklepios are being included in the estimate and upon what evidence the dating is made.

[24] Wickkiser 2008, chapters 1–3. On Greek doctors and medical practice, see Nutton 2005; and Majno 1975, which, although not as recent, is a lively and well-illustrated look at ancient medicine in the Mediterranean and the middle and far east.

occupies an unusual position in the Greco-Roman pantheon: the son of Apollo and a mortal woman, he was trained as a physician by the centaur Cheiron and healed the sick, even bringing the dead back to life until his grandfather Zeus, angered at Asklepios's (mis)use of this power, struck him with a thunderbolt and cast him into Hades. There he remained until Zeus brought him out of Hades and raised him to the position of a god.[25]

What sets the mythic tradition of Asklepios apart from other Greco-Roman gods is his singularity of function. As a deified doctor, his efforts centered solely on healing, whereas other healing gods like his father Apollo served a multitude of functions in addition to curing the sick. Moreover, the earliest sources for his healing describe him employing medical techniques. And so, for example, an early inscription at Epidauros records a cure in which the god performs surgery:

> Arata of Laconia, dropsy....Her mother slept here on her behalf, and she sees a dream. It seemed that the god cut off her daughter's head and hung her body with the neck towards the ground. When a lot of fluid had run out, he untied her body and put her head back on her neck...(*IG* IV² 122.1–5)

Admittedly, surgery in this account is in fact decapitation, and no Greek doctor as far as we know was decapitating his patients; but Asklepios, the doctor-*god* could take a technique like surgery to a superhuman level. It is also remarkable that this account describes Asklepios draining fluid from the girl's body. This corresponds to humoral theory, a cornerstone of Hippocratic medicine. According to this theory, sickness is due to an excess of humor, or fluid, in the body, and so the excess must be removed to restore balance and thereby also health. Techniques like surgery and humoral rebalance differ considerably from the methods of other divine healers, like Apollo, who heal in inexplicable ways, often by their mere presence or touch. Many other accounts of Asklepios's cures, by contrast, have the god applying drugs, such as salves to the eyes, administering purges, excising weapons lodged in difficult places in the body, like the lungs, and so on.

My contention is that, because medicine itself was becoming a more popular form of healing in the 5th century—the period of the earliest

---

[25] The testimonia for Asklepios raising the dead and for his subsequent punishment are collected in Edelstein and Edelstein 1945, vol. 1, T. 1 (esp. lines 54–58), 97, 99–117.

surviving medical treatises and of the famous physician Hippocrates—consequently the cult of the *doctor*-god Asklepios caught on. Over the course of the 5th and 4th centuries, Asklepios cornered a prosperous niche in the ancient healthcare industry that served him well even when other divine healers blazed onto the medical marketplace.[26] And again, it is this modest-looking architectural phase of the sanctuary at Corinth that corresponds to the widespread surge in the popularity of Asklepios cult. Moreover, by virtue of being one of the oldest known Asklepieia anywhere, this sanctuary contains vital, if as yet inscrutable, clues to the early worship of Asklepios.

The Hellenistic Asklepieion

The next major phase of the sanctuary is Hellenistic. It begins at the end of the 4th century with large-scale renovation, which is in keeping with other early sanctuaries of Asklepios such as at (again) Epidauros and Athens.[27] At Corinth, the archaic and classical buildings were razed, the votives carefully buried, and the sanctuary expanded now to cover two levels (fig. 3.3–3.4). The upper level—to the east on both plans—was dominated by a large peristyle court, some of whose colonnades perhaps accommodated the sick and displayed votives.[28] In the center of the court, over the foundations of the earlier cella-like structure, stood a Doric temple, not much larger than its predecessor.[29] A ramp, open to the sky, connected the upper and lower levels.[30] The ramp is an unusual feature for an Asklepieion and may have been used for processions.

---

[26] Other divine healers, like Amphiaraos at Oropos, seem to have adopted Asklepios's methods as a way to attract more patients; Wickkiser 2008, ch. 3.

[27] For Epidauros: Burford 1969; Riethmüller 2005, 1.279–324, with references; Melfi 2007b, 23–63. For Athens: Riethmüller 2005, 1.250–273, with references; Melfi 2007b, 313–433.

[28] The Doric temple measures 6.99 × 13.60 m at stylobate level; the earlier 'cella' measures 5.22 × 7.48 m. Roebuck (1951, 42–64) argues that the rooms behind the west colonnade, as well as the the north colonnade itself, were used for incubation. The colonnades to the west, south, and probably also to the east (no traces remain of an east colonnade, but Roebuck restores one to complete what he calls the architectural border of the precinct, 64) are too shallow to easily accommodate the sick (ca. 0.6–0.7 m deep), and thus are more likely to have been used for displaying dedications.

[29] Roebuck 1951, 30–39. Very few blocks remain from the superstructure, and only one block from the entire building remains in situ (a foundation block for the ramp leading to the temple's east entrance).

[30] Roebuck 1951, 65–84. The walls of the ramp were decorated with light blue stucco, traces of which remain visible to this day.

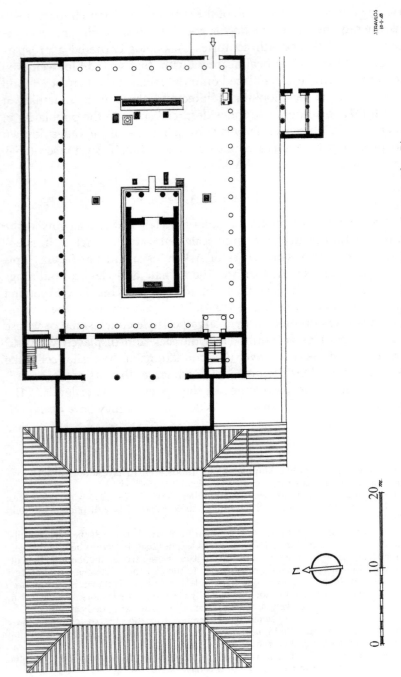

Fig. 3.3. Restoration of the Hellenistic Asklepieion. (Roebuck 1951, Plan B)

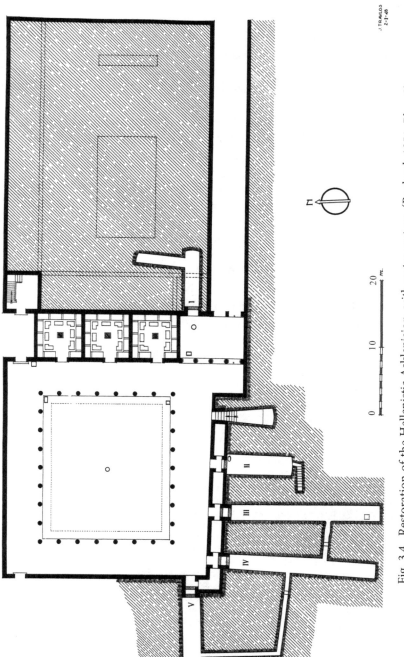

Fig. 3.4. Restoration of the Hellenistic Asklepieion, with water system. (Roebuck 1951, Plan C)

On the lower level stood another peristyle court (fig. 3.4). Behind the east colonnade ran a series of three dining rooms, a common feature of Asklepieia.[31] At the south end of this colonnade, moreover, was a springhouse fed by a subterranean aqueduct, while behind the south colonnade stood a series of five reservoirs cut into the rock and fed from a combination of surface runoff and another, shallower subterranean aqueduct.[32]

Roebuck called this lower level Lerna spring, taking his cue from Pausanias who said that the Asklepieion stood near Lerna (Paus. 2.4.5), but some scholars now place Lerna farther west where another spring, the so-called Fountain of the Lamps, has been excavated.[33] Regardless of its name, it seems that this lower level should be considered an integral part of the Hellenistic Asklepieion and its rituals. The ramp connecting the two levels and the combined dining room (lower level) / abaton (upper level) structure form a clear architectural link between the two.

The most puzzling feature of the Hellenistic phase of the Asklepieion is the extensive provision for water. Not only are there five reservoirs and a spring on the lower level, but on the upper level there is a well near the entrance to the sanctuary, and behind the west colonnade is a room with a waterproof basin equipped with a sophisticated system of in- and out-take pipes, into which one could descend by narrow steps. While water is a common feature in Asklepieia, especially in the form of wells or springs, this latter type of structure is unusual.[34] Perhaps it was used for purification or cures. Nor is this the limit of the provisions for water at this sanctuary; at some later date, a fountain house was added at the top of the ramp.[35]

---

[31] The dining rooms in this Asklepieion are similar in dimension to those of the Hellenistic Asklepieia at Athens and Epidauros (in the SE corner of the Banqueting Hall), and also to the dining rooms of the sanctuary of Demeter and Kore on the lower north slope of Acrocorinth. For comparison of the dining rooms of the Asklepieia at Corinth, Epidauros, and Athens: Tomlinson 1969. On the dining rooms of the sanctuary of Demeter and Kore at Corinth, which date to the 6th through 4th centuries BCE: Bookidis and Stroud 1997, 393–421.

[32] On these water sources, see Landon 1994, 247–64.

[33] Wiseman 1979, 511; Landon 2003, 48, n. 22.

[34] Roebuck 1951, 46–51; Landon 1994, 333–35. Roebuck refers to this structure as a lustral basin; I have visited the Asklepieion with scholars of religion who have remarked in passing that the structure resembles a *mikveh* (a basin used for Jewish ritual bathing). On the availability and use of water at Asklepieia, see Graf 1992, 178–81; Boudon 1994; Ginouvès 1994.

[35] Roebuck 1951, 69–74.

This is the most elaborate waterworks of any Asklepieion yet discovered, and raises many questions about the need for and use of water here. For instance, did the reservoirs, well, and spring serve the needs primarily of the cult, or did people living in the area use the water for their day to day lives? As Mark Landon has shown, a whole series of springs runs along the north wall of Corinth, so there seems to have been no lack of water in the immediate area.[36] If the water served the needs primarily of the cult, then for what exactly was it used? Water for purification, bathing, drinking, and also probably for certain cures (such as Aelius Aristides's famous plunges into cold water at the request of Asklepios, Aristid. *Or.* 47–51 *passim*) would be expected at all Asklepieia, but, as noted above, no other Asklepieion—even at Pergamon and Epidauros, which were both much larger sanctuaries—had such copious provisions for water.[37] Must we therefore conclude that such provisions necessarily reflect a copious supply of water? Betsey Robinson has pointed out to me that the variety and number of water sources may have been designed to compensate for a lack of water in the area, especially in the 4th century when Greece seems to have been hit hard by drought.[38] There is yet another possibility, moreover. Perhaps the extensive water installations were due not to a need for water by the Asklepieion and immediate area but were designed instead as an ostentatious display of the very abundance of water at Corinth in general and in this area in particular.[39]

Any answer to these questions should also take into account the fact that the construction of the system of reservoirs running to the Asklepieion belongs to a larger trend of hydraulic installations in Corinth in the 5th and 4th centuries BCE, including renovations to Peirene fountain and the construction probably of the fountain

---

[36] Landon 2003. Roebuck (1951, 106) remarks that, "It seems unlikely that all this water was necessary for the Asklepieion," and suggests instead that this was the "public water supply for this quarter of the city." However, the multiple provisions for water mapped by Landon across this area beg us to revisit the question.

[37] Aelius Aristides often plunged into icy rivers and sacred wells (the latter at the Asklepieion in Pergamon) at the recommendation of Asklepios, and sometimes in direct contradiction to the recommendation of his doctors. Aristides devotes much of *Or.* 48 to describing "a catalogue of wintry, divine, and very strange baths" (*Or.* 48.24, trans. by C. A. Behr).

[38] Camp (1982) discusses evidence for drought and subsequent famine in the 4th century.

[39] My thanks to Steve Friesen for this suggestion.

of Glauke, all three of which rely on reservoir systems.[40] Although an explanation for the nature of the waterworks at the Asklepieion remains as yet elusive, the sanctuary serves as another example of the many ways by which well-watered Corinth lived up to its epithet.[41]

The Roman Asklepieion

Between 146 when Mummius came through Corinth and the founding of the Roman colony in 44 BCE, the sanctuary suffered some damage, whether through intention or neglect. The colonnades along the south, west, and east sides of the lower court were destroyed and seem never to have been rebuilt.[42] The ramp, moreover, was used now for wheeled traffic, and so the sanctuary became a thoroughfare of sorts.[43]

Beginning shortly after the founding of the Roman colony some of the Hellenistic structures, especially on the upper level, were repaired. The biggest architectural change in the Roman period concerns the ramp. In the 1st century CE, a long, narrow building of uncertain function was constructed over it and thus put the ramp out of use.[44] The lower court may have remained accessible from the upper via stairs to the north, and most of the reservoirs and the dining rooms were reused in the Roman period, but the relationship between the lower and upper levels undoubtedly changed.[45] This change may reflect differences in the worship of Asklepios at Corinth between the Greek and Roman periods. Given that Roman Corinth was founded by Romans,[46] we ought to take into account Gil Renberg's discussion about the lack of any secure evidence for incubation at any Asklepieion in the Latin West, including the god's famous sanctuary on Tiber Island in

---

[40] For the architectural development of the Peirene and Glauke fountains and their relation to other architectural and cultural developments in Corinth, see Robinson 2005. My thanks to Betsey Robinson for sharing with me her thoughts on the Asklepieion's waterworks and on water supplies in Corinth more generally, and for sharing portions of a draft of her forthcoming monograph on Peirene.

[41] Well-watered Corinth: Simonides 720–723 (Page); Plut. *Mor.* 870e; [Dio Chrys.] *Or.* 37 (now attributed to Favorinus); Paus. 2.3.5.

[42] Roebuck 1951, 90.

[43] Roebuck 1951, 82–84; Gebhard and Dickie 2003, 269.

[44] Roebuck 1951, 77–82.

[45] The reconstruction of the north stairway is largely conjectural; Roebuck 1951, 42 and 51. On the use of the lower level in the Roman period, see Roebuck 1951, 54–55 (dining rooms), 91 (court), 99 (spring house), 106 (reservoirs).

[46] On the early colonists, see the contribution of Benjamin Millis to this volume.

Rome.[47] If incubation was not in fact part of Rome's worship of the god, then perhaps the Roman colonists did not incubate at his sanctuary in Corinth, and thus they no longer needed to maintain such ready access to the many facilities afforded by the lower level.

As with the Hellenistic period, almost nothing in the way of votives or inscriptions remains for the Roman period of the cult, with the notable exception of an inscription erected by the city in honor of a doctor and priest of the cult: "The [city] of the Corinthians (hereby honors) Gaius Vibius Euelpistos, the physician, son of Meges (and) priest of Asklepios." This inscription dates to the late 2nd or early 3rd century CE and is valuable for demonstrating both the ongoing popularity of the cult and the continuing ties between doctors and their patron god here at Corinth.[48]

Despite the popularity of Asklepios, we have very little evidence for doctors in Greek and Roman Corinth. Doctors were undoubtedly here, as the Vibius inscription indicates. At least three other inscriptions mention doctors,[49] and there are hints also in literature of doctors practicing at Corinth. Plutarch, for instance, reports that Antiphon, the 5th century orator, came to Corinth and hung his shingle in the agora, claiming to be able to heal those in distress by means of words alone—a sort of proto-psychiatrist. And in the Hippocratic treatise the *Epidemics*, we hear of a doctor who practiced on a patient in Corinth, a certain "eunuch-like son of Scelebreus"—the doctor inserted pepper into the patient's nose to relieve a fever.[50] Galen, physician to Marcus Aurelius, writes about studying medicine under a certain Numisianus in Corinth as a young man, and he later traveled through the city, but

---

[47] Renberg 2006. On the Tiber Island sanctuary, see below.

[48] *Corinth* VIII.3, no. 206: Γάιον Οὐίβι[ον] | ἰατρὸν Εὐέλπισ[τον] | Μέγητος [Ἀ]σκλ[ηπιοῦ] | ἱερέα [------] | ἡ Κορινθ[ίων πόλις]. Trans. by J. H. Kent. Kent dates the inscription to the last quarter of the 2nd century or first quarter of the 3rd. Michael Walbank (personal communication) suggests that the letter forms are more likely to date to the last quarter of the 2nd century.

[49] My thanks to Michael Walbank for bringing these to my attention, discussing them with me, and providing references. Two refer to physicians named Trophimos. The first, *IG* IV 365, Walbank (personal communication) dates to the 2nd or 3rd century CE. The second, published by Pallas in *Praktika* 1965, 163, no. 2, Walbank (personal communication) dates to the late 4th century CE, a century later than Pallas dates it, and believes that it refers to a descendant of the earlier physician Trophimos. The third refers to a physician named Thrasippos (*Corinth* VIII.3, no. 300), which Walbank (personal communication) dates to the 4th or early 5th century.

[50] Hipp. *Ep.* 4.40. The treatise seems to date to the late 5th or early 4th century; W. D. Smith 1994, 10; Jouanna 1999, 388–90.

there is no evidence that he later practiced there.[51] Much as the paucity
of literary evidence for Asklepios would lead us, mistakenly, to believe
that Asklepios had a very limited presence in the city, we should not
assume from the meager evidence for doctors that they were scarce in
Corinth; rather, given the prominence of Asklepios, doctors probably
also flourished here.[52]

To return to the Asklepieion, all its major phases pose a frustrating paradox, as Roebuck observes: in the pre-Hellenistic period, the
architecture is difficult to interpret, but we have a wealth of votives;
by contrast, in the Hellenistic and Roman periods the architecture
is somewhat easier to understand, but the votives scant. And so in
all periods we must rely heavily on analogy to other Asklepieia to
determine the nature of this particular cult. Such assumptions can,
of course, be misleading. Moreover, there remain major gaps in our
knowledge of this cult. For instance, we simply do not know its origin.
Was the early cult founded from Epidauros, as were so many other
cults of Asklepios? Many scholars assume so because of the proximity
of Epidauros to Corinth, but Trikka in Thessaly was another exporter
of the cult and may have had the oldest sanctuary of the god.[53] Moreover, there were still other foundation traditions: at nearby Titane,
for instance, Pausanias reports that the sanctuary was founded by a
grandson of Asklepios (Paus. 2.11.5–7); this tradition is in fact common to other Asklepieia in the Peloponnese.[54] These differing foundation stories almost certainly reflect differences among the various
cults—differences in ritual and administration, as well as in the politi-

---

[51] Galen, *AA* 9 (II.217–18 Kühn). For discussion of Galen and others who traveled
through and/or commented on the landscape of Corinth: Pettegrew 2006, chapters
2–3. Galen studied under Numisianus also in Alexandria.

[52] Moreover, tools found in excavations around the ancient city may have served
as medical instruments; Davidson 1952, 181, and no. 1318–27. These include "ear and
unguent spoons" as Davidson tentatively labels them (note the range of function). For
the difficulty of identifying knives, spatulas, and the like as strictly medical: Wickkiser
2006, 14–15.

[53] For a list of cults reported by ancient sources to have been founded from Epidauros: Edelstein and Edelstein 1945, 2.238–42. The cults at Gerenia in Messenia and
at Kos were said to have been founded from Trikka: Str. 8.4.4, Herodas 2.97. In the
mythic tradition, Trikka and Epidauros both claimed to be the birthplace of Asklepios;
for sources, see Edelstein and Edelsetin 1945, vol. 1, T. 10–20. Strabo also states that
the sanctuary of Asklepios at Trikka is the oldest of the god's sanctuaries (9.5.17).

[54] For example, see Argos (Paus. 2.23.4). According to Pausanias, Asklepios's son
Machaon, as well as his grandsons, had cultic ties to many places in the Peloponnese
including Eua, Gerenia, and Pharae (Paus. 2.38.6, 3.26.9, 4.3.2, 4.30.3).

cal allegiances of the various city-states. Moreover, what happened to Apollo when Asklepios arrived at the sanctuary? Can we be sure the 100-plus anatomical votives were dedicated to Asklepios rather than to Apollo?[55] And when exactly did Asklepios arrive here? Can we be sure that the presence of Asklepios here postdates his presence at Epidauros?[56] The sanctuary continues to hold its mysteries; however, the evidence assembled here indicates that there were important differences between the Greek and Roman facilities and cultic practices.

Other Evidence for Asklepios in Corinth

Apart from his sanctuary and its remains, there are at least two other notable sources for Asklepios in Roman Corinth. Several Corinthian coins minted in the 2nd and early 3rd century CE depict the god (see fig. 6.21 in this volume) and may reflect increased concern over health due to a plague that struck the Roman Empire during the reign of Marcus Aurelius.[57] Concern about this same plague is evident also at Epidauros in a series of 2nd century building projects financed perhaps in anticipation of the plague reaching mainland Greece, as Chrysanthos Kanellopoulos has explored.[58] Another type of material evidence for Asklepios from outside the Asklepieion are two statuettes of the god recovered from recent excavation of a Roman house just southeast of the Forum that was destroyed in the mid-to-late 4th century CE. Lea Stirling, who has published the statuettes, observes that

---

[55] Most scholars assume that anatomical votives continued to be dedicated here in the Hellenistic and Roman periods, although there is no evidence for them. Some have even argued that Paul's use of bodily metaphors in 1 Cor 12:12–31 was influenced by anatomical votives displayed at the Asklepieion; Hill 1980; Murphy-O'Connor 2002 [= 1983], 161–67.

[56] If the Asklepieion at Trikka is indeed older than that at Epidauros, as Strabo claims (9.5.17), then it is possible that Asklepios came to Corinth from Trikka, or even elsewhere, before arriving at Epidauros. Farnell (1921, 249) discusses the possibility that both Corinth and Sikyon had cults of Asklepios before Epidauros did.

[57] BMC Corinth, no. 620, 638, 671 (dating to the time of L. Verus, Commodus, and Plautilla, respectively). In no. 620 and 671, Asklepios appears alongside Hygieia. I thank Aileen Ajootian for bringing these to my attention. For discussion of the plague, see Gilliam 1961; see also Duncan-Jones 1996. On the connection between these coins and the plague, see also the contribution to this volume by Mary Walbank. My thanks to Mary Walbank for discussing these coins with me.

[58] Kanellopoulos 2000, 121–24. Melfi (2007a, 28) believes that the renovations at Epidauros were part of a larger phenomenon of second-century renovation of Asklepieia driven by innovations in the cult, such as performance of sacred songs that required enlarged performance spaces.

they were found together along with statuettes of other divinities in a
room that may have been a domestic shrine at the time the house was
destroyed.[59]

These statuettes and coins, together with the evidence from the long-
lived sanctuary of Asklepios, indicate that his cult at Corinth prospered
through plagues and other health crises until at least the early 5th century CE, despite stiff competition from new healers including Jesus of
Nazareth. By the 5th century, the cult seems to have been in decline
or transition, as suggested by destruction within the sanctuary. During
the 6th century, Christian burials begin to appear inside the sanctuary.[60] Although a series of decrees issued in the late 4th and early 5th
century outlawed pagan cults, there is yet another obvious reason that
the Jesus cult would ultimately eclipse that of Asklepios.[61] Asklepios
typically treated chronic rather than fatal ailments and, according to
mythic tradition, was prohibited by his grandfather Zeus from bringing individuals back to life.[62] The Christian message about Jesus thus
promised a type of cure that Asklepios could not; it promised a cure
for death.

Asklepios in the Early Roman Colony

In order to explore why the sanctuary of Asklepios was rebuilt soon
after the founding of the Roman colony, I would like to move back in
time to the late first century BCE. At least four sanctuaries within the
walls of Greek Corinth were renewed by Roman Corinth: the Archaic
Temple of Apollo in the forum area, the Sanctuary of Demeter and
Kore on the north slope of Acrocorinth, the Sanctuary of Aphrodite
atop Acrocorinth, and the Asklepieion.[63] The Asklepieion, moreover,
seems to have been renovated relatively early in the life of the new
colony. Coins found in a deposit associated with the cleaning and

---

[59] Stirling 2008. My thanks to Lea Stirling for sharing with me an advance draft
of her article. Stirling dates the Asklepios statuettes to the 2nd, and to the 3rd or 4th
centuries CE, respectively. On the *domus* and related finds: Sanders 2005, 420–29.

[60] See n. 3 above. Moreover, I concur with the view expressed by Sanders (2005,
430, n. 17), that the arrival of Christian burial need not signify the end of pagan worship at the Asklepieion.

[61] These decrees are collected in the Theodosian Code validated in 438 CE. For
discussion of the Code, editions, and further references: Matthews 2000.

[62] On the treatment of chronic rather than fatal ailments by Asklepios: Wickkiser
2006.

[63] All four are discussed, with references, in Bookidis 2005.

repair of the upper level indicate that renovations took place sometime after 32 BCE.[64] Furthermore, an inscribed epistyle block from the
temple apparently lists a donor for the renovations, a certain Marcus
Antonius Milesius.[65] John Kent dates this inscription to about 25 BCE,
and both Kent and Roebuck view the period of peace shortly after
Actium as the most likely for the renovations, which would mean that
the sanctuary was rebuilt within about twenty years of the founding
of the colony.[66]

We may now return to the question, why this early interest in
Asklepios? As I suggested earlier, the answer seems obvious: the residents of Roman Corinth, just as of any other town, wanted to secure
the talents of a renowned healer like Asklepios. Besides, there was
a temple already here, in fairly decent condition; all it needed was
repairs. So economic and other practical incentives likely governed the
quick refurbishment.[67] But the appeal of Asklepios at Corinth almost
certainly extended beyond physical health, especially given that the
sanctuary was refounded within a Roman freedman colony during the
reign of Augustus.

Asklepios and Rome

James Walters has emphasized in his discussion of Roman Corinth
that a Roman colony is in many respects a mini-Rome that mirrors

---

[64] Roebuck 1951, 38. Eleven coins were found in a small deposit within an offering
box, and may have been swept there when the sanctuary was cleaned and repaired.
According to Roebuck, the coins date from the period 146–32 BCE.

[65] *Corinth* VIII.3, no. 311; also Roebuck 1951, 39. Roebuck (39) observes that since
the block is broken, and presumably would have continued across the entire length
of the epistyle, another three or four donor names may be supplied. The names are
inscribed in a coat of stucco that was applied at the time of the repairs and are picked
out with the addition of red paint. At some later date, another coat of stucco was
applied to the block, which in turn concealed these names. Both Kent and Roebuck
caution against reading this later act as an instance of *damnatio memoriae*.

[66] *Corinth* VIII.3, 21. Kent gives no reason for the date, but it may be that he is
following Roebuck who dates the renovations by the numismatic evidence mentioned
above. It is important to note, however, that Roebuck (1951, 39) is very tentative about
the date of the renovations: "possibly…in the period shortly after Actium, when more
peaceful conditions afforded an opportunity of building." We need to be careful in
assuming that this sanctuary was thrown back together as soon as the Romans walked
on the scene, as some of the literature on Corinth would have us believe. The best we
can say is that the coins gives us a *terminus post quem* of 32 BCE.

[67] Williams 1987, 32–34. Bookidis (2005, 161) also notes that the canonical architecture of the Hellenistic period of the sanctuary, which would have looked familiar
to the colonists, may have increased its appeal for reuse.

the religious institutions of the city of Rome.[68] The cult of Asklepios at Corinth fits this model well since Rome itself had an active Asklepieion on Tiber Island.[69] But more importantly, Asklepios (or Aesculapius, as the Romans called him) was a popular figure in 1st century Roman culture.[70] The story of Asklepios in the guise of a snake journeying by boat from Epidauros to Rome to cure a plague of the early 3rd century BCE—the foundation myth for the Roman cult of Asklepios—appeared in Livy at this time and shortly afterward in Ovid and Valerius Maximus.[71] The popularity of this story, moreover, is reflected in the very architecture of the Tiber Island. At some point probably in the 1st century with the rebuilding of the adjacent bridges, the southern end of Tiber Island was encased in travertine to resemble a ship's prow, and Asklepios and his serpent-entwined staff were carved in relief.[72]

Given that Asklepios had sparked popular imagination in 1st-century Rome, it should come as no surprise that the colonists at Roman Corinth likewise wanted to honor this god. But this raises another

---

[68] J. Walters 2005.

[69] Ancient testimonia for the cult of Aesculapius in Rome are collected in Edelstein and Edelstein 1945, vol. 1, T. 845–61. For further sources and references, see Riethmüller 2005, vol. 2, no. 586; for a detailed analysis of Asklepios cult within Rome, see Renberg 2006–07. The rituals and architecture of the Asklepieion on Tiber Island are poorly understood, in large part because so little remains of the sanctuary.

[70] We do not know whether the Corinthians ever referred to their god as "Aesculapius". The only inscriptional evidence from the Roman period that mentions the god's name is written in Greek, and there the god is called Asklepios (Ἀσκληπιός; Corinth VIII.3, no. 63, 206). The only literary evidence for the cult in the Roman period (or any period, for that matter) is Pausanias, who consistently refers to the gods of Corinth by their Greek names, even deities known to the Corinthians by their Roman names (for example, he seems to refer to the Roman goddess Venus in the Forum—whose name Venus survives in an inscription found in her temple there—by the Greek name Aphrodite; Paus. 2.2.8).

[71] Liv. 10.31.8–9, 10.47.6–7, per.11, 29.11.1; Ov. Met. 15.622–744; Val. Max. 1.8.2. For these and other sources on the importation: Edelstein and Edelstein 1945, vol. 1, T. 845–854. The Asklepieion at Epidauros had been pillaged by Sulla earlier in the first century BCE (Paus. 9.7.5). Thus when Livy reports (45.27–28) that L. Aemilius Paulus visited Epidauros in 167 BCE, he comments that the Epidauros of his own day "is rich now in the traces of pillaged dedications" (nunc vestigiis revolsorum donorum...dives), whereas at the time of Paulus it was rich with the dedications themselves (tum donis dives erat).

[72] A coin minted by L. Rubrius Dossenus ca. 87 BCE may also refer to the arrival of Aesculapius: its reverse depicts a temple and an altar encircled by a snake, beneath which appears the prow of a ship. Crawford 1974, 348/6; Penn 1994, 121–22. Two medallions minted by Antoninus Pius in the 2nd century CE depict similar scenes; one is inscribed AESCULAPIUS and thus clearly refers to the sanctuary on Tiber Island. See 'Tiber, Tiberinus,' LIMC, no. 23, and 21d; Penn 1994, 37–38. On the travertine embellishment of the southern end of Tiber Island, see Brucia 1990, 18–23.

question: which Asklepios did the colonists establish in their new city? Did they reinstate the Asklepios of Greek Corinth (and it is important to remember in this regard that we do not know whence this earlier Asklepios came)? Or did the colonists import the Roman god Aesculapius, who was himself a Greek import from Epidauros, as the stories circulating in Rome at the time consistently emphasize? It is noteworthy that Pausanias, in his book on Corinth and the Argolid, discusses the foundation of Asklepios's sanctuaries at Sikyon, Titane, Epidauros, and Argos, but not at Corinth. Given the reluctance of Pausanias to discuss Roman artifacts and monuments and his coordinate fervor to discuss things Greek, his silence on this point may reflect that the god of Roman Corinth came most immediately from Rome.[73] And so when Pausanias declares that, "None of the Corinthians of antiquity still live in Corinth, but colonists sent out by the Romans" (Paus. 2.1.2), he may well be including many of the gods among the "Corinthians of antiquity."

Whatever his origin, Asklepios arrived at the Roman colony of Corinth with some hefty cultural baggage because for any Roman of the late first century BCE, Asklepios had strong associations with the *gens Julia*. Asklepios's pedigree alone is telling: he is the son of Apollo, one of the principal divine patrons of Julius Caesar and Augustus, as Stefan Weinstock has studied in detail.[74] But more than that, Romans were conflating the father-son relationships of Julius Caesar and Augustus with Apollo and Asklepios. No one does this more brilliantly than Ovid at the close of the *Metamorphoses*. Here Ovid moves deftly from a lengthy and delightfully detailed story of the arrival of Asklepios in Rome to discussion of Julius Caesar as a god (*Met.* 15.622–870). The two are immediately juxtaposed, and both call attention to father-son relationships. In the story of Asklepios, when the plague hits Rome, envoys travel first to Delphi to consult Apollo. But Apollo tells them, that it is not he (Apollo) whom they need but his son (*Met.* 15.638–639). Only then do the envoys journey on to Epidauros. Ovid is the only source for the importation of Asklepios

---

[73] Sikyon: Paus. 2.10.3; Titane: Paus. 2.11.5; Argos: Paus. 2.23.4. Pausanias's descriptions of Sikyon and Titane, moreover, immediately follow that of Corinth. On the avoidance of *res Romanae* in Pausanias: Hutton 2005a, 296–97 and 316–17, with references.

[74] Weinstock 1971; also Gosling 1992 and J. Miller 2004. Gagé 1955 is the crucial study on Apollo in Rome.

to include the visit to Apollo at Delphi; his narrative thereby invites association between Apollo and Julius Caesar on the one hand, and Asklepios and Augustus on the other. Similarly, when Ovid discusses Julius Caesar, he proclaims immediately that Caesar's greatest achievement was siring a son as noble as Augustus (*Met.* 15.750–51), and he continues to play with these familial relationships in the remaining 150 lines of the poem.[75]

Certainly Ovid was not alone in making these associations. Another story circulated at the time that Augustus's mother had become pregnant with him when she incubated at a temple of Apollo; that is, Apollo in the form of a snake penetrated her while she slept at his sanctuary (Suet. *Aug.* 94.4).[76] According to this story, then, Augustus is Apollo's son (just as Asklepios is Apollo's son), in addition to being Caesar's son by adoption. This story also parallels healing accounts from Epidauros that tell of women who had trouble conceiving and were cured by being penetrated by a snake.[77]

All this is to say that it did not take much in Roman imagination to connect the dots from Apollo and Julius Caesar to Asklepios and Augustus. In the wake of Actium, the medical skills of Asklepios would have served as the perfect metaphor for Augustus's skills at healing a state torn apart by decades of civil war.[78] Moreover, I would contend that in Roman Corinth, these associations were at the forefront of the colonists' minds, especially so close in time to Actium. By resurrecting the sanctuary of Asklepios, the colonists were thus honoring not only Asklepios but by extension also the founders of their city: Julius Caesar and, more immediately, Augustus.

This interpretation suits the abundant evidence for imperial worship in Roman Corinth mentioned by Pausanias and teased from the

---

[75] Ovid precedes the story of Asklepios with an appeal to the Muses (*Met.* 15.622–625), the only appeal to the Muses in the entire poem. This clearly marks the last 250 lines of the poem as a unit. On the relation between the stories of Apollo and Asklepios, and Julius Caesar and Augustus, see Wickkiser 1999 and Papaioannou 2006.

[76] See Lorsch (1997) on the tradition of other historical figures conceived through intercourse with a snake.

[77] *IG* IV² 1.122.129–31 (the god came to the woman with a snake, and she had sex with it; she later bore twins); also *IG* IV² 1.122.117–119 (a snake lay upon the woman's stomach; she later bore five children). Both of these accounts date to the late 5th or 4th century BCE.

[78] On the representation of Augustus as a healer of the Roman state in Augustan art and literature, especially via his ties to Apollo: Wickkiser 2005.

archaeological record by scholars like Charles Williams, Mary Walbank and, in this volume, Margaret Laird.[79] From the Caesarian games, to the temples of Apollo and Aphrodite or Venus, the patron goddess of the *gens Julia*, to the many buildings expressly in honor of the Julio-Claudians, the city teemed with monuments and rituals that celebrated the ruling family. The appeal of Asklepios to the early inhabitants of Roman Corinth must be understood in this context.[80]

Moreover, the colonists built his sanctuary not *de novo*, but instead utilized the same site and even restored earlier Greek buildings. This fact seems to reflect the complex negotiations taking place between Greek and Roman traditions.[81] This is most apparent in the name of the donor preserved on the epistyle block of the Asklepios temple: Marcus Antonius Milesius, presumably a local elite. The name Milesius suggests on the one hand that he was Greek, whereas Marcus Antonius suggests he had received Roman citizenship.[82] By pouring his money into refurbishing the sanctuary of Asklepios, Marcus Antonius indicated his allegiance not to Mark Antony, however, but to the winner of Actium, the combatant favored by Apollo, the new healer of the Roman state.[83]

Asklepios and Manumission

Ties between Asklepios and manumission, the practice of granting slaves their freedom, are also likely to have increased the appeal of Asklepios to the residents of this Roman colony in particular. As we

---

[79] Williams 1986 and 1987; Walbank 1996.

[80] In this vein I would also add that David Romano's recent, although controversial, proposal that a racecourse used for the Caesarian games lay north of the Theater and near the Asklepieion would, if correct, only tighten the ties between Asklepios and imperial cult; Romano 2005. On Corinth's agonistic tradition, especially the Caesarian games, as a means of dialogue between the Greek and Roman identities of the colony, see J. Walters 2005, 407–08, with references.

[81] J. Walters 2005, 405.

[82] Roebuck 1951, 39. Roebuck suggests that M. Antonius was a freedman or son of a freedman of Mark Antony, but there is nothing to indicate that this was necessarily so.

[83] There is a close parallel in Rome for a monument that can be interpreted as an expression both of Augustus's clemency (famously touted in his *Res Gestae*) and his role as healer of the state. C. Sosius, partisan of Antony at Actium, began reconstruction of the temple of Apollo Medicus (or "Doctor") at Rome in the late 30s BCE. Octavian pardoned Sosius, and the rebuilt temple was dedicated ultimately on Octavian's birthdate, while its sculpture celebrated Octavian's military exploits rather than those of Sosius; Wickkiser 2005, 279–280. On Apollo's aid at Actium: Gurval 1995.

know from many ancient sources and as discussed in detail by Benjamin Millis in his contribution to this volume, Roman Corinth was dominated by freedmen. Moreover, by the Hellenistic period if not sooner, Asklepios cult sites had become popular loci of manumission. Epigraphic evidence from Epidauros, as well as Amphissa, Elatia, Stiris, Tithoria, Orchomenos, Thespiae, Naupactus, Cheronea, Gonnoi, Trichonion, and Buthrotum, among others, documents numerous instances of so-called sacred manumission in which a slave was sold by his or her master to Asklepios.[84] As a result, the slave, although now technically the property of the god, was effectively manumitted from service to any mortal master.

Sacred manumission is by no means unique to Asklepios; it occurred widely in the Greco-Roman world in cults of Apollo, Athena, Dionysos, Isis, Sarapis, Nemesis, among others, and within Jewish and Christian traditions.[85] The abundance of evidence from Asklepieia, however, suggests a strong tie between Asklepios and manumission, which makes sense inasmuch as both healing and manumission result in radical changes for the individual. That is, healing is a radical change in physical state from sickness to health, whereas manumission is a radical change in status from slave to freedperson. Aside from sacred manumission *per se*, Asklepios had other ties to freedmen. At Rome, for instance, Claudius in the mid 1st century CE granted freedom to any sick slave abandoned at Asklepios's sanctuary on Tiber Island, and his decree may reflect a longer-standing tradition.[86]

The link between Asklepios and manumission is especially evident at the ancient city of Buthrotum, modern Butrint in Albania, as discussed by Milena Melfi.[87] Buthrotum is fascinating for many reasons, not least for its role in Rome's foundation myth. In the *Aeneid*, Aeneas stops at Buthrotum on his way to Italy and visits with Hellanus and Andromache who established Buthrotum after the fall of Troy (Verg.

---

[84] Deissmann 1965, 319–23, with references; Melfi 2007a, 22–23, with references. On manumission generally in the Greek world, see the recent study by Zelnick-Abramovitz 2005. My thanks to Brent Nongbri for the latter reference.

[85] Deissmann 1965, 319–23, with references.

[86] Suet. *Claud.* 25.2. A Roman inscription from the time of Augustus records a dedication by a freedman to Asklepios in thanks for healing (*IGUR* 105; Girone 1998, 154–56, no. V.1), although dedications by freedmen are by no means unique to Asklepios cult.

[87] Melfi 2007a, 22–23, 27.

Aen. 3.291–505).[88] Buthrotum, moreover, is significant in relation to Corinth because it, too, became a Roman colony under Julius Caesar (*Colonia Iulia Buthrotum*) and may have enjoyed long-standing ties with Corinth because of its proximity to the island of Kerkyra (modern Corfu), which was itself a Corinthian colony. It thus affords interesting opportunities for comparative study, especially as publication of the site accelerates.[89]

Like Corinth, Buthrotum lies in the province of Achaia. Unlike Corinth, Buthrotum was founded primarily as a veteran colony, and some of the locals strongly opposed its foundation, as recorded famously in correspondence between Cicero and his friend Atticus who had a villa near Buthrotum (Cic. *Att.* 16.16).[90]

By the Hellenistic period, a large Theater-Asklepieion complex stood at the foot of the south slope of the acropolis (fig. 3.5).[91] That the Theater and cult of Asklepios had a significant relationship is without question: an inscription from the Theater indicates that the latter was constructed with money from the cult.[92] Moreover, between about 230 and 150 BCE, over 400 manumissions to Asklepios were recorded on the parodos walls, seats, and diazoma of the Theater, as well as in a small building dedicated to Asklepios immediately adjacent to the Theater.[93] These manumissions were all inscribed well before the founding of the Roman colony and indicate that Buthrotum at the time was a member, and perhaps even head, of a regional political association, or *koinon*, known as the Praesebes. Other inscriptions from the Theater record various edicts of the Praesebes; the latest inscription dates to the mid 1st century BCE, just before the founding of the colony.

---

[88] Because of Buthrotum's ties to Rome's foundation myth, Mussolini, who viewed himself as a new Aeneas, funded excavations here in the 1930s and 40s; Gilkes 2003. On ties between ancient Rome and Butrint: Hansen 2007.

[89] Numismatic evidence suggests that the colony was refounded by Augustus as *Colonia Augusta Buthrotum*; Hansen 2007, 47.

[90] Epigraphic evidence, however, indicates that civilians, and possibly also freedmen, were part of the original colony; civilians: Deniaux 2007, with references; freedmen: Patterson 2007.

[91] Ugolini 1942, 91–146; Gilkes 2003; Melfi 2007a; and Riethmüller 2005, 2.318, no. 3 for futher references.

[92] Morricone 1986, 172–74.

[93] The manumission inscriptions are published in Morricone 1986; Bozhori and Budina 1966; Cabanes 1974. Melfi 2007a, 29, n. 21 contains further references. The precise date of these inscriptions remains uncertain.

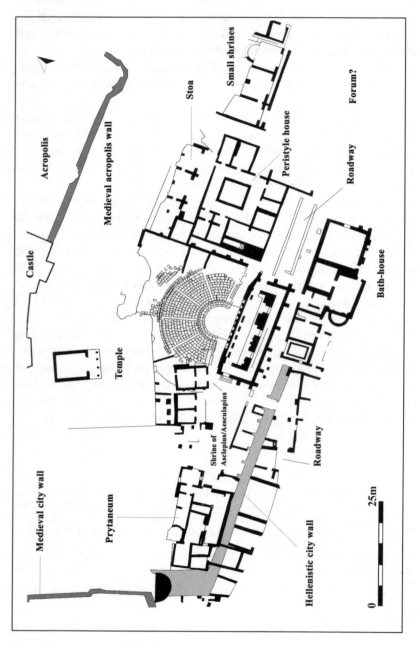

Fig. 3.5. Plan of the Theater-Asklepieion complex at Butrint in the Hellenistic period. (Wilkes 2003, fig. 6.11)

The tradition of inscribing public documents on the Theater apparently stops with the founding of the colony, but it is entirely possible that these documents remained visible for some time afterward and that the role of Asklepios as a manumittor was not to be forgotten, at least in the colony's initial years.[94] Moreover, whether the inscriptions remained visible or not, Romans had long been aware of the Asklepieion and its traditions. As Milena Melfi argues, Roman traders had been visiting Buthrotum possibly as early as the 3rd century BCE, and some of the names recorded in the manumission inscriptions appear to be those of Hellenized Romans.[95] Furthermore, Asklepios remained a prominent figure at Buthrotum even after the founding of the colony, as indicated by coins that depict Asklepios and his attributes. One such coin was minted by the two earliest known *duoviri* of the new colony;[96] another was minted by P. Graecinus ca. 27 BCE–14 CE, whose colleague was a certain Milesius, possibly a relative of M. Antonius Milesius from Corinth who contributed to the restoration of the Asklepieion there at roughly this same time.[97]

At Corinth we have no such records of sacred manumission to any god as far as I know. While there is thus no explicit evidence for sacred manumission at Corinth, the wealth of evidence for this practice from analogous sites raises an important question: might the ties of Asklepios to manumission elsewhere, including Rome, have appealed to the freedmen of Roman Corinth? If so, then the cult of Asklepios complements other links between freedmen and cult activity at Corinth evident, for example, in the benefactions of the Augustales—a group largely of freedmen, whose monuments at Corinth are discussed by Margaret Laird in this volume—and the cult of Ceres, Liber, and Libera, which in the Roman period may have occupied the older sanctuary of

---

[94] A large rebuilding of the Theater sometime in the Roman period would ultimately obscure many of the manumission inscriptions, but the date of these renovations is uncertain and comparative evidence suggests a date in the 2nd century CE; Sear 2003. Melfi (2007a, 26–28) argues for renovations in the 2nd century. A group of Augustan statues found in the Theater was long used to date the Theater renovations to shortly after the founding of the colony, but further analysis has shown that these statues could not have been displayed in the *scaena* of the Theater as Ugolini, their excavator, had thought. Ugolini and Pojani 2003; Gilkes 2003, 178; Pojani 2007.

[95] Melfi (2007a, 27), referencing Cabanes (1976, 399–402). On relations between Rome and Butrint extending well back into the Hellenistic period: Ceka 1999, 12–17.

[96] Coin of P. Dastidius and L. Cornelius, ca. 44–27 BCE: Moorhead, Gjongecaj, and Abdy 2007, 83, no. SF 0433; Hansen 2007, 47.

[97] *RPC* 1.277 no. 1387; Melfi 2007a, 27.

Demeter and Kore on the north slope of Acrocorinth, and which, as Barbette Spaeth has observed, has clear connections with the idea of *libertas*.[98] The cult of Asklepios thus sits firmly within a larger cultic landscape of particular resonance for the city's freedmen population.

FINAL REMARKS

Although the sanctuary of Asklepios lies at the physical edge of the ancient city, I hope to have drawn the god and his cult in from the periphery of Corinth by suggesting two ways we might view his importance to the early colony: first, as another means of articulating Corinth's relationship to Augustus as well as to Rome more generally; and second, as a way of appealing to the social situation of many of the colonists—that is, Asklepios served as a benevolent patron to clients in need, whether in need of healing or of celebrating and perhaps even assimilating to their position as freedmen. Asklepios of Roman Corinth was thus neither a static artifact from the Greek period of the city nor a mere copy of the Roman god, much as the colonists themselves were neither strictly Greek nor Roman but were carving out new cultural identities for themselves.

The appeal of Asklepios to Corinthians in the 1st century BCE, moreover, clearly differs in certain key aspects from his appeal in the 5th centuries BCE or CE, and for many of the thousand years in between. Nor should we assume that his appeal was the same for all Corinthians of the same time. The enduring presence and popularity of Asklepios in Corinth is best understood not simply by generalizations about a universal desire for physical health, but by careful diachronic study of the cult in conjunction with the city's rich and varied history, in all its dimensions, from the political to the religious.

---

[98] Spaeth 1996, 99–100. Bookidis (2005, 162–63), however, argues against identifying Ceres, Liber, and Libera as the inhabitants of this sanctuary in the Roman period. My thanks to Barbette Spaeth and Nancy Bookidis for discussing these and other aspects of the cult and sanctuary with me.

CHAPTER FOUR

THE EMPEROR IN A ROMAN TOWN:
THE BASE OF THE *AUGUSTALES* IN THE
FORUM AT CORINTH

Margaret L. Laird*

A modern visitor to Corinth might notice a prominent base standing in the southeastern sector of the lower Forum. One of the tallest and most complete built features in the area, it is also one of the few honorific monuments preserved *in situ* (fig. 4.1–2). It would have been all the more eye-catching to an ancient viewer when marble or stucco revetment lined its square poros shaft and a bronze statue of deified Augustus stood atop its round marble pedestal. Beneath the statue a large, simple inscription adorned a round marble pedestal and named the monument's commissioners, the *Augustales*. Evidence suggests the monument's longstanding function as a tangible expression of consensus with the imperial system and a popular gathering place; it survived long enough to be incorporated, minus its statue, into a Byzantine wall from which it was finally freed in 1937. Its prominence has paled over the succeeding decades despite the good preservation of both its superstructure and its inscription. Aside from the initial publications of its architecture and text,[1] only Mary E. Hoskins Walbank has examined

* I would like to thank the editors of this volume and the participants of the Corinth in Context conference in Austin for their helpful and stimulating comments, the members of the Classics Department at the University of Washington, where I presented a draft of this paper, and Sandra Joshel, for her invaluable suggestions. Research for this paper was supported by a Council of American Overseas Research Institutions Multi-Country Research Grant and by a travel grant from the Graham Foundation. Parts were written while supported by a Getty Postdoctoral Research Fellowship. I thank these three institutions for their generosity and assistance. My work at Corinth was generously facilitated by Guy D. R. Sanders, Ioulia Tzonov-Herbst and James A. Herbst.

[1] The base was first published by Morgan 1937, 551–52; see also Scranton 1951, 142–43 and pl. 65.1–2. For the inscription, see Kent 1966, 32 no. 53 (I-1750 and I-2140). The base's inscription has provided evidence for the presence of the *Augustales* in the east and for the "Roman" nature of the colony at Corinth; for example, see Price 1984, 88; and Duthoy 1976, 190.

Fig. 4.1. View of the Forum at Corinth, from the east; the Base of the
Augustales is indicated by the arrow. Corinth Excavations.

it in any detail, approaching it as one facet of the imperial cult at
Corinth and as evidence both for the eager devotion of the *Augustales*
to the emperor and for their social prominence at Corinth.[2]

Yet preserved *in situ* in its reconstructable urban and social contexts,
the monument repays sustained attention not only for what it can tell
us about the *Augustales* but for what it says more broadly about the
ways in which inscribed monuments worked in Roman towns. While
scholars have focused on the highly visible and relatively unique imperial commissions in Rome and the ways in which their careful siting
created semantic resonances across time and space, honorific statues
and their inscribed bases made outside of the capital by groups other
than the imperial or senatorial elite have only recently been examined
as protagonists within their civic settings.[3] In part, this is due to the
challenges of reconstructing the municipal contexts in which ancient
monuments were commissioned and viewed; but it is also the result

---

[2] Walbank 1996, 210–11.

[3] For imperial commissions, see, for instance, Zanker 1990, Favro 1996, Davies
2000; and Marlowe 2006. For commissions in Roman towns, see Smith 2006, 4–74;
van Nijf 2000; and Laird 2006.

Fig. 4.2. The Base of the *Augustales*, from the south. Photo by author.

of the ways in which the very ubiquity of inscribed monuments conditions our understanding of the roles they played in their towns.

The combination of monumental support, portrait image, and public lettering was rooted in Classical and Hellenistic honorific practices but was perfected by the Romans to the degree that statues on
inscribed bases became emblematic of Roman public space, even in
antiquity.[4] Honorific statues were everywhere, forming a dense crowd
of body and base, subtly distinguished by differences of costume, attitude, and wording.[5] Constructed supports bearing carved, painted, or
inlaid texts followed standard architectural and decorative patterns
and constituted a common visual language.[6] Inscribed honorific texts
helped define the 'epigraphic habit,' a zeal for public lettering motivated by civic competition and a desire for permanence that peaked
in the 2nd century CE;[7] and in the case of the Corinthian base, its
dedication to *divus* Augustus located it within the empire-wide system
of the imperial cult.[8]

As a hallmark of Roman urbanism and a product of so many overlapping Roman behaviors, contemporary scholarship has included
statues and their bases in what Greg Woolf terms the "ready-made
cultural package" of Roman and Romanizing communities.[9] I have
no debate with this. Dedicators and viewers of an inscribed statue
shared a common understanding of the layers of its symbolism, and
these shared understandings helped to distinguish their community as
Roman.[10] But because these broad cultural patterns are so easy for us
to recognize, they can prompt broad explanations. I have found this
especially true for statues of emperors dedicated by the *Augustales*.
Regardless of their form, date of dedication, placement within a city,

---

[4] For instance, Pliny the Elder speaks of erecting statues in houses to create "fora
in private homes" (*NH* 34.16–17), cited in Stewart (2003, 166).

[5] Smith 2006, 19–39; see also Stewart 2003, 118–83; and Lahusen 1982, 239–41.

[6] For Roman statue bases, see Alföldy 1984, 23–40; and Bonnneville 1984, 132–40.
For the Roman east, see Smith 2006, 31–34; and Tuchelt 1979.

[7] MacMullen 1982; see also Woolf 1996.

[8] For the imperial cult in the eastern Empire, see Price 1984; Friesen 2001, 23–131;
and Gradel 2002; for emperor worship as a facet of Roman-style urbanism in Gaul, see
Woolf 1998, 121, 216–17, and 228. Inscribed portrait monuments also participated in
the system of euergetism; for example, see Veyne 1990, 127–28 and 174 n. 162.

[9] Woolf 1998, 11.

[10] I see the elements of Woolf's 'cultural package' as analogous to sociologist
Anthony Cohen's 'symbols,' whose common understanding helps to bound a particular community (Cohen 1985).

circumstances of donation, or the particular imperial aspect honored, these statues are universally explained as expressions of the loyalty of the *Augustales* to the emperor and their pride in their civic status.[11] While participation in the shared symbolic languages of emperor worship and statuary honors may have been among the motivations of the *Augustales*, the meaning of each monument both for the commissioning *Augustales* and for their audiences were mediated by a set of factors specific to individual dedicatory environments.[12]

Inscribed statues were commissioned by certain people at certain times. As such, they participated in the creation and display of particular networks of individual and communal relationships. Placed in specific sites, they responded to the recent (and past) histories of their built environment. They were permanent, persisting in place yet subject to transformations, desired or not. If, as Woolf argues, there was an active debate about which elements of the Roman 'cultural package' to adopt,[13] we should recognize that this debate extended to include the adaptation or manipulation of the selected elements to make them meaningful to their particular commissioners and audiences. Careful study of the form, location, and dedicatory environment of individual monuments can reveal some of these choices; but this approach is only possible at sites where we can begin to understand the city's monumental core and its material, epigraphic, and numismatic cultures. In the following paper, I will approach the monument of the *Augustales* as a product of the specific contexts in which it was created and to which it responded. I will hope to demonstrate that the monument spoke as much to Corinth's particular past and present dedicatory environments as it did to imperial power.

---

[11] As in Walbank 1996, 210–11. For similar interpretations of other inscriptions made by *Augustales*, see Granino Cecere 1988, 143; Degrassi 1964; and Buonocore 1985. Monuments of the *Augustales* are *a priori* linked to the imperial cult, and *Augustales* are often seen as transmitters of imperial ideology via their commissions; see, for instance, Adamo Muscettola 2000; Zanker 1990, 276. For a critique of scholars' tendency to identify all material related to the *Augustales* as tied to the imperial cult, see Laird 2000.

[12] Cohen 1985, 14–20. It is also important to remember that the *Augustales* were not a universally cohesive group. The organization's title varied from town to town; and the names *Augustales*, *seviri Augustales*, and *magistri Augustales* are joined by over 40 variants (Duthoy 1978, 143–214).

[13] Woolf 1998, 11.

The *Augustales*

This chapter examines Roman municipal monument-making via the commissions of the *Augustales*, self-identifying municipal groups found during the first three centuries CE. The group, which first formed in Italy late in the 1st century BCE, provided an official mechanism to involve wealthy outsiders, both freedmen and freeborn, in municipal life by including them in a series of euergetic liturgies. While the organization is generally considered a freedman's magistracy, the composition varied from region to region. *Augustales* are traditionally identified as municipal organizers of the imperial cult although emperor worship was just one of several public activities undertaken by the organization and its members.[14] Just as often they commissioned or renovated buildings, paid for public statuary, and underwrote games, public banquets, or financial distributions. They constituted a second *ordo* beneath the decurions and seem to have provided a pool from which to replenish the ranks of the town councilmen, much as the equestrians did in Rome. Furthermore, although *Augustales* themselves might be barred from holding public office, their sons could attain the highest magistracies. Like many Romans, *Augustales* enthusiastically embraced the 'epigraphic habit,' and their inscriptions proudly announce their membership in the group, making them a recognizable community within their towns.[15] Moreover, nomenclature and other details recorded in their inscriptions reveal their ties to those of both higher and lower social and political standing. This desire to self-identify, combined with their eager embrace of public commemoration enables comparisons across a large corpus of monuments from the western empire. Moreover, their "in-between"

---

[14] The only literary reference to the group is *Satyricon* 28–79, where Petronius characterizes Trimalchio and two of his dinner guests as *Augustales*. Duthoy (1978, 1254–1309) strongly argues for the group's imperial cult function; see also Fishwick 1991, vol. 2.1, 609–16. Duthoy (1976, 143–214) collects the more than 2,500 inscriptions known up to 1975. This list is updated by Abramenko (1997), who emphasizes the civic, as opposed to cultic, function of the group; see also Beard, North, and Price 1998, vol. 1, 357–58. The earliest dated inscription pertaining to the group (13–12 BCE; *CIL* 11.3200 [= *ILS* 89]) is from Nepet in Eturia. Ostrow (1990, 364–79) sees the foundation of the group as a direct consequence of Augustus's social programs. I discuss the built commissions of the *Augustales* in my dissertation (Laird 2002) and have compiled a current database of all inscriptions related to the group.

[15] It was this quality that prompted D'Arms (1981) to use the *Augustales* of Campania as the basis for his study of the social status of merchants in the imperial period.

status and local focus provides a counterpoint to the imperial and senatorial projects of the imperial center.

A predominantly western phenomenon, *Augustales* are attested epigraphically in Achaia only in the colonies of Corinth and Patrae.[16] At Corinth the epigraphic record is far from stellar. Fragments of six inscriptions naming *Augustales* or the organization can be dated primarily by letter style to the first two centuries CE.[17] This evidence pales in comparison to that from other towns like Ostia, Brixia, Herculaneum, or Misenum, where epigraphic and archaeological evidence has pinpointed the internal structure of the organization, the personal histories of its members, or the meeting places of the group.[18] Nevertheless, we can sketch a rough outline of the Corinthian organization. The base in the Forum dedicated to *divus* Augustus and a second inscription, dedicated to an '*Augustalis Tiberianus Caesaris Augusti*,'[19] suggest that the group was active by the Tiberian period, if not earlier.[20] It seems to have survived at least into the first half of the 2nd century, based on a fragmentary inscription bearing Hadrianic lettering.[21] It is impossible to calculate the size of the organization[22] or to locate a

---

[16] For *Augustales* at Corinth, see the brief note by West (1931, 60–61); further discussion below. Six inscriptions attest to the *Augustales* at Patrae: *CIL* 3.503, 514; *AE* 1991, 1448 [= Rizakis 1998 no. 145]; *AE* 1989, 661 [= Rizakis 1998 no. 50]; and Rizakis *id.* nos. 49 and 128. An *aedes Augustalium* has been identified at Patrae; see Papostolou 1986. Ostrow (1990, 68) summarizes the reasons why the organization was a "Western Imperial phenomenon."

[17] *CIL* 3.6099 and 7268 [= *CIL* 5.8818 = *ILS* 1503]; West 1931, 53 no. 69; and 60–61 no. 77; as well as Kent 1966, 32 nos. 52–53.

[18] For the *Augustales* at Ostia, see Laird 2002, 13–63; at Brixia, see Mollo 1997. For the 'Collegio degli Augustali' at Herculaneum, see Guadagno 1983. For the 'Sacello degli Augustali' at Misenum, see Miniero (ed.) 2000; see also Adamo Muscettola 2000.

[19] West 1931, 60–61 no. 77. The title *Augustalis Ti. Caesaris Augusti* (*Augustalis* of Tiberius Caesar Augustus) is unique to Corinth but may parallel the title *sexvir Augustalis et Tiberianus* (*sexvir* of Augustus and Tiberius) attested elsewhere (West *id.*, 61); see also Duthoy 1978, 1300 and n. 376.

[20] Walbank (1996, 210 n. 36) notes that two examples of pre-mortem honors to imperial women at Corinth suggest that the dedication by the *Augustales* to Augustus could have been made prior to his death.

[21] Kent 1966, 34 no. 59. Elsewhere, *Augustales* were active through the 2nd century and diminish in the 3rd century. The latest dated inscription to mention the group is from Carsulae and dates to 270 CE (*CIL* 11.4589).

[22] Based on a recently published inscription from the 'Sacello degli Augustali' at Misenum, D'Arms (2000, 133–34) calculates a membership of 100 for that town, equivalent to roughly one in 12 male citizens. Numbers from other towns range from around 200 (Ostia and Puteoli) to as low as 20 (Petelia); see Duncan-Jones 1982, 284–87.

collegial *schola* for the group, if indeed it possessed one. A votive base found in Altinum in the Veneto honors Venus and the *'genius collegii Augustalium Corinthus'* (the tutelary spirit of the Corinthian college of *Augustales*), indicating that, like professional *collegia*, the Corinthian *Augustales* celebrated their personified *esprit de corps*.[23]

Based on nomenclature, the organization at Corinth appears to have included both freedmen and freeborn members. Two *Augustales* epigraphically recognize their status as ex-slaves: Q. Cispuleius Q. l. Primus[24] and an unidentifiable *libertinus* ([---] l. Q[---]).[25] The legal status of two others is uncertain. While Ti. Claudius Stephanus[26] may have been an imperial freedman, he might also have been a freeborn descendant with a Greek cognomen. Likewise, Cn. Cornelius Speratus may have been freeborn; but *libertini* also could bear his Latin cognomen.[27] Comparison with the named *Augustales* from Patrae, where we find two freeborn members, one *libertinus* and three *incerti*, suggests the group there was similarly mixed.[28]

Corinth's early history and the varying composition of the 'Augustality' throughout Italy support such an inclusive membership, at least in the decades following the organization's establishment there. Andrik Abramenko argues that the group developed in Italian towns with a significant population of men, either freeborn or ex-slave, whose wealth placed them above the plebs but who lacked the legal status to enter the *ordo decurionum*.[29] One of the most basic legal impediments to the decurionate was freedman status. But in cases where the population of eligible citizen males surpassed the number of spots in the decurionate, an array of qualifications beyond free birth could be introduced to further circumscribe the pool. Emphasizing, for instance, a

---

[23] *CIL* 3.7268 [= *CIL* 5.8818 = *ILS* 1503]. The only comparable gift, dedicated *Augusto sacrum* to the *genius Augustalium*, was found in the apse of the *sacellum* of the *Augustales* at Misenum (*AE* 1975, 211). Duthoy (1978, 1286) sees the worship of a *genius* as an indication that the organization modeled itself on professional *collegia*.

[24] West 1931, 60 no. 77

[25] West *id.*, 53 no. 69.

[26] *CIL* 3.6099.

[27] Kent, 1966, 32 no. 52; see also Kajanto 1965, 77 and 297.

[28] For freedman, see Sex. Aequ[anus] Sex. l. Astius (*AE* 1991, 1448 [= Rizakis 1998 no. 145]). For freeborn, see C. Aurelius C. f. Ia[---]irx[---] Priscus (*CIL* 3.503 and page 1311 [= Rizakis 1998 no. 15]); T. Su(lp)i(c)ius [---] f. Quir. Felix (*CIL* 3.514 [= Rizakis *id.* no. 141]). An *incertus*, see T. Varius Secundus (*AE* 1989, 661 [= Rizakis *id.*, no. 50; Kajanto 1965, 74–75 and 292]); Ti. Claudius Satyrus (Rizakis *id.*, no. 128); C. Varronius Syn[e]ros (Rizakis *id.*, no. 49).

[29] Abramenko 1997, 56–76.

man's origins might bar *incolae* (citizens who had moved to a town as adults), first-generation citizens, or *spurii* (illegitimates) from municipal magistracies, making the *ordo Augustalium* their only avenue to civic prominence. The composition of the *ordo Augustalium* reflects demographic differences between *regiones* in northern and southern Italy. So, in certain regions such as Campania, the *ordo Augustalium* was almost exclusively composed of wealthy freedmen, while in others, such as Cisalpine Gaul, freeborn members predominated among the *Augustales*. Abramenko concludes that the composition of the *Augustales* in any town was not based solely on a 'freedman/freeborn' dichotomy but on a variety of criteria dependent on the status and wealth of its eligible male population. Corinth provides evidence from the provinces to support Abramenko's argument that the *Augustales* were not created as part of Augustus's social planning for freedmen but to address broader social, political, and possibly religious ends.[30]

If the history of the *Augustales* at Corinth is opaque, the social ties of its membership are even more obscure. Inscriptions elsewhere suggest that *Augustales* could be the freedmen or clients of prominent decurions, and that these ties would help the sons of *Augustales* rise to municipal office.[31] At Corinth only one inscription survives to hint at the links between the decurions and the *Augustales*. In the Tiberian period, the *Augustalis* Q. Cispuleius Primus was honored by a certain C. Novius Felix.[32] West identifies Felix as a freedman of the family of the Augustan *duovir* Novius Bassus and the honoree, Cispuleius Primus, as the freedman or father of Q. Cispuleius Theophilus, recipient of decurional and aedilician ornament.[33] This triangle locates at least one Corinthian *Augustalis* within the glow of the local aristocracy.

---

[30] Abramenko 1997, 50.

[31] Mouritsen 1997, 65–70. Abramenko (1997, 331) lists *Augustales* with consular patrons. Laird (2002, 56–62) discusses *Augustales* with patrons who were Ostian *decuriones*.

[32] West 1931, 60–61 no. 77.

[33] West 1931, 87–88 no. 107. Comparison with other inscriptions suggests that it is more likely that Primus was the freedman of Theophilus. Only one son of an *Augustalis* is recorded as receiving decurional ornament (Rizakis 1998 no. 49). In contrast, over 60 sons of *Augustales* were bona fide decurions (and *aediles* or *duoviri / quattuorviri*). It would seem that if the son of an *Augustalis* was wealthy enough to be voted *ornamenta decurionalia*, then he would be wealthy enough and legally qualified to join the *ordo decurionum*, making this the more common honor. On the other hand, two patrons of *Augustales*, both *Augustales* themselves, received decurional ornament and were honored by their freedmen (*CIL* 2.4062 with page 972 [= *ILS* 6955]; *CIL* 3.1426 and *CIL* 3.1425 [= *ILS* 7137] name the same patron and freedmen.

The Monument: Excavation History and Epigraphic Considerations

In contrast to the history outlined above, the base seems reassuringly solid. Excavating a Byzantine wall in 1937, Doreen Canady noticed parts of a cylindrical drum in two large, connecting pieces.[34] Removal of the wall liberated the stones, the smaller of which bore the letters "...*ugus*...," part of the first line of the inscription. The drum was found to be the crowning element of a large statue base of complex design (fig. 4.2–3). At its bottom, four, grey-blue marble slabs, each nearly 3 m long, form a low step.[35] A rectangular bench of local limestone, pieces of which were subsequently united with the base, rests on the step and surrounds a square core of local poros. This was finished either with plaster or revetment, neither of which survive. The base rises ca. 2.20 m above the latest paving of the Forum. Because it was constructed in relation to the earlier (and lower) third paving, the monument could have stood as much as .50 m higher when it was first dedicated.[36]

Two joining pieces of marble bearing a fragmentary inscription above traces of a mutilated bead-and-reel molding had been found the previous year, reused in a nearby wall.[37] Although they do not adjoin the surviving pieces of the marble drum, the orthography and

[34] See Corinth archives, Excavation Notebook 168, "Doreen D. Canaday, Agora N.E., Spring 1937, IV," 51–52. In plans, the base can be seen englobed in the wall, dated between 1059–1210; see Scranton 1957, plan 7, square 9 J, top center. The wall formed the western boundary of a two-room structure that Scranton tentatively identifies as housing for the proprietor of an inn to the west (*id.*, 60–61). Ten smaller fragments of the drum were also found though their findspots were not recorded (West 1931, 32 no. 53).

[35] Three of these were found *in situ* on the pavement of the Forum while the fourth, which lay on the western edge of the base, was found reused in a later wall (Corinth Archives, Excavation Notebook 168, 51).

[36] Scranton (1957, 135–36) does not record the thickness of the final paving, which was composed of marble slabs ranging up to .10 m thick in cement bedding, but its depth is suggested on the reconstruction drawing of the base (*id.*, 143, fig. 69). Scotton (1997, 192–93) provides an unreferenced depth of .60 m between the third and fourth paving in the northeastern corner of the Forum.

[37] See Corinth Archives, Excavation Notebook 157, "R. Scranton, Agora Northeast, 1936," 128–31. The first fragment (I-1750a), reading "...*gusta*...," was discovered by Scranton on May 2, 1936, in the room occupying the upper-left hand corner of square 9 J (Scranton 1957, plan 7). The second (I-1750b), reading "...*ales*..." was found on May 14 in a Byzantine wall running south from the kiln located in 9 I (Scranton *id.*, plan 7).

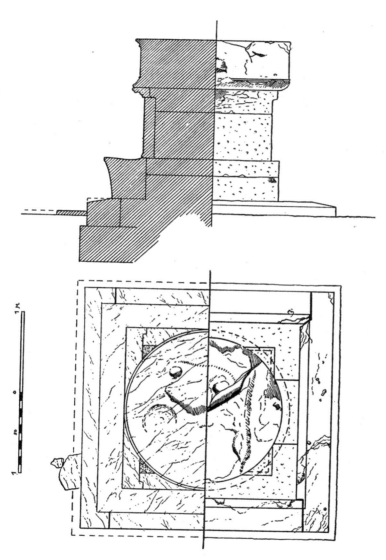

Fig. 4.3. State and restoration drawing of the Base of the *Augustales* from the side and from above. (Scranton 1951, fig. 69)

marble type allowed John Harvey Kent to associate them with the base, and to restore the inscription as follows (fig. 4.4): [divo a]VGVS[to] | [sacrum] | [au]GVSTALES (sacred to the deified Augustus, the *Augustales* [made it].)[38] The preserved fragments constitute roughly two-thirds of the marble drum, most of whose original surface fell victim to fire and post-Classical recutting.[39] The damage is especially severe on the western (inscribed) side, where the original surface is limited to the inscribed fragments (fig. 4.4). The little remaining original surface is preserved primarily along the drum's uninscribed southeast side, which can be seen in fig. 4.2. Despite the poor preservation of the inscription and significant *lacunae* to either side, Kent's reconstruction has been widely accepted. But his reconstruction fails to consider the text as part of the monument's overall design. A close examination of the words in their places suggests a new reading that integrates epigraphic and physical criteria.

LINE 1: Fragment I-2140 preserves four letters across ca. .30 m of the original inscribed surface. To either side, *lacunae* of more than 1 m provide ample space for Kent's restored epithet, *divo*, which finds parallels at Corinth.[40] However, Kent's reconstruction overlooks the design of the monument, which was composed of an inscribed drum, the square base and bench, and a statue. Roman monuments integrate these elements, arranging sculpture and inscription (or inscribed field) so that their vertical axes align along the vertical axis of the base. In this case the center of the bench and the square shaft determine the vertical axis on the monument's front (west) side. Because a significant portion of the drum was found *in situ*, its original position atop the square shaft is secure. Cuttings for the statue's right, weight-bearing foot are preserved on the drum's top and further support this alignment (fig. 4.5). As positioned, the foot turns several degrees to the north (proper right). This is in keeping with a common pose for Greco-Roman pedestrian portraits, whose weight-bearing feet often splay slightly outward. The front plane of the statue would parallel the

---

[38] Kent 1966, 32 no. 53.

[39] The damage and fragmentary nature of the marble drum is noted by Morgan (1937, 551–52). One casualty of the recutting was the stepped molding at the bottom and top of the drum. Both are restored in the reconstruction profile published by Scranton (1957, 143 with fig. 69; see also fig. 3).

[40] For instance, Kent 1966, 32 no. 51.

Fig. 4.4. The Base of the *Augustales*, detail of the inscription on the marble drum. Photo by author.

Fig. 4.5. The Base of the *Augustales* from the west, showing the cuttings on the upper surface of the marble drum. Corinth Excavations.

west face of the base, notwithstanding the gentle twist that a *contrapposto* pose might generate.

Like the statue, the inscription or inscribed field should also center along the monument's front vertical axis. Kent restores a symmetrical inscription whose vertical axis centers on or close to first V of AVGVSTO. However, as carved on the marble drum, this letter falls roughly 15 degrees north (proper right) of the vertical axis of the base and the statue. Because the drum was found *in situ*, and its fragments fit together closely, it cannot be rotated to bring Kent's reconstructed inscription into alignment with the square base. Doing so also would turn the statue to the south, forcing it into an unusual, twisting pose. The vertical axis of the base centers on the second V of AVGVSTO, as carved on the drum in its true position; and it is this letter that establishes the vertical axis for the inscription. To keep the restored '*divo*' at the beginning of the line, we must add a word or abbreviation to balance the line to the right. Spacing permits the restored word '*sacrvm*' or, better, its abbreviation '*sacr(vm)*' to be moved from line 2 to the end of line 1. This wording differs from the more traditional layout, followed by Kent, where the unit '*divo avgvsto*' and the word '*sacrvm*' spread across two sequential lines. However, parallels exist such as a statue base from Narona dedicated by six *seviri magistri mercuriales* (literally, the "six-man magistrates of Mercury"), a group analogous to the *Augustales*.[41] On this inscription it is tempting to see the cognomen of the first donor, Corinthus, as significant. On the other hand, at least one dedication made to Augustus during his lifetime in Corinth honors him simply as *Augusto*, suggesting that this word could have stood alone in line 1.[42] If this reconstruction were acceptable, it would draw the date of the organization's founding securely into the Augustan period. However, as we will see below, the alignment of the text of line 3 excludes this reconstruction.

The restored word *sacrum*, now moved to line 1, finds many parallels throughout the Roman world, including Corinth.[43] The phrase unequivocably sacralizes the monument to Augustus as a god, and

---

[41] *CIL* 3.1770a (= *CIL* 3.*301a = *ILS* 7167a, from Narona); *CIL* 3.1770b (= *CIL* 3.*00301a = *CINar*1, 15b, from Narona); see also *CIL* 6.880 with page 4302, from Rome; *CIL* 8.26517 (= *ILS* 6797 = *AE* 2002, 1682, from Thugga); and *CIL* 13.1642 (= *ILS* 5639 = *AE* 1888, 86, from Forum Segusiavorum).

[42] Kent 1966, 38 no. 69.

[43] At Corinth, see Kent 1966, 32 no. 52, although with *divus* restored. Several of the fragmentary imperial inscriptions from Corinth restore the word *sacrum*, for instance,

resonates with votive meanings.[44] This does not mean that the statue functioned as a cult image although it clearly connects the dedication to emperor worship.[45] If the first line establishes a relationship with the emperor, the following lines complicate the monument by moving beyond demonstrations of loyalty to explain the local motivations for the dedication.

LINE 2: Dedications to deified emperors, *sacrum* or not, are rare among the preserved corpus of *Augustales* inscriptions. Out of 614 'public,' that is, non-funerary, inscriptions dedicated by an *Augustalis*, *Augustales*, or by the *ordo*, only 18 (less than .03%) celebrate a *divus* or a *diva*.[46] Only five of these, including Kent's reconstruction, are initiatives financed by the *ordo* as a collective.[47] More numerous are dedications made by individuals or groups of two or more *Augustales*.[48] The Corinthian monument's size and luxury might argue for the pooled resources of the *ordo*, as reconstructed by Kent; and the preserved text of line 3 clearly indicates several *Augustales* were involved in the project. However, the size of the monument does not mandate a group effort. Elsewhere, wealthy *Augustales* paid for expensive public commissions single-handedly. Assisium's P. Decimus P. l. Eros Merula

---

West 1931 no. 14 (= Kent 1966 no. 69): *Augusto* [*sacrum*]. See also Kent *id.*, no. 50, *Divo Iul*[*io*] | *Caesari* | [*sacrum*], and Kent *id.*, no. 51, [*d*]*ivo* [*Au*]*gusto* [*sacrum*].

[44] Gallus Aelius in Festus, *sacrum est…quod dis dedicatum atque consecratum est.* See also Macr. *Sat.* (3.7.3),…*nam, quidquid destinatum est dis, sacrum vocatur,* cited in Fishwick (1991, 438–39) although the author (*id.*, 442–45) also argues that the formula was at times merely formulaic. For a contrary position, see Clauss 1999, 285–86.

[45] Price (1984, 177), following Blanck (1971, 93), notes that "there is no sign from literary or other evidence that any of the innumerable permanent imperial statues in public spaces, such as the main square or the theater, received cult."

[46] One hundred ninety-four public inscriptions made by *Augustales* or the *ordo* can be assigned to the imperial cult in its broadest definition. These include any type of dedication to an emperor, empress, imperial attribute, or Augustan deity. Of the eighteen dedications to a *divus* or *diva*, half are for *divus* Augustus.

[47] *CIL* 10.1411 (= *ILS* 74a, from Herculaneum); *CIL* 10.1412 (= *ILS* 74, from Herculaneum); *CIL* 9.6258, from Aquilonia Kent 1966 no. 53, from Corinth; and *CIL* 8.305 with page 1198 (= *ILS* 378, from Ammaedara).

[48] For dedications by single *Augustales*, see *CIL* 10.1413, from Herculaneum; *AE* 1979, 172, from Herculaneum; *AE* 1975, 212, from Misenum; *CIL* 3.1947 (= 8566 = *ILS* 219, from Salona); Kent 1966 no. 52, from Corinth; *AE* 1942/43, 18, from Volubilis; *CIL* 2.2778, from Clunia Sulpicia; *AE* 1990, 879 (= *AE* 1999, 1423, from Stobi); *AE* 1939, 113 (= *AE* 1944, 75 = *AE* 1990, 877 = *AE* 1999, 1423, from Stobi). Dedications by two or more *Augustales*: *AE* 1990, 274, from Trebula Suffenatium; *CIL* 2.182, from Olisipo; *CIL* 3.1770a (= *CIL* 3.*301a = *ILS* 7167a, from Narona); and *CIL* 3.1770b (= *CIL* 3.*301a, from Narona).

purchased his freedom for HS 50,000 and paid HS 2,000 *pro seviratu* for the honor of joining the *ordo*. He paved a road (HS 37,000) and provided statues for the temple of Hercules (HS 30,000) and promised the town HS 800,000 on his death (*CIL* II.5400 = *ILS* 7812). At Herculaneum, L. Mammius Maximus built a *macellum* and installed a nine-member imperial statuary cycle, including images of *divus* Augustus and *diva* Livia in the porticus; and at Corinth the *Augustalis* Cn. Cornelius Speratus dedicated a statue of *divus* Augustus, though on a much smaller scale.[49] Because it is less common for the *ordo* to dedicate as a collective, I propose that the lacunose second line records the names of two or more donors.[50]

LINE 3: In its current state and as photographed, inscription fragment I-1750 A–B sits roughly .25 m to the south (right) of its original location (fig. 4.4). In its true position, the surviving text would have centered roughly along the vertical axis assumed in Kent's reconstruction, that is, rotated to the north, with the 'ST' of 'AVGVSTALES' aligned with the first 'V' of 'AVGVSTO' in line 1.[51] Since Kent's vertical axis is north of the monument's overall axis, there is space after the preserved text to restore abbreviations common to public inscriptions. One likely formula would be '*d(ecreto) d(ecurionum)*,' commemorating negotiations with the town council for permission to erect the statue in such a prominent location. This might be accompanied by '*ob h(onorem)*,' an abbreviation found in other inscriptions of the *Augustales*, who were often responsible for public works above and beyond the *summa honoraria* paid for their induction into the organization.[52]

---

[49] On L. Mammius Maximus, see Laird 2002, 114–24; see also Boschung 2002, 119–25; and Rose 1997, 92. On Cn. Cornelius Speratus, see Kent 1966, 32 no. 52. Duncan-Jones (1974, 78–79; 126–127) calculates an average of between HS 4,000–7,000 per statue (with bases). *Augustales* also gave generous gifts to their organization and their towns; two *seviri Augustales* at Ostia donated HS 50,000 to establish foundations [*CIL* 14.367 (= *ILS* 6164); 14.431 (= *AE* 1980, 182)].

[50] With shorter letter heights, line 2 could subdivide into two lines. Compare the HS 60,000 donation to acquire a bath by six *Augustales* at Teanum Sidicinum, *CIL* 10.4792 (= *ILS* 5677).

[51] See Kent 1966, 32 no. 53.

[52] Duthoy 1978, 1266–68 (*seviri Augustales*) and 1281–82 (*Augustales*). The convention is generally expressed *ob honorem Augustalitatis* or *ob honorem seviratus*, although *ob honorem* alone at the end of an inscription is attested. Compare, again, the inscription from Narona *CIL* 3.1770a (= *CIL* 3.*301a = *ILS* 7167a): *Divo Aug(usto) sacr(um)* | *Q(uintus) Sextilius Corinthus* | *C(aius) Stertinius Synegdemus* | *L(ucius) Vibius Amaranthus L(ucius) Aquillius Aptus* | *L(ucius) Titusidius Chryseros C(aius) Valeri(u)s Herma* | *IIIIIIviri(i) m(agistri) m(ercuriales) ob h(onorem)*. See also *AE* 1989,

The restored inscription could read: [divo a]ṾG̣vs[to sacr(um)] | [nomen nomen] | [au]G̣VSTALES [ob h(onorem) d(ecreto) d(ecurionum)]. This new restoration of the inscription proposes that the monument was made by two or more *Augustales* following nego-tiations with the city council. While the first meaning of the statue was to assert publicly the donors' support for the deified emperor, the donation also tangibly represented their membership in the town's second *ordo* and, as we will see, positioned them as members of an elite group of donors actively beautifying the Forum in the early first century CE.

DATE AND URBAN CONTEXT

The restored inscription suggests a date after Augustus's death and dei-fication in 14 CE, a *terminus post quem* supported, though not unam-biguously, by the archaeological record.[53] The base was constructed "in relation to" the Forum's third cement paving, datable to the Augustan period.[54] A fragment of the Forum's final marble paving was found *in situ* against the southwest corner, providing a *terminus ante quem* of the late 1st century (fig. 4.6).[55] The base's location and its orientation refine this window. The monument is positioned slightly northeast of the projected intersections of the *cardo maximus* (the Lechaion road) and the *decumanus*, which met conceptually on the site of the Rostra to the south (fig. 4.7).[56] But the base does not align with the city grid or with the Forum, which follows the east-west line of the Greek South Stoa, although both of these constituted dominant axes for the early colony. Rather, it most closely respects the orientation of the Julian Basilica to the east and Temples D, G, F, the Fountain of Neptune, and the Babbius Monument to the west. These were all built during the flurry of construction that characterized the Augustan and early

---

661 (= Rizakis 1998 no. 50, from Patrae); *CIL* 5.2116 (= *ILS* 5370, from Tarvisium); and *CIL* 9.2439, from Saepinum. If the abbreviation *d(ecurionum) d(ecreto)* were dropped, other formulae that would fit the spacing could include *d(e) s(uis) p(ecuniis) f(aciendum) c(uraverunt)*, as per Kent 1966, 38 no. 69; or *ob iust(itiam)*, in Kent *id.*, 32 no. 52.

[53] But see Walbank 1996, 210 n. 36.

[54] Scranton 1957, 148–49. Bookidis (2005, 152 n. 46) notes that the pottery under the final (fourth) marble paving dates to the first two quarters of the 1st century CE.

[55] Scranton 1957, 149.

[56] Romano 1993, 15–19; see also *id.* 2005, 30; and *id.* 2003, 283–88.

Tiberian periods, and all follow the east-west orientation of the Hellenistic racecourse that occupied this area in the pre-Roman period.[57] The commission of the *Augustales* takes the same orientation—in fact, it stands on the track's southern edge, a point to which I will return later.

While the base and statue were part of the early 1st century building boom, the commission seems to have been one of the latest additions, following the construction, probably in the Tiberian period, of the first Temple E on the graded plateau to the west.[58] This building also followed the orientation of Hellenistic racecourse, and its central east-west axis extends between the Fountain of Neptune and Temple G to bisect the south aisle of the Julian Basilica, providing a major axis for the Roman Forum.[59] The *Augustales* Base stands ca. 2 m north of this line. It is possible that the group was prohibited from building precisely on Temple E's sightline, which was later emphasized with a monumental stairway and a large built base. However, the *Augustales* commission is placed to enjoy the view between the Fountain of Neptune and Temple G towards Temple E, which dominates the western end of the Forum.[60] That the *Augustales* considered Temple E's sightline suggests that they positioned their monument only after the temple was built in the Tiberian period.

The monument's acknowledgment of the orientation and sightlines of Temple E and the other buildings also suggests that the *Augustales* played a part in the coherent urban development of the early

---

[57] Scotton (1997, 109–10) dates the Julian Basilica to ca. 25 CE. On the west end of the Forum, the earliest building, Temple F, was built during the reign of Augustus. It was followed by Temple G and the Fountain of Neptune, the latter underwritten by a local philanthropist, Cn. Babbius Philinus, probably while *aedile* in the late Augustan period. Temple D and the circular Babbius Monument were built shortly after in the Tiberian period; see Williams 1989. For a survey of the building projects of local notables in Corinth over the 1st century CE, see D'Hautcourt 2001, 433–37. For the orientation of these buildings, which deviates by +8 degrees to the east of the Greek orientation established by the Temple of Apollo and the south stoa, see Romano 2003, 33–38. On the Hellenistic starting line, see Morgan 1937, 539–52 and especially 549; as well as Williams 1970 and Williams and Russell 1981, 11–15.

[58] I follow Williams's dating of the first Temple E and its precinct (1989, 156–62). For a date in the Augustan period, see Walbank 1989, 380; and her chapter in this volume (pp. 156–59).

[59] Romano 2003, 36 and fig. 2.5.

[60] Walbank 1989, 364 and 391–93. In particular, the author's fig. 7 (392 with n. 110 for bibliography (…for bibliography; and this volume 172 fig. 68) reproduces a coin of Caracalla that may show the Forum viewed from the east with Temple E looming over the shops.

Fig. 4.6. The southwest corner of the Base of the *Augustales*, showing the corner of the bench and a fragment of the marble paving of the Forum *in situ* against the western side. Photo by author.

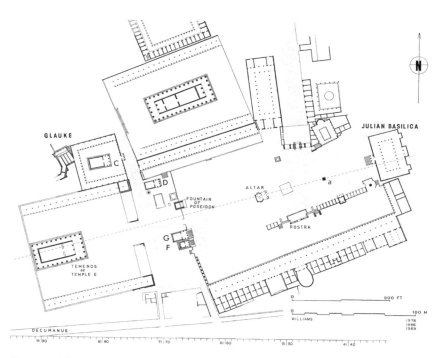

Fig. 4.7. The Forum at Corinth in the mid-first century CE, with dashed line indicating the east-west axis of the Base of the *Augustales* (a).

first century. Thus, the monument provides an index of the improv-
ing fortunes of Corinth's colonists. Only by the Augustan period were
Corinth's colonists wealthy or numerous enough to begin to refine the
rather rough and impromptu civic space of the colonial Forum.[61] That
the *Augustales* participated in this provides an index of the colony's
wealth, which must have extended beyond the members of the *ordo
decurionum*.

THE MISSING STATUE

The cuttings on the upper surface of the marble drum indicate that
the westward-looking statue it supported was made of bronze (fig. 4.3,
4.5). Robert Scranton identified it as that of Athena seen by Pausanias
"in the middle" of Corinth's Forum.[62] Scranton postulated that the
statue was draped although his conclusions about its female identity
may have encouraged this interpretation as much as any cuttings on
the drum itself, whose state of preservation is poor. Recently, Walbank
has argued against Scranton's designation, noting that the dedicatory
inscription does not match the goddess, the monument's site does not
match the area described by Pausanias, and other bases found in the
Forum could just as well have borne the Athena. Instead, Walbank
proposes that the statue represented deified Augustus himself.[63]

The inscription dedicating '*divo Augusto sacrum*' does not necessarily exclude an image of Minerva, as she would have been labeled;
any statue or statuette could be sanctified to the god or goddess of the
donor's choice.[64] Yet while the base *could* have held Pausanias's goddess, two points further support Walbank's proposal. First, although
Athena was connected to Corinth through Bellerophon and Pegasos,
Minerva, or Minerva Augusta, was not a popular goddess among the
Augustales, who honored her overall with only eight dedications.[65]

---

[61] Walbank 1997, 123. The rapid expansion of commercial facilities in the Claudian
period both reflected and drove wealth accumulation; see Williams 1993.
[62] Paus. 2.3.1; see also Scranton 1957, 142–43. Wiseman (1979, 524 with fig. 13)
publishes a drawing of the base topped by a copy of the Athena Parthenos.
[63] Walbank 1996, 210 and n. 37.
[64] See, for instance, a bronze votive statuette of Diana dedicated to Jupiter Doli-
chenus in the Museo Nazionale Concordiese in Portogruaro (Zovatto 1971, 13 no. 28
[= *AE* 1976, 236]).
[65] Out of 188 dedications made by *Augustales* to deities, four honored Minerva: *AE*
1990, 226, from Iuvanum; *CIL* 5.3272, from Verona; *CIL* 3.1079 (= *ILS* 3850, from

Second, the topographical and programmatic context in which the commission was placed favors a statue of *divus* Augustus. This is a dedication that was commissioned to participate in a developing civic program of emperor worship focusing in various forms in Corinth's Forum.[66]

As positioned, the *Augustales* statue and base were nestled among several loci of emperor worship, each celebrating a different aspect of imperial power (fig. 4.7). Behind it to the east rose the façade of the Julian Basilica, which provided a monumental backdrop (fig. 4.8).[67] While the civic function of the Julian Basilica is debated, its contents— one of the most extensive collections of imperial portraits found at Corinth and fragments of two small altars—parallel donations common to many towns throughout the empire.[68] At the time the *Augustales* dedicated their statue, the Julian Basilica would already have contained two of its most famous images, Augustus's heirs, Gaius and Lucius; and perhaps the portrait of the emperor himself.[69] Over the next century, donations by local elites enriched the collection.[70] Inscriptions relating to the office of *agonothetes*, overseers of the Isthmian and Caesarean Games, suggest that the basilica also was a preferred space to honor civic leaders who were involved in this aspect of imperial celebration.[71] The accumulation of sculptures in the Julian Basilica allowed local donors to honor the imperial family, beautify their city, and demonstrate their civic largesse. The *Augustales* donation, honoring a deified emperor, stood in the unofficial forecourt of the Julian Basilica created on the north and south by the Peirene Fountain and

Apulum); and *AE* 1958, 8, from Castulum. Out of 75 dedications made by *Augustales* to 'August' deities, only four honored Minerva Augusta: *CIL* 5.4282, from Brixia; *CIL* 2.4498, from Barcino; *CIL* 3.1426, from Sarmizegetusa; and *AE* 1934, 41, from Bansa. In contrast, 33 dedications honored Jupiter.

[66] The subsequent discussion follows Walbank 1996, 201–14.

[67] Scotton 1997, 159–75 (first phase) and 196–204 (third phase).

[68] For the commissioning of imperial sculptural cycles, see most recently Boschung 2002, 171–79. Scotton (1997, 261–67) identifies the building as the site of the provincial law court, focused on a tribunal flanked by imperial statues in the east side. He also reconstructs a *lararium* to the *lares Augusti* on the north wall. Walbank (1996, 201–14) suggests that the building housed worship of the *genius Augusti*.

[69] For the group, see Boschung 2002, 64–66; see also Rose 1997, 138–39; and De Grazia 1973, 43–48 and 87–108. Boschung summarizes the dates proposed for the Augustus statue, which range from the Augustan to the Claudian period.

[70] For a discussion of these statues and their dedicatory inscriptions, see Scotton 1997, 244–61.

[71] Scotton 1997, 254–55 and n. 567.

MARGARET L. LAIRD

Fig. 4.8. The Base of the *Augustales* seen from the west, with the remains of the Julian Basilica beyond. Photo by author.

the central shops and to the west by the imaginary line of the Lechaion Road as it continued through the propylaea to the Bema.

The base's statue faced west, uniting the eastern Forum with its western half and forming a conceptual pivot between the honorific imperial dedications in the Julian Basilica, a line of small temples dedicated to deities important to the imperial family, and the cult activities of Temple E (figs. 4.7, 4.9). Its central axis passed near an altar that has been reconstructed as a precinct resembling the Ara Pacis and which may have marked the *mundus* (sacred center) of the colony.[72] This altar was razed when the Forum was paved in the late 1st century. The statue should have been tall enough to look west over it towards the smaller temples and Temple E. Several of the former were dedicated to deities meaningful to Augustus and the Julio-Claudian family: Venus (celebrated in Temple F), Clarian Apollo (Temple G), and Tyche/Fortuna (Temple D).[73] Beyond the screen of smaller temples rose Temple E, variously identified as the Capitolium or as the Temple of Octavia and official center of the imperial cult at Corinth.[74] A monumental statue of *divus* Augustus would fit well among these commissions.

While the monument's statue has perished, preserved details and surviving imperial sculpture help suggest its original appearance. The cutting for the right foot measures ca. 0.75 m in length, clearly indicating an over life-size statue whose height could range between 2.5–3.0 m.[75] The *divus* would have stood with his weight on his right foot, a spear or staff resting in a depression to its left. Statues of deified emperors often suggested the subject's divinity with a heroically nude body that could be undraped or modestly swathed in a hip mantle. These employed heroic or divine Greek prototypes, and the overlap between the deified emperor and a particular god could be underscored by the incorporation of specific iconographic elements.[76] For instance, on a relief from Ravenna, a hip-mantled *divus* Augustus cradles the *parazonium* (long, triangular dagger) of Mars Ultor while a bronze statue of Augustus found in a portico at Herculaneum grasps Jupiter's thunder-

---

[72] Walbank 1997, 117.

[73] Bookidis 2005, 153.

[74] The most sustained argument in favor of Temple E as the Capitolium is that of Walbank (1989). For Temple E as imperial cult center, see Williams 1989. Bookidis (2005, 155–56) summarizes the positions of other scholars on this question.

[75] For colossal portraits of Augustus, see Kreikenbom 1992, 61–73.

[76] See Maderna 1988, 18–24; see also Rose 1997, 74–75.

Fig. 4.9. The Base of the *Augustales* seen from the east, with the remains of Temples D, E, F, G, and the Fountain of Poseidon beyond. Photo by author.

bolt.[77] The latter statue with its sharply angled staff and pronounced weight shift may hint at the lost Corinthian statue's appearance, and it has been used as a model for the reconstruction drawing (fig. 4.10). This over life-sized statue would have commanded the Forum, gazing towards Temple E.[78] If this building was the town's imperial cult center, deified Augustus would observe rituals performed in his honor. However, a more complex relationship would arise if Temple E were the Capitolium. In this case the image of a deified emperor in the guise of Jupiter might gaze towards the cult site of the god to which he was assimilated.[79]

DESIGN CONSIDERATIONS

If the monument of the *Augustales* expressed the empire-wide language of emperor worship, it did so within a particularly Corinthian and Achaian framework. It was, after all, the product of a wave of local euergetism, and its strategic position ensured that it became a participant in the private commissions of Corinth's elite. While its subject, a deified emperor, resonated with the imperial center, the nuances of emperor worship were also culturally current on the local stage. The project provided an opportunity for the *Augustales*, a new group composed of men excluded from civic offices, to concretize their presence in the heart of Corinth's developing urban center.[80] The following section reveals how the monument's design responded to current euergetic projects in the town while at the same time creating a fictional pre-Roman history for the commission.

While *Augustales* are considered a 'typically Roman' feature of Corinth, the base they commissioned was anything but typical. Its idiosyncrasies emerge clearly when it is compared with the bases of

---

[77] Rose 1997, 100–02 and pl. 98 (Ravenna relief) and 91–92 and pl. 80 (Herculaneum Augustus).

[78] That the Romans considered the visual sightlines between statues and significant buildings or places to be important is suggested by the positioning of a statue of L. Volusius Saturninus *in aria Apolinis* (sic) *in conspectum* (sic) *curiae*; see Eck (1972, 463), cited in Stewart (2003, 81).

[79] The visual connection between the statue and the west end of the Forum would have been even stronger after the destruction of the altar in the middle of the 1st century CE during the final paving project.

[80] Eck (1994) discusses the social capital that public statuary commissions held for their dedicators.

Fig. 4.10. Reconstruction drawing of the monument of the *Augustales*. Illustration by author.

other imperial statues from Corinth. Their fragmentary remains demonstrate that Corinthian patrons conservatively followed the dominant models, commissioning simple, quadrangular bases. Both monolithic examples and examples with revetment have been found in the city although Corinthians appear to have favored the latter, as their preserved numbers slightly surpass the monolithic examples.[81]

While the revetted shaft of the *Augustales* base nominally fits within this tradition, the monument's height, architectural complexity, and diverse materials set it apart. Standing ca. 2.5 m without its statue, it is the tallest surviving base built specifically for a statue of a Roman emperor in Roman Achaia.[82] Its size is not its only distinguishing feature. Unexpected design elements emphasize its uniqueness. The inscribed marble drum contrasts with the square, revetted pedestal; the step and benches create a monumental molding and a public function; diverse materials—blue-gray and white marble, limestone, bronze—articulate each section of the monument. This combination of size, shape, and materials is virtually unparalleled at Corinth or elsewhere; yet taken individually, each locates the monument in particularly Corinthian and particularly Greek traditions.

The Benches

The four-sided bench at the base's bottom was an intentional feature of the monument's design. A corner of the bench that has been

---

[81] Sixty-eight imperial inscriptions and fragments of inscriptions were worked for adhesion to a secondary surface, identified as 'slabs' or 'revetment' in the publications; West 1931 nos. 13, 17–19, 21, 23–27, 28 a and b, 29–44, 46, and 48–51; see also Kent 1966 nos. 51–52, 55, 59, 66–67, 70–75, 77, 80–82, 84, 86, 88–89, 91–92, 95, 98–106, 109–110, 113, and 115. Remains of 18 monolithic statue bases and their fragments were discovered, identified as 'blocks' or 'bases' in the publications; West *id.* nos. 10, 15–16, 22, 45, 47, and 52; see also Kent *id.* nos. 50, 53, 58, 62, 69, 76, 87, 108, and 116–18. For imperial inscriptions whose original monumental support cannot be determined, see Kent *id.* nos. 83, 85, 90, 93–94 and 97. The Corinthians' preference for revetted bases is surprising. While they were popular on the Italian peninsula, their numbers drop for imperial sculptures of the eastern Roman empire; see Højte 2005, 30–31. In particular, Højte (31, n. 51) comments that revetted bases are found in the Greek East in Pergamum, Ephesus, and Corinth, all towns with strong Italian influence. Perhaps the Corinthians' preference for revetted bases recalls real or imagined Italian origins or reflects economic or material constraints.

[82] Based on measurements collected by Højte 2005, 249–54 (Augustus), 277–80 (Tiberius), 290–91 (Caligula), 307–11 (Claudius), 322–24 (Nero), 337–38 (Vespasian), 350 (Titus), 357–58 (Domitian), 368–69 (Nerva), 386–90 (Trajan), 428–43 (Hadrian), 493–96 (Antoninus Pius), 524–25 (Lucius Verus), 557–60 (Marcus Aurelius), and 580–81 (Commodus).

joined to the monument preserves the top of a curved leg, and the seat's concave profile provides space for feet (fig. 4.6). In addition, the statue's dedicatory inscription has been shifted from its expected place on the monument's square shaft up to the round drum, anticipating the seated bodies that would hide the pillar. These details—combined with the monument's prime location—evidently made the monument a popular gathering place, as indicated by wear across all the treads.

The integration of useful architecture into a simple sculptural support might appear to be at odds with the monument's honorific aims. To my knowledge, there are no Roman imperial statue bases that incorporated benches into their designs.[83] However, bases in the form of *exedrae* with space for seating were found in the Hellenistic east beginning in the 2nd century CE. These bases take the form of a horizontal Π, with statue groups posed across the back. A bench runs beneath the sculptures between two projecting sidewalls. Several examples from Delphi, however, feature quadrilateral shafts whose front and sides are wrapped by benches.[84]

If the *Augustales* recalled Hellenistic *exedrae* bases, they also picked up on a strand of civic philanthropy in early imperial Corinth that fostered an active 'bench culture' in the lower Forum.[85] The flashiest examples are the paired benches flanking the Rostra, located a few meters to the south of the *Augustales'* monument. The speaker's platform, with blue and white marble revetment, dates early in the Forum's development. A *duovir quinquennalis* oversaw the installation of twin *scholae*, ornamented with finely carved marble benches and mosaic floors to either side of the Rostra.[86] Another parallel is the Stepped Base located near the northern entrance to the Forum (fig. 4.7, 4.11).[87] The second course of this large, layered limestone pedestal was designed as a bench with a flat seat above a concave vertical profile to accommodate feet. Above, two more steps were topped by a circular drum of white marble, now missing, whose cuttings suggest a tripod rather than a statue. Scranton dates its construction to the

---

[83] For Roman benches at Pompeii, see Hartnett 2008.

[84] See Schmidt 1995, 124–31 and 499–500 with catalogue nos. 9.15–16.

[85] For benches as euergetism at Pompeii, see Hartnett 2008, 116–17.

[86] The rostra has been dated to the Augustan period; Walbank 1997, 120–22; see also Scranton 1957, 93–110; and Kent 1966, 74 no. 157.

[87] Scranton 1957, 144–45 for the architecture. As with the monument of the *Augustales*, the Stepped Base and the Composite Circle Base (see below) have received little attention beyond their initial discovery and publication.

period of intense building in the Augustan-Tiberian period.[88] Since the orientation of this base more closely follows that of the South Stoa and the Rostra, the stepped base may predate the construction of the western temples and the Julian Basilica, whose orientations so strongly influenced the development of the lower Forum. If the stepped base dates to the early Augustan period, it could have provided a local prototype for the *Augustales* base, built in the Tiberian period.[89] Wear on the lowest step of the Composite Circle Base (fig. 4.12), built to the west of the Stepped Base at around the same time, suggests that it also was used as a seat although this may have been an unintended consequence of its comfortable proportions.[90]

Channeling Greek Corinth

The bench is not the only design element that evokes Greek statue bases. The strikingly complex combination of its round marble drum atop the quadrilateral monument departed from the quadrilateral bases preferred for imperial honorific monuments in Italy and the west. Whether simple or complex, cylindrical bases were used to support imperial statues more frequently in Achaia and Asia Minor, where they recalled a tradition reaching back to the Classical period.[91] By selecting a circular drum, the *Augustales* embraced a regional style of monument. There are similar examples of the Roman absorption of local architectural and building traditions throughout the eastern empire though this practice has mostly been recognized in large construction projects.[92] We should extend it to include statue bases, as

---

[88] Scranton 1957, 150. The Stepped Base appears to have become too crowded with loafers. Cuttings along the lowest step suggest a low fence eventually was installed to limit access.

[89] Scranton (1957, 150) dates the construction of the *Augustales* Base "not much later" than the stepped base.

[90] Scranton 1957, 146–47. For more on this base, see below.

[91] Schmidt 1995, 30–38, 69–79, and 169–75; see also Jacob-Felsch 1969. For round statue bases used for Roman imperial statues, see Højte 2005, 28.

[92] Even at Corinth, a colony with strong Roman identity from its refounding, colonists demonstrated an awareness of Greek styles and an ability and willingness to incorporate them into local projects when desired. The South Stoa and the Apollo Temple were repaired in a manner faithful to their original architectural orders. Among new Roman construction, the first Temple E appears to have been made of poros, a traditional building material of Greek Corinth; and to have featured a very Greek, Doric hexastyle façade atop a three-stepped crepidoma (Williams 1989, 159–60). Elsewhere, the Roman *magistri* of Delos looked to regional Greek orders and styles for three small temples in the Forum of the *competaliastes*; see Hasenohr 2001,

Fig. 4.11. The Stepped Base in the Forum at Corinth.

Fig. 4.12. The Composite Circle Base in the Forum at Corinth.

Corinth provides other examples of this practice. Two other monuments in the Forum echo the historicizing of the Base of the *Augustales*. The first is the Composite Circle Base, a concrete and poros foundation topped by a pieced, round drum of blue marble, finished with a white marble drum large enough for a multi-figure group (fig. 4.12).[93] Like the *Augustales* Base, it uses contrasting colored stones to articulate the various levels, suggesting that Corinth's euergetes were familiar with the form and designs of the complex cylindrical monuments of pre-Roman Achaia. The second, the square Stepped Base, fits within a tradition of tiered bases prevalent in the Archaic and Classical periods.[94] These retrospective bases may reflect a programmatic attempt by the Corinthian colonists to evoke a Greek agora, or at least to evoke the monumental topography of the space now occupied by the Roman Forum.

The central area of the Roman Forum had been the site of a racecourse initially constructed in the fifth century and rebuilt twice, once in the late 5th or early 4th centuries BCE, and again after 270 BCE.[95] Remains of the curved starting platform of the Classical track have been discovered, although its width and length are difficult to determine. More is known about its Hellenistic successor, whose starting platform was straight and whose orientation ran more directly east-west (fig. 4.13). Bases for statues and other monuments lay along its northern and southern sides. On the latter, where a water channel provided the boundary, remains of two broad bases that supported chariot groups have been identified; a third may have stood nearby.[96] Their form was simple: a low euthynteria on a step, topped by a plinth of marble or black limestone that supported bronze figures. The larger of the two predates the Hellenistic racecourse, while the smaller postdates it.

The monuments on the north are more varied. Vestiges of at least twenty-one bases have been identified on top and to the west of the

---

329–40. For the confluence of Hellenistic and Roman building styles in Asia Minor, see Waelkens 1989, 77–88.

[93] Scranton, 1957, 146–47.

[94] Scranton, 1957, 146–47. For Archaic and Classical stepped bases, see Jacob-Felsch 1969, 27–32, 51–52, and 63–64.

[95] For the race course, see Williams and Russell 1981 2–15; Williams 1970, 1–9.

[96] Williams 1970, 6–9. Williams notes that an inscribed base (Meritt 1931, 36, no. 30, commemorating a charioteer) does not match the cuttings on either foundation, suggesting a third monument in the area.

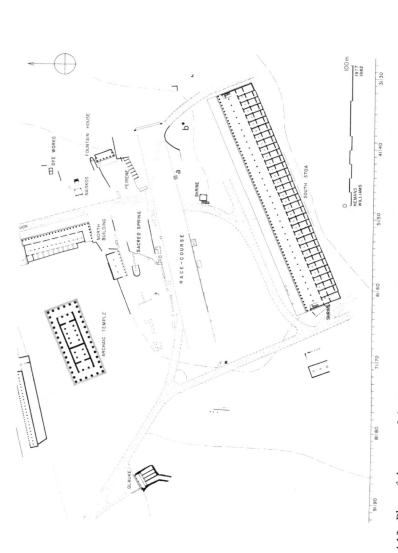

Fig. 4.13. Plan of the area of the Forum ca. 200 BCE, showing the Hellenistic racecourse with statue bases to the north and south, the future location of the Base of the *Augustales* (a) and the Circular Monument (b).

south triglyph wall that delimited the temenos of the Sacred Spring.[97] The date of construction of this wall, in the last quarter of the fourth or early third century BCE, provides a *terminus post quem* for their commissioning.[98] The array included round, columnar, and circular bases for tripods, along with many quadrilateral marble or limestone bases for one or more figures. At least one base appears to have been constructed from stones of contrasting colors or materials. A black limestone block bearing the inscription Λύσιππος ἐπ[όησε] (the work of Lysippos) was found upside down on one of the bases in the row.[99] Its dimensions and traces of cement suggest that it should be assigned to the neighboring base, having been flipped over by the early Roman colonists to free the block beneath, which was more esteemed as building material.

Many of the other monuments met a similar fate: several early Roman walls around the Sacred Spring were built out of spoliated statue bases.[100] By the time of the *Augustales* made their commission, these bases must have largely disappeared. While Roman colonists must have been aware of the racetrack, which provided the orientation for the buildings discussed above, it is difficult to know whether this knowledge would have extended to the bases located on its sides.[101]

One monument from Greek Corinth remained, however, to provide a local model for the *Augustales*. At the eastern limit of the Central Shops stands a massive poros drum 2.1 m in diameter on a square base consisting of four courses of poros ashlars (figs. 4.7, 4.14).[102] It was originally constructed in the 5th century BCE, perhaps in relation to the Classical and Hellenistic racecourse whose starting line was in the area. It is the only Greek monument to survive the systematic grading of the pre-Roman lower Forum. Its base did not match the orientations of any of the Roman buildings in the area; and the colonists integrated it into the design of the eastern Forum only with difficulty,

---

[97] For the bases, see Hill 1964, 123–25; 153; 185–92 and fig. 122.

[98] Williams 1969, 58–60.

[99] The inscription is Meritt 1931, 38–39 no. 34. For the details of its findspot, see Hill 1964, 186–87. The block, found atop base 6 (*id.*, 198, fig. 122) originally topped base 8.

[100] Hill 1964, 148; 150.

[101] Romano 2003, 287 and n. 47, noting that the stairs on the western porch of the Julian Basilica overlap the starting line of the Hellenistic racecourse. See also Scotton 1997, 103–107.

[102] Scranton 1957, 79–85; see also Williams and Russell 1981, 20–21; Broneer 1942, 153–54; and Dinsmoor 1942, 314–15.

first by constructing a circular base around it (ca. 15 BCE) and then by reworking this feature into a rectangle over the ensuing decades. White plaster covered its lower surfaces and perhaps the drum. The reconstruction of the superstructure has been debated. William Dinsmoor limits the circular element to two drums, the upper decorated with a hawk's beak molding above a fascia, although Scranton, following Broneer, extends the monument into a tall column topped with a statue or tripod towering above the Forum (fig. 4.15).[103]

The Circular Monument and that of the *Augustales* stand quite close to each other, with the Base of the *Augustales* echoing—not duplicating—its Greek predecessor. Just as the base's location helped it participate in the Augustan-period commissions to the east and west, it also created a visual and semantic discourse with the Circular Monument (fig. 4.16). The two resonate from nearly every angle of the Forum although the scenography becomes especially complex when viewed from the steps of the Julian Basilica. From this vantage point, the two monuments appear to form a calibrated parenthesis around the twin peaks of Acrocorinth, which rises beyond the façade of the South Stoa (fig. 4.17). While this last vista may be a happy accident, there is evidence that Roman monuments could be purposely inserted into historically or culturally significant settings to create meaningful new ensembles. One need only think of the circular monopteros dedicated to Roma and Augustus built directly in front of the Parthenon in Athens to understand how the addition of a new monument could shift or subvert meanings, or generate new associations.[104]

The Base of the *Augustales* was designed as a Hellenistic statue base and positioned to engage formally and topographically with the sole survivor of Corinth's monumental history. These features cast the Roman commission as a Greek monument of a particular sort: specifically, Hellenistic monumental bases and pillars, made to commemorate successes of the Diadochoi, which could be requisitioned in the

---

[103] Dinsmoor (1942, 314–15) identifies a second drum among blocks reused in modern constructions and connects a sketch by Ittar with the monument. Broneer (1942, 153–54) based his reconstruction on a coin showing a tall columnar monument; see also Scranton (1957, 82–83 and 127) with Plan E, showing the soaring column.

[104] See Baldassarri 2001, 405–06 and n. 11, with prior bibliography; see also Hoff 1996, 185–94. In addition, once completed, monuments could be referenced rhetorically to create personalized significances, as suggested by White (2005, 91–96).

Fig. 4.14. The Circular Monument, from the northeast. Photo by author.

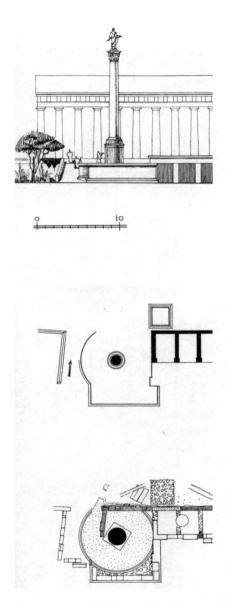

Fig. 4.15. Plan and reconstructed elevation of the Circular Monument.
(after Scranton 1951, Plan E)

Fig. 4.16. The Base of the *Augustales* from the northwest, with the Circular Monument beyond. Photo by author.

Fig. 4.17. Acrocorinth framed by the Circular Monument and the Base of the *Augustales*, as viewed from the north east corner of the Forum. Photo by author.

Roman period for imperial portrait statues.[105] For instance, a round monument in the Pergamene Sanctuary of Athena Polias Nikephoros, originally a victory monument of Attalos I, was enlarged in the early 1st century to accommodate a statue of Augustus dedicated by the demos and its Roman inhabitants (fig. 4.18).[106] In Athens two monumental pedestals originally dedicated to Attalid dynasts, one in front of the Stoa of Attalos, a second west of the propylaea of the Acropolis, were reinscribed for Roman quadriga portraits.[107] Corinth's early colonists probably updated the Circular Monument in a similar manner with a Roman statue. What is extraordinary is that the *Augustales*, a 'quintessentially' Roman organization, built *ex novo* a monument that "deliberately masqueraded as a Greek one,"[108] that not only paid homage to the city's Greek past but Romanized it with an imperial statue.

If this reading is correct, the monument joins a handful of examples where Corinth's colonists sought to create continuities with the town's historical and monumental past. Some scholars assert that Mummius's sack and the difficult conditions in the damaged city over the next century created a cultural rupture that the Roman colonists were not interested in bridging.[109] Others assume that Corinth's freedmen colonists, whether of Hellenic origin or not, would have been reluctant to revive the Greek past now "represented by provincials of inferior status," a status they had recently left behind.[110] Despite these claims, there is evidence that ideas about Greek Corinth played a role in the constitution of the colony's identity even in its early decades. Beyond the renovation of several key structures (the South Stoa, the Theater,

---

[105] On the reuse of statues and bases in general, see Blanck 1969; and briefly Hallett 2005, 139–44. Højte (2005, 37 and 62–63) briefly surveys Greek pillars and bases reused for Roman imperial portraits.

[106] See Stucchi 1984, 198–215, with bibliography.

[107] The pillar in the agora was rededicated to Tiberius (Vanderpool 1959); that on the Acropolis, to Agrippa (Travlos 1971, 483 fig. 91, and also 614, 622). See Goette 1990, 269–74 no. 2, with bibliography.

[108] The words are those of Williams (1987, 34–35), proposing that the present Fountain of Glauke was a Roman creation made to replace the original that had been destroyed by quarrying. Although his arguments have not been accepted (see for example, *contra* this position, Pfaff 2003, 133–34, followed by Robinson 2005, 128–38), they raise the possibility that monuments in Greek style could be consciously recreated in Roman Corinth.

[109] Walbank 1997, 101; Williams 1987, 26–32. Engels (1990, 62) downplays the Greek elements in the Roman colony. For Corinth between the sack of 146 BCE and its refounding, see Gebhard and Dickie 2003, 266–77.

[110] Walbank 1989, 372 n. 29; *id.* 1997, 97; 107.

Fig. 4.18. Victory monument of Attalos I rededicated to Augustus, in the Sanctuary of Athena Polias Nikephoros at Pergamon. (After Stucchi 1984, fig. 9)

the Archaic Temple), this is most clear in the realm of religion, where rituals, cult sites, and perhaps priestly titles were revived though often with a Roman twist.[111] In the urban center, the architecture and the myths surrounding the fountains of Peirene and Glauke were over-hauled to create historiated landmarks of Greco-Roman culture.[112] And much like the Base of the *Augustales*, archaistic and classicizing artworks, including sculpture and pedestals, were commissioned to replace the 'sculptural past' ruined by looting.[113]

The monument of the *Augustales* was probably one of the latest commissions of the early imperial Forum and was commissioned not by the town's most elite citizens, but by a new civic group with signifi-cant resources and a unique opportunity. The design adopted by the commissioning *Augustales* responded to a past and present history: it expressed contemporary values, honoring an emperor within the formal and conceptual currents of local euergetism. At the same time, it anchored that climate in Corinth's past, by creating a fictionalized pedigree. Oriented along the axis of the Hellenistic racecourse, simu-lating a victory monument, the monument proposed itself as an arti-fact of the heroic past, perhaps the last remnant of the racetrack that organized the major axes of the Augustan buildings. With each pass-ing year, the distinction between Roman commission and Greek form would blur, rooting the monument more firmly in the ancient past.

THE LIFE OF THE MONUMENT

The base commissioned by the *Augustales* encapsulated a spectrum of Roman behaviors and attitudes. Most broadly, it can be read as the product of emperor worship and as testimony of the engagement of the *Augustales* in the public life of their town, but details of its com-

---

[111] For the buildings, see Wiseman 1979, 513–21, with bibliography. The revived cults include that of Asklepios, Demeter/Ceres and Kore/Proserpina, and Aphrodite/Venus on Acrocorinth (Bookidis 2005, 159–63). Walbank (1989, 382–83) sees in the title *theocolus Iovis Capitolini* the survival of the title of the Θεοκόλος, or priest, of an unknown cult of Zeus at Corinth. For the return of the Isthmian Games to Corinth's control by 40 BCE, see Gebhard 1993, 78–82. For the addition of *Caesarea* and *Sebastea* to these contests, see Gebhard *id.*, 86–88; as well as West 1931, 64–66; and Kent 1966, 72–73. Generally, see also Wiseman 1979, 494–95.

[112] See Robinson 2005; see also Williams 1987, 34–35. Robinson (*id.*, 133 n. 59) cites Alcock (1997) as a precedent for historical imagination in the Hellenistic period.

[113] See Ridgway 1984, 90. I thank Aileen Ajootian for this reference.

missioning, siting, and design reveal a more specific and temporally complex picture. Probably made as a gift *ob honorem*, it marks an important moment in the public careers of two or more Corinthians. Positioned within an assembly of contemporaneous monuments, it documents early 1st century attitudes towards emperor worship and the blossoming of the town's civic center. Designed as a historiated monument in dialogue with a specific fragment of the past, it brought Greek Corinth into the Roman colony. Standing over time, it demonstrates the anticipated and unanticipated ways in which inscribed portrait monuments—ultimately, public furniture—became protagonists in their own settings.

Over the course of its life, the base and its statue functioned as a testimony to the activities and allegiances of the *Augustales*, admirably fulfilling the long-term goals of commemorative inscribed monuments. It promoted an ongoing civic group and optimistically characterized their continued standing in their community by its enduring presence and the details of the inscription, whose visually consonant words 'Augustus' and '*Augustales*' in lines 1 and 3 underscored the refined ties of 'Augustus's men.' Over time, the monument reasserted this information via its commanding physical presence and its concise text, keeping this message alive and active.[114]

At the same time, its unique design and prime location activated it in unusual and perhaps unintended ways, making it a protagonist both in its own functioning and in the life of the town. As with mile markers, the round drum enhanced legibility, especially for those moving past the monument. But the monument encouraged more than 'spelling out along the road,' or the active engagement a Roman passer-by would expect as she or he moved past the base.[115] It actually halted movement, attracting an audience with the offer of a prime perch.[116] Wear on the treads of the base indicates that it was a popular gathering place (fig. 4.19). From its central location, sitters enjoyed a vista of the Forum, the comings and goings through the propylaea and events taking place at the Rostra. We see a similar tactic at work in the *scholae* tombs of Pompeii, which offered a welcome resting spot to those

---

[114] Sartori 1997, 43.
[115] Susini 1988.
[116] Those familiar with Rome will immediately recall the statue of Giordano Bruno in the Campo de'Fiori, whose base has become a popular hangout spot.

approaching the city.[117] Monuments of this sort and the inscriptions they bear not only sought to stimulate passers-by to remember the commemorated; they actively invited their audience to become participants in the work of the monument.[118] Sitters posed around the base became a living sculptural tableau literally seated at the feet of the emperor. As vocal extensions of the inscription, they might call out to others passing by, encouraging them to approach.

Wear on the western side of the *Augustales* Base is especially extensive, suggesting that this was a favored vantage point. From here, sitters could follow the gaze of *divus* Augustus towards the panoramic façades on the western side of the Forum. In this sense, the base became an inadvertent builder of consensus beyond the norm.[119] As a good imperial monument, it made the deified emperor manifest in the center of town. It further personalized the imperial presence by encouraging sitters to sympathetically see what the *divus* saw. Yet the monument still insisted on the hierarchies of the empire. It placed the emperor above, with an unobstructed view to the end of the Forum and beyond, and the citizenry below, their perspective on local goings-on (the west side also commands the best view of the Rostra). In between, the inscription made the *Augustales* verbally present as donors and orchestrators.

While the functional design of the monument may have encouraged users to congregate, it also paradoxically opened the monument to other, unintended uses at odds with its message of imperial consensus. Roman authorities distrusted unregulated gatherings, which were seen as fomenting unrest. Professional associations in Asia Minor were encouraged to participate in the civic honorific activities of their towns as a way to integrate them into the social fabric.[120] But *collegia*

---

[117] See Kockel 1983. One might also think of the tomb of the fictional *Augustalis*, Trimalchio (Petr. *Satyr.* 71), not because it shares any supposed 'freedman ostentation' with the Corinthian monument but because, like the real *Augustales* of Corinth, Trimalchio's brilliant design—a tomb with sundial—incorporated a functioning public work into an otherwise private monument. Its purpose, as articulated by Trimalchio, was to compel "…anyone who wants the time of day…to read my name."

[118] In a similar way, I have argued that foundation inscriptions compel annual gatherings around the statue that they label on the day when the distributions they record were distributed (Laird 2006); see also Sartori (1997, 51), who cites Pliny (*Ep.* 7.29) on the power of epigraphy to distract a viewer.

[119] Ando 2000, 228–53 characterizes imperial portraits as part of a Roman system aimed at fostering consensus throughout the empire.

[120] Van Nijf 1997, 131–206.

Fig. 4.19. Worn western tread of the Base of the *Augustales*. Photo by author.

and other associations were carefully controlled and periodically suppressed, particularly following riots or civil disturbances. The most famous of these was the crackdown on illicit *collegia* at Pompeii following the riot in the Amphitheater of 59 CE.[121] Likewise, sitting idly was an activity equated by some writers with un-Roman *mores*. A *senatus consultum* in Rome prohibited the erection of benches and sitting to watch *ludi*.[122] Slaves who took their time on errands and returned home late were labeled *errones*, a status that had to be acknowledged at sale.[123] Despite this, there is evidence that some slaves spent their time loafing and lounging, perhaps as an indirect form of resistance.[124]

While *Augustales* have never been accused of these types of misbehavior, the monument they commissioned gently encouraged it, for its benches expressly invited loiterers to gather to pass the time. Many sitters chose the imperial sightline to the west, a viewpoint that also favored the civil activities of the Rostra. But less civic-minded activities took place to the east.[125] The tread of this bench is etched with a rectangular board for the game of *mola* (fig. 4.20). Boards for this game have been found scratched into the pavement of the Basilica Julia in the Roman Forum and onto a roof tile in Cologne.[126] While the board at Corinth is difficult to date, it respects the eastern edge of the bench, indicating that it could have been carved onto the base while the Forum was still functioning as a civic space.[127] Placed on the east side, the gaming would have taken place behind the emperor's back. Yet the base still defused malicious loitering, bringing people into the public eye of the of the Forum, around the emperor's feet.

---

[121] Tacitus, *Annales* 14.17. See also Acts 19:25–27, describing a riot by the silversmiths in Ephesos; and Pliny, *Ep.* 10.94, in which Trajan permits a *collegium* in Amisus as long as it is not factious or disorderly, but orders Pliny to prohibit them elsewhere for the same reason.

[122] Hartnett (2008, 105) citing Valerius Maximus 2.4.1–2; and also Cicero, *Flac.* 15–16.

[123] Dig. 21.1.17.14; I thank Sandra Joshel for this reference.

[124] Bradley 1994, 115–17.

[125] For evidence that benches outside houses at Pompeii were places for romantic trysts, see Hartnett 2008, 95–98.

[126] Salza Prina Ricotti, 1995, 98; Rieche, 1984, 72, fig. 29; von Petrikovits, 1980, fig. 169. Fittà, (1997, 166 and fig. 276) notes *mola* boards inscribed onto two marble slabs reused for the baulustrades of the cloisters of S. Paolo fuori le Mura and S. Giovanni in Laterano.

[127] The Forum appears to have remained clear until the twelfth century; Scranton, 1957, 32.

Fig. 4.20. Board for the game of *mola* on the eastern tread of the Base of the *Augustales*. Photo by author.

The base commissioned by the *Augustales*, complex in design and long-lived, emerges as a monument that combines emperor worship with local and regional styles to create a distinctive piece of urban furniture. I have argued that it can and should be viewed in a variety of overlapping contexts including, but not limited to: formal, regional, historical, urbanistic, and social. Approached in this way, the monument reveals its donors' primary concerns with their place in Roman Corinth expressed through Greek Corinth's monumental past. But the *Augustales* monument reminds us that the donors' original intentions may exert little power over time. While a statue may be constructed in specific dialogue with its site, that discourse will always be changed or even contradicted by those who actively use the monument.

CHAPTER FIVE

GREEK HERITAGE IN ROMAN CORINTH AND EPHESOS:
HYBRID IDENTITIES AND STRATEGIES OF DISPLAY IN
THE MATERIAL RECORD OF TRADITIONAL
MEDITERRANEAN RELIGIONS

Christine M. Thomas

Archaeological remains are an important but sometimes neglected tool for conceptualizing the impact of Roman imperial domination on Greek religion in the Eastern empire. In their visibility and impact on urban space, material objects represent conscious attempts to display the activity of the agents who made them and thus can be valuable for reconstructing the self-representation of ancient subjects.[1] Since Corinth, as a refounded colony, is in many ways an instructive anomaly among the Greek cities of the Roman East, this study will be explicitly comparative, drawing from the evidence at Corinth and contrasting it with a specific example of traditional religion from Ephesos. The material remains will then be contextualized with their descriptions in the account of Pausanias and in the *Ephesiaka*, a second-century CE Greek novel. The literary works open another angle onto the aspirations of the Greek-speaking elite of the eastern Empire, a segment of the population that offers the richest evidence for the phenomenon of identity construction during this period. Literary sources also serve as a reminder that urban space does not consist only of the physical locations through which people moved, but also of the stories they told about them. As will be shown, in their emphasis on a non-hybrid Greek identity, the literary sources sometimes contrasted dramatically

---

[1] Current conceptions of agency in archaeological research derive from Anthony Giddens's theory of 'structuration,' in which each social agent both receives and produces cultural traditions in her individual appropriation of them; Giddens 1979, 69) and 1984. Various theorists of archaeology have sharpened the concept of agency as it can be read from material objects; Barrett 2001; Robb 2005; and Dobres and Robb 2000. Cognitive archaeology employs material objects to make hypotheses about the development of abstract and symbolic thought, which is particularly germane to the study of ancient religion; Renfrew 1998 and 2001; Mithen 2001.

with the public display of the monuments, which tended to present a more complex fusion of indigenous and Roman features.

Corinth, a Greek city that was refounded as a Roman colony in 44 BCE after a long hiatus in its civic life, provides a clear contrast to Ephesos, which never suffered a break in the continuity of its traditions.[2] Even as a Roman colony, Corinth differed from many others.[3] Pisidian Antioch, for example, like other colonies in Asia Minor, had functioning civic institutions at the time that Roman veterans were settled there: the colony represented the addition of formally constituted groups of veterans to an existing Greek city.[4] This was not the case at Corinth, though most signs indicate continued habitation between the 'sack' of the city by Mummius in 146 BCE and its refoundation. Cicero attests people living among the ruins in 63 BCE (*Leg. agr.* 1.5, 2.5.1). Archaeological traces likewise show continued settlement.[5] Graffiti on pottery and the *defixiones* found in the sanctuary of Demeter, which are in Greek, suggest the presence of a Greek population, even if these may have been settlers from outlying regions rather than the "old Corinthians" whom Pausanias no longer found in the Roman city (2.1.2).[6] Economic life also continued. If the land was *ager publicus* as both literary and archaeological testimony suggest,[7] it would then have been leased to tenant farmers. Absent, however, is material evidence of the usual accoutrements of civic life: building programs, organized civic

---

[2] For the date: Walbank 1997, 97–99.

[3] Walters's work on the civic contexts of early Christian mission differentiates first between colonies and cities, and then between types of Roman colonies; 2005, esp. 398–400, which contrasts Corinth with Thessalonike. See also the chapter of Millis in this volume.

[4] Noted by Yegül 2000, 133–34. New evidence has been published in Byrne and Labarre 2006; see also the site survey in Mitchell and Waelkens 1998; and articles in Drew-Bear, Thomas, and Taşlıalan 2002.

[5] D. Romano (2000, 87) notes two roads that traverse the Forum that date from this "dark age" between 146–44 BCE, one along the east end of the south stoa and another parallel to the north of the Hellenistic racecourse.

[6] Walbank 1997, 95–96, 103–7; Gebhard and Dickie 2003, 261–78; confirmed by the study of amphora handles in Grace 1934. Other finds from the east and west ends of the Forum suggest continued habitation through this period; Bookidis 2005, 148–49; I. Romano 1994.

[7] D. Romano (2000, 86–88) cites Cicero, who claims that the *ager publicus* around Corinth was *vectigalis*, that is, a source of income and taxation. Romano criticizes Alcock's theory (1993) of rural abandonment by pointing out that her survey did not take into account patterns of Roman land division that were signs of continued agricultural activity.

cult, and durable votive objects produced in workshops. In terms of its institutional life, Corinth was not a city during this period.

Roman Renewal of Traditional Corinthian Religion

Corinth shows an interesting mix of continuity and discontinuity in its religious sites between the Classical-Hellenistic periods and its Roman colonization. Although a century passed before Corinth was refounded (146 BCE to 44 BCE), many of the most important sanctuaries were rebuilt and rededicated on the very spots that they once occupied in the Greek city. In many cases one can argue for cultic continuity as well. The god or gods honored at some of these temples seem to have been the same, although determining their identity can be more problematic than the simple identification of religious activity at the site. Sometimes clear evidence from inscriptions or dedications exists. The epigraphic record of the sanctuaries of Demeter and of Asklepios, for example, demonstrates that these two divinities continued to be worshipped in their traditional locations even in the Roman period.[8] The most extensive evidence for the identification of religious sites at Corinth in the Roman period is from Pausanias, who visited the city ca. 160 CE. Although he preserved a large amount of useful material, he was describing Roman Corinth more than two centuries after it was refounded. Pausanias also raises a further problem, which is at the heart of this paper: he wrote in Greek, not Latin, the official language of the Roman colony of Corinth, which leads one to question whether he was transmitting the names of the sanctuaries as they were understood by the Roman inhabitants of Corinth.[9] If Pausanias was using Greek equivalents for the official Latin names (*interpretatio Graeca*), one must note that equivalent items are not identical.

Among the traditional Greek sanctuaries at Corinth are four for which clear evidence exists of their reconstruction by the Roman founders and their rededication to the same or an equivalent divinity. The Temple of Apollo north of the Forum dates at least from the

---

[8] See the chapters of Økland and Wickkiser in this volume.

[9] Spaeth (2007) has shown that votive inscriptions, dedications, and priesthoods during the Roman imperial period overwhelmingly name Roman gods and Roman priesthoods despite the common assumption that Greek culture re-emerged as the dominant force by the 2nd century CE.

Archaic period and was seen by Pausanias after it was refounded;[10] the Temple of Aphrodite on Acrocorinth has traces of pre-Roman construction and activity and was seen in the Roman period by Strabo;[11] the Asklepieion to the north near the Classical circuit wall has an archaeological record that spans the Greek and Roman periods;[12] and the Sanctuary of Demeter and Kore, partway up Acrocorinth, was very active in the classical and Hellenistic periods and has clear evidence of reconstruction in the Augustan period.[13] For each of these four sanctuaries, the case for cultic continuity is good.

Strikingly, in all of these cases, the archaeological evidence also suggests architectural discontinuity between the Hellenistic and Roman periods. At most of these sanctuaries, the Hellenistic structures were not reused to build the Roman temples; the exception is the Asklepieion. The temples of Apollo and Aphrodite seem to have been made new in Roman times from the foundation up.[14] Although a number of the existing buildings in the Demeter sanctuary were renovated, it is clear that the focus of the temple changed dramatically. The Roman sanctuary was dominated by three small prostyle temples high on the upper terrace, structures that were absent in the Hellenistic sanctuary.[15]

None of these sanctuaries has durable dedications that date from the period between 146 and 44 BCE, which raises the issue of *ritual* continuity. Did the practices of worship and devotion remain the same between the Hellenistic period and the Roman colonial foun-

---

[10] The Archaic Temple dates to the 6th or 5th century BCE. Its dedication to Apollo is attested by a *pinax*; Bookidis 2005, 142–43. Pausanias 2.3.6 identifies the refounded temple.

[11] Scant evidence for the sanctuary, such as cuttings and blocks for a small temple, dates to the pre-Roman period; Blegen, Broneer, Stillwell and Bellinger 1930, 1–28; Bookidis 2005, 147 and 160. Williams (1993, 32) notes that the presence of Proto-Geometric and Geometric pottery here may suggest a very early cult presence. It was refounded early, since Strabo saw it in 29 BCE (8.6.21).

[12] On the pre-Roman evidence, Roebuck and de Waele 1951, 8–15, 21–64, and 152–59. It was restored in 25 BCE, dated by a painted inscription; Roebuck and de Waele 1951, 156–57. Pausanias attests the sanctuary in the Roman period (2.4.5), as do two Hadrianic inscriptions in Greek; Bookidis 2005, 159 n. 84.

[13] Traces of cult date from the 8th century BCE and proliferate throughout the Classical and Hellenistic periods; Bookidis and Stroud 1997, 13–170. Numismatic and ceramic evidence suggests that the sanctuary returned to use in the Augustan period; Bookidis and Stroud 1997, 272–75.

[14] Williams (1993, 32) suggests that the cult image changed from an armed, warrior-like Aphrodite to one more like Venus.

[15] These date to the 70s CE, most likely after the earthquake of ca. 77; Bookidis 2005, 161–62; Bookidis and Stroud 1997, 337–71.

dation? Archaeological evidence would attest only durable structures and offerings. The overwhelming majority of offerings to the gods in antiquity were, however, perishable. Not only the sacrifices of animals, vegetables, or incense but also votive offerings were usually made of perishable materials: wreaths, garlands, wood *pinakes*, toys, maternity clothes, workmen's tools, wax tablets. These inexpensive gifts were often so numerous at sanctuaries that their clutter would obscure completely from view the cult statue—the one item that is archaeologically 'visible.'[16] It is, therefore, possible that small votives of this sort continued to be offered at sanctuaries by the local population during the interim period.[17]

Surviving architectural evidence, however, suggests changes in ritual practices. The Sanctuary of Demeter offers sufficient published evidence to draw a contrast between the Hellenistic and Roman periods with some specificity. The finds suggest ritual discontinuity, as Barbette Spaeth,[18] drawing on the work of Nancy Bookidis and Ronald Stroud, has emphasized.[19] In the Hellenistic period, the courtyard of the middle terrace, easily viewed from the theater seats on the upper terrace, dominated the sanctuary (see fig. 7.1 in this volume). The Roman sanctuary instead showed greater monumentality, with the temples on the upper terrace axially oriented and facing the long staircase that provided entry to the sanctuary (fig. 5.1). The reorganization of the space suggests that people were doing something different with it; namely, that typical ritual actions had changed. Dining facilities were also dismantled or converted into simple cult rooms with no dining apparatus. The practice of cultic dining prevalent in the Classical period (5th-4th century) was apparently not resumed.[20]

The small finds suggest a similar story of ritual discontinuity. The sanctuary continued to be active in the Roman period, but the nature of the activity seems to have changed dramatically. Bookidis notes the

---

[16] Van Straten 1981, 78, citing Pausanias 2.11.6 and 3.26.1. On types and occasions for votives: Rouse 1902.

[17] Bookidis, however, surveys the evidence and concludes that most sanctuaries were abandoned in this period because of the absence of even small traces of activity such as coins or pottery; 2005, 149–50.

[18] Spaeth 2006; Bookidis 2005, 162–63.

[19] Bookidis 2005, 161–62. The final publication (Bookidis and Stroud 1997) treats the individual aspects of the refoundation; further discussion below. For the preliminary report: Stroud 1993.

[20] The dining rooms were more numerous in the Classical period; Bookidis and Stroud 1997, 393–420; and 277–91 on their abandonment in the Roman period.

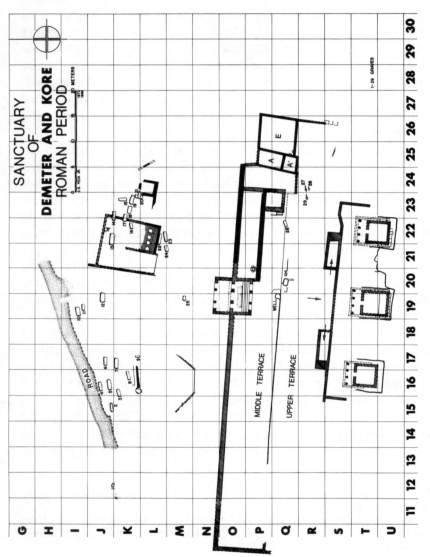

Fig. 5.1. Plan: Sanctuary of Demeter and Kore, Roman period.

radical decline of the votive offerings so common during the earlier periods, such as votive pottery and terracotta figurines. For the Classical and Hellenistic periods, 24,000 such items were recovered. In the Roman period, in contrast, there are only 29 such offerings.[21] At the same time that small votive offerings disappear, fragments of honorific statues and inscriptions in marble make their first appearance. This movement away from small votive offerings and toward the display of honorific inscriptions echoes the construction of the temple buildings, themselves quintessential items of display and the focal point of this sanctuary in the Roman period.

On the whole, the rededication of the sanctuaries in Roman Corinth, although respecting the traditional locations of the temples, shows no architectural or ritual continuity with their previous usage. Charles Williams has noted that, in the cases of the Temple of Apollo and the Temple of Aphrodite, the Roman refoundation made no attempt to preserve the Greek temple plan or its orientation. Instead, the temples were completely rebuilt in Roman style. As he writes,

> ...the Romans knew about and tried to revive the Greek sanctuaries of the city, if possible even on their original sites, but were not concerned to restore them to their original form or recreate their original Greek ritual with any great precision or accuracy.[22]

Instead of 'refoundation,' which suggests cultic continuity, a more accurate term might be 'revival' or 'renewal,' which would parallel the renewals of long-forgotten cults and priesthoods in the city of Rome by Augustus during the same period, renewals that often involved significant changes.[23]

Monumental Display in Traditional Religions of the Roman East

The increase in monumental display noted at the Sanctuary of Demeter in Corinth is a more general phenomenon in the Greek cities of

---

[21] Merker 2000, 311–19.

[22] Williams 1987, 31–32. Gebhard, studying the cult of Melikertes-Palaimon in Isthmia in the Roman period, concludes that despite cultic discontinuity in the Roman refoundation, "the debt to tradition seems to have been greater than previously supposed" (2005, 203).

[23] Scheid 2005; Galinsky 1996, 288–311.

Asia Minor during the Roman period. It is also evident at the Sanctuary of Demeter in Pergamon, where honorific statues and dedications similarly eclipsed other sorts of votive offerings in the 2nd century.[24] In contrast to the Corinthian sanctuary of Demeter, the Pergamene example is an old Greek sanctuary with an uninterrupted history of worship before the Roman period. The increase in display at the Sanctuary of Demeter in Corinth is then not simply a function of its status as a Roman colony, or of its discontinuous history as a sanctuary. It is a characteristic that Greek cities and Roman colonies share. Monumental buildings and the epigraphic record multiply in most Greek cities in the eastern provinces during the early Roman imperial period.

It is on this point that Corinth and Ephesos bear remarkable similarities. In both cases, as will be seen, the archaeological record of traditional cults shows a dramatic increase in epigraphic and architectural dedications during the first two centuries of the Empire, which suggests that urban centers of any size participated in a global market of monumental display. Despite the difference in status between 'Greek' Ephesos and 'Roman' Corinth, the evidence of their traditional cults shows analogous responses to the presence of Roman power.

This should not be surprising. A good quarter-century of studies in colonialism and empire in the modern world has demonstrated that the identities of ruler and ruled are not fixed, pre-scripted roles but are mutually defined in specific historical situations, in a fluid and complex fashion.[25] Greek inhabitants of the eastern provinces were not simply passive objects in a Roman drama of empire; it was a collaborative phenomenon.[26]

At the same time, however, the particular nature of each city's display allows us to differentiate between the particular constellation of social actors in the Roman colony of Corinth and those in the Greek city of Ephesos. No society is divided neatly into two groups, the ruler

---

[24] C. Thomas 1998.

[25] Most scholars mark the beginning of post-colonial theory with Said 1978. Important are Bhabha 1994; Spivak 1987 and 1988. The literature is vast and divides into subfields along disciplinary lines. Recent work has shown more awareness that empires have widely varying institutional structures and cultural effects; Young 2001. Also important is the attempt to devise methods and theories that co-identify the colonizer as an object of scholarly study from an indigenous perspective; Chakrabarty 2000; L. T. Smith 1999.

[26] As R. Robinson writes, "Imperialism was as much a function of its victim's collaboration...as it was of European expansion," quoted by Said 1993, 316; Scott 1986 and 1990.

and the ruled.[27] Power is shared among several groups. The mix of new settlers in early colonial Corinth was diverse, including freedmen, *negotiatores*, some veterans, and Greek notables from outside,[28] in addition to the stock of local Greek inhabitants who had lived at the site even after its destruction in 146 BCE. As is evident from the epigraphic record, Ephesos also had many of the same new inhabitants, especially freedmen and *negotiatores*. Ephesos had begun relations with Rome early, even before it became the provincial capital in 29 BCE. Unlike Corinth, however, it had an entrenched local elite exhibiting considerable power and organization, who, as will be seen below, were able to express themselves as an identifiable group with a distinct profile, and to maintain the practice of their traditional religious institutions even where they most directly incorporated Roman cultural expressions.[29]

Traditional Ephesian Religion in the Roman Period

The association of the Kouretes at Ephesos is a religious institution that sponsored traditional civic festivals and is well-documented from the Hellenistic through the Roman periods.[30] It is attested from the 4th century BCE onward and was centuries old before the Romans came.[31] Though extant for centuries, the association only achieved prominent monumental display under the high Roman Empire in a series of annual lists of Kouretes.

The association of Kouretes at Ephesos is peculiarly local and deeply entwined with the foundation myth of the city. The Kouretes in Greek myth are usually associated with the birth of Zeus on Crete;[32] they

---

[27] The oversimplification of society into two groups is a weakness of Scott's work.

[28] As Spawforth notes, the colony was "dominated socially and politically by wealthy men of freedmen stock and by Roman families with business interests in the east, some no doubt of freedmen stock themselves, and many probably already resident in the east…when Corinth was refounded" (1996, 174). His work is based on the duovir lists of Amandry 1988. Yegül points out the importance of contact between Greeks and Roman *negotiatores*, which had begun in the 2nd century BCE; 2000, 135.

[29] An excellent example is Rogers 1991, 80–151.

[30] Knibbe 1981.

[31] Attested in two early inscriptions; Knibbe 1981, 13–14 no. A1–A2.

[32] In Crete, the myth was bound together with ritual. The Kouretes were young men who performed a dance with weapons in the worship of Zeus, reminiscent of the rites of the Ephesian Kouretes. This was a typical rite of passage. Young men who were about to become citizens went into the wild to be initiated and then returned to

were the helpers of Rhea who banged on their weapons to drown out her birth pangs so that Kronos would not discover and destroy the infant.[33] In the Ephesian myth, however, the din of the Kouretes was not to hide the birth of Zeus but rather that of Zeus's children by Leto, the twins Apollo and Artemis, to shield them from the wrath of Zeus's legitimate spouse, Hera.[34] According to the Ephesian informants of Strabo, Apollo and Artemis were not born on the sacred island of Delos but in a grove of cypress trees in a location called Ortygia, which lay to the south of Ephesos in the valley of the Kenchrios river not far from the coast. Strabo records that an annual festival took place there in which the νεοί, "new men," that is, "new citizens," competed with one another in presenting banquets; and that the ἀρχεῖον ("ancient [association]") of the Kouretes held a symposium with certain sacrifices for initiates (θυσίαι μύστικαι). Epigraphic sources attest that this annual celebration took place on the birthday of Artemis in the month of May when all Ephesians processed from the Temple of Artemis to Ortygia and back.[35]

The sanctuary in Strabo's time comprised several temples, some of them Archaic with old wooden cult images and others, more recent.[36] The presence of wooden statues suggests a cult of some antiquity, corroborated by the early appearance of the association of Kouretes in the epigraphic record. The association thus performed the leading role in a festival that was at once both the founding myth and the 'Christmas' celebration of Ephesos, the festival for the birth of the goddess who gave the city its identity. Epigraphic evidence suggests that this

---

the city as citizens and armed defenders. The myth explicates this: Rhea gives birth in the wilderness to Zeus, who is the symbol of political order; Graf 1999, 259. Strabo emphasizes the ecstatic character of the rites in his comparison of the Kouretes to satyrs and *korybantes*; 10.3.11.

[33] By the early Empire, the dominant myth of the Kouretes had been incorporated into the Roman festival calendar but with a more Anatolian rather than Cretan twist. Lucretius describes the Kouretes as associates of the Magna Mater, an "armed band dancing, fired with blood, leaping in rhythm midst the Phrygian throng, shaking their awful crests with nodding heads" (Luc. *De re. nat.*, 2.600–40, trans. Melville). The Greek Dionysios of Halikarnassos, who lived in Rome in the 1st century, calls "dancing after the manner of the Curetes…a native institution among the Romans" (2.71.3–4).

[34] The myth is transmitted by Strabo 14.1.20, as well as Tacitus *Ann.* 3.61.

[35] The birthday of Artemis is attested epigraphically as the sixth day of *Thargelion*, that is, sometime in May; *Inschriften von Ephesos* no. 1a, lines 224–25.

[36] In the same passage, Strabo lists the sacred olive tree where Leto is said to have given birth to the divine twins.

association, like the more traditional *gerousia*, was also a powerful group that could confer political rights such as citizenship, and that they were located in the Temple of Artemis,[37] near the center of population during the Archaic and Classical periods.[38]

In the Roman period, the association, which was composed of six to nine Kouretes elected annually,[39] continued to comprise male members of the leading families of Ephesos,[40] many of whose careers can be reconstructed from other sources. A recent study of the prominent Ephesian family of the Vedii shows that three of its members—all sons of the famous rhetor Flavius Damianus (135–205 CE) and of Vedia Phaedrina, the daughter of Vedius Antonius III and Papiane—each acquired not only senatorial rank, but also the Roman consulship.[41] The only local office that these three prominent Ephesians seem to have held is membership in the association of Kouretes. It was evidently among the most prestigious local offices a prominent Ephesian could hold, appropriate for anyone of sufficient importance to be not just a Roman senator but even a consul.[42]

---

[37] In one of the inscriptions, the Kouretes are listed prior to the *gerousia* in recommending a foreigner for Ephesian citizenship, involving inclusion in a tribe (φυλή) and in a *chiliasty* (χιλιαστύς), a division of a thousand peculiar to Ephesos, Samos, and Kos; Knibbe 1981, 13–14 no. A2. The inscription notes that it was to be set up within the Artemision, where the other grants of citizenship were recorded.

[38] On the location of the shoreline during this period: Kraft, Kayan, Brückner and Rapp 2000.

[39] The number of Kouretes varies slightly throughout the inscriptions without any steady increase or decrease. The number of cult attendants to the Kouretes, however, expands dramatically around the middle of the 1st century from one σπονδαύλης to a group including that plus a ἱεροσκόπος, ἱεροκῆρυξ, ἱερός ἐπὶ θυμιάτρου, and ἱεροφάντης. Knibbe argues that the increase indicates additional responsibilities, such as sacrifices connected with the Prytaneion; 1981, 76–92. Graf calls this into doubt; 1999, 256. As Rogers notes, these are offices typically associated with mysteries, which tends to affirm that the "initiatory sacrifices" noted by Strabo continued and perhaps expanded; 1999b, 245–47. These mysteries attracted not the marginal but the central members of Ephesian society.

[40] Despite the designation κοῦροι, prosopography indicates that the men who served were generally mature; Graf 1999, 255.

[41] T. Flavius Vedius Antoninus, proconsul of Africa; T. Flavius Damianus; and T. Flavius Phaedrus; Kalinowski 2002, 145.

[42] "The men who held the municipal offices and possessed the power to rule at the local level were Greeks and native Anatolians who had been granted the much-coveted Roman citizenship" (Yegül 2000, 137). In the second half of the 1st century, 17 percent of the senators for whom a provenience is indicated come from Greece and Asia Minor. By the second half of the 2nd century, it was 58 percent. Yegül cites Hammond (1957) and Halfmann (1982).

The most obvious change to this traditional Ephesian cult during Roman times was its location. Previously at home in the Temple of Artemis, the cultic heart of ancient Ephesos, in the Augustan period the center of the association moved to the newly-constructed Prytaneion.[43] This structure, which functioned as a religious and administrative center, was built around the end of the 1st century BCE in a location without a predecessor building. The particular spot, however, had ancient associations with the festivals of Artemis,[44] since it was a stop along the processional way.[45] The connection with Artemis continued after the construction of the Prytaneion. Both the famous statues of the Artemis of Ephesos were found in the Prytaneion, one of them carefully buried within the building,[46] and another of them, in two massive pieces, uncovered by the excavators in 1957. It was found in the forecourt of the Prytaneion where it had fallen face-down near the altar in Late Antiquity, never to be repaired nor replaced.[47]

This particular area, the Upper Agora, was an area of active construction during the early Roman period. Although it seems to have been transformed from a cemetery to a marketplace as early as the 2nd century BCE, the truly monumental constructions are Roman. This

---

[43] Although we do not know exactly when the association of the Kouretes moved to this location, the name of the association changes from an ἀρχαῖον to a συνέδριον around the turn of the millennium, about the same time that the Prytaneion was constructed; Knibbe 1981, 74–76. The earliest inscriptions found in this location date to the early 1st century CE; Knibbe 1981, 15–16 no. B1–B3.

[44] Epigraphic, topographic, and literary evidence suggests that the site of the Prytaneion was the location of traditional altars to Artemis on the sacred way; Knibbe 1999, 450; Knibbe and Langmann 1993, 11 and 21 n. 53. For the report of the excavation of the Prytaneion, Miltner 1959.

[45] The sacred way that ran around Mt. Pion (Panayır Dağ) encircled not only the necropolis but some of the oldest sanctuaries in Ephesos, such as the outdoor sanctuary of the 'mountain mother,' which is epigraphically datable to the 5th century BCE; C. Thomas 2004. The street leading up the slope to the Prytaneion ("Kouretes Street" is the modern name) runs diagonally to the Hellenistic grid system of Ephesos, which suggests that it was an old road predating the foundation of the Hellenistic city and pertaining to the sacred way that was in use before it; Knibbe and Thür 1995, 84.

[46] The 'schöne Artemis,' the smaller of the two larger statues on display at the Efes Museum in Selçuk (inv. no. 718), was found buried along with the 'kleine Artemis' inside the building of the Prytaneion; Knibbe 1999, 451.

[47] Efes Museum inv. no. 712. Miltner writes, "Auf dem Vorplatz des Herdesaales wurde südlich des Postamentsockels eine Statue der Artemis Ephesia in zweifacher Lebensgrösse gefunden, die auf dem Gesicht lag und durch den Sturz in zwei sauber anpassende Stücke zerbrochen war" (1959, 305–07). He states that the base was rather high and that the statue must have faced south, that is, toward the slope of the sacred way leading up to it. Knibbe concludes from this that the altar in the Prytaneion was an element in the sacred processional way; Knibbe and Langmann 1993, 21.

may have been the location of the Temple to the Divus Iulius and Dea Roma mentioned in Dio Cassius (51.20.6).[48] The area was thus already a location with strong Roman associations before the Prytaneion was built and the first extant lists of Kouretes were affixed there in the columns, architrave, and metopes of its entrance hall.

The imperial associations of the Upper Agora only multiplied in succeeding years. The huge Basilike ("Royal") Stoa that fronts the Prytaneion dates to 11 CE and featured a monumental dedicatory inscription in both Greek and Latin, as well as statues of Augustus and Livia, probably in the Chalcidicum on the east end (fig. 5.2).[49] Around 89–90 CE, the Temple of the Sebastoi was built upon its massive terrace overshadowing the Agora.[50] Perhaps because of this context, in lists dating after the Tiberian period, the Kouretes are portrayed not only as εὐσεβεῖς ("properly pious"), as in the earlier lists, but also as φιλοσέβαστοι ("loving the Augusti"), that is, devoted to the Roman emperors.[51]

Since the association of the Kouretes was a civic cult, its relocation to a Romanized part of the city happened at the initiative or at least with the permission of the municipal government. The Ephesians mentioned in the inscriptions seemed eager to engage with Roman culture on other fronts, since they advertised their achievement of

---

[48] The location of this temple is unknown. The structure between the Prytaneion and the Bouleuterion was identified by Alzinger (1974, 55) as a double temple to Roma and Augustus. Scherrer (1990, 87–101) has argued, on the basis of nearby statue finds probably dedicated to Artemis and Augustus, that this structure was not a temple but an altar; this was also Miltner's interpretation.

[49] These statues are on display in the Ephesos museum; inv. no. 1957 and 1-10-75. For their location: Alzinger 1974, 32–33; Jobst 1980; Hanlein-Schäfer 1985, 168–72; Engelmann 1993. On the basilica: Fossel-Peschl 1982; Mitsopoulos-Leon 1991; Mitsopoulos-Leon and Lang-Auinger 2007.

[50] The best and most thorough treatment of this structure and its religious implications is Friesen 1993.

[51] These later lists date from 54–59 CE onward, that is, they begin to use the term even before the dedication of the provincial temple of the Sebastoi in 89/90 CE. As Rogers notes, particularly unusual is the use of the term φιλοσέβαστοι for officials ostensibly dedicated to the service of gods other than the imperial cult; 1999a, 125–36. This may refer to a number of interlocking phenomena: first, the new location of the association of Kouretes in an area of the city in which several gods and goddesses were worshipped; second, the prominence of imperial cult sanctuaries and dedications in this area; and third, the increasing presence of Roman citizens among the personnel of the association of Kouretes. Graf (1999, 261–62) suggests a connection between the Kouretes and the Salii, first noticed by Dionysos of Halicarnassos (*Ant.* 2.70). At Rome the association of the Salii, as well as that of the Arval Brothers, were renewed and fostered as part of Augustus's religious policies.

Fig. 5.2. Statue of Livia found in Basilike Stoa in Ephesos. Courtesy of the
Efes Museum, Selçuk, Turkey. Photograph by author.

Roman citizenship by listing their names with the *tria nomina*, which include the name of the Roman *gens*, or family, into which they were adopted when they achieved citizenship. Nearly half the identifiable individuals on the lists of Kouretes from the 1st century CE are Roman citizens (26 of 58).[52] This leads to a profusion of hybrid names that may have sounded strange to a Greek speaker, such as Publius Vedius Diadoumenos (Πο. Οὐήδιος Διαδουμενός, no. B16),[53] Publius Cornelius Ariston (Πο. Κορνήλιος Ἀρίστων, no. B15), or Tiberius Claudius Nikomedes (Τι. Κλαύδιος Νεικομήδης, no. B22). The very unfamiliarity of these Latin gentilicia is underscored by the variant spellings in Greek: Flavius (Φλάουιος or Φλάβιος), Vedius (Οὐήδιος or Βήδιος), Aurelius (Αὐρήλιος or Αὐρέλιος) and Vibius (Βείβιος or Οὐείβιος).[54]

In a culture that associated the ability to speak Greek with a civilized identity, giving ground on this index of Hellenicity was no small matter. A letter ascribed to Apollonios of Tyana portrays him warning his fellow Greeks not to exchange their traditional Greek names for the new Roman ones lest their ancestors fail to recognize them when they die and arrive in the underworld (*ep.* 71). Change of name meant change of identity. Critically, these hybrid names with which the Ephesian Kouretes introduced their claims to Roman identity appear in the context of the peculiarly Ephesian myth of Artemis's birth, an event fundamental to the identity of the city.

HYBRIDITY IN EPHESOS: TRADITIONAL ELITES AND NEW PATRONS

The association of the Kouretes in the Augustan period thus shows willing and public acceptance by the leading families of Ephesos of a hybrid Greco-Roman identity. This is a fairly common feature of successful situations of political domination, and one can find similar examples throughout the Roman Empire. A number of studies of provincial religion, especially imperial cult, emphasize this *consensual* understanding of hybridity.[55] It is a productive approach in that it

---

[52] The proportion increases over the course of the 1st century from ca. one third of the Kouretes in the Julio-Claudian period (8 out of 25) to more than half in the Flavian period (18 out of 34); Rogers 1999b, 129.

[53] References are to the ennumeration in Knibbe 1981.

[54] For these and similar examples: Knibbe 1981, 119–34 and 138–44.

[55] Price 1984; Friesen 1993; and perhaps Gradel 2002.

assumes agency on the part of the colonized in the construction of their identity, both as a way of avoiding negative sanctions from the more powerful and as a strategy for negotiating benefits from those who dominate them. The assumption of features of Roman culture was advantageous to the powerful families of Ephesos. Roman citizenship in particular brought a number of benefits to the individual and, perhaps more significantly, to his descendents.[56] Offering citizenship was an important mechanism, effected through adoption into a Roman family, by which the leading Roman citizens brought non-citizens into the project of empire and assured their complicity and support.[57]

Part of the importance of the concept of hybridity, however, is its recognition that the colonized, the dominated, are not only active agents in the game of imperialism but also have their own goals. Why should Greek urban elites be judged solely by how many of them received Roman citizenship, and whether they were accepted into the Senate? Was their primary purpose in life to exist in successful collaboration with their dominators?[58] A *consensual* understanding of the Kouretes inscriptions would read the texts as the strategy of a provincial elite to advertise their acceptance and collaboration with the imperial apparatus and its representatives. I would suggest instead that these inscriptions show the leading families of Ephesos in competition with other supraregional benefactors for prominence in the city.

The increase in the epigraphic record for the Kouretes in the Roman period begs for explanation. It is clear that this Ephesian institution existed during the Hellenistic period. The number of Kouretes elected each year remains about the same. Yet the annual lists of Kouretes underwent a dramatic increase in the Augustan period that continued to the beginning of the 3rd century, when all free citizens of the Roman empire were granted Roman citizenship under the *Constitutio Antoniniana*. It is not simply an accident of preservation that we have more Roman inscriptions, for Hellenistic inscriptions from the

---

[56] In addition to the classic studies by Sherwin-White 1973 and Balsdon 1979, see now Noy 2000, and Laurence and Berry 1998. On freedmen: Treggiari 1969; Duff 1958; Weaver 1972.

[57] As Foucault (1980) recognized, power is not something that is owned; it is exchanged dynamically among participants in a society.

[58] One wonders why the largely American and British classical scholars who treat these matters would want to tell the story of acceptance and strategic use of empire by the dominated, rather than narratives of resistance.

Artemision are numerous. Rather, something changed in the Roman period that made public display of membership in the association more desirable.

This punctilious display, year after year, of the names of the Kouretes in the Prytaneion illustrates what Ramsay MacMullen has called the Roman "epigraphic habit."[59] Inscriptions in all parts of the Mediterranean increased during the Roman Empire. Part of this is because the functioning of civic culture in the Roman period depended on the complex economic and cultural system of public benefaction—euergetism—and its recognition through public display.[60] But this is more description than explanation. The Kouretes had played this role of benefactors even in the Hellenistic period. Why the need to monumentalize, at this point in time, a social role that they had played for centuries?

With the arrival of Roman economic and political institutions, a new set of actors entered the municipal playing field. The emperor was the most obvious new benefactor, but other Roman citizens with supraregional connections played this role as well.[61] In the case of the cult of Artemis, a Roman equestrian, Salutaris, left a bequest in 104 CE that funded processions and distributions of money as part of the worship of Artemis.[62] Salutaris was born a Roman citizen and spent much of his career outside Ephesos, with posts in Sicily, North Africa, and Beligica. Though he owned estates in the vicinity of Ephesos, his father is the first member of the family attested in the city, and his primary connections seem to have been with Roman businessmen.[63]

His bequest funded processions on days of civic significance, such as the meetings of the legislative assembly, new moon sacrifices, festivals, and gymnastic games. Within his bequest, however, there was a covert revision of the city's traditions. The processions displayed prominently the statues of members of the imperial family and Roman institutions, such as Trajan, Plotina, the Roman Senate, the equestrian order, the Roman people, and Augustus. These were always paired with an

---

[59] MacMullen 1982; Meyer 1990, who points out the importance of advertising Roman citizenship in epitaphs; Cherry 1995.
[60] Lomas and Cornell 2003.
[61] Eilers 2002.
[62] *Inschriften von Ephesos* 1a.27; Rogers 1991.
[63] Rogers 1991, 16–19.

Ephesian counterpart: the Roman Senate, for example, with the Ephesian Boule.[64] Salutaris also seems to have explicitly reversed the direction of the traditional processions of Artemis (fig. 5.3). Priests would carry the divine statues and images donated by Salutaris from the Temple of Artemis, enter the city through the Magnesian Gate, and give the statues to an escort of *ephebes*. These would traverse the city and leave through the other city gate, the North Gate, located in the northeast corner of the Stadium, at which point they would give the statues back to the priests. The priests would then return alone to the Artemision.

In the older and more traditional direction of the procession, however, the participants would begin at the Artemision but enter the city in the reverse direction, through the North Gate near the Stadium, and exit through the Magnesian Gate.[65] In this fashion, the procession would approach the altar of Artemis and her statue in the forecourt of the Prytaneion from the direction that her temples traditionally faced, that is, from the west as one walked up the street from the Lower Agora. To picture the effect of Salutaris's revision of the processional direction, imagine seeing Christian priests begin a service by processing from the altar out the door of the narthex.[66]

Although Salutaris granted monetary gifts to members of many civic organizations in Ephesos, he left out the two sets of officials most closely tied with the celebrations of the birthday of Artemis: the Kouretes themselves and the Prytaneis, the city elders whose center was

---

[64] Rogers 1991, 83–86, 91–95 and 107–110.

[65] On the extent and direction of the sacred way: Knibbe and Langmann 1993, 16–32 and 55–56. Thür identifies the ἄνοδος ("way up/out") and κάθοδος ("way down/back") and their junctures. One of these is at the *embolos*, where the road to Ortygia joins as a third road, and thus represents a detour from the usual processional way, one which was used only in the procession for the birthday of Artemis; 1999, 164. The other connection between the ἄνοδος and κάθοδος lies on the north slope of Panayırdağ and was found only in 1995 with ground-penetrating radar and is not yet completely published; Thür 1999, 166. In contrast, Engelmann (1995) argues that the direction of the Salutaris procession is the only possible direction for all processions on this road. Knibbe has written a rejoinder which will appear in *Via Sacra Ephesiaca III*.

[66] Rogers, who was not aware of Knibbe's interpretation of the direction of the Artemis procession, notes that it would have been possible and perhaps easier to have begun the procession in the direction opposite to the one that Salutaris chose. Rogers views the direction chosen by Salutaris as one that emphasized the role of Rome in the history of the city, especially by beginning in the Upper Agora, where Roman sponsorship and imagery were clearly on display; 1991, 86–91 and 111–15.

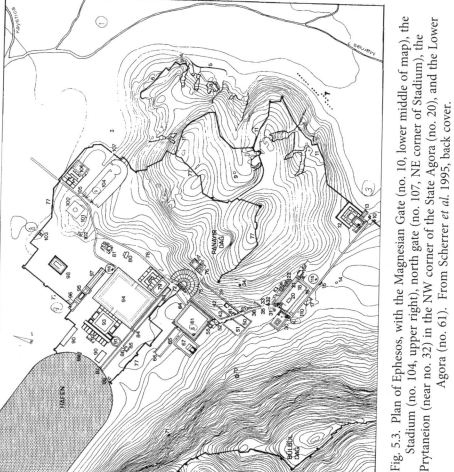

Fig. 5.3. Plan of Ephesos, with the Magnesian Gate (no. 10, lower middle of map), the Stadium (no. 104, upper right), north gate (no. 107, NE corner of Stadium), the Prytaneion (near no. 32) in the NW corner of the State Agora (no. 20), and the Lower Agora (no. 61). From Scherrer *et al.* 1995, back cover.

also the Prytaneion.[67] The other group of people who were neglected was the general population, for Salutaris provided no sacrifices to be shared among the inhabitants of the city as a whole, in contrast to the Kouretes, whose traditional duty was to host the whole population at the traditional feasts during the festival of Artemis. This was consistent with the Roman view that such forms of public benefaction were too 'democratic.'[68] Instead, Salutaris gave gifts to those who were already powerful in the city or to those who would be, such as the *ephebes*. His program seems to have contrasted dramatically with traditional Ephesian celebrations of Artemis, and excluded the leading families whose gifts had funded them. Salutaris was a counter-patron.

In contrast, the inscriptions of the Kouretes that appeared for the first time under the Roman Empire stress the activities of the traditional association, but on a new and more monumental level, and in the very location where the construction projects of the new benefactors were most evident.[69] The display of names from prominent Ephesian families could have performed a number of different functions. It indicated their survival and flourishing as a class, their continued ability to act as sponsors, and their financial support for traditional Ephesian customs. Their espousal of Roman identity is particularly interesting in this context. In addition to presenting a clear appeal to Rome and its institutions, the Roman connection could be seen as an attempt by the urban elite to display their political competence to the eyes of the local inhabitants.

Hybridity in Corinth: The Effect of Roman Rule

Corinth lacks evidence for this sort of interplay between supraregional Roman benefactors and a more locally-based elite, but there is still a significant increase in public display. Not only inscriptions and statues but the entire building plan of the new colony was a calculated pro-

---

[67] Rogers 1991, 65–72.

[68] Woolf 1994, 123–24 with notes.

[69] The Prytaneion was at time of construction directly visible from the plaza of the Upper Agora. The Basilike ("Royal") Stoa, constructed in 11 CE, later obscured it from view. Nevertheless, the altar and statues in its forecourt suggest that the Prytaneion was still employed for sacrifices during festivals of Artemis. Indeed, only the festival officials would have seen the inscriptions of the Kouretes at this point, but they remained an important audience for this sort of display.

gram of display. The establishment of a Roman colony represented the formal foundation of its public religious life, including the determination of a local calendar of festivals and sacrifices, consecrated by priests who came from Rome itself.[70] Land would be allotted and determined for civic sanctuaries, whose divine dedicants would be named in rituals and whose *templa* would be inaugurated by the augurs.[71]

Both Ephesos and Corinth exhibit a hybrid mélange of monumental and architectural styles. At Ephesos the local elite retained the institutional form of a traditional cult association but moved its location to a more strategic, Romanized area, and displayed their identity as Roman citizens. At Corinth, the situation is almost the reverse. The traditional cults retained their historic locations, but the religious practices changed. Sanctuaries were generally rebuilt to facilitate worship in a Roman fashion, both in architectural style and in the arrangement of ritual action.

This would be typical for Roman cults brought from the mother city. It is more surprising for the cults that had local predecessors and that most likely still possessed some visible Hellenistic structures. The evidence from Corinth suggests that, at Roman colonies, not only Roman cults but also the cults of foreign gods accepted into the sacred calendar of Rome, such as Demeter/Ceres, were likewise conducted in a Roman fashion.[72]

The fusion of Roman practice with an appeal to Greek cultural heritage is consistent with Roman ideology. Local gods were to be honored, for they were divine patrons of the city. As at Corinth, Romans generally reconstructed the temples they destroyed. But also evident is a characteristic Roman insistence on honoring in their own way the gods of others. Numerous examples illustrate how the Romans "tamed" or "domesticated" the wilder aspects of foreign cults while still accepting their gods into the pantheon.[73] Sober conduct toward

---

[70] On this aspect of Roman colonial religion, Bookidis (2005, 152–53) cites the *Lex Coloniae Genitivae* for the colony of Urso, Spain, published in Crawford and Cloud 1996, 1:393–454 no. 25. See also the comments by Walters 2005, 400–03.

[71] Beard, North, and Price 1998, 320–39.

[72] This accords with the observation by Bookidis, who has suggested the Greek cults of Roman Corinth be divided into two groups: those for gods and goddesses that had been incorporated into the pantheon of the city of Rome, and those gods or goddesses on the fringe that had not; 2005, 163–64. It is the former, including the cult of Demeter/Ceres, which were most closely monitored in general by Roman officials.

[73] Beard, North and Price 1998, 211–44.

the gods with the consistent performance of orderly ritual characterized the Roman concept of piety.[74] The claim to superior piety was part
of Rome's imperial ideology and part of the legitimation of its right to
rule. This concept of religious superiority lay behind the rite of *evo-
catio*, famously employed at the destruction of Carthage in 146 BCE.
Scipio Aemilianus implored Juno to abandon the city and come live
in Rome, where she would be worshipped with greater honor.[75] Less
attention has been given to another aspect of the story, the renaming of Tanit, the goddess of Carthage, as 'Juno' by the Romans. The
Roman name imposed on the indigenous patron goddess became part
of city's new name, the *colonia Junonia*, a potent symbol of Roman
theological domination of the region.

By reshaping foreign cults and renaming foreign divinities, Roman
officials belied an assumption of cultural superiority. The fact that these
renamings occur in situations of conquest and colonization should
sensitize us to the fact that hybridity is not neutral but can be a factor
in a strategy of domination. Assumptions of imperial superiority can
look very different to those on the periphery. To the rulers, it may
have seemed natural to reward those who mimicked their own cultural
institutions and to prefer doing business with those who 'Romanized,'
just as modern western governments reward foreigners who 'western-
ize' and 'modernize.' For those on the periphery, however, the mere
size, success, economic, and technological strength of the dominant
culture was a potent fact that shaped their lives on a daily basis,
often in dissonance with more familiar, traditional ways of organizing
social life.

Roman attempts to connect with the Greek past co-opted its traditions in part to legitimate Roman power. In her study of the Corinthian fountains of Glauke and Peirene during the Roman period,
Betsey Robinson has written that "the selective appropriation of
ancient 'Greek' Corinthian traditions" is "an important process in the
re-creation of Corinth as a Roman colony and in the formation of its
collective identity."[76] With the example of the Fountain of Peirene,[77]

---

[74] Scheid 2003, 22–38.
[75] Servius *ad Aen.* 12.841; Macr. *Sat.* 3.9.1–13.
[76] Robinson 2005, 113.
[77] Robinson notes that Augustus and Marcus Agrippa were renovating the ancient
springs of Rome during the same period; 2005, 123. These were likewise "historiated,"
that is, associated with historical events in the founding and development of the city.

renovated in a completely Roman fashion in the 20s or 10s BCE, she demonstrates that the Romans adopted and creatively adapted the story of this "historiated" location. The Peirene Fountain is where Bellerophon tamed the winged horse Pegasus with the help of Athena, who at Corinth has the epithet *chalinitis* ("the bridler"). As Robinson notes, Pegasus, known as "the Peirenian colt" in literary sources, often appears alone during the Classical and Hellenistic periods as a symbol of the city. During the Roman period, however, the horse typically appears alongside the man who tamed him, an obvious reference to Roman domination of Greece.[78]

As has been noted, Roman authors often negatively contrasted the present-day Greeks (*Graeculi*) with their illustrious forbears. Roman sources often show great respect for Greek culture, but only as long as it lay in the past. They constructed a narrative of Greek decadence, a decline from greatness, to describe the Greeks with whom they concretely interacted.[79] Greek authors during the Roman imperial period often echoed this narrative, accepting the role that the Romans assigned them. Correspondingly, Roman sources often attributed to the Empire the role of spreading throughout the world the civilized norms, the *humanitas*, developed by the classical Greeks, for which Romans were better equipped because of their superior *mores*. Moreover, whereas they generally characterized their role in the west as creating order among the barbarians, in the Greek East they presented themselves as restoring discipline.[80] What better metaphor for this than bridling a marvelous but wild horse? The story of Pegasus demonstrates how the Romans searched the Greek mythic past for narratives that could legitimate the experience of ruling Corinth.

HYBRID IDENTITIES IN EPHESOS AND CORINTH

The early imperial period at both Ephesos and Corinth thus saw an increase in display and monumentality for traditional cults. In both cases the appropriation of the Greek past provided the starting point for a program of Roman representation within civic space, by integrating the new fact of Roman imperial conquest within the traditional

---

[78] Robinson 2005, 125.
[79] Woolf 1997; Alcock 1997.
[80] Whittaker 1997, 144.

landscape. At Corinth, Roman officials carried this out in the context of the establishment of a formal Roman colony. Their intervention represents a complete restructuring of sanctuaries in a more monumental guise that accorded with Roman perceptions of divine worship and ritual action. The architectural program legitimated this claim to the urban space of Corinth by both employing the traditional locations and identifications of the old Greek sanctuaries and by renovating them according to a supercessionist conception of Roman piety. Roman assumptions of their superior forms of worship and religious institutions were sometimes expressed explicitly in the iconographic program, as with Bellerophon at the Fountain of Peirene. This served the purpose of legitimating Roman domination of a city possessing an august and significant foreign culture.

At Ephesos, on the other hand, the inscriptions of the Kouretes were part of a program of display carried out by a locally-based elite. Rather than restructuring civic space, the Kouretes accommodated themselves to a building program already underway, carried out by Roman citizens with supraregional origins and connections.[81] The lists of Kouretes were advertisements set up in an area of the city that had become a thoroughfare for the wealthy and powerful, such as the *conventus* of Roman citizens who had their temple there, and the adherents of the provincial imperial cult located in the temple of the Sebastoi. The elite Ephesians represented in the Kouretes inscriptions did not themselves structure the space in which they placed their monumental display; they created for themselves a place within it.

The nature of their display was also markedly different. Dedicatory inscriptions, a critical component of monumental building programs, usually only mentioned a single donor and his family. The inscriptions of the Kouretes list hundreds of individuals in organized groups. The names included both Roman names and names from the hereditary clans of the city. Yet as important as were these indications of individual identity, the lists also represented an entire class of people engaged in an ancient cult association. The lists of Kouretes expressed the solidarity of a class and reminded the viewers of their benefactions

---

[81] On the donor of the Royal Stoa: von Hesberg 2002, 149–58. The stoa was dedicated by C. Sextilius Pollio and his wife, Ofillia Bassa, along with his son, Ofillius Proculus, and his other children to Artemis Ephesia, Augustus, and Tiberius ca. 4–14 CE. Pollio and his son were the scions of the wealthiest Roman family in Ephesos in the Augustan period.

to the city year after year in a traditional office that ritualized this particular kind of euergetism. The inscriptions suggest that members of families resident in Ephesos, often with long histories in the city, were presenting a claim for civic honor alongside patrons such as Salutaris, who acted as individuals, spent much of their careers outside the city, and had their family origins and vital connections in Rome or the Italian peninsula.

Thus both in Ephesos and Corinth, monumental display can be read as an index of contested authority. Both the colony and the Greek city were caught in the same web of discourse. The intensity of the contestation can be measured in marble—one of the reasons, I propose, that the Roman East is so opulent.

The Ambiguity of Hybridity as a Site for Resistant Counterstories

The concept of hybridity is useful because it emphasizes the 'in between' and negotiated character of intercultural discourses. Hybrid discourses develop and flourish because they can be read, simultaneously, in different ways by different social actors, and in alternate ways by the same social actors in different contexts. Roman attempts to justify their rule of the Greeks by selectively appropriating the Greek past led to a certain ambiguity, one that could be exploited and transvalued by the very Greeks they ruled. At both Corinth and Ephesos, authors writing in Greek enthusiastically adopted this emphasis on Greek heritage. Their narratives, however, employ the valorization of Greek heritage to depict a world in which most traces of Roman influence have faded from view. Significantly, contemporaneous descriptions of the two cities—by Pausanias for Corinth, and by the anonymous author of the *Ephesiaka* ("Ephesian Tales")—appear in highly literary texts written by native Greek speakers. They remind us that civic space is more than mere buildings on the ground. It also encompasses discourses that produce conceptual spaces, the meaningful *places* equally necessary to human habitation.

If one reads Pausanias's account of the sanctuaries of Corinth, it would seem as if the Roman conquest had never happened.[82] All the

---

[82] The assessment of Pausanias has undergone considerable investigation recently; Alcock, Cherry, and Elsner 2001.

sanctuaries of the Roman city in his account were dedicated to gods with Greek names. Traces of Rome's rededication of these temples have simply evaporated. Particularly suspect is Pausanias's description of a temple to Zeus with the epithet "Capitolios" (Καπετόλιος) in the "language of the Romans," which Pausanias helpfully translated into Κορύφαιος (2.4.5).[83] This Temple of Jupiter Capitolinus was, for Pausanias, a Temple of Zeus. He apparently did not live in the same landscape as the Roman inhabitants of Corinth, whom he contrasted with the "old Corinthians" (Κορινθίων...τῶν ἀρχαίων, 2.1.2) who no longer inhabited the territory but who still remained available to his cultural imagination.

The ambiguity of the *interpretatio Romana* thus ironically facilitates a resistant and subversive understanding of the cults of Corinth by a Greek provincial such as Pausanias, who actively downplayed Roman influence and emphasized Greek continuity. This problematic ambiguity illustrates one of the classic insights of studies of cultural hybridity: ironically, the dominant culture is actually the one more prone to instability. It constantly needs to 'naturalize' itself, to make its exercise of power seem normal, usual, and commonsensical.[84] Roman sources often reflected a deep discomfort with their cultural debt to the Greeks and correspondingly emphasized the need to retain a special sense of dignity and humanity in their treatment.[85] So they, too, like other imperial rulers, covered their exhibitions of power with labels that incorporated and appropriated the culture they dominated. Yet these labels, because they were ambiguous and unstable, became sites of resistance open to diverging interpretations. Architectural style and ritual practice had changed dramatically at most of the refounded Greek sanctuaries, which were henceforth Roman sanctuaries, but Pausanias could still interpret them as continuous with the past and thereby retain a sense of Greek cultural identity.

It is interesting that both Greeks and Romans desired and preserved the Greek past, but in very different ways. Thus, the vexed question of how to refer to the sanctuaries at Corinth, whether with their Latin or Greek names, derives from ancient sources that were formed by a disagreement on this very issue. The proponents of both sides inhab-

---

[83] Walbank 1989, and her chapter in this volume.
[84] Bhabha 1994, 94–131.
[85] Woolf 1994, 118–25; Alcock 1997, 111–12, and 2002, 36–52.

ited the same civic space, but they did not live in the same landscape.[86] Modern scholars are all but forced to take sides, however unintentionally, in a debate that started hundreds of years before.

At Ephesos one can trace similar patterns of ambiguity in the literary record. Alongside the apparent accommodationist display, in which Greek speakers emphasized Roman citizenship, one can find another, more resistant discourse in the Greek novels. The second-century novel, the *Ephesiaka*, begins with a description of the traditional festival of Artemis in Ephesos, the very festival sponsored by the association of Kouretes attested in the inscriptions. At this festival, the young protagonists, the noble Ephesian youths Habrocomes and Antheia, fall in love at first sight.

Because of their focus on the mishaps and eventual happy marriage of their young protagonists, the novels have often been classed as escapist literature for adolescents, women, and the middle class, people uninterested in politics and public life. A more recent consensus, however, based on examination of literary tropes, scribal conventions and the distribution of papyrological witnesses for the novels, suggests that their readership was probably no different from that of other genres of ancient literature—predominantly elite men.[87] If we also assume that at least some of the novels were written in Ephesos or the province of Asia, as the interest in local detail and geography suggests, then the people who were reading the novels were the same ones recording their Latinized names and their devotion to the emperor on the lists of the Kouretes, namely the leading men of Ephesos.

In the world of the novels, however, Rome has disappeared. The *Ephesiaka*, like many novels, studiously avoids direct mention of it, although small details place the novel squarely in the 2nd century.[88] The plotline and the characters focus on traditional Greek civic institutions, such as local temples, gods, and festivals. The heroes of the

---

[86] See Økland's chapter in this volume. For a study of "landscape" in cultural studies and material culture: J. Thomas 2001.

[87] The scanty attestation of the novels is a strong argument that, far from being mass literature, these works were relatively hard to procure. Stephens (1994) has argued that the audience of the novel may have been no different from the readership of works by Thucydides, that is, predominantly elite males. Bowie envisages the readership as "the educated classes of *provincia Asia*" (1994, 451).

[88] The *Ephesiaka* mentions the prefect of Egypt in Alexandria (3.12.6) and Perilaus, an *eirenarch* of Kilikia (2.1.3.3)—the latter office attested only after 116–17 CE; Magie 1950, 1.647 and 2.1514–15.

novels have only Greek names, which emphasizes an ethnic identity free of assimilation, in marked contrast to the display on the lists of Kouretes. As many have noted, these texts are obsessed with Greek identity.[89] Their readers apparently were less attracted to a story that described the Roman Empire than to one in which Romans were not present, and they were alone in their cities.[90]

It is important to realize that both forms of discourse, the novels and the lists of Kouretes, were being practiced by the same people at the same time. Attributing the readership of the novels to callow adolescents or cloistered women eradicates this important connection and fails to see the political consequences of this type of narrative. These texts were not escapist literature but proclaimed the values of their audiences. They form what James C. Scott would call a 'hidden transcript,' a counterstory in which those under domination describe things, not as they are in the 'official transcript' that they share publicly with their rulers, but as they think things ought to be.[91]

As Susan Alcock has stressed, the attitudes evident among the Greek elite in the literary movement known as the Second Sophistic—the emphasis on preserving ancestral traditions, the collection of genealogies and local mythologies, the concern for civic reputation—also have corresponding behaviors and habits in the social and economic realm, such as the maintenance of traditional patterns of land tenure that fostered nucleated settlement around civic centers, even at the expense of optimal agricultural production.[92] As she writes:

> These arguments extend an intense Greek concern about their relationship to the past, long acknowledged in the sphere of high culture, into other aspects of early imperial social organization and relationships. In all its manifestations, this allegiance to the past, rather than being an escapist or antiquarian fantasy, played a vital part in efforts to "stay Greek."... [P]rovincial development, expressed through the medium of a provincial landscape, involves more factors than geography, economics,

---

[89] They have been treated in scholarship as the quintessential product of the Second Sophistic, a movement that valorized the Greek past on many levels. The literature is vast. The classic statement is Bowie 1974. For a recent treatment of Greek identity in the ancient novel: Swain 1996, 101–31.

[90] For this fixation on the Greek past in the *Ephesiaka*, and its broader relationship to religion and culture in Ephesos, see C. Thomas 1995.

[91] Scott 1990, 4–5.

[92] Goldhill 2001.

or administrative stability. It also depends upon negotiations over identity, over the mutual perception of conqueror and conquered.[93]

The cultural world of the novels replicates on a social level the physical pattern of the provincial landscape, in which nucleated settlements gathered around the cultural centers of the Greek cities. The novels do not counsel political careers or activity but rather a domestic strategy of lineage and dynasty through legitimate marriage. The emphasis on marriage highlights the importance of the elite marrying their own kind in order to maintain the social and civic identity of their class.[94]

This feature of the novels finds its echo in the lists of the Kouretes. As Guy Rogers has noted, the lists demonstrate strong kinship ties among the leading families of Ephesos. Nearly half the lists attest relatives serving together as Kouretes during the same year, and members of the Kouretes are often relatives of the prytaneis for that year.[95] The concentration of offices in the hands of extended families illustrates how the alliances formed through intermarriage maintained property and wealth among a few traditional leading families. Perhaps this is one of the reasons that elite Greek women became more prominent in the civic record during the Roman period, often holding offices previously barred to their participation,[96] because women also needed to be enlisted for a strategy of class maintenance dependent on social and biological reproduction. Mere survival as a distinct and non-assimilated class is presented as a sufficient strategy in the novels.

This emphasis on marriage, kinship, and social and biological reproduction stands in direct contrast to another feature of the epigraphic record of the Kouretes, the accommodationist presentation of Roman citizenship. That system, after all, operated on a model of fictive kinship, in which one achieved citizenship by legal adoption into the family of a Roman citizen. The elite men of Ephesos emphasized in the epigraphic record their membership in these new Roman families. In the novels, however, the only families that mattered were those constituted not by foreign adoption and fictive kinship, but by autochthonous marriage and biological reproduction. The novels represent a

---

[93] Alcock 1997, 111–12.

[94] Swain makes the connection between the importance of marriage in the novel and the foundation of elite self-conception in civic identity, which depended on appurtenance to an οἶκος as the basic social unit; 1996, 129–30.

[95] Rogers 1991, 249.

[96] For Ephesos: Friesen 1999; Soldan 1999.

quiet rejection of the new Roman families to which so many of them belonged.

The novels indeed represented a hidden transcript, but one that did not belong to an underclass. They depicted an abstract political world that was the natural and uncontested right of the local Greek elite by inheritance, even if, as the inscriptions show, this view of the world was challenged in public discourse. There should be no doubt, however, about who was *not* represented in this story. Some people—the non-elite classes, merchants, slaves, freedmen, the rural and urban poor—were not part of the visible conflict even in these sources. Previous studies have shown that Roman officials generally neglected the rural poor in the project of imperial assimilation because their control could be left safely to the local propertied classes. Ancient writers stress the dependence of the poorer classes on the aristocracy. If anything, under the Roman Empire the chasm between the rich and the rest of the population became wider and more entrenched.[97] When one realizes that this 'rest of the population' would have been understood in traditional Greek culture as the *demos*, the erstwhile power base of democracy,[98] one sees the social shift that the empire inaugurated. By Late Antiquity 'the rich' and 'the rest' solidified into two permanent legal classes with little chance of migration between the two, the *honestiores* and *humiliores*.

Because of the nature of the evidence, detailed study of hybrid identity formation is necessarily confined to the Greek provincial elite, who also form the focus of a variety of studies of Greeks under Roman rule, particularly through the lens of the Second Sophistic. What this study shows is that there was no single position even among the privileged classes; the levels of discourse were complex and context-specific. Depending on the audience envisaged by the cultural text, elites could appear either more or less Greek. This study also suggests that the phenomenon of hybridity in the Greek East was much more extensive than the literary phenomenon known as the Second Sophistic. It shaped festivals and other forms of worship involving the entire city.

---

[97] de Ste. Croix 1981, 525–28; Whittaker 1993, and 1997, 155; Alcock 1993, 18–20 and 234 n. 23.

[98] Greek sources in the early Empire characterize this economic and social development as a move away from democracy to oligarchy; Brunt 1990, 267–81. One of the effects in religious practice was the Roman tendency to steer Greeks away from the sort of shared civic sacrifice typical of their earlier practice; Woolf 1994, 123–24.

It also played itself out not only in the physical space of the city but also in the contested understandings of this shared space. The literary sources in this study illustrate that there were many possible ways of living in the city. The selfsame monuments and institutions could evoke radically different narratives about them, depending on who was telling their story, and in what situation.

SOCIAL STRATA

CHAPTER SIX

IMAGE AND CULT: THE COINAGE OF ROMAN CORINTH

Mary E. Hoskins Walbank*

INTRODUCTION

Roman Corinth had an active mint from the time it was founded as
a colony in 44/43 BCE until minting ceased in the early years of the
3rd century CE. For 250 years a rich variety of images appeared on the
coins: local myths, architecture, deities and agonistic themes. In this
article I am concerned for the most part with one aspect of the coinage, namely, how does the primary evidence of the coins add to our
knowledge of Roman Corinth and its cults? And with that statement,
I run immediately into a problem familiar to all historians and archaeologists who draw on the evidence of coins. As Duncan Fishwick has
remarked, sometimes the coin image fills, in spectacular fashion, a
huge gap in the source material—it is the equivalent of a photograph.
This view has been forcefully challenged, however, because the details
on the coins often do not match the archaeological evidence. When the
details of a monument or statue differ from one coin type to another,
is it simply artistic license or do the changes have some deeper significance? Did the building or cult statue even exist at the time a particular
coin image was minted?[1] And, if so, how popular was the image? These
problems apply whenever numismatic evidence is used, but at Corinth
there is an additional complicating factor, the *Numismatic Commentary on Pausanias*, which was originally written over a century ago by
two distinguished numismatists, F. W. Imhoof-Blumer and P. Gardner. It is a valuable compendium of coin-types, still widely consulted

* For their assistance and for providing casts and photographs used in the preparation of this article, I am most grateful to M. Amandry, C. Arnold-Biucchi, A. Burnett,
I. Carradice, B. C. Demetriadi, W. E. Metcalf, M. Oeconomides, the late M. J. Price,
H.-D. Schultz, I. Tzonou-Herbst, and O. Zervos. My thanks also to H. Lanz and CNG
for permission to reproduce photographs from their catalogues.
[1] Fishwick 1999, 95. I will not go into the differing opinions here; they have been
ably summarized by Burnett (1999).

today, but the work was published before archaeological investigation at Corinth began. In addition, it contains a number of 'ghost' coins which appear in early numismatic catalogues but whose existence cannot be verified. The authors also assumed that Pausanias was writing the equivalent of a modern travel guide whereas modern scholarship has shown that he was a complex writer with a very different agenda. Their interpretations, which are often repeated by later scholars, must, therefore, be treated with caution.[2]

THE CIVIC COINAGE

First, a brief review of the coinage. Corinth began minting bronze coins almost as soon as it was founded.[3] The right to coin must have been sanctioned by a higher authority— probably at the time the colony was founded—but responsibility for the coinage rested with the city council and the annually elected chief magistrates, the duovirs. Corinth followed normal colonial practice in placing on its first issue the head of the colony's founder, Julius Caesar, but the image on the reverse is of Bellerophon mounted on Pegasus, which refers to one of Greek Corinth's most important founding myths.[4] Other early Corinthian issues between 44–40 BCE included more references to the Bellerophon/Pegasus cycle and to some of the most important deities of the Greek city: a seated Poseidon of archaic aspect, the laureate head

---

[2] Imhoof-Blumer and Gardner's work originally appeared as, "A Numismatic Commentary on Pausanias," *JHS* (1885–87), and was reproduced in an enlarged form as *Ancient Coins Illustrating Lost Masterpieces of Greek Art: A Numismatic Commentary on Pausanias*, Chicago 1964 [= *NCP*]. The literature on Pausanias is enormous. I cite here only recent works: Alcock et al. 2001, with very full bibliography of earlier studies; Knoepfler and Piérart 2001; Hutton 2005.

[3] The economic aspects of the coinage do not come within the scope of this article. The provincial coinages were part of the overall Roman monetary system. They provided small change for local use as well as a medium for self-advertisement and the commemoration of significant events in the life of the city. Corinth's output was always significantly larger than that of other cities in the region, which must reflect its commercial interests and the fact that it was a center for the collection of taxes. However, as Howgego (1989, 199–200) has pointed out, the overall output was tiny in terms of general civic expenditure and there were long periods when the city did not mint at all.

[4] Bellerophon tamed Pegasus with the help of Athena. In some versions of the myth, Bellerophon is descended from the royal house of Corinth, in others he is the son of Poseidon.

of Zeus, Athena with thunderbolt and shield, Kronos and Dionysos (fig. 6.1).[5] Notable by their absence are the foundation types commonly used by colonies on their first coin issues: in particular, the ritual plowing of a furrow to mark the *pomerium* prior to the settlement, which was part of the formal settlement of the colony; and also the military types, such as a legionary eagle between two standards, which were used when veterans formed a significant proportion of the new colonists.[6] Instead, the city magistrates appear to have made a conscious decision to acknowledge the city's antecedents by following the practice of Greek cities, which regularly used types reflecting the city cults. Yet Corinth was refounded as a conventional Roman colony and so its religious institutions mirrored those of Rome itself. The most important public cult would have been that of the Capitoline triad, but other deities would also have been named in the foundation charter as the recipients of cult. By the mid 1st century BCE the major Roman deities had already absorbed many of the characteristics of their Greek counterparts, which would have eased the process, but the Corinthian coin images are clearly based on earlier Greek types.[7]

---

[5] For a detailed description of these and other early issues: Amandry 1988, 23–36, Pl. 1–4; see also *RPC* I, nos. 1116–23. But it is improbable that these early coin images would have been based on statues seen in the Forum by Pausanias 200 years later, as Amandry suggests, since the reorganization of the Roman Forum area would have scarcely begun.

[6] The general and incorrect assumption that veterans were settled at Corinth arises from a misunderstanding of Strabo's comments with regard to the settlement of Carthage and Corinth and the ambiguous evidence of Plutarch. On the literary evidence and origins of the early colonists: Walbank 1997, 97–107; Spawforth 1996, 170–71 on the scarcity of magistrates of veteran stock. On the make-up of the early colony, see B. Millis in this volume.

[7] The foundation charter of *Colonia Laus Iulia Corinthiensis* has not survived, but a useful parallel is the *Lex Coloniae Genetivae Iuliae; ILS* 6087. Urso was a Julian colony of about the same date as Corinth and its foundation charter appears to be typical of those issued to colonies at this time; Crawford *et al.* 1996, 393–454. It is clear that the religious organization of the new colony is based on that of Rome and that the first pontiffs and augurs of the colony were appointed from the colony (contra Bookidis 2005, 152, who thinks that they were sent from Rome). The duovirs were charged with decisions regarding the civic cults, the festivals and public sacrifices (presumably, therefore, they had some choice). Both they and the aediles had to organize and finance shows or dramatic spectacles for the Capitoline triad and "the gods and goddesses," which at Urso included Venus. The charter also required that the duovirs or aediles administer an oath to the scribes handling public monies and records "on a market day (facing) the forum, by Jupiter and the ancestral gods" (ch. 81).

Fig. 6.1. A. *Obv.* Head of Julius Caesar: *rev.* Bellerophon on Pegasus, 44–43 BCE. B. *Obv.* Bellerophon leading Pegasus: *rev.* Seated archaic-style Poseidon, 43–42 BCE. C. *Obv.* Laureate head of Zeus: *rev.* Athena holding a shield and thunderbolt, 42–41 BCE. D. *Obv.* Head of Kronos: *rev.* Dionysos holding kantharos and thyrsos, 40 BCE. BCD Collection (Lanz Auktion 105, 2001, nos. 314, 318, 319 and 322).

The coinage falls conveniently into two distinct periods. From the time of the colony's foundation, coins were issued frequently and the largest issues bear the names of the annually elected duovirs. The coinage is characterized by the assiduous attention paid to the imperial, Julio-Claudian family. The reverse types fall into two broad categories: conventional Roman subjects and local, peculiarly Corinthian images. This duovirate coinage comes to an abrupt end in 68/69 CE. When Vespasian rescinded the freedom from taxation given to Greece by Nero, he also withdrew the right of coinage enjoyed by Corinth and other cities in Achaia.

Under Domitian the Corinthian mint again started issuing coins, beginning with a very handsome series bearing the legend PERM(issu) IMP(eratoris), "by permission of the emperor." The head of the emperor has become standard on the obverse and his title replaces the names of the duovirs. However, the decision to coin was probably always made by the city council, and it is likely that the magistrates or duovirs continued to have responsibility for the actual minting. The reverse types are appropriate for the reopening of the mint: the emperor in a triumphal quadriga; the Isthmian wreath; and the local deities, Ino and Melikertes, who appear together for the first time on the coinage. But the emphasis on the coins has changed. Corinth certainly maintains ties with Rome, but, particularly from the reign of Hadrian, Corinth emphasizes its Greek heritage, as one might expect in the cultural climate of the 2nd century. The hero cult of Palaimon at Isthmia becomes very prominent, and there is an emphasis on personifications, a fashion for panoramic views and also for the pairing of civic deities. In the late 2nd century more militant themes, such as the imperial cavalryman spearing his foe, are added to the repertoire, a response, no doubt, to external military crises. Corinth strikes coins abundantly under Septimius Severus, with portraits of all the imperial family and the familiar Corinthian themes. Then the mint ceases activity abruptly in the early years of the 3rd century.[8]

This second period has not, hitherto, been studied in the same detail as the duovirate coinage.[9] The great majority of the coins can be dated by reign, but not by issue. The imperial title does follow that of the Roman mint, but often in a truncated form with only a rare tribunician or consular date. A rough chronological sequence within the reign can often be worked out by using changes in portraiture, known historical events, and die links. For example, one or two of Domitian's coins do have a consular date, and the die links show all his coins were minted between ca. 85–87 CE. Similarly, some coins of Septimius Severus can be attributed to a specific year. The dating of the issues during Hadrian's reign is notoriously uncertain,[10] but here the changing portrait styles are helpful. On the earliest coins, Hadrian's head is very small and neat, and the imperial title is IMP(erator) CAESAR TRAIANVS HADRIANVS AVG(ustus), often abbreviated. On the latest coins, the emperor is depicted with heavy, fleshy features and a thick neck, evidently a man in late middle age, and following the Roman mint, he is simply HADRIANVS AVGVSTVS or, rarely, HADRIANVS AVGVSTVS P(ater) P(atriae). The combination of die

---

[8] It is not clear why Corinth ceased coining while other cities in the Peloponnese continued for some years. The latest issues depicting the young Caracalla and his wife Plautilla must have been minted during their short-lived marriage and cannot be dated later than her banishment in 205 CE.

[9] On the duovirate coinage: Amandry's detailed study (1988) together with Howgego 1989 and RPC I.249–58, nos. 116–23. For issues under Domitian: RPC II, nos. 101–218. The present article also draws upon my research for a monograph on the coinage from Domitian to the end of the Severans. For a preliminary account and illustrations of the late 1st and 2nd century coinage: Walbank 2003.

[10] Hadrian keeps COS III for most of his reign. He assumed the title Pater Patriae in 128 CE but does not include in his titulature acclamations or tribunician dates which would provide a precise date.

links with changes in portraiture, and technical and historical clues can provide not only a chronological sequence but also a new interpretation of a particular coin image.

How Should We Read Individual Coins?

The gens Iulia *Temple*

The first question is whether the coin is genuine. The question of authenticity does not often arise with the Corinthian coins, but the possibility has to be borne in mind. A well-known Corinthian coin issued during the reign of Tiberius, which has on the reverse a hexastyle temple with GENT(*is*) or (*i*) IVLI(ae) inscribed on the architrave, illustrates some of the problems that can arise. Other versions of the inscription, CAESAR and AVGVSTVS, have led to the assumption that this was a series of coins dating from the time of Augustus, but either the coins can no longer be found or they have been altered in modern times. Nevertheless, they have been used, incorrectly, as evidence for a large temple of the imperial cult dating from the time of Augustus.[11]

The *gens Iulia* temple is unique among the provincial coinages: it was also a very large issue and it must have had a special meaning for the Corinthians (fig. 6.2). It is the only depiction of a Corinthian temple on which there is an inscription, and much effort has been expended in trying to identify the actual building. There are two versions, one with the columns evenly spaced and the other with a wider central opening to indicate the existence of a cult statue. The architectural details on the coin are inconclusive. All one can deduce is that the temple was hexastyle and therefore fairly large (the convention is that the die engraver may reduce the number of columns to simplify the image, but does not increase them). Imhoof-Blumer and Gardner

---

[11] Walbank 1989, 368 and n. 15. The phantom coins with CAESAR and AVGVSTVS on the architrave are listed in *NCP* (22) and have been accepted without question by, among others, Roux (1958, 113) and Williams (1987a, 35–36 and notes 6 and 9). A coin in the British Museum collection (Weber 3774) is inscribed DIVO AVG, but it has been re-engraved in modern times. In the past it was common practice to rework a worn coin in order to improve its appearance or to turn a common specimen into a rare one. The forgery may not have been intentional if the coin in its original state was misread. In any case, the recut coin cannot be regarded as genuine, nor can it be used as evidence.

Fig. 6.2. *Obv.* Augustus radiate, Tiberius laureate, Livia, and Livia veiled as priestess: *rev.* the *gens Iulia* temple, 32/33 or 33/34 CE. Corinth Excavations.

complicated matters by assuming, wrongly, that a seated female figure on another, earlier coin issued under Tiberius (fig. 6.3) was the cult statue in the guise of Octavia; and so the *gens Iulia* temple became the temple of Octavia referred to by Pausanias as "beyond the Agora."[12] Until recently, scholars working at Corinth accepted this interpretation and identified Temple E, which overlooks the Forum and is the largest temple of Roman Corinth, as the *gens Iulia* temple and, therefore, a temple of the imperial cult.

This line of reasoning is untenable. The so-called cult statue of Octavia is a well-known personification of Livia, one of the most widely used coin types under Tiberius, since it was a means of honoring the imperial family while accommodating the well-known reluctance of Tiberius to promote a ruler cult.[13] It cannot be used to connect the reference in Pausanias to a temple of Octavia with the *gens Iulia* temple.

----

[12] Paus 2.3.1.

[13] This Corinthian personification of Livia was issued in 21/22 CE under the duovirs P. Caninius Agrippa and L. Castricius Regulus: Amandry pl. XIX, *RPC* I, nos. 1149 and 1150; *BMC Corinth*, 64, no. 523 and pl. XVI. 4 (where it is wrongly identified as "seated statue of the Julia Gens"). A similar figure at Thapsus is actually identified on the coin as Ceres Augusta and the type is repeated at Rome under Claudius with the legend *diva Augusta*. On some Corinthian coins the seated, veiled figure holds a *patera* and scepter, but on others she holds ears of corn, which must signify Ceres, and I wonder whether a revival of the ancient cult of Demeter and Kore might have been a factor in the appearance of the corn ears instead of a *patera*. Bookidis and Stroud put the earliest use of the Sanctuary by the Romans in the first half of the lst century, perhaps as early as the first quarter; *Corinth* XVIII.3, 271.

Fig. 6.3. *Rev.* Seated female figure holding scepter and three ears of corn, 21–22 CE. BCD Collection (Lanz Auktion 105, 2001, no. 378).

Nor is there any evidence that Pausanias was referring to Temple E when he mentioned the temple of Octavia.[14] There is no reason to think that the latter was a large hexastyle temple. Although ναός is usually translated as temple, it can also mean a shrine or small cult room within a larger structure.[15]

Michel Amandry, in his detailed study of the duovirate coinage, assigned the *gens Iulia* coin issue to 32/33 or 33/34 CE and identified the four obverses as the *domus Augusta*: the reigning emperor Tiberius, the deified Augustus, a portrait of Livia, and Livia (now Julia Augusta) as priestess of the cult of Augustus. The important question is why was this particular coin type issued at such a late date in the reign of Tiberius, well after the concept of the *gens Iulia* had been absorbed into the worship of the *domus Augusta*? There must have been a special reason for the emphasis on the *gens Iulia*. The answer, in my view, is that it was a multiple anniversary issue commemorating the original dedication of a temple early in the life of the colony when the cult of *Divus Iulius* was inaugurated, and that it was combined with other significant dates in the Roman calendar: the 20th anniversary of the death of Augustus and the accession of Tiberius, the 60th anniversary of the *res publica restituta* of 27 BCE, and the 50th anniversary of the *ludi saeculares* of 17 BCE. It is the kind of multiple anniversary that was widely celebrated both at Rome and on the provincial coinages.[16] The Corinthians were assiduous in their attention to the Julio-Claudian family and a large anniversary coin issue in

---

[14] I have argued this in detail elsewhere (Walbank 1989) because use of the numismatic evidence is unsound and also because nowhere else in the Roman world is Octavia known to have been the recipient of a major cult in a Roman colony. I have suggested that there may have been an element of the Temple E complex named after her, but there are other possibilities. Torelli (1986, 222; and 2001, 165–79) argues that the temple of Octavia was at the opposite (east) end of the Forum.

[15] Walbank 1989, 378 n. 46.

[16] Grant 1950.

33/34 CE—a very important year in the Roman calendar—combining portraits of the *domus Augusta* with the *gens Iulia* temple would have been highly appropriate. One would expect that on special occasions, such as anniversaries, the temple would be the focus of celebrations of the local imperial cult.[17]

I have discussed this coin type at some length because it illustrates several important points: in particular, that the image of the *gens Iulia* temple commemorated an event or a number of events rather than the building itself. This is one of the problems in interpreting representations of buildings. It is not always clear whether the die engraver is depicting the actual monument—providing a photograph, as it were—or whether he is recording an event or anniversary that is connected with the monument.

One can, nevertheless, speculate as to the original of this coin image. My own candidate is the Archaic Temple to the north of the Forum, which was almost certainly dedicated to Apollo in the Roman period.[18] It was renovated early in the life of the Roman colony. Given the special relationship between Apollo and Julius Caesar and, later, the adoption of Apollo by Augustus as his patron deity, it is reasonable that the temple would have housed some form of ruler cult. Joint cults between the imperial family and their special gods were not unusual, and a cult of Apollo Augustus at Corinth is attested. Moreover, there was no clearly defined boundary between the imperial cult and other expressions of religion.[19]

The Capitolium

There is another problem with regard to building types. It may be clear that the coin depicts a building, but what kind of building is it? And to what extent is our identification influenced by preconceptions? Two coins of Domitian illustrate the problem. First, there is the depiction of

---

[17] Howgego (1989, 202–03) argues for an earlier date. On balance I think that Amandry's dates are preferable, but Howgego's dating would not affect my argument; rather, it would simply advance the anniversary by a decade; Walbank 1996, 213 for discussion of the dates.

[18] Bookidis and Stroud 2004.

[19] Cult of Apollo Augustus: *Corinth* VIII, 2, no. 120. An article on this inscription is in preparation. For discussion of other manifestations of ruler cult at Corinth: Walbank 1996, 201–12.

Fig. 6.4. O*bv.* Domitian: *rev.* Capitolium, ca. 85–87 CE. British Museum.

A   B

Fig. 6.5. Two versions of the baetyl of Apollo Agyieus on coins issued under Domitian. A. *RPC* II, no. 160; B. BCD Collection (Lanz Auktion 105, 2001, no. 545).

a Capitolium (fig. 6.4). It is obvious that this is a typical representation of a temple of the Capitoline triad. In their well-known study of provincial coins illustrating ancient monuments, Price and Trell thought that this coin was a copy of the Capitolium at Rome. They also identified the image of a conical structure on a base or within an enclosure (fig. 6.5) which appears on other coins as a Corinthian version of the Meta Sudans, the famous fountain in Rome, which can be seen on Roman coins depicting the Flavian Amphitheatre.[20] One identification supported the other, and the idea has been generally accepted that Corinth copied the monuments of the capital city.

However, Price and Trell made this assumption at a time when scholars thought that Roman Corinth had been founded simply as a continuation of Greek Corinth, and it was unlikely, therefore, that the city would have had a Capitolium. The recognition in the 1980s that Corinth was founded as a conventional colony, Roman in organization, government, and religious observances, including the worship of the Capitoline triad, undermined Price and Trell's hypothesis.[21] Moreover, cities normally featured their own monuments. There is no certain instance of the Capitolium at Rome appearing on any provincial

---

[20] Price and Trell 1977, 67, fig. 110.
[21] On the foundation and nature of Roman Corinth: Walbank 1997 (based on a 1986 Ph.D. dissertation).

coinage during the late 1st century BCE and the 1st century CE.[22] The obvious conclusion is that the temple depicted on the Corinthian coin is the Capitolium of Corinth itself. The Corinthian image has a central seated cult figure, Jupiter on a base, flanked by two standing figures, Juno and Minerva. There are only four columns, due to the engraver's need to make room for all three figures, which are crucial to the image.[23] There are acroteria and roof decorations; in the pediment there is a central standing figure flanked by two others with reclining figures in the angles. Further details cannot be made out. The coin is securely dated between 85–87 CE and it is one of the many city images issued when the Corinthian mint resumed coining. This could depict the Capitolium (Temple E) as it was in the mid 80s. It is also possible that the Capitolium had been damaged by the severe earthquake that hit Corinth in the 70s and that the coin represents a decision either to repair the existing building or to replace it with a more impressive structure. There is good evidence that coins were sometimes issued when the work was planned, but before it was completed or in some cases even begun.[24] The archaeological and art historical evidence suggests that the pedimental sculpture on the second Temple E was not completed until the late Hadrianic or early Antonine period, but this would not be unusual for a major building project. Furthermore, at Corinth there is always the possibility that another earthquake, such

---

[22] In making this statement I am drawing on the massive body of research contained in volumes I and II of *Roman Provincial Coinage*, covering the late Republic to 96 CE, which contain over 8,500 coin types. The Capitolium at Rome does appear on a well-known silver *cistophorus* of Ephesus dated 82 CE, but this silver coinage was part of the imperial monetary system, not a civic coinage, and the coins were probably minted at Rome itself (*RIC* II.182, no. 222; Price and Trell 1977, 70, fig. 122). The legend CAPIT RESTIT makes clear that this coin celebrates the planned restoration of the Capitolium in Rome, which had been destroyed by fire in 80 CE. A coin issued by Agrippa I of Judaea has been interpreted as showing the consecration of a treaty between Agrippa and Claudius within the Temple of Jupiter Capitolinus at Rome (*RPC* I, no. 4983). A coin of Cotys I of Bosporus (ca. 45–68 CE) showing a temple and inscribed ΚΑΠΕ may also perhaps refer to the Capitolium at Rome (*RPC* I, no. 333). Both coins were issued by client kings, and the identification of the temple is not certain. There are a few instances of other monuments at Rome being featured on the coins of provincial cities, usually in specific circumstances. Alexandria copied not only Roman monuments but coin images from elsewhere. This seems to have been a peculiarly Alexandrian characteristic. On the depiction of very similar buildings in different cities: Burnett 1999, 145.

[23] Curiously, *RPC* II, no. 194, describes this coin simply as containing a cult figure, but the flanking figures are very clear. I have examined this coin and other specimens, and confirmed the details.

[24] Prayon 1982.

as occurred in the late 130s, might have delayed work on the new Capitolium.[25] In such a case, there may well be discrepancies between the coin image and the temple as actually completed.

I have argued elsewhere that Temple E is the Capitolium of Corinth, and I will not repeat the arguments here except to say that I now think that the temple "beyond the Theater," which Pausanias referred to as that of Zeus Capitolios or Koryphaios, is the same building as the Capitolium (Temple E).[26] I do, however, maintain that the epigraphic evidence for a priest of Jupiter with the specifically Greek title of *theocolus* is best explained by the continuation of a Greek cult of Zeus that was later assimilated into the cult of Jupiter Optimus Maximus. I am tempted to go further and suggest that this is paralleled on the coins: the early issue of 42/41 BCE, which depicts the head of Greek Zeus, is superseded by the seated Jupiter that appears first during the reign of Domitian, then under Hadrian, and from time to time thereafter.

One important piece of information that the Capitolium coin does *not* provide, however, is the date of the original construction. Roman citizens were expected to worship Roman gods, but a precinct (*templum*) and altar would have fulfilled the early colonists' requirements since most rituals, especially sacrifice, connected with the cult took place around an altar which stood outside the temple building. The first Temple E was probably built in the Augustan period, not necessarily in the first decades but when the colony could afford to do so; and it was replaced at some time in the late 1st or early 2nd century.[27]

---

[25] The Capitolium at Pompeii had not been repaired 16 years after the earthquake of 62 CE. The Temple of *Divus Iulius*, decreed in 42 BCE, appears on a coin in 36, but it was not dedicated until 29 BCE. Fishwick (2004, 22–30) discusses a provincial temple at Tarraco authorized by Tiberius, which appears on coins of 15–16 CE, as a projected temple, but was not completed until 69–70. He cites other instances of a lengthy construction period; Fishwick 1999, 102–12.

[26] I made the suggestion some 20 years ago (Walbank 1989) that the temple of Zeus Capitolios or Koryphaios was a different building from Temple E (the Capitolium), housing a Greek cult separate from that of the Capitoline triad, on the then generally held assumption that the descriptions of Pausanias were usually topographically correct. More recent work has shown that Pausanias cannot be regarded as a straightforward travel guide describing the sites in the order visited, but rather that he was concerned with developing themes and associations, in accordance with which he discusses selected monuments, often out of topographical order. Therefore his account does not necessarily reflect the situation on the ground; Osanna 2001, 197–98. See also Hutton (2005, 150–55) who comments that the descriptions of Pausanias (for example, the Forum) can be "topographically disembodied," a nice phrase.

[27] Excavation by Williams in 1989–90 (Williams and Zervos 1991, 14–19) clarified somewhat the dating of the stoas surrounding the precinct. He concluded that analysis of the pottery from the foundation trench of the south stoa placed its construc-

The baetyl *of Apollo Agyieus*

The other Domitianic coin, identified by Price and Trell as a copy of the Meta Sudans fountain in Rome, depicts a conical structure with a finial, set on a high, round base on a shallow step. Sometimes the base is decorated with what appears to be a paling or very narrow arches in relief and other times with wider arches within which are sculptured figures (fig. 6.5).[28] Nothing on the Corinthian coin image identifies it as a fountain.[29] The monument is, however, very similar to the *baetyl*, or sacred stone, of Apollo that appears on coins of Megara, and frequently on coins of Ambracia and Apollonia in both the Greek and Roman periods (fig. 6.6C). Monumental stone *baetyls* of Apollo have been found on Corcyra (fig. 6.6A) and at Apollonia, both of which had close relations with Corinth, and at Nicopolis in Epiros, where a similar monument appears on coins issued under Hadrian.[30] There is also a strong resemblance between the coin images and a terracotta relief of a *baetyl* from the temple of Apollo on the Palatine (fig. 6.6D).[31] I concluded, therefore, that the Corinthian coins depicted the *baetyl* of Apollo Agyieus. Existing monuments and the detail on the Palatine relief may also explain the difference between the Corinthian coin images. The lower section of the base is decorated with wide arches, as on one coin type, while the section above has narrower vertical decoration, similar to the base on the other coin type. It seems that the Corinthian die engravers simplified the image by omitting one or other section in order to fit the monument into the space available.

Apollo Agyieus is the god who guards the road. It is also well-known from literary sources that his symbol stood in the porch of many Athenian houses to protect the household from intrusive evil.[32] Hitherto, there has been no certain evidence of Apollo Agyieus at Corinth, but

---

tion in the reign of Augustus or possibly Tiberius and that the reconstruction of the stoas is probably dated within the 2nd century CE, but the exact date is impossible to determine.

[28] *RPC* II, no. 161, describes it as a "conical monument."

[29] Compare other fountain coins at Rome and Patras illustrated by Price and Trell (figs. 74 and 112), on which the streams of water are very obvious.

[30] On cults of Apollo in northwestern Greece: Tzouvara-Souli 2001. For Corcyra: *SEG* 2002 no. 545. On the Nikopolis monument: Price and Trell (fig. 76), who thought it was a fountain; Oikonomides (1975 no. 29–30) considered it more likely to be a lighthouse.

[31] Other comparanda: 'Apollo Agyieus,' *LIMC* II,1, 327–32 and II,2, 279–83, figs. 1–27.

[32] On Apollo Agyieus at Athens: Parker 2005, 18.

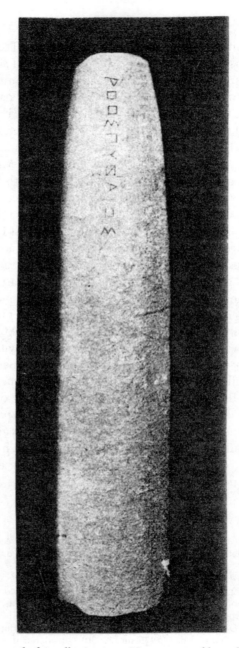

Fig. 6.6A. The *baetyl* of Apollo Agyieus. Upper part of *baetyl* excavated in the sanctuary of Apollo on Corcyra *LIMC* II,2, 280, fig. 8.

Fig. 6.6B. The *baetyl* of Apollo Agyieus. Monument at Cyrene. *LIMC* II,2, 280, fig. 10.

Fig. 6.6C. The *baetyl* of Apollo Agyieus, on coins of I and II) Apollonia; III) Byzantion, Thrace; IV) Megara; V) Ambracia. *LIMC* II,2, 279, figs. 2–6.

Fig. 6.6D. The *baetyl* of Apollo Agyieus. Terracotta relief from the temple of Apollo on the Palatine, Rome. *LIMC* II,2, 281, fig. 19.

we can now add this cult to the worship of Apollo, at least during the Roman period.

Can we identify the actual monument at Corinth? There may have been more than one, of course. A large, truncated marble cone was excavated by James Wiseman in the 1960s in the gymnasium area in a dump just north of the ruins of an apsidal structure.[33] The lower part is missing, and there is a cutting at the top for an attachment, which is also missing (fig. 6.7). It is likely that this is part of a *baetyl* and thus a monument erected to Apollo Agyieus, perhaps similar to that at Cyrene, where the *baetyl* stands on a large semicircular base (fig. 6.6B).[34] But why Apollo Agyieus appeared at this particular time in the reign of Domitian and also on the very early coins of Hadrian is not clear.

The Capitolium and the *baetyl* of Apollo Agyieus are just two of the many images that appeared on the coins issued between 85–87 CE. The wealth of familiar types, as well new images of monuments and local deities, is striking, particularly when contrasted with the paucity of issues elsewhere in Greece at the same time. City coinages owed their existence as much to civic pride as to economic considerations, and the new building types suggest that the ruling class was eager to reassert the image of the city. By this time Corinth had become a flourishing provincial centre, as well as the focus of the provincial imperial cult, attracting both Romans and ambitious Greeks into its administration.[35] Magistrates who would customarily also hold priestly

---

[33] Wiseman 1969, 69–72 and pl. 25a. The 'cone' has been variously identified. Williams (1987c) thought it belonged to a shrine of Diana Nemorensis. He noted "shallow, boss-like protrusions that are visible on one side of the shaft," which I suggest could have been used for the type of attachment or ribbons to be seen in the Palatine relief of Apollo Agyieus. Romano (2005) proposed that the cone was the *spina* of a hypothetical circus, half of which remained unexcavated, but subsequent remote sensing of the unexcavated area produced no evidence of a circus and his hypothesis cannot be sustained. Tzouvara-Souli (2001) recognized that the cone in the gymnasium area was part of a *baetyl*, but she did not make a connection with the coins of Domitian and Hadrian. She also thought that the large circular pedestal on a rectangular base in the southeast area of the Forum was the lower section of a large *baetyl* of Apollo from the classical period. It is an attractive idea, but it cannot be confirmed from the remains. On the circular monument: Williams 1981, 20–21. M. Laird, in this volume, has now observed a relationship between the *Augustales* monument to Augustus and the location of the circular monument.

[34] Reconstruction: *LIMC* II,1,328, fig.10.

[35] Corinth changed its name temporarily during the Flavian period. On most but not all the coins, the addition FLAV(ia) AVG(usta) or sometimes just AVG(usta) is made to the ethnic. The change is thought to be in recognition of imperial assistance

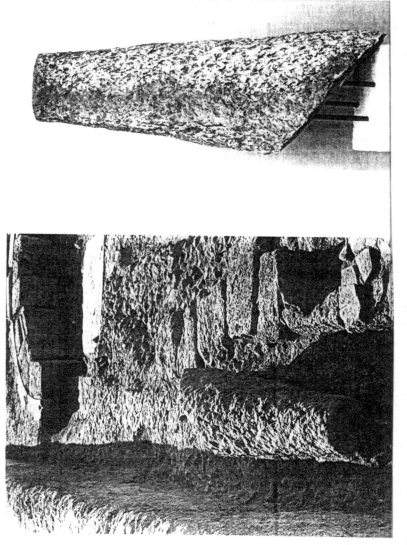

Fig. 6.7. Fragmentary marble baetyl excavated at Corinth in 1968. Corinth Excavations, courtesy J. R. Wiseman.

offices might well have wished to promote the cults in which they had a personal interest.

TEMPLE IMAGES AND THE ARCHAEOLOGICAL EVIDENCE

A number of temples have been excavated in the forum area, which is where we would normally expect the most important public cults to be situated.[36] Yet only one coin image can be said beyond doubt to represent a particular building or cult statue. This is a late coin of the young Caracalla, which shows the Forum defined by shops or porticoes on either side and, at the far end, a monumental flight of steps leading up to a large temple (fig. 6.8). It is schematic in that the Central Shops and South Stoa have been combined, and there is no attempt to represent the small temples along the West Terrace. The flight of steps up to the precinct has been combined with the podium temple. This simplified representation is exactly what one would expect on a coin. The important feature is the way in which the temple dominates the Forum. The large altar that would, in reality, have stood in front of the temple has been moved to the left. What is more, the fish-tailed deities at the base are doubles of those on coins showing the Skylla fountain in the court of Peirene, and their purpose must be to orient the view, that is, depicting the forum, as seen from the east. This may simply be one of the panoramic views that became generally popular in the latter half of the 2nd century or the coin could have marked an event connected in some way with Caracalla.[37]

Almost the opposite problem is presented by a coin of Antoninus Pius showing a large, hexastyle temple with a cult statue of Tyche holding a *patera* over a lit altar (fig. 6.9). There is a distinct crescent moon in the pediment. Pausanias refers to a temple of Tyche and says that there is a cult statue of Parian marble. Several of the temples at

---

following the major earthquake in the 70s. The city reverted to its former name in the reign of Trajan; Walbank 2002, 251–52.

[36] Paus. 2.2.6.

[37] A tantalizing coin, issued at about the same time in the name of the young Caracalla, depicts two mules pulling a sacred cart of the kind used to transport cult images at festivals. It is a coin type popular in the east, but this is, to my knowledge, the only time it was issued at Corinth. It is tempting to associate it with some religious event connected with Temple E and the Forum, but this can be no more than a suggestion. Another very rare coin, issued at Megara under Septimius Severus, shows a similar cart carrying a shrine of Demeter; Price and Trell, fig. 41.

Fig. 6.8. *Obv.* The young Caracalla: *rev.* Corinthian Forum dominated by Temple E. American Numismatic Society.

Fig. 6.9. *Obv.* Antoninus Pius: *rev.* temple of Tyche. BCD Collection (Lanz Auktion 105, 2001, no. 666).

the west end of the Forum have been proposed as the temple of Tyche, but they are all small, tetrastyle buildings.[38] Moreover, the cult statue, reconstructed by Charles Edwards from fragments found in the vicinity, conflates Tyche with Nemesis and does not resemble the image on this coin nor any of the other numerous Corinthian coin representations of Tyche.[39] Does the coin show a temple of Tyche elsewhere, or does it refer to a particular event during the reign of Antoninus Pius when the Corinthians felt it appropriate to associate Tyche with one of their other important public cults?

Another frustrating image is a Domitianic coin depicting a different hexastyle temple with a cult statue (fig. 6.10). The cult figure is standing on a base with the right hand outstretched and the left hand raised, holding what could be either a scepter or perhaps a trident. The stance of the central figure on the pediment is similar to the cult statue, but

---

[38] Scranton (*Corinth* I.3, 64–7) thought the temple of Tyche was Temple F. Williams (1975, 1–50) identified it as Temple D; recent observations by Millis (2003) rule out Temple D as having been built after Pausanias's visit, and he suggests Temple K. All three suggestions presuppose that Pausanias was describing the temples and statues in the Forum topographically, but this is by no means certain. On the problem of identifying monuments at the west end of the Forum: Hutton 2005, 140–55.

[39] Edwards 1990.

Fig. 6.10. *Obv*. Domitian: *rev*. hexastyle temple with standing cult figure. BCD Collection (Lanz Auktion 105, 2001, no. 561).

the details are not sufficiently clear to identify either it or the flanking figures. There are several possibilities: the coin could depict the temple of Zeus that Pausanias mentions near the Asklepieion; if the figure is holding a trident, then it must be Poseidon and the temple at Isthmia is a likely location; there are also sanctuaries at Kenchreai and Lechaion to bear in mind.[40] There is no archaeological or epigraphic evidence, at present, to confirm the identification. All we can say is that, since the coin was minted at the same time as the Capitolium coin of Domitian, it must surely represent a different temple.

Another way of looking at coin images is to consider how the mint responded in times of uncertainty. The types issued during the empire-wide crisis of 68/69 CE included the turreted head of Roma with the legend ROMAE ET IMPERIO ("to Rome and the ruling power") and a three-quarter view of a podium temple (fig. 6.11A and B).[41] These are carefully chosen types signifying loyalty to Rome.[42] At a later time of uncertainty, albeit brief, when Hadrian succeeded Trajan, the head of Roma appears again, as does a podium temple seen in three-quarter view, as well as the façade of a hexastyle temple, which looks remark-

---

[40] Gebhard (1998, 433–35) thinks that the Temple of Poseidon at Isthmia was in a ruined state in the middle of the 1st century and that it was extensively rebuilt in the Flavian period. No evidence has survived of a cult statue at this time, but it could well be shown on this coin of Domitian. Sturgeon (1987, 76–99) dated her reconstruction of the cult statue group of Poseidon and Amphitrite from the surviving fragments to the early Antonine period. This was superseded by the cult group donated by Herodes Atticus and seen by Pausanias.

[41] Roma is the city of Rome personified. The podium temple has been variously identified: for example, in *NCP* (22), as the *gens Iulia* temple seen from a different viewpoint; by Scranton (70), followed by Roux (111), as Temple G (his Pantheon); Amandry (75), as Temple E or perhaps Temple F (Tyche); Torelli (165 n. 140) also cautiously suggests the *gens Iulia* temple.

[42] Other types under the same duovir are: a personification of the Senate with SENATVI P.Q.R., the familiar head of Poseidon with NEPTVNO AVG(usto), Isthmus with two rudders, clasped hands holding a poppy and wheat ears symbolizing peace, and Nike or Victory with wreath and palm. They are all safe types.

Fig. 6.11. A. Head of Roma. B. Podium temple, 68–69 CEP. C. *Obv.* Hadrian: *rev.* façade of a hexastyle temple issued early in the reign of Hadrian. BCD Collection (Lanz Auktion 105, 2001, nos. 501, 489, 630).

ably like the *gens Iulia* temple without the inscription (fig. 6.11C).[43] These temples must have been so familiar to the Corinthians that they did not need identifying, but we can only make intelligent guesses.

The Temple of Palaimon at Isthmia

In contrast with my examples so far, there is one temple that appears with great frequency on the coinage and which does correspond with the archaeological and literary evidence. It is the Temple of Palaimon at Isthmia.[44] It was known from Pausanias that a temple existed, but his account is somewhat ambiguous.

> On the left, within the enclosure, there is a Temple of Palaimon and within it are statues of Poseidon, Leucothea and Palaimon himself. There is also a place called the *adyton* and an underground descent to it where

---

[43] Hadrian's military training and personal links with Trajan's family must have indicated that he was the obvious successor, but he had not been made Caesar nor had he been given the powers enjoyed by previous heirs, for example, Tiberius, Titus, or Trajan himself.

[44] *Isthmia* II, 99–109. In the myth Ino, the mother of Melikertes, fled from her husband, who had been driven mad by Hera, and leapt into the sea with her child. Ino became the goddess Leucothea and Melikertes the boy hero Palaimon. A dolphin carried his corpse to the Isthmus where he was buried and his funeral rites were celebrated in the first Isthmian Games. Different versions of the myth and the cult of Melikertes/Palaimon are discussed in detail by Gebhard (2005).

they say that Palaimon is concealed. Whosoever, Corinthian or stranger, swears falsely there, cannot by any means escape his oath.[45]

When Oscar Broneer excavated at Isthmia, he found a site that corresponded in remarkable detail with the coins. There was the stepped base of a building and beneath it a disused water channel belonging to the earlier Greek stadium. Therefore, Broneer reconstructed the superstructure of the temple according to the coin image (fig. 6.12) with a door in the base giving access to the disused channel, which he concluded was the *adyton*.

There are two images of the temple with the same cult image of Melikertes/Palaimon lying on his dolphin, but one version is shown with the base denoted by a simple line and the other is on a stepped base or podium with an entrance (fig. 6.13). There are small changes in detail. Sometimes there is a pine tree behind the cult image or trees on either side—the pine is important in the cult of Melikertes/Palaimon— but the coins are clearly meant to show the same building. Broneer assumed that the temple without a base, which also appears on coins minted during the reign of Hadrian, was an earlier building replaced by the temple with a stepped base and entrance. But material recovered during Elizabeth Gebhard's excavation in 1989 showed that there could not have been a temple on that particular site as early as the time of Hadrian. She proposed, therefore, that there had been two temples on two entirely different sites (fig. 6.14). She concluded that:

a. a base in front of the large Temple of Poseidon which Broneer had thought was a Roman period altar or perhaps a monument base was, instead, the base of the temple shown on the Hadrianic coin;
b. this temple was dismantled when the precinct of the Temple of Poseidon was enlarged and rebuilt in a more elaborate podium version on Broneer's site, to the south.[46]

Gebhard also thought that "the first temple did not have a passage through the foundation, and it would seem that the rituals it served belonged to a later period of cult practice."[47]

However, there is a problem. Both Marcus Aurelius and Lucius Verus appear separately on the obverse of the coins, and the reverses

---

[45] Paus. 2.2.1. Broneer suggests that the statues of Poseidon and Leucothea were placed in the colonnade of the temple.
[46] Gebhard *et al.* 1998, 440.
[47] Gebhard 1993, 93.

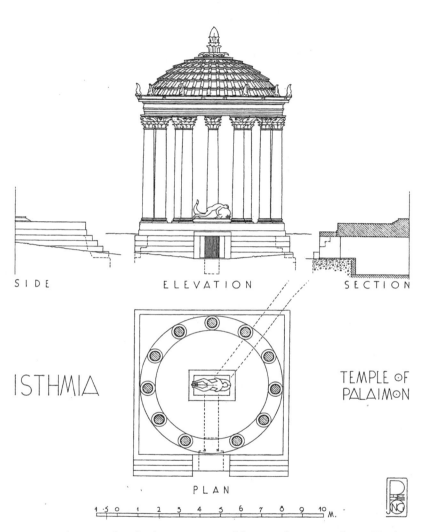

SIDE   ELEVATION   SECTION

ISTHMIA

TEMPLE OF
PALAIMON

PLAN

Fig. 6.12. The Temple of Palaimon restored by Piet de Jong. *Isthmia* II, pl. 73.

Fig. 6.13. Coins showing the Temple of Palaimon issued under Lucius Verus: A, between 161 and 163 CE, and B, after 163 CE. BCD Collection (Lanz Auktion 105, 2001, nos. 754 and 755).

are interchangeable. There is no chronological sequence in which the temple without a podium is earlier in date than the stepped or podium temple. The titulature on many of the coins of Lucius Verus includes CAESAR, which Verus dropped after 163 CE. This suggests very strongly that there was only one Temple of Palaimon, which was dedicated between 161–63, and commemorated on the coinage. My findings do not accord, therefore, with the present dating and understanding of the archaeological remains. It is clear that the hypothesis of two buildings—a temple without a podium, which was dismantled, and another temple built elsewhere in the Antonine period—needs rethinking. Nor can one draw inferences about a change in cult practice. I stress that I am dealing solely with the numismatic evidence, but that is the basis for the archaeologists' current interpretation.[48]

So what were the die engravers doing? In one version, the engraver shows the temple and cult statue in careful detail. In other versions, it is the ritual, the activity connected with the temple, that is important. These coins show the 'doorway' in the podium to draw attention to rituals within. A detail that has not been noted before is that some coins show a small figure standing in this doorway (fig. 6.15A). By

---

[48] There is only space here to give the conclusions of my detailed study, which will be published elsewhere.

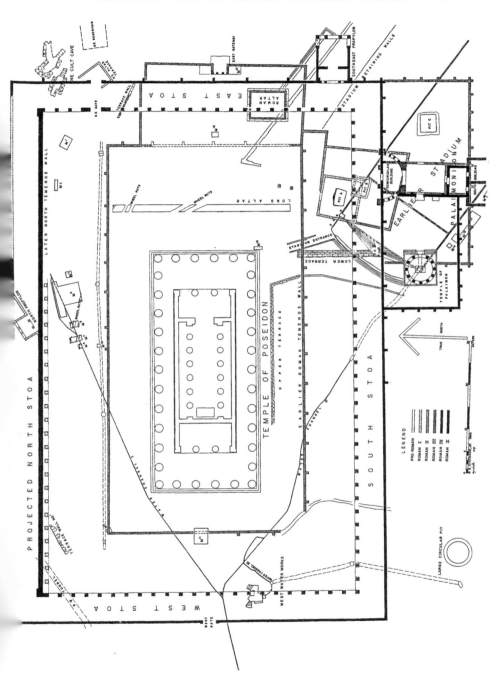

Fig. 6.14. Plan of the sanctuary of Poseidon at Isthmia in the Roman period. *Isthmia* II, plan III.

analogy with a cult statue shown in the centre of a temple façade when it is actually invisible within the cella, this little figure may not indicate that there was a doorway in the podium by which people entered but, rather, it refers to a ritual that took place in the disused water channel which served as the *adyton* below the temple floor.

The podium temple is frequently combined with a bull standing in front of a pine tree or with a bull and priest sacrificing over a lighted altar. These types accord with Broneer's excavation of sacrificial pits, which contained the burnt bones of cattle, and also with the comment of Philostratus that black bulls were sacrificed to Palaimon.[49] Again, these are activities which form part of the cult practice. Subsequently, an extraordinary variety of types referring to the cult of Palaimon and its relationship with the Isthmian festival entered the Corinthian repertoire and continued until the mint ceased production in the early 3rd century (fig. 6.15B–C). The important point here is that we have misunderstood the intention of the die engravers. In one type of image, the emphasis is on the actual temple with its cult statue of Melikertes lying on his dolphin. The other images show the ritual, the cult practices, that were associated with the temple and the worship of Palaimon.

Some specific series of coins can be associated with the emperor. For instance, coins depicting a galley with the legend ADVENTVS AVG(usti) signalled the arrival of Nero and later, Hadrian. There are numerous other types marking the presence of Nero in Greece. So it is worth asking if the presence of Lucius Verus was a factor in the production of the Temple of Palaimon coins. He was certainly in Corinth at about that time en route for the Parthian campaign, and there is a coin issue in his name depicting the emperor on horseback—another type used to announce the arrival of the emperor.[50] It is quite possible that the Palaimon coins were minted to coincide with his visit. The die engraving is unusually good with careful attention to the portrait of the emperor himself (fig. 6.16). It is a suitable, if rather lifeless, portrait of the emperor as commander in chief of the armies in the east.

Issuing coins was normally the responsibility of the city council and magistrates, and evidence from elsewhere shows that members of this

---

[49] *Imagines* 2.16.3.
[50] Verus left Rome in the summer of 162 and is described as "traveling about through Corinth and Athens accompanied by singers and musicians" (*SHA Verus* 6.9) before sailing to Ephesos. No other record of his visit to Corinth survives.

A   B   C

Fig. 6.15. A. *Rev.* Temple of Palaimon with small figure in 'doorway;' to left, priest with bull sacrificing over lighted altar (time of Marcus Aurelius). B. *Rev.* Athlete holding palm and torch, moving away from Melikertes lying on dolphin under pine tree (time of Marcus Aurelius). C. *Rev.* Isthmus raising hand over Melikertes lying on dolphin on altar under pine tree (time of Marcus Aurelius). Bibliothèque nationale de France.

Fig. 6.16. *Obv.* Lucius Verus laureate and cuirassed: *rev.* Melikertes riding on dolphin within Isthmian pine wreath. Bibliothèque nationale de France.

civic elite would sometimes fund a particular issue.[51] An important inscription records the numerous donations made at Isthmia by Publius Licinius Priscus Iuventianus. He came from a distinguished family and was high priest for life of the imperial cult, which was celebrated at Isthmia.[52] Among other projects Priscus constructed at his own expense, "the Palaimonion with its ornaments, the *enagisterion* and sacred doorway." He may also have funded these special coins commemorating his beneficence. The cult of Palaimon is likely to have appealed particularly to the educated classes to which Priscus belonged.[53] The date of the Priscus inscription has been disputed.[54] Given that the

---

[51] *RPC* I.3–4.

[52] Geagan 1989.

[53] Piérart (1998) notes the appeal of the cult to the educated elite, as evidenced, for example, in Plutarch (*Mor.* 576d).

[54] The different dates, ranging from the time of Vespasian to the latter half of the 2nd century, are summarized by Puech (1983), who opts for a Trajanic date, ca. 110. Geagan prefers the latter half of the 2nd century (1989, 358–60), as suggested by Kent on the basis on the lettering but notes that a more exact date is uncertain.

earliest coins showing the temple of Palaimon can be dated to between 161–63, the *stelai* recording the generosity of Priscus must have been erected at, or not long after, that time.

A CULT OF ANTINOUS

We do not know the names of any other magistrates who were responsible and may well have paid for the regular coinage in this later period,[55] but there is a parallel in the very rare and beautiful medallic coins issued in connection with the cult of Hadrian's favorite, Antinous (fig. 6.17). The inscription reads, "Hostilius Marcellus, the priest of Antinous, dedicated (this coin) for the Corinthians."[56] On the obverse is the bust of Antinous, and on the reverse Bellerophon, with the features of Antinous, taming Pegasus—a design that first appeared on the coinage of Nero. Other coins, also the gift of Hostilius Marcellus, depict Antinous either in the guise of the seated Poseidon, save that he holds a *patera* in his outstretched hand and has two dolphins draped limply at his feet, or leaning on a herm and holding the *thyrsus* of Dionysos.[57] These medallic coins can be dated to 134 CE, the fourth year after the death of Antinous, when special games were held in his honor at Mantinea in Arcadia, the center of his worship in Greece.[58] The Corinthian coins suggest that there was also a cult of Antinous at Corinth. Certainly there are sculptures of him in the theater at Corinth and in the Temple of Poseidon at Isthmia.[59] The worship of Antinous was often combined with another cult, and it would have been be easy

---

[55] The latest pair of duovirs known by name is L. Antonius Iulianus and T. Flavius Pompeianus, who supervised a monument to Faustina, the wife of Antoninus Pius (*Corinth* VIII.3, no. 107). They were in charge, but the monument was decreed by the city council at the public expense. In the absence of a benefactor, this was probably also the normal procedure for funding the coinage.

[56] The word ἀνέθηκε is found on coins of Asia Minor. It is also used frequently for other types of benefaction. Bronze, which was the metal used, would not have been expensive, but the cost of employing such a talented engraver might well have been considerable. Similar medallic coins with a race horse on the reverse engraved by the same artist were dedicated by Veturius "for the Arcadians;" Blum 1914, 33–70 and pls. 1–5.

[57] Hostilius also dedicated, that is, paid for coins by the same die engraver "for the Achaians" with Antinous as Hermes, holding a caduceus. As Blum and later scholars have noted, not all the coins showing Antinous can be regarded as genuine.

[58] Paus. 8.9.8.

[59] Sturgeon (*Corinth* IX.3.128–31) has restored statues of Antinous in Apollo Lykeios pose and Dionysos as Katheroidos standing on either side of the *porta regia*

Fig. 6.17. *Obv.* Bust of Antinous: *rev.* Antinous in the guise of Bellerophon restraining Pegasus, 134 CE. CNG 69, 2005, no. 951.

to associate rites for the youth drowned in the Nile with those for the heroized Melikertes.[60]

Although these medallic coins did have a monetary value, they would have been primarily souvenir pieces. Hostilius is known as a *strategos*, as well as the priest of Antinous.[61] He may have been a Corinthian or else he had close ties with Corinth, which were an incentive for him to pay for these special coins. The prospect of the emperor himself attending the festival would have been an added inducement. Both the Greek legend and the outstanding artistic quality distinguish these coins from the ordinary output of the Corinthian mint. They are the work of an exceptionally talented engraver, and the classicizing style is peculiarly appropriate for Hadrian's beautiful young favorite.[62] The Bellerophon and Pegasus reverse is particularly striking, and it does give the impression of having being adapted from a monumental sculptural group, perhaps the fountain which Pausanias describes as the most noteworthy in the city—with a figure of Bellerophon and the water flowing through the hoof of Pegasus.[63]

---

in the theater. At Isthmia fragments of a statue of Antinous were found in the south colonnade of the Temple of Poseidon; *Isthmia* IV.132–35.

[60] On the worship of Antinous: Vout 2005. He also became an element in the imperial cult.

[61] For *strategos*: Bingen 1953; *SEG* 13 (1956) no. 253. For priest: *IG* IV.1554. One of the Corinthian tribes was named Hostilia; *Corinth* VIII.3, no. 349.

[62] Seltman (1948, 77–85 and pls. 27–8) refers to him as "the Alpheios engraver" and identifies him as Antonianos from Aphrodisias in Caria, one of Hadrian's artistic circle, who was responsible for a number of portraits of Antinous.

[63] Paus. 2.3.5.

STATUES AND CULT IMAGES

We come back to figures on coins and how to interpret them. Is it a cult image, a well-known sculpture displayed in the city, or does the image represent something entirely different?

When a figure is shown on a base, as Apollo is in fig. 6.18, we can generally assume that it is a specific statue. The water basin in front of Apollo suggests that it was a fountain or part of a sculptural group with a fountain; the detailing of the herm on which Apollo is leaning would also have identified the sculpture for the Corinthians. It is clear from the representations of the Temple of Palaimon that the figure of Melikertes lying lifeless on his dolphin is a cult image (fig. 6.19A). But is the Melikertes/Palaimon standing upright with his hand outstretched (fig. 6.19B) the same statue that Pausanias saw at Isthmia in the Temple of Poseidon, or is it the one he saw on the Lechaion Road, or neither? And what about this image with the dolphin poised elegantly on its beak (fig. 6.19C)? Melikertes/Palaimon and his dolphin were a favorite subject on the coins of Corinth from early on. There were no doubt a number of different statues in Corinth and at Isthmia, but the variety does suggest that some of them were also creations from the die engraver's own visual repertoire.

The coin image may not even represent a statue at Corinth. One figure (fig. 6.20), which was originally identified as Pan or a satyr with *pedum* is a copy of the statue of Marsyas that stood in the Forum Romanum. This particular Marsyas, which is identified by his stance, the wineskin and the boots, had, by imperial times, come to be associated with civic freedom and the grant of the *ius italicum* with its ensuing tax privileges. Corinth was granted freedom from taxation in the early years of Hadrian's reign, and this was commemorated by a single coin issue depicting the statue of Marsyas.[64]

Sometimes external factors also may have been at work. There is epigraphic and archaeological evidence that the worship of Asklepios, the god of healing, was established or re-established early in the life of the colony, but the god received little attention on the coinage before the Hadrianic period when he appears on coins of both Hadrian and

---

[64] *Corinth* VI.30 no. 26; the *pedum* is the result of corrosion. For the detailed discussion: Walbank 1989. The image of Marsyas in the Forum Romanum appears on the coins of a large number of provincial cities for the same reason.

Fig. 6.18. *Rev.* Statue of Apollo leaning on herm, water basin in front (time of Commodus). BCD Collection (Lanz Auktion 105, 2001, no. 812).

A   B   C

Fig. 6.19. A. *Rev.* Melikertes lying on dolphin with pine tree behind (time of Marcus Aurelius). B. *Rev.* Melikertes standing on dolphin (time of Antoninus Pius). C. *Rev.* Melikertes riding dolphin poised on its beak on a garlanded base or altar (time of Commodus). BCD Collection (Lanz Auktion 105, 2001, nos. 700, 680 and 822).

Fig. 6.20. *Rev.* Marsyas with wineskin (time of Hadrian). BCD Collection (Lanz Auktion 105, 2001, no. 626).

Sabina.[65] But Asklepios could also be equated with Salus, and in this capacity he oversaw not only the health of individuals but also the welfare of the emperor and the state.[66] At Corinth Asklepios (fig. 6.21), often with Hygieia, begins appearing more frequently than hitherto on the coinage at about the time of the Antonine plague, which was

---

[65] Hygieia alone also appears on the smaller coins of Hadrian and Sabina. Pausanias (2.4.5) refers to a temple of Asklepios and cult statues of Asklepios and Hygieia, but there is no indication as to whether the coin images are copies or not.

[66] Dedications were erected at Corinth and also at Isthmia to Callicratea, priestess of the cult of *Providentia Augusta* and *Salus Publica* (*Corinth* VIII.2, nos. 110 and 15, and *ILGR* 116), associated by West with the failed assassination plot against Tiberius by Sejanus in 31 CE, which was widely commemorated in provincial cities.

Fig. 6.21. *Rev.* Asclepios with Hygieia (time of Lucius Verus). Bibliothèque
nationale de France.

carried by the armies of Lucius Verus returning from the east. The
plague was first attested in 165 CE, and it was still an issue in Greece
in the mid 170s. Since Corinth was on an important trade route, the
city would have been susceptible to epidemics. There is no literary
evidence that there was plague in Corinth at this time, but it is a real
possibility and could account for the appearance of Asklepios with or
without Hygieia on the coins.[67]

How then does one identify a cult statue and its location? Take,
for example, Poseidon, one of the most important Corinthian deities.
A naked Poseidon of archaic aspect, seated on a rock and holding
his trident but without a dolphin, was one of the city's earliest coin
images (fig. 6.1B). A seated Poseidon next appears during the reign of
Domitian sometime between 85–87 CE. Now he is semi-draped, seated
on a throne with his trident in the right hand and the left hand outstretched, holding a dolphin (fig. 6.22A). When the city next issues
coins under Trajan in 113 after an interval of almost 30 years, this
seated Poseidon is the only reverse type used on the larger coins, and
it is repeated frequently during the 2nd century (fig. 6.22B).[68] There
are occasional small variations, such the detail of the throne or the
addition of an altar in front of Poseidon, but the images are so similar
that it could be a cult statue. If so, we do not know the location, and
the coins are no help. The obvious place would be in the cella of the

---

[67] For the plague at Athens: the letter of Marcus Aurelius, 174/5 CE. On the Antonine plague in general: Duncan-Jones 1996, 115–34; Jones 2005, 298–301. There could
be a connection with a dedication erected by the city or council of Corinth in the
Asklepieion honoring the physician Gaius Vibius Euelpistus, dated provisionally in
the later part of the 2nd century (*Corinth* VII.3, no. 206). Kent suggests a date in
the last quarter of the 2nd or first quarter of the 3rd century. M. B. Walbank (personal communication) thinks that the letter forms are more appropriate for the earlier
date.

[68] A tiny issue of very small coins with the head of Poseidon and NEP ISTHMI was
probably also issued in 113; Walbank 2003, 340 and fig. 20.3.2.

Fig. 6.22. *Revs.* Seated Poseidon holding trident and dolphin in outstretched hand. A. Issued under Domitian (*RPC* I, no. 189); B. Marcus Aurelius (BCD Collection Lanz Auktion 105, 2001, no. 683).

Temple of Poseidon at Isthmia, but Sturgeon's reconstruction of statues of Poseidon and Amphitrite, and the later donation of a cult group by Herodes Atticus, described in detail by Pausanias, would seem to rule this out. It might have been one of the two statues of Poseidon that Pausanias saw in the pronaos. According to Pausanias, there was also a sanctuary and bronze cult statue of Poseidon at Lechaion, but we have nothing to connect the coin with his comment.[69]

The figure of Poseidon, standing with trident and dolphin, first appears at Corinth on smaller denomination coins under Claudius and regularly thereafter. On later issues he usually has one foot on a rock or prow of a ship (fig. 6.23). This image had been used on Hellenistic coins, and a very similar Poseidon is depicted on coins of Patras, Argos and elsewhere in the Peloponnese. It was probably just a popular coin type, although it may originally have been based on a well-known statue. A similar image appears on two different panoramic views of the Kenchreai harbor issued during the reign of Antoninus Pius (fig. 6.24A). One coin has a standing Poseidon holding a trident and dolphin in the middle of the harbor. On the other coin, Poseidon is replaced by Isis Pelagia holding a billowing sail; the statue of Poseidon is relocated within a temple façade on the coin at left, which does indicate that there was an actual temple of Poseidon. It is to be expected that Poseidon, god of the sea, and Isis Pelagia (fig. 6.24B), who is well-known as mistress of the winds and the guardian of seafarers, would be recipients of cult at Kenchreai, but the images dominating the harbor on the coins are symbolic rather than indicative of a monument. At Kenchreai we have a literary description and archaeological

---

[69] Paus. 2.1.7 (Isthmia) and 2.2.3 (Lechaion).

Fig. 6.23. *Revs.* Standing Poseidon holding a trident and with a dolphin in outstretched hand. A. Issued under A, Claudius (*RPC* I, no. 1185) and B, Hadrian (BCD Collection, Lanz Auktion 105, 2001, no. 633).

Fig. 6.24. A. *Rev.* Kenchreai harbour with statue of Poseidon in centre (time of Antoninus Pius). BCD Collection (Lanz Auktion 105, 2001, no. 667). B. *Rev.* Isis Pelagia (time of Antoninus Pius). Bibliothèque nationale de France.

evidence in addition to the coins, but even so it is difficult to reconcile all three sources.[70]

Personifications

During the 2nd century, personifications become increasingly popular. Some were stock Corinthian types, for instance, the nymphs Leches and Kenchrias, personifying the harbors, and the male deity, Isthmus, portraying the isthmus which separated the two seas. An essentially Roman personification is the *genius* of the colony, which first appears under Claudius and Nero, then later under Hadrian and Marcus Aurelius (fig. 6.25). It is of particular interest because there is epigraphic evidence of a *sacerdos genii coloniae* on a monument in the Forum

---

[70] The Kenchreai harbor coins were issued only during the reign of Antoninus Pius. However, Isis Pelagia, sometimes combined with a lighthouse, appears on several occasions. "In Kenchreai are a temple and a stone cult statue of Aphrodite, after it on the mole running into the sea, a bronze image of Poseidon and at the other end of the harbor, sanctuaries of Asklepios and of Isis," Paus. 2.3. On the harbor-side sanctuaries: *Kenchreai* I.53–90; Hohlfelder 1970; Smith 1977 (on Egyptian cults at Corinth), but his list of Corinthian coins is incorrect. For a wide-ranging discussion of Isis Pelagia: E. R. Williams 1985; *LIMC* (782–84 with figs. 269–97); neither, however, cites the harbor coins. See J. Rife in this volume on more recent investigation of the site.

Fig. 6.25. *Rev.* Genius of colony, 54–55 CE. *RPC* I. no. 1189.

Fig. 6.26. *Rev.* Nike/Victoria writing on a shield which rests on a column (issued in the name of Caracalla). BCD Collection (Lanz Auktion 105, 2001, no. 920).

Fig. 6.27. *Rev.* Tyche/Fortuna (time of Marcus Aurelius). Bibliothèque nationale de France.

dated to the time of Nero.[71] Another Roman type is Nike holding a wreath and palm and sometimes standing on a globe, which had appeared on the very early coinage. The type is also associated with the Isthmian games. Other versions of Nike or Victory were used frequently later in the century, perhaps related to increasing military activity in the eastern empire (fig. 6.26). Tyche or Fortuna is often conflated with other personifications and deities including, at Corinth, Nemesis, but on the coins she retains her simple form (fig. 6.27). She is not to be confused with the turreted head of Roma, which is clearly

---

[71] This Roman type is commonly found in colonies and *municipia*. For the inscription: Martin 1977, 180–83 and pl. 49. For the monument: Williams 1976, 127–32. Another dedication to the *genius*: *Corinth* VIII.2, no. 5. For the *genius* combined with Apollo and another deity, restored as Jupiter Optimus Maximus: *Corinth* VIII.2, no. 4.

identified by the legend ROMA or more usually ROMAE ET IMPE-
RIO. (Neither numismatic nor sculptural representations of Roma do
in themselves imply cult.) Tyche's attributes are a cornucopiae and
rudder. As Dio Chrysostom says, the former illustrates her power to
bestow prosperity, and with the latter, she guides the affairs of men.[72]
Tyche was always popular in public and private life; but given that, as
the 2nd century progressed, there was an underlying uncertainty as to
the future, it is easy to understand why she appears with increasing
frequency on the coinage.

A Diversity of Gods

A notable feature of the 2nd century coinage is the number of Greek
deities who are reintroduced or appear for the first time: Kronos/Sat-
urn and Dionysos, who had been on the very early coinage; a standing
Zeus and Pallas Athena introduced under Domitian; Artemis, Herakles,
Helios, Hermes; Apollo occasionally; and rarely, Ares and Hephaistos
(fig. 6.28A–I). Amid this diversity of gods, I think that one can recognize an increasing emphasis on the worship of eastern deities and
the so-called mystery religions. In addition to Dionysos, there is Isis
holding a *sistrum*, as well as Isis Pelagia, Serapis with Cerberus, and
also a seated Cybele with her attributes of a lion and tympanum, all
personal cults that were concerned with the question of death and survival.[73] An interesting new type issued under Antoninus Pius, Marcus
Aurelius and Geta is a fruiting date palm within an enclosure, which
must be a shrine or altar (fig. 6.29). On the Severan issue, the entrance
has double doors, which suggests that it was quite a large structure,
although its location is unknown. The palm tree has associations with
Artemis and with Apollo, but it is also connected with the worship of
Isis and Anubis.

Personal Types

There is one significant absence from the coinage, namely, any direct
representation of the cult of Demeter and Kore, which we know was

---

[72] Dio Chrys. *Or.* 637.
[73] Sanctuaries of Egyptian Isis, Pelagian Isis, Serapis and a temple of the mother of
the gods (Cybele) are among those on the slopes of Acrocorinth; Paus. 2.4.5. Serapis
appears very rarely on the coinage although there is good evidence of his worship at
Corinth; Milleker 1985.

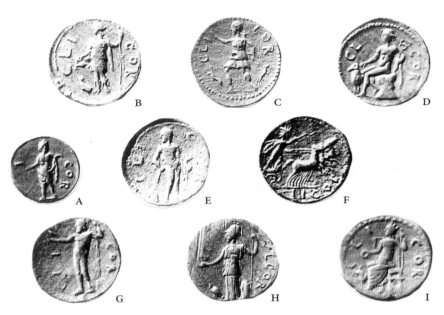

Fig. 6.28. A. *Rev.* Kronos with sickle (time of Antoninus Pius). B. *Rev.* Dionysos holding kantharos and thyrsos with panther (time of Marcus Aurelius). C. *Rev.* Artemis with stag and hound (time of Lucius Verus). D. *Rev.* Mercury holding caduceus and with hand on ram (time of Lucius Verus). E. *Rev.* Herakles with club (time of Marcus Aurelius). F. *Rev.* Helios in quadriga (time of Marcus Aurelius). G. *Rev.* Zeus holding sceptre and with eagle on right hand. (time of Marcus Aurelius). H. *Rev.* Pallas Athena holding Nike, owl at feet (time of Hadrian). I. *Rev.* Cybele seated holding tympanum and with lion (time of Antoninus Pius). Bibliothèque nationale de France.

Fig. 6.29. *Rev.* Date palm in shrine (time of Antoninus Pius). BCD Collection (Lanz Auktion 105, 2001, no. 668).

important at Corinth.[74] There is a single reverse issued during the reign of Hadrian which depicts Triptolemos in his serpent chariot (fig. 6.30).[75] This type is predominantly connected with the Eleusinian mysteries and it also appears at Athens.[76] The Corinthian coins are very rare and an unusual fabric. This must surely reflect the fact that the worship of Demeter and Kore was essentially a private cult in the Roman period. I would put the coin in the context of Hadrian's initiation into the Eleusinian mysteries, and probably a personal issue by one of the city elite, a member of the intellectual circle favored by Hadrian; perhaps the donor was initiated at the same time.

Another rare image refers to the death of the child Opheltes and the slaying of the serpent who killed him by one of the Seven against Thebes. The death of Opheltes is the founding myth of the Nemean Games, which were, in the Roman period, under the control of Argos. Coins with this theme were minted at Corinth under Domitian, Hadrian and also during the reign of Septimius Severus (fig. 6.31). The links between the elites of Corinth and Argos were always strong. The largest and most impressive sarcophagus found at Corinth also has an Argive connection; the principal scene on the front is the departure of the Seven against Thebes and, on the surviving end panel, the death of Opheltes.[77] I suggest that these coins were personal issues by a Corinthian magistrate with strong Argive connections, and that someone from the same family was responsible for commissioning the sarcophagus.

THE CULT OF APHRODITE

I have left to last the cult of Aphrodite. She had been one of the most revered deities of the Greek city, and her worship dates back to at least the 6th century. In the Roman period, she received both public and private cult: she was Venus in her temple in the Forum; Aphrodite

---

[74] In addition to the sanctuary on the slopes of Acrocorinth, there was a Temple of Demeter and Kore at Isthmia, mentioned among the dedications by Licinius Priscus (*IG* IV.203). A recently discovered fragmentary inscription referring to a *sacerdos* of Proserpina has been tentatively dated in the Hadrianic period (Dixon 2000).

[75] It is a pseudo-autonomous coin with the head of Aphrodite on the obverse.

[76] And elsewhere in the Mediterranean, for example, Alexandria in Egypt; and Enna in Sicily.

[77] For example, Cn. Cornelius Pulcher was from Argos; he and his son held high office at Corinth. In *RPC* II.200–03 the Domitianic image is referred to as "Triptol-

Fig. 6.30. *Rev.* Triptolemos in serpent chariot (time of Hadrian). BCD Collection (Lanz Auktion 105, 2001, no. 635).

Fig. 6.31. *Rev.* The Opheltes myth, ca. 85–87 CE. *RPC* I, no. 201.

Melainis, a chthonic deity with a sanctuary on the outskirts of the city; she was also the armed Aphrodite on Acrocorinth.[78] A variety of images appears on the coinage (fig. 6.32A–D). A charming female head with the hair pulled loosely back in a knot, which appears on the very early coinage, is normally identified as Aphrodite although there is no actual proof. The image is repeated on the pseudo-autonomous coinage of Hadrian and briefly under Septimius Severus. Imaginative types issued at the time of Nero's visit celebrate her also as a marine goddess. On one issue she holds up a mirror in a *biga* of hippocamps. One of a pair of coins shows her bust above a galley inscribed LECHAVM and, on the other, above a dolphin inscribed CENCRHEAE (*sic*). Later, she appears with a scepter in one hand and holding out an apple in the other. In the 2nd century, a fashion emerged for the juxtaposing of civic deities: Aphrodite is paired with other major Corinthian deities such as Poseidon, Apollo, Athena, hunting Artemis, and also Ephesian

---

emus fighting snake," but comparison with the coins of Argos makes clear that it is the Opheltes myth. The sarcophagus was found by chance (*Corinth* IX, no. 241; Walbank 2005, 267). It was originally dated loosely to the Antonine period, but Sturgeon now puts it after 180 CE.

[78] On the cult of Aphrodite on Acrocorinth: Williams 1986, where he collates earlier discussions; and 2005. Lanci 2005 questions the much discussed and misunderstood relationship between Aphrodite and sacred prostitution.

Fig. 6.32. A. *Obv.* Head of Aphrodite, 34–31 BCE. BCD Collection (Lanz Auktion 105, 2001, no. 327. B. *Rev.* Aphrodite holding a mirror in a biga drawn by tritons, 54–55 CE; *RPC* I, no. 1197. C. *Rev.* Bust of Aphrodite above a galley inscribed CENCRHEAE, 54–55 CE; *RPC* I, no. 1200. D. *Rev.* Aphrodite holding a sceptre and with an apple in outstretched hand (time of Marcus Aurelius); BCD Collection (Lanz Auktion 105, 2001, no. 689).

Artemis, who had a sanctuary in the Corinthian Forum. Both Corinth and Patras issued coins showing the armed Aphrodite and Artemis Laphria, the principal divinity of Patras, facing over a lit altar.[79] Simply from the number and variety of coin images, one would be justified in thinking that Aphrodite was the most important deity of Roman Corinth.

The most widely produced coin types were those showing Aphrodite on Acrocorinth.[80] There is both literary and archaeological evidence for a Temple of Aphrodite on the summit. Strabo, who visited Corinth in 29 BCE, calls it a *naidion* (a little temple). Pausanias also refers to a temple on the summit which held cult images of armed Aphrodite, Helios (who never appears on these coins) and Eros holding a bow. The archaeological remains, however, are sparse.[81] The temple type without the cult statue was first issued during the reign of Claudius

---

[79] Pairing can signify an economic association or simply the promotion of religious and economic ties. Under Hadrian a very rare coin records Concordia (*Homonoia*) between Corinth and Patras; Walbank 2003, 342 and fig. 20.6.3.

[80] "Acrocorinth is the mountain peak above the city which Briareus as adjudicator assigned to Helios, who then, as the Corinthians say, ceded it to Aphrodite..." (Paus. 2.4.6).

[81] Strabo 8.6.20; Paus. 2.5.1. For archaeological remains: *Corinth* III.1, 4–21.

Fig. 6.33. *Obv.* Claudius: *rev.* temple of Aphrodite on Acrocorinth, 42/43–45/46 CE. BCD Collection (Lanz Auktion 105, 2001, no. 419).

by the duovirs L. Licinius and Octavius, who held office between 42–46 CE (fig. 6.33). The temple is hexastyle in form, and so it must have been fairly large. Aphrodite/Venus, ancestor of the Julian *gens*, was a natural recipient of cult in a Julian colony, but the new temple may also reflect Claudius's antiquarian interests or, given his involvement elsewhere in Achaia, it may even have been a project initiated by the emperor himself.[82]

The distinctive cult image of Aphrodite holding up the shield of Ares to use as a mirror is one of the many types first issued under Domitian. Her last appearance is on coins of Plautilla. The numerous variations in the form of the temple, hexastyle, tetrastyle and distyle, illustrate the fact that the die engraver may alter the building to suit his purpose. There are even more variations in the image of Aphrodite—facing left or right, occasionally balancing the shield on a column, sometimes with one or two *erotes* holding bows or garlands—but she is always immediately recognizable (fig. 6.34A–D). One gets the impression that the die cutters enjoyed playing with the image and introducing new elements. This particular manifestation of Aphrodite must have been immensely appealing, to judge by the number of coin issues, as well as representations on lamps, small-scale sculptures, and figurines; she also appears in an elaborate fresco in a building east of

---

[82] Claudius also had ancestral links in the Peloponnesos. His concern for Achaia and other cities of the East is well-documented; Levick 1990, 178–79. At Athens he was honored as "saviour and benefactor" for his numerous benefactions, which almost certainly included funding the construction of the stairway to the Propylaea; Shear 1981, 367. (However, the rededication of the temple of Nemesis at Rhamnous to the deified Livia, originally dated in 45/6 CE [Dinsmoor 1961], is now put in the reign of Augustus [Lozano 2004].) According to Pausanias (9.27.3) Claudius also returned items looted by Gaius to the cities of Achaia, including an ancient image of Eros to Thespiae. In this context, imperial interest in the restoration of the venerable shrine of Aphrodite on Acrocorinth makes sense.

Fig. 6.34. A. *Obv.* Domitian: *rev.* Aphrodite balancing on a column the shield of Ares used as a mirror. B. *Obv.* Marcus Aurelius: *rev.* Aphrodite in tetrastyle temple. C. *Obv.* Septimius Severus: *rev.* Aphrodite in distyle temple; BCD Collection (Lanz Auktion 105, 2001, nos. 542, 724 and 872. D. *Obv.* Hadrian: *rev.* Aphrodite holding shield of Ares to her left, small Eros with garland behind; Bibliothèque nationale de France.

the Theater.[83] In the later 2nd century, a panoramic view of the great rock of Acrocorinth, crowned by Aphrodite's temple, became popular (fig. 6.35), and it was sometimes combined with other elements of the founding myths such as Pegasus and Bellerophon, Peirene, or the nymphs Leches and Kenchrias, reclining at the base of the rock. This is an essentially Corinthian type. It was also an entirely appropriate image in the 2nd century as the Roman Corinthians succeeded in integrating with their Greek past. This is one coin image of which our understanding is probably the same as that of the Corinthians.

Conclusions

In this brief essay I have had to be selective in my examples and I have discussed only a few aspects of the Corinthian coinage. So, what conclusions can one draw? In what ways do the coins contribute to our understanding of religion and society at Corinth?

---

[83] Williams 2005, 237–40.

Fig. 6.35. *Obv.* Marcus Aurelius: *rev.* Acrocorinth surmounted by temple of Aphrodite. Bibliothèque nationale de France.

Coins are primary sources and they have an immediacy that is often lacking in written sources. They are also official in character. The head of the emperor on the coin obverse is a reminder that Corinth was an integral part of the empire and that the authority to mint came from the imperial government. But it was the local Corinthian magistrates and council who were responsible for actually issuing coins and choosing the designs. The coin images will, therefore, give the form in which people worshipped locally.

Using coins as a primary source is not straightforward. The problem for us is in viewing the coin images as the Corinthians would have done. The evidence loses much of its value—and can be seriously misleading—if the coins are not properly dated and put in context, as has happened with the coins depicting the statue of Livia and the *gens Iulia* temple. It is also important to bear in mind that the coins were intended only for local consumption: the city usually coined when there was a need for small change or to commemorate an important occasion, such as the reopening of the mint or the arrival of the emperor. Other important events may be totally unknown to us, and we may not understand an image that was very familiar to the Corinthians.

Properly interpreted, the coin images add enormously to our knowledge. The value of the coin image as a 'photograph' is evident: the coins present a vivid and sometimes unique picture of the city's places of worship and cult images. This approach has often been criticized because of discrepancies between the archaeological evidence and the representation on the coin. I suggest that the comparison may have more validity now than in the past, since digital photography can alter the original so convincingly to suit a particular need, just as the die engravers altered the image on coins depicting the temple of Palaimon.

The choice of coin designs was made by the city elite—the local council and the magistrates. They are, therefore, an expression of public rather than private cult. In the Roman world official cults were at the heart of public life, and the important priesthoods were public offices. Religious and political duties were often intertwined, cults were powerful social institutions, and prominent citizens would be both magistrates and priests. Civic dignitaries who were priests of a particular cult, when responsible for a new coin issue, may well have favored the cult to which they were attached. There could also have been a political connection between political and religious entities that we are unable to identify.

On the other hand, the elite were also Corinthians who were concerned with promoting the image of their own city, sometimes in the face of intense provincial rivalry. So I think that we should distinguish between two kinds of coin imagery: popular types which signify a common identity, and the choices of the elite. In the former category, I would put the founding myths and types drawn from the Isthmian repertoire, which are used consistently. There may well have been an economic motive in that a good supply of small change would have been needed every couple of years for the Isthmian festivals, but the choice also shows that the worship of the Isthmian gods was very important to the Corinthians. The second category consists of the elite types which may represent the interests of individuals or a particular group, or which were selected to mark specific occasions such as the dedication of a building or an event of unusual significance. In this category I would include the rare Triptolemos and Opheltes types, as well as the appearance of the eastern cults of Isis and Cybele.

The coins are the public face of Corinthian cult. They say little directly about private religious beliefs although some of the imagery found on coins is also familiar in the domestic and funerary contexts. I have already cited Aphrodite in this respect, but the protective deities such as Tyche and Fortuna must also have had a universal appeal. Most ordinary Corinthians would have handled the local small change in the course of their everyday affairs. They may not have been able to read the coin legends, but they would have recognized, perhaps only subconsciously, the coin imagery and the ways in which it mirrored their experience. In particular, the rich variety of temples and cult images depicted on the coins reflects the multiplicity of different religious festivals, sacrifices, and processions that were a part of daily life for the Corinthians. The evidence in this essay does, indeed, convey the sense that it was a polytheistic society, "A World Full of Gods," as Keith Hopkins described it.[84] It is also the context in which the Christian community at Corinth took root and the background against which it has to be seen.

---

[84] The title of Hopkins's provocative study of religious life and the emergence of Christianity in the Roman empire (1999).

CHAPTER SEVEN

CERES, KOPH, AND CULTURAL COMPLEXITY: DIVINE PERSONALITY DEFINITIONS AND HUMAN WORSHIPPERS IN ROMAN CORINTH

Jorunn Økland*

Personality Definition and Anthropomorphism

Do gods have personalities? Definitely, but how these personalities are understood varies. In 19th century Biblical Studies for example, the difference between how God is described in Genesis 1 and 2 gave rise to the hypothesis that the Pentateuch is composed of four separate sources that each had a different understanding of God. Even if this 4-source hypothesis is more questioned and nuanced today, one of its presuppositions is relevant here: how deities are defined says a lot about the social, cultural and temporal location of their worshippers.

In this chapter I focus on how the identities of the goddesses Demeter/Ceres and Kore/Proserpina are also constructed socially, linguistically, and semiotically;[1] that is, I aim to show how the personality definition of the goddesses is dependent on the language in which they were worshiped, on the identity of the worshippers, and on the other deities with whom they were worshipped.[2] If they were worshiped by different social groups, in different languages, or as members of various divine constellations during different periods (or perhaps even

---

* I want to thank colleagues at the 2006–07 Metamorphosis research project at the Center for Advanced Study at the Norwegian Academy of Science and Letters, especially Einar Thomassen, Vigdis Songe-Møller, Denise Buell and the director, Turid Karlsen Seim, for discussions around the issues of continuity, change and categorization, as well as the Center of Advanced Study that hosted us.
[1] This is controversial and depends on perspective. Were these Greek goddesses renamed, appropriated, and put to use by the Romans while retaining some of their ancient features as well as their popularity among Greek audiences; or were they propelled to fame precisely because of the Romans?
[2] This means that if changes take place in one part of the polytheistic system, the relation between all the parts will be affected; Staples 1997, 8. For the semiotic approach to cultural studies: Lotman *et al.* 1975, 57–84.

at the same time), how can this *not* affect the way(s) in which their devotees perceived their respective identities?

Having first noted the dependence, or "vulnerability to change" as Albert Moore calls it,[3] of the divine personality definitions on various factors of human culture, one could, on the other hand, view such vulnerability also as strength and flexibility, as an ability to transform and adjust to new locations, cultural paradigms and ideologies without losing the ability to capture the imagination of sympathizers. Thus the study of divine personality definition becomes not just a study of ancient theology, but engages more actively studies of the worshipping communities. In our case, the communities are found in Corinth, a city where the goddesses Demeter/Ceres and Kore/Proserpina enjoyed joint worship.

These views and questions, as well as the concept 'personality definition,' are further developments of the work of Christiane Sourvinou-Inwood, who has introduced a helpful approach for defining deities through an investigation both of the society that worshiped them and of the larger pantheon to which the deities belonged.[4] In particular, she has also stressed the importance of examining local manifestations of a given deity in order to define it, rather than attempting to rely upon dominant, more generalized conceptions.[5] She offered, in turn, a study of Persephone, who at Locri shared many functions with the goddess Aphrodite and who, therefore, was defined there less in relation to Demeter and more in relation to Aphrodite. Both of these goddesses were perceived as goddesses of love, although Persephone was seen as a local fertility and marriage goddess while Aphrodite was viewed on a more cosmic, pan-Hellenic scale.

Studies of divine characters at Corinth have often been cast in terms of cult continuity or discontinuity between the city's Greek and Roman periods.[6] This essay has, perhaps, been drawn into the gravitation field of such debates in order to ask for more nuance and complexity of these same issues, not least because it seeks theoretical clarification of

---

[3] Moore points out that anthropomorphically conceived and portrayed gods such as the Greek ones, are inevitably also "more involved in and dependent upon the changing ideals of human culture. Just as the surviving Greek images have come through the vicissitudes of history mainly in broken or derivative form, so their anthropomorphic vision itself has been more vulnerable to change;" Moore 1977, 96.

[4] Sourvinou-Inwood 1991.

[5] For a similar argument concerning Corinth: Bookidis 1987; Barringer 2003.

[6] This is certainly true of my own work; Økland 2004, 78–130.

the terms 'continuity' and 'discontinuity.' I pursue this clarification by focusing on the negotiations between the Greek Demeter and Kore and the Roman Ceres and Proserpina at their sanctuary in Corinth.[7] I do so based on the conclusion that the worshipping group to a large extent defines its deity, which inevitably means that analogous developments elsewhere in the Roman Empire will take second place. The hope is still that such an approach at one location may help us explore something more general about cultic Creolization, ambiguity, and contestation elsewhere in the empire.[8]

In its attempts to envisage the worshippers, the current essay will be indebted to earlier essays by Steven Friesen and James Walters on demography and population,[9] especially Friesen's conclusion that the best current economic model for Roman imperial society would posit that most people were poor, living close to subsistence level; and that only about three percent of any urban population was rich.[10] Such an economic theory has radical consequences for how we analyze meanings inherent in the superstructure of Roman society, such as how that economic system contributed to the emergence of religious beliefs such as divine personality definitions and to the emergence of other religious practices like offerings, cultic meals and magic.

One final introductory remark is on the issue of 'religion.' When studying this subject in the ancient world, religious scholars have tended to treat it as too much of an isolated phenomenon in relation to other civic and social issues.[11] This has probably taken place under

---

[7] *Corinth* XVIII.1–4.

[8] As more research is carried out on archaeological remains of the Roman Empire, the variety in the pantheon and in definitions of Roman deities becomes much clearer. One example is the presence of the Germanic deities, Cocidius and the two Alaisiagae, mentioned on altars at Housesteads fort on Hadrian's Wall, northern England. They are mentioned with other Roman deities, Jupiter, Mars, Mercury, and the *numen Augusti*; Collingwood and Wright 1965, no. 1576–78 and 1593–94. Greece, too, has been thrown much more into relief. The Romans had borrowed so much from the Greek pantheon that Greece became their "holy land," to borrow Jaś Elsner's expression. Hence, comparisons are particularly but not exclusively relevant. In short, issues of personality definition of the Roman pantheon look very different when seen from a non-Greek province, a Greek province, or from the imperial center itself; Alcock 1997, 103–16.

[9] Friesen 2005; Walters 2005.

[10] Friesen 2005, 369–70; Friesen 2004, Barclay 2004 and Oakes 2004.

[11] Cf. the definition of religion in the *New Pauly*: "'Religion', the substantive for describing the religious, denotes a system of common practices, individual ideas about faith.... For the academic study of religion, conversely, the word is a purely heuristic category in which those practices, ideas, norms and theological constructs are

influence of modern ideals of the religious sphere, where phenomena such as imperial cults are often presented with a certain bias because they do not conform to the post-Enlightenment idea that 'religion' should be kept separate from the 'state.'[12] In what follows, I will try as far as possible to treat 'religion' as an etic, useful, but ultimately anachronistic category applied to Greek and Roman materials, and thereby aim to avoid any characterization of divine personality definitions in a reductionist way, such as mere functions of social or material factors.[13]

THE GREEK CORINTHIAN DEMETER AND KORE

Myth and Role in Pantheon

The Greek Demeter was the goddess of grain and agriculture, according to the *Homeric Hymn to Demeter*.[14] Her daughter, Kore, also called Persephone, was abducted and raped by Hades, the king of the underworld, when she was out in the fields picking flowers. As revenge, Demeter would not let anything grow until she got Kore back for at least part of the year.[15] The cult myth expressed in the hymn also established Kore as goddess of the underworld and as Hades's wife. The hymn and the myth that it expresses are central in any attempt at personality definition of the Greek goddesses Demeter and Kore, but they are in no way exhaustive for such a project. Some of the findings

---

examined historically; however, the indeterminateness of their content precludes a standard definition of what religion is and who or what gives it legitimacy...Not until the 1st half of the the 17th cent. did religion develop into an abstract noun in the sense of the modern concept of religion;" Salazar 2008, 467. In the field of NT studies, a similar approach to religious studies of the ancient world has been promoted by Hans Dieter Betz (1991).

[12] This idea found its first constitutional expression in the constitutions of the United States of America and France in the late 18th century. It has also colored the way post-Enlightenment biblical scholars have presented early Christians' (non-) participation in civic cults, and their refusal to sacrifice to the image of the emperor. In short, attempts by a ruler to enforce his religion on to his subjects has been viewed in a negative light, whereas this was the rule rather than the exception in the pre-Enlightenment period.

[13] This has sometimes been the perspective chosen by Marxist historians, who have gone to the opposite extreme (i.e. opposite of treating religion as something entirely separate). See a further discussion of this in Boer and Økland 2008.

[14] Foley 1994.

[15] *Hymn to Demeter* (trans. Foley), 398–400, 445–47.

in the Greek sanctuary at Corinth allude to the myth. Dedications of miniature (flower) baskets, for example, may allude to the flower-picking daughter and may also indicate ritual enactment of the same myth (more on this below).[16]

Still, a relatively coherent and well-known myth does not guarantee homogeneity in ritual practice. Bookidis and Stroud observe that "local customs and variations on the traditional myth of the rape of Persephone and Demeter's quest often produced rituals, processions, and sacrifices of widely different types from city to city."[17] From these observations, as well as from the perspective laid out in my introduction, it becomes clear that we cannot assume that we know how the goddesses were defined by various Corinthian worship groups that produced local rituals.[18]

Location

The sanctuary located on the northern slopes of Acrocorinth served for centuries as the center of cult for Demeter/Ceres and Kore/Proserpina (map 2, p. 518), with material evidence dating from the Archaic period well into the 4th century CE.[19] The two best attested periods were the 5th to 4th centuries BCE and the 2nd century CE. There was less activity from 146 BCE until the beginning of the Common Era.

The sanctuary's location outside of the city center is typical of how Greek Demeter sanctuaries reproduced an environment of spatial isolation. Demeter was, thus, defined as a goddess of agriculture, a farmer's goddess, who probably enjoyed the fields more than the dusty city streets where others of her worshippers lived. Susan Guettel Cole, for example, has shown how Demeter sanctuaries that were located inside the city walls, such as that in Corinth, exploited "topographical or geographical features of the site in order to preserve the sense of isolation associated with sanctuaries outside the walls... [T]hey

---

[16] *Hymn to Demeter*, 2–21.

[17] Bookidis and Stroud 1987, 8.

[18] Writing and poetry are seen as belonging to the higher strata of society, together with public space and politics. Even if we allow for an oral tradition existing before the hymn was written down, presumably, the Hymn stemmed from some kind of elite circle; Foley 1994, 97–102; Detienne 1988, 29–82.

[19] I refer to such overviews as Bookidis and Stroud (1987). For an updated view: Bookidis (2005); Økland (2004, 80–91).

are, nevertheless, remote, either removed by distance or because they
occupy an isolated level or terrace of a rising hill."[20] This is important
because the location of the sanctuary was the one thing that was difficult for either the Romans or the changing population to alter. They
could, perhaps, transform the sanctuary space and its 'inhabitants' but
its topography was relatively fixed.

Traces of the Worshippers

Ritual dining by women worshippers was central to the cult. It was an
activity that celebrated the fruits of the earth and female companion-
ship, as well as one that promoted human fertility. Over 40 dining
rooms from the Greek period have been excavated at the site in addition to a theater up the hillside (fig. 7.1). This theater, probably used
for the cult's ritual performances, was cut into the bedrock. One can
assume that cult processions took place in the same area.

Meanwhile, numerous miniature terracotta trays with fruits of the
earth served to define Demeter as the goddess of grain and agriculture
over the course of the same time period.[21] Other contemporary offerings include miniature vases and female terracotta figurines;[22] jewelry;
mirrors; loom weights; scent bottles, a particularly local export product; and combs. To this list can also be added several terracotta pigs
and a large number of children's toys, jointed dolls that may have
been dressed up and brought to the sanctuary. Offerings of water jugs
(*hydriai*) increase in number during the Hellenistic period. Many of
these offerings represent cultural femininity and, thus, could be seen
as confirming the fecund aspect of both the goddesses, as could some
dedications of grotesque figurines caricaturing pregnant women.[23]

---

[20] Cole 1994, 213. For a broader discussion of the location of sanctuaries, not specifically related to Demeter, see Cole 2004.

[21] As concluded by Bookidis and Stroud (1987, 24).

[22] "More than twenty-three thousand terracotta figurines, many of which represent
young female votaries;" Bookidis 1993, 50. Many of the terracotta pieces represent
standing female figures wearing a πόλος (pill-box hat) and carrying a torch in one
hand and a young pig in the other. These last two features were also required by each
individual in the Eleusinian mystery rites. The 40 terracotta statues representing a
young boy found in the area of the theater area are, on these grounds, taken to be
representations of the young Dionysus; but they may also be Triptolemos or simply
votive offerings.

[23] Protruding bellies, more generally, were often seen as a comic bodily feature;
Corinth XVIII.4, H357–361, 195 and pl. 53. The fact that they are exaggerated and,
thus, probably meant to be comical has been seen as an allusion to how the old

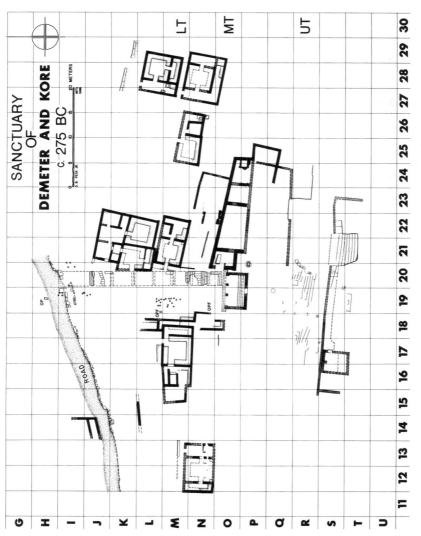

Fig. 7.1. Plan: Sanctuary of Demeter and Kore, Greek period.

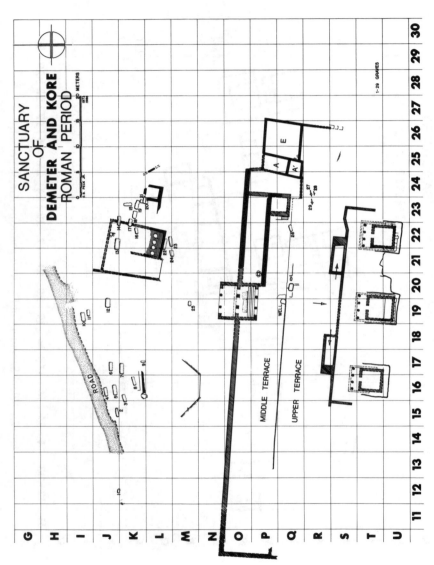

Fig. 7.2. Plan: Sanctuary of Demeter and Kore, Roman period.

All of these miniature offerings would have been inexpensive. Apart from a few terracotta statues, there are relatively few signs of wealthy donors.

Greek Names of the Goddesses

The meaning of the names of the goddesses, too, is significant for personality definition. Kore means simply "the girl." Her other Greek name, Persephone, means "she who beats the sheaves during threshing." Thus, in her hypostasis in Greek cult, she was seen either as Demeter's daughter or as her helper in the process of food production. Both Kore and Persephone, thus, are defined in reference to Demeter. But an interesting complication is that threshing and transforming grain to food (the work of Kore/Persephone) are both specifically human activities, while the production of grain and fertility (the work of Demeter) are not. Thus, Persephone could somehow be seen as closer to human farmers. All they could do with Lady Demeter was to pray for her goodwill.

The name 'De-meter' further includes the mother term. The name thus not only reflects the mythology representing her as the mother of the girl but also allows her to be cast as a goddess of human motherhood, as well as of agricultural fecundity. The first syllable of her name was in antiquity thought to go back to δη/δα ("distribution of land or earth"), an explanation which probably illustrates that the ancients thought her name should reflect their definition of her as "Earth Mother."[24]

THE ROMAN CORINTHIAN GODDESSES

Location and Traces of the Local Worshippers

Mummius's sack of Corinth did not result in destruction of the sanctuary, but the period of the city's abandonment did cause the buildings to deteriorate. When Roman colonists reestablished Corinth in 44 BCE, enough Greek evidence had survived to ensure, for them, a safe

---

woman Baubo, or Iambe, attempts to cheer up Demeter after the rape of her daughter. Humor and laughter played an important role in the Demeter reversal rites elsewhere; Winkler 1991, 188–209.

[24] 'Demeter,' OCD³. 447–48.

identification of the deities worshipped at the site. The great respect Romans showed to ancient cult places has been noted by many, and their care in restoring them has been taken as a strong indication that they understood their own cult in that place as a continuation of the pre-Roman phase. Unfortunately, we do not know how this Corinthian sanctuary was used during the two centuries after the official Greek cult finished and before the Roman refurbishment of the sanctuary some time after 77 CE. It is clear, nevertheless, that there was no clear break between the time of the city's abandonment and the Early Roman period. Finds of pottery and kitchen vessels, for example, in addition to lamps, minor cultic vessels, and coins, indicate that the newcomers to Corinth joined existing activities and may have used the sanctuary's pre-existing buildings when they resumed cult activity.[25] Into the colony's second century then, there was a continuous affirmation of the sanctuary space through various ritual activities and ceremonial forms, but these rituals did not result in a (re)-construction of walls and buildings until probably after the earthquake in 77 CE.

The first signs of rebuilding on the upper terrace involved covering over the theater area and the Hellenistic temple. A new retaining wall was then built below, dividing the earlier 'Greek' sanctuary space more sharply into two areas, an upper and a lower terrace, to which we will continue to refer below. On the lower terrace, none of the former dining rooms was rebuilt in the Roman period as a dining room. The Roman retaining wall excluded the former dining room area from the protected space. The number of kitchen vessels spread over the place may suggest that dining still continued in simplified forms,[26] but it clearly did not take place anymore in a protected space.

There is also a decline in the number of traditional votive offerings during the Early Roman period, but offerings may have taken other forms. For example, Bookidis suggests that the miniature votive offerings were replaced by more occasional, large-scale statues and, for a while, the *thymiaterion*.[27] Large amounts of shells were found in the Roman layers at the end of the Roman middle terrace and within the Roman wall.[28] In the same area and context, an artificial shell made

---

[25] *Corinth* XVIII.3, 273– 76.
[26] *Corinth* XVIII.2, 72.
[27] Bookidis 2005, 162.
[28] Stroud 1993, 72. The lead shell is still unpublished, and I am grateful to Nancy Bookidis for showing it to me.

out of lead was also found. Most likely, an ordinary shell was used as a cast into which the lead was molded, giving it its natural shape and pattern. This lead shell gives more context to the authentic sea shells; they are not coincidental waste but rather appropriate food or appropriate offering to the goddesses. Slane discusses the suggestion that the large amount of lamps and pottery in these fills could have been a new form of votive offering. Given the isolated nature of the sanctuary, Slane does believe that these ceramic pieces were previously used in the sanctuary itself, but rejects the suggestion that they were used as offerings. Apart from some items that were clearly votives, cult furniture or ritual vessels (e.g. over-size lamps, *thymiateria*), she points out that the majority of the material does not differ from what would be found in any domestic or secular context: "The cooking pots...have all been used, suggesting that cooking took place in the Roman Sanctuary, and thus the fine-ware plates and the less numerous cups are probably just what they appear to be, vessels for eating meals prepared in the Sanctuary and for drinking."[29] Thus they demonstrate the use of the sanctuary even before its first rebuilding, with increasing activity around and after the middle of the 1st century.

Finally, the upper terrace was turned into the main center of ritual attention by the erection of three small temples, probably sometime in the late 1st cent CE. The central and largest of these temples lay at the top of a new monumental stairway on the axis of the Roman entrance hall and the Roman well (fig. 7.2).[30] Inside were found the legs and other pieces of an offering table fashioned out of marble.[31] A floor mosaic in the same temple (fig. 7.3), located near the entrance, carries a reference to "Neotera": Οκταβιος Αγαθοπους νεωκορος εψηφοθετησε επι Χαρας ιερειας Νεωτερας ("Octavius Agathopous, *neokoros*, had this mosaic floor laid when Chara was priestess of Neotera.").[32] Above the inscription are depicted two wicker baskets with blue and green snakes curled around them. In between the heads of the snakes, an unknown emblem has been removed.

---

[29] *Corinth* XVIII.2, 6 (see also 2–8). Where Slane includes a similar argument concerning the lamps.
[30] Cut 20 m deep, it must have had some ritual significance.
[31] *Corinth* XVIII.3, 356–57.
[32] *Corinth* XVIII.3, 343–44; they date the mosaic to late 2nd or early 3rd century (350).

Fig. 7.3. Temple floor mosaic with inscription, Sanctuary of Demeter and Kore.

Katherine Dunbabin identifies the missing emblem as a pair of foot-prints (*vestigia*), and contextualizes the mosaic with a body of other monuments in which feet and footprints allude to the presence of a deity or human at a particular place. Together with gates and other signs of transition, these *vestigia* are particularly prominent in Egyp-tian cults.[33] Moreover, Neotera is, according to Dunbabin and many others, Nepthys, "a goddess who has close associations with Isis." Dunbabin, in fact, believes that the missing footprints are those of Isis. Elsewhere, I have extended the argument that it is more plausible the name Neotera refers to both Persephone and Nephtys, just as Demeter and Isis are often identified.[34] For Nepthys is not Isis herself but her younger sister, who plays a different, smaller role in Egyptian mythol-ogy as a funerary goddess who receives the deceased in the otherworld and who guards them there. Thus, in many respects, the personality definitions of Persephone and Nephtys overlap. Wortmann, in fact, has demonstrated the relevance of *vestigia* in relation to Persephone;[35] and Bookidis and Stroud suggest on the basis of evidence from Eleusis that Neotera (meaning "the Younger") was an epithet of Persephone in the Roman period just as Presbytera ("the Elder") was a corresponding epithet of Demeter.[36] Furthermore, the text of the floor mosaic tells us that Neotera was served by a priestess named Χαρά. The donator of this floor is Ὀκτάβιος Ἀγαθόπους, who is described as νεωκόρος, a common designation for an attendant who looked after a sanctuary, especially in Egyptian cults.[37]

There is another significant development at the sanctuary during the Roman period. Curse tablets, found mainly on the lower terrace but with samples spread around the whole sanctuary space, indicate extensive magical practices.[38] In the Roman Building of the Tablets, 10 curse tablets were found.[39] Moreover, in Room 7 and in a building nearby, three tablets were found in layers that possibly predate the

---

[33] See Dunbabin 1990. The official name of Cleopatra was Cleopatra VII Thea Neotera.

[34] Økland 2004, 83; Stroud 1993, 73 n. 7.

[35] Wortmann 1968.

[36] *Corinth* XVIII.3, 365–66.

[37] Dunand 1973, 159–67.

[38] On the map and in parts of the report, it is also called 'Building K-L:21–22;' *Corinth* XVIII.3, 277–91. This building housed the so-called 'Room 7,' where many of the curse tablets were found.

[39] Stroud (forthcoming). Two more were found in disturbed contexts.

rebuilding,[40] thus indicating that the practice of depositing curse tablets did not ultimately depend on the existence of the re-built Room 7. The curse tablets, 18 altogether, will be fully described and discussed in a forthcoming volume by Ronald Stroud.[41]

These curse tablets date from the 1st through 2nd century CE. According to Stroud, the messages are of a common *defixio* type, in which the author calls upon chthonic deities to punish the target of the curse. Among the deities invoked are Demeter, Hermes, Ge (Gaia), and also the *Moirai praxidikai*, the Fates who exact justice and whom Pausanias associated with Demeter on the slopes of Acrocorinth.

The practice of depositing lead curse tablets in Demeter's sacred space was not, however, a uniquely Corinthian phenomenon; it is attested elsewhere.[42] The tablets—illegal according to Roman law—are written in Greek and call the deities by their Greek name.[43] It has been suggested, therefore, that these finds represent a separate cult outside of the Roman sanctuary on the upper terrace, a suggestion to which I will return below.

Names, Language and Translation

Some scholars have argued that the Latin 'Proserpina' derives from a term meaning "to emerge." Others, however, conclude that it is merely a Latinization of the Greek 'Persephone' and hence that no separate meaning should be deduced from it. The meaning of her Greek name 'Kore,' however, was lost in translation. Similarly, the 'mother' aspect of Demeter's name was also lost, although its agricultural connotations were not. These were strongly associated by metonymy with the Latin name Ceres.[44] It is likely then—if we view ancient pantheons as semiotic wholes—that the translation whereby both "the mother" and "the girl" disappeared from their semantic fields reflects the pantheon of a different culture, one in which these two specific goddesses did not represent a woman's world as authoritatively as they had in Hellenic

---

[40] *Corinth* XVIII.3, 282.

[41] Stroud (forthcoming).

[42] *Corinth* XVIII.3, 285–87.

[43] It seems that the early imperial stage of marginalization, including the ban on magicians, concerned only Roman citizens or those rites performed according to Roman custom; Beard, North, and Price 1998, 1.234; Stroud (forthcoming), 92–93.

[44] For a detailed discussion of the emergence of Ceres, including a discussion of her name: Spaeth 1996, 1–4.

pantheon. We must assume, therefore, that other Roman goddesses filled this function,[45] and ask whether this 'loss of meaning' is reflected in the findings in Corinth. The loss of the dining rooms is one indication that the answer to that question would be 'yes.'

What is clear from the outset in the Corinthian material, however, is that there is very little evidence of any use of Latin in connection with these two goddesses. More generally, Cicero, who died in 43 BCE, witnessed a population reappearing in Corinth in his lifetime. There was no formal government before he died. This may suggest that although the local elite may have emigrated or may have been deported from Corinth when Rome sacked the city, its commercial redevelopment engaged the 'native' Corinthians as 'aliens.'[46] Inscriptions from early Roman Corinth are in Latin (with six exceptions), but the situation changed in favour of Greek during the time of Hadrian (117–38 CE).[47] There may be demographic reasons for this, but we should not be surprised, especially in a polyglot empire, that people might have spoken more than one language if external circumstances required.[48] On this more general background, it is striking that virtually all the remaining writing about the Corinthian sanctuary and about its goddesses during the Roman period is in Greek.[49] There is one bilingual inscription from the Forum mentioning a "*sacerdos Proserpinae.*" Dixon suggests that both the Latin and the Greek could be Hadrianic, but he seems to be inclined to think that the Greek was added later on and that this

---

[45] Such developments were quite common. For example, O'Brien (1993, 167–202), studies how Hera developed through various Greek stages and geographical areas "[f]rom soaring life to scheming wife, from life tamer to wife tamer."

[46] *Corinth* VIII.3, 20 n. 10. We know from other such deportations in the ancient world, most notably from Jerusalem, that only members of the elite were deported, that is, those who could threaten the invaders. Others could be put into useful service and did not pose any threat since the ancient social fabric disintegrated from above; Edelman 2005, 290; Barstad 1996.

[47] *Corinth* VIII.3, 18–19. For the more recent additions of Greek inscriptions dated before the reign of Hadrian: Dixon 2000, 338 n. 6.

[48] Williams (1987, 37 n. 20) notes the presence of a Greek-speaking element within the city early in its Roman phase but points out that it is still difficult to know what this signifies. As I try to argue here, I think models of continuity vs. change themselves need revision to allow for more complexity if we want to grasp the meaning of such finds.

[49] An example of this from outside the sanctuary's space: Kent 1966 no. 300. This is a Greek language gravestone from the Roman period of unspecified date with no archaeological context that names Persephone as the receiver of a girl, Kalaino, after death.

originally was a Latin inscription.[50] I will discuss the possible cultural meaning of this towards the end of this chapter. For now, however, it is important to remember that after the refounding of the city as a Roman colony, the official names of the deities worshipped in the sanctuary must have been Ceres and Proserpina since the official language of the colony was now Latin, as numerous inscriptions testify. Whether there ever was an official cult, of course, is another matter. The curse tablets and the absence of coins representing these goddesses or their sanctuary suggest that the cult may have remained private in the Roman period.[51]

The hypothesis that the sanctuary housed a private cult in the Roman period is, however, not the only possible one. In any case, it is still important to remember that Latin never became dominant in the Roman Empire, neither in terms of being the most widely-spoken language nor in terms of functioning as a *lingua franca*. Greek continued to be a crucial language not just for regular communication among Graecophone peoples, but also for elite academic and literary expression in the eastern Mediterranean.[52] This means that even if an official Latin cult had existed, it would not have defined all aspects of the institutions associated with these two goddesses of Roman Corinth, as the Greek-writing authors who describe the period of the Roman sanctuary demonstrate.

The question that arises, then, is how pervasively did official Latin names of these two goddesses affect their personality definitions in the Roman colony? Even if Roman infrastructure meant that cult practices were more assimilated across their own empire than across previous empires,[53] there was still considerable space for variation. Roman sensitivities may have spread from center to periphery. But as Roman marble was placed on top of local stone so that the totality of a building

---

[50] Dixon 2000. The Greek text also includes ναον πλου—[τωνος], as well as 'ΔΗ,' which hypothetically might be an abbreviation for Demeter; or perhaps the text continues elsewhere since it is in the far left corner of the inscription. This might be documentation of the triad also in Corinth. Such documentation already exists for Isthmia, as Dixon points out (2000, 340).

[51] This was Mary Walbank's response to my paper at the conference in Austin (January 2007). She mentioned as a possible exception one coin representing Triptolemos, but this coin is unrelated to the sanctuary. For the curse tablets, see Stroud (forthcoming). I am grateful to the author for access to this manuscript.

[52] Woolf 2001, 314–15.

[53] On the Persian Empire: Edelman 2005; Barstad 1996.

expressed a new aesthetic, so, too, did the blending of Roman beliefs and cult practices with local ones create new, hybrid phenomena.

If we look at the matter from the side of the Roman colonizers, for example, even if they changed the names of the deities into Latin ones and even if changes in personality definition inevitably did occur, Ceres and Proserpina were still viewed as old, Greek deities. In Rome, it was the '*Graecus ritus*' that was observed.[54] The *initia* or *sacra Cereris*, the "initiations or rites of Ceres," belonged to this *Graecus ritus* and were related to the Greek Thesmophoria rituals of Demeter, as well.[55] Moreover, those rituals and festivals that were classified as *Graecus ritus* were organized and celebrated according to gender even as other Roman rituals of Ceres included male and female worshipers together. Still, since the Roman conception of the Greek past was not identical with the Greek past but rather displayed a particularly Roman notion of it, we cannot assume continuity between the older (Greek) and the newer (Roman) rituals—not even in Greece.[56] Nor can we assume that the names and definitions generated from the imperial center were necessarily adhered to beyond the small elites in the colonies. The sanctuary of Demeter and Kore in Corinth gives us particularly good reasons for such an argument.

Listening to the Worshippers: Temple Identification

The question of which deity inhabited the central temple illustrates how different ways of considering personality definitions, and thus the relationship between goddesses and their worshippers, has consequences for how we interpret the archaeological record.

From the outset I reluctantly follow the excavators who think that the main temple in the Roman period might have been dedicated to the daughter and not to the mother.[57] It is right to be cautious about assuming cult continuity between Greek and Roman periods, and Barbette Spaeth argues for a more radical discontinuity in her forthcoming study on "Cultic Discontinuity in Roman Corinth." Spaeth suggests

---

[54] This was the technical term Romans used to denote rites that were exempt from certain Roman religious laws because of their ancient Greek and, hence, noble origin. Less noble Greek rituals were excluded from the Roman cult system from the outset; Scheid 1995.

[55] They were imported to Rome by the 3rd century BCE; Spaeth 1996, 59.

[56] Beard, North and Price 1998, 2 n. 3; Scheid 1995.

[57] *Corinth* XVIII.3, 362–70.

changes not only in names and cult but also in divinities worshipped there.[58] On the basis of a Roman preference for triadic cults and on the existence in North Africa of a complex of temples similar to that one found in Corinth, she proposes that the three temples were dedicated to Ceres, Liber and Libera.

Bookidis has responded to these identifications with a list of counterarguments, one of which is the lack of evidence for the triad in Greece and the eastern Mediterranean.[59] Second, a curse tablet of the late 1st or 2nd century CE, found in the central temple, was addressed to Lady Demeter. Third, a sacred glen at Isthmia is the site of a cult for Demeter and Kore together with Dionysus, Eueteria, and Artemis.[60] Finally, the name of Persephone in its Latin form, 'Proserpina,' is present on the bilingual inscription from Corinth's forum. Bookidis has also pointed to Eleusis for a parallel occurrence of the name "Neotera," prominent in the Corinthian mosaic inscription.

Using personality definition as an interpretive lens, it becomes clear that the basic difference between Spaeth and Bookidis is how and the extent to which they take the local archaeological record into account. It is to be expected that Bookidis, who has worked on Corinthian materials throughout her career, does so more than Spaeth. Still the issue could profit from considering not only the local record, but also the original producers of the archaeological remains: the local worshippers, who also in some sense 'produced' the personality definitions of the Corinthian goddesses.

Spaeth and others have suggested that the central, most prominent temple could not have been dedicated to Proserpina because such a designation would have been an anomaly from the point of view of religious practices in Rome. One could argue, however, that Roman religion (i.e., religion in the Roman empire) in imperial times was a site of conversation and negotiation, in particular, between ancient Roman traditions and ancient local ones in those areas under Roman control. Since religious standards were not strongly reinforced from the top down but rather left to the 'market mechanisms' of benefactions, honor and shame, there was considerable variation between the Roman pantheon worshipped, for example, in England or Greece and

---

[58] Spaeth 2006. I thank the author for access to this manuscript.
[59] Bookidis 2005, 162–63.
[60] *Isthmia* II.113.

that worshipped in Rome or Italy.[61] It therefore makes a difference whether one studies religious dialectics centripetally or centrifugally.[62] What is clear, at least, is that from the perspective of personality definitions, the cult on the lower terrace produced definitions that were alternative, to say the least, from the ones produced on the upper terrace where "well-endowed" would have been a fitting epithet.[63]

The sanctuary further employs a good deal of symbolism associated with both Egyptian cults and the Demeter cult, although the Egyptian cult connection appears more pronounced in the Roman period. Why were Early Roman Corinthians so imprecise according to modern standards in the way they institutionalized their religious activities? I think that is an important question and wish to state from the outset that I do not view syncretism as lack of precision nor as the product of 'dangerous oriental influence.' Rather syncretism reflects the ability of ordinary people to discern divine personality definitions across languages and to connect the wide variety of cultural expressions that surrounded them. Understood in this way, 'imprecision' can be a problem for those with religious authority in each one of the traditions involved, and it explains why the term syncretism has, for some, a negative connotation.[64] A precondition for syncretism, however, is that people see common traits or common functions, and this is where a sharper focus on personality definitions of deities can be instructive.

The name Neotera and the symbolism surrounding the inscription provide a link to Egyptian cults, as discussed above. If Proserpina or even Libera was, in fact, another name for Persephone, why could she not be called Neotera by the Egyptians? As mother goddesses, Demeter and Isis are quite close when seen in regard to their personality definitions. Other points of contact between Egyptian cult and the cult of Demeter and Kore are the symbolism used in the floor mosaic. These baskets with snakes are a particularly strong symbol of the unity of the

---

[61] Provincial imperial cults may be the possible exception.

[62] Boer (2003, 109) describes the tension between these two perspectives in his study of religious and economic centers vs. peripheries as "the fundamental contradiction of the Asiatic mode of production [which] cannot be avoided, namely the centrifugal force of the periphery and the centripetal force of the centre."

[63] The marble present in statuary, offering table and other items on the upper terrace is missing from the Building of the Tablets on the lower terrace. The image produced there is instead of a goddess presiding over magic.

[64] Beard, North and Price 1998, 318 n. 11.

two aspects of the worship of the chthonic gods but also function as important symbols of Isis, as Dunbabin has pointed out.[65]

The shells found in the sanctuary also need to be considered in the context of syncretism. The scallop shell would have been an appropriate offering or food, associated above all with Aphrodite/Venus and Demeter/Ceres, but also with other fertility goddesses.[66] For those layers of the population responsible for the shells in the sanctuary (a free gift), the need to discern exactly for whose honor they were brought may not have been as strong as modern scholars of religion have taken it to be.

Finally, as discussed earlier, the language in which a deity is worshipped or otherwise defined is an integral part of the personality definition of the deity in question, and must be considered also when deciding which temple belongs to whom. Language *can* betray who the worshippers were, but is also significant for personality definition in other respects. Language could be interpreted as both a carrier of continuity or marker of cultural change, although in polyglot empires different languages are often used in different areas of life and their co-existence is thus a marker of cultural complexity.[67] In a Roman colony veering between Greek and Latin, where power issues were intimately linked up with language issues, linguistic definition takes centre stage. If the inscriptions from the first 100 years of the colony's life are overwhelmingly in Latin, this only reflects the public expectations of the stratum of Corinthians who commissioned the inscriptions. It does not mean that there were only Latin-speaking Romans living in Corinth. In fact, we know this was not the case. The letters of Paul and Clement, dating from the 40s to the turn of the 1st century, were written to graecophone house churches in Corinth.[68]

In light of this broader picture it is noteworthy, too, that the documented language in the sanctuary is Greek. Some of the curse tablets found in Room 7 were found in layers that possibly predate the building, which means that this new ritual practice, involving the use

---

[65] Dunbabin (1990) looks beyond the cult of Demeter to make sense of these baskets by pointing to the cult of Isis. DeMaris (1995) uses them as a proof for the heavy focus on the underworld and afterlife of the Roman cult in the sanctuary.

[66] This is a general observation, and already Cook (1925, 302 n. 2) suggested that the association and the symbolism "rests on the resemblance of the shell to the womb."

[67] For example, see the importance of Greek literature for the development of a Roman literary canon in Woolf 2001, 314–5.

[68] See also the chapter by Millis in this volume.

of Greek language and calling the gods by their Greek names, must have been established by the end of the third quarter of 1st century CE.[69] Also, the floor mosaic inscription in the central temple on the upper terrace is in Greek. It is, however, from a period when most inscriptions in the city were in Greek anyway, and thus is not in itself a marker of cultural contestation or different ethnic origins (see the broader discussions of these issues towards the end of this chapter).

Whatever reason lies behind this situation, it demonstrates that by the 2nd or 3rd century at the latest, a wholly Latin/Roman construction of Ceres and Proserpina was not seen as appropriate, even on the upper terrace. This fact raises the question whether Latin/Roman institutions ever were adopted in this Corinthian sanctuary, given that there was no remodelling of the buildings in the colony's earliest and most enthusiastically Roman (Latin-writing) period. Indeed, one could argue that the most Roman element of this floor mosaic with its Greek inscription is its ambiguity, calling upon and, thus, integrating the universes of both Egyptian and Greek cult in a Roman context. If disambiguation means "to remove uncertainty of meaning,"[70] then what the Romans were doing in the provinces was often the opposite—integrating and combining, and then through rhetoric of harmony and unity making it sound as if they had achieved a unified whole.

Bookidis and Spaeth draw from different pools of evidence in support of their respective views. I have complicated this discussion by questioning and blurring notions of continuity and change, by drawing the local worshippers more into consideration, and by stressing (with Sourvinou-Inwood) the importance of examining local manifestations of a given deity in order to define it. This means in the case of the temples that any attempts at identification will have to be built up by many small indications. We must resist the temptation to take as our point of departure a personality definition from another context (e.g. in Rome) and use it to identify structures such as the three Corinthian temples. Our identifications should be based primarily on the evidence for the predilections of local worshippers—what they saw as suitable housing and suitable company for the goddesses. In this section we have not been able to discuss much the semiotic aspect of personality definition, simply because we do not know for certain the

---

[69] Stroud (forthcoming), 3.
[70] See 'disambiguation' in OED².

identity of the third deity in the triad. If we did know, much of the other evidence would have fallen into place.

PERSONALITY DEFINITION AND THE INTERPRETATION OF
CONFLICTING CULTIC DATA FROM ROMAN CORINTH

The discussions about personality definition and its use in interpretation of materials from the Sanctuary of Demeter and Kore belong in a broader, theoretically informed discussion of cultural complexity and what the finds and any attempts at definition might mean in this context. The aim of this broader discussion is not to pin down the 'correct' interpretation of the data in order to decide who is right and who is wrong, but rather to try to display the true complexity of the extant data. They reflect an ambiguous cultural situation that defies attempts at definitive solutions.

Contested Spaces

"Spaces of representation," to use Lefebvre's terminology—or, in other words, dominant, ideal, power- and symbol-heavy spaces—are not easily reproduced elsewhere in a different system of production.[71] This insight from spatial-critical theory has been taken over in postcolonial studies to show how space is contested in (historical and contemporary) societies in transition, often at many levels at once. The instability of such contested spaces in turn results in a dialectics that can be detected in the play of power and in the flow between rural and urban; the production of space in seats of religious and political power and among the poor and the peasants; between repressed, shrinking and expanding, visible spaces; and between the commerce of the sacred and that of space.[72]

---

[71] This refers to the 'father' of spatial-critical social analysis, Henri Lefebvre. According to him 'spaces of representation' are differentiated from plain, material spaces and material flows, from representations of such material spaces that allow the latter to be understood. Spaces of representation are more imaginary or carefully constructed products, such as paintings, or for example the 'Greece' of Pausanias. His work could not have been written within any other cultural set-up. 'Spaces of representation' also include utopian plans and even material constructs such as particular built sacred architecture, museums and other spaces that imagine new meanings or possibilities for spatial practices; Lefebvre 1991.

[72] Along these lines, biblical scholar Roland Boer shows with reference to ancient Israel how shrines and sanctuaries become contested zones, the subject of polemic and theological condemnation; Boer 2003, 88–90.

The hegemonic narrative of the early imperial period is that it should be seen as one of imperial integration not of dissolution. This narrative has, to a large extent, been produced by reading with (rather than against) the grain the empire-wide rhetoric of unity, harmony and integration expressed in letter as well as stone during the Julio-Claudian era.[73] This means that the general patterns of Roman ideology and Roman rule could be reinforced and honored in a variety of areas while still allowing for local color to shine through. Detailed regulation and control is not a viable *modus operandi* for a successful empire; however, it is adamantly clear that not everyone wanted to be integrated. Contestation was still going on, perhaps not as fervently in Corinth as in Jerusalem; we should not assume that tensions were non-existent. The notion of imperial integration, which is undoubtedly adequate when comparing with other more violent periods, nevertheless conceals the complex processes going on under this heading and inhibits us from connecting the dots between those who provided resistance. Contestation is not in and of itself the opposite of integration but rather a necessary condition for its success, as I will show below.

Antoinette Wire commented on this interplay of contestation and integration with respect to Corinth and the apostle Paul.

> The Corinthians contest Paul's ordering, Paul contests the ordering of sanctuary space in Corinth's agora. The Kore worshippers contest the abandonment of her cult through Roman invasion.... Dominant representations may order space, but contestation keeps it alive.[74]

In my view, the Roman wall dividing the former Greek cult area could also be seen as a symptom of contested spaces. The development of the upper terrace must have been expensive and paid for by people with means. Whether the use of Greek there reflects Roman notions of the Greek (*Graecus ritus*) or just Greek-speaking donors is difficult to decide.

Was the development on the lower terrace connected to the development on the upper terrace? The Roman wall dividing the area could indicate independent developments, but we have Stroud's warning. "It is our responsibility as scholars to account for the evidence that excavation has given us, not to try to explain it away on *a priori*

---

[73] For rhetorical value of the Augustan construction projects: Zanker 1988.
[74] Wire 2006. Wire's thinking was influenced by Boer's work, and extended my discussion of the topic (in which I drew on Lefebvre); Boer 2003, esp. 88–90.

grounds."[75] Second, some might want to consider the suggestion mentioned above, that the sanctuary housed a private cult in the Roman period, in which case the presence of the tablets would have been *less* of a problem. But even if magic and religion were kept apart by the lawmakers, we cannot simply presuppose that people, Roman citizens or not, adhered that closely to Roman law.[76]

On the other hand, I am still hesitant to fully endorse Stroud, who says "the location of the building of the tablets on the lower terrace should warn us against any attempt to separate it from the Roman sanctuary." Stroud himself "find[s] it difficult to believe that a large building placed so close to the main line of approach to the upper areas of the sanctuary was not an integral part of the Roman shrine."[77] Instead I want to suggest that the prominent retaining wall was a cultural barrier more than anything else, and that the two areas on each side of the wall could have operated quite separately, still profiting from a joint location. Demeter and Persephone were worshipped on both sides even if sometimes they were perhaps called by different names on the upper side, but it does not follow that there was a single Roman authority overlooking the whole of the former Greek cult area. It is true that emperors as well as slaves made use of curse tablets. Still the financial means needed to erect the temples on the upper terrace were of a different order than the means needed to place a curse tablet on the lower terrace. Where social status indicators are included in the curse tablets, they indicate lower rather than higher socio-economic status.

Contested Languages

Studying Paul has taught me that the contestation of words and the terms used in the construction of reality are as real as reality gets. Language is also contested, more generally, in societies in transition. As suggested already, this could mean that for one layer of the Corinthian population their goddess was Ceres, for another layer, she was Demeter, and there may have been more at stake than just a name. Through Paul's letters we get a glimpse of a poor, Greek-speaking

---

[75] Stroud (forthcoming), 94.
[76] For a slightly different view: Thomassen 1999; and other essays with different takes on this issue in Jordan, Montgomery and Thomassen 1999.
[77] Stroud (forthcoming), 90–91.

underclass in the area, but this group was in a noble company with higher-class Graecophone individuals as well, in the Christ-group as in other Corinthian contexts. As mentioned above, in the longer run, Greek returned as the main language of Corinth.[78] Favorinus, writing in Greek some time during the Hadrianic period, later characterizes the city as "thoroughly Hellenized."[79]

Thus, the increased use of Greek during the 2nd century CE could be seen not just as fashion, but as a successful contestation of the imperial Latin language.[80] Diodorus of Sicily and Plutarch, for example, are two Roman authors writing in Greek who mention Corinthian priestesses of Demeter and Kore.

Diodorus mentions the priestesses of Demeter and Kore who told the Corinthian general and statesman Timoleon that the goddesses had told them in their dreams that they would support him when he sailed off in 344 BCE to rescue his city's old colony, Syracuse, from the Carthaginians. Hence Timoleon called his ship after the two goddesses. Diodorus is interesting because he is from Sicily, part of the Italic peninsula, living from 90–30 BCE, during the very early days of the colony.[81] One could say he is nostalgic, but he does write in Greek and could thus be seen as one example of someone coming from the Italic peninsula to inhabit the new colony. Perhaps his history offers one such perspective on the goddesses. Plutarch relates the same story in a slightly different way:

> When the fleet was ready...the priestesses of Persephone [Kore] fancied they saw in their dreams that goddess and her mother making ready for a journey and heard them say that they were going to sail with Timoleon to Sicily. Therefore, the Corinthians equipped a sacred trireme besides and named it after the two goddesses.[82]

No priestesses of Demeter are mentioned. Kore, instead, is the main focus.

In relation to the bilingual inscription from the Forum mentioning a *sacerdos Proserpinae*, Dixon has suggested that the Greek may have

---

[78] Stroud (forthcoming), 99–100.
[79] Ῥωμαῖος ὢν ἀφηλληνίσθη, ὥσπερ ἡ πατρὶς ἡ ὑμετέρα (Dio Chry. 37.26), written pseudepigraphically by Favorinus, in which he states that the Corinthians have become Greek again and holds up this Hellenization as an ideal for a Roman. The date used here is the one given by White (2005, 66).
[80] See discussions of the Second Sophistic in Goldhill 2001, and Swain 1996.
[81] Diod. Sic. 16.66.
[82] Plut. *Tim.*, 8.1 (trans. by Perrin).

been added at a later time[83] since the Latin inscription is clearly the
primary one (the lay-out of the inscription looks like a Latin main text
with the Greek translation in footnote style at the bottom) and since
Greek inscriptions are rare in Corinth in the period before Hadrian.[84]
If this is the case, then such an act of 'sub-writing' would be an excellent example of contesting the imperial language at a time when it had
once again become politically and culturally possible to do so.

Pausanias also mentions the sanctuary and the goddesses, saying
"[t]hat [the Temple] of the Fates and that of Demeter and Kore do
not have their cult images exposed to view."[85] The fact that Pausanias,
too, describes the sanctuary as that of Demeter and Kore rather than
as dedicated to the triad Ceres, Liber and Libera, suggested to Spaeth
that "[Pausanias] did not wish to call attention to the triadic cult."[86] In
other words, the description by Pausanias is an example of how 2nd
century Graecophone authors would have preferred it to be. A kind
of nostalgia keeps them silent about the changes in their sacred landscape. Spaeth is onto something crucial here, but I think there is more
than a wish "not...to call attention" behind the use of older names
by Pausanias, for Pausanias was not alone in his resentment of the
Roman appropriation of Greek lands, myths and history.[87] If the use
of Greek in the early Roman period may have functioned as a vehicle
of counter-cultural discourse, the 2nd century outcome was that it
turned the tables and confused the (language of the) power of definition. If elite authors and ordinary users of the sanctuary continued to
employ the Greek names of the goddesses, what, then, were the 'real'
names of the goddesses in this period? There must have been enough
of the old personality definitions and characteristics shining through
for these Roman authors still to be able to identify Proserpina/Libera
as Kore in their texts. If these deities could so easily be translated back
into their 'original' Greek names, it means that the supposed discon-

---

[83] Dixon 2000, 336 fig. 1, and 338.

[84] Dixon considers an examination of the relationship between the Latin and Greek
texts as the key issue in dating this inscription, since there is no prosopographical or
historical evidence to assist us in this case. The Greek lettering is post-Hadrianic or
Hadrianic at the earliest, whereas the Latin text, which clearly is the primary text, has
a pre-Hadrianic lettering or Hadrianic at the latest. Still, letter analysis cannot lead
to any safe conclusions, since close parallels for the Latin letter forms do not exist at
Corinth; Dixon 2000, 339.

[85] Paus. 2.4.7 (trans. Jones and Ormerod).

[86] Spaeth 2006, 9.

[87] Swain 1996, 333, 409, 415–16; Alcock 1993, 24–32, 145–49.

tinuity could only be discerned by Latin speakers, who used the new Latin names. From the perspective of the rest, the deities were probably, as always, Demeter and Kore.[88] This means we have a culturally complex situation, neither a new situation discontinuous with an old one, nor an uncontested old tradition still surviving.

Divine Re-Definitions?

Antoinette Wire has made the following response to the excavators' reluctance to reflect on the significance of the amounts, quality and gendered implications of the pottery found in the Roman layers of the sanctuary.

> [T]hough the excavators say that the quantity of lamps are insufficient to prove that the sanctuary was in use before the mid 1st century CE, they also tell us, ironically when speaking about space, that coarsely-made lamps and pottery shards were found in such quantity in the Roman layer that they had to be discarded before analysis for lack of storage space, the very materials that might best show informal or covert use by local women in the time before the sanctuary was deemed worthy of repair.[89]

Wire's synthetic comment refers to Slane's analytical comment that the practice of discarding materials may have affected "coarse and cooking pottery more than lamps and fine wares" and that this means that "it is not possible to give statistics for the totality of finds from the excavation."[90] For the interests of this article, that is regrettable, for as Wire reminds us, the sheer masses of materials that are not accounted for need to be considered as traces of all the invisible people of the ancient world. Wire further reminds us that "the eighteen curse tablets found, illegal by Roman law, begin from this period, almost all written in Greek and directed against women."[91] It is important to speculate who these women might have been. If language was an ethnicity/class issue in Corinth at the time of their production (and I believe it was), it is more likely that these women would be Greek-speaking rather than

---

[88] In this argument I am drawing on recent scholarship, e.g. that of Simon Goldhill, who views the Greek writings of the Roman Empire not as something to be dismissed as they have often been, but rather as "central documents for understanding the pressures and tensions of a society in change;" Goldhill 2001, 17.

[89] Wire 2006.

[90] *Corinth* XVIII.2, 1–2, 5 and 7.

[91] Wire 2006.

Latin-speaking. The Greek curse tablets are some indication of this. Wire further wonders: Does the subsequent rebuilding, then, reflect, not the Roman 'Graecus ritus,' as I have earlier suggested, but some recovery of Greek women's worship space? Could there be a religious parallel between Kore's story of shame and death and a partial revival with that of Corinth?

I find it difficult to respond to this directly. The idea that the myth of Persephone could carry new meaning as expression of the sack, abandonment, and emerging revival of Corinth presupposes quite a bit both in terms of redefinition and of the transference of a myth to a historic, concrete level. On the other hand, it would explain the centrality of Persephone in this period. Scholars of religion have observed how ancient myths and books are often given new, contemporary existential meanings, often in direct contrast to earlier meanings. One example of this in Corinth is how the Julio-Claudian house appropriated Aphrodite, making her its ancestral mother.[92]

Many of the scholarly discussions of the sanctuary referred to so far have tended towards a reading of the sanctuary site as a place of religious integration. But in the extension of such a reading it is also necessary to analyze the traces of contestation of who should be worshipped there, who decided the matter, and whether in the cultural *koine* of the Roman Empire it would have made any difference whether an ancient worshipper called the mother goddess Demeter or Isis, or called her daughter Kore, Proserpina, Nephtys, or Libera, or called her son Dionysus or Liber. Thus, one could conclude that many deities were worshipped there in the Roman period and that both contestation of the sacred space and an attempt to control it are indicative of an enculturation of Roman values and of the process that is called integration. In using the Greek names in this essay, I have, of course, inevitably waded into this area of contestation, but I defend the terminology with reference to the fact that there is no striking evidence of the use of Latin in the sanctuary. Such usage has to be assumed by projection. The temples do speak their own language about their donors, but it is not necessarily Latin. It could also have been upper-class Greek, according to the changes we see also on inscriptions in the period when the temples were erected.

---

[92] Økland 2004, 104–5.

Role in the Pantheon

In the introduction I suggested that the personality definitions of the goddesses depended on the language in which they were worshipped, by whom, and on which functions they filled within the pantheistic system. This means that characterizations of the divine are neither fixed nor given in a vacuum. The complex system of polytheism, especially in its Roman form, allowed for multiple layers within each type of worship. The possibility (and it is only that) that Demeter and Kore could be called by the names of Roman or Egyptian goddesses associated with agricultural and/or human fecundity—together with the Fates, who influence any human undertaking, including motherhood and childbirth—means that these aspects of Demeter's definition might have been retained to some extent. But the forces that looked after fertility and fecundity had also changed. In the Roman imperial period, the emperor and the imperial family were, to a greater degree, seen as protectors of these things. One could even go further and argue on the basis of Spaeth's discussion of the Ara Pacis[93] that an image was being created whereby Ceres was 'demoted' to the level of supplier to and on behalf of the Emperor. This is an experience that the freedmen and freedwomen who originally populated Roman Corinth could probably easily relate to, for they understood that opportunities came from the emperor in a very real way.[94]

The cult of Demeter and Kore was not the only Corinthian cult where cultural memory of the past was preserved in a negotiated version. Other Corinthian goddesses in the Roman period preserved local definitions, and it was not for lack of knowledge of how these deities were understood elsewhere. Rather, we see how cunning Corinthian businesswomen and men converted their local idiosyncrasies into a trademark and commodity: the city of Aphrodite, Athena the Horse-tamer,[95] etc.

---

[93] Spaeth 1996, 34. "The goddess Ceres was frequently used in Roman political propaganda of the imperial period as an important symbol tied to the *princeps* and linking him in turn to her connections with the concepts of fertility and liminality and her associations with the social groups of women and the plebs;" Spaeth 1996, 151.

[94] It is assumed that Corinth got its own local copy of the Ara Pacis altar early on. Located in the forum, it dates from Augustan times; *Corinth* I.3, 139–41 and 150.

[95] The notion of Corinth as the 'City of Aphrodite' was interpreted in different ways in Roman times. Her ancient Greek Corinthian cult was that of the Armed Aphrodite, whereas in the Roman period Corinthian Venus was more or less stripped of clothing and the shield had been turned into a mirror; Williams II 1986; Økland 2004,

It is clear that Demeter and Kore were defined in relation to each other both by Greek and by Latin speakers. On the lower terrace, the goddesses are mentioned in the curse tablets together with the Fates and with other chthonic deities such as Hermes Chthonios; Ge and her children; Ananke, the lord god of the underworld; and the lord, who is perhaps not a chthonic deity but expected to command them, nevertheless.[96] This company, seen in the context of magic, strengthens the chthonic and subversive aspects of the personality definition of the two goddesses.

In this context it is also appropriate to look into the issue of the third Roman temple and to whom it was dedicated since this would also contribute to the definition of the deities on the upper terrace. If it was dedicated to a clearly Roman deity, such as to Liber or Dis Pater, this would also make the goddesses on the upper terrace more Roman. If it was dedicated to Aphrodite, on the other hand, who also had long-standing connections to Acrocorinth, it would strengthen a local perception of the goddesses, similar to that found at Locri. If it was dedicated to the Fates, it would mean that the chthonic aspect of the goddesses really was the dominating one in the Roman period not just in the constellation on the lower terrace. At this stage, however, there are many suggestions and little agreement, and I have little to add beyond my earlier suggestion that it was dedicated to Dis Pater or to Pluto.[97]

CONCLUSIONS

The findings from the sanctuary of Demeter and Kore still produce more questions than answers. Currently, more sophisticated critical thought on empires and cultural complexity is being developed, and it is important to let this critical thought aid us to produce even more adequate questions concerning divine personality definitions specifi-

---

93–96. Similarly, on Roman Corinthian coins Athena continued to be represented as the Horsetamer together with Pegasus, a myth associated with Corinth already in Pindar and which traditionally was more central to her cult in Corinth than elsewhere; Yalouris 1950. The motif was so persistent in the Roman period, and so popular, that it has been suggested that the coins functioned partly as 'souvenirs' from Corinth.

[96] Stroud (forthcoming), 6; for the inscription echoing Christian language, see p. 50.

[97] Økland 2004, 90–91.

cally, and Roman Corinth more generally, rather than just producing new answers to old questions.

Having said this, I still want to conclude by stating that I cannot see why in Corinth the relation and relative strength of Demeter and of Kore would not have fluctuated over time. Kore could well be the most central deity of the two in the Roman period even if this was perhaps perceived differently at Rome.

Further, I hope it is clear by now that I do not see the issue of continuity and change as the most fruitful entryway into the multifaceted, multilayered society of early Roman Corinth. It is a 'conceptual inadequacy'[98] that fails to grasp cultural complexity. Modern studies of contemporary cultures in transition, however, including studies of dying languages, imperial centers, colonies and margins, may turn us into better readers of the material and textual remains of this hybrid city and point out how it is possible for old and new, foreign and local phenomena, to coexist, interact, contest and live off each other.[99] As for deities, we have to ask, who exactly worshipped them, in which language, and what material traces did this worship group leave for us to examine.

Such an approach is perhaps especially close at hand for scholars of Christian scripture because Paul and Clement were writing to Greek-speaking groups who have not left a single material trace that we know of, and yet we do know they were there. Dominant discourse may constrain thought and persuasion. Still, the fact that one layer of the population held the power of architectural and epigraphic definition does not, in and of itself, mean that other layers did not exist, did not use the sanctuary, or did not define the goddesses in their own ways. We only have to track them down via different routes, as Pauline scholars have sought to track down the Corinthian Christ-worshippers, through Paul's letters and through other 1st century remains.

---

[98] Phillips 2000, 140, especially his comment on "theory-challenged classicists covering conceptual inadequacies with 'data overkill.'"

[99] A recent example is Stewart 2007.

CHAPTER EIGHT

THE WRONG ERASTUS:
IDEOLOGY, ARCHAEOLOGY, AND EXEGESIS

Steven J. Friesen*

Writing from Corinth in the mid to late 50s of the 1st century CE, Paul transmitted these salutations: "Gaius, who is host to me and to the whole church, greets you. Erastus, the οἰκονόμος τῆς πόλεως [the city steward], and our brother, Quartus, greet you" (Rom 16:23). Since 1929, many specialists have claimed that Paul's *oikonomos* Erastus was identical to an aristocratic Erastus named in a Latin inscription from Corinth. In this chapter I argue that we can disentangle the inked Erastus from the inscribed one. They were two different individuals, one from the highest sector of elite society and the other from a lower level.

This chapter, however, is about more than a case of mistaken identity. The misidentification of these two 1st century men by 20th century men has been the linchpin in a theory about the growth of Pauline churches. During the last three decades, scholars have used the conflation of these Erasti to support a portrait of Pauline leaders as upwardly mobile men. As a result, the Pauline churches are described as places where entrepreneurial men like Erastus could convert the economic capital they possessed into the spiritual capital they could not acquire in mainstream society. So my attempt to disentangle Paul's Erastus from the inscribed Erastus is also an attempt to disentangle us from the recent history of interpretation and its fascination with upward mobility. It gives us a chance to reflect not only on the social history of the 1st century but also on our own social history.

There is, of course, no view from nowhere. There is no disentangled knowledge, only a choice of entanglements. As we sort out the academic social history, we must position ourselves within some sort of

* I would like to thank several people who helped me think through the issues raised in this study, especially Benjamin Millis, Guy Sanders, Daniel Schowalter, Kathleen Slane, Charles Williams, James Walters, and audiences who heard and responded to early drafts of the argument.

regime of truth. Rather than framing my research within an ideology of privilege and upward mobility, I choose instead to foreground economic inequality, lest we consider only the upward mobility of the few while ignoring the many who were left behind.

THE IMPORTANCE OF BEING ERASTUS

The Erastus inscription was discovered in April 1929.[1] Two years later, Henry Cadbury demonstrated why the inscribed Corinthian should not be identified with Paul's Erastus.[2] Instead of following Cadbury's careful analysis, however, scholars in recent decades have attempted to identify Paul's Erastus with the inscribed Erastus by heaping up possibilities and then supposing that these possibilities prove one's point. The most influential articulation of this identification theory goes back to Gerd Theissen's work in the mid 1970s.[3] Theissen was not deterred by the fact that *agoranomos* was the standard Greek equivalent for the Latin term *aedile*.[4] After approximately six excruciating pages of pros and cons about the possibility that an *oikonomos* might be the Greek translation of *aedile*, he reached this conclusion: "If we weigh the countervailing arguments, the possibility cannot be entirely ruled out that the οἰκονόμος τῆς πόλεως is equivalent to the Corinthian office of *aedile*; but neither can that be satisfactorily proven."[5] There follows another two pages on the possibility that *oikonomos* might be a translation of *quaestor*,[6] after which the author concludes: "...[I]t is conceivable that the office of οἰκονόμος τῆς πόλεως in Rom 16:23 corresponded to that of *quaestor*. We cannot, however, finally settle on this possibility."[7]

Having established nothing, Theissen went on to propose a hypothetical scenario that has become the majority opinion during the last quarter century. He suggested that Erastus had perhaps served first as *quaestor*, which Paul rendered for some reason as *oikonomos* in Greek; then at a later time, Erastus worked his way up to the position

---

[1] *Corinth* VIII.3, 99–100 no. 232.
[2] Cadbury 1931.
[3] Translated and published in Theissen 1982.
[4] Mason 1974, 19.
[5] Theissen 1982, 81.
[6] The normal translation for *quaestor* is ταμίας; Mason 1974, 91; 'ταμίας' in LSJ.
[7] Theissen 1982, 83.

of *aedile*.[8] Notice the speculative character of Theissen's argument for this scenario.

> Thus Erastus, later to be chosen *aedile*, could have occupied the office of οἰκονόμος τῆς πόλεως (perhaps that of *quaestor*) in the year in which Romans was written, an office which did not yet signify the pinnacle of a public career. I can see no compelling argument against this identification of the Christian Erastus.... It is quite possible that he was a freedman, as the inscription does not mention his father. Add to this the fact that he has a Greek name, and we may perhaps imagine him a successful man who has risen into the ranks of the local notables, most of whom are of Latin origin.[9]

On the basis of this speculation, the Erastus of Romans 16:23 was bequeathed an aristocratic status and even a brief biography. He must have been a former slave, one who was successful in some sort of economic activity and who eventually made it all the way into the local decurionate.

Most recent commentators on the topic have accepted Theissen's proposal.[10] The premier study of the social history of the Pauline churches from the last quarter century is certainly *The First Urban Christians*. In that book Wayne Meeks considered the history of interpretation about Erastus and wrote:

---

[8] Another mistaken argument frequently invoked is that the name Erastus was uncommon and that an identification of the inscription with Paul's Erastus is, therefore, somehow more likely. This is also misleading. Fraser and Matthews (1987) list four other Erasti from Sparta and 13 from Attica, all dating from the Classical through Roman period. Justin Meggitt has searched more systematically and found 55 examples of the name in Latin and 23 in Greek. Meggitt also correctly noted (1998, 139–40, n. 345) that this inscription could actually refer to an [...Ep]erastus rather than an Erastus, the former of which is attested 15 times in Latin and 18 times in Greek. So the name, whether Erastus or Eperastus, was not unusual and thus provides no basis for identifying the two men here. After Kent's publication, an inscription naming a Vitellius Erastus came to light from Corinth (Pallas and Dantis 1977, 75–76, no. 19), and it has entered the secondary literature on Christian scripture; Clarke 1991. Rizakis (*RP 1* no. 651) noted that the commentary in Pallas and Dantis was unsatisfactory. The inscription is now lost, so firsthand inspection is impossible. However, the letterforms in the published image suggest that it comes not from the 2nd or 3rd centuries CE but from the 4th century CE or later; Michael Walbank and B. Millis, personal communication.

[9] Theissen 1982, 82.

[10] Some specialists accept the identification as a matter of fact; Orr and Walther 1976, 42. Other scholars are more reserved about Theissen's theory; Dunn 1988, 2.911; Gill 1989. Still others note the problems but consider the identification probable; Fee 1987, 3; Moo 1996, 935–36; Thiselton 2000, 9. Barrett (1968, 57) did not discuss identification issues but simply assumed that Paul's Erastus could not have been poor.

> ... Theissen proposes a new solution.... The Erastus mentioned in
> Romans, in that case, would have been an important official and the
> same person who soon thereafter was elected *aedile*. This conclusion,
> though far from certain, is persuasive. If it is correct, the Christian Eras-
> tus was a person of both wealth and high civic status....[11]

Fast-forward two decades and we see scholars with very different agen-
das recycling this conclusion, still—apparently—because they would
like to believe that it was so.

> This Erastus [named in the inscription] was elected to civic office as
> an *aedilis* in charge of public buildings and facilities.... In his letter to
> Romans, Paul mentions one Erastus, "the city treasurer" (*oikonomos*),
> who sends his greetings from Corinth to Rome (16:23); but an *oikono-
> mos* in Greek or an *ararius* [sic: should be *arcarius*] in Latin is a notch
> below the office of *aedilis*. Maybe it is not the same person, or maybe
> Paul did not know about those civic distinctions. We are inclined to
> think, however, that Erastus was *ararius* [sic] while Paul was at Corinth
> but had sponsored... his way up the ladder to become an *aedilis* by the
> time he laid that pavement.[12]

Jerome Murphy-O'Connor took this line of thought even further. The
identification theory allowed him to reconstruct Erastus's feelings,
Erastus's psychological profile, and even what Erastus imagined other
people thought about him.

> Manifestly, Erastus was one of those energetic freedmen, who flourished
> in the vigorously competitive atmosphere of Corinth and who had the
> surplus funds which enabled him to undertake public office.... Natu-
> rally, to accede to higher office one must have proved oneself in lower
> ones, and inscriptions reveal the office of *quaestor* to be a stepping-stone
> to that of *aedile*, as the latter was to that of *duovir*....
> 　　[T]he figure of Erastus gives us a privileged insight into a section of
> the population of Corinth into which Christianity made inroads. How-
> ever much Erastus may have achieved, he would never have felt fully at
> ease among the free-born. As with others of his class, the stigma of his
> servile origins blighted every pleasure. The fear of being patronized pro-
> voked an injudicious aggressiveness.... Erastus imagined that those who
> looked at him saw not the *quaestor* but merely an ex-slave.[13]

The lack of evidence for such arguments is striking, but more important is the conclusion to which they lead. With no visible means of

---

[11] Meeks 1983, 59.
[12] Crossan and Reed 2004, 329–30.
[13] Murphy-O'Connor 1997, 269–70.

support, these descriptions of Erastus lay out a narrative of Pauline leaders as entrepreneurial men whose social frustrations found compensation in the Pauline subculture.[14] This narrative suggests a modern, Western, male fascination with upward mobility, and a determination to find signs of wealth in the early churches. The primary example of this upward mobility is Erastus, based on the identification theory. He defines the upper end of how wealthy a Pauline believer might have been, and his identification with the *aedile* from Corinth sets the upper end extremely high.

We need to reject an interpretive framework that permits such conclusions. Responsible historical work should be based in an 'ideology of inequality,' by which I mean two things. First, an ideology of inequality starts from the axiom that most people in the ancient world were born into a subsistence lifestyle[15] and stayed there until their deaths, which on average came by age 45 for those who survived childhood.[16] Second, an ideology of inequality should not settle for the assumption that everyone lived in grinding poverty. There was an unimaginably wealthy sector in ancient society, and there were some people who were able to move into that elite minority from lower ranks. When we study the wealthy, however, we should make clear how unusual they were. And when we study individuals like Paul's Erastus, we should question the evidence thoroughly to see whether they were exceptional social climbers or whether they were, like most members of ancient society, living not by choice at the level of basic needs.[17]

---

[14] Meeks 1983, 54–73.

[15] For an elaboration of 'subsistence lifestyle': Friesen 2004.

[16] Here, 'surviving childhood' means reaching the age of 10. Average life expectancy at birth was somewhere between 20 and 40 and probably in the lower half of that range; Frier 1999, 87–88; Scheidel 2001, 13–25. Widespread subsistence living is not a particularly controversial point among economic historians of the Roman Empire, although they do argue about percentages of those who escaped; Scheidel and Friesen 2009. Recently, some have described the early imperial period as a time in which many or most people were safely above subsistence; Jongman 2007.

[17] Meggitt has made the most thoroughgoing, recent dissent about Erastus. He has noted that the actual date of the inscription is uncertain, that an *oikonomos* need not have been a wealthy individual of high status, and that many Erasti are known from the eastern Mediterranean world (1996, 218–23). These arguments are on the right track but need to be taken further. Moreover, his argument was hindered by the untenable conclusion that over 99 percent of the imperial population lived in "abject poverty" (Meggitt 1998, 50 and 135–41).

THE INSCRIPTION OF ERASTUS THE *AEDILE*

The Erastus inscription is preserved on three blocks of white porcellanite that are now located in the plaza southeast of the theater (see map 3 in this volume, and fig. 8.1–2).[18] The three fragments contain the grooves into which bronze letters would have been set using molten lead as the binding agent.[19] A fourth fragment from the beginning of the inscription is missing, and a fifth fragment—originally between blocks B and C—has also never been recovered. Only the large Block A was found here in the plaza in 1929; the smaller Blocks B and C were found in the vicinity.[20] Oscar Broneer apparently reunited the three fragments at this location.[21] With these three extant fragments, we have nearly the entire text of the inscription: "[…]*erastus pro aedilit[at]e | s(ua) p(ecunia) stravit;*" "[…]erastus, in return for his aedileship, paved (this) at his own expense."[22]

---

[18] The inscription was published as *Corinth* VIII.3 no. 232. The publication inaccurately identified the medium as gray Acrocorinthian limestone. It is actually white porcellanite, a hard limestone found in the area. The quarry has not yet been identified; personal communication, Ruth Siddall.

[19] The lead is still visible in two punctuation marks that separate words, and the excavator recorded that the letters 'S' and 'R' from STRAVIT still contained some lead when the inscription was found in 1929; Corinth Notebook 324 (F. J. de Waele 1929), II.891. One unexplained facet of the inscription is that the extant lead shows no signs that bronze was affixed. It is highly unlikely that the whole inscription would have been executed only in lead, and only a little less unlikely that the letters would have been in bronze with the punctuation in lead.

[20] For access to the notebooks I thank Guy Sanders, director of the excavations; and Ioulia Tzonou-Herbst, curator of the Corinth Museum. While the documentation does not give us the precise findspots of Blocks B and C, we have a fairly good idea where Block B was found. De Waele came upon it in 1928, a year before he discovered the fragment we now call Block A. Block B was uncovered above the east *parodos* area of the Theater in the remains of a Byzantine house, less than 50 m from Block A; Corinth Notebook 320 (F. J. de Waele 1928), I.460; Corinth Museum Inscriptions (inv. 2436). According to Kent's publication, Block C was found "in the basement of a late vaulted building southwest of the Theater in August, 1947" (*Corinth* VIII.3, 99), but I have not been able to locate the excavation notebooks that would confirm this. The Corinth Museum Inscriptions inventory records that the late vaulted building was southwest of East Theater Plaza (rather than southwest of the theater itself); but this note could be mistaken since it records, erroneously, that Blocks B and C were found together in 1947 (inv. 2436).

[21] A note added later to the Corinth Museum Inscriptions inventory (2436) indicates that Broneer situated Block B next to Block A.

[22] I have not capitalized 'erastus' in the translation because it is also possible that the original reading was [Ep]erastus; Meggitt 1998, 140.

Fig. 8.1. Overview of the plaza where Block A was found, facing north. Photo
by author.

One rarely noted fact about this inscription is that the official publication is in error. In *Corinth* VIII.3, J. H. Kent wrote that "the pavement
was laid some time near the middle of the 1st century" CE.[23] This, in
turn, has been a crucial argument for identifying the inscribed Erastus
with Paul's Erastus. But Kent's statement about the 1st century context is wrong: there is actually no archaeological evidence that dates
this pavement to the mid 1st century.[24] In fact, we seem to have been
misled by a circular argument on this point. The excavator's preliminary report offered no evidence for the date of the plaza except the
assumed identification of the inscribed Erastus with Paul's Erastus,
which meant that the plaza must have come from the reign of Nero.[25]

[23] *Corinth* VIII.3, 99.
[24] Charles Williams now dates this pavement not to the mid 1st century but to the
mid 2nd century, that is, toward the end of Hadrian's reign or even later. The basis
for the dating is that the pavement covers an apsidal latrine that was used until the
Hadrianic period; personal communication.
[25] De Waele 1930, 54.

Fig. 8.2. The extant Erastus inscription fragments (Blocks A–C, from left to right). Photo by author.

Shear's preliminary report on the same excavations completed the circular argument. Shear claimed without documentation that there was archaeological evidence dating the plaza to the mid 1st century CE and then went on to conclude that this 1st century date meant that the inscribed Erastus was probably the same individual mentioned by Paul.[26] In other words, the identification of the two Erastus references (the inscription and Rom 16:23) proved that the plaza came from the 1st century, and the 1st century date of the plaza proved the identification of the two Erastus references. Critics pointed out that the identification of the two Erasti was unlikely or impossible,[27] and de Waele soon conceded their point.[28] But the damage was done, and

[26] Shear 1929, 525–26.

[27] The identification of the two was already shown to be untenable within a year of the discovery of the inscription; Roos 1930; Cadbury 1931.

[28] De Waele was convinced by Roos (1930) and withdrew his support for the identification theory; Cadbury; 1931, 52 n. 35; de Waele 1934, 226.

this unfounded argument about the date of the plaza still permeates the secondary literature.

A second problem with Kent's official publication, as well as with the preliminary publications, is that the Erastus inscription in its present location has no integral connection to the plaza around it.[29] Even a casual examination reveals that Block A was inserted later into the paved area. The block is not aligned with the slabs of the plaza, it has a different size and shape than the surrounding pavement slabs, and its surface is at a different elevation (fig. 8.3).

The vantage point provided in figure 4 suggests a better explanation for the actual function of Block A in its present location: specifically, it could have been re-used here as part of a long foundation built later than the plaza pavement. The excavation notebooks confirm these suspicions. The plan of the area drawn by the excavator on March 20–21, 1929, shows a Byzantine wall here.[30] The plan drawn on April 8, 1929, after the wall was removed, reveals the foundation that was underneath the wall. Block A was then drawn into the April 8 plan after the block was found on April 15.[31] Thus, the Erastus inscription is not in its original location. It was inserted into this plaza as part of a later foundation.

The Byzantine wall, however, was not the first use of the foundation that brought Block A to this location. Charles Williams is reassessing the area east of the Theater and has established that Block A was moved here first to serve as the foundation for a wall that created a boundary along the south end of the plaza. He has dated this wall to the late 3rd or early 4th century CE.[32] Subsequently, the foundation containing Block A was reused to support the Byzantine wall (perhaps in the 12th century). As a result, the present location of the inscription indicates only that it was created sometime before the mid 4th century CE.[33] But how much earlier? Can we determine the date for the inscription itself?

---

[29] *Corinth* VIII.3, 99–100. Note also that Kent misunderstood Cadbury 1931.

[30] Corinth Notebook 324 (1929), 809–10.

[31] Corinth Notebook 324 (1929), 863–64.

[32] Written communication, August 2008. I thank Mr. Williams for permission to use these materials. They are the basis also for the discussion of the date of the plaza pavement in the next paragraph.

[33] Little attention has been given to the fact that the grooves and fissures in the stone itself indicate reuse between its original display and the reuse of Block A in the latter foundation.

Fig. 8.3. Block A and surrounding slabs. Photo by author.

Fig. 8.4. Overview of plaza facing west. Photo by author.

The evidence for the date of the inscription suggests strongly that it came from the mid 2nd century CE, perhaps late in the reign of Hadrian. Williams developed this argument based primarily on three observations. First, the plaza slabs come from the same porcellanite that was used for the inscription. So the inscription probably (though not certainly) was related to the pavement plaza but was not originally displayed in its present location. Second, the inscription in its original position probably served as a step at a point where people entered the plaza. In that original location, one would have seen the text just before stepping down into the area that had been paved by Erastus.[34] Third, the plaza pavement covers the substructure of an apsidal latrine at the east end of the plaza. The latrine was used until the Hadrianic period, so the pavement can not have been laid earlier than the second quarter of the 2nd century CE.[35] If this argument is accurate, then Erastus the *aedile* was active at least 60 years later than the Erastus mentioned by Paul in Romans 16.

The mid 2nd century date for the Erastus inscription cannot, however, be considered completely certain for two reasons. One is that the original connection between the inscription and the plaza is probable, but not proven. The inscription could have come from some other unidentified paving project in the area. The second reason is that Latin pavement inscriptions tend to come from the Augustan period. If the Erastus inscription comes from the 2nd century, then these comparanda indicate that it was a relatively late example of the genre.

Because there are no other examples of such inscriptions from Corinth, I have compiled references to comparable pieces from else-

---

[34] The original bottom edge of the stone (below the Latin text) is roughly cut, indicating that the block would have been flush with some other stone on this side. However, the original top edge of the stone (above the text) was finely picked, which means that the top edge was meant to be seen in its first location; C. K. Williams, personal communication. The original top edge of the stone is preserved only in Blocks B and C. Block A was cut back at the top in order to be reused in the 3rd/4th century foundation.

[35] Investigation underneath the plaza pavement has revealed no signs that the pavement was laid earlier than the Hadrianic period. In support of the 2nd century date for the plaza, Benjamin Millis noted that public spaces in Corinth tended to remain unpaved until the late 1st/early 2nd centuries; personal communication. The Lechaion Road was apparently paved in the Domitianic period with the same porcellanite used for the East Theater Plaza (stone identified by Ruth Siddall, personal communication), and the Forum was paved with marble around the same time or later; Wiseman 1979, 516–517, 521, 526.

where. The result is a list of 19 other Latin pavement inscriptions, all but one of which is datable (table 8.1).[36] Most of the inscriptions tend to cluster in the early imperial period: 11 of the 18 datable inscriptions come from the reign of Augustus, and three more are either Augustan or Tiberian. The dates of the remaining 4 inscriptions are: the Julio-Claudian period (but probably before Nero); approx. 40–60 CE; 77/78 CE; and the early 3rd century. These examples show that a 2nd century date for the Erastus inscription would be unusual but not unprecedented. If that date is correct, the inscription would have had been an archaizing piece.

The geographic distribution of the comparable evidence shows that the Erastus inscription was part of a Romanizing genre, and that Corinth has the easternmost known example of the phenomenon. Sixteen of the 19 examples come from the Western Empire: 10 from Italy, 3 from Spain,[37] and 3 from North Africa.[38] In fact, the only other comparanda for the Erastus inscription east of Italy are 1 from Albania,[39] and 2 from Olympia.[40]

The comparanda also suggest that the Corinthian pavement was a relatively modest project. Inscriptions for paving projects in a forum, for example, are much longer. The inscription from the Roman Forum measures ca. 12 m. long; one from Veleia, ca. 15 m. long; and that from Terracina, ca. 30 m. long, stretching the length of the town's forum. The Erastus inscription is much smaller, comparable perhaps to one from Scolacium which commemorated a ramp with three steps paved by L. Decimius Secundio. Thus, the size of the Erastus inscription suggests that the *aedile* did not pave a large plaza or forum area.

On the basis of this evidence, then, the probable date for the Erastus inscription is the mid 2nd century CE, which would make it impossible for the *aedile* Erastus to be identical to Paul's Erastus. The date of the inscription based on the archaeology of the plaza and the comparanda,

---

[36] I thank Margaret Laird and Benjamin Millis for the bibliographic leads that initiated this compilation. Charles Williams brought the Buthrotum inscription to my attention. I have not been able to inspect these inscriptions personally and many of the publications include no images (or partial images), so my information for this table depends entirely on the secondary literature.

[37] Sagunto, Segobriga, and Italica.

[38] Lepcis Magna, Hippo, and Madauros.

[39] Buthrotum.

[40] Mallwitz (1988, 45 n. 16) observed that fragment 913a represents a different inscription from fragments 913b–g.

Table 8.1. Latin pavement inscriptions.

	Location	Date	Use	Bibliography
1	Olympia	ca. 16–12 BCE	From Zeus temple porch?	*IvOlympia* 913b–g; Mallwitz 1988, 45 n. 36; Spawforth 2007, 386 and n. 36.
2	Rome	ca. 12–10 BCE	Roman Forum paving	Giuliani and Verduchi 1980: 29 no. 11–12 and fig. 16; Coarelli 1983, 211–18; Lomas and Cornell 2003, 79 n. 28.
3	Assisi	Late 1st BCE	Forum	Binazzi 1981, 31–35.
4	Olympia	Late 1st BCE?	(Unknown)	*IvOlympia* 913a; Mallwitz 1988, 45 n. 36; Spawforth 2007, 386.
5	Buthrotum	Late 1st BCE?	Prytaneion paving?	Melfi 2007, 27–28 and fig. 2.13.
6	Lepcis Magna	5/6 CE	First use at temple?	Aurigemma 1940, 20 and fig. 11; Flower 2006, 137 and fig. 23.
7	Saepinum	6 CE	Forum	Gaggiotti 1990, 259, and 1991, 501-02; Cianfarani 1959, pl. 48 fig. 1
8	Scolacium	Augustan	Ramp between forum and *decumanus*	Lattanzi 1998, 683–84; Arslan 1998, 98–101; *AE* 1999, 542; Spadea 2005, 72–73.
9	Pompeii	Augustan	Forum	Zanker 1998, 104; Coarelli 2002, 61.
10	Sagunto	Augustan	Forum	Alföldy 1977, 7–13 and pl. 1–6; Aranegui *et al.* 1987, 94–96 and fig. 22.
11	Segobriga	Late Augustan	Forum	Abascal *et al.* 2001.
12	Terracina	Augustan–Tiberian	Emiliano Forum	Coppola 1984, 357–59.
13	Italica	Augustan–Tiberian	Theater orchestra	Corzo 1993, 168; Rodríquez 2001, 248; Gutiérrez 2004, 128–30.
14	Atena Lucana	Early Empire	Forum	*AE* 1927, 4 no. 12; Weltin 1953, 84.
15	Veleia	Julio-Claudian (1–54 CE?)	Forum	De Maria 1988, 55; Calvani 2000, 542-44.
16	Iuvanum	40–60 CE?	Forum	Iaculli 1990, 88–89; Lapenna 2006, 67 and 71.
17	Hippo	77/78 CE	Forum	Benario 1959, 496–98; Eck 1970, 90, 124.
18	Madauros	Early 3rd CE?	Forum	Gsell and Joly 1922, 58–59 and pl. 17.
19	Ferentinum	(Undated)	(Unknown)	*CIL* I².2.1527; Hoare 1819, 313 no. 4; Egger 1863, 370.

however, is only probable. To demonstrate that we are certainly deal-ing with two different individuals, each named Erastus, we need to consider the positions of *oikonomos* and *aedile*.

Erastus the *Oikonomos*

Paul's use of the Greek term *oikonomos* presents us with a crucial problem of interpretation, for Corinth was a Roman colony and its civic offices had Latin titles.[41] My argument in this section is that the Greek phrase '*oikonomos* of the city' cannot be used as an equivalent for the Latin *aedile* because the latter was one of the highest offices in the colony.[42] An *oikonomos*, on the other hand, would have been a low to mid level functionary in the city's financial administration, not a Roman citizen, and probably a slave. He may have had social and economic resources beyond most of the population but not nearly equal to those of the colony's elite. So, Paul's Erastus would have been neither an *aedile* nor a member of the Corinthian decurionate.[43]

---

[41] There are two other references in Christian scripture to an Erastus. Neither plays a role in this discussion. One is 2 Timothy 4:20, where the author notes that Erastus had remained in Corinth. Since 2 Timothy is generally taken to be a pseudonymous letter, I consider this to be hagiographic, creative fiction. The other reference is from Acts 19:22, where the author says Paul sent Timothy and Erastus to Macedonia while Paul remained for a time in the province of Asia. Although the author of Acts tends to have more reliable traditions about Paul's apostolic activities than does the author of 2 Timothy, we can not be certain of the accuracy of this particular narrative. More-over, if the Acts 19 tradition is reliable, we would still need to establish that this was the same individual since Erastus was not an uncommon name; see above, note 8. Commentators such as Dunn (1988, 1.911) and Schlier (1977, 451) did not think the Erastus of Romans 16 was the same individual mentioned in Acts. Wilkens, how-ever, has asserted (1982, 146) that they were different individuals precisely because he thought that the Erastus of Rom 16:23 was a high-ranking official who would not have made the trip with Paul described in Acts. My interpretation here relies on what we find in Paul's undisputed letters.

[42] Most scholars now recognize that *oikonomos* is not the technical translation for *aedile* because the only possible example would be Erastus, based only on the assump-tion that the inscription and Romans 16:23 refer to the same person. Unfortunately, the mistaken equation of the Greek and Latin titles has been canonized in the impor-tant reference work of Mason (1974, 71). Rizakis (*RP 1* no. 254), however, suggests that the identification is improbable and perhaps impossible.

[43] There is likewise no evidence for Theissen's suggestion that οἰκονόμος τῆς πόλεως could conceivably translate the word *quaestor*, which was a prominent administrator a little lower than an *aedile*. Theissen's suggestion was special pleading, generated by the theory that the two Erasti considered here had to have been the same individual (1982, 82–83).

Even though the colonial charter of Corinth has not survived, we can reconstruct some of its offices from Corinthian coins and inscriptions and from surviving charters from other colonies.[44] The highest office in the colony was that of *duovir*. Every year, two men held this office simultaneously and had responsibilities in what we would call the executive, judicial, and legislative sectors of municipal life. Second to the *duoviri* was the office of *aedile*, also held by two men elected annually from the ranks of the local elite. An *aedile* had a range of duties as well, but this office focused especially on the management of municipal business and the maintenance of public buildings, markets, and streets.[45] The normal Greek translation of this title would have been 'agoranomos.'[46]

Someone in Corinth whose job could be described as an *oikonomos* of the city would have been lower in the socioeconomic hierarchy than an *aedile*. Municipal *oikonomoi* are known from inscriptions from the Greek cities of the eastern Mediterranean. In those civic contexts, an οἰκονόμος τῆς πόλεως was normally a subordinate financial manager who was not a decurion or even a citizen. He was usually a slave, sometimes with economic resources above subsistence and, hence, better off than the majority of the population in financial terms if not in legal terms. Three inscriptions illustrate my point, although one should remember that these do not come from Achaia nor from Roman colonies.

The first inscription provides a typical reference to *oikonomoi* of cities in Asia Minor as officials who dispersed funds for statues and honorary decrees from the municipal accounts. This damaged inscription from Hierapolis, for example, names two *oikonomoi* who were ordered to pay for a statue of a man who had served as treasurer (τάμιας, l. 3), city magistrate (δήμαρχος, l. 4), and judge (l. 7–9), and who had been appointed as *strategos* (l. 5–6).

---

[44] The best preserved colonial charter is still fragmentary: the *Lex Coloniae Genetivae* from Urso in Spain. For text, translation, and commentary, Crawford 1996, 1.393–454. I thank James Walters for calling this to my attention. For a summary: Lintott (1993, 137–41). Levick (1967, 68–91) discusses government institutions after the transition from *polis* to *colonia* further east.

[45] *Corinth* VIII.3, 27–28; 'Aediles' in *NP* 1.168–69.

[46] Mason 1974, 19.

[...] | τα[...] | [τ]αμίαν[...] | δήμαρχον, | στρατηγὸν ‖ ἀποδεδειγμένο[ν] |
τὸν ἁγνὸν κα[ὶ] | δίκαιον καὶ ἀγα– | θὸν δικαστὴν, | προνοησαμένων τῆς
‖ ἀναστάσεως τοῦ | ανδριάντος τῶν | οἰκονόμων | τῆς πόλεως Τατιανοῦ
| καὶ Διοκλέους κατὰ κέ– ‖ λευσιν τῆς πόλεως.

The *oikonomoi* of the city, Tatianus and Diokles, took care of the erection of the statue according to a command of the city (lines 10–15).[47]

Note that the two *oikonomoi* of the city were not Roman citizens, for *nomina* and *praenomina* are absent in a context where citizenship would be noted.[48] These men are, however, mentioned by name, which means that their service was more prestigious than that of the masons who carved the stone or the laborers who transported and installed the statue and its base.

A second inscription (from Stobi) also illustrates cases where an *oikonomos* was a slave, albeit a slave with financial and social resources that were above average.

Διαδούμενος οἰκονόμος τῆς Στοβαίων πόλεως καὶ οἳ σύνδουλοι τὰς Νύμ-
φας ἐποίησαν.

Diadoumenos, *oikonomos* of the city of the Stobians, and [his] fellow slaves commissioned the [statues of] the nymphs.[49]

A modest dedication like this statue group would put Diadoumenos and his colleagues well below the economic level of the local decurionate but above subsistence and, therefore, above most of the population. The dedication also suggests social connections beyond those of a normal slave, for he had the desire and the permission to engage in this benefaction with the assistance of his fellow slaves.

A third inscription, originating in Thessaloniki, reminds us that an *oikonomos* could also have very few resources. The text is poorly cut and carved on a damaged Ionian epistyle block. The *oikonomos*

---

[47] *IGR* 4.813.

[48] Mason (1974, 71) listed this inscription as evidence that οἰκονόμος τῆς πόλεως was equivalent to *aedile*, but his interpretation is clearly mistaken. He also cited two other inscriptions as evidence: *IGR* 4.1630 (Philadelphia) and 1435 (Smyrna). Both of these, however, also mention *oikonomoi* who were not citizens. Thus, Mason has no evidence that equates the two terms and several inscriptions equating *oikonomos* with *actor* (agent), *vilicus* (manager), and *dispensator*.

[49] *SEG* 24 (1969), 174 no. 496, cited by Plekett (1985, 194). For another *oikonomos* dedicating a statue: *SEG* 1997, 483 no. 1662 (a correction of *SEG* 1989, 448 no. 1316).

recycled this fractured architectural piece to use it as a grave marker for his wife

Λονγεῖνος οἰκονόμος τῆς πόλεως Ἀρτεμιδώρᾳ τη συμβίῳ μ(νεί)ας χάριν.

Longeinos, *oikonomos* of the city, in memory of his wife Artemidora.[50]

The kinds of men described as municipal *oikonomoi* in these inscriptions do not fit the profile of a Corinthian *aedile*. Titles such as *dispensator* or *arcarius* would provide a better Latin translation for *oikonomos*. A *dispensator* was a man in charge of the physical disbursement of funds. He was normally a slave, which gave his owner greater control over financial transactions because the owner had the right to torture him for information about serious discrepancies in the accounts.[51] The status of a *dispensator* varied depending on the bureaucracy within which he worked—a business environment, a family estate, coordinating civic finances (as in this case), or even as a member of the emperor's private bureaucracy, managing his imperial estates as part of the *familia Caesaris*.

Paul's Erastus was not a member of an imperial bureaucracy, for Paul specifically called Erastus the *oikonomos* of the city. However, *dispensatores* of the imperial family may provide a general comparison for us. In the *familia Caesaris* these were mid-level financial officials, usually slaves but sometimes also freedmen, roughly 30–40 years old, who could normally expect manumission by age 45. They could accumulate significant wealth as slaves and lead households.[52] By analogy to the evidence from the *familia Caesaris*, then, a *dispensator* in Corinth's administration could have been an "intermediate level cleric" (Weaver's term) or a paymaster in the colony's financial bureaucracy.

Arcarius is another possible meaning for *oikonomos* since the Vulgate translates Paul's phrase (οἰκονόμος τῆς πόλεως) as *arcarius civitatis*. An *arcarius* was also an office in various financial bureaucracies but one located a level or two down from that of *dispensator*. *Arcarii* sometimes appear in the historical record as assistants to a *dispensator*, and they were normally slaves. *Arcarii* may have had responsibilities

---

[50] *SEG* 1988, 214 no. 710, cited by Meggitt (1998, 139 n. 337).
[51] '*Dispensator*,' *KlPauly* 2.105; '*Dispensator*,' *NP* 4.558.
[52] Weaver 1967, 6 and 13; Weaver 1972, 7 and 241.

for particular accounts. They might have been cashiers who actually handled payments.[53]

Corinth probably had *dispensatores* and *arcarii*, but no references to them have survived. Their absence from the epigraphic and numismatic record indicates that they were less prominent than the upper echelon offices of *duovir*, *aedile*, and *agonothete*. Thus, if Paul's Erastus was indeed an *arcarius* or *dispensator*, he was further down the hierarchy than the aristocratic men who filled the elite offices mentioned above. Moreover, he would most likely have been a private or civic slave, either of which would normally have disqualified him for life from the decurionate.[54] Although he could never have served as *aedile*, such a slave could still have had working relationships with the city's well-placed families.

In sum, the epigraphic record makes it impossible to identify Erastus the *aedile* with Erastus the *oikonomos*. The former would have been one of the wealthiest men in the early Roman colony. The latter would have been a low to mid-level financial officer in the city's bureaucracy who was probably not a Roman citizen. He was likely a slave, and he may have had financial resources beyond that of most people. In the final section, moreover, I suggest that Erastus the *oikonomos* was not even a participant in Paul's churches.

ERASTUS THE *OIKONOMOS* AND THE CHURCHES OF CORINTH

In our rush to describe Paul's Erastus as a wealthy believer, we have also overlooked issues in Romans 16. A more careful examination of the text indicates that the *oikonomos* Erastus was not a believer. The wording of Paul's reference and a comparison with the rest of the chapter demonstrates that Erastus was not a participant in the assemblies at Corinth.[55]

---

[53] 'Arcarius,' *KlPauly* 1.498; 'Arcarius,' *NP* 1.971.

[54] Freedmen were usually barred by law from entering the decurionate although this was not always the case during the early years of colonies founded by Caesar; Spawforth (1996, 169–70). Freedmen did serve in the highest offices in Corinth also, but this practice seems to have come to an end during the reign of Tiberius; Laird in this volume. In any event, a slave or former slave in the time of Paul could not have served as *aedile*.

[55] Thus, he was clearly not the host of a house church, as argued by Clarke (1993, 56).

First, the wording of the reference. Romans 16:23b is constructed to identify only Quartus, not Erastus, as a brother: ἀσπάζεται ὑμᾶς Ἔραστος ὁ οἰκονόμος τῆς πόλεως καὶ Κούαρτος ὁ ἀδελφός ("They greet you, Erastus the city *oikonomos*, and Quartus the brother;" my translation). Paul could easily have designated both of these men as brothers with a plural noun. Earlier in the chapter, for example, three pairs of individuals are listed with a plural noun or participle: Prisca and Aquila are called "coworkers" (τοὺς συνεργούς μου, 16:3); Andronikos and Junia, "relatives" (τοὺς συγγενεῖς μου, 16:7); and Tryphaina and Tryphosa, "those laboring in the Lord" (τὰς κοπιώσας ἐν κυρίῳ, 16:12). In 16:21, moreover, Paul refers to three men jointly as "relatives" or "fellow countrymen" (οἱ συγγενεῖς μου). Verse 23b, however, sets up a contrast between Quartus as believer and Erastus as *oikonomos*. In this context the omission of the term 'brother' in reference to Erastus must be deliberate.[56]

This is confirmed when the reference to Erastus is compared to the rest of the chapter. In fact, Erastus is one of three persons mentioned in Romans 16 who are not described as believers. The other two, Aristoboulus (16:10) and Narcissus (16:11), appear only because some people in their households were believers while they were not.[57]

> Greet Apelles, who is approved in Christ. Greet those who belong to the family of Aristoboulus (τοὺς ἐκ τῶν Ἀριστοβούλου). Greet my relative Herodion. Greet those in the Lord who belong to the family of Narcissus (τοὺς ἐκ τῶν Ναρκίσσου τοὺς ὄντας ἐν κυρίῳ, Rom 16:10–11).

Peter Lampe has shown that these believers were probably some of the slaves or freedpersons from within the households of the two non-believers.[58]

The peculiar position of Aristobulus, Narcissus, and Erastus is clarified by table 8.2, which lists the 37 individuals in Romans 16.[59] As

---

[56] If this argument is correct, then Paul is treading a difficult line in his rhetoric. Erastus was known to him and to the letter's recipients. Erastus asked Paul to send greetings, so Paul had to find a way to describe Erastus positively. Yet Paul had no spiritual terminology at his disposal because Erastus was not a participant in the assemblies. Paul's solution, apparently, was to reference Erastus by his occupation. This allowed him to identify Erastus to his audience without embracing him as a 'brother' but also without expressing disapproval.

[57] Fitzmyer 1993, 740–41; Jewett 2007, 966–68.

[58] Lampe 2003, 164–65.

[59] There are significant questions about the unity of this chapter, but these arguments do not affect my point here. Specialists agree that we are dealing with Pauline

the table makes clear, Paul uses a wide variety of terms to express spiritual affinity in this chapter, describing people in the following ways: "beloved" (16:5, 8, 9, 12), "co-worker in Christ" (16: 3, 9, 21), "my relative/compatriot" (16:7, 11, 21), "laboring in the Lord" (16:12), "laboring among you" (16:6), "deacon of the church" (16:1), "sister" (16:1), "like a mother" (16:13), "brother" (16:14, 23), "my benefactor" (προστάτις, 16:2 NRSV), "first fruit in Christ" (16:5), "fellow prisoner" (16:7), "in Christ" (16:7), "in the Lord" (16:11), "esteemed among the apostles" (16:7), "approved in Christ" (16:10), "chosen in the Lord" (16:13), "saints" (16: 15), and "host of the whole church" (16:23). For Erastus, however, there is no effusive praise as with Prisca and Aquila; no strong support as with Phoebe; no fictive kinship as with Quartus, Phoebe, and the mother of Rufus; no common labor as with Prisca, Aquila, Tryphaina, Tryphosa, Urbanus, and Timothy; no church titles like Phoebe, Andronikos, Junia, and Gaius; no reference to "being in Christ" or "in the Lord" as with Andronikos, Junia, and some members of the household of Narcissus. Instead, with Erastus Paul only mentions a vocational title.

So the wording of Romans 16:23 and the rhetorical patterns of the chapter indicate that Erastus did not participate in the Corinthian assemblies. The evidence suggests instead that Erastus the *oikonomos* was someone who was not a believer but who had positive, ongoing contact with Paul and his assemblies. It would make him an example of people we know existed but who are rarely attested in Paul's letters: specifically, one of many who knew Paul and who were not persuaded by his gospel.

The close grammatical connection between Erastus and Quartus (Rom 16:23) might indicate that Quartus himself was the link between Erastus and the believers.[60] If that was the case, then we can suggest two possibilities. One is that Quartus and Erastus were members of

---

texts, whether directed toward Rome or toward Ephesus, and Pauline authorship is sufficient for my purposes. For surveys of the issues: Fitzmyer 1993, 55–65; Jewett 2007, 8–9.

[60] Jewett (2007, 983–84) rightly notes the unusual reference to Quartus as "*the* brother," rather than *my* brother or *your* brother, but has difficulty explaining Paul's wording. Jewett suggests that the καί connecting the two names might actually mean "his" (that is, Erastus's) brother. We do not need to settle for this strained explanation. If we conclude that Erastus was not a participant in the churches, then the wording makes sense. Paul was distinguishing the believer Quartus from the (non-believing) *oikonomos* Erastus.

Table 8.2. Individuals from Romans 16.

	Name	Verse(s)	M/F	Participant terminology
1	Phoebe	1–2	F	Our sister; deacon; προστάτις
2	Prisca	3–4	F	My co-workers in Christ
3	Aquila	3–4	M	My co-workers in Christ
4	Epainetos	5	M	My beloved; first fruit of Asia to Christ
5	Marcia	6	F	Labored greatly among you
6	Andronikos	7	M	My relatives; my fellow prisoners; prominent among the apostles; before me in Christ
7	Iounia	7	F	My relatives; my fellow prisoners; prominent among the apostles; before me in Christ
8	Ampliatos	8	M	My beloved in the Lord
9	Urbanus	9	M	Our co-worker in Christ
10	Stachys	9	M	My beloved
11	Apelles	10	M	Approved in Christ
12	Aristobulus	10	M	
13	Herodian	11	M	My relative
14	Narcissus	11	M	
15	Tryphaina	12	F	Labored in the Lord
16	Tryphosa	12	F	Labored in the Lord
17	Persis	12	F	The beloved; labored greatly in the Lord
18	Rufus	13	M	Chosen in the Lord
19	(Mother of Rufus)	13	F	Also my mother
20	Asynkritos	14	M	(The brothers with them)
21	Phlegon	14	M	(The brothers with them)
22	Hermes	14	M	(The brothers with them)
23	Patrobas	14	M	(The brothers with them)
24	Hermas	14	M	(The brothers with them)
25	Philologos	15	M	(All the saints with them)
26	Ioulia	15	F	(All the saints with them)
27	Nereus	15	M	(All the saints with them)
28	(Sister of Nereus)	15	F	(All the saints with them)
29	Olympas	15	M	(All the saints with them)
30	Timothy	21	M	My co-worker
31	Lucius	21	M	My relatives
32	Jason	21	M	My relatives
33	Sosipater	21	M	My relatives
34	Tertius	22	M	In the Lord (written apparently by Tertius, not Paul)
35	Gaius	23	M	My host; host of the whole church
36	Erastus	23	M	
37	Quartus	23	M	Brother

the same household, perhaps as fellow slaves or as freedmen of the same patron. I am inclined, however, toward a second possibility: that Quartus may have been a slave or freedman in the household of Erastus. This seems somewhat more likely because it would reflect a family structure already mentioned twice in the chapter, such as existed in the households of non-believing Aristobulus and Narcissus, both of which contained Pauline believers. The difference in this case would be that Erastus was known both to Paul and to Paul's addressees whereas we have no evidence of direct contact between Paul and either Aristobulus or Narcissus. In either scenario, however, the reconstruction takes account both of Paul's reference to Erastus and Paul's reserve in his description of Erastus.

Some specialists whose work is framed by an ideology of upward mobility do not take account of Paul's reserve here and suggest instead that Paul was proud to have a convert with significant civic accomplishments[61] or even that he was presenting Erastus as a model civic benefactor for other rich 'Christians' to follow.[62] This is unconvincing for two reasons. First, on the basis of what Paul writes in Romans 16, we see that he emphasizes service to the assemblies. In fact, with the exception of Erastus, there is no reference to anyone doing anything except in service to the assemblies or to Paul himself. All that matters to Paul in this epistolary setting is life in Christ.

Second, when we look at Paul's corpus of letters, it is clear that his theology and his activism were framed in contrast to social status, not in praise of contributions to society. There are many texts we could consider here; for the sake of brevity I give two examples, both from 1 Corinthians. Early in this letter, Paul emphasizes that his gospel focuses on the crucified Christ, which he characterizes as the wisdom of God that reveals the foolishness of human wisdom.

> Consider your own call, brothers and sisters: not many of you were wise by human standards, not many were powerful, not many were of noble birth. But God chose what is foolish in the world to shame the wise; God chose what is weak in the world to shame the strong; God chose what is low and despised in the world, things that are not, to reduce to nothing things that are, so that no one might boast in the presence of God. He is the source of your life in Christ Jesus, who became for us

---

[61] Theissen 1982, 75–76.
[62] Winter 1994, 195.

wisdom from God, and righteousness and sanctification and redemption, in order that, as it is written, "Let the one who boasts, boast in the Lord" (1 Cor 1:26–31).

The repeated formulation "not many wise, not many powerful..." is tantalizingly ambiguous; and specialists who embrace an ideology of upward mobility have emphasized the possibility that a few believers might have been wealthy, and have ignored the majority who certainly were not. But whatever the demographic implications of this text might be, this is neither the rhetoric nor is it the theology of a man who would brag about his acquaintance with someone in a municipal position.[63] The accomplishment of Jesus and the calling of the assemblies are described in direct contrast to the values of mainstream society.[64]

Another section of the same letter shows that Paul's eschatology provides an important reason for his rejection of the standard markers of social status. After a discussion of slavery and of marriage, Paul summarizes the rationale for his advice on the renunciation of mainstream social values.

> I mean, brothers and sisters, the appointed time has grown short; from now on, let even those who have wives be as though they had none, and those who mourn as though they were not mourning, and those who rejoice as though they were not rejoicing, and those who buy as though they had no possessions, and those who deal with the world as though they had no dealings with it. For the present form of this world is passing away (1 Cor 7:29–31).

In Paul's view, history was coming to its surprising, divinely appointed denouement. The markers of social interaction that had made up the pattern of lived experience, τὸ σχῆμα τοῦ κόσμου τούτου ("the present form of this world"), were coming to an end.[65] Since Paul downgraded the value of familial, economic, and social ties, it would be contrary to Paul's worldview to brag about someone's civic status.

I think we must conclude that Paul's Erastus was not a participant in the Corinthian assemblies. He was, rather, an outsider related in some way to an active church participant who had significant, posi-

---

[63] The rhetoric is more likely an attempt by Paul to explain why people like Erastus, Narcissus, and Aristobulus, were not convinced by his gospel.

[64] The foundational study here is Mitchell 1991, 207–13, which places Paul's text within the context of deliberative rhetoric; Barrett 1968, 56–57; Fee 1987, 87–88; Thiselton 2000, 147.

[65] Fee 1987, 337–42; Mitchell 1991, 123–25 and 237; Thiselton 2000, 578–86.

tive contact with the Corinthian assemblies over the course of time. He may have been a non-believing member of a household that also included believers, like those from the household of Narcissus, or he may have been, like Narcissus, the patriarch of a household that included some believers.

This interpretation accords well with evidence from other letters of Paul. Of the 56 individuals we know about from the writer's undisputed letters,[66] Erastus is the only one with any kind of civic title. Scholars operating with an ideology of upward mobility have taken this one example as evidence for a tendency that Pauline leaders were men of ambiguous standing whose economic resources outstripped the other markers of social status. It seems to me, however, that one out of 56 is not a trend. Erastus is an exception, an outlier, an anomaly that requires a different explanation. I propose that the best explanation is that Paul's Erastus was on the margins of the Corinthian assemblies. He was not a brother in Christ; he was an acquaintance whose occupation was *oikonomos* of the city.

CONCLUSION

I have argued that inaccurate archaeology, inattentive New Testament interpretation, and an ideology of upward mobility among modern interpreters have prevented scholars from recognizing that the inscribed Erastus at Corinth[67] and the Erastus of Paul's letter were two different individuals. Several aspects of the archaeological record were recorded inaccurately: the plaza does not come from the mid first century, the inscription is not in its original location, and the inscription was probably commissioned in the mid 2nd century CE.

Inaccurate arguments have also clouded our understanding of the roles of *aedile* and *oikonomos*. If we put aside circular arguments and special pleading, we see, in fact, that an *oikonomos* would never have been an *aedile* in Corinth. The epigraphic and textual record is clear. A city *oikonomos* would have worked in the city's financial administration at a low or mid-level position, would usually have been a slave, and would rarely have been a Roman citizen. In some cases, an *oikonomos* would have lived around subsistence while others who served

---

[66] This number does not include Jesus Christ or Paul himself.
[67] Or, perhaps, '[...Ep]erastus.'

in this capacity had economic resources that placed them above most people but below elite levels.

A careful examination of Romans 16 also leads to a more nuanced understanding of Paul's reference to Erastus. The title he used and evidence from the rest of the chapter indicate that Paul did not consider Erastus to be a brother. The most likely explanation for this is that Erastus was someone with whom Paul and other believers had ongoing positive contact but who was not a participant in their assemblies.

All of this raises an important question: Why have we identified Paul's Erastus with the inscribed Erastus on the basis of so little evidence? I suggest we have been more interested in the wealthy elites of antiquity than in the rest of the ancient population. In Pauline studies, in particular, there has been a persistent tendency in recent decades to highlight a few believers who might have been wealthy, accompanied by a similar tendency to ignore the majority who were not. In cases like that of the Erastus who knew Paul, we have often employed an ideology of upward mobility, asking only whether he might have been a powerful aristocrat and never considering whether he might have been an exploited slave. That is peculiar since there were many more exploited slaves than powerful aristocrats in the Roman Empire. The odds should be on the side of an ideology of inequality.

In fact, an ideology of inequality might have saved us from this lengthy detour in Pauline studies. It might have made us suspicious of scholarship that ran roughshod over text and material evidence in order to focus on possible wealth. We would have been looking for evidence of the unequal distribution of material and spiritual goods and for religious solutions to those phenomena. Instead of hypotheses about entrepreneurial leaders in Pauline assemblies, we would have been building theories about the nearly complete absence of wealth in Paul's churches. We have barely begun to ask what congregational life was like when nearly everyone lived near the level of subsistence, or why some of the poor were attracted to Paul's gospel at the same time that their superiors—people like Aristobulus and Narcissus—were not impressed by the apostle and his assemblies. We have spent too much time searching for the wrong Erastus.

CHAPTER NINE

WHERE HAVE ALL THE NAMES GONE?
THE CHRISTIAN COMMUNITY IN CORINTH IN THE
LATE ROMAN AND EARLY BYZANTINE ERAS

Michael B. Walbank

INTRODUCTION

This study is based upon inscriptions, many fragmentary, dating from the late 4th through the early 7th centuries CE. Most are from Christian gravestones, but I have included some of the few secular or official documents from the same period, where they include personal names. A little more evidence derives from non-funereal inscriptions, which tend to provide information about the city's elite, the upper levels of the official and ecclesiastical establishments, and there are a few literary references naming inhabitants of Corinth during these times. The study has yielded 390 names and 107 trades, occupations, or ranks, preserved whole or in part or whose existence can be inferred from their contexts.[1] In addition to the basic names, there are also several words that may be occupational names or nicknames, evidently used to identify specific individuals. Since most burials in and around Corinth are anonymous, these gravestones provide evidence of a substantial number of relatively prosperous members of Corinthian society at this time, who had both the will and the wherewithal to purchase and to mark out as their property the graves in which they or their relatives were interred over a period of about 300 years. A much larger portion of the population is anonymous, lying in unmarked graves and with few, if any, grave-goods in the vast cemeteries along the northern scarp of the lower plateau of the city, as well as in other, smaller cemeteries elsewhere in the city and its environs.

---

[1] See the appendix.

HISTORY OF THE CHRISTIAN INSCRIPTIONS OF CORINTH

Apart from a very few earlier finds, the Christian gravestones of Corinth and its surrounding areas first came to notice in the late 1890s. Andreas N. Skias published several of these inscriptions, chance finds around the village of Old Corinth,[2] and these were subsequently collected together in the *Corpus*.[3] The American excavations at Corinth began in 1896, and a report of early finds of Christian gravestones was published in 1903.[4] In 1931 Benjamin Meritt collected, edited and published the inscriptions from the first thirty years of excavation.[5] In 1941 Nikos A. Bees re-edited many of these, together with some of the inscriptions collected in *IG* IV.[6] In 1966 John H. Kent edited all the Corinthian inscriptions found between 1926–50.[7] This volume was reviewed in the same year by Louis Robert, who suggested many changes and re-interpretations of the texts.[8]

Since 1950 scattered finds have been made, both in excavations and by chance, and some of these have been published or mentioned in the Greek journals. In particular, during the late 1960s, James Wiseman discovered a large number of Christian graves in excavations in the Gymnasium area of Corinth, along with several fragments of gravestones, some of which he published. Many other fragments have yet to be edited and published.[9] Further revisions of the inscriptions published by Meritt, Bees, Kent, and Wiseman were made in 1985 by Dennis Feissel, recognizing that some of these included firm dates.[10] Both Robert and Feissel were working from the publications, not from the actual stones. I have now examined all the stones in the Corinth

---

[2] *ArchEph* 1893; *Prakt.* 1906.

[3] *IG* IV.3, no. 402–13.

[4] Powell 1903, 26–71; the Christian gravestones are no. 42–60 of this article.

[5] *Corinth* VIII.1; the Christian gravestones are no. 135–331.

[6] *Isthmos: Korinthos* 1, the first entry in what was planned as *Die Corpus der griechisch-christlichen Inschriften von Hellas*, went to press in 1941; but the beginning of World War II meant that it was never properly circulated. No further volumes were completed. A photographic reproduction was produced in Chicago (1978); *SEG* 11, 1954, no. 92–119.

[7] *Corinth* VIII.3; the Christian gravestones are no. 522–721. Kent included many inscriptions that were found in or near the Asklepieion and Lerna and which had been mentioned but not published by Roebuck (*Corinth* XIV, 165–67).

[8] Robert 1966, 761–70.

[9] Wiseman 1967, 1969, and 1972. I am extremely grateful to Professor Wiseman for permission to include names and occupations appearing in his unpublished material.

[10] Feissel 1985a–b, 267–369.

Museum inventory, both published and unpublished, and have made several new readings and interpretations.

LIMITATIONS OF THIS STUDY

In all, around 660 fragments of Christian gravestones from the period under study here have been found, of which about 100 remain unpublished. Most of these are now stored in the Old Museum at Corinth, where I have been able to examine them in detail. A few early finds are in the Epigraphy Museum, Athens, and I know of these only from published reports and photographs. I have not had access to finds at Kenchreai and Isthmia, nor to those uncovered in the excavations carried out at various places in the Corinthia by the Greek Archaeological Service, particularly at the Lechaion, Skoutela and Kodratos Basilicas, except where I have been able to draw upon published texts and/or photographs of those that accompany these texts.[11] I have taken note of but not included here individuals who are mentioned in literary texts but for whom I have not been able to discover any epigraphic evidence. Apart from the ecclesiastics mentioned by Limberis, notably Saint Kyriakos the Anchorite,[12] one literary source provides the name of a Prefect of Illyria, Andreas,[13] and another mentions a holy man, Elias of Corinth. During the plague of 542/3, the monk Barsanouphius, appealed to by a correspondent who had expressed anxiety over recent natural disasters, assured him that there were certain holy men, who would intercede with God and, by the agency of their extreme piety, prevent a universal catastrophe. Barsanouphius mentioned three such persons, "John, at Rome, Elias, at Corinth, and another in the province of Jerusalem."[14]

DATING THE INSCRIPTIONS

A major problem in this study has been the almost complete absence of external dates. The gravestones often provide the date, even the day

---

[11] For instance, in *Prakt.* 1961, 1962, and *ArchEph* 1977.

[12] Limberis 2002, 443–57, especially 455–56.

[13] *Anth. Pal.* 7.162.

[14] Barsanouphius, *Correspondance,* 569 (cited by Peter Brown, *CAH* 14.781). One Corinthian Elias is recorded on a gravestone; Wiseman 1969, 423. Its date is much too early for the Elias mentioned by Barsanouphius.

of the month, death or deposition, but the year is seldom given and when it is, only in a fashion that is largely incomprehensible today. Thus, reference will be made to the year within the indiction, but the number and hence the date of the indiction is never provided. (The indiction was a 15–year cycle introduced in 297 CE for the purposes of taxation and made obligatory after 537 for the dating of documents.) Occasionally, a reference is provided to an external event, such as the name of the ruling emperor, or, better still, to a precise year in his reign, but such references themselves are not always as exact as we might wish.[15] All too often a date has to be established by study of the script employed, and this can be a highly subjective process, particularly since, in the period from which these inscriptions derive, there was enormous variety in script, a process accentuated by the frequent employment of relatively unskilled stonemasons. This process is made even more difficult because of the extraordinarily fragmented nature of much of the epigraphic evidence. The reasons for this are unknown, but causes must surely include earthquakes and the recycling of the debris in new buildings or in limekilns. I have attempted, nevertheless, to provide a date for each gravestone, using as criteria the script, material and content of each stone, based on autopsy, along with such other evidence as the graves themselves provide. Study of the huge number of lamps found with them, as well as associated pottery, indicate that the greatest number of burials, particularly in the regions of the Fountain of Lamps, Lerna Court, and the Asklepieion, occurred from the mid 5th through the mid 6th centuries. To go by the evidence of their script and their materials, this period produced the greatest number of inscribed gravestones.[16]

TYPES OF GRAVESTONES

At Corinth the gravestones that survive display certain basic information: always the name and almost always words, phrases and symbols that emphasize the Christianity of the deceased. Sometimes, too, his or

---

[15] Feissel 1985a, 269–98.

[16] On these criteria, see now Walbank and Walbank (2006, 267–88) on the script and materials, and Sanders (2005, 430–37) on pottery and lamps. Unfortunately, only a very small number of gravestones can be associated with specific tombs, as Roebuck noted (*Corinth* XIV, 165) regarding the Asklepieion and Lerna Court, where the exact numbers are three out of a total of sixty-five. The same is true of other burial places.

her occupation and/or characteristics appear, as well as the ownership and provenance of the tomb, its cost, the date of death or deposition, and occasionally strictures against trespass or usurpation of the tomb. A basic epitaph is Meritt 148 (fig. 9.1):

> + Κοιμητίρι|ων διαφέ|ρον τὰ Μαυ|ρικίου γου|ναρίου +
> (*Cross*) A sepulcher owned by Maurikios the furrier. (*Cross*)

The needs of the deceased to be known for who and what he was, for his title to the tomb to be published, and his Christianity to be emphasized, are all met; the opening and concluding crosses prevent any encroachment or alteration. This opening formula is found in the majority of Corinthian epitaphs (ca. 73 published). It seems to have been particularly favored in Corinth but is less common in other places.

A fuller epitaph is Kent 541:

> + Κοιμητήριον διαφ|έροντα τῷ τὴν μα|καρίαν μνήμην | Συμφέροντος
> ἐξ|κ(ουβίτορος) γεναμένου, ὅσ|τις ἀνεπαύσατ[ο]| μηνὶ Ἰουλίῳ [ἡμ]|έρα
> τρίτῃ ἰ[νδικτι]|όνι δευτ[έραι +]
>
> (*Cross*) A sepulcher owned by Sympheron the guardsman, who has achieved blessed memory, who died on the third day of the month of July, in the second year of the indiction. (*Cross [restored]*)

The indiction cycle of 15 years is undated by reference to external factors, so that the year of Sympheron's death is unknown, despite the apparent precision of the wording.

A different type of epitaph identifying the place of burial, usually combined with the word "sepulcher," is Kent 582:

> Κοιμητήριον. | ἔνθα κατακῖτε | Ἀδαμάντιος | ὁ μακάρ(ιος), τελευτήσας
> μη(νὶ) | Αὐγούστῳ ῑγ | ἐπιν(εμήσεως) ῑ.ὅυτιν(ος) | καὶ διαφέρι +
>
> Sepulcher. Here lies the blessed Adamantios, who died in the month of August on the 13th day, in the 10th year of the indiction, who also owned the sepulcher. (*Cross*)

Here, the normal formula for ownership was tacked on at the end, as if someone had forgotten to write it in at the beginning.

The third most common formula is with the word *MNHMA* or *MNHMION*, "memorial." A very simple example is Kent 563 (fig. 9.2):

> + Μνημῖον | Ἰωάννου | κραμβιτᾶ +
>
> (*Cross*) Memorial of Ioannes the vegan. (*Cross*)

Fig. 9.1. Maurikios the furrier gravestone; Meritt 148.

Fig. 9.2. Ioannes the vegan gravestone; Kent 563.

This epitaph is unusual in that it is carved in relief.

When title to the grave was purchased from someone else, as is known to have happened in 35 cases,[17] sometimes the simple phrase 'purchased from' is used, as here in Kent 561 (fig. 9.3):

+ Κυμητήριον | διαφέρον Ἀνδρέα | [κ]αὶ Εὐγενία. ἔνθα | [κα]τακίτε ἡ τούτων | [θυ]γάτηρ Ἀναστάσια. |̣[ἀγ]οράσθὲν πα | [[{πα}]]ρὰ Κυριακοῦ | φασαναρίου μη(νὸς) | Ἰουνίου δ ἰνδ(ικτιῶνος) | η +

(*Cross*) A sepulcher owned by Andreas and Eugenia. Here lies their daughter Anastasia. It was bought from Kyriakos the breeder of pheasants in the month of June on the fourth day, in the eighth year of the indiction. (*Cross*)

In a few cases, this same formula is amplified by the addition of the price, almost always one-and-a-half gold pieces (*nomismata*), as here in Kent 556:

+ Κοιμητήριον διαφ(έρον) | Γεωργίω τῶ μακαριωτ(άτω) | δεκανῶ καὶ Εὐτυχιανῆ. | ἠγοράσθη ἐπιν(εμήσεως) αῑ παρὰ | Τρύφωνος αἰγιαρίου | νό(μισμα) ᾱ<.

(*Cross*) Sepulcher owned by Gheorghios the most blessed gravedigger and Eutychiane. It was purchased in the 11th year of the indiction from Tryphon the dealer in goatskins for one-and-a-half *nomismata*.

The price seems to be an addition since it is in a different hand; also, the adjective "most blessed" may indicate that Gheorghios was already dead at the time that the gravestone was erected.

Another, more elaborate example of such formulae is the gravestone of Maria, Kent 530 (fig. 9.4):

+ | + Ἐνθάδε κῖτε Μαρία, | σώφρων γυνὴ Εὔπλου | ἡνιόχου, ς ἀγοράσας | τὴν ληνὸν Εὔπλους παρὰ | Ἀναστασίου ὑπηρέτου | χρισίνου ἑνὸς ἥμυσυ καὶ | δοὺς τὰς τιμὰς Ἀναστασίω | καὶ λαβὼν ἐξουσίαν παρ' αὐτοῦ | ἐπέθηκα τὸν τίτλον. ἐτελεύ|τησεν δὲ ἡ μακαρία τῆ | πρ(ὸ) ῑα καλανδ(ῶν) Σεντενβρ(ίων) | +

(*Two crosses, one above the text*) Here lies Maria, the modest wife of Euplous the charioteer. I, Euplous, bought the grave from Anastasios the

[17] Henceforth, Meritt, *Corinth* VIII.1 [= M.]; and Kent, *Corinth* VIII.3 [= K.]. M. 193. K. 522–23; 530; 551–52; 556; 558; 561; 573; 579; 584; 595; 687; 605; 611; 625; 636–37; 639; 643; 669; 674–75; 695; 707; *IG* IV.404 and IV.411; *ArchEph.* 1977, no. 2 and no. 8; *ArchEph* 1977, Προσθήκη; *Hesperia* 1969, 423; *Hesperia* 1972, no. 35; and two unpublished inscriptions. Five more unpublished instances are too fragmentary to be certain.

Fig. 9.3. Anastasia gravestone; Kent 561.

Fig. 9.4. Maria gravestone; Kent 530.

sub-deacon for one-and-one-half gold pieces. I gave the purchase price to Anastasios, received full rights from him, and put the epitaph in place. My blessed wife died on the 11th day before the Kalends of September [August 22]. (*Cross*)[18]

Another feature of these gravestones is that several of them bear *anathemata*, injunctions against trespass, misuse or appropriation of a grave. The purpose of these is to further reinforce the claims of the owners or occupants of graves to sole ownership. An implication of these *anathemata* is that the practices of trespass, misuse or appropriation were widespread in Corinth, where, of course, the graves not only of the former Greek inhabitants of the city but also of earlier Roman and pagan inhabitants were frequently re-used for Christian burials. I have found 19 examples of *anathemata*.[19] In a few cases, the simple warning against trespass is accompanied by a ferocious curse. This well-known example is Kent 644 (fig. 9.5):

+ Κοιμητήριον διαφέρο[ν] | Μακεδονίας τῆς τὴν μακ|αρίαν μνήμην γεναμένης. ἤ τις δὲ δοκειμάσιει τοῦτο ἀνῦξ<ε> χωρὶς τ|ῶν <τ>ούτου <δ>εσποτῶν, | ἔστω αὐτῷ τὸ ἀνάθεμα Ἄν/να κ(αὶ) Καιάφα +

(*Cross*) Sepulcher owned by Makedonia, who has become a woman of blessed memory. If anyone attempts to open this without the consent of its owners, may the curse of Annas and Kaiaphas be upon him. (*Cross*)

Here, the "curse of Annas and Kaiaphas" refers to the fate that later Christians thought these two High Priests of Jerusalem suffered: they went to Hell and stayed there forever because they had successfully argued for the execution of Jesus.

Another type of grave-monument is a cenotaph, a stone erected to commemorate someone who had died and been buried elsewhere but who for one reason or another was remembered at Corinth. A probable example is Meritt 157, the memorial of Irenaios (fig. 9.6):

+ + + | Μνῆμα τοῦ εὐλαβεστάτου | χριστιανοῦ Ἰρη|ναίου τοῦ τὴν | αἰδέσιμον μνήμην ἀπὸ ἐπάρ|χων Διογενία[νος]. (*Hedera*)

(*Three crosses, set above the text*) Memorial to the most pious Christian Irenaios, in revered memory of whom the ex-prefect Diogenianos [set this up]. (*Three ivy leaves, set below the text*)

---

[18] Walbank and Walbank 2006, 267–88.
[19] M. 135–36, 171, 197, 324. K. 535, 539, 620, 631, 636, 638, 643–44, 660, 676; as well as *IG* IV.410; and *Prakt.* 1961, 132.4; *Prakt.* 1962, 54; and *ArchEph* 1977, no. 9.

Fig. 9.5. Makedonia gravestone; Kent 644.

Fig. 9.6. Irenaios gravestone; Meritt 157.

Irenaios was probably the Count and Bishop of Tyre. In 449 he lost his position as Bishop of Tyre on the specious grounds that he had been married twice. His accuser, Dioskouros, Patriarch of Alexandria, achieved this at the Council of Chalcedon, when he enjoyed the favor of the Emperor Theodosius II. After the unexpected death of Theodosius, his sister Pulcheria married the leading general Markianos; and a new regime ensued, unfavorable to Dioskouros' ambitions. As a result at the Council of Nicea in 451, Dioskouros was himself deposed and his victims reinstated. I suggest that Irenaios was one of those reinstated, albeit posthumously, and that this monument was then set up in Corinth by Diogenianos in a public place, perhaps the Forum. I believe that Count Irenaios was a Corinthian by birth, but that his career was spent elsewhere. The stone is small, but very carefully laid out. The ivy leaves are an unusual feature at so late a time.[20]

These are the most common types of epitaph found at Corinth. There are other variations, as might be expected, but, on the whole, these epitaphs are pretty formulaic.

OCCUPATIONS AND RANKS IN CORINTHIAN SOCIETY[21]

Public Officials

Public officials constituted an important element in Corinthian society at this time. Since Corinth was the capital of the Province of Achaia, the official establishment included both high officials posted there from the Imperial capital or from other provincial centers, who were

---

[20] M. 157, ca. 451 CE. Find-spot: Unknown. For a description of Irenaios's situation: Frend 1984, 764–73. My interpretation of this inscription links it to a known historical event, at a time suggested by the letterforms. Furthermore, the adjective αἰδέσιμον is, as Feissel noted, generally applied to bishops; it would be appropriate in this context. Meritt suggested that the term ἀπὸ ἐπάρχων means "ex-prefect." I believe that this applies to Diogenianos, that he was the son of Irenaios and that Irenaios died first. Thus, I restore the name of Diogenianos in the nominative, as the dedicator of this monument. However, Feissel (1985a, no. 21), while assuming that the term 'ex-prefect' described Diogenianos, argued that he died before his son Irenaios; therefore, he restored the lost end of Diogenianos's name in the genitive. He was not aware of Irenaios's identity. The word order of the original Greek text is convoluted and there is no punctuation, so precise interpretation is difficult.

[21] The Fountain of the Lamps. The following list expands considerably upon those published by Bees (1941, 56); and Avraméa (1997, 134–35). The latter lists 35 examples, not including officials and ecclesiastics. She groups her examples as follows: *Service de collectivitè; Secteur d'alimentation; Secteur de l'habillement*; and *Secteur de la construction*. My categories differ slightly from hers, and I have added entertainers, public officials, and religious officials.

not necessarily born and bred in Corinth and might expect to move as their careers progressed, and lesser officials who lived out their lives in the same city. Thus, the evidence for the presence of these persons derives both from gravestones and from official documents of one sort or another.

Table 9.1. Public officials. Total 27 (22 names, plus 5 unknown);
e. = early, *l.* = late.

Occupation	Name	Date
Adjutant (*vir clarissimus*)[22]	Paulos	mid 5th c.
Assessor[23]	Atheneos	*e.* 5th c.
Bathhouse keeper[24]	Julianos	*e.* 6th c.
Beadle[25]	Alexandros	6th or 7th c.
Beadle[26]	G(aius) Ioulios	*e.* 5th c.
City weight inspector[27]	Unknown	6th c.
Clerk[28]	Neikies	*l.* 5th c.
Councillor[29]	Romanos	*l.* 4th c.

---

[22] Παῦλος δομέστικος λαμπρότατος, K. 509 and *CIG* 8824 [= Bees, no. 2A; *SEG* 11, 115; *SEG* 22, 222; and Robert 1960b, 21–39, no. 1]. Find-spot: Lerna Court. Feissel (1985a, no. 34) adds *CIG* 8824 to this with its correct interpretation.

[23] Ἀθήνεος πρῶτος, K. 553 [= Bees, no. 46; *SEG* 11, 176]. Find-spot: Asklepieion.

[24] Ἰουλιανὸς βαλνικάριος, K. 534 [= Feissel 1985b, no. 55]. Find-spot: Asklepieion.

[25] Ἀλέξανδρος ῥάβδουχος, Pallas and Dantis, *ArchEph* 1977, no. 10 [= *SEG* 29, 307; Feissel 1985b, no. 101]. Find-spot: Unknown.

[26] Γ. Ἰούλιος ῥάβ[δουχος], K. 518. Find-spot: Unknown. Kent made no attempt to restore this man's occupation; however, I think it very likely that he was a beadle or wand-bearer, a ῥάβ[δουχος].

[27] An unknown ζυγοστάτης τῆς πόλεως, M. 158 [= de Waele 1936 *ap.* Bees, no. 56; and *SEG* 11, 158; see also Robert and Robert 1961, no. 6; and Feissel 1985b, no. 16]. Find-spot: Lechaion Road Shops.

[28] Νεικίης ὀρθόγραφος, K. 305 [= de Waele 1936, 90–92; *SEG* 11, 153]. Find-spot: Kraneion Basilica. The occupation of Neikies has generated considerable discussion; de Waele suggested that he had won spelling contests while still a schoolboy; Kent remarked "it is fully as probable that he served for a short time as an army clerk while in his late teens." Robert (1966, 754), however, citing other examples of this word, demonstrated that he was, in fact, "*un fonctionnaire*," that is, an official, a junior civilian clerk. Kent's restoration σιγγ(όνου) was shown by Robert (1966, 762) to be incorrect. Kent dates this inscription to the late 3rd century, but a coin found in this grave is of Valentinian II (375–92). Thus, the inscription cannot be earlier than the late 4th century; its script, however, is more characteristic of the 5th. This is one of several metrical epitaphs from Kraneion; since the basilica was not built until the late 5th or early 6th century, this grave should probably be dated here, not earlier.

[29] Ῥωμανὸς βουλευτής, K. 657. Find-spot: Old Corinth. Feissel (1985b, no. 79) felt that Kent's date, the beginning of the 4th century, was too late; and he followed Kent in suggesting that Romanos might be a non-Christian. On the basis of the script, however, I am inclined to place Romanos towards the end of the 4th century when he was more likely to be a Christian.

Table 9.1 (*cont.*)

Occupation	Name	Date
Ex-prefect[30]	Diogenianos	mid 5th c.
Guardsman[31]	Sympheron	e. 6th c.
Guardsman[32]	Loukas	e. 6th c.
Guardsman to the prefect[33]	Boudis	e. 7th c.
Guardsman to the prefect[34]	Ioannis	e. 7th c.
Guardsmen to the prefect[35]	Unknown	e. 7th c.
Palace steward[36]	Theodoros	6th c.
Palace steward[37]	Unknown	e. 6th c.
Provincial filing clerk[38]	Petros	5th or 6th c.
Provincial financial official[39]	Polychronios	431
Provincial financial official[40]	Unknown	5th or 6th c.
Public muleteer[41]	Theodoros	6th or 7th c.

---

[30] ἀπὸ ἐπάρχων Διογενία[νος]; see note 20.

[31] Συμφέρων ἐξκ(ουβίτωρ), K. 541 [= Feissel 1985b, no. 58]. Find-spot: Lerna Court.

[32] Λουκᾶς ἐξκ(ουβίτωρ), K. 558 [= Bees, no. 36; SEG 11, 171b; Feissel 1985b, no. 39 and 58.] Find-spot: Lerna Court.

[33] Βούδις βουκελλάριος, M. 207 [= Feissel 1985b, no. 22]. Find-spot: Northwest shops. Opinions differ over the date of inscriptions deriving from the prison in the northwest shops. Kent was inclined to place them in the 9th or 10th century but "emphasizes the uncertainties involved in dating mediaeval inscriptions by letter forms" (Scranton 1957, 46, n. 25). On the basis of autopsy, I believe that the date is probably the early 7th century.

[34] Ἰωάννις βουκελλάριος, M. 207; see note 33.

[35] Unknown βουκελλάριοι, M. 208. Find-spot: Northwest Shops.

[36] [Θεό]δωρος δομ[έστικος τοῦ θίου] παλατίου κ(αὶ) βασιλικ[οῦ ἐξκουβί]του τοῦ γνησ[ίως δουλεύο]ντος, SEG 11, 52a [= Bees, no. 3; Feissel 1985b, no. 27]. Find-spot: Isthmia.

[37] An unknown [δομέστικος τοῦ θίου] παλα[τίου], K. 615. Find-spot: South Stoa. Kent's restorations are based on those of a contemporary Isthmian inscription for another *domestikos* of the imperial palace; see note 36.

[38] [Πέ]τρος ταξε[ώ]τ[ης], M. 153 [= Robert and Robert 1961, 50, no. 5; Feissel 1985b, no. 14]. Find-spot: Unknown.

[39] Πολυχρόνιος σινγουλάριος, Pallas and Dantis in *ArchEph* 1977, no. 2; SEG 29, 319. Find-spot: Near the Amphitheater. On the term σινγουλάριος, see Robert and Robert 1960, 357–59; Robert 1966, 762; and Feissel 1985b, no. 96; see also 'Σινγουλάριος' in Lampe 1961.

[40] An unknown σινγ(ουλάριος), K. 536. Kent printed this as the epitaph of an unknown man and his brother (or sister). Robert pointed out (1966, 762) that the letters σινγ- in line 4 were the beginning not of the word σινγ(όνου) but of σινγ(ουλαρίου). Kent restored the end of another man's name in line 3, followed by a linking κ[αὶ], but I believe this reconstruction is unlikely. The letters -ουκ- must be from the middle of the name of the *Singoularios*, and the line length considerably shorter than Kent supposed.

[41] Θεόδωρ(ος) μωλίων, IG IV.437 [= Pallas and Dantis in *ArchEph* 1977, Προσθήκη, 82–3; Robert and Robert 1958, 264–66, no. 301; Robert and Robert, 1961, 29 n. 2; and Feissel 1985b, no. 104]. Find-spot: Stimanga.

Table 9.1 (*cont.*)

Occupation	Name	Date
Servant (high official)[42]	Victorinos	527–65
Steward[43]	Andreas	*e.* 6th c.
Vir clarissimus[44]	Gratos	4/5th c.
Vir clarissimus, ex-consul[45]	Mnaseas	*e.* 6th c.
Wife of a Vir clarissimus[46]	Unknown	*e.* 6th c.
Vir illustris, patrician[47]	Ianouarios	*e.* 5th c.
Vir illustris, patrician?[48]	Theodosios	*e.* 5th c.

ADJUTANT (*VIR CLARISSIMUS*; δομέστικος λαμπρότατος). This man was a high official, a *vir clarissimus* (λαμπρότατος [m.]), but less senior than Ianouarios, the patrician and *vir illustris*, for whom he worked.

---

[42] Βικτωρῖνος δοῦλος αὐτοκράτορος, K. 508 [= Bees, no. 1]. Find-spot: Hexamilion. Βικτωρῖνος γνησίως δουλεύων, *IG* IV.205 [= Bees, no. 2; *SEG* 11, 52]. Find-spot: Hexamilion. The first is a prayer to God to preserve the Emperor; the second, a prayer to the Virgin Mary to preserve the empress. This man was evidently a senior official during the reign of the Emperor Justinian; the term δοῦλος here by no means indicates that he was a slave; see *LGPN* III.A, no. 1. Another inscription relating to Victorinos, apparently his gravestone, was found at the Kodratos Basilica; see Stikas 1964 in *Prakt.* 1961, 132, *εἰκ.* 3γ [= see Appendix, note 60].

[43] Ἀνδρέας [οἰκ]όνομος, K. 558 [= Bees, no. 35–36; *SEG* 11, 171]. Find-spot: Lerna Court. A question that arises from this opisthographic text is who bought what from whom? Bees clearly thought that Andreas bought the tomb from Loukas, but this interpretation creates problems that are complicated by Bees's erroneous restoration of [κοιμητήρ]ltον in lines 1–2 of what Kent styles "Face *b*." Kent's explanation is the correct one, "that one of the texts reversed the names of the buyer and seller, and that when this error was discovered, the stone was given a quarter turn and the correct text was cut on the opposite side." Thus, Loukas was the purchaser and Andreas the seller.

[44] Γράτος λαμ(πρότατος), Stikas 1966 in *Prakt.* 1962 no. 52 [= Feissel 1985b, no. 84]. Find-spot: Kodratos Basilica.

[45] Μνασέας [λαμπρό]τατος ἀπὸ [ὑπάτων], K. 673 [= Feissel 1985b, no. 82]. Find-spot: Old Corinth. Kent suggested that this was the epitaph of Ato[- -]tes son of Apo[llo] and conjectured that these were Jewish names; but Robert (1966, 770) demolished Kent's interpretation. This man must have been an ex-consul or holder of a similar high magistracy.

[46] An unknown [λαμπρο]τάτη, K. 627 [= Feissel 1985b, no. 75]. Find-spot: Temple J. Kent left the last line unrestored. Robert (1966, 768) suggested the restoration [λαμπ]ροτάτη.

[47] Ἰανουάριος πατρίκιος ἐνδοξότατος, K. 509; see note 22.

[48] Θεοδόσ[ιος πατρίκιος ἐνδοξότατος?], M. 245 [= Bees, no. 2A; *SEG* 11, 115; Feissel 1985a, no. 33]. Find-spot: Kenchreai? Robert and Robert (1961, 20–39, no. 1) discuss this inscription extensively, including Theodosius's rank as "*un haut fonctionnaire*" (22).

The wife of such a man would be styled Λαμπροτάτη (f.). Another *clarissimus*, styled ἀπο ὑπάτων, was an ex-consul.

ASSESSOR (πρῶτος). Kent, following Roebuck,[49] thought that this occupation was civilian rather than military, a minor fiscal official or an assessor. Thus, Atheneos (or Athenaios?) was a member of the provincial administration.

BATHHOUSE KEEPER (βαλνικάριος). This term is translated by Kent as "bath attendant," but, as with many other of Kent's translations, this may undervalue the activities of Ioulianos. He could be the manager or even the owner of a bathhouse.

BEADLE ('ράβδουχος). A beadle (wand bearer) was a minor court official of the provincial or ecclesiastical administration (the equivalent of a *lictor*). But Feissel suggests[50] that a *rhabdouchos* might be not a court official but a keeper of beasts of burden, thus a colleague of the *moulion*, working in the public transportation system, the *cursus publicus*.

CITY WEIGHT INSPECTOR (ζυγοστάτης τῆς πόλεως). An important member of the local administration with the right to inspect weights and measures used in the markets and shops.

CLERK (ὀρθόγραφος). Neikies was a clerk in the provincial administration.[51]

COUNCILLOR (βουλευτής). A member of the city council and thus a local rather than a provincial official.

EX-PREFECT (ἀπὸ ἐπάρχων). Most likely, a recent governor of the province.

GUARDSMAN TO THE PREFECT (βουκελλάριος). These men acted as a police force and, as such, were often cursed by their victims.

GUARDSMAN (ἐξκουβίτωρ). The term refers to a member of the imperial guard and derives from the Latin *cubiculum* (bed chamber). Thus, an *excubitor* was originally "one who stands outside the bed-chamber."

PALACE STEWARD (δομ[έστικος του] θίου παλατίου κ(αὶ) βασιλικ[οῦ ἐξκουβί]του τοῦ γνησ[ίως δουλεύο]ντος). This man had responsibility for the running of the governor's mansion and for protecting his person. As such, he was a senior imperial official.

---

[49] *Corinth* XIV, 167, n. 37.
[50] See Feissel (1985b, no. 101) on the evidence of 4th century papyrus documents.
[51] Robert 1966, 754.

PROVINCIAL FILING CLERK (ταξεώτης). The word derives from τάξις, that is, "rank" (as a "taxi" is a vehicle that waits in rank for customers) and thus means 'one who puts files in order;' i.e., a clerk in the office of the governor or another official.[52]

PROVINCIAL FINANCIAL OFFICIAL (σινγουλάριος). This man was an orderly or courier, employed in the *officium* of the governor and sometimes involved in financial matters at a senior level.

PUBLIC MULETEER (μουλίων). This man was not just a muleteer or teamster but in charge of the *cursus publicus*, the system of official transportation within the province.

SERVANT (δοῦλος αὐτοκράτορος and δουλεύων γνησίως). Victorinos was evidently a senior imperial official during the reign of the Emperor Justinian. The term δοῦλος here by no means indicates that he was a slave.

STEWARD (οἰκόνομος). Kent's translation "overseer" is inadequate. This word can mean merely 'steward,' but here, as Kent points out, it refers to an imperial employee. Thus, he may have been a palace steward in charge of the administration of the imperial household. As such, he would be in a position to acquire and to sell a tomb, perhaps having accumulated a few perks from his position. The difference in rank between an οἰκόνομος and a δομέστικος is unclear and depends upon context, but at least one of these δομέστικοι was of high rank, a *vir clarissimus*. Perhaps all were.

VIR ILLUSTRIS, PATRICIAN (πατρίκιος ἐνδοξότατος). Ianouarios was a high official in charge of a building project, probably in the 5th or 6th century. His adjutant (δομέστικος) Paulos probably oversaw the actual work.

Religious Officials

The ecclesiastical establishment constituted another important element in Corinthian society at this time. Since Corinth was the seat of a bishopric, senior officials would be posted there from the capital or from other provincial dioceses, and, as with public officials, moved on as their careers progressed. Limberis points out that there was a growing ecclesiastical upper class in Corinth during the 5th century.[53]

---

[52] Robert and Robert 1961, 50–1. Its military meaning of "sergeant" or "member of the *militia palatina*" seems unlikely in a Corinthian context.

[53] Limberis 2005, 455.

Lesser ecclesiastics who lived out their lives in the same city perhaps also improved their social position.

It is interesting that three of the ecclesiastical officials listed here were in a position to sell tombs: Anastasios the sub-deacon may have acted as the bishop's representative in Corinth, empowered to sell off parts of an estate owned by the church. Perhaps Andreas, the gravedigger at the site of the unexcavated 'Pallas' Basilica, was likewise so empowered. But the role of Theodoros the bishop's muleteer remains enigmatic. Had he accumulated funds with which to purchase real estate through his job, or was he, too, acting as an agent for the church? Note also the reference to one office that could have been for the Jewish community.

Table 9.2. Religious officials. Total 21 (17 names, plus 4 unknown);
e. = early, l. = late.

Occupation	Name	Date
Bishop[54]	Eustathios	5th c.?
Bishop[55]	Photios	6th or 7th c.
Bishop's (?) muleteer[56]	Theodoros	6th or 7th c.
Deacon[57]	Loukianos	5th or 6th c.
Deacon?[58]	Zenon	l. 6th c.
Deaconess[59]	Unknown	5th or 6th c.

[54] Εὐστάθιος ἐπίσκοπος, Stikas 1964 in *Prakt*. 1961, 131–32, *εἰκ*. 3α. Find-spot: Kodratos Basilica. Stikas published this with a drawing and minimal commentary. Feissel (1985a no. 35) suggested that the bishop's epitaph was inscribed in two disparate styles: line 1 in the style of the 4th or 5th century; line 2 in the style of the 5th or 6th century. M. E. H. Walbank believes (*Corinth* XXI, forthcoming) that the bishop died and was buried in the 4th or 5th century, and that his tomb was later moved after construction of the basilica in the late 5th or early 6th century. On the episcopal record at Corinth, see Limberis 2005, 443–58. I have omitted any reference to the bishops and other ecclesiastics mentioned by Limberis unless, as here, epigraphic evidence survives.

[55] Φώτιος ἐπίσκοπος, Pallas and Dantis in *ArchEph* 1977, no. 7 [= *SEG* 29, 302]. Find-spot: Acrocorinth. Although the script suggests a later date for this prayer, the editors speculate that this man was the Bishop Photios of Corinth, documented for 536–53 CE.

[56] Θεόδωρος μουλίων τοῦ ἐπισκοπιανοῦ, Pallas and Dantis in *ArchEph* 1977, no. 8 [= *SEG* 29, 311; and Feissel 1985b, no. 99]. Find-spot: Kraneion.

[57] [Λου]κίανος δηάκον[ος], Pallas 1961 in *Prakt*. (1956), 154, πιν. 101β. Find-spot: Lechaion Basilica.

[58] Ζήνων [διάκονος?], M. 192. Find-spot: Unknown. Feissel (1985b, no. 17) suggests that Zenon was "*peut-être un diacre de l'église de Corinthe.*"

[59] An unknown [Διακόν]εσσα, K. 629. Find-spot: Kraneion Basilica.

Table 9.2 (*cont.*)

Occupation	Name	Date
Gravedigger[60]	Gheorghios	*e.* 6th c.
Gravedigger[61]	Andreas	431
Housekeeper?[62]	Deutera	*e.* 5th c.
Intendant (f.)[63]	Unknown	5th or 6th c.
Intendant (m.)[64]	Ioannes	5th or 6th c.
Presbyter[65]	Valerianos	5th c.
Presbyter[66]	Tasios	*e.* 5th c.
Presbyter[67]	Paulos	*e.* 6th c.
Presbyter[68]	Thomas	6th c.
Reader (ecclesiastic) [69]	Unknown	525

---

[60] Γεώργιος δεκανός, K. 556 [= Bees, no. 37; *SEG* 11, 172]. Find-spot: Lerna Court. Kent, while recognizing that Gheorghios was an ecclesiastic, called him a "deacon." Robert (1966, 764–65) corrected this. He was a δεκανός, a "sexton" or "gravedigger;" as Bees (1941, 81–2) had already suggested. Note that this term can also have a military meaning.

[61] Ἀνδρέας δεκανός, Pallas and Dantis in *Prakt.* 1977, no. 2.431 [= *SEG* 29, 319]. Find-spot: South of the Amphitheater. Previous editors proposed that the year was 581; but Feissel (1985b, no. 96) pointed out that May 18, 581, was a Sunday. Since the date given on this gravestone was Monday, May 18, in the 14th year of the indiction, the year must be 431. There was, in fact, no year in the 6th century when May 18 was a Monday. In my view, the script is much more suited to the 5th than to the 6th century despite what Pallas and Dantis thought (1977, 64).

[62] Δεύτε[ρα δού]λη Ἁγίας T[ριάδος], K. 583. Find-spot: South Stoa and/or Bema.

[63] An unknown μιζοτέ[ρα], K. 604. Find-spot: Central Shops. Kent's text for line 2 ended with the letters εὐθ[- -]. However, the last partly preserved letter is a 'Λ,' not a 'Θ.' I believe, therefore, that the epithet εὐλ[αβεστάτη] should be restored in line 2, thus identifying the deceased as an ecclesiastic; see Robert (1966, 767–68) on the restoration of the first line.

[64] ['Ιωάν]νης μιζότερος, Pallas and Dantis in *ArchEph* 1977, no. 11 [= *SEG* 29, 317; and Feissel 1985b, no. 97]. Find-spot: Kraneion.

[65] Βαλεριανὸς πρεσβύτερος, Stikas 1964 in *Prakt.* 1961, 131–32, no. 3β, *εἰκ.* 3β [= Feissel 1985b, no. 83]. Find-spot: Kodratos Basilica. Stikas published this with a drawing and minimal commentary, mentioning that also very many fragments of Christian gravestones were found in the excavation of the basilica that later came to be known as the Basilica of Saint Kodratos. These remain unpublished; see 'Πρεσβύτερος' in Lampe 1961.

[66] Τάσιος πρεσβύτερος, *Hesperia* 38, 85, no. 84. Find-spot: Lerna Hollow, painted on the wall of a tomb.

[67] Παῦλος πρεσβύτερος, *Prakt.* 1956, 171. Find-spot: Lechaion Basilica, painted on a wall.

[68] Θῶμα πρεσβύτερος, *Prakt.* 1956, 173. Find-spot: Lechaion Basilica, carved on the cover of a tomb.

[69] An unknown ἀναγν(ώστης), K. 548. Find-spot: Asklepieion. Kent tried to restore this as the epitaph of Klara, who permitted her (secular) reader to be buried with her. Robert (1966, 763–64) rejected this, commenting that this text "*n'est pas encore*

Table 9.2 (*cont.*)

Occupation	Name	Date
Servant (m., in church)[70]	Demetrios	5th or 6th c.
Servant (m., in church?)[71]	Isidoros	5th c.
Sub-Deacon[72]	Anastasios	*e.* 6th c.
Supervisor (of synagogue?) and Teacher[73] (Jewish official?)	Unknown	4th c.
Vegan cultist[74]	Ioannes	*e.* 7th c.?

BISHOP (ἐπίσκοπος). In charge of a diocese, the bishop of Corinth resided at Lechaion.

BISHOP'S(?) MULETEER (μουλίων τοῦ ἐπισκοπιανοῦ). This man may be the same Theodoros who is mentioned as the seller of a tomb at Stimanga (see note 41), which lay on a major road that formed part of the road-system served by the *cursus publicus*, but this man is specifically called a μουλίων τοῦ ἐπισκοπιανοῦ, as if the intention was to differentiate him from any other Theodoros. The epithet implies not a connection with a place or even a private individual but with a bishop; he was the "bishop's muleteer."

DEACON (διάκονος, δηάκον[ος]). A middle-ranked male ecclesiastic, junior to the presbyter.

---

clair." Feissel (1981, 493–94 [= *SEG* 31, 288]) established that this text, in fact, was the epitaph of an unknown ἀναγνώστης who died during the final three months of the second consulship of Justin I. This man, as the epithet εὐλ[αβ](εστάτου) indicates, was an ecclesiastical reader.

[70] Δημήτριος δοῦλο(ς) Χ(ριστο)ῦ, M. 196 [= Bees, no. 10; and *SEG* 11, 106a]. Find-spot: Propylaia.

[71] Ἠσή[δ]ορος δοῦλος, Waage 1935, 88–90 [= *SEG* 11, 142]. Find-spot: Western Shops. This is a bronze plate, inscribed with a prayer for help from God. Isidoros referred to himself as a δοῦλος. Whether this meant that he was an actual servant in a church or whether it is merely a figure of speech is impossible to say, but I think that it is the former.

[72] Ἀναστάσιος ὑπερέτης, K. 530 [= Bees, no. 30; *SEG* 11, 154; and Feissel 1985b, no. 34]. Find-spot: Cheliotomylos. For an extensive discussion regarding the date and interpretation of this inscription, see Walbank and Walbank 2006; see also "Ὑπερέτης' in Lampe 1961.

[73] An unknown ἀρχ[ισυνάγωγ]ος? and διδάσ[καλος], Pallas and Dantis in *ArchEph* 1977, no. 30. Find-spot: Acrocorinth. Stroud (*SEG* 29, 300) notes that "the restorations and length of line are very dubious." To judge by the script, the date offered by Pallas and Dantis in the 3rd or 4th century is much too early.

[74] Ἰωάννης κραμβιτᾶς, K. 563 [= Robert and Robert 1950, 135; Robert 1966, 765–67; and Feissel 1985b, no. 67]. Find-spot: Asklepieion.

DEACONESS (διακόνεσσα). A middle-ranked female ecclesiastic, especially concerned with women and with baptism.

GRAVEDIGGER (δεκανός). A sexton or gravedigger.

HOUSEKEEPER (δούλη Ἁγίας Τριάδος). The term δούλη ([f.] ("servant," not "slave") probably indicates that the deceased woman held some kind of official position in the church, and I have translated it here as "housekeeper." Alternatively, it may be merely a figure of speech, implying Deutera's extreme piety.

INTENDANT (μιζότερος [m.] and μιζοτέρα [f.]). Minor officials of the church. The terms μιζότερος and μιζοτέρα are found in both secular and ecclesiastical contexts,[75] but here the epithet εὐλ[αβεστάτη] indicates that the woman, at least, was an ecclesiastic.

PRESBYTER (πρεσβύτερος). A priest in a specific church, senior to a deacon, junior to a bishop.[76]

READER (ἀναγνώστης). A minor, unordained ecclesiastical official, not a secular one.

SERVANT (δοῦλο(ς) Χ[ριστο]ῦ). The term Δοῦλος probably indicates that these men held official positions in the church as 'servants of God.' This term is often applied to a bishop, priest or deacon.

SUB-DEACON (ὑπερέτης). Kent translated this word as "servant," but he was rather more than just that. He was an official in the ecclesiastical hierarchy, albeit a minor one, and may have been responsible for the sale of church property, in this case, the grave sold to Euplous the charioteer for his wife, Maria.

VEGAN CULTIST (κραμβιτᾶς). Kent, following the 1950 discussion of Robert and Robert, translated this term as "vegetarian," a word that has led some to think that Ioannes was a seller (or grower) of vegetables. However, as Robert's later discussion (1966; added to by Feissel) makes clear, this term relates to a follower of a semi-medical sect that pursued the *methodos* of eschewing all but a vegetable diet, especially vegetables of the cabbage family, in the interests of good health. Today such a regime might be construed as combating the effects of free radicals.

A JEWISH (?) OFFICIAL: SUPERVISOR? AND TEACHER IN THE SYNAGOGUE (ἀρχ[ισυνάγωγ]ος? and διδάσ[καλος]). If these readings are

---

[75] See 'Μιζότερος, Μιζοτέρα' in Lampe 1961.

[76] See Lampe 1961, 'Μιζότερος, Μιζοτέρα,' on these terms. The precise difference between a πρεσβύτερος and διάκονος at this time is unclear and depends on the context.

correct, this man would be both the head of the synagogue at Corinth and the expounder of Jewish doctrine. The restorations and line length, however, are very questionable.[77] The existence of a synagogue at Corinth is attested by a much earlier inscription.[78]

Entertainers, Physicians, Teachers, etc.

Some of these people, such as Euplous and Korinthas, may not have been permanent residents of Corinth but passed through it in the course of their careers. Most of the others probably lived and worked there throughout their whole lives.

Table 9.3. Entertainers, physicians, teachers, etc. Total 7 (7 names);
e. = early, l. = late.

Occupation	Name	Date
Bard[79]	Themistokles	5th or 6th c.
Charioteer[80]	Euplous	e. 6th c.
Teacher of grammar[81]	Andreas	5th c.
Trainer in the gymnasium[82]	Demetrios	5th or 6th c.
Physician[83]	Trophimos	l. 4th c.

---

[77] SEG 29, 300; see note 73.

[78] M. 111. Meritt comments that this is probably not the synagogue from the time of the apostle Paul but it may well have been in the same area. Its script puts it "considerably later" than Paul's time, but it is not so late as SEG 29, 300 [= see note 73].

[79] [Θεμι]στοκλῆς [μου]σοπόλος. Find-spot: Kraneion Basilica. See Pallas 1977 (Prakt., no. 2; and SEG 29, 308) where the name is restored incorrectly as [Ἀρι]στοκλῆς. This is one of several metrical epigrams from the Kraneion Basilica. Feissel (1985b, no. 92), on the basis of the script, places this in the 6th century.

[80] Εὔπλους ἡνίοχος; see note 72 [= Bees, no. 30; SEG 11, 154; Walbank and Walbank 2006, 281–83]. Find-spot: Cheliotomylos.

[81] Ἀνδρέας γραμματικοδιδάσκαλος, Hesperia 41, no. 30, and unpublished. Find-spot: Fountain of the Lamps. A joining fragment completes his name and provides this man's occupation.

[82] Δημήτριος ἁλίπτης, unpublished. Find-spot: Temple E, South Decumanus. The square script suggests a fairly early date.

[83] Τρόφιμος ἰατρός, Pallas 1967 in Prakt. (1965), 163, no. 2 and pl. 208β. Find-spot: Near the site of the later Lechaion Basilica. This does not seem to be a gravestone. Its script places it in the late 4th century not the late 3rd, where Pallas dates it. Trophimos may have been a descendant of an earlier Trophimos, also a physician, who was honored in the early imperial era for his services to the guild of θηρεύτορες (gladiators who specialized in wild beast fights in the arena); IG IV.365.

Table 9.3 (cont.)

Occupation	Name	Date
Physician and poet[84]	Thrasippos	e. 5th c.
Veterinarian[85]	Korinthas	e. 6th c.

BARD ([μου]σοπόλος). According to the epigram, this man came from a distinguished family (of poets?), wrote poetry himself and perhaps, therefore, made a living as a bard. He was the only son of his mother and a comfort to his blinded father. Since he is referred to in terms that suggest that he was very young, and the term μουσοπόλος can just mean "serving the Muses," this may merely mean that he composed poetry rather than that he earned a living as a poet.

CHARIOTEER (ἡνίοχος). Kent translated this word as "teamster." This usage accorded with his feeling that this inscription was a late, crude, and semi-literate production, which would be appropriate for a lowly carter. The more usual translation of Ἡνίοχος is "driver," especially of horses, not mules; and in this sense it has the much grander meaning, going back as far as Homer, of "charioteer." Chariot racing was a mass spectator sport in the late 5th and early 6th century, and Euplous probably plied his trade wherever there was a hippodrome, thus at several locations, not just at Corinth.

PHYSICIAN (Ἰατρός). Trophimos, who is named in an inscription found at the site of the later Lechaion Basilica.

PHYSICIAN AND POET (ποιητάς and ἰητῆρ). A later inscription named another physician, Thrasippos. He composed this metrical epitaph for his deceased patient, referring to himself as both a "poet" and a "physician." He clearly had a high opinion of himself since he says he is "second to none of the Greeks" at these trades. It is not clear whether

---

[84] Θράσιππος ἰητῆρ καὶ ποιητάς, K. 300 [= Robert 1966, 753]. Find-spot: Unknown. This is the epitaph of a young woman, Philista, daughter of Timarchos (LGPN III.A, no. 50). It consists of four elegiac couplets. I believe that the date hitherto generally accepted for this gravestone, the late 3rd century, is too early. To judge by the script, a date in the late 4th or early 5th century is preferable. There is no indication, however, that any of these persons was Christian; in fact, the reference in the epigram to Persephone suggests that they were not unless this is merely a literary device.

[85] Κορινθᾶς ἱπποιατρός, SEG 35, 256. Find-spot: Agora Southwest. Another ἱπποιατρός from Phthiotic Thebes was an ecclesiastical functionary; Robert and Robert 1961, 363.

Trophimos and Thrasippos worked in private practice or were public doctors, such as existed in many cities.

TEACHER OF GRAMMAR (γραμματικοδιδάσκαλος). A "teacher of grammar," but the term seems to have wider connotations, such as schoolmaster, teacher of rhetoric, or textual scholar.

TRAINER IN THE GYMNASIUM (ἀλίπτης). This man worked in the gymnasium, where his job was to apply oil to the bodies of athletes. Hence, this term came to mean trainer. In a medical context, it can mean masseur.

VETERINARIAN (ἱπποιατρός). Korinthas specialized in diseases and injuries to horses. As such, he may have been part of the sporting establishment of the hippodrome where Euplous the charioteer performed, and like Euplous he may have plied his trade at several other hippodromes in central and southern Greece. His name implies that he was a Corinthian, but I wonder whether this was, in fact, a nickname.

Skilled Workers and Artisans

These men may have worked away from Corinth but are not likely to have gone far.

Table 9.4. Skilled workers and artisans. Total 9 (4 names, plus 5 unknown); e. = early, l. = late.

Occupation	Name	Date
Arborist?[86]	Epiphanios	e. 6th c.
Blacksmith?[87]	Unknown	5th or 6th c.
Marble worker[88]	Nikostratos	6th or 7th c.
Metalworker?[89]	Pleuratos	5th or 6th c.

---

[86] [Ἐπι]φάνιος ἀποδρεπ[αντής], *Hesperia* 41, no. 34 and unpublished. The root of this word may be the verb ἀποδρέπειν ("to pluck or prune"). Hence it could mean "one who prunes trees," that is, an arborist.

[87] [- - -]χος σιδ[ηρουργός?], K. 707. Find-spot: Unknown.

[88] Νικόστρατος μαρ[μαράριο]ς, *IG* IV.537 [= Pallas and Dantis in *ArchEph* 1977, Προσθήκη, 82–83]. Find-spot: Stimanga.

[89] Πλ[ευρᾶ]τος? χευ[ματοποιητής?], K. 653. Find-spot: Temple Hill East. Kent suggested that the name was Πλευρᾶτος. This name is not attested for Corinth. He also suggested that the reading might be Π<α>[ύλω]ι τῷ, but this would involve the assumption that the mason inscribed a Λ for an Α. However, Kent's comment, that the letters τω at the beginning of line 4 might be a definite article, has merit; and I wonder

Table 9.4 (*cont.*)

Occupation	Name	Date
Road builder?[90]	Unknown	5th or 6th c.
Marble cutters[91]	Unknown (guildsmen)	e. 5th c.
Quarrymen[92]	Unknown (guildsmen)	e. 5th c.
Stone polishers[93]	Unknown (guildsmen)	e. 5th c.
Stucco renderer[94]	Leonidios	mid 5th c.

ARBORIST (ἀποδρεπ[αντής]). In the original publication of fragment *a*, this man's name was read as Phanios. The new, joining fragment makes it clear that his name was, in fact, Epiphanios and also provides the central part of the occupational name. This term is not so far attested.

BLACKSMITH (σιδ[ηρουργός?]). Kent left this unrestored. I believe that line 3 contains the genitive ending of a man's name followed by the beginning of an occupational name σιδ[ηρουργός], "iron worker" or "blacksmith."

GUILDSMEN. Quarrymen (ἀκον[ηταί]), stone polishers ([λ]ιθόξο-[ο]ι), and marble cutters ([μαρ]μαράριοι) were all members of a guild or guilds, probably working at Kenchreai or on the Hexamilion Wall. Just what the difference was between ἀκονηταί, λιθόξοοι, and μαρμαράριοι is difficult to define. This document was a collective dedication by them to their patron the *vir illustris*, Theodosius, in gratitude for his employment of them.

MARBLE WORKER (μαρ[μαράριο]ς). The deceased, Nikostratos, was a marble worker, but what the term μαρμαράριος implied here is unclear. He was buried at Stimanga by his father and brothers, who perhaps plied the same trade as a family business.

---

whether a more suitable interpretation might be Πλ[ωτίου]ι τῷ. The name Plotios is attested for Corinth in the 1st century; *LGPN* III.A, 365.

[90] An unknown σιλικά[ριος?], unpublished. Find-spot: Old Corinth. This man along with his wife was the owner of a tomb in which were buried their son and daughter (?), [Ste]phanos and Stephania. Thus, his name might also be Στέφανος since ca. eight letter spaces are available before the occupational name. The script is appropriate to a relatively early date.

[91] (Guildsmen) [μαρ]μαράριοι, M. 245; see note 48.

[92] (Guildsmen) ἀκον[ηταί], M. 245.

[93] (Guildsmen) [λ]ιθόξο[ο]ι, M. 245.

[94] Λεονίδιος λευκαντής, K. 522 [= Bees, no. 31; Robert 1966, 761; and Feissel 1985b, no. 35].

METALWORKER (χευ[ματοποιητής]?). Kent also suggested χευ[μα-τοπωλητής] ("seller of metal bowls"). This is, I think, less likely than χευματοποιητής ("one who moulds metal," that is, a metal worker). Χεύματα are cast vessels or bowls, not necessarily metal, but also pottery and glass. In an Early Byzantine context, however, they would be most likely metal, that is, bronze or copper.

ROAD BUILDER? (σιλικά[ριος]?). This word is a transliteration of the Latin word *silicarius*, one who paves roads with pebbles, a "pavior," thus, perhaps, a "road builder."

STUCCO RENDERER (λευκαντής). Kent, following Bees, translates this term as "fuller." Robert, however, pointed out that it is actually a Greek translation of the Latin word *dealbator*, "one who applies plaster or whitewash to walls." Feissel added further documentation on the different categories of such artisans.

Shopkeepers, Manufacturers, etc.

Most of these people probably spent their entire lives in Corinth or moved temporarily only a short distance from it in the course of their careers. The occupations indicate more than just labels. These were people of some substance. They include dealers and manufacturers of basic subsistence goods, as well as providers of luxury goods. This is hardly surprising in a flourishing provincial capital such as Corinth.[95] Of these occupational names, the ending -άριος (Latin -*arius*) seems to indicate that these people were more than mere retailers. Several of them processed things, as well.

Table 9.5. Shopkeepers, manufacturers, etc. Total 34 (27 names, plus 7 unknown); *e.* = early, *l.* = late.

Occupation	Name	Date
Barber[96]	Unknown	*e.* 7th c.
Butcher[97]	Unknown	mid 5th c.
Butcher[98]	Unknown	*e.* 6th c.

---

[95] On the range of such trades and activities in the Late Roman and Early Byzantine eras, see Jones (1986, 824–72). Many of the occupations discussed by Jones have not appeared in the epigraphic record at Corinth so far.

[96] An unknown κουρεύς, K. 722. Find-spot: Northwest Shops.

[97] An unknown μακελ[λάριος], unpublished. Find-spot: Near the Amphitheater.

[98] An unknown [μ]ακελλάριος, Pallas and Dantis in *ArchEph* 1977, no. 9 [= *SEG* 29, 327; Feissel 1985b, 368 no. 100]. Find-spot: Asklepieion. The script and type of

Table 9.5 (*cont.*)

Occupation	Name	Date
Buyer of secondhand clothes[99]	Mnaseas	*e.* 5th c.
Buyer of secondhand clothes[100]	Eusebios	mid 5th c.
Buyer of secondhand clothes[101]	Eusebios	*e.* 6th c.
Candle maker?[102]	Solomon	*e.* 7th c.
Cloak maker[103]	Unknown	*e.* 6th c.

stone suggest a date early in the 6th century, rather than a century later, as Pallas and Dantis posited.

[99] Μνασέας καμι[σαγοραστής?], M. 191. Find-spot: Agora West. Meritt published this without comment or restoration except to surmise that it was "apparently part of a Byzantine grave stele." The first line contains a name in the genitive; I believe that the occupation καμισαγοραστής appears in line 2. Line 4 probably refers to another member of this family, the brother of Mnaseas (κασίγ[νητος]), who is otherwise unknown.

[100] Εὐσέβιος καμισαγοραστής, K. 522 [= de Waele 1933, 436, n. 4; Bees no. 31; *SEG* 11, 168]. Find-spot: Lerna Court. This grave, not that of Eusebios but of (his son?) Noumenis, contained four skeletons. Lamps found beside this tomb have now been dated to the late 6th or even early 7th century; see Sanders 2004, 10; and Sanders 2005, 434–35). Was this tomb, therefore, re-used in the late 6th or early 7th century when the lamps died, and so were they deposited when the other burials occurred? Or do they come from another nearby tomb? Bees believed that Eusebios came from Soloi in Cyprus. Kent's interpretation is the correct one; he was a σολίτης, a seller of shoes, as well as a buyer of secondhand clothes. Feissel (1985b, no. 35) called him a *"fabricant de sandals (?) et acheteur de chemises,"* a maker of sandals and a buyer of clothing. He also called him a *"fripier,"* a buyer of old clothes. His nickname Ἀνατολικός may mean that he came originally from somewhere in Asia Minor or that he dealt in clothing from that area. Was he originally a peddler who settled down in Corinth and died there?

[101] [Εὐσέβιος] καμισα[γοραστής?], M. 193 [= Powell 1903, 67]. Find-spot: Northwest Shops. Meritt left this unrestored. The deceased's role as a καμισαγοραστής was recognized by Feissel (1985b, no. 35). I believe that he was Eusebios the Anatolian, owner of a separate tomb from that of K. 522 in which he had buried Noumenis; see note 100.

[102] Σολομῶν πολυκα[νδήλους?], K. 614 and 618. Find-spot: (*a*) Northeast Agora and (*b*) South Stoa. I have identified K. 614 as the upper part of K. 618. Combined, these prove this to be a gravestone (μνῆμα). Kent left both fragments mostly unrestored except for the name Solomon. Robert (1966, 768) suggested that Solomon may have made a gift of ten candles (πολυκα[νδήλους]| δέκα) to some institution, perhaps a church, a synagogue, or an important secular building. Even with the longer line length, this may still be the case; Feissel 1985b, no. 113. We might restore with a longer line πολυκα[νδήλους ὁλιοκοτίνων]| δέκα "a gift of candles worth ten gold pieces." Apart from the name, which might suggest Jewish connections, there is no indication as who this Solomon was. It seems that Robert thought of him as Jewish since he calls him "Salomon," but the cross at the start of K. 614 makes it clear that he was a Christian.

[103] An unknown [εἱματικ]άριος, unpublished. Find-spot: Unknown. This appears to be the stone referred to by Feissel (1985b, no. 48) as remaining unedited but mentioned by Bees (1941, 56), who was apparently told about it by de Waele. Feissel notes

Table 9.5 (*cont.*)

Occupation	Name	Date
Confectioner[104]	Kyriakos	*e.* 6th c.
Dealer in goatskins[105]	Tryphon	*e.* 6th c.
Dealer in goatskins[106]	Tryphon	*e.* 6th c.
Dealer in goatskins[107]	Ioulianos	*e.* 6th c.
Eel fisherman[108]	Andreas	mid 5th c.
Fattener of poultry[109]	Anias	*e.* 6th c.
Fattener of poultry[110]	Paulos	*e.* 6th c.
Fattener of poultry[111]	Paulos	*e.* 6th c.
Fireman?[112]	Andreas	*e.* 6th c.
Frankincense dealer[113]	Nikeas	*e.* 6th c.

that Bees had intended to include it as number 68 in his collection. I have, so far, been unable to track down this inscription.

[104] Κυριακὸς [πλακουντ]άρ(ιος ?), Pallas and Dantis in *ArchEph* 1977, no. 5 [= *SEG* 29, 316; Feissel 1985b, no. 98.]. Find-spot: Kokkinovrysi.

[105] Τρύφων αἰγιάριος, K. 556. Find-spot: Lerna Court. For the likely meaning of Αἰγιάριος and a discussion of its origins, see Feissel 1985b, no. 40.

[106] Τρύφων ἐγιάρ<ι>ος, *Hesperia* 41, no. 32, and unpublished. Find-spot: Fountain of the Lamps.

[107] Ἰουλιανός ἐγιάριος, K. 587 [= Feissel 1985b, no. 69]. Find-spot: South Stoa. The spelling ἐγιάριος is the phonetic equivalent of αἰγιάριος.

[108] Ἀνδρέας κυρτᾶς, K. 551 [= Bees, no. 32; *SEG* 11, 169; and Feissel 1985b, no. 36, citing Robert and Robert (1966, 39–46); and Robert (1966, 764). Find-spot: Lerna Court.

[109] Ἀνίας σιτευτάριος, K. 542; see note 111. Find-spot: Lerna Court. Kent, misunderstanding lines 6–8, suggested that Anias, son of Paulos, inscribed this text. Robert (1966, 763) showed that he merely oversaw its engraving, ensuring that the ownership of the tomb was legally validated.

[110] Παῦλος σιτευτάριος, K. 542; see note 109.

[111] Παῦλος σιτιστάριος, K. 559 [= Feissel 1985b, no. 54]. Find-spot: Asklepieion. Kent restored this man's nickname as Μ[α]κρόχει[ρ], "Long Hand." The nickname was used here to distinguish this man from others bearing the same name or even having the same trade. Σιτιστάριος has the same meaning as σιτευτάριος; see K. 542; see note 110.

[112] Ἀνδρέας πυρόξαλλ[ος?], M. 154 [= Bees, no. 54; *SEG* 11, 98; and Feissel 1985b, no. 15]. Find-spot: Unknown. Bees read this word as Πυρόμαλλ[ος], "Yellow Haired." Meritt read πυρόγαλλ[ος] without suggesting a translation. As for the second half of this word, a Γάλλος was a eunuch priest of Cybele, which seems unlikely in a Christian context. According to *LGPN* III.A, no. 1, Πυρόμαλλ[ος] is a patronymic. However, the correct reading is πυρόξαλλ[ος].

[113] Νικέας [Λί]βανος (?), K. 550. Find-spot: Lerna Court. Kent believed that the correct reading in lines 1–2 was κατὰ [κλί]βανον. This he interpreted from the find-spot in reservoir four of Lerna as meaning "down near an underground channel." But the correct reading, for which Robert (1966, 764) cites several parallels, is κατὰ [Λί]βανον, "nicknamed Libanos;" Feissel 1985b, no. 62. Frankincense was viewed with distrust among early Christians but by the 5th century was much in demand; Harvey 2006.

Table 9.5 (*cont.*)

Occupation	Name	Date
Furrier[114]	Maurikios	*e.* 6th c.
Innkeeper/shopkeeper[115]	Kosmas	*e.* 6th c.
Manufacturer of silk cloth[116]	Gheorghios	*e.* 6th c.
Meat cutter[117]	Helenos	e. 6th c.
Miller[118]	Unknown	6th or 7th c.
Miller[119]	Artemon	5th or 6th c.
Money changer[120]	Gheorghios	mid 5th c.
Pheasant breeder[121]	Kyriakos	*e.* 6th c.

---

[114] Μαυρίκιος γουνάριος, M. 148. Find-spot: Lechaion Road Shops. Meritt published this without comment or translation. Bees (no. 56) translates γουνάριος as "furrier" but also raises the possibility that this word derives from γουνός ("high ground"). If so, it might be a nickname, "Highlander," rather than an occupational name. Robert and Robert (1965, 72) and Feissel (1985b, no. 12) opt for furrier, and I think that this is correct.

[115] Κοσμᾶς κάπηλος, K. 525. Find-spot: Lerna Court. Robert (1966, 762) makes no comment regarding Kent's translation of this term as "innkeeper." Feissel (1985b, no. 53), citing several examples, translates it as "*cabaretier*," which means "tavernkeeper."

[116] [Γεώρ]γιος σ[ιρικο]π(ο)ιός, unpublished. Find-spot: Fountain of the Lamps. The Σ of the occupational name survives, with space for three-to-five letters to right of it. Since the second half of the deceased's name projects a little into the left margin, it is quite possible that the initial letters of the occupational name likewise project into the right margin. Thus, σ[ιρικο]π(ο)ιός may be preferable to σ[υρο]π(ο)ιός.

[117] ["Ε]λενος χρε[α]τοκοπ[οιός?], unpublished. Find-spot: Unknown. The available space makes any other restoration of this man's name impossible. The first letter of the occupation is definitely a X; after the P, the upper left curve and a trace of the bar of an E are preserved; the combination of letters that follows in the next line makes this restoration extremely likely, even though the usual spelling is κρεατοκοποιός.

[118] An unknown μυληνός, unpublished. Find-spot: West of the Amphitheater. This may be the name of the owner of the tomb or of his occupation, a "miller" (μυληνός). Since there does not seem to be any personal name with this ending, I believe that this is a hitherto unknown form of the word μυλινάριος (or of μουλίων [?], "muleteer"). There is another name in the genitive here, perhaps that of the seller of the tomb. This is definitely a Christian gravestone; the last line ends with a cross. The script is very close to that of *Prakt.* 1977, no. 8, the early 7th century gravestone of Zoe. I have assigned a similar date to this stone.

[119] Ἀρτέμων μυλινάριος, ArchEph 1893 (Skias), 126, no. 18 [= IG IV.411; now EM 4971; Bees, no. 41; and Feissel 1985b, no. 6.] Find-spot: Old Corinth.

[120] Γε[ώργι]ος τραπεζίτης, K. 640 [= Bees, no. 61; SEG 11, 183]. Find-spot: East Lechaion Road. Robert (1966, 769) corrected Kent's text for line 4 to τὸ ἐπίκλην. The nickname is discussed at length by Bees, suggesting that it may be Κοδρυ[ληνός], a variant of Κορδυληνός, the ethnic of Kordyla in Cappadocia; or else Κοδρυ[ᾶς]. Kent felt that it might be a transliteration of a Latin name such as Quadratus.

[121] Κυριακὸς φασανάριος, K. 561 [= Bees, no. 34; SEG 11, 171]. Find-spot: Asklepieion. On the meaning of this word, see Feissel 1985b, no. 38, citing Robert and Robert (1961, 48–49; and 1974, 229, n. 302).

Table 9.5 (*cont.*)

Occupation	Name	Date
Pickle merchant[122]	Unknown	mid 5th c.
Pickle merchant[123]	Andreas	e. 6th c.
Pickle merchant[124]	Unknown	e. 6th c.
Shoemaker[125]	Andreas	e. 6th c.
Shoe seller[126]	Eusebios	mid 5th c.
Seller of quinces and fruit[127]	Glaukos	mid 5th c.
Tailor[128]	Paulos	e. 6th c.
Tailor[129]	Sotiris	e. 6th c.

[122] [- -]ας σαλγα[μάριος?], unpublished. Find-spot: East Old Corinth. An unknown man, a *makellarios* ("butcher"), sold a tomb to a *salgamarios* ("merchant of pickled goods"), whose name should be between three-to-four and six-to-seven letters long, probably the former.

[123] Ἀνδρέας σαλγαμάριος, K. 551; see note 108.

[124] [- -]ανος σαλγαμάριος, K. 540 [= Robert and Robert 1960, 39–46; Robert 1966, 762–763; Feissel 1985b, no. 57]. Find-spot: Asklepieion. The owner of this tomb, an unknown man who was a *salgamarios* ("pickle merchant"), seems to have allocated a corner (γωνία) of his tomb to Maximos. His name might be [Φλαβι]ανός, which was quite common in Corinth in imperial times (see *LGPN* III.A, 466). Another possibility is [Ἐρωτι]ανός, known in Achaia in imperial times (*LGPN* III.A, 156).

[125] Ἀνδρέας [κ]αλλιγάριος, K. 547 [= Bees no. 51; *SEG* 11, 178]. Find-spot: Lerna Court. The correct reading in line 3 is not, as Bees proposed, [σ]αλμ(α)γ(άριος), or, as Kent thought, [β]αλνι(κάριος). Feissel (1985b, no. 44), working from Kent's photograph, pointed out that it must be [κ]αλλιγ(άριος), "*cordonnier*," a cordwainer or shoemaker. Autopsy shows that this reading is correct.

[126] Εὐσέβιος σολίτης, K. 522; see notes 100–01.

[127] Γλαῦ[κος] [κ]υδώ[νιας?], K. 648 [= Bees, no. 62; *SEG* 11, 184]. Find-spot: Temple Hill North. Bees believed that the deceased was a woman, Glauke, and that line 3 contained a date by indiction. Kent showed that the letters partly preserved in this line might be Κ, Λ, and Ω. Of these, however, only the Ω is certain. Only the tops of the other two letters survive, so they could be, respectively, Κ or Υ; and Α, Δ, or Λ. There are two possible interpretations of these: one, that Kent's readings are correct, in which case the text might read [ἐπί]κλ(ην) Ω[- -], thus indicating a nickname beginning with Ω; two, that these letters are, in fact, Υ, Δ and Ω, part of an occupational title such as [κ]υδώ[νιας], or a nickname. The line length is likely to be that preferred by Bees, ca. 10–11 letters. Thus, if either of my conjectures is correct, the deceased is probably a man, Glaukos, rather than a woman. The marble used for this epitaph is of a type that seems to have been popular in the mid 5th century. See M. 145; see Appendix, note 222.

[128] Παῦλος ῥάπτης, *Hesperia* 41, no. 33 [= Feissel 1985b, no. 90]. Find-spot: Fountain of the Lamps.

[129] Σωτηρὶς ῥάπτης; see note 128. The wording suggested to Wiseman that the grave was that of Sotiris, the son of Paulos, rather than the other way round: the word υἱος ("son") is repeated twice, once in the nominative, the second time in the genitive. In the latter case, it is set off to the side, as if an afterthought, to remove ambiguity as to who was buried here.

BARBER (κουρεύς). A barber looked after the facial hair as well as the coiffure of his customers. Whether, as in medieval Europe, he also served as a surgeon is unknown.

BUTCHER (μακελλάριος). A μακελλάριος, whose name derives from the Latin *macellum* ("meat market") was a "butcher." As I have suggested (see note 121), a *makellarios* was perhaps a wholesaler, providing a range of meat products.

BUYER OF SECONDHAND CLOTHES (καμισαγοραστής, καμισογοραστής). While the meaning of the word καμίσιον is "shirt," Eusebios seems to have been a buyer of secondhand clothes in general. He also sold shoes.

CANDLE MAKER (πολυκα[νδήλους]?). I wonder whether, in fact, this word identifies Solomon's trade—that of candle making—as well as a gift made by him to some institution.

CLOAKMAKER ([εἱματικ]άριος). Cloaks were outer garments usually worn over other clothing.

CONFECTIONER ([πλακουντ]άριος?). This restoration is somewhat questionable. If correct, it describes one who made little cakes and sweets. But another occupational name that would fit the available space is [Παπυλιων]άριος, "tent maker," an alternative to the term σκηνοποιός used to describe the apostle Paul in Acts 18:3.

DEALER IN GOATSKINS (αἰγιάριος, ἐγιάριος). Tryphon is presumably the man who sold a grave to Gheorghios the gravedigger and his wife (see note 59). This is his own gravestone. Kent, followed by Avramea (134), believed that the meaning of αἰγιάριος was "goatherd," but this translation probably undervalues the occupation. Skins and hair were valuable commodities and had a wide range of uses.

EEL FISHERMAN (κυρτᾶς). Kent translates this word as "trapper of lobsters and fish." In conjunction with the term *salgamarios*, a *kurtas* is, perhaps, not merely an eel-fisherman but one who farms and processes eels. Andreas may have owned stew-ponds, perhaps in the marshy ground near the sea where he raised eels.

FATTENER OF POULTRY (σιτευτάριος, σιτιστάριος). Kent translates this term as "one who fed grain (σῖτος) to animals or poultry in order to fatten them for eating," thus an intermediary between the breeder and the butcher. The same term is found in K. 559 but spelled σιτιστάριος. It is a possible indication that these two Pauloi are different men, as, indeed, the nickname M[α]κρόχειρ ("Long Hand"), given to K. 559, may imply since they may be of about the same date.

FIREMAN? (πυρόξαλλ[ος]). Earlier readings, πυρόμαλλ[ος] and πυρόγαλλ[ος], are incorrect. The correct reading is πυρόξαλλ[ος]. I think that this may be a nickname, based upon the materials with which this man was concerned, πῦρ ("fire"), πυρός ("wheat"), or ὀξαλίς ("sour wine," hence, "vinegar"). Thus, he may have been a fireman or a merchant dealing in wheat or in vinegar.

FRANKINCENSE DEALER ([λί]βανος?). The correct reading, for which Robert cites several parallels, is κατὰ [Λί]βανον, "nicknamed Libanos." Robert regarded this word as being merely a nickname, but λίβανος means "frankincense." I suspect that the nickname of Nikeas was a little like the modern Welsh use of an occupation as an additional surname to distinguish several persons having the same surname from one another—for instance, Jones the Bank, Jones the Bread, Jones the Teach. Since Nikeas is a common name, I suggest that Nikeas the Frankincense was a dealer or importer of frankincense.

FURRIER (γουνάριος). Furs from all kinds of animals were used for hats, cloaks, wraps, shoes, and so forth.

INNKEEPER/SHOPKEEPER (κάπηλος). This word means "tavern-keeper." There are examples from several sites elsewhere in the Roman world. However, *kapelos* can also mean "shopkeeper" since inns sold other goods besides alcoholic beverages.

MANUFACTURER OF SILK CLOTH (σ[ιρικο]π(ο)ιός, rather than σ[υρο]π(ο)ιός). Gheorghios manufactured silk fabrics rather than Syrian-style clothing.

MEAT CUTTER (χρε[α]τοκοπ[οιός]?). The usual spelling is κρεατοκοποιός. What was the difference between a μακελλάριος ("butcher") and a χρεατοκοποιός ("meat cutter")? I am inclined to see the μακελλάριος as a wholesaler, providing a range of meat products, whereas a χρεατοκοποιός may have been a retailer, concentrating on fresh, unprocessed meat.

MILLER (μυληνός?). This may be a hitherto unknown word for a miller, or even for a muleteer?

MILLER (μυλινάριος). This is the usual spelling of the Greek word for a miller.

MONEYCHANGER (τραπεζίτης). A *trapezites* was one who set up a table (τράπεζα) in the market or elsewhere in order to change foreign currency for local currency. From this simple beginning, the *trapezites* evolved into something more resembling a modern banker, taking deposits, making loans, and providing surety.

PHEASANT BREEDER (φασανάριος). Pheasants evidently were reared for the market, as poultry is today.

PICKLE MERCHANT (σαλγαμάριος). These three men preserved foodstuffs by pickling them in brine or vinegar. Robert, however, finds parallels from elsewhere that show *salgamarioi* operated village-stores (*pantopoleia*), the ancestors of today's corner store or supermarket, that sold all kinds of foods and also medicines in an age when refrigeration was unknown. One *salgamarios*, Andreas, was also an eel fisherman (K. 551; see notes 108 and 122).

SELLER OF QUINCES AND FRUIT ([κ]υδω[νιᾶς]?). This seems to be a nickname, either referring to the man's origins in Kydonia in Crete or used as an occupational name. I think that the latter explanation may be the correct one. The word κυδωνιᾶ means "quince;" therefore, this man was, perhaps, a seller of quinces, and thus a fruit merchant.

SHOE MAKER ([κ]αλλιγάριος). Ancient shoes were often similar to sandals, a leather sole bound to the foot with woven cords. In this instance, the shoes made by Andreas were made with beautiful (καλλι-) colored cords, therefore dress-shoes. Andreas may have supplied the likes of Eusebios the Σολίτης, who sold all kinds of shoes.

SHOE MAKER (σολίτης). A σόλιον is a "slipper." Thus, this man probably sold or made slippers or shoes, as well as buying used clothing.

TAILOR ('ράπτης). Paulos and his son Sotiris were both tailors, in the usual fashion of sons following in their father's trade.

Unknown Occupations

Table 9.6. Unknown occupations. Total: 9 unknown occupations or ranks (2 names, plus 7 unknown); *e.* = early, *l.* = late.

Occupation	Name	Date
Unknown[130]	Unknown	*e.* 6th c.
Unknown[131]	Unknown	*e.* 6th c.
Unknown[132]	Unknown	*e.* 5th c.

---

[130] [- - -]τος Ε[- - -], M. 149. Find-spot: Near Hagios Ioannes. Perhaps an Ἐ[λαιοπώλης?] (oil merchant) or an Ἐ[ριουργός?] (wool worker). There are several other possibilities.

[131] [- -]νος Λα [- -], K. 625. Find-spot: South Basilica. Perhaps a Λα[νάριος] (wool worker or weaver of wool). As such, he was likely to be a moderately wealthy individual, having the wherewithal to own a tomb.

[132] An unknown Υ[- - - -], M. 156. Find-spot: Agora East. Perhaps a Ὑ[περέτης?] (sub-deacon) since, as Meritt recognized, the adjective εὐλα[βέστατος] appears in line 2.

Table 9.6 (*cont.*)

Occupation	Name	Date
Unknown[133]	Unknown	*e.* 6th c.
Unknown[134]	Unknown	mid 5th c.
Unknown[135]	Unknown	*e.* 6th c.
Unknown[136]	Klementios	*e.* 6th c.
Unknown[137]	Unknown	*l.* 4th c.
Unknown[138]	Poulos	*e.* 6th c.

Total Number of Ranks, Trades and Occupations

There is a total of 107 ranks, trades and occupations, including 26 "doubles" and nine unknown, identified with 79 names, plus 28 unknown.

---

[133] An unknown [- - -]λοπ(ο)ιός, K. 708. Robert (1966, 770) pointed out that Kent had failed to notice that de Waele had restored this as τὸ ἐπίκ[λην - | - -]λοπιου[- -]. Thus, the word in line 2 may be a nickname. I wonder, in fact, whether it is part of an occupational name, following a nickname (line 1), which has perished. One possible restoration is [πι]λοπ<ο>ιός, "felt maker."

[134] An unknown [....]νάριος, unpublished. Find-spot: Fountain of the Lamps. Perhaps a [σα(ρ)γα]νάριος, (basket maker) or a [σιππι]νάριος (wool worker). The second restoration is more likely to be correct since it does not involve an abbreviation.

[135] An unknown [...]άριος, K. 523. Find-spot: Asklepieion. This man's occupation was given in lines 3–4; this word must be short, such as [λαν]άριος (wool worker) or [νοτ]άριος (notary).

[136] Κλημ[έντιος (?)....ά]ριος, K. 646 [= Bees, no. 60; *SEG* 11, 182]. Find-spot: Theater. The owner of this tomb may have been Κλημ[έντιος], as Kent suggests; but a shorter name would be preferable, given the space available, perhaps Κλήμ[ης]. His occupation was given in lines 3–4. This word, too, must be quite short, eight-to-nine letters in all. Two possible restorations are [λιβρά]ριος ("secretary") and [ὀστιά]ριος (bone setter).

[137] [- - -]λιδος [- - -]Λησ(τής?), K. 579. Find-spot: Central Shops. In line 1 the end of a man's name survives in the genitive followed by the beginning of a definite article. Either a patronymic follows or an occupational name although it is probably both in the genitive. At the end of what I believe to be an occupational name, there survive a trace of a letter before the H, the base of the diagonal of a Λ or a Χ; if the latter, this word might be [ὀρ]χησ(τής) (pantomime dancer).

[138] Πούλ[ος?] [- -]ξα[- -], K. 621. Find-spot: South Stoa. The letters ΧΑ at the start of the second line might be part of a patronymic, such as [Ἀλε]ξά[νδρου]. This seems the likeliest conjecture, but it is worth thinking of an occupation. I suggest [πα]ξα[μᾶς] (baker) or [μετα]ξά[ριος] (silk merchant).

The Economic and Social Implications of these Gravestones

Since so many graves are anonymous, it is reasonable to suppose that graves for which gravestones survive are those of relatively prosperous individuals or families. There is, however, a discernible sub-category of 34 individuals, persons wealthy enough to purchase one or more graves, either for themselves or for members of their family. In a few cases, an individual owned two or more graves, one of which he sold on to members of other families. Where the price of a grave is given, it becomes likely that, throughout the period studied here, the going rate for a grave was one-and-a-half gold pieces, a considerable sum of money. Moreover, the gravestone itself was an object of value, as well as constituting a record of legal title to the real property represented by the grave itself. In every instance at Corinth where the price is preserved, with the exception of the grave of Polychronios the *singoularios,* the price is one-and-a-half *solidi*.[139] Polychronios's grave was situated near the unexcavated 'Pallas' Basilica at the eastern edge of the city, and it is likely that the price of two *solidi* that Polychronios paid was related both to his senior position in the official establishment and to the proximity of his tomb to the new basilica.

Names, Nicknames, and Families

Generally individuals bore only one name, and these were drawn from a relatively small stock so that, as a result, many names occur several times over. Personal names were sometimes survivals from pagan times, such as Artemon, Euplous, Mnaseas, Neikias, Tryphon; or were derived from the names of saints, such as Andreas, Demetrios, Gheorghios, Maria, Paulos. When ambiguities arose, nicknames might be used to differentiate one man from another of the same name, such as

---

[139] Ivison (1996, 106) makes a serious error in an otherwise extremely useful study of burial and urbanism at Corinth by misreading Kent (no. 584), where he apparently believes that the clause [ἠγο]ράσθη ἀ[πὸ—χρυσίνων ἡμισέων] τρειῶν means "purchased from...for [an exceptional] three and a half *solidi*." In fact, this means "for three half pieces of gold," that is, one-and-a-half *solidi*. In every instance where the price is preserved, with the exception of the grave of Polychronios, the price is one-and-a-half *solidi*; Pallas and Dantis in *ArchEph* 1977, no. 2; see note 39.

Paulos "Long Hand." Also, for reasons that may have to do with pride or prestige, names were often accompanied by a word denoting rank, profession, or trade. It is sometimes difficult to determine whether such a word is actually a nickname or surname as, for instance, a man who may have sold orchard-fruits was called "Quince." Another, who may have dealt in frankincense, was named "Frankincense," and another, who may have been a maker of candles, was apparently known as "Many Candles."

Many nuclear families can be identified (husbands, wives, children male or female, brothers and sisters), but there is no evidence of extended families (uncles, aunts, grandparents) and little evidence of families persisting over several generations.

CONCLUSIONS

The 662 fragments of inscriptions that I have studied represent the achievements and aspirations of a small but relatively prosperous sub-group of Late Roman and Early Byzantine society at Corinth, one that was willing both to identify itself as Christian and to vaunt its prosperity. For want of a better definition, I label this group as 'middle-class.'

The trades and occupations recorded upon the gravestones indicate that during this period of the city's existence, there existed a range of commercial and manufacturing activities, both of basic commodities and of more 'up-market' products. Since Corinth was the capital of the province of Achaia, this spread is not altogether surprising although it gives lie to the opinions expressed elsewhere that the city was in decline during this period. Decline, if it occurred, came later, after the natural and other upheavals of the 7th century—earthquakes, plagues, and invasions—when tombstones of this kind were no longer being made and set up.

Most of these gravestones derive from the cemeteries along the north scarp of the lower city from the Asklepieion and Lerna Court in the east to the Gymnasium and the Fountain of the Lamps in the west; that is to say, from the cemeteries near the commercial center of the city and thus close to where the deceased had probably lived and worked. However, a significant proportion comes from such places as the great basilicas—the Kraneion, Skoutela, Kodratos, and Lechaion Basilicas and the unexcavated 'Pallas' Basilica—with a few examples scattered throughout the environs of the city. Basilicas were popular as burial places because of their sanctity and the prestige that proximity to them conferred. Thus, the elite seem to have chosen to be buried there rather than in the popular burial places along the northern scarp of the lower plateau.

The primary function of these gravestones was to establish ownership of the grave, a piece of real property to which legal title attached, either to the occupant(s) or to the living relative(s) of the deceased. In other words, the epitaph was a legal document. But a secondary purpose was to indicate to all who read it that the occupant(s) of the grave or their living relative(s) were persons of substance. They were wealthy enough both to own a grave and to pay for a gravestone, and they expected to be known and to be remembered by posterity. In some sense, they have achieved their expectations, though not quite as they could have imagined.

The kind of information that the gravestones provide is not very different from that found in contemporary gravestones elsewhere in Greece, for instance, at Thessalonika. The purpose was to show who an individual was, what he had achieved in his life, and to advertise this to his contemporaries. Most of the deceased were minor officials and ecclesiastics, professionals, entertainers, artisans, manufacturers, and tradesmen. At these levels of society there seems to have been no aspiration to public service of any kind; they were merely taxpayers, not aspiring to make donations to the state or city or to set up public monuments. In a period of relative prosperity, they believed it appropriate to advertise their success. There are a few cases of families in the old Roman sense,[140] but these are early in date, fragmentary, and not found *in situ*, in or on a tomb.

These people, for the most part, had no history; that is, they seem to have been self-made men whose economic and social status were not inherited. They may have hoped to pass on their status and wealth to future generations, but there is no evidence that they were able to do this. The city's outlying areas are still mostly unexcavated or unreported, and thus the picture is incomplete. Certainly there was an aspect of mourning and personal remembrance in these epitaphs,

---

[140] K. 689 is a Greek version of the standard Latin (Roman) epitaph for an extended family; see Appendix, note 52. M. 243 (and M. 174?) may be another; see Appendix, note 265.

but the simple formulae employed do not provide much scope to go beyond this. The emphasis was upon ownership of the grave as a resting place for the dead; that is, the wording is a statement of legal title in perpetuity to the grave which was clearly thought of as a piece of real property that needed protection against appropriation by others.

The implication of the title of this paper is that the names of the ordinary Christians of Corinth have disappeared. This examination has shown that this is not the case. In fact, not only have many names survived, they can also be seen as those of individuals with specific occupations and expertise. They provide ample evidence for the existence of a prosperous Christian community at this stage in the long history of Corinth.

APPENDIX

THE CORINTHIAN CENSUS

There is a total of 390 names (including 77 'doubles,' 111 incomplete or uncertain, and 67 unknown), plus 205 gravestones for which no evidence survives of the person's identity, rank or occupation (127 published and 78 unpublished). The total number of inscriptions analyzed is 662 (557 published and 105 unpublished). Thus, there is evidence for a minimum of 595 individuals from the period under study.

In this compilation, I have employed the Greek spelling found in the actual inscriptions. *LGPN* generally converts this to the standard spelling, a procedure that sometimes leads to ambiguities. I have indicated where *LGPN* differs. Also, *LGPN* records nicknames and occasionally ethnics, as if they were personal names. I do not follow this practice.

Key to abbreviations: b. = brother; d. = daughter; f. = father; g.- = grand-; h. = husband; m. = mother; sis. = sister, s. = son, w. = wife.

A

Ἀγαθοκλῆ[ς].[1]   Agathokle[s?]
Ἀγαπωμένη? sis. of Κέρδων and Ἀγαπώμενος.[2]   Agapomene?
Ἀγαπώμενος? b. of Ἀγαπωμένη and Κέρδων.[3]   Agapomenos?
Ἀγαθοκλῆς s. of Ἀφοβία and b. of Ἰωάνης.[4]   Agathokles
Ἀγαθοκλία.[5]   Agathoklia

---

[1] *ArchEph* 1893, no. 22 (Skias), dated to the 5th or 6th century [= *IG* IV.409; now EM 4973; and Bees, no. 44]. Find-spot: Old Corinth. According to *IG*, the name is restored as Ἀγαθο[ς]; Bees thought that it was Ἀγαθόπ[ους]. This was accepted by Feissel (1985b, no. 5). However, the photograph published by Bees makes it clear that neither of these suggestions can stand. The bases of three letters survive following the 'O'; the first of these could be a 'K, N, or a Π'; the second a 'Λ'; and the third, perhaps, an 'H.' Thus, the name is probably Ἀγαθοκλῆ[ς].
[2] M. 136 [= Bees, no. 15; Feissel 1985b, no. 10; *LGPN* III.A, no. 1], dated to the early 5th century. Find-spot: Southwest of the agora, Old Corinth. My interpretation of lines 1–3 differs from Meritt's.
[3] M. 136; see note 2.
[4] K. 531 [= Feissel 1985b, no. 54; *LGPN* III.A, no. 46], dated to the 5th century. Find-spot: Lerna Court. Kent printed Φοβία as the mother's name. For the correct name and relationship: Robert (1966, 764–65).
[5] K. 659 [= *LGPN* III.A, no. 5–6, with spelling Ἀγαθόκλεια], dated to the 4th or 5th century. Find-spot: Asklepieion.

Ἀγαθοκλία m./d. of Ἐπαγαθῶ.[6]	Agathoklia
Ἀδαμάντιος.[7]	Adamantios
[Ἀδαμ]άντιος (?) f. of ?[8]	[Adam]antios(?)
Ἀθη[ναῖος?].[9]	Athe[naios?]
Ἀθήνεος Πρῶτος.[10]	Atheneos
Ἀθηνόδωρος h. of Ἐπαφροδίτη.[11]	Athenodoros
Ἀκάκι[ος?] s. of Ἰουλίανος Ἐγάριος.[12]	Akaki[os?]
[Ἀ]λεξα[νδρ- -?].[13]	[A]lexa[ndr- -?]
[Ἀλ]εξανδρία?[14]	[Al]exandria?
Ἀλέξανδρος f. of Νεικίης Ὀρθόγραφος.[15]	Alexandros
Ἀλέξανδρος Ῥάβδουχος.[16]	Alexandros
Ἀλέξαν[δρος?].[17]	Alexan[dros?]
Ἀλέξ[ανδρος] h. of Εὐτυχ[ιανή].[18]	Alex[andros]

---

[6] K. 532 [= Bees, no. 45; SEG 11, 175; Feissel 1985b, no. 41; and LGPN III.A, no. 5–6, with spelling Ἀγαθόκλεια], dated to the early 5th century. Find-spot: Asklepieion. Epagatho owned this tomb and buried Agathoklia in it. She herself must have been interred elsewhere. The deceased was probably a close relative, to judge by her name.

[7] K. 582 [= Feissel 1985b, no. 42; LGPN III.A, no. 1], dated to the early 6th century. Find-spot: South stoa.

[8] Unpublished; see note 118. This is the third name on this stone, perhaps that of the deceased.

[9] M. 140 [= Bees, no. 47; SEG 11, 94], dated to 4th century. Find-spot: West Lechaion Road.

[10] K. 553 [= LGPN III.A, no. 8, with spelling Ἀθηναῖος]; see preceding essay, note 23.

[11] IG IV.405 [= M. 161; Bees, no. 66; Feissel 1985b, no. 3; LGPN III.A, no. 5], dated early 7th century. Find-spot: Old Corinth. This was first seen in Old Corinth when it was complete (Ross 1834, 62). Subsequently, it disappeared and was rediscovered in 1900 without its upper right side in the Northwest Shops.

[12] K. 587; see preceding essay, note 107. In line 6 Kent printed dotted 'A, I, and I' in the third, fourth and fifth spaces respectively; in fact, the tops of five letters are preserved, the only certain one of which is the 'K' in the fourth space. This name may be a transliteration of the Latin Acacius, attested elsewhere in Roman and Byzantine times, for example, in Messenia and Southern Italy (LGPN III.A, 21), in Cyrene and Thasos (LGPN I, 22), and in Macedonia and Thrace (LGPN IV, 12).

[13] Unpublished, early 6th century. Find-spot: South Oakley. Perhaps [Ἀ]λέξα [νδρος]?

[14] K. 678 [= LGPN III.A, no. 6], dated 5th century. Find-spot: Hagia Anna.

[15] K. 305 [= LGPN III.A, no. 77]; see preceding essay, note 28.

[16] ArchEph 1977, no. 10 [= LGPN III.A, no. 143]; see preceding essay, note 25.

[17] K. 526 [= LGPN III.A, no. 141], dated early 6th century. Find-spot: Asklepieion. Kent assumed that this person was male. Since the ending has not survived, it is equally possible that the name is feminine, that is, Ἀλεξαν[δρία].

[18] K. 650 [= LGPN III.A, no. 142], dated 5th century. Find-spot: Temple Hill East. Kent restored the husband's name as Ἀλέξ[ανδρος]. This is not the only possible restoration; for example, the name Ἀλεξιάδης is also attested for Corinth earlier in the imperial era; LGPN III.A, 25).

[Ἀ]μμιανή?[19]	[A]mmiane
[Ἀμ]μιανή?[20]	[Am]miane?
Ἀναστασία d. of Ἀνδρέας and Εὐγενία.[21]	Anastasia
Ἀναστασία w. of [- - -?].[22]	Anastasia
Ἀ[ναστα]σία d. of Α[- - -?] and Νεῦ[να?].[23]	A[nasta]sia
Ἀναστάσιος Ὑπερέτης.[24]	Anastasios
Ἀναστάσιος.[25]	Anastasios
[Ἀνα]στάσ[ιος?].[26]	[Ana]stas[ios?]
Ἀνδρέας.[27]	Andreas
Ἀνδρέας.[28]	Andreas
Ἀνδρέας Δεκανός.[29]	Andreas
Ἀνδρέας Σαλγαμάριος, Κυρτᾶς.[30]	Andreas
Ἀνδρέας Γραμματικοδιδάσκαλος.[31]	Andreas
Ἀνδρέας [Κ]αλλι(γάριος).[32]	Andreas
Ἀνδρέας [Ὀικ]όνομος, seller of a tomb.[33]	Andreas
Ἀνδρέας Πυρόξαλλ[ος?].[34]	Andreas
Ἀνδρέας h. of Εὐγενία.[35]	Andreas

---

[19] Unpublished, early 6th century. Find-spot: FoL. Ammiane owned this tomb and probably was buried in it.

[20] K. 588 [= Bees, no. 49; SEG 11, 177; LGPN III.A, no. 1], early 6th century. Find-spot: Agora Southwest.

[21] K. 561 [= LGPN III.A, no. 1]; see preceding essay, note 121. This gravestone was found in the grave to which it belonged, one of the few stones that can be associated with a particular burial.

[22] K. 671 [= ArchEph 1893 (Skias), no. 15; IG IV.412; Bees, no. 50; SEG 11, 186; LGPN III.A, no. 2], early 6th century. Find-spot: Old Corinth.

[23] K. 666, early 6th century. Find-spot: Unknown. This text presents many problems. Kent believed that Anastasia was both the owner of the tomb and the person buried in it, but I can detect no trace of the dotted 'A' that Kent prints in line 2. It is equally possible that the persons named in lines 1–3 are a husband and wife and, thus, Ἀναστασίου κὲ (= καὶ) Νευ[- -]; the Anastasia of line 6 would then be their daughter. If I am correct, the wife's name could be Νεῦ[να]. This name is attested for Epidamnos in Illyria in the Hellenistic-Roman era; LGPN III.A, 314.

[24] K. 530 [= LGPN III.A, no. 2]; see preceding essay, note 72.

[25] Hesperia 31, 117, dated early 6th century. Find-spot: 650 m. southwest of the Odeon.

[26] K. 611, early 6th century. Find-spot: Central Agora.

[27] K. 552 [= LGPN III.A, no. 19], early 6th century. Find-spot: Lerna Court.

[28] M. 164 [= Bees, no. 53; SEG 11, 102; LGPN III.A, no. 14], early 7th century. Find-spot: Agora East.

[29] ArchEph 1977, no. 2 [= LGPN III.A, no. 22]; see preceding essay, note 39.

[30] K. 551 [= LGPN III.A, no. 18]; see preceding essay, note 108.

[31] Hesperia 41, no. 30 [= LGPN III.A, no. 13] and unpublished; see preceding essay, note 81.

[32] K. 547 [= LGPN III.A, no. 17]; see preceding essay, note 125.

[33] K. 558 [= LGPN III.A, no. 20]; see preceding essay, note 43.

[34] M. 154 [= LGPN III.A, no. 14]; see preceding essay, note 112.

[35] K. 561 [= LGPN III.A, no. 21]; see preceding essay, note 121.

Ἀνδρέας s. of Γεώρ[γιος].³⁶   Andreas
Ἀ[νδρέας?].³⁷   A[ndreas?]
Ἀνθίαν[ος?].³⁸   Anthian[os?]
Ἀνθοῦσα.³⁹   Anthousa
[Ἀ]νθοῦσ[α] w. of [- - - -?] and m. of [Μα?]ρία.⁴⁰   [A]nthous[a]
Ἀνίας Σιτευτάριος s. of Παῦλος Σιτευτάριος.⁴¹   Anias
Ἄννα.⁴²   Anna
Ἄννα.⁴³   Anna
[Ἄ]ννα.⁴⁴   [A]nna
[Ἄνν]α? widow of [. .]ώδιος.⁴⁵   Anna
Ἄννα? m. of [Ἐρατο]σθ[ένης?].⁴⁶   Anna?
Ἀν[να?].⁴⁷   An[na?]
[Ἄν]να w. of [- - - -?].⁴⁸   [An]na

---

³⁶ M. 206 [= *LGPN* III.A, no. 16], early 7th century. Find-spot: Northwest Shops.

³⁷ *ArchEph* 1977, no. 15, dated to the 7th century (?). Find-spot: Old Corinth. Only the initial 'A' of this name survives, so the editors' restoration must be regarded as questionable.

³⁸ *Hesperia* 41, no. 31, dated to the 5th or 6th century. Find-spot: FoL. Part of a second name survives in line 3.

³⁹ K. 578 [= Bees, no. 55; *SEG* 11, 180; Feissel 1985b, no. 45; *LGPN* III.A, no. 3], dated early 6th century. Find-spot: Near the Bema in the Agora.

⁴⁰ Unpublished, dated 6th century. Find-spot: Old Corinth. The name of the husband is lost. The hand is the same as that of K. 532; see note 6.

⁴¹ K. 542 [= *LGPN* III.A, no. 1]; see preceding essay, note 109.

⁴² K. 613 [= *LGPN* III.A, no. 2], early 6th century. Find-spot: Bema in agora. Anna owned this tomb; but someone else, her husband or a child, may have been buried in it.

⁴³ Unpublished, early 6th century. Find-spot: FoL. This name is placed in the line immediately above the date of death, so must be that of the deceased. It may be part of the inscription published as *Hesperia* 41, no. 34 (see note 208) since the type of stone and the script seem identical.

⁴⁴ K. 625 [= *LGPN* III.A, no. 3], early 6th century. Find-spot: South Basilica. This Anna was either a single woman or a widow when she purchased this tomb.

⁴⁵ K. 533, early 6th century. Find-spot: Lerna. Kent suggested that this Anna was a widow since she is referred to here as "the wife of the blessed [- -]odios."

⁴⁶ *ArchEph* 1977, no. 29 [= *SEG* 29, 309; *LGPN* III.A, no. 1], dated late 6th century. Find-spot: Hagia Panayia. Pallas and Dantis's restoration of the second name, Anna, is questionable since the last letter of this name in the genitive (Ἄννα[ς]]) is missing. Likewise, their restoration of the first name is highly doubtful since so little of it survives. What is certain, however, is that final line contains the word '*mishkab*' ("tomb"), inscribed in Hebrew letters; thus, we can be certain that these two persons were Jewish.

⁴⁷ K. 672, dated 5th century. Find-spot: Unknown. Bees (no. 57) reported the upper left corner of a second 'N,' but Kent's photograph makes it clear that this does not exist. I have confirmed this by autopsy. Thus, the restoration is questionable as is the sex of the deceased.

⁴⁸ *ArchEph* 1893 (Skias), 126, no. 20 [= *IG* IV.413; EM 4975; Bees, no. 56], dated to the 5th or 6th century. Find-spot: Old Corinth.

Ἀντιοχία m. of Μάξιμος and Μάννους.[49]   Antiochia
Ἀρέτη w. of Ἡσή[δ]ορος.[50]   Arete
Ἀριάγνη w. of Τρύφων.[51]   Ariagne
Ἁρπαλ[ύκη].[52]   (H)arpal[yke?]
Ἀρτέμων Μυλινάριος, seller of a tomb.[53]   Artemon
Αὐ[ρηλίανος?] s. of Διονύσιος and [.....η].[54] Au[relianos?]
Ἀφοβία m. of Ἰωάννης and Ἀγαθοκλῆς.[55]   Aphobia

B (V)

Βαλεριανὸς Πρεσβύτερος.[56]   Valerianos
Βενενᾶτος.[57]   Venenatos
Βικτωρῖνος Δοῦλος Αὐτοκράτορος.[58]   Viktorinos
(Βικτωρῖνος) Δουλεύων Γνησίως.[59]   (Viktorinos)
[Βικτ]ορῖν[ος?].[60]   [Vikt]orin[os?]
Βούδις b. of Ἰωάννις Βουκελλάριος.[61]   Boudis

---

[49] Unpublished, early 6th century. Find-spot: FoL. Antiochia owned this tomb. Her sons Maximos and Mannous were the deceased.

[50] *SEG* 11, 142 [= *LGPN* III.A, no. 4]; see preceding essay, note 71.

[51] *Hesperia* 41, no. 32 [= *LGPN* III.A, no. 1] and unpublished; see preceding essay, note 106. A joining fragment provides the name of Ariagne's husband, Tryphon, and his occupation.

[52] K. 689 [= *LGPN* III.A, no. 1], early 5th century. Find-spot: Hagios Ioannos. This woman was one member of a family or extended family who seem to have been interred in what appears to be a family tomb of the older Roman type. This is one of the few known from Corinth in this period (see also *IG* IV.404; see note 54). Line 4 evidently extends rights to occupancy of the tomb to the offspring and descendants of the persons listed in the first three lines, as if this were a Greek version of the normal Roman epitaph. The other persons listed are Istuleia, [Hos?]tilius, Herm[ione?], and at least one more individual.

[53] *IG* IV.411 [= *LGPN* III.A, no. 16]; see preceding essay, note 119.

[54] *ArchEph* 1893 (Skias), no. 17 [= *IG* IV.404; EM 4972; Bees, no. 42], dated 5th or 6th century. Find-spot: Old Corinth. This is another of the very few Corinthian family tombs known from this period; see note 52.

[55] K. 531 [= *LGPN* III.A, no. 1]; see note 4.

[56] *Prakt.* 1961, 132, εἰκ. 3b [= *LGPN* III.A, no. 1]; see preceding essay, note 65.

[57] *Hesperia* 38, 93 [= Feissel 1985b, no. 89], dated 5th or 6th century. Find-spot: FoL.

[58] K. 508; see preceding essay, note 42.

[59] *IG* IV.205 [= *LGPN* III.A, no. 1]; see preceding essay, note 42.

[60] *Prakt.* 1961, 132, εἰκ. 3γ, 527–65. Find-spot: Kodratos Basilica. The inscription has not been published except in a photograph printed by Stikas (1964). Of the name of the deceased, the middle four letters are partially preserved. I think that this man may be Biktorinos; see notes 58–59.

[61] M. 207 [= *LGPN* III.A, no. 1, with the spelling Βούδιος]; see preceding essay, note 33.

Γ

[Γε]νεθλία.[62]   [Ge]nethlia

[Γεν]εθλί[α?].[63]   [Gen]ethli[a?]

Φλ(άβιος) Γενεθλίδ(ιος) Ἰοῦστος.[64]   Genethlid(ios)

Γεόργιος h. of Εὐμορφία.[65]   Gheorghios

Γερ[μα]νός.[66]   Ger[ma]nos

Γεωργία d. of Κλημ[- -?].[67]   Gheorghia

Γεώργιος Δεκανός h. of Εὐτυχιανή.[68]   Gheorghios

Γε[ώργι]ος Τρα[πεζί]της Κοδρυ[- -?].[69]   Ghe[orghi]os

Γεώρ[γιος] f. of Ἀνδρέας.[70]   Gheor[ghios]

[Γεώρ?]γιος Σ[ιρικο]π(ο)ιός.[71]   [Gheor]ghios

[Γεώρ?]γιος h.? of [- -]ολια?[72]   [Gheor?]ghios

Γλαῦ[κος?] [Κ]υδώ[νιας].[73]   Glau[kos?]

Γράτος Λαμ(πρότατος).[74]   Gratos

---

[62] M. 170 [= Bees, no. 58; *SEG* 11, 103; *LGPN* III.A, no. 1] and *SEG* 11, 103. Dated early 5th century. Find-spot: Unknown.

[63] K. 527 [= Bees, no. 58A; *LGPN* III.A, no. 2], 6th century. Find-spot: Lerna Court.

[64] K. 516 [= Feissel 1985b, no. 50; *LGPN* III.A, no. 1], 5th or 6th century. Find-spot: Hagia Ioannes.

[65] M. 200, early 7th century. Find-spot: Northwest Shops.

[66] K. 575 [= Bees, no. 59; *SEG* 11, 181], dated mid 5th century. Find-spot: South Stoa. Kent noted, correctly, that the word missing in line 3 was likely to be the name of this man's occupation rather than a patronymic although he left open the question whether the wife of Germanos may have been named here instead (if there is sufficient space). Both the script and the type of stone suggest a date in the mid 5th century. The marble from which this gravestone was made is a distinctive blue with white streaks, probably imported as decoration for some public building, and was employed for several other Corinthian gravestones, all of which are therefore likely to be of much the same date; M. 145, note 222, securely dated to 445/6 CE; *LGPN* III.A, no. 2.

[67] K. 646 [= Bees, no. 60; *SEG* 11, 182; *LGPN* III.A, no. 1], early 6th century. Find-spot: Theater. Kent's text supersedes Bees's unlikely restorations.

[68] K. 556 [= *LGPN* III.A, no. 4]; see preceding essay, note 60.

[69] K. 640; see preceding essay, note 120.

[70] M. 206 [= *LGPN* III.A, no. 1]; see note 36.

[71] Unpublished; see preceding essay, note 116.

[72] Unpublished, late 6th or early 7th century. Find-spot: Unknown. The available space demands that this man's name is either [Γεώρ]γιος or [Κυνή]γιος. The next line probably contains the name of his wife.

[73] K. 648; see preceding essay, note 127.

[74] *Prakt.* 1962, 52 [= *LGPN* III.A, no. 1]; see preceding essay, note 44.

Δ

[Δα]μασεῖος.⁷⁵   [Da]maseios
Δεύτε[ρα?] [Δού]λη Ἀγίας Τ[ριάδος].⁷⁶   Deute[ra?]
Δημήτριος Δοῦλος Χ(ριστο)ῦ.⁷⁷   Demetrios
Δημήτριος Ἀλίπτης.⁷⁸   Demetrios
Διογενία[νος?] ex-prefect and s. of Ἰρηναῖος.⁷⁹   Diogenia[nos?]
Διονοί[σα] d. of Διονύσιο[ς].⁸⁰   Dionoi[sa]
Διονύσιος h. of [.....η].⁸¹   Dionysios
Διονύσιος f. of Διονοί[σα].⁸²   Dionysios
Διονύσιος s. of Διονύσιος & [.....η].⁸³   Dionysios
[Δι]ωνυσίς.⁸⁴   [Di]onysis

E

Εἰριῶν, seller of a tomb.⁸⁵   Eirion
Ἑλένη d./sis. of Ῥουφῖνος and Μαρία.⁸⁶   (H)elene
[Ἔ]λενος Χρε[α]τοκοπ[οιός?].⁸⁷   [(H)]elenos
Ἐλπιδιανός h. of Θωμαδία.⁸⁸   Elpidianos

---

⁷⁵ *Prakt.* 1961, 154, εἰκ. 101β. Dated to the 5th or 6th century. Find-spot: painted on a wall of the Lechaion Basilica.

⁷⁶ K. 583; see preceding essay, note 62.

⁷⁷ M. 196 [= *LGPN* III.A, no. 44]; see preceding essay, note 70.

⁷⁸ Unpublished; see preceding essay, note 82.

⁷⁹ M. 157 [= *LGPN* III.A, no. 1]; see preceding essay, note 20.

⁸⁰ *IG* IV.404 [= *LGPN* III.A, no. 1, with the spelling Διόνυσα]; see note 54.

⁸¹ *IG* IV.404 [= *LGPN* III.A, no. 1]; see note 54.

⁸² *IG* IV.404 [= *LGPN* III.A, no. 169]; see note 54.

⁸³ *IG* IV.404; see note 54.

⁸⁴ K. 544 [= *LGPN* III.A, no. 2, with the spelling Διονυσίς], early 6th century. Find-spot: Lerna Court. Kent noted that this text did "not correspond to any other Corinthian sepulchral text." He made no attempt to restore anything except the standard formula [μα]κ̣αρίαν [μνήμην] in lines 2–3. Robert (1966, 763) restored a name, [Δι]ωνυσίς, in line 3.

⁸⁵ K. 551 [= *LGPN* III.A, no. 1, under Σιριῶν]; see preceding essay, note 108. Bees read the seller's name as Σιρίων; Kent read it as Γιρίων. In fact, the initial letter is an 'E' and the name is Εἰρίων.

⁸⁶ K. 564 [=*LGPN* III.A, no. 2; Feissel 1985b, no. 68], dated early 5th century. Find-spot: Lerna Court. I think that Kent is too sanguine in suggesting that the three deceased "presumably died at different times." Either this is a family tomb, as Kent's interpretation implies; or the deceased are the three children of Mattheas; or his son, daughter, spouse, and grandchild. In any case, all died from the same cause, perhaps plague or earthquake.

⁸⁷ Unpublished; see preceding essay, note 117.

⁸⁸ K. 664 [= *IG* IV.403; Bees 126, no. 64; *SEG* 11, 186; Feissel 1985b, no. 1], dated to the 6th century. Find-spot: Acrocorinth. Since the script is much like that of K. 597 (see note 89), I wonder whether this man is the same Elpidianos; *LGPN* III.A, no. 1.

['Ελπι]διανό[ς?].[89]   [Elpi]dianos
['Εό]ρτιος h. of [Πρ]ονία.[90]   [(H)eo]rtios
Ἐπαγαθώ m./d. of Ἀγαθοκλία.[91]   Epagatho
Ἐπαφροδίτη w. of Ἀθηνόδωρος.[92]   Epaphrodite
Ἐπιφάνιος.[93]   Epiphanios
Ἐ[πι]φάνιος Ἀποδρεπ[αντής]?[94]   E[pi]phanios
['Ερατο]σθ[ένης?] s. of Ἄννα?[95]   [Erato]sth[enes?]
Ἐρμ[ίονη?].[96]   (H)erm[ione]
Εὐγένια w. of Ἀνδρέας and m. of Ἀναστασία.[97]   Eugenia
[Ε]ὐγένια w. of [- -]τια[- -?].[98]   [E]ugenia
Εὐγένιος.[99]   Eugenios
Εὐκάρης.[100]   Eukares
Εὐμορφία w. of Γεόργιος.[101]   Eumorphia
Εὐόδ[ιος?].[102]   Euod[ios?]

_____

[89] K. 597 [= Bees, no. 64A], dated 5th or 6th century. Find-spot: Central Shops. The hand is virtually the same as that of K. 664; see note 88. Thus, this should be of or about the same date.

[90] *ArchEph* 1893 (Skias), no. 14 [= *IG* IV.406; EM 4974; Bees, no. 65], dated 5th century. Find-spot: Old Corinth.

[91] K. 532 [= *LGPN* III.A, no. 1]; see note 6.

[92] *IG* IV.405 [= *LGPN* III.A, no. 1]; see note 11.

[93] K. 568 [= Bees, no. 7; *SEG* 11, 159; Feissel 1985b, no. 28], dated to 5th century. Find-spot: South Stoa. This is not a gravestone but a prayer. Kent noted that its top bore a circular relief or insert. I wonder whether this bore a *christogram* within a wreath. Epiphanios calls himself a δοῦλος, a term that very likely implies that he held some sort of official position in the church. de Waele, quoted by Bees (20) thought that he might have been a bishop, but Bees himself thought that unlikely; *LGPN* III. A, no. 2.

[94] *Hesperia* 41, no. 34 and unpublished; see preceding essay, note 86.

[95] *ArchEph* 1977, no. 29; see note 46.

[96] K. 689; see note 52.

[97] K. 561 [= *LGPN* III.A, under spelling Εὐγένεια]; see preceding essay, note 121.

[98] K. 686 [= *LGPN* III.A, no. 1, under spelling Εὐγένεια], dated to 5th century. Find-spot: Temple E. Kent's text is misleading. The leaf carved at the bottom lies below the 'E' of Eugenia's name and is thus centered on the stone, as normal. Thus, there was no second leaf as Kent prints in brackets at the left. The name of Eugenia's husband (?), whose surviving letters lie in line 1 above the 'Γ, E, and N' of her name in line 2, is considerably longer than Kent's text implies. The husband's name may well be one of those ending in -τίανος.

[99] *Prakt.* 1962, 54, εἰκ. 50 [= Feissel 1985b, no. 87], dated 4th or 5th century. Find-spot: Kodratos Basilica. This man was a native of Nikopolis but died at Corinth. As Feissel remarked, it is impossible to say from which city named Nikopolis he came. His epitaph ends with an *anathema*, restored by Robert and Robert (1965, 162); *LGPN* III.A, no. 1.

[100] K. 684 [= *LGPN* III.A, no. 2, under the spelling Εὐχάρης], early 7th century. Find-spot: Asklepieion.

[101] M. 200 [= *LGPN* III.A, no. 2]; see note 65.

[102] Unpublished, dated early 5th century. Find-spot: Panayia south. The elegant script and the use of the older 'Roman' system of dating suggest a relatively early date.

Εὔπλους Ἡνίοχος.[103]   Euplous
Εὐσέβιος Καμισογοραστής, Σολίτης.[104]   Eusebios
[Εὐσέβιος?] Ἀνα[τολικὸς] Καμισα[γοραστής].[105] [Eusebios?]
Εὐστάθιος Ἐπίσκοπος.[106]   Eustathios
Εὐστάθ[ιος?].[107]   Eustath[ios?]
Εὐτυ[χαί]α w. of [...]ιος.[108]   Euty[chai]a
Εὐτύχη w. of Χρυσέρως.[109]   Eutyche
Εὐτυχ[ιανή] w. of Ἀλέξ[ανδρος?].[110]   Eutych[iane]
Εὐτυχιανή w. of Γεώργιος Δεκανός.[111]   Eutychiane
Εὐφρασία w. of Κωνστά[ντιν]ος.[112]   Euphrasia
Εὐφ[ρασία?].[113]   Euph[rasia?]

Z

Ζήνων [Διάκονος?].[114]   Zenon
Ζοή.[115]   Zoe
Ζοή d. of [- -?].[116]   Zoe

---

[103] K. 530 [= *LGPN* III.A, no. 2]; see preceding essay, note 72.

[104] K. 522 [= *LGPN* III.A, no. 2, where Ἀνατολικός is listed as a patronymic]; see preceding essay, note 100.

[105] M. 193; see preceding essay, note 101.

[106] *Prakt.* 1961, 131–32, εἰκ. 3α [= *LGPN* III.A, no. 2]; see preceding essay, note 54.

[107] M. 189 [= *LGPN* III.A, no. 1], dated 5th or 6th century. Find-spot: Hagia Paraskevi.

[108] K. 543 [= *LGPN* III.A, no. 1], early 6th century. Find-spot: Asklepieion. Kent suggested that the husband's name in line 3 might be [Παῦλ]ος but admitted that "there are a few other possibilities." However, the trace of a letter visible on the stone before the 'Ο' of this name cannot be part of a 'Λ.' It is the top of a central vertical, probably therefore of an 'Ι.' Even so, there are not "few" but many possibilities.

[109] M. 160 [= *LGPN* III.A, no. 2], early 7th century. Find-spot: Unknown.

[110] K. 650 [= *LGPN* III.A, no. 4]; see note 18.

[111] K. 556 [= *LGPN* III.A, no. 3]; see preceding essay, note 60.

[112] K. 589 [= Feissel 1985b, no. 70; *LGPN* III.A, no. 1], dated mid 5th century. Find-spot: South Stoa. This tomb held three interments to judge from its text: Konstantinos; his wife, Euphrasia; and their child, whose name has not survived (line 6) but who was probably a boy. The marble of this gravestone is of the same type as M. 145 (see note 222) and should probably be placed at about the same time.

[113] *ArchEph* 1977, no. 6 [= *SEG* 29, 310; Feissel 1985b no. 15]. Find-spot: Kokkinovrysi. This gravestone is securely dated to 533. The green schisty marble from which this gravestone is made is an exotic stone that was brought to Corinth late in the 5th or early in the 6th century for the decoration of important public buildings. Thus, this and the many similar plaques probably date to the early 6th century; Walbank and Walbank 2006, 286.

[114] M. 192 [= *LGPN* III.A, no. 16]; see preceding essay, note 58.

[115] K. 660 [= Bees, no. 22; *SEG* 11, 164; *LGPN* III.A, no. 1, under the spelling Ζώη], early 5th century. Find-spot: Old Corinth.

[116] *ArchEph* 1977, no. 8 [= *LGPN* III.A, no. 2, under the spelling Ζώη], dated 6th or 7th century. Find-spot: Kraneion.

H (E or I)

'Ηλίας h. of Φιλοξένα.[117]   Elias
'Ησή[δ]ορος Δοῦλος h. of Ἀρετή.[118]   Isi[d]oros

Θ

[Θεμι]στοκλῆς [Μου]σοπόλος.[119]   [Themi]stokles
Θεοδόρο[ς].[120]   Theodoro[s]
Θεωδοσία.[121]   Theodosia
[Θε]ωδ[οσία?].[122]   [The]od[osia?]
Θεοδόσ[ιος Πατρίκιος ἐνδοξότατος].[123]   Theodos[ios]
[Θεο]δόσ[ιος?] s. of [- -]νίανος.[124]   [Theo]dos[ios?]
Θεοδοῦλος.[125]   Theodoulos
[Θ]εόδωρα.[126]   [Th]eodora
Θεόδωρος Μωλίων.[127]   Theodoros
Θεόδωρος Μουλίων Ἐπισκοπιανοῦ.[128]   Theodoros
[Θεό]δωρος Δομ[έστικος τοῦ θίου] παλατίου κ(αὶ)
    βασιλικ[οῦ ἐξκουβί]του Γνησ[ίως Δουλεύο]ντος.[129]   Theodoros
Θεόμνισθος f. of Θεοσέβια.[130]   Theomnisthos

---

[117] *Hesperia* 36, 423. Dated 522 or 597 CE. Find-spot: FoL. Feissel (1985b, no. 88) pointed out that the script and archaeological context of this inscription rule out any date before 522; *LGPN* III.A, no. 1. This is the only gravestone found *in situ* in this area.

[118] *SEG* 11, 142 [= *LGPN* III.A, no. 1, under the spelling Ἰσίδωρος]; see preceding essay, note 71.

[119] *Prakt.* 1977A, 173–75 no. 2 [= *LGPN* III.A, no. 1, under the spelling [Ἀρι]στοκλῆς]; see preceding essay, note 79.

[120] Unpublished, dated 5th or 6th century. Find-spot: Acrocorinth. This is a fragment of a panel on which an intaglio cross is surrounded by an inscribed roundel.

[121] K. 562 [= Feissel 1985b, no. 66; and *LGPN* III.A, no. 1, under the spelling Θεοδοσία], dated early 6th century. Find-spot: Asklepieion. The marble of this gravestone is of the same type as *ArchEph* 1977 no. 6 (see preceding essay, note 113) and should probably be placed at about the same time.

[122] *ArchEph* 1977, no. 14, dated 6th or 7th century. Find-spot: Old Corinth.

[123] K. 509 [= *LGPN* III.A, no. 3]; see preceding essay, note 22.

[124] Unpublished, dated early 6th century. Find-spot: Near the Amphitheater.

[125] K. 661 [= Feissel 1985b, no. 81; *LGPN* III.A, no. 1], early 6th century. Find-spot: Unknown.

[126] K. 705 [= *LGPN* III.A, no. 11], dated 6th or 7th century. Find-spot: New Corinth.

[127] *ArchEph* 1977, Προσθήκη; see preceding essay, note 41.

[128] *ArchEph* 1977 no. 8 [= *LGPN* III.A, no. 61, listing Ἐπισκοπιανός as this man's father]; see preceding essay, note 56.

[129] *SEG* 11, 52a; see preceding essay, note 36.

[130] *IG* XII.5.565 [= *LGPN* III.A, no. 3, under Θεόμνηστος], 4th or 5th century; a Corinthian whose daughter died abroad.

Θεοσέβια d. of Θεόμνισθος.[131]	Theosebia
Θράσιππος Ἰητῆρ, Ποιητάς.[132]	Thrasippos
Θῶμα Πρεσβύτερος.[133]	Thomas
Θωμαδία w. of Ἐλπιδιανός.[134]	Thomadia

I (Hɪ, or J)

Ἰανουάριος Πατρίκιος ἐνδοξότατος.[135]	Ianouarios
Ἰουλιανός Ἐγιάριος.[136]	Ioulianos
Ἰουλιανός Βαλ[νι]κάριος.[137]	Ioulianos
Γ(αῖος) Ἰούλιος Ῥάβ[δουχος].[138]	Ioulios
[Ἱπ]πόλυτος.[139]	(H)ip]polytos
Ἰρηναῖος f. of Διογενία[νος?].[140]	Irenaios
Ἰσ[οκράτης?].[141]	Is[okrates?]
Ἰστληία[142]	Istleia
Ἰωάνης s. of Ἀφοβία.[143]	Ioanes
Ἰωάννα d. of Ἰωάννης and Μαρία.[144]	Ioanna
Ἰωάννης.[145]	Ioannes
Ἰωάν[νης], seller of a tomb.[146]	Ioan[nes]
Ἰωάννης Κραμβιτάς.[147]	Ioannes
[Ἰωάν]νης Μιζότερος.[148]	Ioannes
[Ἰω]άννης b. of Λο[ύκιος] and Ὠφέλιμος.[149]	[Io]annes

---

[131] IG XII.5.565 [= LGPN III.A, no. 3, under Θεοσέβεια]; see note 130. Married daughter of a Corinthian who died at Kartheia on Keos.

[132] K. 300 [= LGPN III.A, no. 4]; see preceding essay, note 84.

[133] Prakt. 1956, 173; see preceding essay, note 68.

[134] K. 664 [= LGPN III.A, no. 1]; see note 88.

[135] K. 509 and CIG 8824; see preceding essay, note 22; LGPN III.A, no. 1.

[136] K. 587 [= LGPN III.A, no. 5]; see preceding essay, note 107.

[137] K. 534 [= LGPN III.A, no. 4]; see preceding essay, note 24.

[138] K. 518; see preceding essay, note 26.

[139] Unpublished, dated 6th or 7th century. Find-spot: Near the amphitheater.

[140] M. 157 [= LGPN III.A, no. 1, under the spelling Εἰρηναῖος]; see preceding essay, note 20.

[141] ArchEph 1977, no. 4, dated 5th century. Find-spot: Cheliotomylos.

[142] K. 689; see note 52.

[143] K. 531 [= LGPN III.A, no. 14, under Ἰωάννης]; see note 4.

[144] ArchEph 1977, no. 3 [= SEG 29, 315; Feissel 1985b, no. 99; LGPN III.A, no. 1], dated early 6th century. Find-spot: Kraneion Basilica.

[145] K. 721 [= Robert 1966, 770; LGPN III.A, no. 11], dated 6th or 7th century. Find-spot: South of South Basilica.

[146] IG IV.404 [= LGPN III.A, no. 12]; see note 54.

[147] K. 563 [= LGPN III.A, no. 9]; see preceding essay, note 74.

[148] ArchEph 1977, no. 11; see preceding essay, note 64.

[149] ArchEph 1893 (Skias), no. 16 [= IG IV.408], dated 5th or 6th century. Find-spot: Old Corinth, now apparently lost.

Ἰωάννης h. of Μαρία and f. of Ἰωάννα.[150]   Ioannes
Ἰω[άννης?].[151]   Io[annes?]
Ἰωάννις b. of Βούδις Βουκελλάριος.[152]   Ioannis

K

Καλλίστη.[153]   Kalliste
Καλωγενήτης f. of Λαυρέ<ν>τιος, and g.-f.
  of Παῦλα.[154]   Kalogenetes
Κέρδων b. of Ἀγαπωμένη? and Ἀγαπώμενος?[155]   Kerdon
Κλεοπ[άτρα?].[156]   Kleop[atra?]
Κόκκος f. of Πανχάριος.[157]   Kokkos
Κορινθᾶς Ἱπποιατρός.[158]   Korinthas
Κοσμᾶς Κάπηλος.[159]   Kosmas
Κο[σμόδωρος?], seller of a tomb.[160]   Ko[smodoros?]
Κυριακὸς Φασανάριος.[161]   Kyriakos
Κυριακὸς [Πλακουντ]άριος.[162]   Kyriakos
Κωνστά[ντιν]ος h. of Εὐφρασία.[163]   Konst[antin]os

---

[150] *ArchEph* 1977, no. 3 [= *LGPN* III.A, no. 13]; see note 144.

[151] K. 605 [= *LGPN* III.A, no. 10], early 6th century. Find-spot: Central Shops.

[152] M. 207 [= *LGPN* III.A, no. 8, under the spelling Ἰωάννης]; see preceding essay, note 33.

[153] K. 557 [= Feissel 1985b, no. 63], dated mid 5th century. Find-spot: Lerna Court. For another fragment of streaky, blue and white marble, and possibly of comparable date, see M. 145 (see note 222) and *LGPN* III.A, no. 2.

[154] K. 560 [= Feissel 1985b, no. 65; *LGPN* III.A, no. 2, under spelling Καλογένητος], early 6th century. Find-spot: Asklepieion. See Robert (1966, 765) for a parallel from Beroia for this name.

[155] M. 136 [= *LGPN* III.A, no. 24]; see note 2.

[156] K. 685, dated 6th or 7th century. Find-spot: Old Corinth. Kent noted that the letter-traces permit restoration of the name Κλεοπ[άτρα], as here, or Κλεογ[ένης]; however, the last surviving letter in this line is almost certainly a 'Π,' not a 'Γ.'

[157] *SEG* 13, 228 [= *SEG* 22, 223; *LGPN* III.A, no. 1], dated early 6th century. Find-spot: Kraneion. This is another metrical epigram from the Kraneion Basilica.

[158] *SEG* 35, 256 [= *LGPN* III.A, no. 2]; see preceding essay, note 85.

[159] K. 525 [= *LGPN* III.A, no. 2]; see preceding essay, note 115.

[160] K. 595 [= *SEG* 11, 173; *LGPN* III.A, no. 2], dated 5th or 6th century. Find-spot: Agora. Bees (no. 39) restored this name as Κο[σμᾶς]. The more likely restoration is that of Kent.

[161] K. 561 [= *LGPN* III.A, no. 3]; see preceding essay, note 121.

[162] *ArchEph* 1977, no. 5 [= *LGPN* III.A, no. 5]; see preceding essay, note 104.

[163] K. 589 [= *LGPN* III.A, no. 1]; see note 112.

Λ

Λαυρέ<ν>τιος s. of Καλωγενήτης and f. of Παῦλα.[164]	Laurentios
Λεων[ί]ας.[165]	Leon[e]as
Λεονίδιος Λευκαντής.[166]	Leonidios
Λουκᾶς Ἐξκ(ουβίτωρ), purchaser of a tomb.[167]	Loukas
Λουκίανος Δηίκονος.[168]	Loukianos
Λο[ύκιος] b. of ['Ιω]άννης and Ὠφέλιμος.[169]	Lo[ukios]

Μ

Μαθθέας f. of 'Ρουφῖνος and Μαρία.[170]	Mattheas
[Μ]αθθ[έας?].[171]	[M]atth[eas?]
Μακεδόνια.[172]	Makedonia
Μακεδόνιος.[173]	Makedonios
Μάννους s. of Ἀντιοχία.[174]	Mannous
Μάξιμος.[175]	Maximos
Μάξιμος s. of Ἀντιοχία.[176]	Maximos
Μαρία w. of Εὔπλους.[177]	Maria
Μαρία w. of 'Ιωάννης and m. of 'Ιωάννα.[178]	Maria
Μαρία w./sis. of 'Ρουφῖνος.[179]	Maria
[Μα?]ρία d. of [- - -?] and [Ἀ]νθούσ[α].[180]	[Ma?]ria

---

[164] K. 560 [= *LGPN* III.A, no. 1]; see note 154.

[165] M. 200 [= *LGPN* III.A, no. 5, under spelling Λεωνᾶς]; see note 65. Feissel (1985b, no. 19) suggested Λεων(τι)ανό(ς).

[166] K. 522 [= *LGPN* III.A, no. 1]; see preceding essay, note 94.

[167] K. 558 [= *LGPN* III.A, no. 3]; see preceding essay, note 32.

[168] *Prakt.* 1961, 154, πιν. 101β; see preceding essay, note 57.

[169] *IG* IV.408; see note 149.

[170] K. 564 [= *LGPN* III.A, no. 1]; see note 86.

[171] Unpublished, early 5th century. Find-spot: Unknown. The surviving letters in the second line appear to derive from a name such as [Μ]αθθ[έας].

[172] K. 644 [= Bees, no. 17; *SEG* 11, 160; Feissel 1985b, no. 29; *LGPN* III.A, no. 1], dated 5th or 6th century. Find-spot: Theater; see preceding essay, note 19.

[173] K. 602 [= Feissel 1985b, no. 71; *LGPN* III.A, no. 1], early 6th century. Find-spot: Temple H.

[174] Unpublished; see note 49.

[175] K. 540 [= *LGPN* III.A, no. 4]; see preceding essay, note 124. The relationship between the *Salgamarios* and Maximos is unknown; possibly, they were relatives; equally possibly, the *Salgamarios* sold this corner of his tomb to Maximos.

[176] Unpublished; see note 49.

[177] K. 530 [= *LGPN* III.A, no. 3]; see preceding essay, note 72.

[178] *ArchEph* 1977, no. 3 [= *LGPN* III.A, no. 4]; see note 150.

[179] K. 564 [= *LGPN* III.A, no. 2]; see note 170.

[180] Unpublished; see note 40.

Μάρινος s. of [- - -?] Κουρεύς and b. of [- - -]ωρος.¹⁸¹   Marinos
Μάρινος.¹⁸²   Marinos
[Μ]άρινο[ς?].¹⁸³   [M]arino[s?]
Μαρκέλλινος.¹⁸⁴   Markellinos
Μάρκελλος h. of Χαρίσση.¹⁸⁵   Markellos
Μαρτ[υρία] w. of ['Ιωάν]νης.¹⁸⁶   Mart[yria]
Μαρτύρ[ιος] h.? of Κα[- - - -?].¹⁸⁷   Martyr[ios]
Μαυρίκιος Γουνάριος.¹⁸⁸   Maurikios
Μνασέας [Λαμπρό]τατος ἀπὸ [ὑπάτων].¹⁸⁹   Mnaseas
Μνασέας Καμι[σογαραστής?].¹⁹⁰   Mnaseas
[Μοδέ?]στος.¹⁹¹   [Mode?]stos

N

Νεικίης Ὀρθόγραφος s. of Ἀλέξανδρος.¹⁹²   Neikies
Νεῦ[να?] w. of Α[- - -?] and m. of Ἀ[ναστα]σία.¹⁹³   Neu[na?]
Νικέας [Λί]βανος?¹⁹⁴   Nikias
Νικόστρατος Μαρμαράριος.¹⁹⁵   Nikostratos
Νόννο[ς?].¹⁹⁶   Nonno[s?]
Νουμένις s. of Εὐσέβιος Ἀνατολικός.¹⁹⁷   Noumenis

---

¹⁸¹ K. 722 [= *LGPN* III.A, no. 2]; see preceding essay, note 96.
¹⁸² M. 215 [= *LGPN* III.A, no. 1], early 7th century. Find-spot: Northwest Shops.
¹⁸³ K. 601, early 6th century. Find-spot: Agora Northeast. Kent left this name unrestored. I suggest that the correct reading here is [δι]αφ[έρον|τα Μ]αρίνο[υ]. For the probable date, based on the stone, see M. 145 (see note 222).
¹⁸⁴ *ArchEph* 1977, no. 10 [= *LGPN* III.A, no. 1]; see preceding essay, note 25.
¹⁸⁵ Unpublished, dated early 6th century. Find-spot: Fountain of the Lamps.
¹⁸⁶ *ArchEph* 1977, no. 11; see note 148.
¹⁸⁷ K. 576, late 5th century. Find-spot: South Stoa. Kent restored [το]ῦ μάρτυρ[ος]. Since this is a gravestone, a reference to a martyr seems unlikely; and I suggest that the reading is, in fact, [ἡ γύνη το]ῦ Μαρτυρ[ίου]: "the wife of Martyrios."
¹⁸⁸ M. 148 [= *LGPN* III.A, no. 1]; see preceding essay, note 114.
¹⁸⁹ K. 673 [= *LGPN* III.A, no. 12]; see preceding essay, note 45.
¹⁹⁰ M. 191 [= *LGPN* III.A, no. 11]; see preceding essay, note 99.
¹⁹¹ *Prakt.* 1961, 154, πιν. 101β, dated 6th century. Find-spot: Lechaion Basilica.
¹⁹² K. 305; see preceding essay, note 28.
¹⁹³ K. 666; see note 23.
¹⁹⁴ K. 550 [= *LGPN* III.A, no. 16]; see preceding essay, note 113.
¹⁹⁵ *ArchEph* 1977, Προσθήκη [= *LGPN* III.A, no. 67]; see preceding essay, note 88.
¹⁹⁶ K. 707, dated early 6th century. Find-spot: Unknown. Kent left this unrestored. However, it appears to be a gravestone on which parts of two or three names are preserved. The script is almost identical to that of K. 550 (see preceding essay, note 113); and this should therefore be of about the same date. The name Νόννος is attested for Corinth only so far in the Hellenistic era but is also found in Late Roman and Byzantine times in Karpathos and in Cyrenaica; *LGPN* I, 340.
¹⁹⁷ K. 522; see preceding essay, note 100. Robert (1966, 761–62) corrected Kent's suggestion that the name of Eusebios's son (?) Νουμένις might be of Jewish origin.

O

[Ὁσ]τίλιος.¹⁹⁸   [(H)os]tilios

Π

Πανχάριος s. of Κόκκος.¹⁹⁹   Pancharios
Πασκασία.²⁰⁰   Paskasia
Παῦλα d. of Λαυρέ<ν>τιος and g.-d.
  of Καλωγενήτης.²⁰¹   Paula
Παύλινα.²⁰²   Paulina
Παῦλος Δομέστικος Λαμπρότατος.²⁰³   Paulos
Παῦλος Πρεσβύτερος καὶ Δοῦλος.²⁰⁴   Paulos
Παῦλος Ῥάπτης f. of Σωτηρὶς Ῥάπτης.²⁰⁵   Paulos
Παῦλος Σιτευτάριος f. of Ἀνίας Σιτευτάριος.²⁰⁶ Paulos
Παῦλος Μ[α]κρόχει[ρ] Σιτιστάριος.²⁰⁷   Paulos
Παῦλος, seller of a tomb.²⁰⁸   Paulos
Παυσ[ίμαχ?]ος.²⁰⁹   Paus[imach?]os
Πέτρος s. of Σέργιος.²¹⁰   Petros
[Πέτ]ρος Ταξε[ώ]τ[ης].²¹¹   Petros

This name is merely a phonetic rendition of Νουμήνιος; *LGPN* III.A, no. 2, under spelling Νουμήνις.

¹⁹⁸ K. 689; see note 52.
¹⁹⁹ *SEG* 13, 228; and 22, 223; see note 157.
²⁰⁰ K. 545 [= Feissel 1985b, no. 61; *LGPN* III.A, no. 1, under spelling Πασχασία], early 6th century. Find-spot: Asklepieion.
²⁰¹ K. 560 [= *LGPN* III.A, no. 3]; see note 154.
²⁰² *Prakt.* 1962, 53 [= Feissel 1985b, no. 85; *LGPN* III.A, no. 1], dated 5th century. Find-spot: Kodratos Basilica.
²⁰³ K. 509 and *CIG* 8824; see preceding essay, note 22; *LGPN* III.A, no. 7.
²⁰⁴ *Prakt.* 1956, 171; see preceding essay, note 67.
²⁰⁵ *Hesperia* 41, no. 33 [= *LGPN* III.A, no. 4]; see preceding essay, note 128.
²⁰⁶ K. 542 [= *LGPN* III.A, no. 6]; see preceding essay, note 109.
²⁰⁷ K. 559 [= *LGPN* III.A, no. 5]; see preceding essay, note 111.
²⁰⁸ *Hesperia* 41, no. 34; see preceding essay, note 86. Wiseman noted "traces" in line 5. In fact, the tops of six letters survive and can be read as the name Παῦλος in the genitive.
²⁰⁹ K. 535 [= Bees, no. 25; *SEG* 11, 166], dated early 5th century. Find-spot: Asklepieion. Since the stone breaks at right on the curve of a circular or semicircular letter in line 1, Bees's conjecture Παῦ[λος] is impossible. Kent suggests "Παυσ[ίμαχ]ος, Παυσ[ίλυπ]ος, *vel sim.*"
²¹⁰ Pallas 1980 in *Prakt.* (1977), 174–75 [= *SEG* 29, 318], 5th century. Find-spot: Kraneion Basilica. This is metrical epigram for Petros, dead of plague at the age of twenty, far from his home, somewhere in the East, where he had gone alone. It was set up by his father Sergios; see also *LGPN* III.A, no. 4.
²¹¹ M. 153 [= *LGPN* III.A, no. 2]; see preceding essay, note 38.

Πέτρ[ος?] f. of an unknown child.[212] Petr[os?]
Πετρουνία?[213]   Petrounia(?)
Πλ[ευρᾶ]τος? Χευ[ματοποιητής?].[214]   Pl[eura]tos(?)
Πολυχρόνιος Σινγουλάριος.[215]   Polychronios
Πολυχρ[όνιος?].[216]   Polychr[onios?]
Πούλ[ος?] [- -]ξα[- -?].[217]   Poul[os?]
[Πρ]ονία w. of [Ἑό]ρτιος.[218]   [Pr]onia

P

Ῥουφῖνος s. of Μαθθέας and h./b. of Μαρία.[219]   Rouphinos
Ῥωμανὸς Βουλευτής.[220]   Romanos

Σ

Σεκουνδῖνος.[221]   Sekoundinos
Σελή[νη?].[222]   Sele[ne?]
Σ[ερα?]πίων.[223]   S[era?]pion
Σέργιος f. of Πέτρος.[224] Serghios

---

[212] K. 595 [= LGPN III.A, no. 3]; see note 160.

[213] M. 215 [= LGPN III.A, no. 1, under spelling Πετρωνία]; may be either a personal name or a place-name.

[214] K. 653; see preceding essay, note 89.

[215] ArchEph 1977, no. 2 [= LGPN III.A, no. 2]; see preceding essay, note 39.

[216] M. 183, dated early 6th century. Find-spot: Agora East. Meritt offered no restorations but clearly thought that a name began in line 2. The name is probably Polychr[onios]; LGPN III.A, no. 1.

[217] K. 621; see preceding essay, 138.

[218] IG IV.406; see note 90.

[219] K. 564 [= LGPN III.A, no. 3]; see note 86.

[220] K. 657 [= LGPN III.A, no. 1]; see preceding essay, note 29.

[221] ArchEph 1977, no. 1 [= SEG 28 390; LGPN III.A, no. 2], dated 5th or 6th century. Find-spot: Tenea. This inscription was found near Tenea in the southern Corinthia and first published by Wiseman (1978, 91–93 and 96). Pallas and Dantis were unaware of the earlier publication.

[222] M. 145, dated 445/6 CE. Find-spot: Agora East. Feissel (1981, 491–93; 1985a, no. 13) discusses lines 4–7 at length, concluding that the date is probably the postconsulate year of the Emperor Flavius Valentinian III, consul for the sixth time in 446 (?). The marble from which this gravestone was made is a distinctive blue with white streaks, probably imported as decoration for some public building and was employed for several other Corinthian gravestones, all of which are therefore likely to be of much the same date; LGPN III.A, no. 1.

[223] Unpublished, dated 6th century. Find-spot: Unknown. This is an unlikely name to be found in a Christian epitaph; and it is not, so far, attested at any time in Corinth.

[224] SEG 29, 318 [= LGPN III.A, no. 1]; see note 210.

Σολομὼ[ν] Πολυκα[νδήλους?].[225]   Solomo[n]
[Σπ]άρτη.[226]   [Sp]arte
Στεφάνις.[227]   Stephanis
Συμφέρων Ἐξκ[ουβίτωρ].[228]   Sympheron
Συμφέ[ρων?].[229]   Symphe[ron?]
Συριανός.[230]   Syrianos
Σωσίδημος.[231]   Sosidemos
Σωτηρὶς Ῥάπτης s. of Παῦλος Ῥάπτης.[232]   Soteris

T

Τάσιος Πρεσβύτερος.[233]   Tasios
Τίμαρχος f. of Φιλίστα.[234]   Timarchos
Τρόφιμος Ἰατρός.[235]   Trophimos
Τρύφων Αἰγιάριος.[236]   Tryphon
Τρύφων Ἐγιάρ<ι>ος h. of Ἀριάγνη.[237]   Tryphon
Τύχη, seller of a tomb.[238]   Tyche
[Τ]ύχη?[239]   [T]yche?

---

[225] K. 618 [= Feissel 1985b, no. 113; LGPN III.A, no. 2]; see preceding essay, note 102.

[226] M. 151 [= Feissel 1985b, no. 13; LGPN III.A, no. 1], early 6th century. Find-spot: Peirene North.

[227] M. 147 [= LGPN III.A, no. 2], mid 5th century. Find-spot: Agora Northwest. Meritt printed "Στεφάνι = Στεφάνη, the name of the deceased"; but Feissel (1985b, no. 11) corrected it and identified the date (May 15).

[228] K. 541 [= LGPN III.A, no. 1, classifying him as a resident but non-Corinthian]; see preceding essay, note 31.

[229] Unpublished, dated 5th or 6th century. Find-spot: Anaploga. For another Sympheron: K. 541 (see note 228). The fragment is definitely a gravestone, but the position of the name does not rule out the possibility that the man was the seller of the tomb—not the deceased. Nor can Συμφέρουσα, the feminine version of this name, be ruled out, either.

[230] M. 74 [= Corinth XII, 366 no. 2884; LGPN III.A, no. 2], 6th century. Find-spot: Agora East. Stamped lead votive disc.

[231] Prakt. 1956, 167, πιν. 67α, dated 6th century. Find-spot: Lechaion Basilica.

[232] Hesperia 41, no. 33 [= LGPN III.A, no. 9]; see preceding essay, note 128.

[233] Hesperia 38, 85, no. 84; see preceding essay, note 66. This inscription is not carved but rather painted on the wall of a tomb.

[234] K. 300 [= Robert 1966, 753; Peek 1988, no. 2020; LGPN III.A, no. 9, following Peek in listing his daughter as Φιλίστα, not Καλαινώ]; see preceding essay, note 84.

[235] Prakt. 1965, 163 no. 2 [= LGPN III.A, no. 2]; see preceding essay, note 83.

[236] K. 556 [= LGPN III.A, no. 6]; see preceding essay, note 105.

[237] Hesperia 41, no. 32 and unpublished; see preceding essay, note 106.

[238] Hesperia 36, 423 [= LGPN III.A, no. 6]; see note 117.

[239] K. 709, dated 5th or 6th century. Find-spot: Agora Southeast. Kent left this unrestored. The letters -υχησ- probably derive from the end of a woman's name in the genitive, such as Tyche.

Φ

Φθόγγος.[240]	Phthongos
Φιλίστα d. of Τίμαρχος.[241]	Philista
Φιλοξένα w. of Ἡλίας.[242]	Philoxena
Φιλοστράτη.[243]	Philostrate
Φιλούμε[νος?] or Φιλουμέ[νη?].[244]	Philoume[nos?] or Philoume[ne?]
Φώτιος Ἐπίσκοπος.[245]	Photios

X

Χαρίσση w. of Μάρκελλος.[246]	Charisse
Χρυσέρως h. of Εὐτύχη.[247]	Chryseros
[Χ]ρυσόγο[νος?] f.? of [- - -?].[248]	[Ch]rysogo[nos?]

Ω

Ὠφέλιμος b. of [Ἰω]άννης and Λο[ύκιος].[249]	Ophelimos

---

[240] Unpublished, 5th century. Find-spot: Agora Southwest. This is a very simple epitaph in which the name of the deceased is given without any other details. This name occurs earlier at Corinth during the 2nd and 3rd centuries CE on a lamp; *LGPN* III.A, no. 1.

[241] K. 300; see preceding essay, note 84.

[242] *Hesperia* 36, 423 [= *LGPN* III.A, no. 7]; see note 117.

[243] K. 658 [= *LGPN* III.A, no. 1], dated late 4th century. Find-spot: Unknown. On the basis of the language of lines 5–7, Kent thought that this was a Christian epitaph. Feissel (1985b, no. 80) regarded it as pagan, calling Kent's interpretation of the word ποιμήν (line 7) as "the Good Shepherd" pure conjecture.

[244] K. 628 [= Feissel 1985b, no. 76; *LGPN* III.A, no. 7], early 6th century. Find-spot: Temple K. The deceased might be male or female. Robert (1966, 768) expands Kent's text to show that the deceased died at the age of eighteen in an unspecified year of the current indiction.

[245] *ArchEph* 1977, no. 7 [= *LGPN* III.A, no. 1]; see preceding essay, note 55.

[246] Unpublished; see note 185.

[247] M. 160 [= *LGPN* III.A, no. 3]; see note 109.

[248] K. 612 [= Feissel 1985b, no. 73; *LGPN* III.A, no. 3], early 6th century. Find-spot: Central Shops. Kent left line 2 unrestored. Robert (1966, 768) identified this as part of a name [Χ]ρυσόγο[νος] or [Χ]ρυσογό[νη].

[249] *IG* IV.408 [= *LGPN* III.A, no. 3]; see note 149.

INCOMPLETE NAMES

A[- - -?] h. of Νεῦ[να?] and f. of Ἀ[ναστά]σια.²⁵⁰   A[- - -?]

Ἀλ[- - -?] [κυρ]τᾶς?²⁵¹   Al[- - -]

Ἀν̇[- - - - ?].²⁵²   An[- - - -?]

Ἀνδρα[- -?].²⁵³   Andra[- -?]

Αὐρ[- - - -?] w. of [- - - -?].²⁵⁴   Aur[- - - -?]

Γλαυ[κ- -?].²⁵⁵   Glau[k- -?]

Δημ[- - -?].²⁵⁶   Dem[- - -?]

[Θ]εο[- -?].²⁵⁷   [Th]eo[- -?]

Κ[- - -?].²⁵⁸   K[- - -?]

Κ[- - -?] w. of [- - -]ωρος.²⁵⁹   K[- - -?]

Κα[- - - -?] w.? of Μαρτύρ[ιος].²⁶⁰   Ka[- - - -?]

Κλημ[- -?] [. . . . ἀ]ριος.²⁶¹   Klem[- -?]

Κο[. . . . . .?], seller of a tomb.²⁶²   Ko[. . . . . .?]

Κο̇[- -?].²⁶³   Ko[- - -?]

---

²⁵⁰ K. 666; see note 23. This man's name might be Ἀ[ναστάσιος].

²⁵¹ K. 570, dated early 6th century. Find-spot: Agora Northeast. There may be as many as four names here: that of the owner of the tomb Ἀλ[- - -], his father's name [- -]αμεν[- -], and that of the man or woman buried in this tomb, Χεν[- - -]. In addition, line 3 may contain the end of the owner's occupation, perhaps [κυρ]τᾶς. It is also possible that line 5 contains part of the deceased's patronymic: [- -]μων[- -]. None of these can be restored with any certainty. The first name may be Ἀλ[εξάνδρος] or, more likely because of the space available, Ἀλ[εξᾶς]. The father's name might be [Ἀλεξ]άμεν[ος]; and his occupation, perhaps [κυρ]τᾶς. As for the name of the deceased, in the imperial era I can find only Χέν[ος], a name of a Cretan; see *LGPN* I, 485. This man's patronymic is likely to be one of those names ending in -μων.

²⁵² K. 592, dated 6th century. Find-spot: Agora.

²⁵³ K. 586 [= Bees, no. 52; *SEG* 11, 179], early 6th century. Find-spot: South Stoa. Kent points out that the deceased is definitely a woman (lines 4 and 6, *contra* Bees). However, the grave itself did not necessarily belong to her.

²⁵⁴ K. 647, dated early 5th century. Find-spot: Theater.

²⁵⁵ K. 648 [= Bees, no. 62; *SEG* 11, 184], mid 5th century. Find-spot: Temple Hill North. This name is probably Γλαῦ[κος], a name attested for Corinth in the imperial era; *LGPN* III.A, 99.

²⁵⁶ M. 152 [= Bees, no. 63; *SEG* 11, 97], early 6th century. Find-spot: Unknown. Perhaps Δημ[ήτριος] in the genitive or dative?

²⁵⁷ K. 651, dated 5th or 6th century. Find-spot: Temple Hill.

²⁵⁸ M. 150, dated early 6th century. Find-spot: Hagios Ioannes.

²⁵⁹ M. 169, dated 5th or 6th century. Find-spot: Unknown. Meritt recognized that two names appeared in line 2 but made no attempt to identify these people. I believe that it is most likely that they are a husband and wife.

²⁶⁰ K. 576; see note 187.

²⁶¹ K. 646; see preceding essay, note 136.

²⁶² K. 573, dated early 6th century. Find-spot: South Stoa.

²⁶³ K. 632, dated early 6th century. Find-spot: Kraneion Basilica.

Κορν[ηλι-].²⁶⁴   Korn[eli-?]

Κορν[ηλι-?].²⁶⁵   Korn[eli-?]

Κυρ[- - - -?], seller of a tomb.²⁶⁶   Kyr[- - - -?]

Ο[- - -?].²⁶⁷   O[- - -?]

Πε[- - -?].²⁶⁸   Pe[- - -?]

Πο[- - - -?].²⁶⁹   Po[- - - -?]

Στε[- - -?] s./d. of [?] Σιλικάρ[ιος].²⁷⁰   Ste[- - -?]

Τ[- - -]η w. of [- - -]ος.²⁷¹   T[- - -]e

Φ[- - -?].²⁷²   Ph[- - -?]

Φαρ[- -?], seller of a tomb.²⁷³   Phar[- -?]

Φιλου[- -?].²⁷⁴   Philou[- -?]

Χεν[- - -?] s.? of [- -]μων[- -?].²⁷⁵   Chen[- - -?]

[...]ολια? w. of [Γεώρ]γιος.²⁷⁶   [...]olia?

[- -]ιμια.²⁷⁷   [- -]imia

---

²⁶⁴ M. 174, dated 4th or 5th century. Find-spot: West Glauke.

²⁶⁵ M. 243, dated 4th or 5th century. Find-spot: Unknown. This is another Corinthian family tomb, possibly linked with M. 174; see note 264.

²⁶⁶ K. 579, late 4th century. Find-spot: Central Shops. In line 3 Kent printed Κυ[- -]; but the vertical of another letter, probably a 'P,' survives in the break at right. Thus, the name of the seller may be Κυρ[ιακός], a name attested several times in Corinth; *LGPN* III.A, 262.

²⁶⁷ K. 537, early 6th century. Find-spot: Asklepieion.

²⁶⁸ M. 139, early 5th century. Find-spot: Unknown. Perhaps Πέ[τρος] in the genitive? But there are many other possible restorations of this name.

²⁶⁹ K. 577, dated 5th century. Find-spot: South Stoa.

²⁷⁰ Unpublished; see preceding essay, note 90. The name is perhaps Στε[φάνια].

²⁷¹ K. 539 [= Bees, no. 20; *SEG* 11, 163], dated mid 5th century. Find-spot: Lerna Court. The name of the husband occupied ca. seven-to-eight spaces; that of his wife, also ca. seven-to-eight spaces. The daughters' names were not listed.

²⁷² K. 619, early 6th century. Find-spot: Agora Northeast.

²⁷³ K. 637 [= Bees, no. 38], dated 5th century. Find-spot: Apollo Peribolos. This name may be Φαρ[νάκης], a name attested for Corinth during the imperial era; *LGPN* III.A, 444.

²⁷⁴ K. 717, early 6th century. Find-spot: Lerna Court. This fragment, which may be part of a gravestone, seems to contain parts of two names: [- - -]λίων, probably the owner of the tomb; and Φιλου[- -], the deceased.

²⁷⁵ K. 570; see note 251. Χέν[ος]?

²⁷⁶ Unpublished; see note 72. Unless these letters are part of an occupational name, they will be the end of a woman's name, perhaps [Εὐ]πωλία, spelled here with an 'O' rather than an 'Ω.'

²⁷⁷ K. 687 [= Bees, no. 48], dated 6th or 7th century. Find-spot: Unknown. Kent noted that Bees printed 'AMIA' "without a single letter dotted." He prints instead -λκισα-, dotting each letter. In fact, Bees' reading was correct except for the first letter, which is a vertical stroke, probably an 'I.' Kent prints a dotted 'Γ' in the next line where Bees printed nothing. In fact, the tops of A, Γ and O are visible and probably, therefore, form part of the word ἀγο[ρασθέν]. This may be a record of the purchase of a grave from an unknown person.

[- -]ηνία.²⁷⁸   [- -]enia

[- - -]ρία d. of [Ἀ]νθούσ[α?].²⁷⁹   [- - -]ria

[- - -]αρία w./d. of Ἀνθίαν[ος?].²⁸⁰   [- - -]aria

[- - -]μα d. of [- -?].²⁸¹   [- - -]ma

[.....]η w. of Διονύσιος.²⁸²   [.....]e

[....]κη w. of [?] Σιλικά[ριος].²⁸³   [....]ke

[- - -]δων.²⁸⁴   [- - -]don

[- - -]λίων.²⁸⁵   [- - -]lion

[....]ς, seller of a tomb.²⁸⁶   [....]s

[- - - -]ς, relative of [- - -]δων.²⁸⁷   [- - - -]s

[....]ας Σαλγ[αμάριος].²⁸⁸   [....]as

[- -]γωθᾶ[ς?].²⁸⁹   [- -]gotha[s?]

[- - ⁚ -]λίδης [Ὀρ]χησ(τής)?²⁹⁰   [- - -]lides

[....]ος h. of Εὐτυχαία.²⁹¹   [....]os

[.....]ος s. of Κωνστά[ντιν]ος and Εὐφρασία.²⁹²   [.....]os

---

²⁷⁸ K. 596, dated early 6th century. Find-spot: Agora West. Kent published this with little restoration. I believe that part of a name survives in line 2, namely, that of the owner of this tomb; and that the end of another name survives in line 3, where Kent read [ἔνθα κατ]ακιτε. In fact, these letters are –ηνιαε and, thus, the end of the name of the deceased, followed by the usual formula ἔ[νθα κατακίτε]. The thin, square lettering is a mark of an early date.

²⁷⁹ Unpublished; see note 40. A name such as Maria seems likely in view of the space available.

²⁸⁰ *Hesperia* 41, no. 31; see note 38.

²⁸¹ *ArchEph* 1977, no. 13 [= *SEG* 28, 381], dated early 6th century. Find-spot: Aetopetra, Old Corinth. First published by Wiseman (1978, 100–11), this is an opisthographic fragment. The face published as Face A carries the end of an epitaph while the other face seems to bear a longer text; the section discussed here derives from the middle part of the epitaph. Also, the script of Face A seems later than that of Face B. Thus, I should be inclined to suggest that Face B should actually be 'Face A' and *vice versa*. In the second line, the base of the slightly sloping right vertical of a M survives followed by an A; thus, this name may be something like Zosima. The name is followed by the words ἡ θυγ[άτηρ]. Her father's name has not survived.

²⁸² *IG* IV.404; see note 54.

²⁸³ Unpublished; see preceding essay, note 90. This woman's name probably occupied ca. six-to-seven letter spaces.

²⁸⁴ K. 680, dated early 7th century. Find-spot: Unknown. The lettering, layout, and type of marble suggest that this may be part of the same monument as K. 643 and perhaps also K. 685; see note 156. There is another name of an unknown deceased in line 4.

²⁸⁵ K. 717; see note 274.

²⁸⁶ K. 675, 5th or 6th century. Find-spot: Unknown.

²⁸⁷ K. 680; see note 284.

²⁸⁸ Unpublished; see preceding essay, note 122.

²⁸⁹ K. 649, dated early 6th century. Find-spot: Temple Hill North.

²⁹⁰ K. 579; see preceding essay, note 137.

²⁹¹ K. 543; see note 108.

²⁹² K. 589; see note 112.

[- - - -]ος h. of [- - -?].²⁹³   [- - - -]os

[- - - -]ος h. of Τ[- - -?].²⁹⁴   [- - - -[os

[- - -]ιος.²⁹⁵   [- - -]ios

[. .]ώδιος h. of Ἄννα.²⁹⁶   [. .]odios

[- - -]λόπιος?²⁹⁷   [- - -]lopios

[- - - -]τέριος.²⁹⁸   [- - - -]terios

[- - -]φιος.²⁹⁹   [- - -]phios

[- -]νος Λα[- -?], seller of a tomb.³⁰⁰   [- -]nos

[.....]ανος Σαλγαμάριος.³⁰¹   [.....]anos

[- -]νίανος f. of [Θεο]δόσ[ιος?].³⁰²   [- -]nianos

[- -]φανος s. of [- -?] Σιλικάρ[ιος].³⁰³   [- -]phanos

[- - - -]ος? seller of a tomb.³⁰⁴   [- - - -]os?

[- - -]ωρος s. of [- -?] Κουρεύς and b. of Μάρινος.³⁰⁵   [- - -]oros

[- - -]ωρος h. of Κ[- - -?].³⁰⁶   [- - -]oros

[- - -]τος Ε[- - -?].³⁰⁷   [- - -]tos

[....]τος Μακελ[λάριος], seller of a tomb.³⁰⁸   [....]tos

[- -]νοστος h.? of [- -?].³⁰⁹   [- -]nostos

[- -]λωτος.³¹⁰   [- -]lotos

---

²⁹³ K. 554, dated mid 5th century. Find-spot: Lerna Court. I read this line as the end of a man's name, followed by κα[ί]. If, however, the letters -OY are part of the word [τ]ου, the next two letters, KA-, might be the beginning of a patronymic. Again, if -OY is the end of a name in the genitive, the next two letters might be the beginning of an occupational name.

²⁹⁴ K. 539; see note 271.

²⁹⁵ M. 176, early 7th century. Find-spot: Unknown.

²⁹⁶ K. 533; see note 45.

²⁹⁷ K. 708; see preceding essay, note 133.

²⁹⁸ Unpublished, dated 4th or 5th century. Find-spot: Agora Southwest.

²⁹⁹ M. 177, 5th or 6th century. Find-spot: Unknown.

³⁰⁰ K. 625; see preceding essay, note 131.

³⁰¹ K. 540; see preceding essay, note 124.

³⁰² Unpublished; see note 124. Perhaps [Εὐγε]νίανος, a name attested in the 3rd or 4th century at Corinth; K. 512.

³⁰³ Unpublished; see preceding essay, note 90. The name is perhaps [Στέ]φανος.

³⁰⁴ Unpublished, dated 5th or 6th century. Find-spot: Unknown. This fragment seems to be the record of the purchase of a [κυμη]τήριο[ν] in the month of January (or February?) from a man whose name ends –ος.

³⁰⁵ K. 722; see preceding essay, note 96. Kent read [- -]ηρου in line 4. The first letter is definitely not an 'H' but a clumsily rendered 'Ω.' The name may be Theodoros, but there are other possibilities.

³⁰⁶ M. 169; see note 259.

³⁰⁷ M. 149; see preceding essay, note 130.

³⁰⁸ Unpublished; see preceding essay, note 97.

³⁰⁹ K. 697, dated early 6th century. Find-spot: North Shops. The end of a man's name linked, probably, to that of his wife. The second vertical of a 'N' is preserved at left before the first 'Ω.'

³¹⁰ M. 188, dated 5th or 6th century. Find-spot: Unknown.

[- - -]χος Σιδ[ηρουργός?].³¹¹   [- - -]chos
[- - -]χος.³¹²   [- - -]chos
[- - -]ώρευς.³¹³   [- - -]oreus
[- - -]ὼ.³¹⁴   [- - -]o
[..]αιι[- -?] f. of Ἰουλιανὸς Ἐγιάριος.³¹⁵   [..]aii[- -?]
[- -]άτιμε[- -?].³¹⁶   [- -]atime[- -?]
[- -]αμεν[- -?] f.? of Ἀλ[- -?].³¹⁷   [- -]amen[- -?]
[- -]μων[- -] f.? of Χεν[- - -?].³¹⁸   [- -]mon[- -]
[- -]ουκ[- -?] Σινγ[ουλάριος].³¹⁹   [- -]ouk[- -?]
[- - -]στοδο[- -?].³²⁰   [- - -]stodo[- -?]
[- -]τια[- -?] h. of [E]ὐγενία.³²¹   [- -]tia[- -?]
[- -]ξα[- -?] f.? of Πούλ[ος?].³²²   [- -]xa[- -?]

Lost Names Whose Existence Can Be Inferred from Context

unknown f. of Νικόστρατος Μαρμαράριος.³²³
unknown f. of Ζοή.³²⁴
unknown f. of [- - -]μα.³²⁵
unknown w. of [- - - -]ος.³²⁶
unknown w. of [- -]νοστος.³²⁷
unknown parents of [Θεμι]στοκλῆς [Μου]σοπόλος.³²⁸

---

³¹¹ K. 707; see preceding essay, note 87.

³¹² M. 144, early 6th century. Find-spot: Peribolos of Apollo. Meritt printed [- -]χου τοῦ εὐ[- -]. I believe that a name in the genitive is followed by some such adjective as εὐ[λαβεστάτου]; this, in turn, suggests that the man named here was an ecclesiastic. See M. 157; see preceding essay, note 83.

³¹³ K. 565, dated 5th or 6th century. Find-spot: Lerna Court.

³¹⁴ M. 174; see note 265. An unknown woman.

³¹⁵ K. 587; see preceding essay, note 107.

³¹⁶ K. 596; see note 278.

³¹⁷ K. 570; see note 251. [Ἀλεξ]άμεν[ος]?

³¹⁸ K. 570; see note 251.

³¹⁹ K. 536; see preceding essay, note 40.

³²⁰ M. 166, dated 5th or 6th century. Find-spot: Agora Northwest. The letters ΣΤΟΔΟ in line 1 are probably part of a name, such as Aristodoros.

³²¹ K. 686; see note 98.

³²² K. 621; see preceding essay, note 138. A patronymic, such as [Ἀλε]ξά[νδρου], or an occupational name, such as [Πα]ξα[μᾶς] or [Μετα]ξά[ριος].

³²³ ArchEph 1977, Προσθήκη; see preceding essay, note 88.

³²⁴ ArchEph 1977, no. 8; see note 116.

³²⁵ ArchEph 1977, no. 13; see note 281.

³²⁶ K. 554; see note 293.

³²⁷ K. 697; see note 309.

³²⁸ Prakt. 1977A, 173–75, no. 2; see preceding essay, note 79.

unknown w. or child of Πέτρ[ος?].[329]

unknown children of [- - -]ω and Κορν[ηλι- -].[330]

unknown d. of [.....]νάριος?[331]

unknown daughters of Τ[- - -]η and [- - -]ος.[332]

unknown s. of Διονύσιος.[333]

unknown s.? of [Χ]ρυσόγο[νος?].[334]

unknown s. of [- - -?] Ζυγοστάτης τῆς πόλεως.[335]

unknown s. of [- - -?] Σιλικάρ[ιος].[336]

unknown h. of Ἀναστασία.[337]

unknown h. of [Ἀ]νθούσ[α] & f. of [Μα?]ρία.[338]

unknown h. of [Ἄν]να.[339]

unknown h. of Αὐρ[- - -?].[340]

unknown h. of Τ[- - -?].[341]

unknown child of Κωνστά[ντιν]ος and Εὐφρασία.[342]

unknown h. or child? of Ἄννα.[343]

unknown w. or child of Νικέας [Λί]βανος.[344]

unknown w. or child of Πέτρ[ος?].[345]

unknown child of the owner of a tomb.[346]

unknown b. of Μνασέας Καμι[σογοραστής].[347]

unknown brothers of Νικόστρατος Μαρμαράριος.[348]

unknown Ἀκον[ηταί].[349]

---

[329] K. 595; see note 212.
[330] M. 174; see note 264.
[331] Unpublished; see preceding essay, note 134.
[332] K. 539; see note 271.
[333] *IG* IV.404; see note 54.
[334] K. 612; see note 248.
[335] M. 158; see preceding essay, note 27.
[336] Unpublished; see preceding essay, note 90.
[337] K. 671; see note 22.
[338] Unpublished; see note 40.
[339] *IG* IV.413; see note 48.
[340] K. 647; see note 254.
[341] K. 539; see note 271.
[342] K. 589; see note 112.
[343] K. 613; see note 42.
[344] K. 550; see preceding essay, note 113.
[345] K. 595; see note 212.
[346] K. 606, early 6th century; see note 373. Find-spot: South Stoa West.
[347] M. 191; see preceding essay, note 99.
[348] *ArchEph* 1977, Προσθήκη; see preceding essay, note 88.
[349] M. 245; see preceding essay, note 92.

unknown Ἀναγν(ώστης).³⁵⁰
unknown Ἀρχ[ισυνάγω]γος?³⁵¹
unknown Βουκελλάριοι.³⁵²
unknown [Διακόν]εσσα.³⁵³
unknown Διδάσ[καλος].³⁵⁴
unknown [Δομέστικος τοῦ θίου] παλα[τίου?].³⁵⁵
unknown Ζυγοστάτης τῆς πόλεως.³⁵⁶
unknown [Εἱματικ]άριος?³⁵⁷
unknown Καμισα[γοραστής?].³⁵⁸
unknown Κουρεύς f. of Μάρινος and [- - -]ωρος.³⁵⁹
unknown [Λαμπρο]τάτη.³⁶⁰
unknown [Λι]θόξο[ο]ι.³⁶¹
unknown [Μ]ακελλάριος.³⁶²
unknown [Μ]ακελλάριος.³⁶³
unknown [Μαρ]μαράριοι.³⁶⁴
unknown Μιζοτέ[ρα].³⁶⁵
unknown Μυληνός.³⁶⁶
unknown Σιλικάρ[ιος].³⁶⁷
unknown Σιβύ[ρτιος?].³⁶⁸
unknown Σινγ(ουλάριος).³⁶⁹

³⁵⁰ K. 548; see preceding essay, note 69.
³⁵¹ *ArchEph* 1977 no. 30; see preceding essay, note 73.
³⁵² M. 208; see preceding essay, note 35.
³⁵³ K. 629; see preceding essay, note 59.
³⁵⁴ *ArchEph* 1977, no. 30; see preceding essay, note 73.
³⁵⁵ K. 615; see preceding essay, note 37.
³⁵⁶ M. 158; see preceding essay, note 27.
³⁵⁷ Unpublished; see preceding essay, note 103.
³⁵⁸ M. 193; see preceding essay, note 101. Perhaps [Εὐσέβιος]?
³⁵⁹ K. 722; see preceding essay, note 96.
³⁶⁰ K. 627; see preceding essay, note 46.
³⁶¹ M. 245; see preceding essay, note 93.
³⁶² Unpublished; see preceding essay, note 97.
³⁶³ *ArchEph* 1977, no. 9; see preceding essay, note 98.
³⁶⁴ M. 245; see preceding essay, note 93.
³⁶⁵ K. 604; see preceding essay, note 63.
³⁶⁶ Unpublished; see preceding essay, note 118.
³⁶⁷ Unpublished; see preceding essay, note 90. Perhaps [Στέφανος]?
³⁶⁸ *Prakt.* 1977A, 172–75 [= *SEG* 29, 322], 5th century. Find-spot: Kraneion Basilica. This is a metrical epigram apparently for a native of Sibyrtos, Crete, who died at Corinth and was buried there.
³⁶⁹ K. 536; see preceding essay, note 40.

unknown Y[- - - -?].[370]

unknown [....]άριος, seller of a tomb.[371]

unknown [.....]νάριος?[372]

unknown owner of a tomb, f. of an unknown child.[373]

unknown purchaser of a tomb.[374]

unknown purchaser of a tomb.[375]

unknown purchaser of a tomb.[376]

unknown purchaser of a tomb.[377]

unknown purchaser of a tomb.[378]

unknown purchaser of a tomb.[379]

unknown purchaser of a tomb.[380]

unknown purchaser of a tomb.[381]

unknown seller of a tomb.[382]

unknown seller of a tomb.[383]

unknown seller of a tomb.[384]

unknown seller of a tomb.[385]

unknown seller of a tomb.[386]

unknown man?[387]

unknown man.[388]

---

[370] M. 156; see preceding essay, note 132.

[371] K. 523; see preceding essay, note 135.

[372] Unpublished; see preceding essay, note 134.

[373] K. 606; see note 346.

[374] Unpublished; see note 304.

[375] K. 573; see note 262.

[376] K. 687; see note 277.

[377] K. 674, dated 5th or 6th century. Find-spot: Old Corinth.

[378] K. 687; see note 277.

[379] K. 675; see note 286.

[380] Unpublished; mentioned in preceding essay, note 17.

[381] K. 523; see note 371.

[382] K. 552; see note 27.

[383] K. 584 [= Bees, no. 40], 5th or 6th century. Find-spot: Central Shops.

[384] K. 674; see note 377.

[385] K. 687; see note 277.

[386] K. 605; see note 151.

[387] *Prakt.* 1961, 132–33, εἰκ. 3δ, dated 5th century. Find-spot: Kraneion Basilica. Stikas (1964) published a photograph without commentary. The text, so far as it can be restored, ends with an *anathema*.

[388] *Prakt.* 1977A, 174 [= *SEG* 29, 323], dated 5th or 6th century. Find-spot: Kraneion Basilica. This is metrical epigram for an unknown man who died at Corinth and was buried there; see note 368.

unknown family member.[389]
unknown person(s)?[390]

---

[389] K. 689; see note 52.

[390] One hundred twenty-seven published fragments of Christian gravestones survive from which no names or personal identification can be gleaned. In some instances, only parts of one or two lines survive; on others, parts of several lines are preserved. I list them here by publications: *IG* IV.402, 407, and 410; M. 135, 137–38, 141–434, 146, 155, 159, 162–63, 165, 167–68, 171–73, 175, 178–79, 181–82, 184–85, 187, 190, 197; Bees, no. 29 and 38; K. 524, 528–29, 538, 546, 549, 555, 566–67, 569, 571–72, 574, 580–81, 585, 590–91, 593–94, 598–600, 606–10, 616–17, 620, 622–24, 626, 631, 633–36, 638–39, 641–43, 645, 652, 654, 656, 662–63, 665–67, 670, 677, 679, 681–83, 692, 694–96, 698–702, 704, 706; 710–16, 718, 720; *Hesperia* 36, 424; *Hesperia* 38, 92–94 (10 fragments); *Hesperia* 41, no. 29; *ArchEph* 1977, no. 12, 16, and 18. In addition, there are 78 unpublished fragments in the Corinth Museum inventory that lack names or other means of personal identification.

LOCAL RELIGION

CHAPTER TEN

SEEKING SHELTER IN ROMAN CORINTH: ARCHAEOLOGY
AND THE PLACEMENT OF PAUL'S COMMUNITIES

Daniel N. Schowalter

One of the most intriguing postcards sold near the archaeological site
of ancient Corinth features an image of the Roman *bema* located in
the center of the Forum with a drawing of Paul superimposed on the
archaeological remains. Not only does this cartoon apostle look out
of place in the picture, but the super-sized version of Paul completely
obscures the archaeological remains. This postcard serves as a symbol
of the difficulties modern scholars face when they attempt to reconcile
literary evidence from the early Jesus movement with material remains
from the 1st century CE world. As use and abuse of archaeological
material becomes more common in New Testament studies, scholars
must consider how to make such a comparison without allowing what
we 'know' from the text to overshadow what we can learn from either
new archaeological evidence or a fresh reading of the archaeological
record.

The organizers of this conference try to approach this question by
combining a passion for material remains and ancient culture with
excavation experience and a desire to enhance our knowledge of the
social situation and religious perspective of early believers in Jesus. My
own work as co-director of the excavations at Omrit in northern Israel
has made me conscious of the difficulty of reading the archaeological
record in a constructive and responsible way. The various stages of
interpretation involved cannot be ignored or taken lightly, and even
archaeologists are cautious when drawing conclusions. For the non-
specialist, this difficulty becomes even more poignant, especially when
trying to make a connection with a cherished religious text.

This paper seeks to probe the extent of our archaeological knowledge related to domestic space in ancient Corinth and to evaluate how
that knowledge informs our study of Paul's communities there. The
variety of approaches applied to this latter question is truly impressive,

as one would expect given the interest generated by its connection to Pauline and other New Testament studies. While this paper cannot claim to be based on a review of all the work that has been done on domestic space in Roman Corinth, much less in the broader Roman world, it does focus on several recent approaches to the subject with the hope of assessing the current state of the question and where we might best go from here. This paper also serves as a case study of some of the ways that New Testament scholars try to relate archaeological evidence to the earliest churches.

The starting point for this endeavor is a word of caution about the paucity of evidence for domestic space at Corinth. It is safe to say that without the influence of Paul's Corinthian letters, there would be far fewer attempts to draw major conclusions about where and in what manner people lived in mid 1st century Corinth. Due to the scope and nature of excavations to this point, we simply do not have a sufficient range of evidence to talk about Corinthian domestic space in a comprehensive way. Betsey Robinson, who has excavated at Corinth and written about the history of the Peirene Fountain,[1] speaks to these concerns.

> A few things are crucial to keep in mind about Ancient Corinth. In 1898, the American archaeologists located the Roman Forum. Thereafter, the focus of the excavations was on this civic and political center (rather than religious and domestic), and the excavations have not strayed very far. Now, 110 years into the venture, our access to the past is increasingly channeled (and constrained) by the development of the modern village on the site.[2]

The sample size of domestic space in 1st century Corinth is simply too meager to generalize about where and how the majority of the population would have lived. The evidence is even less suitable to answer questions about how and where specific groups of people (whether designated by socio-economic status, occupation, or religious affiliation) would have resided.

Since the study of the early Jesus followers is often an attempt to isolate just such a group within the context of the ancient city, this effort would seem to be fraught with difficulty, if not doomed to failure. Yet these bleak prospects have done nothing to deter a string of

---

[1] Robinson 2005 and forthcoming.
[2] Robinson 2006.

New Testament scholars from attempting to draw conclusions based on the limited data. While these efforts have led to some creative connections between the material remains of ancient Corinth and Paul's communities there, they have also revealed the difficulties of trying to apply archaeological material that is out of date, that is subject to reinterpretation, or that does not relate to the archaeological evidence from ancient Corinth.

In 1983, Jerome Murphy-O'Connor, published *St. Paul's Corinth: Text and Archaeology*. O'Connor's book was an early attempt to do what many scholars working in New Testament studies today are trying to accomplish: applying the results of archaeological research to New Testament studies. When *St. Paul's Corinth* first appeared, very few people had attempted to take archaeological material seriously in studying Paul's letters or other New Testament documents. In the mid-1980s, when some of us were working with Helmut Koester to publish the slides and data sheets that today take the form of the *Cities of Paul* CD, a colleague gave me a photocopy of pages from Murphy-O'Connor's newly published work as a possible model for our project. Any disagreements I may have with Murphy-O'Connor's book need to be tempered by an appreciation for his early and important contribution.

In a chapter called "House Churches and the Eucharist," Murphy-O'Connor focuses on the remains of the Anaploga villa, which was excavated in the 1960s. After comparing the layout and size of this structure with villas at Pompeii, Ephesus, and elsewhere, Murphy-O'Connor declares that the Anaploga villa is a "typical house," by which he means typical in size and layout.[3] Murphy-O'Connor suggests that "Gaius, a wealthy member of the Christian community at Corinth" who is mentioned at the end of Paul's letter to the Romans, might have owned just such a house.[4] Further, he encourages the reader to imagine how meeting in a space like the Anaploga villa would have affected the assembly of believers in Corinth when 'the whole church' gathered (1 Cor 14:23).[5]

After calculating that the approximate size of the Corinthian community of believers at the time of 1 Corinthians was around 50 people,

---

[3] Murphy-O'Connor 2002, 178.
[4] Murphy-O'Connor 2002, 182.
[5] Murphy-O'Connor 2002, 182.

Murphy-O'Connor notes that the physical layout of the villa would have allowed for only a limited number of diners to be in the dining room (*triclinium*). The rest, he suggests, gathered in the atrium where they were subjected to over-crowding, bad weather, and probably a lesser quality of food. In Murphy-O'Connor's reconstruction, this separate and unequal meal space along with possible discrepancies in menu depending on social status, may have exacerbated divisions in the community that eventually led to the *schismata* which Paul mentions explicitly in 1 Corinthians 1 and criticizes implicitly throughout the letter.[6]

Murphy-O'Connor's approach is a typical method of comparing literary and material remains. In it, the scholar interprets the archaeological record with an eye to explaining some aspect of the biblical text. This type of connection can be misinterpreted and extended by other readers as a kind of 'proof texting,' where the veracity of the biblical text is said to be verified by archeological discovery. For those who are seeking to demonstrate the accuracy and even inerrancy of the biblical text, Murphy-O'Connor's interpretation of the archaeological data can become 'material evidence' or 'proof' for the factions mentioned by Paul. Even if this is not the intention of Murphy O'Connor, it may be an unavoidable side effect of this approach.[7]

In 2003 David G. Horrell challenged some aspects of the reconstruction offered by Murphy-O'Connor. Horrell acknowledges that Murphy-O'Connor's discussion has been very influential, citing works by Peter Lampe, Carolyn Osiek and David Balch, Gordon Fee, and Anthony Thiselton to illustrate some of the ways in which scholars have built on Murphy-O'Connor's suggestion that the Jesus followers of Corinth met in a structure like the Anaploga villa.[8] For the most part, these scholars also follow Murphy-O'Connor by describing the socio-economic composition and structure of the communities based on this villa model. In the end, however, Horrell questions both the descriptive work of Murphy-O'Connor, and those who have built on that description. While the Anaploga villa remains an important resource for understanding aspects of Roman Corinth, Horrell points out that uncertainty about dating and layout of the villa, along with a

---

[6] Murphy-O'Connor 2002, 184–85.
[7] Often, when I give a public lecture related to archaeology, someone will ask me if I have "found anything to prove the Bible."
[8] Horrell 2004, 352–53.

general difficulty in connecting space as described in literary texts with actual material remains make it very difficult, and ultimately unadvisable, to base significant conclusions about the gathering of Jesus followers on such a tentative and limited base of evidence.[9]

This observation would seem to be supported by findings from Monika Trümper. In her study of Delos, Trümper reports that the island boasts 91 completely excavated houses, many of which feature wall and floor treatment in a good state of preservation. Even with this relative abundance of evidence, Trümper claims that "the use and consequently the name of a specific room can rarely be determined."[10] If this is true in the case of Delos, where evidence for some types of domestic space is abundant, how much more must it relate to Corinth where the opposite is true.

Horrell's concerns about the archaeological basis for Murphy-O'Connor's claims are reinforced by the nature of the archaeological evidence for the Anaploga Villa. Partially excavated in 1962–64, the results from the villa were never published in a systematic way. In 1972 Stella Miller published an article dealing with the mosaic from the villa, in which she dates that mosaic to the last quarter of the 1st century.[11] When Murphy-O'Connor published *St. Paul's Corinth* in 1983, he was primarily dependent on Miller's mosaic article for his archaeological information.[12] Since that time, there has been no further work on the site and almost no scholarly analysis of the architecture and dating based on more recent methodologies and chronologies. In fact, the villa site now lies reburied underneath a modern olive orchard. At the Corinth conference in Austin, current excavators from Corinth were surprised to learn that the so-called villa had come to play such a prominent role. In the ensuing discussion, they raised questions about both the architectural identification and the dating of the Anaploga site. Without conducting further research, it is impossible to be certain, but there is a definite possibility that the site may not have been a villa at all in the mid 1st century CE.

---

[9] Horrel (2004, 355–56) cites Allison (2001, 189), who argues in general that "it is extremely subjective to interpret the domestic behavior in these villas through room functions for which there is no material evidence."

[10] Trümper 2003, 22.

[11] S. Miller 1972, 332. Horrell (2004, 354) cites more recent analysis which dates the mosaic much later.

[12] Murphy-O'Connor also cites Wiseman (1979).

How can New Testament scholars make use of archaeological materials when results are not fully published, or when even final publications can be subject to criticism and revision long after being released? It would seem that the results of such a comparison need to be tentative. On the one hand, it is likely that there would have been villas in the region during the time of Paul, and so Murphy-O'Connor is right to speculate about how a meeting of early Jesus followers might have filled possible spaces in a hypothetical villa. It goes beyond the scope of evidence, however, to connect the assemblies of believers with particular rooms or spaces. Further speculation about how a hypothetical space might have affected the unity of Paul's community may be interesting, but should not be taken as definitive.[13]

Horrell's own ideas about locating the house churches in Corinth advance the discussion, but also bring to light another set of difficulties. He concludes his article by suggesting an alternative location for the assembly in 1st century Corinth based on excavations of buildings east of the theater.[14] The results of excavations in this area were published in preliminary form by Williams and Zervos in a series of articles in *Hesperia* in the late 1980s.[15]

Horrell comments on buildings 1 and 3 of the East Theater Street complex, which appear to have been in operation from the early 1st century. This space is composed of rooms with ovens and was found to contain large deposits of animal bones. It is interpreted as a site for food production most likely in association with the Theater. Horrell's interest in the structures, however, is not with the production of food on the first floor but with the suggestion of a second and possibly third floor above. In the preliminary report, the excavators posit that these hypothetical upper floors could have been used for domestic space. Horrell, in turn, sees the supposed second story as evidence of another type of structure in Corinth that could have housed an *ekklesia* of believers during the mid 1st century. In fact, he prefers the lower-rent option of the East Theater Street buildings because space

---

[13] Penelope Allison (2001, 202) argues that Roman historians should not "wait for archaeologists to do the job properly. Rather they need to take into account the often already interpretative nature of the available information, and the significance of this to their own inquiries." The same is certainly true for New Testament scholars who may be eager to find specific connections between text and material remains, and unfortunately unfamiliar with the 'interpretive nature' of archaeological results.

[14] Horrell 2004, 360–65.

[15] Horrell cites Williams and Zervos 1986 and 1988.

of this type and in this area would have been more affordable than the putative villa described by Murphy-O'Connor. Horrell argues on economic grounds that the East Theater Street location is more likely to have been the type of space utilized by Jesus followers who probably did not count many villa owners as members. Horrell describes the residents of this sort of housing as "non-elite, though not the most impoverished urban residents."[16]

Horrell admits that his scenario of a meeting of Jesus followers in space similar to the supposed second floor above the East Theater Street 'shops' is "entirely imaginative." He does add, however, that his suggestion is "no more so unlikely (and probably a good deal less so) than imagining them meeting in the villa at Anaploga."[17] Horrell should be commended for his restraint in drawing implications from his discussion of these upper rooms. He is very careful to state that there is little evidence for the rooms themselves, even less indication of the decor and layout of the hypothetical upper stories, and there is absolutely no evidence that the rooms were ever used by followers of Jesus.[18] His point, however, is that "NT studies should pay more attention to the varieties of domestic space in the urban setting of Corinth and other cities of the Roman empire, and consider these as possible settings for early Christian meetings."[19]

With these cautions in place, Horrell would seem to have achieved the kind of tentative approach suggested above for connecting material remains with New Testament texts. His observations remain valid, even in the face of challenges to the specific archaeological findings on which he has based his suggestion. In fact, such challenges have come to light. In discussions at the Austin conference, Charles Williams reported that the final publication of the East Theater Street buildings

---

[16] Horrell 2004, 356–59 and 367–68.
[17] Horrell 2004, 368.
[18] Horrell 2004, 364–65.
[19] Horrell 2004, 369. I have no argument with this conclusion, since the early believing communities certainly did meet in many different configurations, and in varied places. In a session reviewing Jorunn Økland's book (2004) at the 2006 SBL meeting in Washington, D.C., one of the panelists stressed that there is no reason to assume that the believing assembly always met in the same place or even the same kinds of places. She was responding to a question about whether ritual activities of the assembly could have taken place anywhere, even outdoors. We will return to this point and to Økland's approach.

would not include evidence for a second story.[20] Williams noted that
the propensity for earthquakes in the area around Corinth meant
that multi-story buildings were simply not practical. Fortunately, this
development does not change the thrust of Horrell's main argument:
scholars should focus on a broader spectrum of options for domestic
space at Corinth. It only means that the second-story space should be
removed from the spectrum of housing options in Corinth. Unfortunately, Horrell's closing comments serve to distract from his main
contribution, and to create the same opportunity for misinterpretation
that was possible with Murphy-O'Connor's work.

Horrell calls for "disciplined imagination" when thinking about the
supposed second-story meeting spot on East Theater Street,[21] but not
everyone is able to view these possibilities with such discipline. There
are some, both within and especially outside the scholarly community,
who might read Horrell's article and simply substitute the imaginative placement of the communal meeting above the East Theater Street
shops for a meeting spot in the Anaploga villa. In either case, readers
can continue to assume that archaeology has discovered the location
of the house churches. In the end, this is not Horrell's fault since he is
very clear about the tentative nature of his hypothesis, but the potential for this kind of interpretation still exists.

Horrell does undermine some of his own discipline with a final
reference from Acts 20, the account of a young man who fell to his
death from an upper story window during a sermon by Paul.[22] Horrell
cites the text from Acts in support of his argument that meetings of

---

[20] "Four arguments countering a multiple-storied theory are, first, no evidence
exists to restore a stairway to either building; secondly, the 0.45 m wide walls and the
long free span of the rooms, especially in the original design, argue against a second
story; thirdly, the pottery in the debris recovered from the south room of Building 1,
upon closer examination, appears to have fallen from shelves set against the south wall
of the south room of Building 1 and from the kitchen of Building 3, both ground-
floor rooms. Finally, the wall with yellow-ground fresco decoration, which initially
had been thought to have collapsed from the second floor of Building 3 in reality
had decorated the north wall of a ground-floor room of Building 5, which had been
constructed above the terrace wall against which Building 3 had stood. It should also
be noted that Roman contractors would have been familiar with the frequency and
strength of earthquakes in Corinth and would have known that multi-storied constructions such as those in Rome and Ostia would not have been feasible in Corinth."
I thank Charles Williams for allowing me to use this preliminary text from a forthcoming volume in the Corinth series.

[21] Horrell 2004, 366–67.

[22] Horrell 2004, 368.

the *ekklesia* could be held in an upper story. Horrell claims in a note that debates about the historicity of Acts are not relevant here, but I would argue that they are indeed relevant. A significant portion of New Testament scholars recognize differences in the dating, approach, and details of Acts and Paul's letters.[23] There is a danger here that a less-than-disciplined imagination might take the Acts account as a 'proof text' and quickly move beyond the hypothetical. In spite of Horrell's cautions, some will undoubtedly see his analysis of the supposed second floor space on East Theater Street as archaeological evidence proving the accuracy or even inerrancy of the Acts 20 account. If Acts 20 is taken to prove that the believers sometimes convened in an upper room, the location of the community could become just as fixed on the non-existent East Theater Street second story, as it was in the Anaploga villa.[24]

In light of the cautions and uncertainties associated with the proposals of Murphy-O'Connor and Horrell, how can New Testament scholars proceed? Based on Horrell's call to pay attention to the varieties of domestic space, does it make sense to say that any newly discovered domestic space or space of any sort can be evaluated as a potential meeting spot for the early Jesus followers in Corinth? If this is the case, what can we hope to learn from such a pursuit? Is it time to admit that our ability to distinguish potential *ekklesia* space in 1st century Corinth is compromised for the immediate future by a lack of specific archaeological evidence and an imperfect knowledge of who

---

[23] While 1 Corinthians is usually dated somewhere between 50–60 CE, the book of Acts does not appear to be written until close to the end of the 1st century. This means that in telling the story of Paul's mission, the author of Acts is addressing a very different situation and audience than Paul himself did. The purpose of the book of Acts is to tell a cohesive and relatively harmonious story about how the early Jesus followers in Jerusalem developed into a predominantly Gentile movement that was spreading rapidly around the Mediterranean world. Acts also attempts to address a late 1st century concern on the part of Roman officials about the people they have started to recognize and label as "Christians," a term not used in the Pauline letters. These differences of chronology and content between Paul's letters and Acts are regularly ignored in the context of many modern Christian churches and certainly by most of the students in my classes. If we in the academy are really interested in promoting a better understanding of the world in which the New Testament documents were written, then we ignore these differences of time, audience, and purpose at our peril.

[24] Most readers of Horrell's essay will not be aware that the proposed second story of the East Theater Street shops has been dropped by the excavators and will not appear in the final report. In fact, Horrell's summary of the preliminary reports will be the only exposure most readers have to the archaeological material.

actually made up those *ekklesiai*? Three additional studies bring these questions into higher relief.

In their book, *In Search of Paul: How Jesus's Apostle Opposed Rome's Empire with God's Kingdom*, John Dominic Crossan and Jonathan Reed also make observations about a potential meeting place for the community of Jesus followers in Corinth.[25] A previous book by these authors[26] attempted to use archaeological evidence to demonstrate Jesus' mission against the oppressive forces of Roman society.[27] A similar agenda is clearly stated to be the purpose of the Paul study.[28] One may agree or disagree with the modern social commentary that Crossan and Reed include in their book, but there should be unanimity in saying that discussions of archaeology and ancient society should not be manipulated in order to support particular viewpoints about modern society.

For Reed and Crossan, the examination of Paul and the house churches of Corinth comes as part of the chapter entitled, "Who and What Controls Your Banquet."[29] Here the authors pay special attention to what they consider to be architectural evidence for the interplay between social levels in the Roman world. In this particular case, they argue that in Roman cities such as Herculaneum and Pompeii, the standard architectural forms include a second-story luxurious villa combined with shops and workshops on the street level below and more modest apartments above. Based on this layout, they suggest that the Roman system of patron-client relationships and the proximity

---

[25] Crossan is a well-known scholar in the field of New Testament and Gospel studies. Reed is an archaeologist and a New Testament scholar who has excavated at Sepphoris in the Galilee.

[26] See Crossan and Reed 2001.

[27] "When, therefore, Jesus announced the Kingdom of God in the 20s in Lower Galilee, he and his companions taught, acted, and lived in opposition to Herod Antipas's localization of the Kingdom of Rome among his peasantry;" Crossan and Reed 2001, xix.

[28] Crossan and Reed explicitly state that one purpose of the book is to answer the question, "To what extent can America be Christian?" (2004, xi). Other modern sociopolitical issues mentioned include a challenge to the 'new world order' of American foreign policy, an allusion to the 'shock and awe' approach of U.S. military action, questions about the possible admission of Turkey to the European Union, a suggestion that the modern label 'obscene' should be used to condemn war rather than sexual material, and the assertion that destruction awaits modern humans unless they reject a culture of violence. They write: "Is it not clear by now that the safety of the world and the security of the earth demand the unity not of global victory, but of global justice? Otherwise, God will still be God, but only of the insects and the grasses" (403).

[29] Crossan and Reed 2001, 292–348.

of entrances to these different areas of the building must have provided the opportunity for interaction between people from different strata of society.[30] Crossan and Reed suggest that this combination of spaces provided the kind of architectural crossroads in which people from different social levels could have found themselves involved in the same community of Jesus followers.[31]

David Balch has also pointed out this tendency for Roman housing in Pompeii and Herculaneum to be the point of intersection for people of different social levels. "Both *domus* and *insulae* incorporated shops, again placing owners, freedmen and slaves in the same domestic spaces..."[32] Balch bases his comments on the analysis of archaeological evidence for housing in and around Rome, Pompeii and Herculaneum by Andrew Wallace-Hadrill,[33] and he suggests that these findings can provide a broader view of possible locations for Christian assemblies. "Archaeological investigation of *domus* in Pompeii and Herculaneum does not sustain the current consensus that early Pauline house churches were necessarily small or that they were private."[34] He does not, however, attempt to apply these findings to specific communities where this evidence is not attested.

Crossan and Reed take the 'household as crossroads' model[35] based on *domus* and *insulae* remains from Italy and try to apply it in Corinth where no evidence for this kind of housing has been found. In effect, the authors use the good state of preservation caused by the Vesuvius eruption as a rationalization.[36] They transport this architectural style from Herculaneum and elsewhere and employ it to explain the social environment in Corinth, where they argue that Paul was exposed to "more elevated circles" than he had known before.[37] Since this housing pattern is attested elsewhere, but not at Corinth, it is not clear why

---

[30] Crossan and Reed 2001, 316–30.
[31] Crossan and Reed 2001, 328–29.
[32] Balch 2004, 42.
[33] Wallace-Hadrill 1994 and 2003.
[34] Balch 2004, 41.
[35] Wallace-Hadrill 2003; Balch 2004, 42.
[36] "You are in Campania because volcanic horror preserved there far more, far better, and far fuller examples of those villa-and-shop combinations than you can see at Corinth or Ephesus" (Crossan and Reed 2004, 319). Charles Williams's warning that the potential for earthquake damage made multi-story housing impractical at Corinth is again relevant here. It is not that evidence for multi-story housing has been lost, according to Williams, but rather that it never existed.
[37] Crossan and Reed 2004, 329.

Corinth would be the first place where Paul would have encountered it. For Crossan and Reed, the need to have some architectural form to explain the social diversity of the believing community in Corinth and the apparent social conflicts discussed in the first letter is so great, that they import a locally unattested form. There is an interesting contrast here to the aforementioned work of Murphy-O'Connor, who is not cited in the Crossan and Reed book, but who also used an architectural pattern to explain the social conflict. In Murphy-O'Connor's case, however, the villa form that he utilized was at least attested at Corinth.

Once again, the attempt to connect specific architectural evidence with meeting places for the early Jesus movement in Corinth seems to lead to speculative and indefinite conclusions. At the 2006 Society of Biblical Literature meeting in Washington, D.C., one of the participants in a panel review of Jorunn Økland's book (2004), suggested that 30 years of work on the question of housing in Corinth had not proved fruitful in significant ways. Does this mean we should give up? Does it mean that the search for actual, physical, specific space is not worth the effort? While it is tempting to simply answer 'yes' to this question, I believe that Økland herself provides a helpful approach to the question.

Økland moves away from the attempt to locate the physical place where the communities might have met, and instead suggests that *ekklesia* space is determined by ritual, not vice versa. She argues:

> With a spatial-ritual approach to 1 Corinthians 11–14 it is possible to see the contours of a particular, historically situated and discursively defined ritual space which was quite different from the modern reality of the institutionalized Christian churches.[38]

Along the way, her study is certainly enhanced by reviewing the range of physical space available within the Corinthian context. Her approach, however, is not dependent on any particular physical location and can be applied to whatever space the believing community or some group within it might have utilized.

---

[38] Økland 2004, 166.

> *Ekklesia*, in the meaning of ritual gathering, should be a space properly set off from daily life. Clear verbal boundaries must be constructed in order to avoid overlapping between the two kinds of space.[39]

It is possible to read Økland's work, especially the chapters entitled "Placing the Corinthian Gatherings" and "Corinthian Order," as attempts to utilize both textual and archaeological evidence without resorting to unwarranted entanglement with a specific physical place for the gatherings. "In Paul's text, it seems that the material space where the *ekklesia* gathers is rather irrelevant: in his question it does not seem to be a problem that the material text housing the ekklesia space is the same as that of the household."[40]

Økland's work may signal the best way forward, by taking the archaeological material seriously while admitting the limitations of both the evidence and our ability to interpret it. Thinking of the *ekklesia* as ritual space and not just physical location provides a good intellectual framework for Horrell's challenge to "pay more attention to the varieties of domestic space in the urban setting of Corinth and other cities of the Roman empire."[41] Rather than trying to locate the communities in a particular physical venue, scholars are challenged to think about how the ritually defined community made use of different places. This approach serves to enhance our understanding of the context for Paul's communities without creating an artificially certain connection between archaeology and text. In the case of Økland's work, this interplay between physical space and ritual context is especially important for understanding gender roles in the early believing community.[42]

One final source may help to fine tune this approach even more. Carolyn Osiek and Margaret Y. MacDonald invite the reader to take very seriously the real world events, especially events involving women, that would have taken place in domestic space where this ritually defined *ekklesia* was established. While Økland, argues that "[c]lear verbal boundaries must be constructed to avoid overlapping between

---

[39] Økland 2004, 166.
[40] Økland 2004, 142.
[41] Horrell 2004, 369.
[42] "Further, 1 Corinthians 11–14 structures the *ekklesia* space in a way analoguous to the sanctuary spaces of early Roman Cointh, and genders this space as male....The male, unified body of Chirst is *the* representation of the ritually constructed *ekklesia* in this section. Proper ritual is dissociated from disorder, *glossolalia*, lack of unity, women out of bounds, and so on;" Økland 2004, 224.

the two kinds of space,"[43] Osiek and MacDonald contend that such overlap would have been unavoidable:

> The sounds of a woman in labor somewhere in the background, the crying of infants, the presence of mothers or wet nurses feeding their children, little toddlers under foot, children's toys on the floor—all could have been part of the atmosphere.[44]

While the interruptions would have been different if the believers were gathering in a shop, a warehouse, or in a more pastoral setting, it is a helpful reminder that even the best ritual definition of space as *ekklesia* would not have eliminated the natural sounds, the smells, the sights, and the other distractions of the *oikia* and the real world. While Horrell encourages us to use disciplined imagination to think about a variety of spaces, and Økland highlights the importance of ritual definition of *ekklesia*, Osiek and MacDonald emphasize the noise and messiness of real people living and dying in real places.

Having reviewed these different approaches to the question of Paul's community or communities and domestic space in Corinth, albeit in summary fashion, is it possible to draw conclusions or set up standards by which the interpretation of lodgings in Roman Corinth should be undertaken? It is obvious that even those who dig in Corinth cannot snap their fingers and address the lack of evidence for domestic space. But if new material remains are brought to light, how should they be approached by those who seek to understand the early Jesus movement in Corinth?

We might start with the analysis of Crossan and Reed, whose work on housing in Corinth should caution us not to go beyond the local evidence by importing non-existent material remains to support a particular finding or presupposition. Learning from Murphy-O'Connor, we are encouraged to take the material remains seriously, but not to set up a paradigm that limits our understanding of where and how these first 1st century believers would have gathered. They could have met in a villa, and we can consider how the physical realities of that space might have influenced the community. At the same time, basing a reconstruction on one particular space must be called into question since archaeological evidence for that space is subject to reinterpretation. As Horrell points out, there were other locations where

---

[43] Økland 2004, 166.
[44] Osiek and MacDonald 2006, 67.

people lived and we "should pay more attention to the varieties of domestic space in the urban setting of Corinth and other cities of the Roman empire."[45] The fact that the imaginative domestic space on East Theater Street disappears with the second story, does not lessen the importance of Horrell's observations. Økland enriches this broader approach with clear discussion of how ritual definition meant that *ekklesia* was not dependent on any one type of physical space. Finally, Osiek and MacDonald offer a positive model for consideration of how new evidence for domestic space might be related to the real lives of all members of the community regardless of age, status or gender. These steps allow scholars to ask how the realities of the surroundings might have affected attempts to establish *ekklesia* in a particular space, but to let the archaeological evidence speak to us rather than vice versa.

The first use of building imagery in 1 Corinthians comes in the third chapter where Paul refers to his own work as laying a foundation on which other apostles have later come to build. In his mind this makes perfect sense, given his early influence on the community and the universal truth that a strong foundation is necessary to create a solid and long-lasting building. Archaeological study, however, is largely dependent on the analysis of foundations to determine the layout of ancient buildings. By its very nature, the process of re-creating the space above the foundation is more speculative since it is usually based on scattered and fragmentary evidence. "Archaeological remains are as physical as one can hope to get, but their interpretation is up to the scholar, and that never is as solid as the material being discussed."[46] It may very well be that finding ways of talking about the 1st century assemblies of believers without attempting to tie them to particular locations may provide a foundation for advancing the subject in the future. As Robinson puts it, "[W]ith continued cross-disciplinary communication, we can better understand the ancient city, the spaces into which it was divided, by walls or ritual, and the people therein."[47]

---

[45] Horrell 2004, 369.
[46] Charles K. Williams, personal communication.
[47] Robinson 2006.

CHAPTER ELEVEN

PAUL AND THE POLITICS OF MEALS IN ROMAN CORINTH

James C. Walters

In this essay I will argue that Paul's rebuke of the Corinthians for their meal practices in the setting of the Lord's Supper and his corrective instructions (1 Cor. 11:17–31) are best understood as an attempt to limit the power that Paul's rivals could exert through meals. This thesis depends on recognizing the utility of meals as contexts within which hosts were able to wield considerable influence, the crisis of leadership Paul faced at Corinth, and the potential effects of Paul's instructions on those hosting meals in the Corinthian *ekklesia*.

The Utility of Meals for Exerting Political Influence

The connection between meals and civic political influence is explicit in a law contained in the *Lex Coloniae Genetivae*, the colonial charter of Urso in Spain, a colony that was—like Corinth—founded in 44 BCE under Julius Caesar.[1] It is widely assumed that the *Colonia Laus Iulia Corinthiensis* was founded on the basis of a similar charter.[2] Though fragmentary, most of Urso's charter has survived on bronze tablets engraved in the Flavian period. The surviving tablets begin with the authority and rights of magistrates (ch. 19–29), followed by those of the decurions (ch. 30–48). The next section deals with elections (ch. 49–60) followed by sections dealing with public administration (ch. 61–83), the administration of justice (ch. 84–94), and various other matters.[3]

The law that concerns us here forbids what might be called 'general' or 'indiscriminate' hospitality in the setting of the election of

---

[1] For the text of this charter with English translation and commentary: Crawford 1996, 393–454.
[2] For details of the colonization process: Salmon 1969, 13–28.
[3] Crawford 1996, 397. The first tablet is missing but is believed to have dealt with religion.

magistrates.[4] The law clearly seeks to limit bribery or influence peddling though banquets and gifts:

> No candidate in the *colonia Genetiva* after the granting of this statue,
> whoever shall seek a magistracy in the *colonia Genetiva Julia*, with a view
> to seeking a magistracy in that year, in which year each such person will
> seek or will be about to seek a magistracy as a candidate, is to offer ban-
> quets [with a view to] seeking a magistracy or invite anyone to dinner
> or hold a banquet, nor is he knowingly with wrongful [deceit] to see that
> anyone hold a banquet with a view to his candidature or invite anyone to
> dinner, except insofar as the candidate himself in that year [in which] he
> may seek a magistracy may have invited up to nine men a day and may
> have held a banquet, if he shall wish, without wrongful deceit. Nor may a
> candidate give or distribute a gift or present or anything else with a view
> to his candidature knowingly with wrongful deceit. Nor is anyone with
> a view to candidature of another to give dinner or hold a banquet,[5] nor
> is anyone with a view to the candidature of another to give or grant or
> distribute any gift or present or anything else knowingly with wrongful
> deceit. If anyone shall have acted contrary to these rules, he is to be con-
> demned to pay 5,000 sesterces to the colonists of the *colonia Genetiva
> Iulia* and there is to be action, suit and claim for that sum according to
> this statute by whoever of them shall wish in a recuperatorial trial before
> the *IIvir* [or] prefect and there is to be right and power.[6]

The numbing repetitions in the wording of this law contribute to the
common view that the larger charter is an "ill-drafted and ill-organised
document."[7] Crawford, however, argues that on the whole the charter
is coherent and intelligible and that such repetitions "result from an
obsessive desire to leave no room whatsoever for doubt in the mind
of the reader."[8] What this law seeks to make clear is the boundary
between hosting an innocent meal—or giving an innocent gift—and
electoral bribery. Most importantly, the law provides the grounds for

---

[4] Crawford 1996, 453.
[5] Similar concerns regarding the strategic use of dinners to influence elections can
be seen in Gellius's comment that the law of Antius, in addition to curtailing extravagant spending for dinners, "contained the additional provision, that no magistrate or
magistrate elect should dine out anywhere except at the house of stipulated persons"
(*Attic Nights* 2.24.13). This provision must have been put in place to stop candidates
from getting around previous laws by having friends give dinners on their behalf.
[6] Crawford 1996, 431–32.
[7] Crawford 1996, 395. Although it is possible that some changes were made to
the charter when it was published in the Flavian period, it is very likely that these
electioneering restrictions go back to the foundation of the Colony in 44 BCE and to
electioneering reforms during the late republic.
[8] Crawford 1996, 396.

an interested party to bring legal action against a rival who may have used meals unlawfully—or other favors—to garner votes.

The three main sources that shed light on electoral bribery during the late Republic are two speeches by Cicero defending candidates charged with electoral bribery, *Pro Murena* and *Pro Plancio*; and the *Commentariolum Petitionis* (or, *Handbook on Electioneering*).[9] The latter purports to be a letter from Quintus Cicero to Marcus Cicero offering advice for a successful political canvass.

Pro Murena offers perhaps our best ancient commentary on the concerns addressed by the colonial charter from Urso. Cicero denies that Murena broke the law of Calpurnius forbidding candidates from paying men to meet them, hiring companions, and indiscriminately giving places at gladiatorial games and invitations to dinner. In the speech, Cicero responds to Cato's charge of *ambitus* (bribery) by blurring the distinction between traditional favors and bribery. He claims that the large crowds that followed Murena did so out of good Roman manners, not because they were paid: "There is no penalty that can prevent men of the lower class from showing their gratitude in this old-established way of fulfilling their obligations."[10] To the charge of giving gladiatorial seats and dinners indiscriminately he also appeals to tradition calling such favors the "rewards and bounties that poorer men receive from their fellow-tribesmen by ancient custom." Mockingly, Cicero asks:

> The Senate does not think that it is illegal to go out to meet a candidate, does it? No, only if payment was made. Prove that it was. To be escorted by a large crowd? No, only if they were hired. Show that they were. To provide a seat at a show or give an invitation to dinner? Not at all, unless it was given indiscriminately throughout the city.[11]

Fortunately, Cicero defines what he means by 'indiscriminately' as "given to everybody."[12] Moreover, in the same context he offers a tangible example:

> If a Vestal Virgin, a relative and friend, has given Murena her seat at the gladiatorial games, her gift is a mark of affection and his acceptance of it

---

[9] Brunt 1988, 43.
[10] *Mur.* 71. 4–16 (trans. MacDonald 1976).
[11] *Mur.* 73.15–16.
[12] *Mur.* 73.17–18.

above reproach. All these acts are the obligation of friends and relatives, the services of poorer men and the duties of candidates.[13]

Cicero concludes this part of his argument with another appeal blurring the distinction between traditional favors and bribery:

The Roman commons, therefore, should not be robbed of the enjoyment it gets from games, gladiatorial shows and banquets, which were all established by our ancestors, nor should candidates be prevented from displaying an open-handedness which is the token of liberality rather than bribery.[14]

Commenting on Cicero's rhetoric in this speech, Lintott writes:

Clearly, one's concept of bribery depends on whether one is the offender, the offender's friend or the victim. To bribe is an irregular verb: 'I take appropriate care of my friends, you are recklessly generous, he bribes.' Yet there is an objective element too in Cicero's attitude. The traditional care of dependents is honourable, the separation of people from their former connections by throwing money about is immoral—a conservative paternalist view very much in harmony with Cicero's general approach to politics.[15]

By 'conservative' Lintott means that it was aristocrats who sought these laws in order to restrict the power newcomers ('new men') could exert to gain office through excessive expenditures associated with their electioneering.[16]

Although the quotations from Cicero's defense of Murena seem to suggest that meals and other favors were offered by candidates to attract votes from the lower classes, the dominant view among historians of the Late Republic has long been that aristocratic families determined the outcomes of elections, not the poorer classes.[17] However, in recent studies of electioneering there has been a decided trend to take popular participation in elections in Rome more seriously. The change can be traced back to Fergus Millar's three *JRS* essays in the mid to late 1980s and to his 1998 book.[18] Also important is the work of Alexander

---

[13] *Mur.* 73.25–30.
[14] *Mur.* 77.16–21.
[15] Lintott 1990, 11.
[16] Lintott 1990, 11. In the case of Corinth, a colony settled by freedmen, 'new men' would be persons campaigning for office who were not descendants of the wealthy freedmen appointed to office when the colony was originally settled.
[17] See, for example, the influential study by Gelzer 1912, 134–35.
[18] Millar 1984, 1986, 1989, and 1998.

Yakobson.[19] Yakobsen challenges the common view that the very rich dominated the centuriate assembly and electoral bribery is central to his argument. He writes, "If massive electoral bribery is hard to account for in an 'oligarchic assembly,' should we not conclude that the assembly was less oligarchic than is often thought, rather than doubt the testimony of the sources?"[20] Building on Brunt's earlier critique, he disputes the notion that electoral success was routinely achieved by the delivery of votes via patronage ties, arguing instead that public support was required. "The more the concept of patronage covers," he writes, "the less it explains."[21] Therefore, instead of discussing the census qualifications—which would require considerable speculation regarding qualifications for the respective classes, and especially regarding the distribution of citizens among the classes—Yakobsen chooses to focus on the behavior of the candidates as the key to understanding the election system during the Late Republic. He claims that issues mattered in elections and that the secret ballot effectively drove up the price of tangible rewards sought by voters; namely, banquets, feasts, shows and bribes.[22]

That popular participation was a real concern to candidates seeking office can be seen in the *Handbook on Electioneering*. Although it is questionable whether it is a letter from Quintus to Marcus Cicero, as it purports to be, Roman historians take its knowledge of Republican election practices seriously.[23] The advice for appealing to the 'people' is telling. The candidate must conduct himself "...so that they say and believe that you know people well, solicit them courteously, canvass continuously and thoroughly, are a gracious and generous person;

---

[19] Yakobson 1999.

[20] Yakobson 1999, 25.

[21] Yakobson 1999, 81.

[22] Lintott argues that sumptuary laws enacted during the Republic should be read in light of concerns regarding electoral bribery (*ambitus*) rather than merely attempts to restrain extravagant indulgence, as some Roman writers would have us believe. From the *Lex Orchia* of 182 BCE to the *Lex Antia* of 68 BCE, at least five such laws were enacted, including the *Lex Fannia*, the *Lex Didia*, and the *Lex Licinia*. References to bribery become more common during the Late Republic and additional laws (Sulla, 81 BCE; C. Cornelius, 67 BCE; Pompey 52 BCE) sought to regulate electioneering practices. References to improper influence through seats at gladiatorial shows, entourages and dinners are commonplace; Lintott 1990, 1–16.

[23] For bibliography on both sides of the authenticity debate: Shackleton Bailey 2002, 402–03.

and so that your house is full long before dawn with crowds of all
classes…"[24]

A successful canvass of the people depends, according to the Handbook, on (1) knowing people, especially their names; (2) ingratiation;
(3) attendance; (4) and generosity.[25] And it is banquets that are featured as the best means of displaying a candidate's generosity. The
Handbook explains that generosity is shown "in the use of one's private means, for although this cannot reach the masses, the masses like
hearing it praised by your friends; it is shown in banquets, to which
you and your friends should often convoke the people at large or tribe
by tribe."[26]

The last phrase, "banquets, to which you *and your friends* should
often convoke people at large or tribe by tribe," should remind the
reader of the Urso charter's attempt to regulate these very actions;
"Nor is anyone with a view *to the candidature of another* to offer banquets or invite anyone to dinner or hold a banquet."[27] As Cicero's
defense of Murena makes clear, banquets could be given and defended
if those invited had natural connections to the one hosting the banquet (for example, belong to the same tribe). This made the personal
connections of candidates extremely important because through these
connections a variety of networks could be exploited—reaching even
to the poorer classes. Moreover, because the *Handbook on Electioneering* explicitly offers advice on how a 'new man' can break into the consular ranks through meals and other favors, it supports Lintott's claim
that regulating these practices was the concern of elites who sought to
limit the rise of new men.[28]

Before turning to Paul's mission, I would like to anticipate three
objections that might be brought against using electioneering materials as comparanda for the Pauline mission: these sources and these
elections involved the wealthy and are, therefore, not relevant to the
Pauline mission; one cannot use materials from Republican Rome
to imagine behaviors across the Empire; and, it is not appropriate to
extrapolate from influence peddling in the setting of elections to other
areas of life.

---

[24] *Comment. Pet.* 50.8–12 (trans. Shackleton Bailey 2002).
[25] *Comment. Pet.* 41–44.
[26] *Comment. Pet.* 44.4–8.
[27] Crawford 1996, 432.
[28] *Comm. Pet.* 2.1–3; 13.1–3; Lintott 1990, 11.

Although those who competed in these elections were the wealthiest of the wealthy, their concern was not only to influence their peers but also the lower classes as well. This is, in fact, why recent studies of electioneering in Rome are so central to my thesis. If the votes of the lower classes mattered in Roman elections, attempts to win those votes tell us something about these classes as well. In fact, Yakobson notes that seats at gladiatorial games and banquets would have appealed especially to the lower classes; "It seems more than probable that the *proletarii*, too, benefited from the *largationes*—especially such as games and feasts—which were aimed primarily at the humbler sort of *assidui*."[29] Moreover, although most of the evidence involves candidates competing for the highest offices in Rome, Cicero's defense of Plancius concerned bribery charges in an election for the office of an *aedile*. L. R. Taylor has noted that because *aediles* put on games and theatrical performances for the people, this was an important post for Romans who were climbing the ladder of Rome's *cursus honorum*.[30]

Although the utility of banquets for exerting influence in the competition for votes is commonplace in literary sources from the Late Republic, can electioneering practices in Rome—the political center of the empire—be used to imagine conduct in provincial cities? The colonial charter from Urso indicates that the answer is yes. Rome's *cursus honorum* was replicated in Roman colonies so that even under the empire, elite males contended for office in an 'honors race' that involved competing in and winning elections.[31] Moreover, because magistrates served only one-year terms, elections—and electioneering—were a non-stop feature of civic life in Rome and in its colonies.

These canvassing regulations no doubt made their way into Caesarian colonial charters because the task of establishing and maintaining a stable elite in a new colony—keeping the reins of power in the 'right' hands—could be undermined through gifts and banquets. Lintott's observation that such restrictions had a conservative character—that they sought to prevent newcomers from breaking into the ranks of the elite by means of wealth—informs my argument here.[32] The Romans had only recently learned this lesson the hard way, and the Urso

---

[29] Yakobson 1999, 26.
[30] L. R. Taylor 1949, 30–31.
[31] Hellerman 2005, 51–109.
[32] Lintott 1990, 11.

charter indicates that they perceived a need for regulations not only in Rome but also in Rome's colonies.[33]

Finally, is it possible to extrapolate from election canvassing to influence peddling in other arenas of life—like, for example, the Pauline mission in Corinth? The best ancient evidence may be the prologue to Plautus's *Amphitryon*. Mercury addresses the audience with a petition from Jupiter asking that inspectors be appointed to insure fairness in theatrical competitions. Such inspectors, he asserts, would protect against undue influence by actors and their agents on the outcome of the competitions. Plautus has Mercury say:

> Now here is the favour Jove bade me ask of you: (*with great solemnity*) let inspectors go from seat to seat throughout the house, and should they discover claqueurs planted for the benefit of any party, let them take as security from all such in the house—their togas. Or if there be those who have solicited the palm for actors, or for any artist—whether by letter, or by personal solicitation, or through an intermediary—or further, if the *aediles* do bestow the said palm upon anyone unfairly, Jove doth decree that the selfsame law obtain as should the said party solicit guiltily, for himself or for another, public office. Tis worth has won your wars for you, saith he, not solicitation or unfairness: why should not the same law hold for player as for noblest patriot? Worth, not hired support, should solicit victory. He who plays his part aright ever has support enough, if it so be that honour dwells in those whose concern it is to judge his acts. This injunction, too, did Jove lay upon me: that inspectors should be appointed-for the actors, to the end that whosoever has enjoined claqueurs to clap himself, or whosoever has endeavoured to compass the failure of another, may have his player's costume cut to shreds, also his hide. I would not have you wonder why Jove is now regardful of actors; do not so: he himself, Jove, will take part in this comedy.[34]

By comparing actors seeking to sway theatrical judges with *aediles* running for office, Plautus has Mercury accusing actors of unfair electioneering. Because the passage contains a number of legal terms found in Republican laws that attempted to check electoral bribery, the passage has been central to interpolation theories that seek to exploit the apparent tension between dates for the career of Plautus and specific

---

[33] Concerns over illicit political influence through banquets are traceable to the turmoil of Late Republican Rome. As Millar notes, "the much greater prominence of electoral bribery in our sources for the last two decades of the Republic reflects the real power of the electorate, whose support had to be gained by all possible means" (1998, 69).

[34] Plaut. *Amph.* 64–96 (trans. Nixon 1938).

ambitus laws.[35] What concerns us here, however, are not interpolation theories but the obvious assumption in the play that the audience would have no difficulty making the move from illicit influence in electioneering to illicit influence in other areas of life.

My interpretation of chapter 132 of Urso's colonial charter in light of other laws governing electioneering in Republican Rome leads to four conclusions: (1) hosting meals—by a candidate or a candidate's supporter—was perceived as a formidable means of swaying votes in an election; (2) concerns about using meals to bribe voters resulted not only in laws being enacted in republican Rome, but also laws being inscribed in colonial charters; (3) meals were viewed as especially effective for influencing the poorer classes either because the poor benefited directly by dining, or because word of mouth advertised the candidate's generosity to poor persons even if they were not present for the meal; (4) limiting who could host a meal did not simply level the playing field, it limited the rise of newcomers. Lintott's summary of Cicero's 'conservative paternalist view' bears repeating: "The traditional care of dependents is honorable, the separation of people from their former connections by throwing money about is immoral."[36]

PAUL'S POLITICAL CRISIS AT CORINTH

The general narrative of Paul's interactions with the Corinthian Christ-believers that emerges from reading the extant correspondence vividly illustrates the crisis of leadership the apostle faced in Corinth.[37] Although we do not have the first letter Paul wrote to Corinth, the allusion to it in 1 Cor. 5:9 indicates that the letter failed in its aim to regulate community interactions with immoral persons who belonged to the Jesus movement in Corinth. Paul's responses in 1 Corinthians to the various reports and letters he received from Corinth reflect continuing confusion, developing schisms and a waning of Paul's influence

---

[35] For example, McDonnell 1986.

[36] Lintott 1990, 11.

[37] Stamps (1993) explores the rhetorical situation of 1 Corinthians by transforming the letter into a narrative of Paul's interactions with the Corinthians as inscribed in the letter.

over his converts.[38] Most revealing is the conclusion of Paul's call for concord in the opening argument (1 Cor. 4:14–21):[39]

> I am not writing this to make you ashamed, but to admonish you as my beloved children. For though you might have ten thousand guardians in Christ, you do not have many fathers. Indeed, in Christ Jesus I became your father through the gospel. I appeal to you, then, be imitators of me. For this reason I sent you Timothy, who is my beloved and faithful child in the Lord, to remind you of my ways in Christ Jesus, as I teach them everywhere in every church. But some of you, thinking that I am not coming to you, have become arrogant. But I will come to you soon, if the Lord wills, and I will find out not the talk of these arrogant people but their power. For the kingdom of God depends not on talk but on power. What would you prefer? Am I to come to you with a stick, or with love in a spirit of gentleness?

In 4:18–21 Paul clearly zeros in on a group within the community (not outside agitators) who have actively challenged Paul's authority and influence. Verses 14–17 indicate that Paul fears their influence on the larger community. Fee writes:

> The problem, of course, is that they have had considerable influence on the entire community, so that the majority, it seems likely from the tenor of the argument throughout, are on the side of these malcontents, or at least are being influenced by them.[40]

Although Paul claims that allegiance to teachers is misplaced in chapters 1–4 (see especially 1:10–17), in the conclusion to the opening argument of the letter he asserts that allegiance to him as their 'father' is quite in order. As Elizabeth Castelli has argued, Paul's call in 4:16 for his converts to "be imitators of me" should be read in connection with this patriarchal image as an attempt to assert his authority: "That Paul would exhort the Corinthians twice in this one document to become his imitators, when he is dealing with problems of social diffusion and dispersed authority, is both striking and telling."[41] Especially important is her observation that the call to mimesis in 4:16 is

---

[38] Fee 1987, 7–15.

[39] M. Mitchell (1991, 184–225) has argued persuasively that the entire letter of 1 Corinthians is an appeal (deliberative rhetoric) urging concord and that 1:18–4:21 censures Corinthian factionalism and establishes the need for Paul's advice. Unless otherwise noted, quotations of Paul's letters are taken from the NRSV.

[40] Fee 1987, 190.

[41] Castelli 1991, 98. Although some have emphasized ancient parallels that make care and affection the central features of the 'father metaphor' (Fiore 1982, 325–26),

connected to the call for unity in chapters 1–4 in the face of a crisis of leadership in the community. It is in this context that Paul offers him-self as the "singular authoritative model" and announces his planned dispatch of Timothy to offer them a refresher course in how to imi-tate Paul.[42] The face-to-face showdown Paul claims he would relish with "some…who have become arrogant" in 4:18–21 does not turn out in the apostle's favor when the day finally arrives.[43] According to his own reflections on the 'painful visit' in 2 Corinthians, many from whom he expected support did not take Paul's side and the result was his humiliation before them (2 Cor. 2:1–5, 12:20–21). Although Paul faces different rivals in 2 Corinthians (including outside agitators), his failure to find broad support during this visit confirms the waning of Paul's authority detectable already in 1 Corinthians.[44] The lack of back-ing he received during the "painful visit" indicates that the escalation of opposition forces and the weakening of his own position may have caught Paul somewhat off guard. Nonetheless, he was not completely in the dark. Paul stops short of naming Apollos as the problem in 1 Corinthians, but it seems apparent that he is one former community leader that some of Paul's rivals looked to instead of Paul. Two brief texts stand out:

> For as long as there is jealousy and quarreling among you, are you not of the flesh, and behaving according to human inclinations? For when one says, 'I belong to Paul,' and another, 'I belong to Apollos,' are you not merely human? What then is Apollos? What is Paul? Servants through whom you came to believe, as the Lord assigned to each. *I planted* [that is, founded the community], *Apollos watered* [that is, nurtured the com-munity], but God gave the growth (3:3–6; emphasis added).

Paul refers to Apollos again in the following chapter:

> I have applied all this to Apollos and myself for your benefit, brothers and sisters, so that you may learn through us the meaning of the saying,

---

others, like Castelli, have noted the assertion of patriarchal authority; Holmberg 1980, 77–79.

[42] Castelli 1991, 111 and 114.

[43] Stamps emphasizes the way Paul uses threats to visit as a means of creating an "aura of authority" in 1 Corinthians (1993, 204–08).

[44] On Paul's opponents in Corinth—with warnings against assuming that the oppo-nents in 2 Corinthians were the same as those in 1 Corinthians—see Sumney 1990.

'Nothing beyond what is written,' so that none of you will be *puffed up in favor of one against another* (4:6; emphasis added).[45]

When these references to Apollos are read in light of Paul's assertion of his own authority in 4:14–21, it becomes apparent that Paul is concerned not only about discord in the Corinthian *ekklesia* but also about his role as a leader of the community. Mitchell is correct in my view that 1 Corinthians is from beginning to end a call for concord addressed to a community plagued by factionalism.[46] However, Paul is not a neutral observer writing a treatise on concord. Rather, he is the community's founder, and wants to be its patriarch (4:15). He indeed argues for concord, but concord on his terms.[47]

POLITICAL RIVALRY AND MEALS IN THE *EKKLESIA*

Although the utility of meals for exerting electoral influence coupled with the challenges to Paul's leadership at Corinth would be sufficient grounds for reconsidering the import of Paul's instructions in 1 Cor. 11:17–34, there is another important reason. The introduction to the 'Lord's Supper' pericope (11:17–19) explicitly raises the issue of factions as the prelude to the rebuke and instructions that follow.[48]

> Now in the following instructions I do not commend you, because when you come together it is not for the better but for the worse. For, to begin with, when you come together as a church, I hear that there are divisions (σχίσματα) among you; and to some extent I believe it. Indeed, there have to be factions (αἱρέσεις) among you, for only so will it become clear who among you are genuine (11:17–19).

Noting that 11:18 is the first time the word σχίσματα ("divisions") occurs in the letter since 1:11, Welborn draws attention to the political rivalry in Paul's rhetoric by comparing the slogans, "I am of Paul, I am of Apollos, I am of Cephas, I am of Christ," to political slogans that

---

[45] For approaches and bibliography explaining Paul's reference to Apollos, especially in 4:6, see Thiselton 2000, 344–56.

[46] M. Mitchell 1991, 67.

[47] Paul's authoritative tone and rhetoric are central to Hurd's (1965, 82) well-known reconstruction of Paul's interactions with the Corinthians.

[48] According to M. Mitchell, Paul introduces the discussion by unmistakable political *topoi*: σχίσματα and αἱρέσεις. In addition, Mitchell demonstrates that συνέρχεσθαι (used 5 times in the pericope) commonly carries political connotations in contexts seeking reconciliation of divided persons (1991, 151–55).

have survived among the graffiti at Pompeii."[49] Moreover, comparing Paul's argument in chapters 1–4 with ancient *homonoia* speeches and the reference to the humiliation of the 'have-nots,' he relates Paul's strategy to that of Cicero. Paul's actions, according to Welborn, "bear a remarkable resemblance to Cicero's attempt in the eleventh hour of the republic to capture the lower classes for his own faction by means of a political fiction, the idealization of class affiliation (*pro Sestio* 96–98)."[50] It should also be noted that candidates routinely competed for office by exploiting the rhetoric of concord, claiming to be more committed to the "common advantage" (*to sympheron*) than their rivals who only sought their own interests.[51]

Whether or not class conflict is the best theoretical framework for interpreting 1 Cor. 11:17–34 is open to debate. However, it is apparent that both economic and status issues are salient factors in this context. Since the influential work of Gerd Theissen on the social context of 1 Corinthians, scholars have increasingly read 11:17–34 in light of Greco-Roman meal traditions in order to illuminate how the conduct of the banquet might have humiliated the have-nots.[52]

> When you come together, it is not really to eat the Lord's supper. For when the time comes to eat, each of you goes ahead with your own supper, and one goes hungry and another becomes drunk. What! Do you not have homes to eat and drink in? Or do you show contempt for the church of God and humiliate those who have nothing (11:20–22a)?

Note the contrast between "the Lord's supper" (κυριακὸν δεῖπνον) and "your own supper" (ἴδιον δεῖπνον) indicating that all were not eating the same food—or at least the same amounts of food. This interpretation is confirmed by Paul's comment that "one goes hungry and

---

[49] Although Hurd does not make the connection to political slogans at Pompeii, he does make a strong connection between this text and the slogans in 1 Cor. 1:10 and following. He writes, "the information which 11.17–34 presupposes is simply another aspect of the news which Paul explicitly said he had heard from 'Chloe's people' (1965, 82).

[50] Welborn 1987. D. Martin also sees class divisions as central to the factionalism at Corinth and notes that Paul consistently sides with the 'weak' (1995, xv–xvi).

[51] Cicero, *Off.* 3.28.101. Kei Eun Chang is finishing a dissertation at Boston University that compares the rhetoric of *to sympheron* in Cicero with Paul's use of this term in 1 Corinthians.

[52] Theissen 1982, 145–74. There is a lively debate regarding the social/economic status of the Pauline communities. However, there is broad agreement that Paul's house churches were populated largely with persons who were poor and of low status (1 Cor. 1:26). On the larger debate, see Friesen 2004.

another becomes drunk." The fact that the conduct of the meal communicated status distinctions is apparent in the concluding accusation that their behavior during the meal results in the humiliation of "those who have nothing."[53]

Because meals provided a tangible context in which status differences could be clearly demarked (invitations, posture, seating location, amount of food, quality of food, etc.), they provided an important arena for both showing honor and competing for honor.[54] Such competition is clearly seen in specific rules that attempted to regulate the behavior of association members when they dined together. Dennis Smith, in his study of Greco-Roman meal conventions, listed seven common regulations:[55]

1. Injunctions against quarreling and fighting.
2. Injunctions against taking the assigned place of another.
3. Injunctions against speaking out of turn or without permission.
4. Injunctions against fomenting factions.
5. Injunctions against accusing a fellow member before a public court.
6. Specifications for trials within the club for inter-club disputes.
7. Specifications for worship activities.

Because these associations provided opportunities for non-elites to compete for status and offices independent of the civic arena in which elites competed, it is not surprising that such regulations were necessary for maintaining group concord. Ascough writes, "Participation in an association allowed for the attainment of honor, prestige and authority through the replication of the organizational structure of the *polis*."[56] Therefore it seems unlikely that the competition for status

---

[53] The interpretation of the phrase τοὺς μὴ ἔχοντας is disputed. The NRSV's "those who have nothing" takes it in an absolute sense (that is, they are destitute), but its referent may be "houses/homes" from the previous sentence; Horrell 2005, 108, n. 35.

[54] D. Smith 2003, 42–46.

[55] D. Smith 1981, 323.

[56] Ascough 1997, 25. Although there were differences in the goals of association meals (conviviality) and electioneering meals (winning votes), there was also considerable overlap. This is true because the competition for offices in an association paralleled that of the civic arena. Moreover, candidates sought votes through the associations themselves. In *Comm. Pet.* 30 Cicero is encouraged to cultivate the leading men of *collegia* because they are the means by which to deliver the votes of the "rest of the multitude."

between members of an association was typically between rich and poor, even though the social makeup of associations was not always as uniform as is often supposed.[57] More often than not it would have been between persons who were only somewhat better off than others. However, we should not doubt that competition for status could be keen among people who may have lived only somewhat above subsistence.[58] Because the group life of associations centered on convivial dining at regular community banquets, these meals could easily become flashpoints for the very issues the regulations noted above attempted to manage.[59]

In Paul's mission, and in the communities he founded, it is also clear that meals were settings in which competition between rivals resulted in factions requiring the management of competing interests. I am persuaded by Dale Martin's interpretation of 1 Cor. 5:1–13 as reflecting a larger conflict between the 'weak' and the 'strong' within the Corinthian *ekklesia*.[60] Paul sides with the 'weak' who are concerned about the spread of pollution through sexual intercourse and he pressures the community to move against the immoral brother who enjoys the support of the 'strong.' Paul demands that the gathered community expel him (5:5, 13) and that they bar him from community meals (5:11b). According to Galatians 2:11–14, it was in the context of the community meal at Antioch that representatives from Jerusalem dispatched by James brought pressure on Paul's missionary companions and his Gentile converts, even influencing his coworker Barnabas to change sides.[61] In Rom. 14:1–15:13 Paul sought to regulate decisions about the food eaten at community meals so that those who were "weak in faith" might not be pressured to eat foods their faith did

---

[57] Harland (2003, 25–53) emphasizes that associations of Christ-followers were not unique in including persons of differing social locations because they often were composed of networks of individuals that were in themselves diverse (for example, households).

[58] Much more work needs to be done on the implications of what appear to us to be minor differences in economic level. Friesen (2004) in his 'poverty scale' attempts to quantify differences between persons who lived above subsistence.

[59] Eight of the 15 by-laws from a burial association at Lanuvium (136 CE) address matters related to the community's meals (*CIL* 14.2112).

[60] D. Martin 1995, 169–74.

[61] Nanos (2002) argues that what was at issue in Antioch was not the food that was eaten, but the manner in which the meal was conducted: dining so that Gentiles were treated as equal in status without becoming proselytes.

not permit.[62] Meals became flashpoints because they enacted contested issues in the community, issues that were seldom far removed from the rivals who were contesting them.

Because Paul founded the Corinthian *ekklesia*, early leaders who hosted meals were no doubt loyal to Paul—persons like Gaius (Rom. 16:23).[63] However, as the power dynamics changed at Corinth and as Paul continued his work in other locales, community meals became politically charged contexts that threatened Paul's influence. If, as Ronald Hock has argued, the rivalries at Corinth were between households who competed for status by hosting teachers who entered into their households according to the conventions of philosopher-teachers, one should expect that these rivalries were reflected in community meals hosted by the heads of some of these same households.[64] This is consistent with Stephen Barton's argument that in 1 Cor. 11:17–34 Paul sought to reorder "social relations in the church by restricting the intrusion of household-based power."[65]

If Paul's rivals were hosting community meals, or if Christ-followers of relatively higher status and financial means were hosting them on their behalf, these meals provided numerous opportunities to increase their influence in the community. The host was in an especially strong position to increase his/her status by displaying generosity.[66] As the *Handbook on Electioneering* noted, banquets were the best means of displaying a candidate's generosity.[67] Not only were they offering favors to the larger community that were experienced directly (meeting space and at least some of the resources), their generosity would be talked about even to persons who were not present for the meal.[68] Moreover, meal hosts were in a position to honor—and therefore to elevate—selected members of the community by executing their duties as host according to common meal conventions. These could include

---

[62] J. Walters 1993, 84–92.

[63] Although Paul calls Gaius "host to me and to the whole church," he certainly would not have been the only meal host at Corinth (Rom. 16:23)—though Paul no doubt wishes he was! Paul clearly attempts to elevate the status of Stephanas in the letter's final greetings, referring to his household as "the first converts in Achaia" and urging the Corinthians "to put yourselves at the service of such people, and of everyone who works and toils with them" (1 Cor. 16:15–16).

[64] Hock 1980, 62–65.

[65] Barton 1986, 243.

[66] On the role of meal hosts: D. Smith 2003, 33 and 100–101.

[67] *Comm. Pet.* 41–44 (trans. Shackleton Bailey 2002).

[68] These benefits were explicitly noted in *Comment. Pet.* 44.4–8.

invitations, variations in the amount and/or quality of food served to individual guests, whether those present could recline or had to resort to sitting or standing, who might be invited to 'first tables,' as well as how the participation in teaching and worship were managed.[69] If Paul was no longer able to determine that Gaius (Rom. 16:23)—or others sympathetic to him—would host the community meals at Corinth, he could at least attempt to limit the utility of these meals as contexts for his rivals to curry favor—or, in his view, to foment factions.

Paul's Instructions in Light of the Urso Charter

How would Paul's instructions have impacted the influence that hosts could exert through meals? First, by sharply distinguishing the community meal from other meals, Paul is able to challenge the appropriateness of meal conventions that reinforced the host's status and power in other settings. Second, by underscoring that Jesus himself is the host of the community meal, Paul rhetorically supplants the Corinthian hosts who might use meals to supplant him.

Paul had a meal problem because a community meal was central to the identity and organization of the *ekklesia* and because the meal conventions that permitted his rivals to consolidate and extend their influence in the community were common household conventions that were broadly assumed. Because they were assumed, they required neither explanation nor defense. The problem is so great that Stephen Barton wonders whether Paul's community organizing efforts would have been better served if he had distanced himself from the household pattern rather than attempting to modify it.[70] Barton is convinced that differences over the boundaries between church and household stand behind the conflict between Paul and at least some of the Corinthians regarding women speaking in the assembly (1 Cor. 14:33b–36) and

---

[69] D. Smith (2003, 200–14) makes a strong connection between 1 Cor. 11 and chapters 12–14 so that status issues reflected in the meal are not isolated from status issues reflected in worship—which he thinks also happened in the dining room. "First tables" refers to the possibility that some of the Corinthians were invited to have "appetizers" before others arrived for the meal. This reading is more plausible if προλαμβάνειν in v. 21 is translated "goes ahead with" rather than "shares in" because this invites an interpretive connection between v. 21 and the exhortation to "wait for one another" in 11:33; D. Smith 2003, 191–93.

[70] Barton 1986, 243.

regarding the conduct of the community meal (1 Cor. 11:17–34).[71] The situation is complicated by the fact that Paul generally embraces the image of the church as a household. Therefore when he believes that practices and assumptions belonging to the household are inappropriate for the church, he must delicately differentiate the two—especially since the church is meeting in a house. In his anthropological analysis of 1 Cor. 11:17–34 Barton highlights seven ways Paul works to distinguish the church meal from an ordinary household meal.[72]

1. By giving it a distinct 'spatio-temporal location' indicated by the special use of the verb συνέρχεσθαι ('to gather together') in 11:17, 18, 20, 33 and 34 (as well as ἐν ἐκκλησίᾳ [11:18] and ἐπὶ τὸ αὐτό [11:20]).
2. By giving it a sacred name: 'Lord's meal' (κυριακὸν δεῖπνον, 11:20).
3. By linking the meal with holy tradition 'received from the Lord' (11:23–25).
4. By contrasting it to a mundane meal 'at home' (11:34a, 11:21)
5. By using the traditional citations over the 'breaking of bread' at the beginning of the meal and 'the cup' after the meal to encourage solidarity—beginning and ending together.
6. By emphasizing the dangerous quality of the meal as a potential source of guilt and judgment (11:27–32, 34b).
7. By structuring the meal as a *ritual of incorporation,* a ritual means of renegotiating patterns of allegiance among separate and competing household groups (emphasis retained).

Because household meal conventions were the norm, the power that a host wielded in the setting of a meal was largely "veiled" because their roles and the choices they made were conventional.[73] By differentiating this meal from ordinary meals, Paul argues that normal meal conventions do not apply. He hopes that such a move will undermine the

---

[71] Barton 1986, 225.

[72] I have attempted to condense these using Barton's language (1986, 240–42) whenever possible.

[73] "Veiled" in the sense that Gordon claims the emperor's power was veiled by the association between the practice of euergetism and his position as sacrificer and priest after Augustus became *pontifex maximus;* Gordon 1990. In this case it would be the association between the practice of euergetism and the position of head of the household/host of the meal.

advantages that hosts might have extending their influence via meals while he is away from Corinth.

Like Barton, Jorunn Økland also thinks Paul is working hard in this text to distinguish the community meal from a household meal. She emphasizes the role ritual plays in making the distinction. Drawing attention to 1 Cor. 11:22 where Paul writes, "do you not have houses (οἰκίας) in which to eat and drink…or do you despise the church (ἐκκλησίας) of God," she writes:

> Since the places where the Christians gathered functioned simultaneously as someone's house, it follows that from the perspective of many of those present, the material space of the *ekklesia* and that of their *oikia* was identical. If they followed Paul's advice, ritual constructed the sanctuary space on the place that already had strong connotations of household and home for them. They had no other place to go to eat or drink. These people did not leave the room to 'go to' *ekklesia*, they simply changed discourse or dimension when they gathered as *ekklesia*. The gatherings were marked out through ritual actions as opposed to the daily life between the Christians.[74]

Because this meal is eaten in *ekklesia* space—not *oikia* space—different codes apply: "Codes of veiling, silence and speaking, and of meal patterns are different in household space and *ekklesia* space."[75]

What makes Økland's argument of special interest to me is her claim that Paul makes the distinction principally by connecting the κυριακὸν δεῖπνον at Corinth with Jesus' last supper.[76] She writes:

> By drawing on the words of Jesus on the occasion of the Pesach meal (according to Christian oral tradition 'Jesus' last meal') in this context, Paul communicates that the last supper is in a way paradigmatic for the Christian meal. In that meal in Jerusalem with his friends, Jesus 'took'—

---

[74] Økland 2004, 142.

[75] Økland 2004. Similarly, Hofius writes: "This celebration is constituted as 'the Lord's meal' by 'the bread of the Lord' and the 'cup of the Lord,' i.e., by the two sacramental acts that enclose the common meal and thus give it, too, its essential character" (1993, 96).

[76] The rhetorical structure of the pericope supports this claim. The pericope has four rather straightforward rhetorical moves: a rebuke of the Corinthians (11:17–22); the recital of the Lord's Supper tradition (11:23–26); Paul's application of this tradition to the Corinthian situation (11:27–32); and, concluding exhortations (11:33–34). The second move is clearly where the weight of the argument rests. For a rhetorical analysis of the passage that outlines the text in a similar way: Eriksson 1998, 174–96.

'said grace'—'broke'—'said'—and finishes with a commandment to 'do this in remembrance of me' (11.25).[77]

Thus *oikia* space becomes *ekklesia* space through recollecting and reenacting Jesus' last supper. Drawing on Jonathan Z. Smith's theories of space/place and ritual, Økland claims that in *ekklesia* space:

> Corinth and Jerusalem are simultaneously 'here.' *Ekklesia* 'recollects' an idealized and stylized Jerusalem happening. This remembrance, and imitation of what is remembered through ritual, makes the *ekklesia* different from *oikia*.[78]

Økland is correct, in my view, that by connecting the meal with the Jesus' last supper Paul uses temporality to construct *ekklesia* space on top of *oikia* space. What she does not underscore, however, is that by doing so Paul makes Jesus the host of the community meal—the very reason he calls it the "Lord's Supper." Thus it is not only the 'codes' that change when *ekklesia* space is constructed on top of *oikia* space, the host changes as well. The name Paul uses for the meal (κυριακὸν δεῖπνον) is not the only indication that Paul views Jesus as the host of the meal. If, as Økland argues, Paul's evoking of the words of Jesus makes Corinth and Jerusalem "simultaneously 'here,'" there can be little debate about the identity of the host of this meal—at least from Paul's point of view.

There are, however, other indications in 1 Corinthians. Paul's exclamation, "You cannot drink the cup of the Lord and the cup of demons. You cannot partake of the table of the Lord and the table of demons" (1 Cor. 10:21), indicates whose table Christ-followers gather around when they eat a meal in *ekklesia* space regardless of which *oikia* might be hosting the gathering. Moreover, the phrases "drink the cup of the Lord" and "partake of the table of the Lord" suggest that for Paul whatever food and drink might have been provided by those with relatively greater resources for the poorer members of the community

---

[77] Økland 2004, 146. Clearly the paradigm to be transferred is the sort of 'other regard' exemplified by Jesus, the host, who in the words over the bread at the Last Supper said, "This is my body that is *for you*" (Horrell 2005, 108).

[78] Horrell 2005, 147. As J. Z. Smith has argued, "It is through the structures of temporality, as ritualized, that the divisiveness and particularity of space are overcome" (1987, 94).

should not highlight their generosity, but Christ's.[79] This conclusion is adumbrated by the source of the "spiritual drink" the Israelites consumed in the wilderness: "For they drank from the spiritual rock that followed them, and the rock was Christ" (1 Cor. 10:4).[80] Of course, even though Paul's rhetoric and the ritual practices he enjoins underscore that Jesus is the proper host of the meal, human hosts—some as his rivals—will continue to exert influence as meal hosts in Corinth. Nonetheless, by placing their roles in tension with that of Christ, Paul attempts to undermine the power of local meal hosts, which is not a bad strategy for an absent apostle.

CONCLUSION

In 1 Cor. 11:17–34 we do not find the same legal vocabulary we read in *Lex Coloniae Genetivae* 132, but we do have a banquet, restrictions on banqueting, and a lively context of competition between Paul and his rivals over who will lead the Corinthians. Moreover, the reference to factions in the introduction of the text suggests that the community meal was a locus for dissensions between rivals and that Paul viewed this as a threat to the *ekklesia* and to his continuing leadership. Paul responded by sharply differentiating this meal from conventional meals and by underscoring—or perhaps installing—Jesus as the host.[81] Paul's regulations for the community meal in Corinth sought to accomplish something quite similar to what the colonial charter from Urso sought to accomplish: individual candidates—or their supporters—would not be able to use their status as meal hosts to tilt 'voters' toward their aspirations of leadership in the colony. Such an attempt on Paul's part—as the self-proclaimed patriarch of the community—to

---

[79] As Hofius puts it, "That Christ himself is the one who distributes the sacramental gifts emerges from 1 Cor. 10:4" (1993, 102, n. 146). See also Klauck 1993, 70.

[80] This would not have been lost on the Corinthians. The best ancient parallel appears to be the cult of Sarapis; Klauck 1993, 69–70. According to Aelius Aristides, Sarapis was present at cultic meals and served as the host: "And mankind exceptionally makes this god [Sarapis] alone a full partner in their sacrifices, summoning him to the feast and making him both their chief guest and host" (Or. 45.27, trans. Mitchell). Aristides even has Sarapis extending the invitations to banqueters, a claim that is backed up by papyrus invitations; Or. 45.28, POxy 110, and PKoln 57.

[81] Hofius (1993, 76) thinks Paul merely cites a fixed tradition, but others think Paul may have adapted the tradition for his mission (for example, placing the cup after the dinner in order to ritualize the whole meal setting).

maintain his position of authority while impeding the rise of new men (or new women) would seem to reflect Cicero's paternalist view of electoral bribery noted earlier: "The traditional care of dependents is honorable, the separation of people from their former connections by throwing money about is immoral."[82]

---

[82] Lintott 1990, 11.

CHAPTER TWELVE

THE SACRED SPRING: LANDSCAPE AND TRADITIONS

Guy D. R. Sanders

Science must begin with myths, and with the criticism of myths.... The
theories are passed on, not as dogmas, but rather with the challenge to
discuss them and improve upon them.[1]

INTRODUCTION

Although excavation has revealed several ancient sanctuaries and
temples within Corinth and its surroundings, it has proven difficult to
identify the divinities to which they were dedicated. Inscriptions are
rare, and the material culture is usually too obscure or generic to be of
assistance. Furthermore, the literary record is either absent or tainted
by cultural bias; and most of the received evidence for pre-Roman
religion, traditions and monuments has been extrapolated from Attic
institutions, vase painting, satire and drama. These Attic sources portrayed Corinthian deities, including those named or renamed Medea,
Medusa, Sisyphus, and Cotyto, as frightful, promiscuous, tragic or
even comic figures. With so few tools at hand, it may be profitable
to isolate these sanctuaries and examine them in their unique urban
and mythological landscapes in order to gain a better appreciation of
them in their Corinthian contexts. Similarly, something may be sal-
vageable from the Athenian stereotypes and the traditions developed
from them by searching for the Doric Peloponnesian prototypes which
the Athenians perverted for the benefit of humor, political satire and
propaganda.

[1] Popper 2002, 66–67. This chapter represents a departure from my usual academic
interests, and so I am especially grateful to Benjamin Millis, Stephanie Larson, Betsey
Robinson, and Sarah James for their critiques and encouragement. Alicia Carter, Jan
Sanders, Betsey Pemberton and Ian McPhee also read the text and offered advice.
Despite their help, I retain the right to claim factual and methodological errors as
my own.

I intend here to concentrate on the Sacred Spring and some of the deities scholars have associated with it. I omit the earlier suggestions that worship of Apollo, Dionysos, or Zeus Chthonios was a feature of the precinct.[2] Instead, my discussion will focus on the three candidates who have emerged after a more reasoned consideration of the material evidence: Artemis, Hellotis and Cotyto.[3] Although the evidence is circumstantial, the three are not mutually exclusive and there is good reason to believe that Artemis was an aspect of worship at the Sacred Spring.

While mythological tradition associates Artemis with Corinth, crucial to understanding the nature and function of the Sacred Spring is its relationship to the adjacent racetrack. Analogies to Spartan festivals involving Artemis, athletic competition and watery spaces, suggest that the Sacred Spring is connected with that goddess. In addition, two Corinthian festivals—the Helloteia and that of Artemis Eukleia, both of which I would argue can be associated with Artemis—included races which would have taken place next to the sanctuary of the Sacred Spring. Overall, I would argue that the evidence strongly favors Artemis as a strong presence in the Sacred Spring.

THE SACRED SPRING

The Sacred Spring lies in the Peirene Valley at the southeast corner of Temple Hill at the edge of what many scholars once assumed to be the Agora.[4] This identification of the Roman Forum as the successor of the Greek Agora probably arose because the idea of continuity of the area's public functions seemed obvious.[5] In the Classical period, the

---

[2] On Apollo: Elderkin 1941; and the Robinson Open Meeting of ASCSA (1969; cited in Williams 1978b, 89, n. 4). For Dionysos, see Bonner 1929; for Zeus Chthonios, see de Waele 1932.

[3] On Hellotis, Athena and Poseidon: Broneer 1942, 150–53. On Cotyto: Lisle 1955, 117 and 153–55, n. 168; and Williams 1978b, 131–36. For Artemis Cotyto, see Herbert 1972, 70–75; and 1986, 32–35.

[4] Excavation of the Sacred Spring was first described in Richardson 1902; *Corinth* I.6, 116–99.

[5] *Corinth* I.6, 116–8; Winter 1963. The belief that the Forum succeeded the Agora was so strong that a Classical decree (*Corinth* VIII.1, no. 5), found in two non-joining fragments, one at the northwest corner of the Forum and the other near the Roman propylaia near Peirene, was restored to read καὶ ἀναθέμεν εἰς [τὰν εἴσοδον τᾶς] ἀγορᾶ[ς τὰν ἐ]πὶ Πειρήναι. The editors suggested that it should be set up "at the entrance of the agora by the Peirene (fountain)." Even if the inscription is restored

area under the Forum was a large, open public space with a stadium running up the middle.[6] In the Hellenistic period, a stoa formalized the south side and the racetrack was realigned. This building program leveled the entire upper part of the Peirene Valley. The remodeling may have prompted Robert Scranton to suggest that the Agora originally lay to the north of Peirene and had later been expanded to include the area under the Forum.[7] After reviewing the architectural, inscriptional and historical evidence and after testing pre-Roman strata in both areas, however, Charles Williams has argued that the Agora must lie elsewhere. He proposed that it lay unexcavated under part of the modern village on the lower terrace to the north of Temple Hill.[8]

It matters little for this study whether or not one believes in a northerly or southerly site for the Corinthian Agora; Peirene Fountain and the Sacred Spring were located at the most liminal point of Corinth's topography. The Peirene Valley is practically the only place in the two km long, 15 m high terrace where a natural break permits wheeled traffic to ascend easily from the lower plateau towards Acrocorinth. The valley and its springs were clearly of considerable significance to the Corinthians for several centuries, and in recent years the Peirene Fountain has been comprehensively discussed.[9] The complicated history of the Sacred Spring, however, has challenged scholars who have tried to make sense of the site. Only Williams, who excavated a

---

differently, the stone still juxtaposes the Agora with Peirene. This suggests that the Agora was not far from the fountain. The full thickness of neither fragment is entirely preserved, but the stone and letters are identical. They are considered to be from the same inscription. No alternate reading has yet been proposed. Indeed, the inscription has never been subsequently discussed.

[6] *Corinth* XX, plans II–III.

[7] *Corinth* I.3, 134.

[8] Williams (1970, 32–39; 1978a, 39–40; 1987, 473–74) reasoned that prior to the late 4th century BCE, the slopes of the valley area south of Temple Hill sloped quite steeply and that the terrain was unsuited for an agora. The principal water source, Peirene, was approached from and overflowed towards the north whereas the surviving early roads began to branch out from the north end of the Peirene valley. There were very few civic inscriptions and no civic buildings found in the forum area. Williams (Williams and Fisher 1971, 173), however, offers the Strategeion in Athens as a parallel for Building II, which he describes as an office building in the Forum Southwest. When Xenophon (*Hell.* 4.3.2–3) described the Spartan slaughter of Corinthians at the festival of Artemis Eukleia in 393 BCE, those in the Theater sought sanctuary at the altars of the gods in the Agora. Williams suggested that they went to the Agora because it was convenient and concluded that the Agora must lie to the north of Temple Hill under the modern village. The argument for the date 383 BCE is presented in Buckler 1999, 310, n. 1.

[9] Robinson 2001 and 2005.

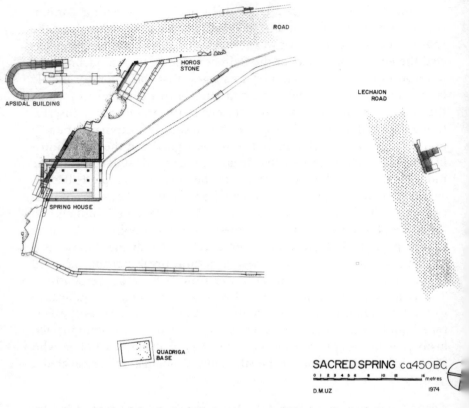

Fig. 12.1. Plan of the Sacred Spring area ca. 450 BCE. Corinth Excavations.

sizeable portion of it, can truly claim to understand it.[10] Several architectural modifications probably reflect gradual and occasionally radical changes in the nature of the worship conducted in the area. Rather than attempt a description of all its phases, I will focus my architectural discussion on the early 5th century BCE.

The ancients enhanced the natural spring by undercutting the marl from beneath the conglomerate ledge above, much as they had done with the Peirene spring. This space was then paved with slabs and interior piers. Walls on three sides supported the bedrock ceiling. Two lion head spouts projected the spring water from a reservoir into a

---

[10] Williams 1978b.

channel and draw basin. The tristyle in antis façade supported a pediment. Next to a road on the terrace above the Sacred Spring there was a small apsidal building, also tristyle in antis. Inside, a circular base probably supported a *perirrhanterion*. A short triglyph and metope frieze defined part of the low, vertical terrace between the two buildings, and a low flight of rock-cut steps connected the two platforms. One of the metopes of this frieze acted as a door, opening onto a concealed passage and water channel which drained water from the apsidal building down to the terrace. Later, when the springhouse façade was demolished, the triglyph and metope frieze was reset and extended southwards over the spring. The spring remained accessible from a higher level by a staircase. Traces of paint preserved on the plaster coating of the frieze blocks indicate that monument was highly decorated.

An inscription set up at the east end of the north leg of the triglyph and metope wall reads ἄσυλος μή καταβιβασσκέτω ζαμία IIIIIIII.[11] The use of καταβιβασσκέτω indicates that the inscription reads, "Inviolable place. Do not descend into. Fine: eight (coins)." The unfinished surface of the back of the stone indicates that it was originally set against a wall and later relocated to the position in which it was uncovered.[12] The verb ("descend into") is consistent with the stone having been placed either at the end of the tunnel or near the entrance to the springhouse.

The excavated finds, the bulk of which the excavator believed to derive from the activity in the precinct, are somewhat suggestive.[13] A cursory survey shows that excavations in and around the Sacred Spring produced pin heads, at least 12 earrings, two finger rings, several loom weights, three alabaster alabastron fragments, five arrow heads, a bone tube (perhaps from a *syrinx*), and numerous terracotta figurines. Among these figurines were many female figures, including jointed dolls, *korai*, a miniature Nike, a *kourotrophos*, several seated females, reclining humans, a sphinx, and a satyr. Animal figures include dogs,

---

[11] This was originally translated, "Forbidden to enter. Fine: eight (coins)." It was compared with a stone from Tralles (Ὅρος ἱερος ἄσθλος Διονύσου Βάχου...). Consequently, an initial ὅρος ἱερός was restored here. According to Millis, citing Eran Lupu, who examined the stone, there is no indication that the inscription was truncated. The addition is, therefore, erroneous.

[12] Smith 1919, 354 credits Hill with the observation that the stone was moved.

[13] Williams 1978b; Steiner 1992.

doves, a rooster, horse and riders, a possible bear, a possible deer and a crouching animal. Many of these have little to distinguish them from those found in funerary areas such as the North Cemetery or in the context of chthonic cult in the area of the Roman Forum, the Peirene Valley and the Panayia Field. Many of the small finds show a feminine bias—even the five arrowheads, if, as Sharon Herbert suggests, we are dealing with Artemis.[14] The possible deer, bear and the *kourotrophos* that are present among the figurines, certainly would not contradict this conclusion. The ceramic finds include Archaic, Classical, and Hellenistic miniature vessels, unusually large proportions of sherds from vessels that held oil, and several fragments of red-figure pottery.

In addition, earth altars were found in the immediate vicinity of the Sacred Spring. The large quantity of cut bones associated with them was initially believed to be from sacrificial animals. David Reese, however, has observed that the unburned condition of the bones is inconsistent with sacrifice and that the preserved cut marks derived from the process of fashioning bone artifacts.[15] The altars may, therefore, have served some purpose other than sacrifice, such as the lighting of torches.

Ann Steiner observed that in the Sacred Spring, the architectural and spatial elements of public cult practices were mixed with a ceramic assemblage normally associated with private funerary practices.[16] She suggested that this mixture is consistent with the commemoration of mythical figures who died in civic space, such as Cotyto, whose story is discussed below.[17] Steiner also noted parallels with assemblages outside Corinth that included large proportions of funerary oil vessels. Specifically, these are the Corycian Cave sacred to Pan and the nymphs; and a hypaethral shrine in the Athenian Agora, sometimes identified as the Leokorion but perhaps sacred to the nymphs. The few published details of the Pitsa Cave, also sacred to the nymphs, suggest it may be another. Steiner may also have added, had it been published at the time, an Archaic votive deposit found on a terrace below the Temple

---

[14] Herbert 1986, 32–35.

[15] Personal communication; Steiner 1992, 385, n. 2.

[16] Steiner 1992, 399–400 notes that although a similar range of vessels was present at the Sanctuary of Demeter at Corinth, the numbers were much fewer and the chronological range for their use was of shorter duration. The oil vessels, however, appear evocative of the funerary assemblages found in the North Cemetery.

[17] For a discussion of the sources: Will 1955, 130–43; Williams 1978b, 44–46; Wiseman 1979, 530.

of Helen (the 'Menelaion') at Therapne, in which the most common, closed-vessel shape were *aryballoi*.[18] These parallels to votive deposits from other sites suggest that the Sacred Spring was sacred to a female chthonic deity associated with nymphs.[19] Such a goddess may well have been Artemis, whose retinue comprised scores of nymphs.[20]

Although it was not found in the precinct, Williams suggested that an Archaic inscription from the west side of the Peirene Valley may have originally derived from the Sacred Spring. It is a stuccoed, lime-stone, Doric column shaft with the retrograde inscription 'ΑΡΤΑΜΩ' cut on one flute.[21] Williams understood this to be the name of the dedicator.[22] Of the earlier commentators, Jeffrey suggested the column was either dedicatory or funerary, and Merritt expressed no opinion.[23] In this case, the fullest discussion of the inscription is also the oldest. Smith suggested that it was either a female name ending in 'Ω' or part of a longer inscription, such as Αρταμώ[ν....ἀνέθηκε].[24] Although uncommon, second declension feminine words such as Κόρινθος, Κόριθος and, indeed, the names of most islands were declined as mas-culine. The use of the word ἄρταμος is masculine when it is (rarely) found in literature or in inscriptions. Like ὁ/ἡ τροφός or ὁ/ἡ θεός, it could have been plausibly both masculine and feminine. The inscrip-tion may, thus, be the feminine dative of ἄρταμος, ("cutter in pieces," "murderer," "butcher," or "cook"). Some but not all consider this word to be the probable root of the name Artemis. If so, then ΑΡΤΑΜΩ would read "to the murderess," or simply "to Artemis."[25] While this object

---

[18] Catling 1992, 66–68.

[19] Steiner 1992, 399–406.

[20] Kopestonsky 2009 treats the roadside shrine at Kokkinovrisi, west of the Theater, and discusses the importance of the nymphs at Corinth.

[21] *Corinth* VIII.1, no. 37.

[22] Williams 1970, 26–27. Bookidis and Stroud (2004, 410) follow this reading.

[23] Jeffrey 1990, no. 22 with n. 4; *Corinth* VIII.1, no. 37.

[24] Smith 1919, 358–59, no. 71.

[25] Plato (*Kraty.* 406b) offers a derivation from *artemis* ("safe"). Drawing on the Doric form *artamis*, Preller and Robert (1894, 296) connect the name with *artamos* ("butcher," or "cutter in pieces"). Chantraine (1990) doubts the derivation. Szemerényi (1994) reviews these attempts and offers his own solution. The female name Artemo is attested, for instance as the name of the sister of Seleukos II. Catling writes, "Mor-phologically, I cannot see how [the inscription] could be derived from Artamis, the Doric name for the goddess. More likely, it is a personal name, either ΑΡΤΑΜΟ, the female name; or ΑΡΤΑΜΟ[Ν], a male name ('Ο' for 'Ω' in both cases). However, I can-not find any parallel for names in ΑΡΤΑΜ—in Doric cities of the Peloponnese (always ΑΡΤΕΜ-) though they do occur in Boiotia (Aiolic dialect) and in Corinthian colonies

cannot unequivocally be associated with the Sacred Spring, since it could equally have fallen from Temple Hill, it does suggest that Artemis was a presence in the Peirene Valley.[26]

The iconography of the red-figure pottery from the Sacred Spring favors dining and komastic scenes.[27] Other pieces portray a reveler, a satyr, and bearded Thracians, perhaps listening to Orpheus. Two fragments portray individuals holding a torch.[28] One of the torchbearers is identified by a partial *dipinto*, frustrating in that it only preserves the last four letters of a woman's name. Ian McPhee suggested the name [ΦEPEΦ]ATTA, that is, Persephone; but [IΦIAN]ATTA or [TEΛEΦ]ATTA are equally possible. We may be able to identify the torch racer as Iphianassa (that is, Iphigenia or Iphimede), a follower of Artemis.

A fourth inscription is equally problematic yet offers further possibilities. An Archaic cup handle inscribed EYKΛE came from the fill below the level of the triglyph and metope facade.[29] There is clearly no space before the first E for another letter, suggesting that the beginning of the word is complete although there may have been a word preceding it, placed lower on the handle. There is no space between the final E and the rim for more letters. If the cup originally had a second handle, the graffiti may well have continued on it to read EYKΛE[—]. A dedication by someone called Eukles (*Eukles anetheken*) is possible.[30] Another reading may be a dedication to [Artemis] *Eukle[ia]* or, simply, *Eukle[ia]*.

Architectural parallels to the Sacred Spring sanctuary in its early 5th century form, though few, are informative. The tristyle Doric façade of the springhouse and the apsidal building is by no means unique. At Corinth, the Fountain of Glauke and perhaps an earlier manifestation of Peirene with piers between the water storage tunnels had a similar tristyle separation. Elsewhere, the Archaic Bouleuterion at Olympia and an apsidal monument of about the same date on the Athenian

---

in Sicily (Syracuse and Kamarina: Artamidoros), which might well be relevant" (personal communication).

[26] Bookidis and Stroud (2004, 410) suggest the column and a *pinax* preserving what may be the Archaic form of Apollo's name found nearby may have come from Temple Hill.

[27] McPhee 1981, no. 2, 14, 27(?), 28, 37, 38(?), 39, 49. Female flutists (no. 10d, 16, 27) may well be part of a komastic scene.

[28] McPhee 1981, no. 6 (reveler); no. 25 and 36 (satyrs); no. 29 (bearded Thracians). See also Pease 1937, no. 6 (fig. 4), no. 7 (fig. 5), and no. 22–23 (torchbearers).

[29] Corinth inv. CP 3118; Richardson 1902, 318; and 1903, 28–29.

[30] Wachter (2001, 350, DOC 5) preserves the name Eukles.

Acropolis had an identical arrangement.[31] On a much smaller scale, a votive temple model from Artemis Orthia at Sparta preserves part of its apsidal end and a Doric frieze.[32] A Corinthian kylix shows the departure of an anonymous warrior who armors up outside a tristyle façade building as his chariot waits.[33] This scene was doubtless one easily recognized in antiquity, but is not so obvious to modern viewers. It plausibly derives from a Homeric or other heroic tradition, such as the preparations of one of the Seven against Thebes. A very close parallel to the fountain of the Sacred Spring, even down to the lion head waterspouts, is portrayed on the François Vase. Here, Achilles fills pots while Apollo looks on. The story is clearly not the ambush of Troilos. It may refer to later events at the same fountain in the sanctuary of Thrymbian Apollo when Achilles went out to meet Polyxena and his own death. In Hades, Achilles and Helen, Medea or Iphimede ruled Leuke, the isle of the blessed.[34]

Triglyph and metope friezes on altars and miniature altars are well-attested, for instance, at Perachora, but as part of a terrace they are almost unknown. The only example of which I am aware is that of the Temple of Helen (the so-called Menelaion) at Therapne. The temple consists of a small *oikos*, oriented north-south, on a tall knoll. Access to it was by a ramp ascending the west and north sides to a platform.[35] In the 6th century, a massive limestone terrace carrying a triglyph and metope frieze was added to the south and east side.[36] The frieze was designed to be seen from the open ground to the east, where presumably the worshippers congregated. The location of the frieze at this level raises the possibility that the viewers were intended to understand it as the upper part of a subterranean chthonic temple.[37]

---

[31] Building B on the Athenian Acropolis, the blocks of which were built into the foundations of the 5th century propylaia; Hurwit 1998, 134, fig. 109.

[32] Dawkins 1929, 194, no. 60 and pl. 72.

[33] Payne 1931, 114–15, no. 994 and fig. 40.

[34] For Helen: Paus. 3.19.13. For Medea, see *schol.* Apollonius (4.814–5), citing Ibycus (PMG 291) and Simonides (PMG 558). See also Apollod. *Ep.* 5.5. Iphigeneia (Iphimede) married Achilles and was the mother of Neoptolemos; Duris *FGrHist.* 76 F 88; and *schol.* Lycoph. 183 and 325.

[35] It was originally thought that the oikos dated to the late 7th century, and the ramp to the 6th century. Tests by Richard Catling in 2005 demonstrated that both belong to the third quarter of the 7th century; Whitley *et al.* 2006, 37.

[36] Once dated to the 5th century, this can now be placed in the mid 6th century; Whitley *et al.* 2006, 37.

[37] Such an interpretation would be in line with Harrison 1899, who would have had no problem in identifying the hillock at Therapne as a tholos or omphalos which had been monumentalized.

The architectural remains of the Sacred Spring suggest a chthonic deity associated with an underground springhouse and an above-ground apsidal structure. In the area in front of the Sacred Spring, altars were used for some purpose other than animal sacrifice. The fragmentary pottery and minor objects, discussed above, from dumped fills possibly related to the Sacred Spring are suggestive of nymphs and perhaps Artemis. Two inscriptions, albeit tentatively associated with the complex, further strengthen this hypothesis. The iconography of the decorated pottery in the same contexts hints at revelry, dance, fire and the association of a female, perhaps called Iphianassa. Moreover, the use of the triglyph and metope frieze in the sanctuary is reminiscent of the Temple of Helen and Menelaus at Sparta and, with the Archaic temple model from Artemis Ortia, connects the architecture of the Sacred Spring with Laconian tradition.

This evaluation of the archaeology of the Sacred Spring provides some data which suggests that Artemis may have been a significant figure at the sanctuary. A further examination of the spring's relationship to other monuments in the immediate vicinity offers additional evidence for the nature of its religious context.

The Sacred Spring in the Context of its Physical and Mythological Landscape

The Roman monuments covering the Peirene Valley make it difficult to visualize how it must have appeared in earlier centuries. Before the erection of the first buildings, steep bluffs of white marl clay, overlain by a thick deposit of limestone, flanked the valley on either side. In some places the marl had probably eroded or was cut to form shallow caves. Two springs near the head of the valley emerged at the interface between the marl and the limestone. In summer, when the surrounding landscape and vegetation were parched and yellow, the water from these two springs irrigated a perennially green meadow. Deciduous trees are uncommon in the arid landscape of coastal Corinthia, yet the Peirene valley may well have supported a grove of phreatophytic trees such as planes (*Platanus orientalis*). Beginning with the first rains in September and especially in springtime, the meadow would have been a variegated carpet of wildflowers and vegetation. It is easy to imagine this lush green oasis as the setting in which the Corinthians placed events associated with their gods.

Fig. 12.2. Reconstructed view of Sacred Springs. James Herbst, Corinth Excavations.

Inasmuch as the two springs watered the same small meadow, the traditions associated with the meadow logically pertain to both springs and not just to Peirene. Since we know the name of one spring, Peirene, her story may provide clues to the identity of the other. One version of Peirene's parentage makes her the daughter of the river Achelous, while in another she is the child of the river Asopos and Metope.[38] One other daughter of these river gods appears to be a suitable candidate for the Sacred Spring—Aegina, who does have a mythological connection to Corinth. When Zeus abducted her, the Corinthian king Sisyphos told her father Asopos what had happened. As a reward, Asopos endowed a spring on Acrocorinth; but in revenge, Zeus set Thanatos on Sisyphos, whose final punishment was to roll a stone uphill in perpetuity. An Archaic Lakonian cup from Samos which shows Sisyphos rolling a stone up the back of a fountain house seems to refer to this

---

[38] Paus. 2.2.3; Diod. Sic. 4.72.

tradition.[39] According to Pausanias, the gift of Asopos was Peirene on Acrocorinth.[40]

An older tradition identifies Peirene as a daughter of Oibalos and, presumably, of his wife Gorgophone, the daughter of Perseus.[41] Her full siblings, therefore, included Tyndareos and Ikareos,[42] and she was, thus, the aunt of Helen, Klytemnestra, Timandra, Penelope and the Dioscuri, and half aunt to Idas, Lynkeos, Phoebe, Hilaeira and the Hippokoontidai.[43] The significance of this familial relationship bears on the discussion of the Sacred Spring as an adjunct to the dromos, which I will discuss below. Poseidon fathered one or both of Peirene's sons, Kenchrias and Leches, the eponyms of Corinth's two harbors.[44] When Artemis accidentally killed Kenchrias, Peirene wept so copiously that Artemis transformed her into a spring.[45] This tradition places Artemis firmly within the context of the Peirene Valley at Corinth.

Viewing the sanctuary in its topographical context, Henry Robinson and others believed that the Sacred Spring complex could be understood in its relation to the Archaic temple on Temple Hill.[46] From the southeast, where the public assembled to witness the proceedings, the tristyle façade of the Sacred Spring may refer to that of the apsidal building. Steps, the disguised tunnel and the water channel physically connected these two planes. From this viewpoint, the congregation in the temenos in front of the Sacred Spring saw the Archaic Temple as a visual backdrop to the action which took place below. A ramp ascending from the road past the apsidal building led to the general region where the altar associated with the Archaic temple once stood and physically connected the two zones. The consensus is that this was the Temple of Apollo although some have speculated that it was

---

[39] Pipili 1987, 35–36 with fig. 50.

[40] Pherecides *FGrHist.* 3F57; Paus 2.5.1.

[41] Paus. 2.2.3.

[42] Also Icareus and Arene. Her half brothers were Leucippus and Aphareus.

[43] Also Idas and Lynceus. According to Apollodorus (3.10.6), Timandra and Philonoe were also daughters of Leda and Tyndareus.

[44] If Peirene can be identified with Arene, also a companion of Poseidon, then Cenchrias and Leches are versions of Idas and Lynceus. Pausanias (2.1.9) identifies the Dioscuri, saviors of ships and seafarers, on the statue base of Poseidon at Isthmia, but it is also possible to see them as Poseidon's sons Leches and Cenchrias.

[45] Paus 2.3.3.

[46] Williams (1978b, 89, n. 4) mentions that Robinson considered that the spring related to Apollo (mentioned at the American School of Classical Studies at Athens Open Meeting, spring 1969). Elderkin (1941) thought the spring was sacred to Apollo and Dionysos.

dedicated to both Artemis and Apollo.[47] One possibility is that Apollo occupied the temple above, and Artemis the spring below. As suggestive as these related topoi are, the activity in the Sacred Spring must also be considered in the context of the racetrack (*dromos*) immediately to the south.

In the Classical period, the dromos stood on a terrace of the southeast bank of the upper Peirene Valley. This site was less than ideal for the construction of a 200 meter horizontal monument. Presumably, other considerations, such as an extant religious festival, dictated its location. With the construction of the South Stoa at the end of the 4th century BCE, the racetrack had to be realigned. The starting line (*apheteria*) retained its location, perhaps because it was of special significance. The track itself was reoriented northwards at the expense of the southern part of the Sacred Spring enclosure. This shift required a leveling operation which partially obscured the west extension of the triglyph and metope wall. The fact that the track could invade the enclosure suggests that the functions of the two were very closely related, and the encroachment made relationship between the Sacred Spring and the dromos still more intimate.

One find near the racetrack may help identify some of the activities taking place in the general area. A 3rd century bronze figurine base found against the north temenos wall of the underground shrine, south of the track, bears a dedication to Artemis Corithoe.[48] This Artemis can be identified with Artemis Corithalia, in whose Spartan festival boys performed wearing masks and girls danced.[49] According to Athenaeus, this took place at the time of the *Tithenidia*, a Spartan *kourotrophic* event for the preservation of infants and youth festival. Nurses of male children presented their charges at the sanctuary of Artemis Corithalia where they sacrificed pigs. The temple stood near a sanctuary of the Charites (Cleta and Phaenna) on the banks of the

---

[47] Stroud and Bookidis (2004) summarize all the evidence supporting this suggestion. Apollo was also the god of the Agora below, where he had a sanctuary close to the Bouleuterion; Plut. *Cleom*. 19.1–2, and *Arat*. 40). Although very different in detail, the two versions can be read together to make coherent sense. It is probable that Plutarch accurately associated the Corinthian Bouleuterion with the Apollonion and that this was located in the Agora and not on Temple Hill. Such an interpretation would clearly explain the epithet "Prytanis of the fair dancing Agora," given by Simonides to Apollo at Corinth; *Greek Anthology* 6.212 (= 'Simonides' 62, 284–85).

[48] Williams 1972, 153, no. 16.

[49] Polemon in Athen. 4.139b. These masks were perhaps reminiscent of those terracotta masks from Artemis Orthia; Carter 1987, 356, n. 7; Hesychius K3689.

river Tiassa on the road from Sparta to Amyclae.[50] Other minor Laconian connections are a temple of Apollo Cori(n)thos near Corone in Messenia.[51]

Pausanias's description of two different festival racetracks at Sparta further articulates close parallels for what seems to have been happening at the Sacred Spring. An early center for Spartan agonistic activity existed south of the Acropolis between "Another" Street and Aphetais Street of Pausanias's itineraries.[52] Here, he describes the site of the original race in which Odysseus competed for the hand of Penelope. The starting line stood at the statue of Aphetais, the starting god, near the house of Krios, in which the Spartans worshipped Karneos, the son of Europa and Zeus. Later, these races became associated with the Karneian festival in which unmarried youths ran and with races run by the Leucippidae, who were the young, unmarried priestesses of Dionysos, Phoebe, and Hilaeira. A Temple of Dionysos was also situated near the race track, opposite an altar dedicated to four deities, specifically Zeus, Athena, and two starting gods, Kastor and Polydeukes In the time of Pausanias, this track seems to have functioned strictly in the context of religious festivals, such as the Karneia and Dionysia. Another track at Sparta seems to be a later development because Pausanias mentions a gymnasium built in the Roman period nearby.[53] This second track had watery and agonistic activities similar to those around the Sacred Spring and Peirene Fountain at Corinth. Like the first track, this was also a setting where young unmarried men and women engaged in athletic activities in an area where the Oebalids were honored.

Further evidence for the association between rituals for young men and women and watery spaces at Sparta comes from Pausanias's description of the *Platanistas* in the Mousga valley, northwest of the theater.[54] The sanctuaries in the vicinity were of divinities associated with water and included Thetis, Poseidon and Artemis Limnaea (Issoria). Situated next to the spring at the Platanistas were a Sanctuary of Helen and the tomb of Alkman, whose poems concentrated on dances of young women. Nearby, there was a race track, outside of which was

---

[50] Athen. 4.139a-b; Paus. 3.18.6.
[51] Luraghi 2002, 45–69.
[52] Paus. 3.12.10–3.13.9. Sanders 2009 places the monuments mentioned by Pausanias between the round building on the Acropolis and the so-called Tomb of Leonidas.
[53] Paus. 3.14.6, Sanders 2009, 199–200.
[54] Paus. 3.14.2–3.15.5. This topography is discussed in Sanders 2009.

the house of Menelaus where the poet Theokritos had set his marriage to Helen.[55] Theokritos portrays Helen's attendants dancing in a watery meadow wearing hyacinth wreaths. They wove garlands, which they then hung in Helen's sacred plane tree, and poured libations of oil at its roots. During the performance, Helen transformed from a maidenly companion to a married woman. The chorus bade her farewell and promised to reassemble at dawn. Significantly, the scholiast on Theocritus 18.39–40 and 44 placed Helen's sacred plane tree in the gymnasium next to the race track.

In Spartan tradition, the *Platanistas* was where the Dioscuri slew their cousins, the sons of Hippocoon, in a contest for the daughters of Leucippus. Pausanias locates many of their tombs, scattered as if they had been erected where the Hippocoontidae fell.[56] This was also the venue for a mass watery pankration for boys. The festival began with the sacrifice of a puppy at the Sanctuary of Phoebe below the Temple of Helen at Therapnae. The boys then processed to the Sanctuary of Achilles and thence to the *Platanistas*, where they joined battle.[57]

Unfortunately, this part of Sparta remains unexcavated, and there is no architectural basis for comparison with Corinth. Nevertheless, the setting of the Sacred Spring, Peirene and the dromos at Corinth complements the juxtaposition of ephebic contests, sacred marriage and maiden dance in a water meadow next to the dromos at Sparta. It lends credence to the archaeological evidence of the Sacred Spring; namely, that the spring was the domain of a deity such as Artemis, who as Corithoe or Kourotrophos at Corinth governed ephebic activities such as athletics, song, dance and marriage and who was also present in the Spartan Platanistas. Since the Helloteia is an attested Corinthian athletic festival and may relate to the activity in the Peirene valley, it is worth examining its complicated literary tradition to see if there is a connection between this festival and Artemis and the Sacred Spring.

---

[55] *Idyll* 18.
[56] Alternately, Herakles killed the Hippocoontidae.
[57] With good reason, West (1963, 161–63) considered that this fight may have been a reenactment of a struggle described in the cosmogony of Pherecydes between the Chronidae and the Ophionidae. After the battle there was a sacred marriage in which Zas married Chthonie-Ge, draping her in a cloak embroidered with symbols of the earth and ocean.

THE HELLOTEIA

Oscar Broneer, Sharon Herbert, and Charles Williams also recognized the significance of the link between the Sacred Spring and the dromos but in a different context from that already discussed. Broneer observed that the starting blocks of the earlier dromos had grooves so close together that the runners had to adopt an upright starting posture, perhaps because they carried torches. He suggested that the racetrack was for the Helloteia, a festival mentioned in Pindar's thirteenth Olympian Ode. Following an etymology proposed by an ancient Pindaric scholar, that the Helloteia derived its name from the bridling (εἷλεν) of Pegasus at the Peirene fountain nearby, Broneer placed the worship of Athena Hellotis and Poseidon in the Sacred Spring.[58] Herbert, who thoroughly discussed the significance of the torch races represented on pottery at Corinth, including pieces found in the Sacred Spring excavations, placed the festival in the context of another scholion on Pindar 13. She concluded that at Corinth the cult in the Sacred Spring was that of Artemis Hellotis and not Athena Hellotis.[59] Williams suggested that the Helloteia belonged on the dromos, and that Cotyto, the alleged sister of Hellotis, governed the Sacred Spring.[60]

Pindar's *Ol.* 13.40 (56) refers to the seven victories of Thessalos in the Helloteia. The scholia on this passage preserve different opinions about the etymology of the word Helloteia and the origin of the festival. The simplest version appears to be the prototype of a more embroidered version. It places the festival in a mythological setting reminiscent of the Leokorion in Athens, named after the daughters of Leos who were sacrificed to end a plague.[61] This version relates that when the Heracleidae attacked Corinth, several women including Eurytione, Hellotis, and an unidentified infant, took refuge in the Temple of Athena. Eurytione, Hellotis, and the child died when the temple burned. A plague followed, and Athena advised that the temple should be rebuilt and that a festival be instigated.[62]

---

[58] Broneer 1942. Although the etymology is weak, the association of the Helloteia with the bridling of Pegasus at the Peirene fountain demonstrates that the scholiast associated the festival with this specific part of Corinth.

[59] Herbert 1986.

[60] Williams 1978b and 1970.

[61] Paus. 1.5.2.

[62] *Scholia* to Pind. *Ol.*, 13.40 [56c].

The fuller version tells us that Hellotis, Eurytione, Chryse, and Cotyto were the daughters of King Timander of Corinth. When the Heracleidae returned to Corinth, Hellotis and Chryse perished in the temple fire; and Aletes subsequently introduced purification rites for the deaths of Hellotis and Chryse.[63] The introduction of an otherwise unknown Corinthian king, Timander, and his daughters, Cotyto and Chryse, is suspect and is perhaps a later addition. Cotyto also appears in a scurrilous play written by Eupolis, called the *Baptai*. It portrays Cotyto, as a lyre-playing goddess, logically a variant of Artemis, being worshipped by effeminate men.[64] For some scholars, the play's title suggests a form of watery baptism into the rites of Cotyto. Others have suggested that in the context of Eupolis's work, it refers to homoerotic activity because the voice of the title, *Baptai*, is active and not passive; and because baptism is unknown in pre-Christian Greek religion.[65] According to one tradition, Alcibiades killed Eupolis in revenge for the way the latter portrayed him in the play. That a certain Timandra, mother of the Corinthian courtesan Lais, was the mistress of Alcibiades suggests that the depiction of Cotyto in the Baptai may have more to do with the negative portrayal and death of Alcibiades than with Corinthian religion.[66] It may also explain why Hesychius alleged that the *Baptai* "represented a certain deity (Cotyto/Artemis) out of hatred for the Corinthians."[67] By discounting the Cotyto of the Baptai, and by suggesting that the fuller version of the Hellotis myth is a fabrication,

---

[63] *Scholia* to Pind. *Ol.*, 13.40 [56]

[64] Eupolis *Baptae* test. ii.

[65] Storey 1990, 20.

[66] The reputation of Alcibiades was embroidered after his death in 404 BCE. Some accounts state that he died at the hands of assassins hired by the Spartans. They set fire to his home, perhaps in Phrygia, and killed him with darts and arrows. According to another version of the story, his mistress Timandra buried him in her clothes. Timandra was said to be the mother of Lais. Since Cotyto was the Thracian equivalent of Phrygian Cybele, the death of Alcibiades in a Phrygian house fire and his burial in Timandra's frock suggest that King Timander, Cotyto, and perhaps Chryse as well, were all additions to a Corinthian myth in which Hellotis and Eurytione were the original protagonists. In this context the Heracleidae may represent the Spartans; Cotyto, the Phrygian Artemis; Timander, Timandra without drag; and Chryse perhaps Alcibiades as Chryseis the daughter of Apollo's priest at Troy, who was seized as she sacrificed to Artemis (*Cypria* fr. 28, edited by Barnabé). For such allegorical readings of late 5th century material, Vickers 1997 (note the review in Parker 1997).

[67] Hesychius K3820 (Eupolis fr. 93). For a discussion of the sources, Will 1955, 130–43; Williams 1978b, 44–46.

we can disassociate Cotyto from the Sacred Spring and continue the search for a deity connected to the Helloteia.

The etymology offered for the Helloteia by yet another scholion is that it derives from ἕλος ("marsh" or "meadow"), specifically, the marsh at Marathon where there was a festival of Athena Hellotis.[68] More than any other battlefield on which they shared victory, the Athenians justifiably made Marathon their own, and it came to shape the way in which they projected themselves to the outside world. Yet many of the gods and traditions of eastern Attica seem to be alien to mainstream Athenian tradition. At Marathon there was a Temple of Herakles, a very Doric divinity, near the battlefield. After the battle, Pan, who is strongly associated with Arcadia, received the honor of an annual torch race.[69] Tradition associates all of these with the region: Theseus of Troezen; Hellotis, also associated with Crete and Corinth; Marathonus, a Sikyonian; Pelops, the Pisan sire of the house of Atreus; and Medea, a Corinthian.[70] A Temple of Nemesis was built at Rhamnous north of Marathon near Trikorinthos, and Theseus brought Helen to Aphidnae a similar distance to the northwest. To the south Taurian Artemis had temples at Brauron and Halae, the former of which can be related to Artemis Ortheia at Sparta. Since these gods and heroes all have strong Peloponnesian and Dorian associations, a Dorian version

---

[68] *Scholia* to Pind. *Ol.* 13.40 [56a]. *IG* II².1358. Richardson 1895 suspected the stone was originally set up in the *deme* of Marathon and that it was later moved to the slopes of Mount Pendeli.

[69] Hdt. 6.108.1, 6.116 (Herakles); 6.105.1 (Pan).

[70] Paus. (2.3.9 and 2.1.1) credits Eumelos with the information that Helios bequeathed Asopia to Aloeos and Ephryraia to Aeetes. He cites the *Corinthian History* of Eumelos; and he identifies the grandson of Aloeos as Marathonos, who fled to the coast of Attica to escape the tyranny of his father. Aeetes left Ephyra in the hands of his regent Bunus, and departed for the Black Sea where he founded Kolchis. Later, the Ephyrians sent for Medea, who brought her husband, Jason. When Medea concealed her children in the Sanctuary of Hera, hoping to immortalize them, they died. Jason was unable to forgive her and departed for Iolcos. Medea herself then departed for an unspecified destination, leaving Corinth for Sisyphos. Euripides portrays Medea as a *pharmakopoios*, coerced by Aphrodite to love a foreigner and taken from home, a Peloponnesian queen who was the nemesis of all, the companion of Achilles in the isle of the blessed. Medea, therefore, has much in common with Helen. At home in Kolchis, Medea was a priestess of Hecate, the underworld companion of Persephone. This conjunction of Attica with a wicked 'oriental' queen, Medea; her son, Medus, the eponymous namesake of the Medes; her aunt Circe, the seducer of Odysseus; her other aunt Pasiphaë, the seducer of the Cretan (Marathonian) bull and mother of the Minotaur all suggest a xenophobic authorship. Since the identity of the all-conquering hero is Theseus, we must suppose that the fabrication or embellishment of this story was Athenian.

for the identity of Hellotis at Corinth may be Europa rather than the Athena identity favored in Attica.

On Crete the Helloteia was a chthonic festival of Europa in which celebrants carried and cremated a garland believed to incorporate the body of the goddess.[71] Although we tend to associate Europa with Crete and with Thebes through her brother Kadmos, she also has strong ties to the Peloponnese. As the mother of Karneos, she was connected to Lakonia.[72] As a woman abducted by a bull, she is similar to Io.[73] In one tradition, Io is the daughter of an Argive called Peiren.[74] Eumelos of Corinth wrote an epic entitled the *Europeia*, perhaps referring to a local tradition of Europa in the region. Neighboring Sikyon portrayed Europa on their treasury at Delphi, and Praxilla of Sikyon was sufficiently acquainted with her to write that she and Zeus were the parents of Karneos. This Karneos was probably worshipped at Corinth in the Kraneion grove, glossed as 'Karneian,' where Pausanias saw the tomb of Lais.[75] Another possible Peloponnesian version, preserved in the drama of Euripides, Sophocles, Aeschylus, and in later sources is that Europa, if the name can be derived from Aerope, was the daughter of the Cretan king Katreos. Nauplios saved her from death by drowning and brought her to the Argolid. After the death of his first wife, the result of his failure to sacrifice a promised golden lamb to Artemis, Atreus married Europa. Their children were Agamemnon and Menelaus. She became the lover of her brother-in-law, Thyestes, and by him was the mother of Aegisthus. The action is set in Mycenae, Sikyon and Midea.[76] This last version of Europa's tale ties her to traditions beyond her royal Cretan parentage.

In addition, Europa has a strong mythical connection to Artemis. The rescue of Europa from drowning is analogous to the rescue of Britomartis, the "honey maiden" favorite of Artemis, from a similar fate.[77] At Sparta Europa was actually worshipped as Artemis Issoria, surnamed

---

[71] Athen. 15.678a–b, citing Seleukos the grammarian.
[72] Mitchell 2001, 344 and 351.
[73] Mitchell 2001, 351.
[74] Apollodorus 2.5.
[75] Paus. 2.2.4.
[76] Eur. *Ores.*, 995–1012 with *scholia*; *Elec.*, 699–742 with *scholia*; and *Hel.*, 390–92. See also Soph. *Aj.*, 1293–98; *id. Thy.*; and Aes. *Ag.*, 1583–95; Hyginus *Fab.*, 86–88, 97; Apollod. 2.4.6; and *id. Epitome* 2.10–14.
[77] Elderkin 1939, 203–13.

Limnaia, whose temple overlooked the grove at the Platanistas.[78] In
the Peloponnese, the epithet Limnaia for Artemis is common; and in
addition to the Issorion, there was a second sanctuary at Sparta called
Artemis Orthia in the Limnaion, named after a sanctuary at Kalamai
on the Messenian border.[79] The Spartans claimed that their xoanon
of Orthia was the authentic Taurian image brought home by Iphigenia and Orestes. Iphigenia is also credited with having brought the
worship of Artemis and the xoanon to the sanctuary at Brauron from
Tauris, and she served as the first priestess.[80] Like the Sacred Spring,
the temple of the kourotrophic Artemis at Brauron is located at the
base of a rock by a spring in a meadow. Closer to Corinth at Sikyon,
the Temple of Artemis Limnaia stood between the Temple of Dionysos and the Agora.[81] The strong mythological and cultic association
between Europa and Artemis in the Peloponnese, which can be seen
clearly in these examples, thus allows parallels to be drawn between
the Cretan festival of the Helloteia and Europa and the Corinthian
Helloteia and Artemis.

The last scholion to Pindar states that the Helloteia was a festival of
Athena at Corinth during which youths ran *lampadodromies* ("torch
races").[82] For reasons already discussed, there is no particular reason to

---

[78] Paus. 2.30.3 and 3.14.2.

[79] For Calamae: Paus. 3.2.6, 3.7.4, 4.4.2, 4.31.3, 3.14.2, and 7.20.7–8; Tac. *Ann.* 4.43; *IG* V.1.1431 line 38; Strabo 8.4.9; Plut. *Agis.* 32.3; Polyaenus *Strategemata* 2.1.14; 'Isso-rion' in Stephanus Byzantius; 'Issoria' in Hesychius; *IG* V.1.226 (= *SEG* 34.306), and V.1.225. See also Limnaea at Epidauros Limera, north of Monemvasia (Paus 3.23.10), nine *stades* from the walls of Tegea on the road to Sparta; Paus 8.53.11; a temple of Heleian Artemis at Alorium; Strabo 8.3.25; at Epidaurus, Paus. 3.23.3; at Lomboth-ekra, Sinn (1981); and at Patras the Temple of Artemis which contained an image stolen from Sparta (Paus. 7.20.7–9).

[80] The association between Iphigenia and Artemis was widespread in the Pelopon-nesos. Lloyd Jones (1983, 95–6) provides evidence for the Megarian tradition (Paus. 1.43.1–2). Four ancient authors—Pausanias (2.22.6–7, citing the Argive tradition), Euphorion of Chalcis (fr. 90 Powell), Alexander of Pleuron (fr. 2 Meineke), and Ste-sichorus (*PMG* 191)—record that Helen dedicated the sanctuary of Eilethyia near the Temple of the Dioscuri at Argos after she gave birth to Iphigeneia in the period between her return from Aphidna and her marriage to Menelaus. She gave the child to her sister Clytaemnestra to foster. Also adjacent to the sanctuary of Eilethyia was a Temple of Hecate. Paus 2.35.1 describes a temple dedicated to Artemis Iphigenia at Hermione (incidentally the name of another daughter of Helen), which demonstrates a clear connection between the two figures. At Aegira a statue of Iphigeneia stood in the Temple of Artemis, which Pausanias (7.26.5) speculated had originally been dedicated to Iphigeneia.

[81] Paus. 2.7.6.

[82] *Scholia* to Pindar *Ol.* 13.40 (56c).

believe that the Corinthian Helloteia honored Athena rather than some other deity. Herbert may well be correct in believing that the scholiast transposed 'Athena' for 'Artemis' because he knew of the Attic Athena Hellotis.[83] Torch races were common enough in the ancient world. In Athens, for instance, torch races for Athena, Prometheus and Hephaistus were supplemented after the Persian wars by races for Pan and Artemis Bendis. A relief from Rhamnous in Attica shows a victorious team presenting their torch to three goddesses whom Ashmole identified as Demeter, Persephone, and a winged Nike.[84] Contextually, however, the goddesses portrayed on the torch race stelai should be Nemesis, Helen, and a winged Nike (Eukleia?).

The torches used in these races have various regional names including *heleni*, which is directly comparable to the name of the goddess Helen.[85] The concept of eukleia and Artemis Eukleia are strongly connected with torches and torch races throughout Greece after the Persian wars. In Boeotia, torches were known as *daidhes* and *lampadhes*. After Plataea, the Boeotian hearths were extinguished and rekindled from the flame at the communal hearth at Delphi; the runner who brought the flame died and was buried in the sanctuary of Artemis Eukleia.[86] In an inscription from Plataea, which records a long list of dedications by women,[87] the number of torches (*daidhes* and *lampadhes*) listed is almost as great as the number of more usual offerings put together and suggests the gifts were for Eukleia.[88] Plutarch relates that

---

[83] A similar error made by the scholiast on Lycophron's *Alexandra* (858) states that the epithet *Phoinike* at Corinth belonged to Athena rather than Artemis.

[84] Ashmole 1962, 234. A herm also dedicated by torch racers at Rhamnous portrays a goddess whom Ashmole considered to be Persephone.

[85] Clader (1976, 63) reviewed a long list of possible associations strictly concentrating on the name Ἑλένη: Ἑλένη....λαμπάς, δέτη (Hesychius E1995). See also Hes. E1993 (Ἑλένιον, ἑλένειον), a festival in which (Hes. K675) girls were carried to the festival in carts called *cannathra*, decorated with images of griffins and *tragelaphon*.

[86] Schol. Pind. *Pyth* 3.77 (137) and Paus 9.25.3. See Paus (9.17.1) for a Temple of Artemis Eukleia at Thebes with the statue of a lion outside. See Plut. *Arist.* (20.4–6) for the marriage sacrifice. He also recounts how after Plataea the Delphic oracle ordered all fires to be extinguished because they had been contaminated by the Medes. Sacrifice could only resume when the flames had been rekindled with a flame brought from the public hearth at Delphi. Euchidas, the runner who brought the flame, died on arrival and was buried in the Plataean Sanctuary of Artemis Eukleia.

[87] Richardson 1891.

[88] For the objects, Richardson 1891, 413–16. Faced with three possibilities, Hera, Artemis and Demeter, Richardson chose Hera because *boukephali* were among the dedications. Bulls' heads among the dedications at Orthia and Serapna indicate that these were also appropriate for Artemis.

in his time the Boeotian custom was for engaged couples to sacrifice at the altar of Artemis Eukleia in the agora.[89] The worship of Artemis Eukleia with contests (*agones*) at Corinth is attested from the early 4th century BCE.[90] Athletic competitions in honor of Artemis Eukleia also occurred at Delphi and in or close to the agora at Athens in thanks for the victory at Marathon. Moreover, Athenian playwrights frequently juxtaposed Artemis and the concept of *eukleia*.[91]

Clearly, the Helloteia has a very complicated tradition and a fuller discussion is not possible within the scope of this essay. At its core, however, we can say that the festival seems to have had regional variants which developed through time. The Peloponnesian protagonists identified are Oebalids and Pelopids, Europa, Karneos and Artemis; in Attica Athena joined the cast. The Helloteia also pulled together the traditions of three of the four women, Medea, Io, Europa, and Helen, whose abductions were identified with the origins of the Persian War. The Greeks celebrated their victories in this war with torch races for Artemis Eukleia in which the name of the torch itself bore the name of the Oebalid Helen.

CONCLUSION

Archaeologically, the Sacred Spring in Corinth appears to have been a sanctuary of a chthonic deity with watery associations. Although the evidence is circumstantial, it points to a goddess who was a protector of the young. This deity was an important figure at various stages in life, nurturing them from conception until adulthood, through marriage, and again at their death. In a balanced, orderly family and civil society, governed by *eunomia*, she was 'safe' (*artemis*). Like Dionysos, this goddess had an angry, violent, and vengeful side. When the natural order was overturned and injustice prevailed, she became a ruthless

---

[89] Plut. *Arist.* 20.6. See Braund (1980) for references to Euklaia and the dedication of hair in Aristophanes *Hipploytus*.

[90] Xen. *Hell.* 4.2.

[91] *SIG*² 438 indicates that the festival took place in the second half of the month Bysios or the first half of the month Theoxenios. Roux (1979, 235) dates Bysios to January/February or February/March and Theoxenios to February/March or March/April. At Vergina a relief from the sanctuary portrays Kybele with an anonymous male and a snake; Blackman 1998, 79; 1999, 88. For Athens, see Paus. 1.14.5. This has not yet been identified in the excavated area, although the Hephaisteion is a candidate; Braund 1980, 184; Soph. *OT*, 159–61; Eur. *Hipp.*, 47, 405, 423, 489, 687, 717, 1028, 1299.

homicidal avenger, *Artamos*, a nemesis to the enemies of peace and concord. In the Peloponnesos this goddess was known as Limnaia, Orthia, Kordax, and even Erinys; and elsewhere, as Adrasteia, Nemesis, Bendis, and Cybele. Secondary figures in the Sacred Spring and its environs are murkier, but as at Sparta they seem to include the extended family of Oebalid Peirene, such as Helen, her siblings, cousins, and relations by marriage.

There is no reason to believe that worship at the spring remained static throughout its history. Indeed, we should envision a gradual evolution of form, function, and practice occasionally punctuated with innovations that were more radical. If we accept the statement that the Corinthian Helloteia derived from Marathon, the natural conclusion is that this festival was the Corinthians' torch race to celebrate their part in the victories and the restitution of *eunomia* after the Persian Wars. Such celebrations of Eukleia (literally, "well renowned") flourished after the wars, and at Corinth the festival Helloteia was well established by 393 BCE. The Corinthian festival included events which took place in the Theater, and its athletic component surely took place in and around the dromos next to the Sacred Spring.

To Steiner, pottery from the Sacred Spring suggested a public commemoration of death, normally a domestic preserve. The presence of Artemis and others do not contradict this conclusion. It suggests, however, that the Corinthians celebrated other, usually private, human transitions publicly in this space. A death and a funeral with its purification rites, garlands, a torchlight procession by night to the grave, and the funerary feast itself was a transition from the oikos of the living to that of the dead. In much the same way, a marriage was a transition of a bride from her paternal oikos to the marital *oikos*. The bride cut and dedicated her hair to the goddess, removed her maidenly girdle to adopt matronly dress, and took a purification bath in (sacred) spring water to induce fertility. At the wedding the couple wore floral wreaths and traveled by night in a torchlight procession to their home.[92] Although much of the extant evidence for marriage ceremonies comes from Athenian literature and iconography, the *Epithalium of Helen* and several other fragments from Sparta permit the reconstruction of a very similar wedding ceremony in Lakonia. Corinthian weddings may not have been radically different. Plutarch relates that in his time

---

[92] Seaford 1987, 96–130, for discussion and bibliography.

the Locrian and Boeotian custom was for engaged couples to sacrifice at the altar of Artemis Eukleia. At Delphi the festival of Artemis
Eukleia took place in March or April, probably about the same time
when Helen's nuptials were celebrated and when, in myth, Persephone
was abducted. Such various activities in the Sacred Spring precinct in
Corinth may explain the paucity of finds ascribable to any particular
activity or deity. Water was drawn, oil poured, torches lit, hair and
perhaps clothes, wreaths and trinkets (such as earrings) were dedicated. Few of these materials survive in the archaeological record.

Two unique features of the Sacred Spring—the inscription forbidding people to descend into the asylum and the secret tunnel—may
now require reassessment if Artemis was the god worshipped there.
The Homeric Hymns, Homer, and Kallimachos repeatedly tell us that
Artemis was a patron of dance.[93] The injunction μή καταβιβασσκέτω
may somehow relate to the *bibasis*, an unusual dance whose performance the Spartan woman Lampito tells the Athenian Lysistrata is
responsible for the strength of her thighs.[94] More directly, it probably
was an injunction not to enter the springhouse or the secret tunnel.
The tunnel itself was perhaps an entrance to the underworld of the
kind taken by Dionysos at Lerna to recover Semele/Thyone or that
from which they emerged with his mother at the Temple of Artemis at
Troezen.[95] Alternately, the tunnel may have played a role in the initiation of Corinthians into the rites of Artemis.

Helen, whose name has recurred constantly in this discussion, raises
new avenues of inquiry in relation to the Sacred Spring. Her horsey
brothers, the oath of her suitors on the corpse of a horse, and the bestial
transformation of her parents relate her to both Arcadian (Demeter)
Erinys and the Indo-European Saranyu.[96] Both goddesses have names
that are thought to be cognates of Helen's name. Both transformed
themselves into mares to escape solar divinities intent on rape. In turn,
these gods became stallions and covered the mares. Saranyu bore the
Aśvins, certainly variants of the Dioskouroi, to Vivasvant; and Erinys
bore Despoena, a human daughter, and Arion, a horse, to Poseidon. It
may also relate Helen to the once beautiful, horse-headed, uber-Erinys

---

[93] Homeric Hymn 5 to Aphrodite; 27 to Artemis; 3 to Pythian Apollo; Iliad 16.181;
Callimachus, Hymn 3 to Artemis.
[94] Aris. *Lys.*, 82.
[95] Paus. 2.37.4–5 (Lerna); 2.31.2 (Troezen).
[96] Skutsch 1987, 189–90.

Medusa, who lay with Poseidon in a flowery meadow, plausibly the one in the Peirene Valley. Peirene's grandfather, Perseus, delivered the twin children of this union, Pegasus and Chrysaor. Pegasus, of course, was bridled in the meadow at Peirene, and Chrysaor became an epithet of Artemis at Kynosura.[97] Given these links, a future line of inquiry may take up the observation of Frothingham, who identified Medusa as the mountain mother Artemis, mistress of the animals, and that of Crowfoot, for whom Medea was Cybele and consider possible Near Eastern connections to the rituals in the Sacred Spring.[98]

---

[97] Hdt. 8.77.
[98] Frothingham 1911; Crowfoot 1900, 124.

CHAPTER THIRTEEN

RELIGION AND SOCIETY AT ROMAN KENCHREAI

Joseph L. Rife*

INTRODUCTION

Kenchreai, Corinth's prosperous port on the Saronic Gulf (fig. 13.1), is best known for its religion during the Roman Empire. Paul visited Kenchreai, perhaps regularly, during his Corinthian sojourn in the middle 1st century, and he spent time there before his departure to Ephesos with Aquila and Prisca (Acts 18:18). He most likely founded a house church there, and the deacon Phoebe delivered his letter to the Romans (16:1–2). Apart from the Christian presence, Roman Kenchreai was the home of several traditional cults. Pausanias observed sites and images sacred to Aphrodite, Poseidon, Isis, and Asklepios during his tour in the second half of the 2nd century (2.2.3). Around the same time, Apuleius wrote arguably the most important ancient account of personal conversion. The concluding chapter of his novel, set at Kenchreai, narrates how Lucius undergoes a physical transformation from asinine back into human shape and is initiated into the mysteries of Isis (*Met.* 10.25–11.25). In addition to this literary testimony, the archaeological and epigraphic records have produced evidence for cults of Dionysos and Pan and for magical practice. Although disparate and tantalizingly brief, these sources together reveal a vibrant religious life in the port.

* I compiled this study as director of the Kenchreai Cemetery Project (2002–06) under the auspices of the American School of Classical Studies, with the permission and oversight of the Hellenic Ministry of Culture and the sponsorship of Macalester College. I express my sincere gratitude to Tim Gregory, Betsy Gebhard, and Guy Sanders for helping me over several years to understand Corinthian religion better. For their thoughtful responses to this paper I thank the editors and the learned audience at the University of Texas at Austin. The drawings and photographs used as figures for this chapter are the work of the author (no. 1, 2, 5, 8–10, 13), C. Mundigler, D. Edwards and M. Nelson (no. 2), and members of the staffs of the Kenchreai Excavations (no. 3–7, 11–12) and the Corinth Excavations (no. 8).

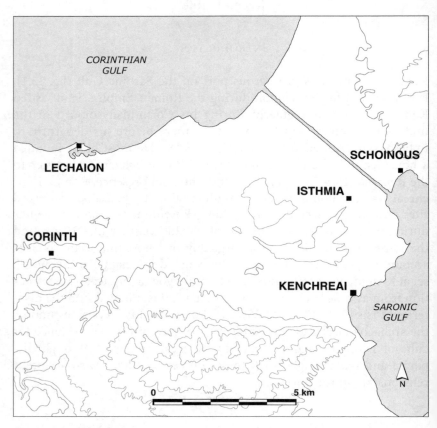

Fig. 13.1. The Isthmus of Corinth (contour interval 100 m). Courtesy of the Kenchreai Excavations.

The broad topic of religion and society at Roman Kenchreai has never received systematic study, although scholars have discussed at length specific problems of religious and social history at the site. The first sustained investigation of Kenchreai was the excavation program by the American School of Classical Studies from 1962–69, sponsored by the University of Chicago and Indiana University under the general direction of Robert Scranton.[1] This exploration concentrated on the dense structures of the north and south moles, where Scranton and his colleagues aimed to validate Pausanias's brief account (fig. 13.2). In the end, they argued that they had found the sanctuaries of Aphrodite and Isis, although Scranton openly professed that the identifications were at best reasonable conjectures. In addition to these studies, excavation and extensive survey in the 1960s along the harborfront and in the broader area of settlement led to the discovery of two churches and a small corpus of inscriptions associated with both the pagan cults and the Christian congregation.

In 2002–06 I directed a second campaign to explore Corinth's eastern port, the Kenchreai Cemetery Project (KCP) under the auspices of the American School.[2] KCP was a program of interdisciplinary research to investigate systematically the burial grounds surrounding the ancient harbor. We concentrated on the main cemetery on the Koutsongila Ridge, which overlooks the harbor and extends northward ca. 350 m (fig. 13.2). The primary goal of KCP was to understand social structure and cultural identity in the local community through the study of funerary ritual, mortuary space, and sepulchral design. Another goal was the synthesis and reconsideration of findings by previous investigators in the cemeteries and the harbor, including not only Scranton's team but also various other American and Greek researchers throughout the 20th century.[3]

---

[1] Full-scale excavation ran from 1963–68 with an intermission in 1966, but preparatory and supplementary fieldwork was conducted in 1962 and 1969. The major publications of this project relevant to the present study are Hohlfelder 1970 and 1976, and *Kenchreai* I–VI.

[2] Barbet and Rife 2007; Faraone and Rife 2007; Rife 2007; Rife *et al.* 2007; Sarris *et al.* 2007; Ubelaker and Rife 2007 and 2008. I started KCP as a complement to my broader research on urban and rural society and mortuary landscape in the Corinthia during Roman to Early Byzantine times: Rife 1999, 199–332; Tartaron *et al.* 2007, 461, 510; *Isthmia* IX.

[3] Georgiades 1907 with plate 2; Lampakis 1907; Pallas 1957, 54; Robinson 1966 and 1972; Kristalli-Votsi 1984; Rothaus and Rife 1996.

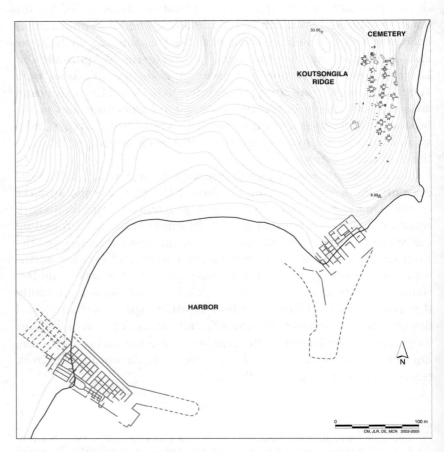

Fig. 13.2. Kenchreai and its vicinity (contour interval 1 m). Courtesy of the Kenchreai Excavations.

KCP has collected important evidence for burial forms and practices in the Roman Corinthia, which is addressed in separate publications. The continuing exploration of burial sites and the revision of old discoveries have also led to new perspectives on Christianity and magic. Furthermore, KCP laid the groundwork for a large-scale excavation that began in 2007 as a collaboration between the Directorate of Prehistoric and Classical Antiquities of the Ministry of Culture and the American School.[4] This Greek-American expedition in 2007–09 has explored an area from the cemetery on Koutsongila southward to the dense residential and commercial zone, leading up to the harbor and connecting with Scranton's trenches. The new project should uncover important new evidence for religion at Kenchreai, contributing to a sharper comprehension of long-standing problems while undoubtedly generating unforeseen ones.

On account of the varied sources at our disposal, the prospect of new discoveries through excavation, and the congenial interchange of the Texas colloquium, the time is ripe for a general assessment of religion and society at Roman Kenchreai. The evidence is fragmentary, and much is still under study. Nonetheless, it will be useful to frame certain problems in Corinthian religious history, even if in an exploratory manner, and to consider what can and cannot be reasonably said about them. We can at present discuss the local worship of Aphrodite, Isis, Poseidon, Asklepios, Dionysos, and Pan, as well as magic and the evidence for Christianity. Beyond the mere existence of these beliefs and practices, we can address their history, their place in an evolving landscape, and their significance in the life of a provincial community, especially their connection to social and cultural identity. In examining such questions of history, topography, and identity, we should address the relationship between Cenchrean religion and Corinthian religion, that is, how the deities, cults, and sacred spaces at the port responded to or diverged from those at Corinth and at other sites in the region, especially the Isthmian Sanctuary. Although the port never achieved political independence from the city, Kenchreai supported Corinth as a booming center of trade and travel. Residents of both the city and its countryside would have visited Kenchreai and would have known

---

[4] I represent the American School in this endeavor. I thank Elena Korka, Head of the Directorate of Prehistoric and Classical Antiquities, and Panagiota Kasimis, supervising archaeologist for the 37th Ephoreia of Prehistoric and Classical Antiquities in Archaia Korinthos, for their continuing support and collaborative spirit.

its cults. This experience and the memory of it must have shaped how they conceived of themselves as Corinthians.

THE ORIGINS OF ROMAN KENCHREAI

Kenchreai as we know it was largely a formation of the Roman era. Exploration immediately around the harbor has uncovered no consistent evidence for widespread settlement before the Empire, with only a slight representation of earlier sherds and architecture in scattered contexts. Most significant were fragmentary walls found beneath the Roman buildings at the base of the north mole, but a pre-Roman date for them has not been proven by artifactual associations.[5] Scranton was surely correct to locate the core of the Classical and Hellenistic settlement further inland to the west (fig. 13.2). That is the only area where buildings and artifacts of early date have been found, on the high ground over a low plain that once contained a broad inlet from the Saronic Gulf but now underlies the village of Kechrees.[6] This shallow basin seems to have filled with alluvial sediment during the Hellenistic era, shifting the shoreline eastward to near its current location.

The various writers who mentioned the operation of the port during the Classical and Hellenistic eras only described it as a fortified naval station, and none cited cults.[7] To be sure, early residents of the harbor must have participated in religion of some form, but no testimony concerning which deities were worshipped at Kenchreai survives from before the Roman era. The site's only known mythological associations were recorded by post-Classical writers: Diodorus (4.74) and Pausanias (2.2.3, 2.3.2) noted that Corinth's two ports were named after Leches and Kenchrias, the children of Poseidon and the nymph

---

[5] *Kenchreai* I, 20, 27, 34, 36, 44, 51, 53, 70, 79–81, 87; Hohlfelder 1976, 220. Recent exploration on the Koutsongila Ridge has found little material predating the Roman era, although numerous ashlar blocks raise the possibility of monumental architecture here during the Classical and/or Hellenistic eras; Rife *et al.* 2007, 149–50 with fig. 5; Sarris *et al.* 2007, 20.

[6] Early remains on the high land northwest of the Roman harbor: *Kenchreai* I, 4, 6–10, fig. 4–6 with plates IV:A and V–VIII:B (buildings); Kristalli-Votsi 1984, 64–65 with plate 57:α–δ (burials).

[7] F. Bölte, "Kenchreai" 2, *RE* XI (1921) coll. 167–170; Thuc. 4.42.4, 4.44.4, 8.10.1, 8.20.4, 8.23.1; Scylax 55 ed. Müller; Xen. *Hell.* 4.5.1, 6.5.51, 7.1.17, 7.1.41; Polyb. 2.59.1, 2.60.7–8, 4.19.7, 5.29.5, 18.6.4.

Peirene (see Philostr. Jun. *Imag.* 2.16.4). This tradition also appeared in numismatic iconography of Roman date.[8]

With the Caesarian foundation and the subsequent revival of Corinthian commerce, the eastern port was slowly reborn around the crescent-shaped bay. Builders improved the anchorage within by erecting sturdy quaywalls and constructing the massive north and south moles (fig. 13.2–4). When exactly these developments took place is unknown, but associated deposits consistently point to an Augustan date.[9] Thereafter, abundant utilitarian artifacts began to appear in public contexts during the early 1st century, and the earliest burials in the port's main cemeteries appeared around the middle 1st century.[10] Thus, while the harbor surely received ships, traders, and travelers from the earliest days of the Corinthian colony, it seems that the town did not flourish until the early to middle 1st century. Since the Games returned to the Isthmus in the 40s or 50s,[11] this seems to have been a time of revitalized activity in the eastern Corinthia generally. The preponderance of archaeological remains around the harbor shows that Kenchreai grew into a busy hub during the middle and late Roman centuries. Apuleius (*Met.* 10.35, 11.7–17) and Favorinus ([falsely attributed to Dio Chrys.] *Or.* 37.8) portrayed a town thronging with diverse residents and visitors. But it was never a city in the sense of an autonomous municipality: Kenchreai did not produce its own coinage, and there is no evidence for magistracies or the monumental elements of urban planning, such as an amphitheater. It was, however, a substantial settlement with a dense population that sustained regional networks of exchange and communication.[12]

All known cult sites, except for perhaps those of Dionysos and Pan (see below), were located in the immediate vicinity of the harbor, at

---

[8] A coin struck at Corinth under Hadrian bears two nymphs as the reverse type with the legend LECH CENCH; Head 1889, 75 with plate XXI:15; Imhoof-Blumer 1923, 410–11, no. 577 and tab. 18.20. The gender of Kenchrias in this tradition seems to have been variable; 'Kenchreai, Kenchrias,' *LIMC* 5.1.

[9] *Kenchreai* I, 22, 25, 34, 36–38, 43, 51, 70, 87; *Kenchreai* III, 2; *Kenchreai* IV, 44–45 and 106–07. This is the same period when Strabo wrote his geographical treatise, which identified Kenchreai as a "town and harbor" (κώμη καὶ λιμήν, 8.6.22).

[10] Pottery of the early 1st century: *Kenchreai* IV, 44–45. Burials around mid-century: Pallas 1957, 54, fig. 1; Pallas 1959, 213–14, fig. 29; Pallas 1975, 7–9, fig. 10; Robinson 1965, 80 with plate 92:e; Robinson 1966 and 1972 (south of harbor); Rife *et al.* 2007, 151, 153–54, 162, 167–69 (north of harbor).

[11] Gebhard 1993, 87–88 and 2005, 185, n. 76; Kajava 2002.

[12] For such towns in the colonial sphere of Achaia: Rizakis 1996, 290–97.

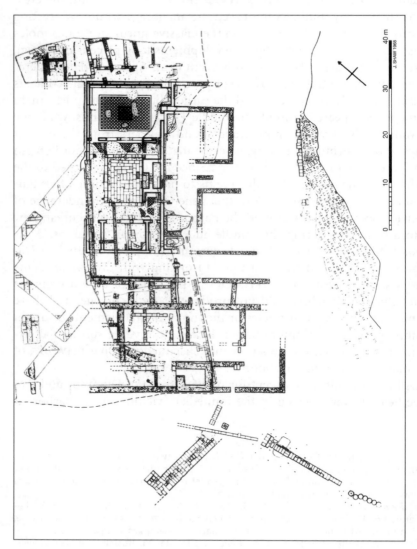

Fig. 13.3. Structures at the base of the north mole. Courtesy of the Kenchreai Excavations.

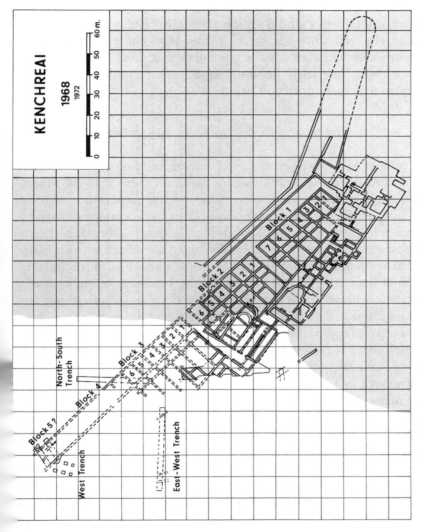

Fig. 13.4. Structures on the south mole of the harbor. Courtesy of the Kenchreai Excavations.

the heart of the settlement during the Roman Empire. It is uncertain when exactly these cults were established. The literary, epigraphic, and numismatic evidence dates no earlier than the late 1st century CE. Even so, at least one house church must have formed in Kenchreai during the 50s, and by that time the town must have had a lively atmosphere. Since no dominant cultic tradition seems to have existed before the Roman era, and since the sacred places were clustered around the harbor, we should consider the possibility that these cults were local innovations of the Early Roman period, perhaps imported from the Isthmian Sanctuary or from Corinth.

The Major Cults: Aphrodite and Isis

The cults of Aphrodite and Isis predominate in discussions of religion at Kenchreai because more evidence exists for them than for others. Although it is difficult to ascertain the relative importance of these two cults at the port, we can reasonably propose that they played a central role in the religious life of the community on the basis of their establishment in highly visible locales, their identification with maritime activity, and the elaborate public rituals attached to the worship of Isis at least. The best testimony for the sanctuary of Aphrodite is Pausanias, who recorded that a "temple and a stone statue" (ναὸς καὶ ἄγαλμα λίθου, 2.2.3) were located before the north mole with respect to the traveler approaching the harbor from the north. From this short description, it is reasonable to infer that the building, as a dwelling place for the deity that also housed a cult statue, was a monumental structure in a conspicuous location where sacrifices and offerings were made.

The excavators in the 1960s found a building complex at the base of the north mole that Scranton identified as the sanctuary cited by Pausanias (fig. 13.2–3).[13] He admitted, however, that this identification rested on tenuous grounds. I submit that the evidence cannot support it. Scranton presented no positive evidence on which to base his theory, noting only the general location of the complex at the harbor's north end, the presence of common lamps and other ceramic objects with gladiatorial, erotic, Dionysiac, and mythological imagery (which hardly connote cult activity), and the observation that sanctuaries of

---

[13] *Kenchreai* I, 87–90.

Aphrodite do not seem to follow a standard plan in classical architecture. Among the rich finds from this area, none could be identified as an offering like those found in the cult facilities east of the theater at Corinth, namely, assorted figurines and statues, several depicting Aphrodite.[14] Furthermore, nothing about the building complex, which passed through several phases of design and use from the Early to Late Roman periods, indicates a religious function. It contained several rooms in an axial arrangement facing the sea, including a heated chamber, a peristyle, and a spacious *atrium* or *aula* with wall-painting, mosaic pavement, and molded marble revetment. This plan and decor suggest that the building served as an opulent residence, most likely a seaside villa bordering the harborside—Scranton himself proposed this alternative interpretation.[15] If the Temple of Aphrodite was not situated right at the base of the north mole, it should be sought somewhere nearby but further to the west or north, in areas that have not yet been fully explored.[16]

Apart from the presence of a temple, there is no evidence for the cult's history or character. Aphrodite was of course a central deity of Corinth from early times,[17] proposed a Roman date for the Cenchrean cult of Aphrodite, and perhaps the Corinthians established a corollary cult at Kenchreai near the renewed harbor in the first century. Of the goddess's many attributes, Aphrodite Euploia would have been particularly appropriate to the maritime setting of Kenchreai. This aspect of Aphrodite was worshipped at the Piraeus at least as late as the 1st century BCE.[18] In her survey of Aphrodite in Classical Attica, Rachel Rosenzweig stressed that, though separate cult sites were devoted to the goddess's specific forms, worshippers at any place could revere the

---

[14] C. K. Williams 2005.

[15] *Kenchreai* I, 88; Rothaus 2000, 66–69.

[16] Geophysical survey conducted by KCP in 2004 identified a rectangular wall measuring ca. 17 m × 25–30 m and enclosing a smaller building, both aligned roughly southwest-northeast, in the flat meadow directly overlying the vertical exposure of limestone that borders the northern harborside (fig. 13.2); Sarris *et al.* 2007, 12–14, 20, fig. 12–13). In its basic outline this plan resembles a structure like a podium-temple inside a *peribolos*, or perhaps an enormous peristyle. The building is under investigation by the new Kenchreai Excavations. If it is the Temple of Aphrodite seen by Pausanias, we can confirm that he entered the port along the coastal ridge directly to the north.

[17] C. K. Williams 1986; Bookidis 2003.

[18] Garland 1986, 112, 150, 154; Rosenzweig 2004, 90. Pausanias (1.1.3) recorded that Konon erected a temple in her honor after the victory off Knidos in 394. *IG* II² 2872 is a dedication to Aphrodite Euploia by Argeios, *stratêgos* of the Piraeus, dated 97/6 BCE.

divine presence in all her incarnations.[19] Visitors to the temple by the Cenchrean harbor presumably invoked Aphrodite as protector of seafaring. If the building was situated at the south end of the Koutsongila Ridge in the high meadow above the harbor, not unlike the Aphrodision on Eëtioneia above the main harbor of the Piraeus,[20] the Temple of Aphrodite would have literally watched over the port's activities.

Complementing Aphrodite at the south side of the harbor was the place of another goddess associated with the sea, Isis. Pausanias only wrote that a "sanctuary" (ἱερόν) of Isis was situated opposite the Temple of Aphrodite. Apuleius gives invaluable testimony concerning the local cult, but his narrative contains only evocative imagery, no specific details that help reconstruct sacred topography.[21] The archaeological remains likewise provide little concrete evidence. Scranton tentatively interpreted the maze of walls that he excavated on the south mole as the famous Iseion cited by Pausanias and attended by Apuleius's protagonist Lucius. His argument was based on three sources: a series of rooms that he identified as a temple-complex; a group of glass panels in *opus sectile*; and an inscribed column.[22]

When Scranton excavated the surface of the pier at the base of the south mole, he uncovered rooms arranged in blocks that apparently constituted *horrea*, or warehouses (fig. 13.2, 13.4). During the 1st century CE, these buildings were fronted by walkways that probably served both as platforms for unloading moored boats and as promenades for residents and visitors alike. At some point in the Early Roman period, the southwestern end of the pier was altered by the erection of several walls. These spaces evolved dramatically from the 1st to 6th centuries, culminating in the building of a Christian basilica (see below).[23]

The stratigraphic and structural sequences in this patently confusing area would repay fresh study for several reasons. Our understanding of ceramic chronology has progressed greatly since the 1960s. Moreover, the phasing proposed by Scranton is often speculative or controvertible, depending as it does on the synchronic association of certain

---

[19] Rosenzweig 2004.
[20] Garland 1986, 150. *IG* II² 1657 records the presence of the Aphrodision on Eëtioneia in 394/3. This might be the Aphrodision that Themistocles founded after the victory at Salamis; Schol. *ad* Hermogenes, *Rhet. Gr.* IV.393 ed. Walz.
[21] Gwyn Griffiths 1975, 17; D. E. Smith 1977, 209, n. 28.
[22] *Kenchreai* I, 71–78 is Scranton's fullest interpretative discussion.
[23] *Kenchreai* I, 53–71 and VI, 5–8.

blocks or walls that lie in superposition to one another.[24] This is not
the place for revising complicated architectural problems, which will
require close scrutiny of the excavation records and the finds.[25] We can
state confidently that, beginning in the 1st century CE (though perhaps
the end) and continuing until the major seismic event or events in the
late 14th century, this area was occupied by a corridor leading to an
apsidal court faced with marble, paved in mosaic, and adorned with
an octagonal font. Scranton also traced a rectangular enclosure at the
corner of the block immediately west of this Fountain Court, and he
reconstructed a prostyle podium temple along its southeast wall.

Scranton interpreted these buildings as the Sanctuary of Isis. It is a
clever interpretation, but ultimately it is unpersuasive on architectural
grounds. Besides the well-preserved apsidal court, the only surviving adjacent structures are the lowest courses of walls or the footing
trenches, and, as has been noted, the basic relationships between the
fragmentary foundations are open to debate. Little fallen superstructure survives to clarify our understanding of function, especially in the
case of the putative temple building.

Richard Rothaus has given a simpler explanation of this area, one
not motivated by a compulsion to substantiate Pausanias and Apuleius.
The court and its entrance corridor might have comprised an opulent
nymphaeum, either a wing of a larger residence like the one at the
base of the north mole, or a fountain erected by private funds as a
public benefaction with a spectacular Saronic vista.[26] The identification of these structures as part of a lavish residence would fit a recur-
rent pattern at major ports, such as Ptolemaic Alexandria, Herodean
Caesarea, and Imperial Portus, where palatial complexes were situated
prominently alongside busy harbors. On the other hand, Wilma Stern,
who has studied the copious wood and ivory furniture that decorated
the apsidal court during the 4th century, has suggested that this space
was a luxurious dining room used by scholarly and political leaders.[27]

---

[24] Noteworthy in this regard are the walls of the structures that predate the Christian basilica; *Kenchreai* I, fig. 25–30.

[25] During the early 1990s, R. Rothaus surveyed the stratigraphy and artifacts of this
area with reference to the original notebooks. While I cannot endorse all conclusions
in this cursory study as published (2000, 69–76), Rothaus offers some keen observations concerning the plan and chronology of the south mole.

[26] Rothaus 2000, 64–71.

[27] *Kenchreai* VI, 308–11.

In the end, we should recognize the circumspection and rigor with which Scranton and his able architect, Joseph Shaw, among many others, explored this challenging area over forty years ago, often employing pioneering underwater techniques. Scranton's theory about the Iseion still deserves serious consideration, and we cannot decisively disprove it without fuller evidence. But we cannot uncritically accept it either, and we should examine alternative interpretations that account for the topography of comparable Mediterranean harbors.

In addition to these problematic buildings, the excavators in the 1960s made an astounding discovery. On the floor of the apsidal court they found a cache of over 120 large glass panels in *opus sectile*. These were stored in wooden crates, where they seem to have been off-loaded in the middle or late 4th century and then buried under a dense stratum of debris when the court collapsed in a massive earthquake.[28] The panels were intended for parietal display, presumably somewhere nearby. They are distinguished not only by their intricate artistry in the vitreous medium but also by their vivid iconography (fig. 13.5). Apart from usual geometric and floral forms, the panels portray three main subjects: scenes of bustling harbor life; scenes of teeming Nilotic flora and fauna; and full-figural portraits of Imperial or civic officials, winged divinities, and intellectual luminaries (Homer, Plato, and Theophrastus).[29]

Scranton and Leila Ibrahim, who studied and published the panels, argued that the Nilotic imagery and the 'hieratic' portraits were most suitable to an Egyptian cultic setting. Therefore, they proposed that the panels were sacred ornaments for the supposed Iseion.[30] In contrast, the recent evaluation of these panels by Katherine Dunbabin stressed that there is nothing specifically religious or even Egyptian about them. Nilotic scenes were ubiquitous in Roman paintings and mosaics, regardless of the origin of production or location of display. The panels should be viewed foremost, Dunbabin asserted, as brilliant creations of a nascent Late Antique visual sensibility that was distinguished by multiplicity of perspective, variable scale, two-dimensionality,

---

[28] *Kenchreai* II, 1–11 discusses the depositional context of the panels; see *Kenchreai* VI, 6–8 on the furniture among the debris.

[29] *Kenchreai* II, 30–224.

[30] *Kenchreai* I, 73; *Kenchreai* II, 266–69; Rothaus 2002, 206–07.

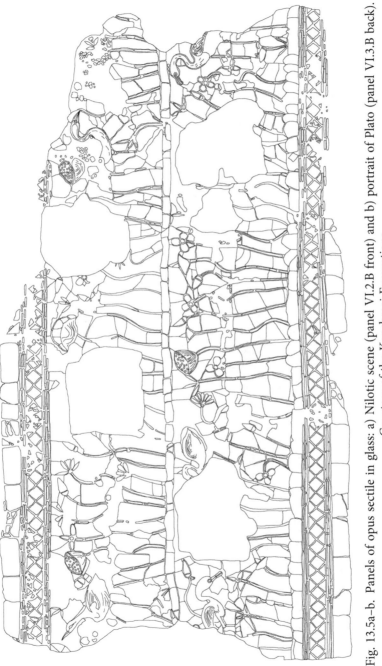

Fig. 13.5a–b. Panels of opus sectile in glass: a) Nilotic scene (panel VI.2.B front) and b) portrait of Plato (panel VI.3.B back). Courtesy of the Kenchreai Excavations.

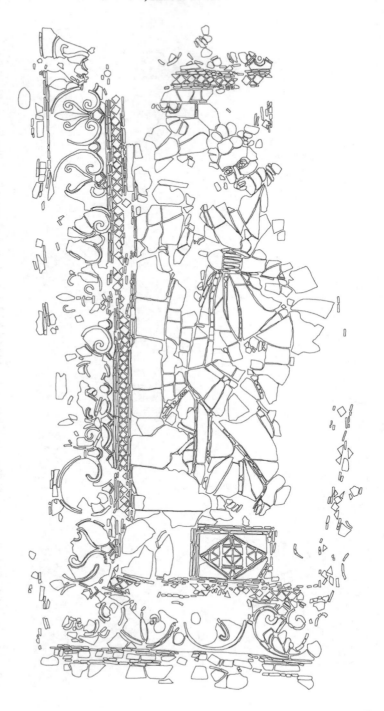

and repeated schematic forms.[31] Hector Williams has further argued that the seascapes were imaginary but essentially realistic, and thus provide a valuable source for nautical design and navigation in the 4th century.[32]

Finally, the portraits represent an intellectual and cultural climate that deeply valued the classical heritage, particularly in the embodiment of Homer, the epic poet and theologian, and early philosophers. Visu-ally literate elites would have recognized the images as belonging to a wider body of iconography that communicated certain shared moral and cultural values.[33] Rothaus has even speculated that the glass panels were intended for a Neoplatonic school housed in the *nymphaeum*, not unlike the contemporary mansion-*cum*-school at Aphrodisias, which exhibited the collection of intellectual-portraits that R. R. R. Smith has insightfully studied.[34] Whether practicing philosophers or educated elites gathered at the building, it is attractive to imagine that it belonged to a wealthy residence. The remarkable glass panels at least reveal that some structure in this part of the harbor was to be deco-rated with rare elegance and *au courant* sophistication. We cannot know exactly what the purpose of that building or buildings was, but the panels themselves do not require that it was a Sanctuary of Isis.

There is one piece of direct evidence for the Egyptian cult. Excava-tors found an inscribed column amid the destruction debris over the Christian basilica, just west of where the apsidal court had stood. The fragmentary column in fine, blue-veined, white marble was found in a secondary depositional context, and it did not originally belong to the basilica. Inscribed on the column was a single word, Ὀργία, in sharp, clean letters, though the epigrapher mistakenly cut the diagonal *hasta* for the final alpha before completing the vertical stroke of the iota (*SEG* XXVIII 387; fig. 13.6).[35] The meaning of this word is *prima*

---

[31] Dunbabin 1999, 266–68. For the Egyptian imagery in its Roman artistic context and the panels from Kenchreai, see generally Versluys 2002, 217–19, no. 117.

[32] H. Williams 2004.

[33] See the apposite discussion by R. Leader-Newby (2005, 236) concerning personi-fications in eastern mosaics during Late Antiquity.

[34] R. R. R. Smith 1990, 151–52; Rothaus 2000, 79–83, 2002. For similar assemblages of figures, see the statues of Greek poets and philosophers in the hemicycle in the Sarapeion at Memphis (Lauer and Picard 1955) and Ps.-Plut., *de vita et poesi Homeri* 120 (Homer, Plato, Aristotle, and Theophrastus). R. Lamberton (1986) explores the Late Antique figure of Homer as theologian in the context of Neoplatonic allegory.

[35] Inventory no. KE 837. *Kenchreai I*, 73, 125 with plate XXVIII:C; Pallas 1987–89, 301, fig. 4; Bricault 2005, 35, no. *102/0201. Preserved dimensions of the column:

Fig. 13.6. Column inscribed with a cult epithet of Isis. Courtesy of the Kenchreai Excavations.

facie obscure. It could be the neuter plural ὄργια, meaning "mysteries" or "sacred cult objects" (see Theoc. 26.13, *GVI* 1344, and Clem. Alex. *Protr.* 2.22). That interpretation should be rejected, however, because the isolated use of the abstract noun without a concrete referent on an architectural member would make little sense.

On the other hand, the inscription of divine names on columnar stones, whether pillars or altars, was a common dedicatory practice. Scranton recognized that Ὀργία was used as an epithet for Isis in the priestly dedication of an altar in the 2nd century at the Sarapeion in Thessalonica (*IG* X.2.1 103), and Laurent Bricault has noted that Plutarch called the Greek cults of Isis and Osiris ὄργια (fr. 212 ed. Sandbach *ap.* Theodoret, *Cur. Gr. aff.* 1.468a).[36] This epithet echoes two rare substantives in the Imperial Greek lexicon: ἡ ὀργίας and ὁ ὀργιαστής, meaning "mystic" or "ecstatic," or more specifically a participant in the sacred ritual (see Plut. *Mor.* 417A, App. *BC* 4.47, Manetho astrol. 4.63). The appellation Ὀργία identified Isis as the goddess of the mystery-cult or overseer of initiation, not unlike the appellation of Osiris as μύστης on another dedication from the Thessalonican Serapeion (*IG* X.2.1 107).[37] The column from Kenchreai might have exhibited the name Isis higher up, on the part that is now lost, because it seems unlikely that a solitary epithet was written on the stone. The inscription thus would have read ["Ἶσις] Ὀργία or ["Ἴσιδι] Ὀργίαι, "Isis (inscribed or understood) of the Mysteries," or "To Isis (inscribed or understood) of the Mysteries."

We cannot know how this column functioned as a dedication, or what was its original architectural setting. But it does confirm both the proximity of the Iseion to the harbor's southern limit and the existence of the mysteries. The use of the unusual epithet exemplifies the bountiful polynymy that characterized this popular Egyptian goddess, a multiform deity especially susceptible to representation in different guises.

The final book in the novel by Apuleius paints a vivid picture of the cult's place in the local community. Although this picture is embedded in a fictional narrative replete with fantastic events, the story's setting, as Fergus Millar has demonstrated, was drawn with historical

---

1.270 m height; 0.370 m diameter at the level of the text. Letter height: ca. 0.060 m. The stone now resides on the back patio of the Isthmia Museum.

[36] Bricault 2005, 156–57, no. 113/0552.

[37] Dunand 1975, 32; Bricault 2005, 138 and 157.

realism. Lucius's world is unmistakably the world of Antonine Thessaly and Achaia.[38] Apuleius studied at Athens as a young adult (*Apol.* 72.5; *Flor.* 18.15, 20.4), at which time he probably would have visited Corinth, and he sailed across the Aegean (*Flor.* 15; *Mund.* 17.7), presumably leaving from either the Piraeus or Kenchreai. Some scholars have even suggested that he was a young initiate into the mysteries at Kenchreai.[39] Regardless of his personal history, both Apuleius's knowledge of the Corinthia and the verisimilitude with which he colored his novelistic world would have informed his portrayal of the Isiac cult at Kenchreai.

The highlight of the episode is the procession to the sea (*Met.* 11.8–17). Devotees launched the sacred ship of Isis laden with offerings, an annual rite in early March that inaugurated the sailing season. Gian Franco Gianotti and Ian Moyer have elucidated the sociocultural setting of Apuleius's account.[40] Moyer in particular has observed that the constituents of the seaward procession adopted variegated dress and behavior reflecting structural relations within the community. The ordered, uniform, and austere actions of the cult initiates at the center of the parade (*religiosi*) identified them as members of a special class possessing a certain prestige and power that cross-cut other identities, such as political, familial, or economic status. In contrast, the diverse people who marched at the front of the procession (*profani* or *populi*) wore outrageous costumes as animals or mythic figures, and their attitude was colorful, individualized, and playful. This element of the carnivalesque was a dynamic channel for the participation of non-initiates in a major public ritual with a perceived impact on the community's livelihood. The festival of the *navigium Isidis* at Kenchreai, which presumably attracted not only local residents but also crowds from elsewhere in the region, illustrates the multivocal nature of religion at Kenchreai.

There are few secure chronological indices for the history of the cult. Certainly it was operating when Pausanias and Apuleius wrote, and a

---

[38] Millar 1981.

[39] P. Veyne (1965, 248) and J. Gwyn Griffiths (1975, 1–7, 14–20) proposed that the Kenchreai episode was based on personal experience. F. Millar (1982, 64) said only that he had probably been to Corinth. The elaborate account in the *Metamorphoses* of the horrific spectacle in the Corinthian Amphitheater, the flight to Kenchreai, the theophany, and the initiation into the cult of Isis (*Met.* 10.18–11.25) implies that Apuleius also knew the Isthmus.

[40] Gianotti 1981; Moyer (in preparation). I thank Ian Moyer for kindly sharing his unpublished manuscript and for his enlightening discussions of this episode.

rare Corinthian bronze coin issued under Antoninus Pius showed a semicircular harbor, apparently Kenchreai, around the mantled figure of Isis grasping a billowing sail to the right as goddess of the sea (Πελάγια).[41] Since imperial coinage, Pausanias (2.4.6) and perhaps a now-lost inscription (*CIG* I, 575 = *SIRIS* no. 34) attest to the worship of Isis Pelagia at Corinth,[42] it is quite possible that the cult was exported thence to Kenchreai during the port's 1st-century revival. On the other hand, Isis in her various forms spread widely in Attica and southern Greece during the Hellenistic and Roman eras, and the cult of Isis Pelagia at Kenchreai can be viewed within a constellation of Aegean cult sites that were active during the Roman Empire, including Athens, Mytilene and Iasos.[43] The cult at Kenchreai probably did not persist as late as the 6th century, when the Christian Church had become the dominant institution in local communities, and the Corinthians no longer made monumental dedications to traditional cults. In this regard, the date of the marble column to Isis of the Mysteries is striking: the letter forms, especially the alpha with its steep diagonal hasta and triangular loop, are typical of Late Roman Corinthian inscriptions.[44] The column can therefore be identified as a sacred dedication of the 4th or 5th century, a transitional age when old sanctuaries across the Greek world were defunct or declining.

---

[41] Bricault and Veymiers 2007, 394–96 with fig. 3 (Type 3) and 406–13. The best known example is in the Staatliches Münzkabinett, Berlin: Lehmann-Hartleben 1923, 238, 259 with plate 11; Leipoldt and Regling 1925, 129–30 with plate 5.3; Hohlfelder 1970, 326, n. 2 with plate 80:c; Gwyn Griffiths 1975, 18; D. E. Smith 1977, 202–03. M. J. Price and J. L. Trell (1977, 83, fig. 146) cited another well-preserved example in London. On the numismatic iconography of Isis Pelagia: 'Isis' IV.D *LIMC* 5, no. 274–94, in particular no. 275 and 278 (Alexandria 2nd century CE).

[42] On Isis at Corinth in general: D. E. Smith 1977; *Corinth* XVIII.3, 5–8; Bookidis 2003, 257–58, and 2005, 146–47. L. Bricault and R. Veymiers (2007) discussed Corinthian coins of Isis Pelagia issued from Antoninus Pius to Plautilla. Jean-Baptiste-Gaspard d'Ansse de Villoison, who visited Corinth in late May, 1785, apparently found a dedication to Isis in the courtyard of a house there; Famerie 2006, 143–44. Although A. Boeckh and L. Vidman considered Villoison's reference to this discovery unambiguous, some have questioned its meaning and doubted the existence of the Corinthian inscription; Dunand 1973, 157–58 n. 1; Bruneau 1974, 337; D. E. Smith 1977, 216–17.

[43] On the diffusion of the Isiac cult in Attica and the Peloponnese: Bricault 2001, 2–9. On Isis in Athens and at the Piraeus: E. R. Williams 1985; Garland 1986, 126–28. On Isis Pelagia in the Aegean: Bricault 1996, 60; *IG* XII.2 113 (Mytilene); *Iasos* 241. The settlement history at Kenchreai renders it improbable that the Isis cult was established in Hellenistic times, *pace* Dunand 1973, 17–18.

[44] For the form of the alpha, see *Corinth* VIII.3, no. 542, 552, 586 (epitaphs, 4th through 6th centuries). I thank Eli Weaverdyck for discussing the paleography of this inscription.

OTHER CULTS: POSEIDON, ASKLEPIOS, DIONYSOS, AND PAN

Next to Aphrodite and Isis, other gods occupied the port's sacred spaces, but little evidence exists for their attributes and cults. Pausanias wrote that a "bronze image" (χαλκοῦν [ἄγαλμα]) of Poseidon was situated after the Temple of Aphrodite "on the mole [extending] out into the sea" (ἐν τῷ ἐρύματι τῷ διὰ τῆς θαλάσσης, 2.2.3). An uncommon coin struck at Corinth under Antoninus Pius shows a semicircular harbor around a statue of Poseidon, quite possibly the one cited by Pausanias, as Robert Hohlfelder proposed.[45] We cannot know what exactly this statue looked like, and how it related to other figural depictions of Poseidon, though Pausanias saw four in Corinth and at Lechaion (2.2.5, 2.3.4, 2.3.5).[46] One possible location for this statue would have been the broad, rectangular platform at the extremity of the north mole.[47] The statue was a sacred object but probably not a locus for veneration or ritual performance. Like many other colossal statues of gods displayed at ports across the Mediterranean, the image of Poseidon at Kenchreai, especially if it was perched on the waves some 100 m off the headland, would have been as much a symbol of the sea's divine force as it was an impressive work of art and a monumental point of reference for seafarers. Moreover, as a Corinthian landmark, it prefigured the religious history and landscape of the region for travelers arriving from the East. We know nothing about the sanctuary (ἱερόν) of Asklepios, except that Pausanias said it joined the Iseion at the south end of the harbor (2.2.3). It is significant that Poseidon and Asklepios had well-established cults at the Isthmus and at Corinth.[48]

---

[45] Hohlfelder 1970. The coin was first illustrated at Imhoof-Blumer and Gardner 1887, 17 with plate D:LX.

[46] E. Walde-Psenner (1979) discussed possible connections between this statue and other images of Poseidon, particularly in Roman Italy.

[47] Hohlfelder 1970, 331; *Kenchreai* I, 18–19, fig. 7 with plate XI:A, which describes the remains at the end of the north mole.

[48] On Poseidon: *Isthmia* I; Bookidis 2003, 253. On Asklepios: *Corinth* XIV; Wickkiser in this volume. A miniature marble relief depicting Asklepios, Hygieia, and Telesphoros, probably dating to the 2nd century, was found in a possibly domestic context of the late 4th century in the East Field at Isthmia; *Isthmia* VI, 43–48, no. 40 with plate 32:a.

The epigraphic corpus from Kenchreai has produced evidence for an overlooked cult of Dionysos. A rupestral inscription, published in 1936 by Markellos Mitsos and commented on soon thereafter by Margherita Guarducci, recorded that a former *agoranomos*, Cn. Pompeius Zenas, donated a tithe "to Zeus' son Dionysos" (Διὸς Διονύσῳ, *SEG* XI 50).[49] The inscription was found in an area ca. 1 km northwest of the harbor called Spilia Voli, near an ancient north-south road and just west of the expansive limestone quarries that lay outside the port-town to the north.[50] But the exact location of the cult site is uncertain because such dedications could be made in visible places, like roadsides, separate from the place of ritual activity. The presence of Dionysos at Kenchreai is not surprising when one considers that he was also worshipped at the Isthmus and at Corinth.[51] Certain Dionysiac cults with marine associations involved festivals celebrating the god's advent from the sea, such as the City Dionysia at Smyrna.[52] It is, however, unknown whether Dionysos joined Aphrodite and Isis at Kenchreai as a divine overseer of seaborn traffic.

A previously unpublished inscription found in 1963 in the wall of a modern farm building attests to an unnamed cult that was most probably devoted to Dionysos (fig. 13.7).[53] The text is carved on a now battered block of very hard, blue-grey limestone with a thin *cyma reversa* delimiting the lower edge of the inscribed face. The letters are sharply but unevenly cut on the smooth side of what was once a base.[54] The inscription is of interest from the viewpoints of philology, onomastics, and religious history:

---

[49] Mitsos 1936, 146, fig. 7; Guarducci 1939. The text was first noted at Lampakis 1907, 78, n. 2.

[50] I have searched in vain for this inscription.

[51] On Dionysos at Isthmia: *Isthmia* II, 113–16; *IG* IV.203 (Sacred Glen); Seelinger 1998. On Dionysos at Corinth: Paus. 2.2.7; Bookidis 2003, 255, n. 69, and 2005, 153–59, n. 83.

[52] Philostr. *VS* 1.531; Aristid. *Or.* 17.5, 21.4 ed. Keil. The major Dionysia at the Piraeus do not seem to have carried marine associations; Garland 1985, 124–26.

[53] Inventory no. KE 811: *Kenchreai* I, 72–73. The stone now resides on the back patio of the Isthmia Museum.

[54] Preserved dimensions of the base: 0.267 m height, 0.230 m width, and 0.310 m thickness. Letter height: 0.030–0.040 m.

Fig. 13.7. Inscription commemorating a sacred dedication by C. Heius Agathemerus and Terentia. Courtesy of the Kenchreai Excavations.

Γ(αἰος) Ἥιος Ἀγαθήμερος καὶ Τε-
ρέντια πῶμα θιάσῳ ἀρτο-
κρεωνικῷ ὑπὲρ Ἥιας Παυ-
λείνας θυγατρὸς αὐτῶν λι-
κναφόρου ἀνέστησαν. hedera

C. Heius Agathemerus and Terentia
set up the cup for the ritual of
distributing bread and meat
on behalf of Heia Paulina,
their daughter, the basket-bearer.

This inscription records the dedication of a sacred object (πῶμα) by C. Heius Agathemerus and his wife, Terentia, in honor of their daughter Heia Paulina, who was a ritual-participant with a special role (λικναφόρος). Although these persons are otherwise unattested, the Gaii Heii were an eminent Corinthian family who enjoyed a close connection to the duovirate during the colony's first generations and appeared across central and southern Greece into the 2nd century.[55] The letter forms are Early or Middle Roman, and the known histories of both the port and the family would favor a date in the 1st or 2nd century. We cannot say whether Agathemerus and Terentia were residents of Kenchreai, though it is possible that, on account of the family's prominence, they lived in the city but participated in cult activity at the port. The epigraphic commemoration of sacred dedications on behalf of relatives was a common practice among urban elites in the eastern provinces. It not only advertised their generous contribution to civic life but also celebrated familial devotion and religious piety, which were common aristocratic virtues.

This text raises several basic questions: which role did Paulina play in which cult, and what did her parents dedicate for what purpose? Paulina was a λικναφόρος. The λίκνον was a broad, fan-like basket for winnowing grain that was a standard instrument in Dionysiac mysteries from the Classical to the Roman eras. The cult festival involved a procession in which a devotee carried a covered winnowing-basket containing fruit and an erect phallus.[56] The rich nomenclature

---

[55] RP I, 326–28, COR 305–11 (Corinth); FD III.4 92, 96 (Delphi, 2nd century), IG V.1 659 (victor at Sparta, early 2nd century), SEG III 335 (victor at Thespiae, 2nd century). I thank Benjamin Millis for discussing this inscription within the larger frame of Corinthian epigraphy.

[56] On the winnowing-fan and Dionysiac mysteries: Nilsson 1952, and 1957, 21–37, 44; Burkert 1987, 95–98. A Hellenistic epigram by one Flaccus (AP 6.165) colorfully

for the functionaries of this cult in the Imperial Greek world shows that there were several separate duties of bearing. The other known instances of the term λικναφόρος appear in inscriptions commemorating Dionysiac cults from Thracian Apollonia (Roman; *IBulg* I² 401) and Philoppopolis (241–44 CE; *IBulg* III.1 1517), and in the famous Bacchic inscription of Pompeia Agrippinilla from Torre Nova, now in the Metropolitan Museum of Art (ca. 160 CE; *IGUR* I 160, face I.1, col. B.3, line 11).[57] Paulina, therefore, seems to have been an initiate into local mysteries of Dionysos, and she played a central role in the public procession. Furthermore, members of this cult comprised an association for the distribution of bread and meat, presumably sacrificial (θίασος ἀρτοκρεωνικός).[58] Banqueting, whether by associations or by the civic community, was of course an integral part of ancient religious life. The adjective ἀρτοκρεωνικός is a *hapax legomenon*. The very rare neuter noun ἀρτόκρεας, however, occurs in one text listing sacred dedications in the cults of Artemis and Apollo at Roman Didyma (*IDidyma* 387) and in another from west of Sardis honoring a man who contributed to the Imperial cult (*IGR* IV 1348),[59] while the Latin transliteration (*artocreas*) seems to have had some currency (Pers. 6.50 and *CIL* 9.5309). How, where, and for whom exactly this distribution occurred remain unknown, but the sharing of sacrificial offerings among worshippers was a usual practice.

We turn to the object that Agathemerus and Terentia set up (ἀνέστησαν).[60] The word πῶμα occurs most commonly in the Roman

---

depicts the roles and properties (including the λίκνον) of a Bacchante; Page 1981, 46–49. The λίκνον was also used in the Eleusinian mysteries, and there are Archaic-Classical replicas of this tool in terracotta from the Sanctuary of Demeter and Kore on Acrocorinth (*ThesCRA* I, 306), but there is little evidence for the attachment of the term λικναφόρος/λικνοφόρος to cults of Demeter beyond Callimachus (*Hymn to Demeter* 126; Hopkinson 1984, 42–43, 177). *Pace* Scranton (*Kenchreai* I, 72–73), there is nothing about this text that associates it with the Isiac cult, notwithstanding the reference by Apuleius to a *vannum* in the procession at Kenchreai (*Met.* 11.10).

[57] Nilsson 1957, 45–61; Scheid 1986. Note that the alternative spelling λικνοφόρος is not attested in known Greek inscriptions.

[58] While the commonest meanings of θίασος are "Bacchic frenzy or revel" and "association or group of worshippers," the word could also mean "banquet or feast" in Imperial Greek prose (see entries at III in LSJ and 4 in Lampe 1969). This explains the ambiguous translation of lines 2–3 in the dedication from Kenchreai.

[59] Robert 1960, 480–81.

[60] The use of the aorist active ἀνέστησαν connotes not merely dedication but rather the establishment of something substantial, as in the erection of statues, *stelai*, trophies, or altars; see the entry at A.15 in LSJ. But all possible meanings of πῶμα in this context could not indicate a sizable, substantial object. Perhaps the epigrapher was using the verb as a synonym for ἀνέθηκαν, which would have been an easy semantic leap.

era meaning "cover for a burial" or "stone slab,"[61] but obviously that definition cannot apply here. However, the word ἔκπωμα meaning "beaker" or "drinking-cup" was used to describe vessels dedicated at Classical Athens and Delos,[62] and a shortened form of the same word, without the prepositional prefix (πῶμα), has been found on cups from Late Antique Scythia Minor (*IGLRom* 63, 106, 217 ed. Popescu).[63] The dedication of a drinking-cup would be particularly appropriate for a Dionysiac ritual involving the distribution of food. In general, the use of such rare terms in this condensed statement obscures the precise nature of the rituals to which they refer. We can only conclude that a cult involving elaborate ceremonies, in all probability a mystery cult of Dionysos, attracted devotees to Kenchreai, perhaps including citizens of status from Corinth.

The last deity known to have been venerated at the port is Pan. The only source for his cult is a votive-relief that was donated to the Corinth Museum in 1953, presumably by a villager who happened upon it (fig. 13.8).[64] The sculpture is a substantial but portable piece of fine-grained, pure white marble that is broken along the left edge and abraded and gouged across the face.[65] It depicts a reclining Pan inside a somewhat elliptical grotto rendered with an irregular, blunt edge that closely surrounds the figure. Pan fully reclines on a bench covered with grooves that suggest a textile. The god leans on his left arm and holds the syrinx in a dangling hand; his right arm rests lightly on his right knee cradling the *lagobolon*, which curves up to his shoulder. This Pan has a grotesque head with short horns, a rounded forehead and cheeks, tall ears, a large nose, and a dense beard that seems to hang in two corkscrews or plaits. His arms and chest are muscular, his torso is mostly covered by an animal skin draped in thick folds with a head hanging from a lappet at his left shoulder, and his caprine

---

[61] Luc. *DMar.* 2.2, *SEG* XLV 793 (Philippi, Roman); *Perinthos-Heracleia* 103 (Roman); *IEph* 1625B (note the diminutive form); *TAM* III 574 (Termessus) and V.2 1157 (Thyateira); *IMT Kyz Kapu Dağ* 1578 (Cyzicus, 113/4 or 114/5 CE) and 1840 (Roman).

[62] *IG* I³ 342; *IG* II² 1382, 1407, 1408, 1409, 1643, 1644; *IDélos* 103, 104, 104(2), 104(12), 1417.

[63] The word πῶμα refers to a draft from Lethe in a verse-epitaph from Kerkyra dating to the late 2nd to early 3rd centuries (*IG* IX.1 883).

[64] Inventory no. S 2607: Wiseman 1978, 51–52, 76, n. 50, fig. 48. I thank Ioulia Tzonou-Herbst for her kind assistance in studying this sculpture at the Corinth Museum.

[65] Preserved dimensions of the stone: 0.112 m maximum height front, 0.196 m maximum width front, 0.174 maximum thickness front, 0.055 m maximum height back strut.

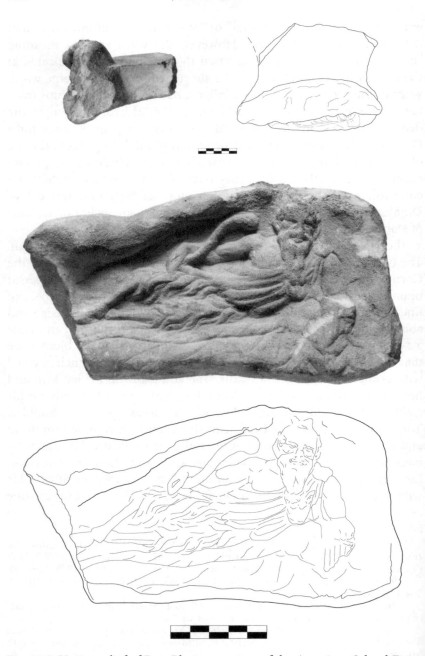

Fig. 13.8. Votive-relief of Pan. Photos courtesy of the American School Excavations at Corinth; drawings courtesy of the Kenchreai Excavations.

legs are crossed at the ankles. This image represents the uncommon Classical type of the reclining Pan, similar examples of which can be found on Late Classical to Hellenistic Arcadian coinage.[66] The quality of the sculpture is detailed but almost schematic, showing a figure with thick but fluid contours, an almost languid posture, an oversized head, and hair that parts in broad strands. These stylistic traits compare with sculpted depictions of Pan dated broadly to the 2nd to 3rd centuries,[67] and we should likewise place the votive-relief from Kenchreai in the Middle Roman period.

Unfortunately no record of this piece's provenience exists. One clue to its depositional setting is the granular concretion that evenly encases the sculpture up to two mm thick. This calcareous shell indicates that the stone most likely rested in a place where water pooled. There are two areas that would furnish such an environment in the vicinity of the archaeological site: the flat, well-watered plain that directly under-lies the modern village and probably represents an infilled embayment, and a cave situated in the area of Spilia Voli, where Zenas inscribed his tithing to Dionysos (fig. 13.9). Although the cave has never been scientifically investigated and its age is unknown, it would have been a typical place for votive offerings to Pan. This scenario is especially attractive, because the relief itself takes the form of a grotto, and numerous votives-reliefs for Pan and the nymphs have been found in caves, such as the famous series from Classical Attica.[68] The back of the relief from Kenchreai (fig. 13.8) has a flat, projecting strut with curved sides that must have served to attach and to stabilize the stone against an architectural member or, more likely, a wall.

If this votive-relief was originally affixed inside an ancient cave at Spilia Voli, it would have been displayed on the outskirts of the Roman Kenchreai. The full northern extent of the settlement has not been determined, but this area seems to have belonged to a suburban zone bordering both the limestone quarries and an ancient road that prob-ably communicated with the Isthmian Sanctuary across higher ground to the north. This liminal setting between travel routes, residential

---

[66] 'Pan,' *LIMC* suppl., no. 124–25 (4th to 3rd centuries); Marquardt 1995, 304 with plate 31.2, citing Gardner (1887, 173–74, tab. 32.10/11, Arcadian coins, ca. 363–280 BCE).

[67] For example, see 'Pan,' *LIMC* suppl., no. 118, 139 (Roman), 218 (early 3rd cen-tury) and 227 (190s); Marquardt 1995, 32–33, no. 36 with plate 4.3 (Severan).

[68] Edwards 1985, 19–27; Wickens 1986, 1.168–210.

Fig. 13.9. Cave at Spilia Voli northwest of Kenchreai, viewed from south-southeast. Courtesy of the Kenchreai Excavations.

space, industrial activity, and the countryside was appropriate to a cult of Pan, in which devotees would have contemplated the intersection between human experience and the wilderness.[69] The god inhabited other Corinthian sites too, but not always at the margins. Sculpted images of Pan were displayed in more central locales at Corinth and at the Isthmus during the Empire.[70]

Magical Practice in Daily Life

Religious experience at Roman Kenchreai was not confined to public ritual, mystic initiation, and the veneration of popular deities. Residents of the port also practiced magic, or the limited manipulation of supernatural forces according to personal or group needs, often through technical assistance with materials and language. At Kenchreai the best evidence for this dimension of religious experience comes in the form of lead tablets, four of which have been found in burial contexts of the late 1st to middle 3rd centuries CE. These tablets are typical: small rectangular strips of lead inscribed by stylus in cursive scripts, though none from Kenchreai w pierced with nails. All were found on Koutsongila in the subterranean chamber tombs arrayed in rows facing seaward (fig. 13.2), carefully situated either at the base of an altar or near the edge of a grave. The tombs were used for several generations by families and their dependents, and they were opened on multiple occasions for burial and commemoration.[71] On these occasions, visitors would have left the tablets in places advantageous for sending a message to the chthonic deities concerning a personal offense or a source of tension within the community.

The best preserved tablet was found near the edge of a brick-lined, tile-covered cist set into the floor in the southeastern part of Tomb 22 (fig. 13.10).[72] The text begins with a call to Violence (Βία), Fate

---

[69] The Classical shrine probably to Pan and the nymphs that existed in the area of Kokkinovrysi, near the road heading out of Corinth toward Sikyon, might have held a similar place in the city's religious landscape; C. K. Williams 1981, 409–10; Merker 2003, 237; Bookidis 2004, 147–48.

[70] *Corinth* XVII, 77, no. 106 with plate 29 (small head of Pan, Great Bath on the Lechaion Road, Roman); *Isthmia* IV, 123–25, no. 45, with plate 58–59 (group of Pan and the Muses [?], Palaimonion, 2nd century CE). Bookidis (2003, 254, n. 64) also notes reliefs of Pan and the nymphs from Hellenistic deposits in the city.

[71] Rife *et al.* 2007, 154–63.

[72] Inventory no. KM043: Faraone and Rife 2007. I thank Christopher Faraone, who s studying the Cenchrean tablets, for sharing his observations.

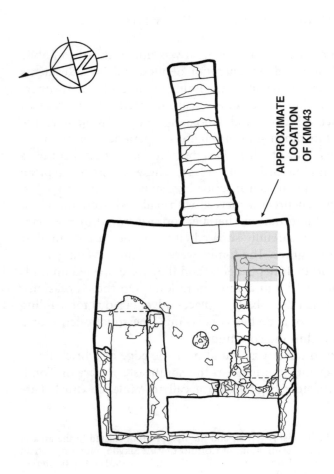

Fig. 13.10 Tomb 22, plan showing the location of the lead curse tablet KM043. Courtesy of the Kenchreai Excavations.

(Μοῖρα), and Necessity (Ἀνάνκε) and concludes with an invocation of Lord Chan Sereira Abrasach, a *vox mystica* of Egyptian origin. The writer of the tablet wanted to "overshadow" (σκιάσδω) the entire body of the offender, a son (or perhaps slave or freedman) of one Caecilius, because he allegedly stole a valuable garment of some kind. The text belongs to a popular subset of prayers for justice in which a victim acts as plaintiff in a divine court and urges the god(s) to mete out punishment.[73] The date of this and the other tablets cannot be ascertained with precision, but their depositional associations point to the 2nd or 3rd century.

The tablet from Tomb 22 has several notable features. It reflects how prayers for justice furnished an extra-legal instrument of social control in a close community. It reminds us of the multitude of otherwordly forces that played a role in the daily experience of local residents. It also demonstrates a link to religion at Corinth. The chthonic triad named at the opening of the tablet is unique in such texts. The three do, however, show up in the sanctuaries on Acrocorinth. One curse from the sanctuary of Demeter and Kore, which will be published by Ronald Stroud, names the Fates and Necessity, and Pausanias recorded that Violence, Necessity, and the Fates all had shrines on Acrocorinth (2.4.6–7).[74] Furthermore, prayers of justice with a similar format have been found at Corinth, in Roman tombs north of the city and in the buildings east of the Theater.[75] As research progresses on this growing corpus of Roman Corinthian tablets, we may be able to trace further connections between texts, and to explore the process of their manufacture and the circulation of magical knowledge.

THE CHRISTIAN COMMUNITY

Any survey of Cenchrean religion is incomplete without consideration of the Christian community, for which we have both textual and archaeological testimony. The first archaeologists to investigate Kenchreai, Georgios Lampakis and Anastasios Orlandos, were compelled

---

[73] Versnel 1991 is the fundamental study on this class of curse tablets.

[74] Bookidis 2005, 147. Faraone and I thank Ron Stroud for kindly sharing his unpublished catalog and commentary on the curse tablets from Demeter and Kore.

[75] Walbank 2005, 277–78, n. 48 (north tombs); Williams and Zervos 1987, 31, n. 43 (East of Theater). For a full listing of known curse tablets from the Corinthia, excluding the four so far found at Kenchreai: Jordan 1985, 166–67, and 2000, 12, no. 25.

by the site's Pauline association.[76] An abiding interest in the apostle's personal presence is a familiar phenomenon at many sites across Greece and Asia Minor. At Kenchreai this fascination has been sparked not just by the well-known passages in the New Testament but also by the plainly visible ruins of the Christian basilica at the south mole, which generated the toponym Vasiliki. One old legend of the eastern Isthmus, possibly a survival from the Byzantine era or before, has identified a system of grottos high on nearby Mount Oneion as 'Paul's Cave.'[77] Behind these durable traditions we can trace in vague outline two features of Christianity at Kenchreai during the 1st to 7th centuries: the early years of the community, and the use of basilicas in Late Antiquity.

The Acts of the Apostles records that Paul visited Kenchreai from Corinth during the middle first century (18:18). According to Romans 16:1–2, he worked closely with a deacon (διάκονος) named Phoebe, an early leader of the port's Christian assembly (ἐκκλησία), which would probably have convened at a house. In his short introduction, Paul used honorary language to commend her as a "leader" or "patroness" (προστάτις)[78] who helped many people, including himself. The identity of Phoebe has been much discussed, most profitably in comparison with the wealthy Lycian Junia Theodora, an approximate contemporary of Phoebe's who also lived near Corinth and was distinguished by her patronage.[79] A range of personal qualities can be inferred from Paul's brief characterization of Phoebe and from the comparison with Theodora: generous support, protection, hospitality, and benefaction. As Steven Friesen has observed, Phoebe was surely not among the wealthiest Corinthians.[80] But she was probably a woman of means who wielded authority within her group and enjoyed a measure of influence at the port.

---

[76] Lampakis 1907; Orlandos 1935.

[77] Georgiades 1907, plate II. The upper slopes of Mount Oneion not far from Kenchreai have several cavities and niches, such as those documented at Caraher and Gregory 2006, 339–40, fig. 10.

[78] This word is the feminine counterpart of προστάτης. The usage of these Greek terms during the Roman era seems to have been the equivalent of the Latin *patronu* and *patrona*; 'προστάτης, προστάτις,' III.3 in LSJ.

[79] Walters 1993, 168–85; Kearsley 1999; Murphy-O'Connor 2002, 84, 198. The testimony for Junia Theodora comes from a stone inscribed with five decrees that was found in 1954 near Solomos; Pallas, Charitonides, and Venencie 1959; *SEG* XVIII 143.

[80] Friesen 2005, 368–69.

Christianity at Kenchreai grew from Paul's foundation and Phoebe's leadership. If we consider the prominent references to Kenchreai in Paul's writings, it should come as no surprise that the port is listed as a episcopal seat in the *Apostolic Constitutions* (7.46.10). This work was compiled from diverse sources probably in the area of Antioch in the late 4th century.[81] Some ecclesiastical historians have asserted that the bishop at Kenchreai never existed, questioning this passage as an invention and pointing out that Kenchreai was a mere satellite of Corinth, which already possessed a powerful bishop.[82] The possibility, however, should not be rejected outright. Communities of all sizes and ranks in the eastern provinces acquired bishops, even villages and minor settlements of strategic import.[83] Kenchreai was a sizable community with an established church located ca. 8 km from Corinth, all conditions that would have been conducive to local episcopal authority. In addition, the so-called 'iconoclast' *notitia* composed at Constantinople in the 8th century lists a suffragan bishop at Kenchreai (*NEEC* 3.736).[84] Although this late document gives a corrupted place-name (Κικνιπέως), the identification with Kenchreai seems certain.[85] Regardless of the historicity of these sources, the presence of Kenchreai in two prominent episcopal lists purporting accuracy suggests that the notion of a bishop at Kenchreai was plausible in the Late Roman and Early Byzantine periods, presumably on account of the port's apostolic past as well as its vitality.

Little evidence exists for the interaction of Christianity and Hellenic polytheism at Kenchreai. We do, however, possess substantial archaeological evidence for the Christian community in its most developed form. Excavation at the base of the south mole in the 1960s uncovered a Christian basilica to the west of the Fountain Court and above its level (fig. 13.11). Our understanding of the building's history has

---

[81] Metzger 1985, 54–60; Mueller 2004, 35–126.

[82] Von Harnack 1924, 790; R. Janin, 'Cenchreae,' *DHGE* XII, 1953, col. 135. Fedalto 1988, 483 lists known Corinthian bishops during the Roman Empire.

[83] Jones 1964, 874–79.

[84] Bees 1915, 242–43; Gritsopoulos 1973, 119–20; Phougias 1997, 201, n. 85. Some scholars have questioned the validity of this testimony: Bon 1951, 24; Kordosis 1981, 347, n. 6.

[85] The corruption of the nominative Κεγχρεαί, genitive Κεγχρεῶν to genitive Κικνιπέως can be reconstructed through a series of scribal errors and phonological shifts that typify the text (*NEEC* 3 [20–21]): de-aspiration, iotacism, epenthesis of *iota*, substitution of *pi* for *rho*, transposition, and singularization. Alternatively, Kountoura-Galaki (1996, 59–64) retraces the toponym's formation as a translation into Greek from a lost Latin text with mixed Latin and Greek orthography.

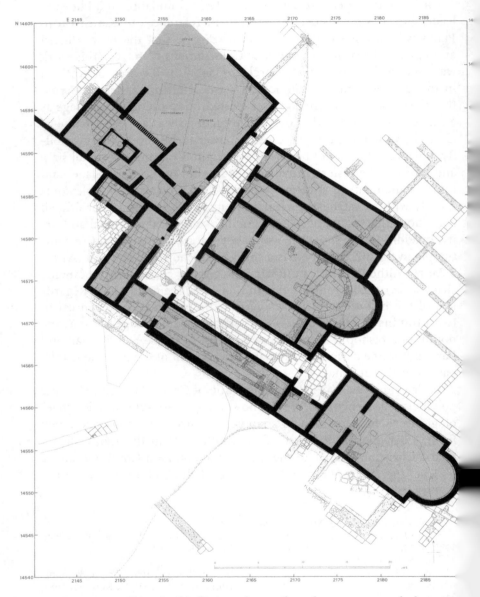

Fig. 13.11. Christian basilica on the south mole, reconstructed plan.
Courtesy of the Kenchreai Excavations.

benefitted from the architectural studies of Anatasios Orlandos and Demetrios Pallas.[86] More recently, Rothaus has surveyed the excavated contexts and devised a fundamentally reliable depositional sequence. According to his reading of the evidence, the building was erected at the end of the 5th or early 6th century.[87] At our present stage of knowledge, we cannot know whether the basilica immediately succeeded the worship of Isis and Asklepios somewhere in the vicinity, or whether the traditional cults were long since defunct when the church-building was founded. The late date of the columnar dedication to Isis, however, raises the possibility that Isiac and Christian worship were on some level contemporaneous. The basilica was used until the early 7th century, when it suffered destruction either at the hands of the invaders, because of seismic catastrophe, out of disuse, or through some combination of these factors. After the collapse of sections of the roof and walls and the dispersal of several interior members, worshippers cleared debris from certain central spaces including the aisles, where they resumed the burial of the dead until around the middle 7th century, when activity seems to have ceased.[88]

Unlike the underlying buildings that, Scranton argued, comprised the Iseion, the form of the small and lavishly appointed basilica is more or less clear.[89] The nave was flanked by two north and two south aisles, it was fronted by an atrium and baptistery, and it was accompanied by a *parekklêsion*. The interior was decorated with finely carved marble columns, imposts, and screens (fig. 13.12), and the floors were carpeted with mosaics and cosmatesque. To be sure, the building resembles the great basilicas of Corinth in neither scale nor workmanship. It did, however, exhibit a coordinated program of attractive decoration in relatively compact spaces, a certain preciosity. One templon fragment bears an inscription announcing that members of the church (their names do not survive) "beautified" (ἐκαλ[λιέργησαν) the building (fig. 13.13).[90] This formulaic dedication, which occurs in

---

[86] Orlandos 1935; Pallas 1987–89.

[87] Rothaus 2000, 76–79.

[88] Rothaus and Rife 1996 and Rothaus 2000, 78, n. 53 list as ceramic evidence for activity in the 7th century an Early Byzantine lekythos, combed and banded-combed amphoras, coarseware jugs with wave decoration, an African red-slip form 105 or 106 ring foot, and a Phocaean ware form 10 type A rim.

[89] *Kenchreai* I, 65–68, 71, 77–78, 107–131, fig. 30, 41 with plates XXII-XXIII, XXVII–XXVIII, XL–XLII, XLVI–XLVIII, LIV.

[90] Inventory no. KE 500: *BullÉp* 1965, no. 163. *Kenchreai* I, 126, no. 27 with plate XLVII:B; *SEG* XXVIII 388; Feissel 1985b, 369, no. 103*.

Fig. 13.12. Interior decorative members from the basilica: mosaic pavement around the baptistery (left); panel with ... (lower right). Courtesy of the Kenchreai Excavations.

Fig. 13.13. Inscribed screen from the basilica.
Courtesy of the Kenchreai Excavations.

Greek basilicas of the 5th and 6th centuries, pertains to donations of interior décor, usually mosaic pavement, by eminent persons, often clergy.[91] Such inscriptions attest to the importance of the church in Late Antique Greek society as the new locus for the public display of piety and wealth, and even for competition in the arena of construction. By at least the 5th or 6th century, leading benefactors had emerged within the Christian community at Kenchreai, though they did not control the same resources as building patrons and church officials at contemporary Corinth.

The placement of the basilica was also important. Stratigraphic, architectural and geological evidence indicates that one or more catastrophic earthquakes struck the harbor during the Roman era, and co-seismic subsidence led to the submergence of at least a portion of the moles by the 6th century.[92] Once the buildings further out on the south mole were fallen and sunken, the basilica would have stood out as the most prominent monument at the harbor's southern end. The placement is reminiscent of modern Greek harbors, which often have seaside *ekklêsakia*; Late Antique ports sometimes also possessed churches in conspicuous places around their harbors, such as Knidos.[93] The situation of the basilica at Kenchreai reflects the centrality of the church in the life of the community. The enduring presence of the Christian god at the waterfront might have even conferred on sailors a sense of reassurance, if not overt protection, as had Isis and Aphrodite in earlier times.

The vitality of the church at Kenchreai around this time is also evident in the presence of another small basilica outside the main settlement. Scranton discovered but only partly excavated this building, which was located ca. 500 m northeast of the north mole on a plateau set back from the sea. While its complete form remains unknown, the elements of a standard basilical plan are unmistakable, and cist graves were found concentrated at the east end of the north aisle and apse.[94] This building occupied the area of a vast burial ground and

---

[91] For example, see *IvO* 656 (beginning of the 5th century); *RIChrM* 208 (Mount Athos, 5th to 6th centuries); *IPriene* 218 (Late Roman). For similar dedications but different wording: Bandy no. 67A-C (Elounda, Crete, Late Roman); *SEG* XV 141 (Athens, 5th century?) and XIX 552 (Mastichari, Kos, Late Roman).

[92] *Kenchreai* I, 144–47; Sarris *et al.* 2007, 9–10.

[93] Parrish 2001, 31–32, 34–35, fig. 1–14.

[94] Scranton and Ramage 1967, 184–86, fig. 16 (but the excavators did not identify it as a basilica; Rothaus 2000, 65, n. 3). T. Gregory (1986, 163) reported the discover

probably a coastal road that stretched northward from the Koutsongila Ridge at least 1 km up the coast. The basilica's peripheral location is reminiscent of many Greek cities, including Corinth, where churches along routes ringed the urban core. Moreover, the northern basilica at Kenchreai, which might have served chiefly as a burial chapel, was situated alongside a massive tomb constructed in the 1st century CE in the form of a towering altar sheathed in exquisite marble.[95] Any visit to the church would have involved the viewing and consideration of the old tomb. The same spatial arrangement can be found at the Kodratos Basilica on the northern limit of Corinth, an imposing burial church that was erected amid a pre-existing cemetery and aligned on axis with and directly behind an impressive Early Roman mausoleum.[96] Such striking juxtapositions between grand sepulchral forms of disparate eras points to a meaningful continuity in mortuary behavior. Christian Greeks in Late Antiquity transformed the monumental landscape by building churches while they respected, and even appropriated, the memory of earlier structures.

Conclusion

This critical examination of the literary, epigraphic, and archaeological sources for Roman Kenchreai has provided insights into certain problems in religion and society that I raised at the outset. First, a rich pluralism of Greek and eastern deities both large and small deepened religious experience at the port, as in so many other provincial communities. The relatively narrow space of the harbor settlement would have ensured that their cult sites existed in close proximity, comprising a diverse but circumscribed sacred landscape. Among the known deities, two for certain (Poseidon and Isis) and possibly a third (Aphrodite) were associated with the port's maritime activity. This association was underscored by the harbor's particular monumental context, because sanctuaries and statues were situated prominently at its limits

---

of an apsidal structure during an early surface survey of the Koutsongila Ridge and tentatively identified it as a Christian church; Rife *et al.* 2007, 152. The excavation of this building by the Greek-American team in 2007 confirmed that it was not an early church but rather a turret or artillery emplacement erected during the Second World War.

[95] Cummer 1971.

[96] Stikas 1964, 133–34, fig. 1 with plate pl. 88, and 1966, 51–52 with plate 45:β.

(Aphrodite and Isis) and somewhere on the north mole (Poseidon), which was the forward jetty for most approaching ships. Moreover, the attested cults, apart from perhaps the mysteries of Dionysos and the worship of Pan, can be reasonably (if not decisively) identified as foundations of the 1st century CE, or slightly earlier. The evidence from Kenchreai points to the Early Roman period as an age of cultic innovation, amplifying the picture already drawn by Elizabeth Gebhard at Isthmia and Nancy Bookidis at Corinth.[97]

The port's cult sites and festivals allowed residents to communicate their social identity through religious performance. Some rituals were exclusive (the mysteries of Isis and Dionysos), while others were open to all (the use of lead tablets and votive offerings to Pan). Certain duties (λικναφόρος) must have expressed and corroborated an individual's distinction within the community. The dedication of ritual implements or structures was a channel for the elite display of piety and status as well as a venue for competition. These conditions are shared by cities, towns, and ports across the eastern provinces. In this respect, Roman Kenchreai furnishes a vivid example for the study of larger phenomena.

Finally, religious experience at Corinth, the Isthmian Sanctuary, and the port seems to have been integrated. People from different parts of the region would have travelled to all three sites. While the deities at Kenchreai could be found throughout the Greek East, the consistent correspondence between the local gods and those at Corinth and the Isthmus points to a certain unity of belief and practice across the Corinthia, possibly reflecting a history of cult foundations after the establishment of the colony. Since religion was a central component in what it meant to be a Corinthian in the Empire, we should conceive of 'Corinthian' as a multilocal identity, not strictly bound to urban public life. So it would have been for Paul, who spent time at both Corinth and Kenchreai and probably visited the Isthmus. The residents of the port recognized a specific range of cults, but they shared these with Corinthians from the city and the countryside. On one level, Kenchreai was a place apart, Lucius's refuge; on another, it was part of a larger yet interconnected landscape.

---

[97] Bookidis 2005; Gebhard 2005.

CHAPTER FOURTEEN

RELIGION AND SOCIETY IN THE ROMAN EASTERN CORINTHIA

Timothy E. Gregory*

INTRODUCTION

The broader Corinthia, outside the city itself, is an area not well known either historically or archaeologically.[1] The eastern part of the Corinthia, however, was always one of the more important suburban regions of Corinth, and recent archaeological work carried out in the area should shed light on the Pauline mission and its historical development (fig. 14.1). Two important archaeological sites, Isthmia and Kenchreai,[2] have been significantly explored, but the results of this have not been systematically integrated into issues of importance for an understanding of the growth of Christianity in the region. The broader Corinthian countryside, between ancient Corinth itself and the Saronic Gulf, has been explored by important but unsystematic studies,[3] and these have been expanded by the Eastern Korinthia Archaeological Survey, which carried out a systematic surface survey there between 1999 and 2003.[4]

---

* I wish to acknowledge here my debt of gratitude my colleagues Charles Williams and Guy Sanders, Nancy Bookidis, Daniel Pullen and Thomas Tartaron, and especially to R. Scott Nash, Elizabeth Gebhard, Joseph Rife, Bill Caraher, Dimitri Nakassis, and David Pettegrew. The latter three younger scholars are already making their mark on the landscape of the eastern Corinthia, and they currently have in press several studies that will contribute in many ways to our understanding of this important area. My observations here have profited from work with all of them; but I will try, as best I can, not to tread on their territory and to leave them to draw their own conclusions from the evidence without undue interference from me. Much of the original manipulation of the survey data was done by Caraher, Nakassis, and Pettegrew and I thank them for that. Readers of Caraher et al. 2006, and Pettegrew 2007 will be aware of my debt to them. I especially want to thank Bill Caraher for his always patient willingness to help with illustrations.
[1] Sakellariou and Faraklas (1971) and Wiseman (1978) provide the best general overview to the topography, archaeology, and history of the eastern Corinthia.
[2] See the *Isthmia* and *Kenchreai* series.
[3] On centuriation: Doukellis 1994; Romano 2003 and 2005a.
[4] Tartaron et al. 2006.

This paper will examine this wide area in Roman and Late Roman times (1st to 7th centuries CE) at the Sanctuary of Poseidon on the Isthmus and its rural hinterland. It will not touch significantly on the port of Kenchreai since this is the subject of a chapter here by Joseph Rife. The major theme of this chapter is to discuss phenomena from the area of the eastern hinterland of Corinth and how it can contribute to our understanding of social and religious interactions in the broader region in the first few centuries CE. Central to this is an understanding, as far as we can have it, of the social and religious conditions in the area and of the relationships between polytheism and Christianity over the same time.

First, a few definitions. The eastern Corinthia, for the purpose of this work, is geographically the area bounded by the Xeropotamos (Lefkon) River in the west, the Saronic Gulf in the east, the shortest line across the Isthmus (that is, the line of the modern canal) in the north, and the mountains in the south.[5] For various reasons, the Sanctuary of Poseidon, where excavation and study has been ongoing for over half a century, will form a major focus of my investigation, but beyond that I wish to look more broadly at the entirety of the landscape.

THE EARLY ROMAN PERIOD

Since this book had its origins in a conference that sought to bridge disciplinary boundaries between religious history and archaeology, it is appropriate to begin this chapter at Isthmia and to examine some of the major observations that have already been made. Elizabeth Gebhard, of course, already set an admirable standard with a series of important articles that focus on the history of the site in Roman times, including her significant contribution to the volume from the conference in 2002.[6] Her work has shown, for example, that the return of the Isthmian Games to the sanctuary at Isthmia was delayed long

---

[5] For this area see Tartaron *et al.* 2006. The southern boundary of this area is somewhat vague, in part, because the original plan of the Eastern Korinthia Archaeological Survey was to venture well into the mountainous area of the southeastern Corinthia (the region of Sophiko); but restrictions imposed by the Greek Ministry of Culture limited our work essentially to the area north of the Oneion mountain chain.

[6] Gebhard 1993; Gebhard, Hemans, and Hayes 1998; Gebhard and Dickie 2003; Gebhard 2005; Seelinger 1998.

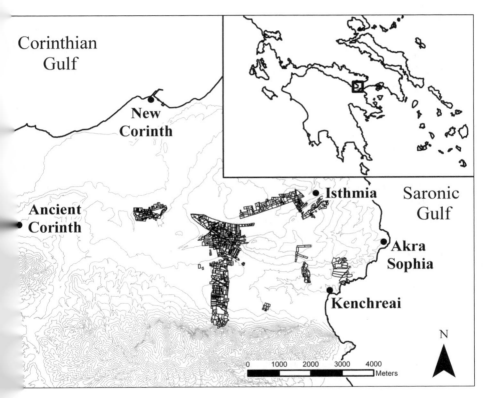

Fig. 14.1. The Corinthia, showing the area intensively investigated by the
Eastern Korinthia Archaeological Survey.

after the refounding of Corinth in 44 BCE and that this did not, in fact, take place until around the middle of the 1st century CE, probably during the reign of Nero.[7] In addition, she has redated construction of the first Roman *temenos* in the center of the sanctuary to a Flavian or Hadrianic date and has proposed that the structure identified by Broneer as the Roman altar was actually a temple to Palaimon built under Hadrian.[8] These are all important chronological markers we need to bear in mind. Recent interest in the cult of Palaimon and controversy over the date of its origin have led to further analyses.[9] Koester, in particular, most clearly makes the argument that worship of the boy-god was, in fact, a mystery cult, a phenomenon whose ramifications and full implementations have not yet been fully explored.[10] Gebhard discusses the mystery cult in the Roman period,[11] and Gebhard and Dickie show, convincingly, I think, that the hero cult was not an invention of Roman times but that it went back at least to the time of Pindar.[12]

In 1962 Oscar Broneer suggested another connection between text and archaeology, namely, that the apostle Paul may have witnessed the games in the Sanctuary of Poseidon at Isthmia during his visits to the Corinthia and that the victory crowns of dried celery may have inspired his famous statement about the immortal crown awaiting Christians.[13] Following the detailed study of Pfitzner, most scholars have dismissed this connection.[14] Some recent commentators, however, have now come to accept the possibility of a general relationship between Paul's vocabulary in 1 Corinthians and the revived games at Corinth and Isthmia.[15] Richard DeMaris's article on the theme of the

---

[7] Gebhard 1993.

[8] Gebhard 1993, 89–93; Gebhard, Hemans, and Hayes 1998, 433–44.

[9] Fundamental for all this is Hawthorne 1958.

[10] Koester 1999; Seelinger 1998.

[11] Gebhard 2005.

[12] Gebhard and Dickie 1995; Gebhard 2005.

[13] Broneer 1962.

[14] "Since the metaphor is widespread, and since sport is an everyday feature in the life of every Greek city, there is no need to think particularly of the isthmic games at Corinth and the pine-wreath as prize" (Conzelmann 1975, 162, n. 31). Conzelmann bases his observations on Pfitzner (1967), who provides an exhaustive discussion of the subject; see also Papathomas 1997. I owe these references to R. S. Nash, whom I warmly thank.

[15] For example, Thiselton 2000. See also Murphy-O'Connor: "Paul could not have been unaware of the Isthmian games, and was probably in Corinth when they took place; they were celebrated in the spring of AD 49 and 51" (2002, 16–17). Athletic

'baptism for the dead' (1 Cor. 15:29) should be mentioned here as well since he argues, using primarily the archaeological material at Isthmia, that the controversy over such baptisms may have come from practices perhaps carried on in the contemporary Corinthia.[16]

All this information and discussion represent important contributions from Isthmia to our understanding of basic conditions and tensions in the Corinthia overall. Further contributions to our understanding of society and religion in the Corinthia in the Roman period will certainly be provided by the ongoing research on Palaimon and the Palaimonion, Rife's contribution to the present volume and his full-scale publication on the Roman and Byzantine burials at Isthmia,[17] and the final publication of the Roman Bath at the site.[18]

An important issue that has not been investigated fully is how the study of the Corinthian countryside might help inform our discussion of society and how this might fit into our consideration of the reception of Christianity into the area. As is already well known, one significant branch of research on the Corinthian epistles focuses on the social and economic situation in Corinth and how the young Christian movement and the Pauline epistles fit into this framework. Virtually all the research in this regard has focused on the urban aspect of this phenomenon even though everything we know about the ancient city shows how closely tied it was to the countryside. The exception to this is the controversial book by Donald Engels on Roman Corinth, a study that has certainly found its way into the interpretation of Corinthian society by many scholars of Christian scripture.[19] This is not the place to enter into debate about the validity of the view of Engels regarding the Corinthian economy as one based significantly on manufacturing, trade, and services in the city. Engels certainly demonstrates considerable knowledge of the texts and the published material from

---

metaphors were a commonplace in the popular philosophy of the period (Pfitzner 1967, 23–37); but it can hardly be coincidental that Paul's first sustained development of this theme occurs in a letter to the Corinthians (1 Cor 9:24–27).

[16] DeMaris 1995a and 2008.

[17] *Isthmia* IX (forthcoming).

[18] For now, see Gregory 1995. The final publication, written by Gregory, F. Yegül, and J. Marty, will appear in the Isthmia series.

[19] Engels 1991. As one example of the acceptance of Engels's sometimes quite remarkable conclusions, see Winter (2001b, 220) with a figure of 100,000 for the population of Roman Corinth. Winter also cites Engels as support for phenomena such as the cult of Antonina as Aphrodite in Corinth (274), the institution of the Caesarean Games, and the victory of Nero at the Isthmian Games (276–77).

the excavations at Corinth and his ideas are interesting and stimulating. Nevertheless, there is very little evidence that he used any of the
information from the countryside that was readily available when he
wrote the book. His appendix, "The Use of Archaeological Surveys,"[20]
is an indication that he did not really understand what archaeological
survey had become by the time he wrote the book, even though he
cites information from modern surveys published in 1981 and 1984.
This much is probably understandable: many people who write about
archaeological surveys even today do not quite seem to know what
they are (Engels calls them "site surveys"). But it seems peculiar that
although he points out that he was involved in the work of Sakellariou
and Faraklas and Wiseman, he never makes use of any of the information these works provide.[21]

The research of the Eastern Korinthia Archaeological Survey should
shed significant light on the nature of society and economy in the
Corinthia in all periods. This project, which carried out fieldwork
between 1999 and 2003, was an intensive, systematic archaeological
survey of stratified areas of the eastern Corinthia (fig. 14.2).[22] This
investigation of the rural Corinthia has a 'prehistory' in the sense that
it draws on the tradition of over a century of topographic work in
the area.[23] In addition, David Romano has contributed important evidence to our understanding of the influence of Rome on the Corinthia although, to date, the issue of centuriation and land division has
really not been brought into the larger question of society in the Early

---

[20] Engels 1991, 186–88.

[21] To be fair, most of the large, modern surveys were published after Engels's book
appeared, but one can cite the following major publication of surveys before that date:
McDonald and Rapp 1972; Renfrew and Wagstaff 1982; van Andel and Runnels 1984.
In addition, many preliminary reports on intensive survey projects had been published well before 1990.

[22] The term 'stratified' refers to the common practice in archaeological survey of
investigating what one might refer to as a cross-section of the landscape, investigating
in detail a sample of the different landforms and settings that can provide us with an
idea of what the whole of the area might contain. Some might think that this approach
is unreasonable since the project could not examine every agricultural field in an area
of some 265 sq. km. But the idea of intensive, systematic, stratified archaeological
survey has the potential of providing significant information within the limitations
of present financial and staffing abilities. For the theoretical bases of this approach:
Tartaron et al. 2006. Many scholars, it must be admitted, remain unconvinced about
the validity of survey as an approach to understanding of the past. Sanders (2004,
163–68) provides a recent, thoughtful critique.

[23] Corinth I.1; Sakellariou and Faraklas 1971; Wiseman 1978; Stroud 1971a and
1971b.

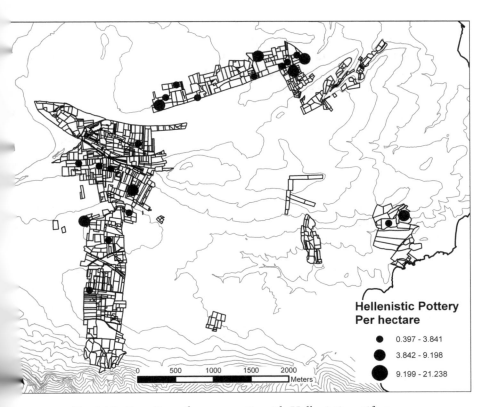

Fig. 14.2. Location of survey units with Hellenistic artifacts.

Roman Corinthia.[24] Moreover, systematic archaeological surveys have been carried out in Greece now for well over 25 years, and there has been significant discussion and often strong disagreement about methods and interpretative strategies.[25]

Furthermore, for the Early Roman period, Susan Alcock provided a model derived in large part from the evidence of archaeological survey.[26] It had already long been accepted that the Hellenistic period, especially the 2nd and 1st centuries BCE, was characterized in Greece by difficulties and likely by population decline as a result of the wars among Hellenistic states and piracy and because of the effects of Roman conquest and even Roman civil wars, fought largely on Greek soil.[27] One would naturally expect an improvement of the situation after the battle of Actium and the establishment of peace and a relatively regular system of imperial administration. Alcock argued, however, partly on the basis of the evidence from survey, that the difficulties continued in part because of the imposition of an imperialistic scheme of manipulation in which land in Greece was given over to the production of cash crops for absentee Roman landowners.[28]

The evidence from the Eastern Korinthia Archaeological Survey (EKAS) would, therefore, seem to have much to bring to the discussion. At first sight the information from the survey seems to support Alcock's argument for population stagnation in the Early Roman period or at least the control of the land by relatively few owners who presumably exploited that land by using agricultural workers who were not resident on the land. Figure 14.3 shows the location of places where EKAS identified surface material that could be assigned to the Hellenistic period, here defined as 232–31 BCE).[29] Figure 14.4 shows the location of places where Early Roman material was found (here defined as 31 BCE–250 CE).[30] The contrast between the picture one

---

[24] Romano 2005a and 2003; Doukellis 1994.

[25] Examples of such projects can be found in van Andel and Runnels 1984. See also Cherry, Davis, and Mantzourani 1991; and Alcock and Cherry 2004. The first and the third of these are synthetic and non-technical while the second is a full-scale presentation of a survey, and the last a comparison of various survey projects.

[26] Alcock 1989a, 1989b, and 1993.

[27] For example, Larsen 1938.

[28] Alcock 1993, 8–92.

[29] This uses only objects identified through systematic survey in what are called 'discovery units.' For the methods and terminology of EKAS: Tartaron et al. 2006.

[30] One may argue that this period of 300 years is overly long to pick up significant changes in the Roman Corinthia, but this is one of the problems with survey archaeol-

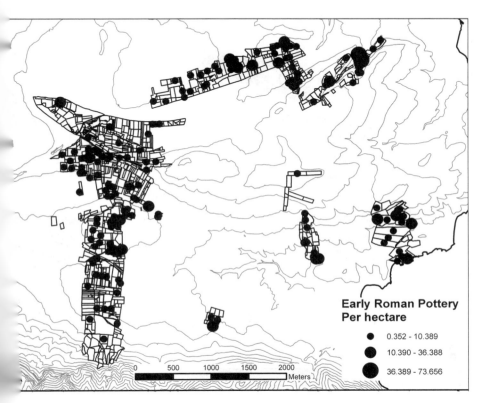

Fig. 14.3. Location of survey units with Early Roman artifacts.

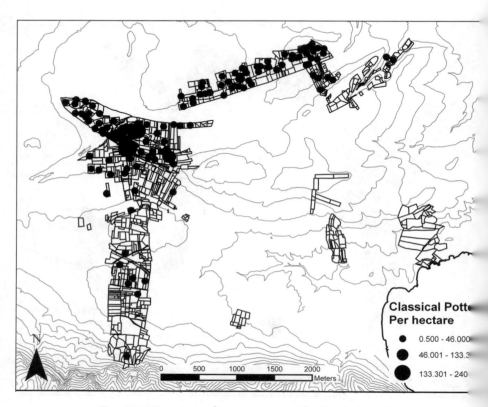

Fig. 14.4. Location of survey units with Classical artifacts.

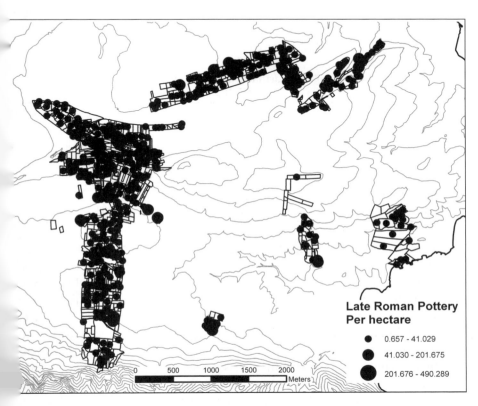

Fig. 14.5. Location of survey units with Late Roman artifacts.

gets from these two periods and the immediately preceding Classical period is striking (fig. 14.5).

Similar information can be seen in table 14.1, which shows the raw numbers for artifacts assigned to several periods.[31] The numbers turn down dramatically from the Classical to the Hellenistic period and then rise only very slowly in the Early Roman period before peaking dramatically in the Late Roman period (250–700 CE). This can also be shown graphically (fig. 14.6).

Table 14.1. Number of artifacts assigned to EKAS narrow periods (total 38,654).

	Artifacts	% of all
Classical	539	1.39%
Hellenistic	22	0.06%
Early Roman	334	0.86%
Late Roman	1737	4.49%
Early Medieval	19	0.05%
Late Medieval	57	0.15%

Further, one has to consider the nature of the evidence and how our ability to identify various ceramic wares affects the number of objects assigned to specific periods.[32] It is already well known that Early Roman coarse wares are not particularly diagnostic, and, therefore, we have to ask ourselves whether the apparent decline in evidence for habitation/use in the Early Roman period is the result of a real economic/social/political change or whether it is significantly affected by our ability to identify with precision the material from that period. Table 14.1 would, nevertheless, seem to support the conclusions that there was a decided decline in activity on the land from the Classical period onward, and this is in keeping with a theory that the land was largely in the hands of a relatively few individuals who presumably rented out the land or utilized it with hired or semi-servile labor.

---

ogy, a process in which even the relatively short periods one must use are rather long by historical standards.

[31] Only objects that could be dated to these relatively narrow periods are included here. Artifacts dated to earlier (prehistoric through Archaic) and later (Ottoman through Modern), as well as objects that could be assigned only to broader periods (such as Archaic-Classical or Roman; see discussion below) are not included in these figures.

[32] Caraher *et al.* 2006; Pettegrew 2007.

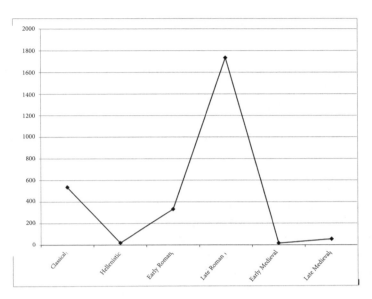

Fig. 14.6. Raw number of artifacts per period.

These raw numbers, however, may also be otherwise affected by our frequent inability to assign objects to precise periods. In order to deal with varying levels of chronological precision, EKAS developed a complex chronological scheme involving a hierarchy of overlapping periods. Thus, for example, one object could be assigned to 'narrow periods,' such as Hellenistic or Early Roman; but another artifact might be identified by a 'broad period,' such as Classical-Hellenistic or Roman, each of which would include objects that could not be identified any more precisely than this.[33] Table 14.2 provides the same information for three of the broad periods associated with the narrow periods listed in Table 14.1.

Table 14.2. Number of artifacts assigned to EKAS broad periods
(N = 38,654).

	Artifacts	% of all
Classical-Hellenistic	1030	2.66%
Roman	2233	5.78%
Medieval	175	0.45%

---

[33] There also were broader periods, such as Ancient or Archaic-Classical, but these re not considered here.

If our knowledge of pottery and other material were perfect, the arti-facts assigned to one of the broad periods should have been assigned to one of the narrow periods. We can, therefore, extrapolate the arti-facts assigned to the broad periods into the narrow periods, based on the proportion of the number of years in each.

These extrapolated numbers can be seen in Table 14.3 and in graphic form in fig. 14.7. The two curves in fig. 14.7 are similar; but there are significant differences, especially in the extrapolated numbers for the Hellenistic and the Early Roman periods where the drop from Clas-sical to Hellenistic is not as sharp and the rise in the Early Roman is greater. Again, one of the more significant observations is that, using the extrapolated figures, the Early Roman number is higher than that of the Classical period. This is important since many characterizations of the survey evidence for the Early Roman period do so in relation to the Classical age, which is often taken as one of the high points of economic activity in the ancient world. There is no doubt that both curves in fig. 14.7 are overshadowed by the high numbers from the Late Roman period, a peak that David Pettegrew and others have sought to soften.[34] Moreover, the apparently great drop-off of Medieval material is another phenomenon that needs to be discussed further at consid-erable length. Nonetheless, the evidence as we have it, even when we compare the raw data, does suggest an up-turn in the Early Roman period from a low-point in the Hellenistic period,[35] rising to a figure that is, in fact, higher than that of the Classical age.

Table 14.3. Extrapolated numbers for artifacts.

	Artifacts	% of all	Years in period	Extrapolated artifacts	% of all
Classical	539	1.39%	157	900	2.33%
Hellenistic	22	0.06%	291	691	1.79%
Early Roman	334	0.86%	281	1192	3.08%
Late Roman	1737	4.49%	450	3112	8.05%
Early Medieval	19	0.05%	500	136	0.35%
Late Medieval	57	0.15%	250	115	0.30%

---

[34] Caraher et al. 2006; Pettegrew 2007.

[35] One should, of course, remember that the Hellenistic period included the sack of Corinth by Mummius in 146 BCE and a 100-year period in which Corinth had no urban standing. For a recent consideration of this period in the Corinthia, see Geb-hard and Dickie 2003.

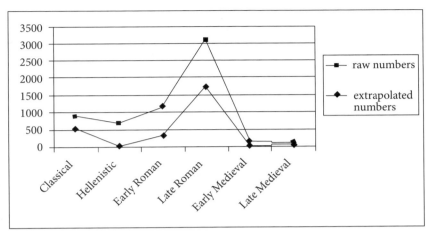

Fig. 14.7. Raw numbers per narrow period along with extrapolated numbers when the artifacts from broad periods are added proportionally to the number of years in each broad and each narrow period.

The finds from intensive archaeological survey can be measured not only as simple numbers but also as evidence of activity in a given survey unit, much in the same way as one could say that, for example, certain artifacts are present in individual excavated sites. Table 14.4 displays some of the evidence from EKAS in this way, arranged, as before, by the EKAS narrow and broad periods. The second column shows the number of units in which finds for each period were found and the area represented by the total of those units. The third column shows the percent of areas in which finds for each period were found, first, in terms of the total number of units and, then, in terms of the total area investigated in the survey.

A quick look at these figures reinforces the observations already made: the Hellenistic, narrow period is poorly represented, and the Late Roman narrow period is the best represented of those considered. Probably the most significant of these figures is the percent of the area covered by the finds from each period (the number in parentheses in the third column of table 14.4). Figure 14.8 plots these percents for ease of comparison.

Probably the most important observation is that, again by this analysis, the Early Roman period is, although, slightly, still more strongly represented than the Classical period. Little can be done at this point with the area figures for the broad periods except to note that the

Table 14.4. Finds from Classical to Roman periods shown in terms of areas represented by EKAS individual survey units ('discovery units').[36]

Narrow Periods	Units (and area in ha.)	% of units (% of total area)
Classical	179 (83.7 ha.)	16.0% (24.3%)
Hellenistic	29 (13.8 ha.)	2.6% (4.0%)
Early Roman	197 (95.0 ha.)	17.6% (27.6%)
Late Roman	574 (218.7 ha.)	51.4% (63.5%)
Broad Periods		
Classical-Hellenistic	321 (126.5 ha.)	28.7% (36.8%)
Roman	593 (227.9 ha.)	53.1% (66.2%)

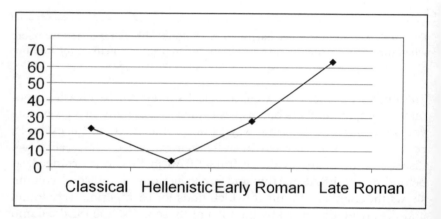

Fig. 14.8. Percents of the total EKAS survey area represented by the areas of survey units in which finds of individual narrow periods were identified.

broad Roman period has an overwhelmingly stronger signature than the Classical-Hellenistic period. One must stress that this analysis is still only preliminary, and we should be careful not to assume that any of these numbers be seen as direct indications of population, wealth, or general social well-being. Nonetheless, it should be seen that the data from archaeological survey in the eastern Corinthia is not easily compatible with a view of the Early Roman period as one of downturn or of continued socio-economic difficulties that began in the Hellenis-

---

[36] One may note that the figures given here are slightly different from those in Caraher *et al.* 2006, 26 and tab. 5. The reason for this is that in order to stress internal comparability of the data, I am here using the information only from the central transect in the Examilia-Isthmia basins of the eastern Corinthia. The broader conclusions from the figures, however, are the same.

tic age. Rather, they can best be understood as evidence of recovery and of an agricultural and economic system spread broadly across the landscape. In any case, one hopes that these data will ultimately be useful to scholars attempting to understand the social background and the religious developments in the first centuries CE in the Corinthia.

The Middle Roman Period and the End of Paganism

Thus, while we hope that the information from survey will allow us to say more about the situation in the whole of the Corinthia in the 1st and 2nd centuries, at Isthmia the main consideration from later centuries would seem to be the issue of transformation from the 'pagan' (polytheistic/Hellenic) sanctuary of Poseidon (and other gods) to a settlement astride one of the most important military constructions in Byzantine Greece. The main lines of this development are clear, but the details are enormously complex and controversial (fig. 14.9).

One of the key issues is the date of the end of the pagan sanctuary. Elizabeth Gebhard has argued that there is no evidence for cult activity in the area of the Temple of Poseidon after the mid 3rd century, between 220 and 240, remarkably early for most studies of the phenomenon elsewhere, which generally date the closing of the sanctuaries to the last years of the 4th century CE.[37] The basis for her argument is the absence of ceramic material in the area around the Temple of Poseidon and a lack of significant repairs or rebuildings in the central sanctuary from the mid 3rd century onward.[38] This includes the Palaimonion, which, as Gebhard has now argued, was constructed in its finest and final phase only in the Antonine era, possibly between 161–69 CE.[39] In this view 'Palaimonion V' would have functioned only for a period of 50–80 years before being abandoned. The insertion of a single, presumably Christian burial (5th to 6th century) within the foundation of the temple, therefore, raises difficult questions about the degree to which individuals in this period were aware of the ancient use of the sanctuary and the ways in which they sought to react to it.[40]

---

[37] Trombley 1993, especially volume 1; Saradi 2006, 355–56.

[38] Gebhard, Hemans, and Hayes 1998, 446: "Old finds from the site suggest a cessation of cult activity around AD 220–240; the 1989 pottery adds no further precision to this date."

[39] Gebhard 1993, 89–93; Gebhard, Hemans, and Hayes 1998, 438–41; Gebhard 2005, 197.

[40] See the detailed discussion in Rife, *Isthmia* IX (forthcoming). The question here is whether the people who went to the trouble to cut the grave into the solid masonry

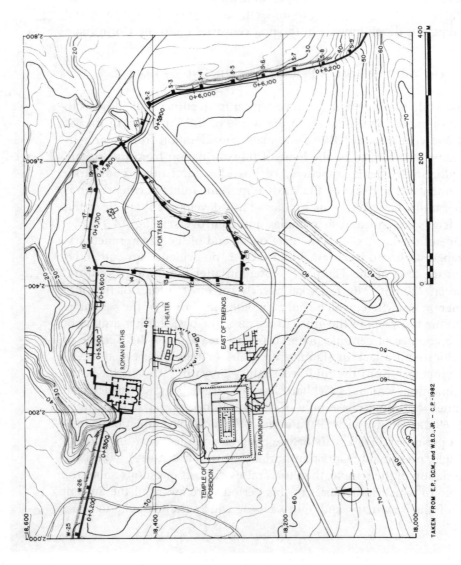

Fig. 14.9. Isthmia.

Richard Rothaus points out that Libanius's *Oration* 14 (362 CE) mentions that the Corinthian aristocrat Menander went to the Isthmus and took part in the mysteries (ἐλαύνων δὲ εἰς Ἰσθμὸν ὑπὲρ τῶν τοῦδε μυστρίων), contributing also to the expenses thereof, an event that Rothaus dates to 328–38.[41] Certainly, this is significant evidence to argue that the cult of Poseidon on the Isthmus was still functioning in the second quarter of the 4th century CE. Rothaus sought to resolve this apparent contradiction between the archaeological and the written evidence. He provides a good discussion of the difficulty in deriving information about religious practices from the archaeological record and even suggests that much of the ceramic material from the mid 3rd to the mid 6th century in the central sanctuary could have been washed away by the winter rains, a phenomenon that is not impossible to imagine.[42]

In any case, the general historical probability suggests that the sanctuary at Isthmia and the games associated with it continued to function at very least until the end of the 4th century. This was certainly the opinion of Oscar Broneer, who thought that the Temple of Poseidon stood until the 6th century. It is interesting to note that he published a total of 219 lamps in his categories XXVIII–XXXIII, which date from the 4th through the 6th century, as well as another 182 lamps of Type XXVII, bringing the total to 401 for lamps that one can reasonably assign to the period after Gebhard's suggested date for the end of the sanctuary.[43] An interesting exercise in this regard is to examine the findspots of the lamps that Broneer assigns to Types XXVII–XXXIII (table 14.5).[44] It is true that this analysis does not take into account the stratigraphic details of the findspots, whether these were in layers of the 3rd to 6th centuries, or whether they were surface finds; and this consideration must wait for further research.

---

of the temple foundations were aware that this had been an important polytheistic cult building, and, if so, whether they did this as a means to continue that tradition or to defile it by the placing of a corpse in the holy place.

[41] Rothaus 2000, 84–86; see also Lib. *Or.* 14.5.

[42] Rothaus 2000, 87–90; in n. 25 he credits F. Hemans with the idea about the loss of the Late Roman layers in the central sanctuary. Gebhard points out that the late levels in the Palaimonion are intact, which seems to contradict this hypothesis (personal communication with Gebhard).

[43] *Isthmia* III.73–83. Lamps are particularly diagnostic at Isthmia because Broneer inventoried all of the fragments. Thus, his publication does not represent a sample of what was found but rather a reasonable approximation of the total.

[44] *Isthmia* III does not assign provenience to all the lamps, so the total number that appears in table 14.3 will be well below 219.

Table 14.5. Findspots assigned to Type XXVIII–XXXIII lamps in *Isthmia* III.

	Th	LS	SEH	NER	WS	T	Pal	Tem	OCE
Type XXVIII	42	9	2	2	1	7	1	2	3
Type XXIX						2			
Type XXX									
Type XXI						3		3	2
Type XXXII	1					2	4		
Type XXXIII	1					2	1	1	
Totals	44	9	2	2	1	16	6	6	5

Th   = Theater area   T   = Temenos
LS   = Later Stadium   Pal = Palaimonion
SEH = Southeast House   Tem = Temple
NER = Northeast Reservoir   OCE = outside central area
WS   = West Stoa

The fact that 401 lamps were found in the general area of the central sanctuary does not tell us anything directly about the continuation of cult, but it does show that there was activity of some kind there at least through the 6th century.[45] The findspots are interesting, especially for Type XXVIII, and the lamps and other artifacts indicate some activity in the Theater, the later Stadium, and the broader area of the *temenos*.[46] This is suggestive of something more than simple stone robbing, but one cannot be certain.

At Corinth there seems to be good reason to think that Hellenic cult survived at least until the end of the 4th century in most places and considerably later than that in others. Thus, in considering the evidence of the area east of the theater in Corinth, C. K. Williams writes that "... the private and semi-private religion of the Roman Corinthians started to loose ground, but slowly and gently, toward the end of the second century. It seems that it is only in a later period, and well after the second quarter of the third century, that the reaction

---

[45] Again, one should note that although table 14.5 lists only 91 lamps by findspot area, Broneer publishes a total of 401 lamps of Types XXVII–XXXIII, all, or nearly all, of which must have come from his excavations in the broader area of the sanctuary.

[46] For discussion of possible late activity in the Theater: Rothaus 2000, 143–44. It is true that little of the Stadium was excavated and that one may, therefore, question the number of lamps found there. The positive evidence, however, does remain since the lamps were found in that area.

to paganism started to turn militant."[47] Significant information comes from the Sanctuary of Demeter and Kore on Acrocorinth, which certainly continued in use through much of the 4th century and where Aristophanes, the son of Menander (mentioned above in connection with Isthmia), may have contributed to its upkeep in the middle of the same century.[48] Destruction debris from the Roman stoa contained pottery and lamps of the second half of the 4th century. Among this debris were eight coins dating from 355 onward, the last of which can be dated 383–92, allowing the excavators to conclude that "the destruction of the stoa ought to be placed no earlier than the last two decades of the 4th century after Christ."[49] Similar destruction debris was found at several places, including "the marble heads of two priestesses and the female cult statue that had been broken from their bodies and hurled down the well."[50] In the end, the most likely scenario is that the destruction of the Sanctuary of Demeter and Kore was the result of a violent attack by Christians at the very end of the 4th century.[51]

Sanders, meanwhile, discusses the same set of questions largely through the lens of the new excavations in the Panayia Field at Corinth. He makes note of the painted decoration of the spacious *domus* located there, including a representation of Aphrodite, and a small collection of sculpture found within the house. The sculpture included a Farnese-style Herakles, Pan, Europa, Dionysos, two statues of Artemis, two of Asklepios, and a seated Roma. In Sanders's view, "they may be considered to be copies of cult images" and probably "... represent the

---

[47] Williams 2005, 246. For an overview of Christianity at Corinth, see Meeks and Fitzgerald 2007, 21–23 and 44–46 for the Pauline period; Engels 1991, 116–20 on the 2nd-4th centuries; Trombley 1985 and 1993 on conflict between pagans and Christians.

[48] Lib. *Or.* 14.7; see also *Corinth* XVIII.3, 438.

[49] *Corinth* XVIII.3, 327. "Worship and other activities apparently continued undiminished until the end of the 4th century after Christ" (*Corinth* XVII.3, 437). Kathleen Slane (2008) has recently published a detailed reassessment of the evidence for the end of this sanctuary, and she concludes that the original date of the destruction is correct (ca. 380 CE).

[50] *Corinth* XVIII.3, 438; Rothaus 2000, 123, n. 59 (written before publication of *Corinth* XVIII.3).

[51] *Corinth* XVIII.3, 438–40; and 379–91 for a discussion of the remains built over the destroyed sanctuary, including 29 graves; and the fascinating suggestion that those who dug the graves must have known that they were doing so on the site of the sanctuary, reflecting perhaps "the survival of the Sanctuary of Demeter and Kore in folk memory as an ancient holy place that was particularly hospitable to women and children" (391).

personal and civic divinities revered by the household.[52] Sanders compares the sculpture to a similar group of three small sculptures found possibly in a 4th century context in a nearby building in 1947. These included a small marble Aphrodite of the Capua type, two terracotta sculptures, a Dionysos and a bearded god, possibly Zeus or Hades. The latter are published as coming from Egypt.[53] Comparison of these two sets of finds with the sculpture group from the Sanctuary of Demeter and Kore is also apt. The destruction of the *domus* in the Panayia Field at the end of the 4th century put an end to this phase of occupation; and the building constructed above it in the 5th century took no account of the walls of its predecessor, suggesting, perhaps, that the new inhabitants had no connection with the former occupants and that they might not have shared the same religious sentiment. Sanders concludes that for the continuation of the cult of the Hellenic deities, "the destruction of the Panayia *domus* sculptures ca. 370 is as far as we can push at present."[54] Hard archaeological evidence for Christian worship, on the other hand, "appear[s] no earlier and plausibly much later than ca. 475. Only in the sixth century is there a sense that Christianity has prevailed."[55]

Hellenic religion certainly continued in Corinth beyond 400 CE in one form or another, and the laws against the old religion and the accounts in literary sources make it clear that this phenomenon was common throughout the eastern Mediterranean.[56] In Corinth there is reason to see such continuity in the Asklepieion and even more in the nearby underground shrine of the Fountain of the Lamps[57] and perhaps elsewhere.[58]

In addition, archaeological evidence at other Panhellenic sanctuaries now demonstrates at least some continuation at the ancient sites well past the 3rd century. Perhaps most spectacular in that regard is the inscribed bronze plaque (ca. 0.75 m high by 0.40 m wide) found in the athletes' guild building south of the Leonidaion at Olympia.[59] The plaque is of a type that is otherwise attested, and it had been used in the 1st century by a competitor in the *pankration* to commemorate

---

[52] Sanders 2005, 424.
[53] Broneer 1947.
[54] Sanders 2005, 441.
[55] Sanders 2005, 441–42.
[56] Trombley 1985; Irmsher 1981.
[57] Garnett 1975; Jordan 1994.
[58] Rothaus 2000, 137–40.

his participation. In the 4th century, however, a remarkable inscription was engraved in large letters, commemorating two brothers from Athens, Marcus Aurelius Eukarpidis and Marcus Aurelius Zopyros, both of whom competed in the boys' competition, Eukarpidis winning the *pankration* in the 290th Olympiad (381 CE) and Zopyros winning at boxing in the 291st Olympiad (385 CE). In between the two inscriptions were wreaths, each inscribed with the winner's name. The last line may be translated, "May the brotherly love of Eukarpidis and Zopyros only increase." This discovery shows clearly that the Olympic contests were still being held in the 380s.[60]

One can draw similar conclusions at Delphi, where the last known victor was Aurelius Apollinaris, whose accomplishment was honored by the emperors Valerian and Gallienus (dated 253–59 CE).[61] At least some of the athletic buildings at Delphi were repaired in the 4th century, and Aupert noted that the *xystos* was kept clear until the late 5th century when debris began to build up, and that the Stadium was apparently still being used at least until that same time.[62] This may give greater weight to a law of 424 that makes financial arrangements for the contests, indicating that they were still going on at that time.[63] Lastly, for Nemea, of course, the date of the end of the sanctuary is moot since the games were transferred from the ancient site to Argos in 271 BCE. By the time Pausanias visited Nemea in the mid 2nd century CE (2.15.2), the roof of the Temple of Zeus had already collapsed.[64]

All of this discussion is simply to place the end of Hellenic cult at Isthmia into its broader historical context. To return to the actual archaeological evidence from the site, we should consider those areas

---

[59] Ebert 1994; Sinn 2002, 194.

[60] Sinn (2002, 190–91) confirms this conclusion and strengthens it by discussing a small bath built around 300 CE north of the athletes' guild building with an innovative heating system showing, in his view, that "Olympia in that age continued to be full of life."

[61] Weir 1998, 322.

[62] Aupert 1979, 139–42, 179, and 264.

[63] *C.Th.* 15.5.4 (22 April 424) from Theodosius II to the prefect of Illyricum. The law does not say specifically that the games were still being celebrated at Delphi, but it refers to a report by the prefect that apparently said that the city council of Delphi was having financial difficulties because of its 'losses.' The emperor's remedy was to exempt all the cities of Illyricum from contributing to the expenses of spectacles in Rome.

[64] For the Christian community and basilica, see discussion below.

explored by the OSU/UCLA project. These, as we shall see, include architectural restorations and refurbishment that go up to the end of the 4th century, some 150 years later than the evidence adduced from the area around the main temple. Naturally, such observations are subject to changes in ceramic chronologies, especially in Corinth,[65] but at present we continue to believe that there was significant activity in the Roman bath down to its partial collapse around 400 and that construction in the nearby area east of the *temenos* can be documented well after that point.

The date of the end of polytheistic cult in the sanctuary is, of course, of crucial importance if we want to investigate the transformation between the two religious traditions. On the one hand, if pagan religious ceremonies came to an end at an early time and the site was either abandoned or used for purely 'secular' purposes before Christianization became a common phenomenon, then one would not expect much in the way of continuity between the two religions.[66] Clearly, there was continuity of a certain kind in the area of the sanctuary since there was significant construction and military activity in the area after 400 CE.[67] Thus, nearly all of the visible blocks from the temples, stoas, and other buildings found their way into the construction of the Hexamilion (the eight km barrier wall across the Isthmus)—sometime early in the 5th century.[68] This, however, tells us little about religious continuities/discontinuities in the area. As already mentioned, there is considerable evidence to show that the Roman Bath at Isthmia continued to function until its partial destruction at the end of the 4th or possibly the beginning of the 5th century CE.[69] The evidence for use throughout the 3rd and 4th centuries is provided, first, by the fill beside the furnace under Room III of the baths.[70] This fill is composed of several levels, the uppermost of which is largely ash from the functioning of the furnace. Under that is a soil that contained among other things a

---

[65] Slane and Sanders 2005.

[66] The argument that Hellenic religion at many sites had died out well before Christianity came to dominance was made, for example, by Frantz (1965) and followed by Spieser (1976, 309–20).

[67] Such structural 'continuity' is discussed at length by Kardulias (1995, 2005).

[68] *Isthmia* V.

[69] See the general discussion by Rothaus 2000, 144–46.

[70] Gregory 1995, 293 and fig. 7. For some reason Rothaus does not cite this article in his treatment although he makes reference to the proper original evidence.

coin of Aurelian (IC 78–4: 270–75 CE).[71] The coin provides a *terminus post quem* for the use of the furnace. In the ash level was pottery that extends down to the end of the 4th century (Isthmia Lot 08–024), providing secure evidence that the baths were functioning through that time. Like the furnaces, the drains of the baths provide evidence for how long the building continued to be used and kept in repair. Thus, the fill in the drain in Room VI contained two coins, one of Constantine II (dated 330–35 CE)[72] and one of Gratian (dated 383 CE),[73] and lamps that date to the late 4th or early 5th century.[74] Likewise, the pottery and the lamps on the floors, especially of the northern rooms of the Bath, date to the same period although the fill is not as chronologically 'clean' as the more closed contexts just mentioned.[75] The coin of Gratian is especially good evidence since it can be dated quite precisely to a single year, and this provides a *terminus post quem* for the silting up of the drains, showing that they were still being kept clean at least until the middle of the 380s.

Similarly, the area east of the *temenos* at Isthmia, formerly called the East Field, demonstrates considerable continuity of use from the 2nd to at least the 6th century CE.[76] The precise sequence and absolute chronology of the buildings are still being studied, but it is clear that this area is key to understanding the topography and the broader fabric of the sanctuary at Isthmia since it lies at the meeting point of

---

[71] See also the evidence for filling of the central drain of the Theater at Isthmia in the third quarter of the 3rd century CE. The evidence in the Roman Bath, however, shows that it continued to be used after that date.

[72] 'GLOR. IAEXERC. ITVS,' IC 90–2 (two soldiers with standards); *LRBC* 1.1224.

[73] 'VOTXX MVLTXXX,' IC 90–3; *LRBC* 2.1957.

[74] IPL 90–001 (Athenian post-glazed, early 5th century); IPL 90–004 (join with IPL 76–164, Athenian glazed, late 4th century); IPL 90–005/007 (Athenian glazed, late 4th to early 5th century); and IPL 90–006 (pre-glazed, early 4th century). IPL 76–049 (Athenian pre-glazed, first half of 3rd century) is from the drain of Room I. It is a small fragment, and too much should not be made of it. However, this could suggest that the drain of that room may have gone out of use earlier than those elsewhere in the building. One might also mention IPL 76–002 (Athenian post-glazing, mid 5th century) from the end of the drain of Rooms I–II although probably from a funerary context. The dates for the lamps given above are those provided by B.L. Wohl; Slane would presumably provide a slightly earlier date.

[75] Wohl (1981) published this material as an "open deposit," and some have taken exception to this term. See, for example, Slane in *Corinth* XVIII.3, 20, n. 82; and Karivieri 1996, 55.

[76] The area, excavated during 1970–73, has not been fully studied or published. The best summary is Peppers (1979, 215–71) although the annual reports of Clement in the Αρχαιολογικόν Δελτίον provide significant information.

the Temple of Poseidon, the later Stadium, the Roman Baths, and the Theater. The building sequence in the area is complex; but the first structures were erected in the 2nd century CE and that there were several phases, lasting until at least the 7th century.[77]

A particularly intriguing feature is an underground tunnel, running roughly east-west for 11 m, and at some point in its history equipped with steps and an entranceway on either end. Near the west entrance to the tunnel, a hoard of 97 coins was found, the latest of which date to 393.[78] The excavator, Paul Clement, connected the loss of the hoard with Alaric's invasion of the Peloponnesos in 396 CE. Near the hoard was also found a cache of some six small pieces of sculpture, all in good condition. These were as follows: a small, probably female head, maybe a maenad (mid 2nd century CE);[79] a bearded god, possibly Poseidon but more probably Zeus (2nd century, possibly Hadrianic);[80] a head of Hermes (second half of the 2nd century);[81] a relief stele with twin Cybeles and a "Mother of the gods" inscription (late Hellenistic [?]);[82] a three-figure stele of Asklepios, Hygeia, and Telephoros, unfinished (2nd century CE);[83] and, lastly, a three-figure stele of nymphs (probably from the Imperial age).[84]

All of these pieces are religious in nature and they have reasonably been connected with cult, possibly centered in the nearby tunnel or associated with an altar also found in the vicinity. Thus, Birgitta Lindros Wohl has recently argued that the unusual lamps, 'snake vase,' incense burner, and the sculpture are all to be associated with cult within the tunnel, characterizing worship there of perhaps a syncretistic or chthonic nature.[85] In addition, all the pieces of sculpture are notable in their relatively small size (none larger than 29 cm high),

---

[77] Peppers (1979, 273) drew up an especially useful chronological list of the Roman coins from the area east of the *temenos*: before 50 CE, one; 50–100 CE, four; 100–150 CE, five; 150–200 CE, 10; 200–217 CE, 10; 217–270 CE, three; 270–300 CE, 16; 300–350 CE, 14; 350–400 CE, 128 (including 97 from the hoard mentioned below); 400–500 CE, two; and 500–600 CE, seven.

[78] Beaton and Clement 1976.

[79] *Isthmia* VI no. 3, IS 71–3.

[80] *Isthmia* VI no. 4, IS 71–2.

[81] *Isthmia* VI no. 6, IS 71–1.

[82] *Isthmia* VI no. 89, IS 71–4.

[83] *Isthmia* VI no. 90, IS 71–5.

[84] *Isthmia* VI no. 91, IS 71–6; Peppers 1978.

[85] Wohl 2005; Peppers 1979, 268–69.

their possibly 'exotic' nature, and their relatively early date (mainly 2nd century CE). There is no certain date for the loss of this sculptural group, but it seems reasonable to connect it with the nearby coin hoard and assign a date in the final decade of the 4th century CE. In her forthcoming publication of the lamps from the UCLA/OSU excavations at Isthmia, Wohl observes that those from the tunnel date from the 2nd-4th century (or very early 5th century) with the bulk of the lamps assigned to the late 3rd or early 4th century, and that one may, therefore, reasonably assign the use of the tunnel to this range of dates.[86]

There is, of course, a possible discrepancy of date between the manufacture of the sculpture and its loss since none of the pieces have been dated later than the second half of the 2nd century CE. This is also the case with a sculptural group from Antioch, concerning which Hannestad recently suggested that the small-scale sculpture has been improperly dated and that they should, in fact, be assigned not to the Middle Roman period but to the period between 350–450 CE.[87] Of course, the loss of both the coins and the sculpture at Isthmia may have been caused by earthquake or, as suggested by Clement, the attack of Alaric, but it is also possible that it was caused by violence associated with Christian attempts to put an end to the observance of the ancient Hellenic rites. In this case we can connect the loss of the Isthmian sculpture to the three similar cases in Corinth.[88] This is to some extent in keeping with the claim made by Clement in 1976 (in his usual laconic manner) that the Hellenic cult at Isthmia ended in the 390s, although he saw the 'culprit' as Alaric while Christians might have been the actual agents. Of course, it should be remembered that Alaric was an Arian Christian and that Eunapios specifically says that the monks helped him pass through Thermopylae to devastate Greece in 396. The importance of such a possible association with Christian violence cannot be underestimated since it goes against Allison Franz's

---

[86] Wohl (forthcoming).
[87] Hannestad 1994, 117–49; Wohl 2005, 214.
[88] So Rothaus 2000, 123–24. In the context of sculpture caches in Late Roman Greece, we should remember the two 6th century sculpture hoards in the Athenian Agora apparently thrown down wells in an attempt to preserve them from Christian desecration (*Agora* XXIV, 41 and 88–89).

theory about the essentially peaceful transition between the two religions, at least in Greece, that has held sway from the time of its publication in 1965.[89]

LACK OF A CHURCH AT ISTHMIA

There is no evidence whatsoever that the pagan sanctuary at Isthmia was replaced by a place of Christian worship after it went out of use. This is highly unusual since most other major sanctuaries in Greece already had, at least by the 6th century, a Christian church either within the earlier *temenos* or, more commonly, in the vicinity of the pagan holy place.[90] The list that follows is only a sample of some of the sanctuaries that attest to the phenomenon: at Olympia, in the so-called workshop of Phidias;[91] in the vicinity of Delphi but apparently not within the *temenos*, the remains of at least three early Christian churches;[92] at Nemea a basilica constructed on the remains of the *xenon*;[93] just northeast of the sanctuary at Eleusis, the remains of an early Christian church within which is the modern church of the Prophet Elias (Elijah);[94] close to the entrance to the Sanctuary of Asklepios at Epidauros, a six-aisled early Christian church;[95] and finally, near the sanctuary of Apollo at Delos.[96]

Thus, as mentioned above, Isthmia stands apart from virtually all the major sanctuaries of Greece in that we cannot document a Christian church there before the end of the 6th century. Certainly, this cannot be explained by arguing that the area was abandoned since there is plentiful evidence for settlement and considerable activity in the vicinity of the former sanctuary. An intensive survey carried out

---

[89] Frantz 1965; Gregory (1986b) on the situation at Epidauros, at the Asklepieion in Athens, and elsewhere.

[90] There is considerable scholarship on the 'conversion' of pagan temples to churches, beginning with Deichmann (1939, 105–36). For Greece, Frantz (1965) is fundamental; see also Spieser 1976; and Gregory 1986b.

[91] Mallwitz 1972, 107–119; Mallwitz and Schiering 1964; Adler 1892, 3–105.

[92] Pallas 1977, 19–21; Laurent 1899, 206–79; Petridis 1997.

[93] Kraynak 1992, 99–187; note also the basilica on the nearby hill of the Evangelistria (Orlandos 1952, 401 and 571).

[94] Sotiriou 1929, 183–84; Orlandos 1952, 135, 203–05, 400, 451 and 505.

[95] Sotiriou 1929, 198–201; Orlandos 1952, 50–51, 98–101, 106, 125–30, 140, 154–55, 162, 175–79, 202, 400–01, and 570.

[96] Orlandos 1936.

in 1981–83 within the Byzantine fortress at Isthmia (see below) had as one of its goals the identification of a Byzantine basilica[97] that was believed certainly to have existed there.[98] Reports of the remains of Byzantine churches within the fortress and the near certainty that a Byzantine fortification, dating to the early 5th century with significant rebuilding in the 6th century and later, would contain a church made us expect to find such a Christian religious center.[99] The survey involved intensive surface examination, collection and geophysical prospecting over nearly the whole of the fortress. Nonetheless, despite this intensive effort, absolutely no evidence of such a church was found.[100] None of these methods of exploration were, of course, effective in the immediate vicinity of the modern church of Ayios Ioannes Prodromos because of both the existence of the modern building and the fact that the churchyard itself is now covered with concrete. The shape of the modern church is a cross set within a square, and a building of this shape is shown on early plans of the site so it may be that this was the location of a Middle Byzantine church within the fortress and one may easily argue that a predecessor (possibly of the 5th–6th century) lies buried below the modern structures. Nonetheless, early Byzantine basilicas normally leave a very strong archaeological signature, even when they have been completely destroyed. Leaving aside the large architectural footprint, their normally lavish building decoration, fragments of which can usually be found on the ground, traditionally remain behind and, thus, would likely have turned up in the excavations carried out in and around the fortress over the past seventy years. Common markers of Christian basilicas include elements such as *thorakia* (that is, chancel screen slabs or slabs between columns), roughly datable capitals, and impost blocks, all combined with the Christian builders' habit of marking nearly everything with

---

[97] In order to conform with usage common in New Testament Studies, in this chapter the term 'Byzantine basilica' or 'Early Byzantine basilica' is used, instead of 'Early Christian basilica,' which is found more commonly in archaeological studies of this period for churches of the 4th through the 7th centuries.

[98] Gregory and Kardulias 1990; Kardulias 2005.

[99] Leake 1830, 3.286–96 and pl. 3. Leake does not specifically mention churches within the fortress, which he thought was the Sanctuary of Poseidon; but he does quote Wheeler, who mentions "several old churches." Both Monceaux (1884, 273–85, 354–63; and 1885, 205–14, 402–12) as well as Staïs (1903) refer to churches. Monceaux says specifically that there were three Byzantine chapels; see the discussion in *Isthmia* 7.130.

[100] Gregory and Kardulias 1990, 503, n. 35; Kardulias 2005, 57–93.

crosses. Yet during the years of intensive investigation at Isthmia, not a single fragment of this type has been found that can reasonably be connected with a Christian church.

How are we to explain such a situation? As we have seen, this cannot have been because no one lived in the vicinity. The Christianity of those living in the vicinity is, of course, difficult to demonstrate, and one must admit that few of the many lamps found at Isthmia have Christian symbols. In *Isthmia* III Broneer published only a handful of lamps with such Christian symbols. The UCLA/OSU excavations have arguably identified more: some 18 in all, virtually all of them from the fortifications (a total of 10) and the Roman baths (six). Christian symbols on lamps, however, appear universally late throughout Greece, and their absence cannot be taken as an indication of pagan sentiment. On the other hand, attention has already been called to the inscription of a fish, perhaps a Christian symbol, in the wet plaster of tower 15 of the Byzantine fortress, dating from the time of its construction or, more likely, from its reconstruction in the 6th century. Likewise, the numerous graffiti crosses cut in the blocks of the fortress, especially near the gates, indicate Christian sentiment, although these cannot be dated with any certainty and they may well be Medieval.[101]

The well-known Victorinus inscription, however, is both reasonably well-dated and a certain indication of Christian sentiment.[102] This stone, and probably another like it, was undoubtedly built into the wall of one of the gates of the Isthmian fortress. The stone itself, which almost certainly came from a circular building in the Sanctuary of Poseidon, was inscribed on the order of the imperial official Victorinus. Moreover, its text had strong liturgical connections that linked the well-being of the people of Greece to the emperor Justinian and their faith in the Christian God.

---

[101] *Isthmia* V.98 with fig. 26 and pl. 31a; and *id.* V.125, with ill. 23; Sanders 2005 428 with fig. 166.

[102] *IG* 4.204; discussion and bibliography in *Isthmia* V.12–13 and pl. 1a. We are pleased that this inscription has now been returned to Isthmia where it is displayed in the Archaeological Museum.

TRANSFORMATION TO A CHRISTIAN WORLD

We leave these issues now and turn to the broader framework of what had become a largely Christian society on the Isthmus of Corinth. Clearly, the most important development in the eastern Corinthia in the 5th-6th centuries was the abandonment of pagan cult and the construction of the Hexamilion, the great defensive wall across the whole of the Isthmus, and its large eastern fortress just 200 m east of the Temple of Poseidon.[103] As is well known, Nick Kardulias has argued for significant continuity in the transformation from sanctuary to fortress. In both phases Isthmia was a place of interaction and exchange, the entrance to the Peloponnesos, and a source of economic wealth.[104] Thus, in the Byzantine period the Isthmus remained a central focus of transport, and significant resources were devoted to the maintenance and repair of the Hexamilion at various times. Troops were certainly stationed at the fortress and along the Hexamilion at least at times of threat, and so the area of the fortress developed into a significant population center. The focus had certainly changed, from religion and athletics to defense and agricultural production, but the geographical location of Isthmia meant that the area would retain its economic and strategic importance throughout the ages.

Beyond the site at Isthmia itself, we may look more broadly at transformation in the countryside surrounding the sanctuary at Isthmia, the region that was intensively explored between 1999 and 2003 by EKAS.[105] This is not the place to deal with the complexities of the enormous quantity of information from the systematic survey. David Pettegrew and others are working on this, and their discussions will be available shortly.[106]

One of the important indications of activity in the Late Roman and Early Byzantine periods elsewhere is the presence of churches. Even when the location of a church is known, however, the interpretation of the evidence for churches is not a simple matter since one can rarely know why individual churches were built, how they were used, or why

---

[103] *Isthmia* V.
[104] Kardulias 2005 and 1995.
[105] Tartaron *et al.* 2006.
[106] Caraher *et al.* 2006; Pettegrew 2007.

they were rebuilt or refurbished. Nonetheless, the geographical location of churches and their chronology, at least on a general level, is a
first line of evidence that can play a significant role in our investigation
of an area. It was, therefore, a surprise, if not a disappointment, that
the EKAS project did not initially discover clear evidence of early Byzantine churches in the study area other than those that were already
known, despite (as we shall shortly see) the enormously strong signature of artifacts from the Late Roman phase.

An early Byzantine basilica has long been known on the south mole
of the harbor of Kenchreai, and another is located north of the harbor
close to a monumental tomb of Early Roman date.[107] At Almyri, south
on the coast of the eastern Corinthia, Fowler mentions marble architectural fragments including column shafts in the courtyard of the old
church, and these have been thought to be from an early Byzantine
church in the area although they are nowhere to be found now.[108] This
latter is not at all certain, but at most these three are the only early
churches published to date in the rural eastern Corinthia.

One possible site of another early Byzantine church is at a place
called Ayia Paraskeve, located between Xylokeriza and Kenchreai,
where local informants consistently reported the remains of such a
church until fairly recently (fig. 14.10). The site was also connected in
local lore with the seasonal habitation of transhumants, who suppos-
edly used the church. Recent bulldozing and construction have now
destroyed any traces of such a church, but intensive survey recorded
high levels of artifacts ranging from the classical through the modern period with significant quantities of Late Roman (otherwise common in the survey area) and Middle Byzantine material (otherwise
very rare). No architectural pieces that can be associated with an early
Byzantine church were found at the site, however, and the identification of such must, therefore, remain problematic.

Surface survey attested considerable activity in the early to Late
Roman phase in a large field east of Examilia (Perdikaria, EKAS 'LOCA
9221'). Interestingly enough, the same field contained large quantities of Middle Byzantine pottery. Geophysical investigation, mainly
recording of magnetic anomalies, was carried out in 2002 by Dr.

---

[107] *Kenchreiai* I.75–78; Pallas 1977, 170–72; Scranton and Ramage 1967, 185–86
with fig. 16; Hawthorne 1965, 197; and J. Rife's chapter in this volume.
[108] *Corinth* I.1, 99.

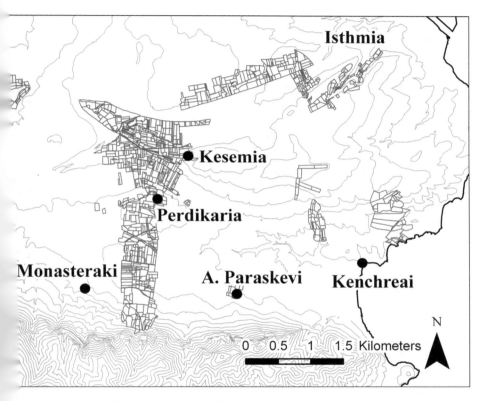

Fig. 14.10. Churches and Possible Churches in the Eastern Corinthia.

Apostolos Sarris of the Institute for Mediterranean Studies (FORTH, Rethymno). This work produced strong evidence of architectural remains ca. 1.0–1.5 m below the surface. These seem to represent at least two complexes of buildings at slightly different orientations (but roughly east-west), perhaps indicating two different phases of occupation. One of these complexes appears to be dominated by a large, east-west trending structure, which may well be a church, perhaps of an early Byzantine date. The other complex could be of a later (possibly middle Byzantine) era, and it could be an agricultural establishment or perhaps a monastery.

After the completion of EKAS fieldwork in 2003, information provided by local residents suggested the existence of an early church in an area approximately half a kilometer north of the site mentioned above in an area called Kesimia. Surface survey produced no significant indication of a church here; but recent visits to the area produced an intact, imitation African lamp of the 6th century along with large fragments of rooftiles of Late Roman date. Reliable informants say that over two decades ago two intact, unfluted, green marble columns were found at the site and dragged off to houses in the vicinity where they are still located and known to local archaeological authorities. There is no certain proof that these came from a church, but the available information makes this likely.

Likewise, after completion of fieldwork, we visited a site to the west of Xylokeriza, suggestively known as Monasteraki, where intensive survey had not been carried out. There, a small platform on the northern foothills of Mt. Oneion has a remarkable view over the whole of the central Corinthian plain with south-north ravines on either side. The surface is covered with broken rooftiles, pottery of Late Roman date, and an amazing selection of marble revetment and broken marble slabs. In the northern part of the site, a small section of east-west wall of rubble and mortar construction is still preserved, apparently *in situ*. The different colors and types of marble suggest a building of considerable sophistication and wealth. One of the fragmentary slabs is clearly a *thorakion*, and the molding along the outside of the slab suggests a date in the 6th century. This building is all but certainly a basilica of that date.

This information allows us to posit the location of several possible or probable early Byzantine churches in the EKAS survey area, all of them interestingly located along or just below the lowest foothills of the Oneion mountain chain in the land just above the fertile central corridor of the eastern Corinthia. The location of these churches can perhaps serve as one approach to the question of settlement and land use in the period from the 5th–7th century. Obviously, we cannot speak of a precise chronology either of construction or abandonment, although the apparent activity in the areas of Ayia Paraskeve and Perdikaria might suggest either continuity of use or reuse of the presumed churches in the Middle Byzantine period.

FURTHER SURVEY EVIDENCE

Villas in the Roman Corinthia

To this information we should add the location of the presumed villa complex at Akra Sophia (Kavo Isthmias; for location see fig. 14.1), previously published.[109] This series of buildings, partially preserved and generally understandable without excavation because of deflation and erosion from the sea, seems to have been a luxurious seaside villa, one arguably involving actual agricultural production as well as residential facilities. It was presumably built on a series of terraces stepping down toward the sea, and it seems not to have been fortified in any way. As is generally known, there is surprisingly little evidence of Roman rural villas in the Corinthia. The Akra Sophia example is, therefore, relatively significant.[110]

The EKAS project identified a number of other locations that might represent villa sites in the eastern Corinthia. One of these is on a hill that overlooked the harbor and the urban area of Kenchreai from the northwest and is identified by EKAS as 'LOCA 9216.' A partially surviving structure there was identified by Wiseman as a Hellenistic tower, and the EKAS investigation of the area seems to support that identification. A dense but broad spread of artifacts of Classical through Late Roman date, marked by a predominance of early and Late Roman material, however, suggests settlement in this period, and the appearance of marble revetment, storage jars, and millstones would be appropriate for a villa of the Roman period. Likewise, the density of Roman

---

[109] Gregory 1985.
[110] Among the few known rural villas are those at Pano Magoula near New Corinth (Pallas 1955); at Varela near ancient Kleonai (Moutzale 1984); another near Dervenakia (Αρχαιολογικόν Δελτίον 1972, 212) and the spectacular lavish villa at Koudounistra above Loutraki (Aslamatzidou-Kostourou 1996).

and Late Roman material, including high quality building material, suggests the existence of a villa in the Oneion foothills ('LOCA 9228'). Finally, at a spot just west of the probable church at Perdikaria ('LOCA 9221'), the density and type of finds suggest another villa of Roman date. It is possible that concentrations to the east and west of this may be the remains of one or more other similar complexes.

All of these possible villas had fragments of Late Roman pottery extending, at least, into the first half of the 7th century. They are, too, like the churches, concentrated in the broad area of interface between the foothills of Oneion and the plain to the north. The location of the Akra Sophia villa, with its presumably agricultural production; as well as that of the other presumed villas, and evidence of coastal activity along the Saronic Gulf all remind us of the important connection of this region to the sea.

Pottery

Beyond this we can look briefly at a few of the distributions of material from the EKAS area and what we might be able to say from them. One with real possibilities is the kitchenware that can be reasonably assigned to the period of Late Antiquity. According to the EKAS records, 180 pieces of such pottery were identified in some 94 different sampling units. It is reasonable to suggest that kitchenware would have been connected with residential activity and that its distribution would give a clue to that in individual periods. But we can also be more chronologically precise by looking at the readily identifiable cooking pots with triangular rims that can be assigned to the period after 550 CE.[111] Some 25 of these pots were discovered in 20 different survey units, and these are shown in fig. 14.11 along with the course of the modern roads.

These roads are constrained by the natural environment as much as the ancient roads, which they mainly follow. It is, therefore, presumably significant to note that the distribution of these Late Roman cooking pots is related to the location of some of these roads. This is just one example of the sorts of analysis that can be done with the information gathered by the survey in the eastern Corinthia. This chapter,

---

[111] As shown by the comparison with examples published by Slane and Sanders (2005).

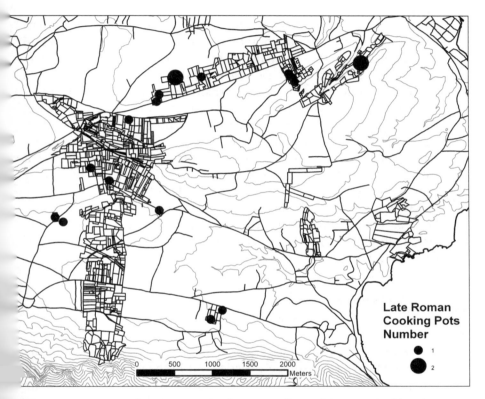

4.11. Late Roman/Early Byzantine Cooking Pots (late 6th century and later) against
the background of the modern road network.

however, is not the place to attempt such a detailed examination of the survey data. The example cited does show a significant correlation between the location of one class of pottery found in intensive survey and the proposed location of one important class of features, namely, the road system. Further examination and study will allow us to make more significant observations about the nature of life in the eastern Corinthian landscape.

The work of EKAS and earlier topographic studies show the Eastern Corinthia to have been a vibrant and active place in the Roman and Late Roman periods, what many scholars have called a "busy country-side."[112] Previous estimates had suggested that the early Roman period witnessed economic depression, perhaps partly as a result of imperial policies dictated by Rome, but more recent work indicates that in this period the countryside may have been more prosperous and more economically and socially diverse than previously thought. This situation certainly continued into the late Roman period, although recent work by Pettegrew suggests some caution in this assessment. Just as important, while until recently our knowledge of the sacred landscape of the eastern Corinthia in the 4th–7th centuries had been severely limited, recent discoveries have begun to put place names on the map, which allows us to examine archaeological evidence for the spread of Christianity into the countryside.

ISLANDS AND THE POSSIBILITY OF NEW PEOPLE IN THE LATE ROMAN CORINTHIA

The islands located offshore arguably played a significant role in the exchange that was presumably carried out in the eastern Corinthia in this period and that drew the area into the broader currents of the Saronic, the Aegean, and beyond. These islands have, of course, been the subject of considerable debate and have frequently been described as 'isles of refuge,' connected with the invasions and difficulties of the second half of the 6th century.[113]

---

[112] Pettegrew 2007.
[113] Hood 1970; Gregory 1984; Gregory, Kardulias, and Sawmiller 1995; Rosser 1996.

In earlier publications I have argued that the archaeological evidence from these islands does not primarily reflect refugee settlements but rather continuing economic activity common to both the land and the sea. I continue to find such an explanation most convincing although one must admit the possibility that some of the islands, at least, could have been used occasionally as refuges, while many more seem to have served as naval stations, especially from the middle of the 7th century onward.

As just mentioned, many scholars have argued that the settlements on these 'desert islands' were connected with the invasions by Avars, Slavs, and possibly other people, beginning in the later years of the 6th century. This is not the place to discuss this difficult question in depth, but we put it into context with information from Isthmia about the period of the early Byzantine 'dark ages' of the 7th and 8th centuries.

After the initial collapse of the Roman Bath at Isthmia, ca. 400 CE, the western two-thirds or so apparently remained standing and were utilized. The floors of most of the rooms appear to have been cleared of debris, and at least some of that material was thrown indiscriminately through the doorway at the southeast corner of the building. Clearly, at least some of the heating facilities of the bath were out of service; and the hypocaust system of Room IX was used as storage for (or, less likely, disposal of) amphorae, funnels, and drinking cups. It is conceivable, however, that in this phase parts of the baths continued to be used although on a severely limited level. The fact that the Roman baths were not significantly redesigned and divided up into small bathing areas, as happened in many contemporary bathing establishments, suggests that even in the 5th and early 6th centuries bathing was not a primary activity at Isthmia.

Sometime after the middle of the 6th century, the rest of the Roman Bath at Isthmia seems to have collapsed. The earthquake of 551 is a tempting candidate, but other phenomena may have been the actual cause. After a period that allowed for the accumulation of considerable debris, a settlement was constructed above the ruins of the Roman Bath.[114] Buildings of the settlement, presumably dating to the 7th or 8th century, were mainly small rectangular houses sometimes featuring an apsidal end, and they were apparently scattered over the entire

---

[114] Gregory 1993.

area once occupied by the bath. Some of the material associated with these buildings was the so-called 'Slavic pottery,' a poorly made, frequently hand-shaped ware that has been found in significant quantities at various sites in Greece, for example, at Argos (where it was discovered primarily in the large baths built under the height of the Larissa), Tiryns, Olympia, Messene, and Demetrias.[115] Interestingly, most of this material was apparently associated with burials while the remains at Isthmia definitely suggest habitation. Likewise, this rare pottery is known at Corinth and turns up in many contexts throughout the site at Isthmia.

Small-scale excavations to the south of the Roman Bath carried out between 2002 and 2007 brought to light the remains of two further buildings of this period, one of them apsidal, and a large, roughly paved floor, suggesting that the settlement extended beyond the area of the baths. The discovery of millstones associated with the structures had already indicated that the inhabitants of this settlement were involved in small-scale farming activities.[116] The rough pavement discovered in 2006 was covered with a thick deposit of rich black soil that was thought at first to have been ash from the furnace of the Bath. Closer examination suggests that it was, instead, decomposed organic material and that it had no connection with the functioning of the facilities. Rather, it was a place either where decomposing material was stored or perhaps, more likely, the floor of an area where animals were kept, again an indication of the agricultural character of the settlement.

The settlement around the ruins of the Roman Bath may be connected with a few very late houses in the vicinity of the Temple of Poseidon on the upper terrace of the Sanctuary and with others in the area East of Temenos. In the same context one may mention the hoard of coins found in the debris of the foundation trench of the north colonnade of the Temple of Poseidon.[117] This included 270 coins, of which the earliest was struck in 538/9. There were 23 coins of Tiberius II Constantine, and the latest was a coin of Maurice Tiberius, dated to

---

[115] Aupert 1980; Anagnostakis and Poulou-Papademetriou 1997; Poulou-Papademetriou 2001; Vida and Völling 2000.

[116] Gregory 1993.

[117] MacDowall 1965; Avramea 1983, 56–57 and 75–76; Avramea 1997, 74; and comparison with hoards found at Athens (Metcalf 1962), Corinth (Avramea 1983, 52–56), Kenchreai (Hohlfelder 1973), and elsewhere.

year 2 (583/4). Avramea concludes that this hoard, which represents an apparently systematic 'collection' of coins from the time of Justinian to that of Tiberius II, but which ends dramatically in 583/84, presents strong evidence of a disturbance, probably an invasion, and perhaps even the one mentioned by the Chronicle of Monemvasia (in 587/8) as responsible for the flight of the Corinthians to the island of Aegina.[118]

The settlement around the ruins of the Roman Bath and the houses at various points on the upper terrace may be dated to the 7th century and perhaps later. It is possible that some of the people who lived in this settlement may have been newcomers to the Corinthia, but this issue remains an open question. In any case, there is presently no firm evidence that this settlement continued in use into the middle Byzantine period. By that time a new, much larger settlement had been established in and around the fortress on the Hexamilion.

CONCLUSIONS

I hope that this brief tour through some complex and difficult information will help to indicate the kinds of information that Isthmia and the eastern Corinthia can provide to help us understand society, economy, and religion in the Roman period, and the relationship of this information both to what we read in Christian Scripture and to what we know about the development of Christianity in the region. First, we can see that the archaeological material from the Sanctuary of Poseidon at Isthmia has frequently been used by scholars of Christian Scripture to investigate social and religious trends at the time of the Pauline mission. This is a natural and reasonable endeavor, but considerable care must be exercised in making use of the archaeological data, in part, because of well-known problems of chronology, scale, and specificity. Thus, as we have already seen, changes in chronology, both of pottery and of construction phases, are crucial to both

---

[118] Avramea 1997, 72–75. She also correctly points out that the main road from Athens and central Greece into the Peloponnesos ran directly north of the find spot of the hoard, and she also seems to suggest that the deposit may also (somehow) have been connected with the robbing of the temple for the rebuilding of the Hexamilion by Justinian—although the date for this would obviously have been well before the deposit of the coins.

the historical and the archaeological debate. Related to this, but even more fundamental to the discussion, is the fact that the archaeological data will not normally provide us with direct evidence about specific historical events, such as the date or the local conditions at the time of Paul's visits to Corinth. Indeed, the old idea that archaeology's main contribution to historical discourse is to confirm or contradict individual narratives is certainly simplistic and probably false.

This is not to say that the archaeological evidence from Isthmia cannot be useful to those interested in considering the social, economic, and political background of the Corinthia in the New Testament period. The importance of the sanctuary, in the mind of the Romans and the leadership of the colony at Corinth is obvious, although this does not seem to have been their earliest priority, and if we are correct in our understanding of the chronology, the apostle Paul would only have been aware of preparations to reconstitute the ancient celebrations in their original location. Presumably, however, he would have fully understood the relationship between the civic government of Corinth and the organization and operation of the games, a topic that must have been much 'in the air' at the time. He would also presumably have known about the worship of Palaimon (even though we know little about this in the 1st century CE), and recent work on the cult and its physical manifestation at Isthmia certainly contributes to our understanding of it in the broader context.

Likewise, the information from archaeological survey (in this case EKAS) has the potential to provide significant new views of the countryside and of society in the broader Corinthian area. Analysis of the EKAS data is still underway, but preliminary interpretations already suggest some modification of earlier characterizations of the Roman countryside. It is true that the Hellenistic period in the survey area is not at all well represented, but the Early Roman period may be one of significant upturn. Further analysis of this question will help clarify the situation. This issue is, however, of considerable importance since one would imagine a very different social reality if the countryside had been occupied mainly by independent farmers rather than by a few landowners who farmed the land for profit.

Another significant observation, from a slightly later period, is how different parts of the site at Isthmia provide divergent views on the viability of 'pagan' religion in the 3rd and 4th centuries. This is not in itself surprising since it may be the result of changes in the cult, the place it was conducted, or in our understanding of the evidence

In any case, it is important to determine how long the Hellenic cult survived, with or without its athletic trappings, since that is crucial to our understanding of the relationship between the old and the new religions and the connections and antagonisms between the two. Evidence on this issue elsewhere in Greece is divided, but generally most scholars accept some form of continuation of the ancient cult at least until the end of the 4th century CE. Although the evidence for cult activity at Isthmia, in and around the Temple of Poseidon, seems to come to an end by the middle of the 3rd century, activity continued in other areas (such as in the Roman baths) at least until the end of the 4th century. Furthermore, even though previous scholarship suggested a peaceful transition between paganism and Christianity in Greece, evidence examined here suggests significant religious violence at various times in the Corinthia, especially at the end of the 4th century.

A particularly striking observation is that we cannot find any evidence of an early Byzantine church at Isthmia even though a Christian community was established there at least from the early 5th century and we know that all other major Hellenic sanctuaries had churches by the 6th century. Presumably, this is an accident of how the site has been preserved, and one must expect a church will be found at Isthmia at some point. Nevertheless, even outside Isthmia only three Christian basilicas had previously been identified in the eastern Corinthia, a remarkably small number, given the large numbers identified in Attica, on the islands, and at nearby Corinth. Preliminary work of EKAS at first failed to find any 'new' churches in the survey area, but follow-up research allows us to posit a significant number of churches in the countryside by the 6th century.

Overall, we should note that a major change in the landscape of the area of Isthmia was the construction and use of the Hexamilion and the fortress. We already know something about the road network in the region, with its primary artery running from central and northern Greece through the great Roman arch at the northeast corner of the sanctuary, past the Temple of Poseidon, and on to Corinth and the rest of the Peloponnesos. Beyond this, we know of several other roads to Kenchreai, to the so-called 'sacred glen,' and elsewhere, but much research on this question is still needed. Finally, although the central part of the sanctuary at Isthmia has certainly been identified, much of the broader complex remains unexcavated and the location of many of its important buildings are still unknown.

Beyond this we may note the remarkable contrast between what we learn from excavation at Isthmia and what we can deduce from survey in the countryside. Thus, at Isthmia we have evidence of a modest Christian settlement that apparently had a close relationship with its ancient past but one that seemingly lived at a rather low economic level, as suggested by the burials. Indeed, it can be argued that newcomers arrived in the area probably in the 7th century and that they lived an agricultural, rather basic life, apparently in close contact with the local residents in the broader area. In the countryside, however, we find what appears to be a rich and vibrant society with some of its members apparently living in luxurious buildings amid a number of Christian churches. Further, as mentioned above, there is at Isthmia plentiful evidence of new kinds of pottery, such as the so-called 'Slavic' or 'low technology' wares, while virtually no trace of that is found in the countryside.

Overall, the information from this part of the Corinthia is rich and complex, and it invites exploration by those interested in the relationship between religion and society in the first few Christian centuries. The archaeological evidence, as we have seen, clearly informs the broader questions better than the more specific ones—issues such as the 'popularity' of various cults and the maintenance of the structures associated with their celebrations, or the nature of land use and the social and economic repercussions of this. The investigation of such evidence and its manipulation to shed light on historical and textual problems is difficult and challenging, but certainly well worth doing.

BIBLIOGRAPHY

Abascal, J. M., G. Alföldy, and R. Cebrián. 2001. "La Inscripción con letras de bronce y otros documentos epigráficos del foro de Segobriga." *Archivo español de arqueología* 74: 117–30.

Abramenko, A. 1997. *Die munizipale Mittelschicht im kaiserzeitlichen Italien. Zu einem neuen Verständnis von Sevirat und Augustalität.* Frankfurt: Peter Lang.

Adamo Muscettola, S. 2000. "Miseno: culto imperiale e politica nel complesso degli Augustali." *MDAI(R)* 107: 79–108.

Adler, F. 1892. "Die byzantinische Kirche." In *Die Baudenkmäler von Olympia (Olympia volume 2)*, 3–105. Edited by F. Alder *et al.* Berlin: A. Asher and Co.

Alcock, S. 1989a. "Archaeology and Imperialism: Roman Expansion and the Greek City." *JMA* 2: 87–135.

———. 1989b. "Roman Imperialism in a Greek Landscape." *JRA* 2: 5–34.

———. 1993. *Graecia Capta: The Landscapes of Roman Greece.* Cambridge: Cambridge University Press.

———. 1997a. "The Heroic Past in a Hellenistic Present." In *Hellenistic Constructs*, 20–34. Edited by P. Cartledge, P. Garnsey, and E. Gruen. Berkeley: University of California Press.

———. 1997b. "Greece: A Landscape of Resistance?" In *Dialogues in Roman Imperialism: Power, Discourse, and Discrepant Experience in the Roman Empire*, 103–15. Edited by D. J. Mattingly and S. E. Alcock. Portsmouth: JRA.

———. 2002. *Archaeologies of the Greek Past: Landscape, Monuments, and Memories.* Cambridge: Cambridge University.

Alcock, S., and J. Cherry (eds.). 2004. *Side-by-Side Survey: Comparative Regional Studies in the Mediterranean World.* Oxford: Oxbow.

Alcock, S., J. Cherry, and J. Elsner. (eds.). 2001. *Pausanias: Travel andMemory in Roman Greece.* Oxford: Oxford University Press.

Alföldy, G. 1977. *Los Baebii de Saguntum.* Valencia: Servicio de Investigación Prehistórica.

———. 1984. *Römische Statuen in Venetia et Histria. Epigraphische Quellen.* Heidelberg: Carl Winter-Universitätsverlag.

Allison, P. 2001. "Using the Material and Written Sources: Turn of the Millennium Approaches to Roman Domestic Space." *AJA* 105: 181–208.

Alzinger, W. 1974. *Augusteische Architektur in Ephesos.* Vienna: Österreichisches Archäologisches Institut.

Amandry, M. 1988. *Le monnayage des duovirs corinthiens.* Paris: de Boccard.

Anagnostakis, I., and N. Poulou-Papademetriou. 1997 "Η πρωτοβυζαντινή Μεσσήνη (5ος–7ος αιώνες) και τα προβλήματα της χειροποιητής κεραμεικής στη Πελοπόννησο." *Σύμμεικτα* 11: 229–322.

Ando, C. 2000. *Imperial Ideology and Provincial Loyalty in the Roman Empire.* Berkeley: University of California Press.

Aranegui, C., E. Hernández, M. López, et al. 1987. "El Foro de Saguntum: La planta arquitectónica." In *Los Foros romanos de las provincias occidentales*, 73–97. Edited by C. Aranequi. Madrid: Ministerio de Cultura.

Arslan, E. A. 1998. "Urbanistica di *Scolacium*." *Journal of Ancient Topography* 8: 79–110.

Ascough, R. 1997. *Paul's Macedonian Associations.* Tübingen: Mohr Siebeck.

Ashmole, B. 1962. "Torch Racing at Rhamnus." *AJA* 66: 233–34.

Aslamatzidou-Kostourou, Z. 1996. "Θέση Κατουνίστρα." Αχραιολογικόν Δελτίον 55: 94–95.

Aupert, P. 1979. *Fouilles de Delphes: Tome II, topographie et architecture*. Two volumes. Paris: de Boccard.

———. 1980. "Céramique slave à Argos (585 ap. J.-C.)." In *Études argiennes: Bulletin de correspondance hellénique*, 373–95. Athens and Paris: Diffusion de Boccard.

Aurigemma, S. 1940. "Sculture del Foro Vecchio di Lepcis Magna raffiguranti la Dea Roma e principi della casa dei Giulio-Claudi." *Africa italiana* 8: 1–94.

Avi-Yonah, M. 1939. "Abbreviations in Greek Inscriptions." *QDAP* 9: 9–125.

Avraméa, A. 1983. "Νομισματικοί «Θησαυροί» και μεμονωμένα νομίσματα από την Πελοπόννησο." *Σύμμεικτα* 5: 49–90.

———. 1997. *Le Péloponnèse du IVᵉ au VIIIᵉ siècle: Changements et persistances*. Paris: Publications de la Sorbonne.

Balch, D. 2004. "Rich Pompeiian Houses, Shops for Rent, and the Huge Apartment Building in Herculaneum as Typical Spaces for Pauline House Churches." *JSNT* 27: 27–46.

Baldassarri, P. 2001. "Lo specchio del potere: programmi edilizi ad Atene in età Augustea." In *Constructions publiques et programmes édilitaires en Grèce entre le IIᵉ siècle av. J.-C. et le Iᵉʳ siècle ap. J.-C*, 401–25. Edited by J.-Y. Marc and J.-C. Moretti. Athens: Ecole française d'Athènes.

Balsdon, J. 1979. *Romans and Aliens*. Chapel Hill: University of North Carolina Press.

Barbet, A., J. L. Rife, and F. Monier. 2007. "Une tombeau peint de la nécropole de Cenchrées-Kenchreai, près de Corinthe." In *Proceedings of the IX Congreso internacional de la "Association internationale pour la peinture murale antique,"* 395–99. Edited by C. Guirla Pelgrin. Saragossa: Government of Aragón, Department of Territorial Politics, Justice, and Interior.

Barclay, J. 2004. "Poverty in Pauline Studies: A Response to Steven Friesen." *JSNT* 26: 363–66.

Barrett, C. K. 1968. *A Commentary on the First Epistle to the Corinthians*. New York: Harper & Row.

Barrett, J. 2001. "Agency, the Duality of Structure, and the Problem of the Archaeological Record." In *Archaeological Theory Today*, 140–54. Edited by I. Hodder. Oxford: Polity Press.

Barringer, J. 2003. Review of Christiane Sourvinou-Inwood (1991). *BMCR* 14.04, accessed online.

Barstad, H. 1996. *The Myth of the Empty Land: A Study in the History and Archaeology of Judah during the "Exilic" Period*. Oslo: Scandinavian University Press.

Barton, S. 1986. "Paul's Sense of Place: an Anthropological Approach to Community Formation in Corinth." *NTS* 32: 225–46.

Beard, M., J. North, and S. Price. 1998. *Religions of Rome*. Two volumes. Cambridge: Cambridge University Press.

Beaton, A., and P. A. Clement. 1976. "The Date of the Destruction of the Sanctuary of Poseidon on the Isthmus of Corinth." *Hesperia* 45: 267–79.

Bees, N. 1915. "Beiträge zur kirchlichen Geographie Griechenlands in Mittelalter und in der neueren Zeit." *OChr* 5: 238–78.

Bees, N. 1941. *Die griechisch-christlichen Inscriften des Peloponnes I: Isthmos-Korinthos*. Athens: Christlich-Archäologische Gesellschaft. Reprinted Chicago: Ares, 1978.

Behr, C. 1968. *Aelius Aristides and the Sacred Tales*. Amsterdam: Hakkert.

Bell, C. 1998. "Performance." In *Critical Terms for Religious Studies*, 74–75. Edited by in M. Taylor. Chicago: University of Chicago Press.

Benario, H. 1959. "C. Paccius Africanus." *Historia* 8: 496–98.

Betz, H. D. 1991. "Christianity as Religion: Paul's Attempt at Definition in Romans." *JR* 71: 315–44.

Bevan, E. 1940. *Holy Images: An Inquiry into Idolatry and Image-Worship in Ancient Paganism and in Christianity.* London: George Allen and Unwin, Ltd.

Bhabha, H. 1994. *The Location of Culture.* London: Routledge.

Binazzi, G. 1981. "Iscrizione pavimentale nel c.d. foro di Assisi." In *Scritti sul mondo antico in memoria di Fulvio Grosso,* 29–38. Edited by L. Gasperini. Rome: Giorgio Bretschneider.

Bingen, J. 1953. "Inscriptions du Péloponnèse." *BCH* 77: 641–42.

Bird, P. 1991. "Israelite Religion and the Faith of Israel's Daughters." In *The Bible and the Politics of Exegesis,* 311–17. Edited by D. Jobling *et al.* Cleveland: Pilgrim Press.

Blackman D. (ed.). 1997. "Archaeology in Greece 1996–97." *AR* 44: 1–125.

———. 1998. "Archaeology in Greece, 1997–98." *AR* 44: 1–128.

Blanck, H. 1969. *Wiederverwendung alter Statuen als Ehrendenkmäler bei Griechen und Römern.* Rome: L'Erma di Bretschneider.

———. 1971. "Review of *Studien zur statuarischen Darstellung der römischer Kaiser* (H. G. Niemyer)." *GGA* 223: 93.

Blegen, C., O. Broneer, R. Stillwell and A. Bellinger. 1930. *Acrocorinth: Excavations in 1926.* Cambridge: Harvard University Press.

Blum, G. 1914. "Numismatique d'Antinoos." *JIAN* 16: 33–70.

Boer, R. 2003. "Henri Lefebvre: The Production of Space in 1 Samuel." In *Marxist Criticism of the Bible,* 87–109. Edited by R. Boer. London: Continuum.

Bon, A. 1951. *La Péloponnèse byzantin jusqu'en 1294.* Paris: Presses universitaires de France.

Bonner, C. 1929. "A Dionysiac Miracle at Corinth." *AJA* 33: 368–75.

Bonneville, J.-N. 1984. "Le support monumental des inscriptions: terminologie et analyse." In *Épigraphie hispanique. Problèmes de méthode et d'édition,* 117–40. Paris: E. de Boccard.

Bookidis, N. 1987. "The Sanctuary of Demeter and Kore: An Archaeological Approach to Ancient Religion." *AJA* 91: 480–81.

———. 2003. "The Sanctuaries of Corinth." In *Corinth XX,* 247–59.

———. 2005. "Religion in Corinth: 146 B.C.E. to 100 C.E." In *URRC,* 141–64.

Bookidis, N., and R. Stroud. 1987. *Demeter and Persephone in Ancient Corinth.* Athens: ASCSA.

———. 2004. "Apollo and the Archaic Temple at Corinth." *Hesperia* 73: 401–26.

Boschung, D. 2002. *Gens Augusta: Untersuchungen zu Aufstellung, Wirkung und Bedeutung der Statuengruppen des julisch-claudischen Kaiserhauses (Monumenta Artis Romanae 32).* Mainz: Philipp von Zabern.

Boudon, V. 1994. "Le role de l'eau dans les prescriptions médicales d'Asclepios chez Galien et Aelius Aristide." In *L'eau, la santé et la maladie dans le monde grec,* 157–68. Edited by R. Gionouvès *et al.* Athens: Bullétin de correspondance hellénique.

Bowersock, G. 1965. *Augustus and the Greek World.* Oxford: Clarendon Press.

Bowie, E. 1974. "Greeks and Their Past in the Second Sophistic." *Studies in Ancient Society,* 166–209. Edited by M. I. Finley. London: Routledge.

———. 1994. "The Readership of Greek Novels in the Ancient World." In *The Search for the Ancient Novel,* 435–59. Edited by J. Tatum. Baltimore: Johns Hopkins University.

Bozhori, K., and D. Budina. 1966. "Disa Mbishkrime të Pabotuara të Theatrit të Butrintit." *Studime Historike* 20: 143–91.

Bradley, K. 1994. *Slavery and Society at Rome.* Cambridge: Cambridge University Press.

Braund, D. 1980. "Artemis Eukleia and Euripides' Hippolytus." *JHS* 100: 184–85.

Bricault, L. 1996. *Myrionymi: Les Épiclèses grecques et latines d'Isis, de Sarapis et d'Anubis.* Stuttgart: Teubner.

———. 2001. *Atlas de la diffusion des cultes isiaques (ive s. av. J.-C.–ive s. apr. J.-C.).* Paris: Académie des inscriptions et belles-lettres.

——. 2005. *Recueil des inscriptions concernant les cultes isiaques*. Paris: Diffusion De Boccard.

Bricault, L. and R. Veymiers. 2007. "Isis in Corinth: The Numismatic Evidence. City, Image and Religion." In *Nile into Tiber: Egypt and the Roman World. Proceedings of the IIIrd International Conference of Isis Studies*, 392–413. *Religions in the Graeco-Roman World* 159. Edited by L. Bricault, M. J. Versluys, and P. G. P. Meyboom. Leiden: Brill.

Broneer, O. 1942. "Hero Cults in the Corinthian Agora." *Hesperia* 11: 128–61.

——. 1947. "Investigations at Corinth, 1946–1947." *Hesperia* 16: 233–47.

——. 1962. "The Apostle Paul and the Isthmian Games." *BA* 25: 1–31.

Brown, P. 1995. *Authority and the Sacred*. Cambridge: Cambridge University Press.

——. 2000. "Holy Men." *CAH* 14: 781–810.

Brucia, M. A. 1990. "The Tiber Island in Ancient and Medieval Rome." Ph.D. diss., Fordham University.

Bruneau, P. 1974. "Existe-t-il des statues d'Isis Pélagia?" *BCH* 98: 333–81.

Brunt, P. 1988. *The Fall of the Roman Republic*. Oxford: Oxford University Press.

——. 1990. *Roman Imperial Themes*. Oxford: Clarendon Press.

Buckler, J. 1999. "A Note on Diodorus 14.86.1." *CP* 94: 210–14.

Buell, D. and C. Hodge. 2004. "The Politics of Interpretation: The Rhetoric of Race and Ethnicity in Paul." *JBL* 123: 235–51.

Buonocore, M. 1985. "C. Marius Atys *sevir Augustalis* di Venafrum." *ArchCl* 37: 290–92.

Burford, A. 1969. *The Greek Temple Builders at Epidauros: A Social and Economic Study of Building in the Asklepian Sanctuary During the Fourth and Early Third Centuries B.C.* Toronto: University of Toronto Press.

Burkert, W. 1985. *Greek Religion*. Cambridge: Harvard University Press.

——. 1987. *Ancient Mystery Cults*. Cambridge: Harvard University Press.

Burnett, A. 1999. "Buildings and Monuments on Roman Coins." In *Roman Coins and Public Life under the Empire*, 137–64. Edited by G. M. Paul and M. Ierardi. Ann Arbor: University of Michigan Press.

Burrus, V. and R. Lyman. 2005. "Shifting the Focus of History." In *A People's History of Christianity. Late Antique Christianity*, 1–23. Edited by V. Burrus. Minneapolis: Fortress Press.

Byrne, M. and G. Labarre. 2006. *Nouvelles inscriptions d'Antioche de Pisidie: d'apres les Note-books de W. M. Ramsay*. Bonn: Habelt.

Cabanes, P. 1974. "Les inscriptions du théâtre de Bouthrotos." In *Actes du colloque 1972 sur l'esclavage*, 105–209. Paris: Belles Lettres.

Cadbury, H. J. 1931. "Erastus of Corinth." *JBL* 50: 42–58.

Calvani, M. M. 2000. "Veleia." *Aemilia: La cultura romana in Emilia Romagna dal III secolo a.C. all'età costantiniana*, 540–46. Edited by M. M. Calvani. Venice: Marsilio.

Camp, J. 1983. "Drought and Famine in the 4th Century B.C." In *Studies in Athenian Architecture, Sculpture and Topography Presented to Homer A. Thompson*, 9–17. Princeton: American School of Classical Studies.

Caraher, W., D. Nakasis, and D. K. Pettegrew. 2006. "Siteless Survey and Intensive Data Collection in an Artifact-rich Environment: Case Studies from the Eastern Corinthia, Greece." *JMA* 19: 7–43.

Caraher, W., and T. E. Gregory. 2006. "Fortifications of Mount Oneion, Corinthia." *Hesperia* 75: 327–56.

Castelli, E. 1991. *Imitating Paul: A Discourse of Power*. Louisville: Westminster/John Knox.

Catling, R. 1992. "A Votive Deposit of Seventh-Century Pottery from the Menelaion." In *ΦΙΛΟΛΑΚΩΝ: Lakonian Studies in Honor of Hector Catling*, 57–75. Edited by J. Sanders. London: British School at Athens.

Ceka, N. 1999. *Butrint: A Guide to the City and its Monuments*. London: Butrint Foundation.

Chakrabarty, D. 2000. *Provincializing Europe: Postcolonial Thought and Historical Difference*. Princeton: Princeton University Press.

Chantraine, P. 1990. *Dictionnaire étymologique de la langue grecque: Histoire des mots*. Paris: Klincksieck.

Cherry, J., J. Davis, and E. Mantzourani. 1991. *Landscape Archaeology a Long-term History: Northern Keos in the Cycladic Islands from Earliest Settlement until Modern Times*. Los Angeles: UCLA Institute of Archaeology.

Cherry, D. 1995. "Re-Figuring the Roman Epigraphic Habit." *AHB* 9: 143–66.

Chuvin, P. 1990. *A Chronicle of the Last Pagans*. Cambridge: Harvard University Press.

Cianfarani, V. 1959. "Vecchie e nuove iscrizioni sepinati." *Atti terzo congresso internazionale di epigrafia greca e latina (Roma 4–8 Settembre 1957)*, 371–80. Rome: Bretschneider.

Clader, L. 1976. "Helen: The Evolution of Divine to Heroic in Greek Epic Tradition." *Mnemosyne* 42: 90.

Clark, G. 2004. *Christianity and Roman Society*. Cambridge: Cambridge University Press.

Clarke, Andrew D. 1991. "Another Corinthian Erastus Inscription." *TynBul* 42: 146–51.

——. 1993. *Secular and Christian Leadership in Corinth: A Socio-Historical and Exegetical Study of 1 Corinthians 1–6*. Leiden: Brill.

Clauss, M. 1999. *Kaiser und Gott: Herrscherkult im römischen Reich*. Leipzig: Teubner.

Clement, P. A. 1980. "Korinthas, Veterinary." In *Panhellenica: Essays in Ancient History and Historiography in Honor of Truesdell S. Brown*, 187–89. Edited by S. Burnsetin and L. Okin. Kansas: Coronado Press.

Coarelli, Filippo. 1983. *Il Foro romano: Periodo repubblicano e augusteo*. Rome: Quasar.

——. 2002. "Government and the Forum." In *Pompeii*, 53–73. Edited by F. Coarelli. New York: Riverside.

Cohen, A. P. 1985. *The Symbolic Construction of Community*. London: Routledge.

Cohen, S. 1999. *The Beginnings of Jewishness: Boundaries, Varieties, Uncertainties*. Berkeley: University of California Press.

Cole, S. G. 1994. "Demeter in the Ancient Greek City and Its Countryside." In *Placing the Gods: Sanctuaries and Sacred Space in Ancient Greece*, 199–216. Edited by S. Alcock and R. Osborne. Oxford: Oxford University Press.

——. 2004. *Landscapes, Gender, and Ritual Space: The Ancient Greek Experience*. Berkeley: University of California Press.

Collingwood, R. G., and R. P. Wright. 1965. *The Roman Inscriptions of Britain: Inscriptions on Stone*. Oxford: Clarendon.

Collins, R. F. 1999. *First Corinthians*. Collegeville, M.N.: The Liturgical Press.

Conzelmann, Hans. 1975. *1 Corinthians: A Commentary on First Epistle to the Corinthians*. Translated by J. W. Leitch. Philadelphia: Fortress.

Cook, A. B. 1925. *Zeus: A Study in Ancient Religion*. Two volumes. Cambridge: Cambridge University Press.

Coppola, M. R. 1984. "Il Foro Emiliano di Terracina: Rilievo, analisi tecnica, vicende storiche del monumento." *MEFRA* 96: 325–77.

Corzo, R. 1993. "El Teatro de Italica." In *Teatros Romanos de Hispania: Cuadernos de Arquitectura Romana*, 2: 157–71. Murcia: Universidad de Murcia.

Crawford, M. et al. (eds.). 1996. *Roman Statutes*. Two volumes. London: University of London.

——. 1974. *Roman Republican Coinage*. Two volumes. Cambridge: Cambridge University Press.

Crossan, J. D., and J. L. Reed. 2001. *Excavating Jesus: Beneath the Stones, Behind the Texts*. New York: Harper San Francisco.

——. 2004. *In Search of Paul: How Jesus's Apostle Opposed Rome's Empire with God's Kingdom (A New Vision of Paul's Words and World)*. San Francisco: Harper San Francisco.

Crowfoot, J. 1900. "The Lions of Kybele." *JHS* 20: 118–27.

Cummer, W. 1971. "A Roman Tomb at Korinthian Kenchreai." *Hesperia* 40: 205–31.

Curta, F. 2005. "Female Dress and 'Slavic' Bow Fibulae in Greece." *Hesperia* 74: 101–46.

D'Arms, J. 1981. *Commerce and Social Standing in Ancient Rome.* Cambridge, Mass.: Harvard University Press.

——. 2000. "Memory, Money, and Status at Misenum: Three New Inscriptions from the *Collegium* of the Augustales." *JRS* 90: 126–44.

Davies, Penelope. 2000. *Death and the Emperor: Roman Imperial Funerary Monuments, from Augustus to Marcus Aurelius.* Cambridge: Cambridge University Press.

Davis, J. L. 1991. *Sandy Pylos: An Archaeological History from Nestor to Navarino.* Austin: University of Texas Press.

Dawkins, R. 1929. "Carvings in Soft Limestone." In *The Sanctuary of Artemis Orthia at Sparta*, 187–95. Edited by in R. Dawkins. London: Macmillan.

Degrassi, A. 1964. "Una dedica degli Augustali Brindisi a Tiberio." *Athenaeum* 42: 299–307.

Degrassi, D. 1986. "Il culto di Esculapio in Italia centrale durante il periodo repubblicano." In *Fregellae 2: Il Santuario di Esculapio*, 145–52. Edited by F. Coarelli. Rome: Quasar.

De Grazia, C. E. 1973. "Excavations of the American School of Classical Studies at Corinth: The Roman Portrait Sculpture." Ph.D. diss, Columbia University.

D'Hautcourt, A. 2001. "Corinthe: Financement d'une colonisation et d'une reconstruction." In *Constructions publiques et programmes éditilaires en Grèce entre le IIe siècle av. J.-C. et le Ier a J. C.*, 427–38. Edited by J.-Y. Marc and J.-C. Moretti. Paris: De Boccard.

Deichmann, F. 1939. "Frühchristliche Kichen in antike Heiligtümern." *JDAI* 54: 105–36.

Deissmann, A. 1965. *Light from the Ancient East: The New Testament Illustrated by Recently Discovered Texts of the Graeco-Roman World.* Translated by L. Strachan. Grand Rapids: Baker.

De Maria, S. 1988. "Iscrizioni e monumenti nei fori della Cisalpina romana." *MEFRA* 100: 27–62.

DeMaris, R. E. 1995a. "Corinthian Religion and Baptism for the Dead (1 Corinthians 15:29): Insights from Archaeology and Anthropology." *JBL* 114: 661–82.

——. 1995b. "Demeter in Roman Corinth: Local Development in a Mediterranean Religion." *Numen* 42: 105–17.

——. 1999. "Funerals and Baptisms, Ordinary and Otherwise: Ritual Criticism and Corinthian Rites." *BTB* 29.1: 23–34.

——. 2008. *The New Testament in its Ritual World.* London: Routledge.

Deniaux, E. 2007. "La structure politique de la colonie romaine de Buthrotum." In *Roman Butrint: An Assessment*, 33–39. Edited by I. L. Hansen and R. Hodges. Oxford: Oxbow.

de Ste. Croix, G. 1981. *The Class Struggle in the Ancient Greek World: From the Archaic Age to the Arab Conquests.* Ithaca: Cornell University Press.

Detienne, M., with G. Camassa. 1988. *Les savoirs de l'écriture en Grèce ancienne (Cahiers de Philologie 14).* Lille: Presses Universitaires de Lille.

de Waele, F. J. 1930. "Die Korinthischen Ausgrabungen, 1928–1929." *Gnomon* 6: 52–57.

——. 1932. "Ancient Corinth." *Gnomon* 8: 366–67.

——. 1933. "The Sanctuary of Asklepios and Hygieia at Corinth." *AJA* 39: 417–51.

——. 1934. Review of Rhys Carpenter, *Ancient Corinth: A Guide to the Excavation.* (second edition). *Gnomon* 10: 225–30.

——. 1936. "Ὀρθόγραφος and Προικοφάγας on Corinthian Inscriptions." In *Classical Studies Presented to Edward Capps on His Seventieth Birthday*, 90–93. Princeton: Princeton University Press.

Dickie, M. 2001. *Magic and Magicians in the Greco-Roman World*. New York: Routledge.

Dinsmoor, W. B. 1942. "Note on a Circular Monument in the Corinthian Agora." *Hesperia* 11: 314–15.

———. 1961. "Rhamnountine Fantasies." *Hesperia* 30: 179–204.

Dittenberger, W., and K. Purgold. 1896. *Die Inschriften von Olympia*. Berlin: A. Asher.

Dixon, M. D. 2000. "A New Latin and Greek Inscription from Corinth." *Hesperia* 69: 335–42.

Dobres, M.-A., and J. Robb (eds.). 2000. *Agency in Archaeology*. London: Routledge.

Doukellis, P. 1994. "Le territoire de la colonie romaine de Corinthe." In *Structures rurales et sociétés antiques: actes du colloque de Corfou (14–16 mai 1992)*, 359–90. Edited by P. N. Doukellis and L. G. Mendoni. Paris: Les Belles Lettres.

Drachmann, A. 1903. *Scholia Vetera in Pindari Carmina*. Leipzig: Teubner.

Drew-Bear, T., C. M. Thomas and M. Taşlıalan (eds.). 2002. *Actes du Ier congres international sur Antioche de Pisidie*. Paris: de Boccard.

Duff, T. 1999. *Plutarch's Lives: Exploring Virtue and Vice*. Oxford: Clarendon.

Duff, A. 1958. *Freedmen in the Early Roman Empire*. New York: Barnes and Noble.

Dunand, F. 1973. *Le culte d'Isis dans le bassin oriental de la Méditerranée*. Three volumes. Leiden: Brill.

———. 1975. "Les Mystères égyptiens aux époques hellénistique et romaine." In *Mystères et syncrétismes*, 9–62. Edited by F. Dunand. Paris: P. Geuthner.

Dunbabin, K. M. 1990. "*Ipsa deae vestigia...*: Footprints Divine and Human on Graeco-Roman Monuments." *JRA* 3: 85–109.

———. 1999. *Mosaics of the Greek and Roman World*. Cambridge: Cambridge University Press.

Duncan-Jones, R. 1982. *The Economy of the Roman Empire: Quantitative Studies*. Cambridge: Cambridge University Press.

———. 1996. "The Impact of the Antonine Plague." *JRA* 9: 108–36.

Dunn, J. 1988. *Romans*. Dallas: Word.

Duthoy, R. 1976. "Recherches sur la répartition géographique et chronologique des termes sevir Augustalis, Augustalis et sevir dans l'empire Romain." *EpStud* 11: 143–214.

———. 1978. "Les *Augustales." *ANRW* 2.16.2, 1254–1309.

Ebert, J. 1994. "Die beschriftete Bronzeplatte." In *Bericht über das Forschungsprojekt 'Olympia während der römischen Kaiserzeit und in der Spätantike (III. Die Arbeiten im Jahr 1994)*, 238–41. Edited by U. Sinn, G. Ladstätter, A. Martin, and T. Völling. *Nikephoros* 7: 229–50.

Eck, W. 1970. *Senatoren von Vespasian bis Hadrian: Prosopographische Untersuchungen mit Einschluss des Jahres und Provinzialfasten der Statthalter*. Munich: Beck.

———. 1972. "Die Familie der Volusii Saturnini in neuen Inschriften aus Lucus Feroniae." *Hermes* 100: 461–84.

———. 1994. "Statuendedikanten und Selbstdarstellung in römischen Städten." In *L'Afrique. la Gaule, la Religion à l'époque romaine. Mélanges à la mémoire de Marcel Le Glay (Collection Latomus 226)*, 650–62. Edited by Y. Le Bohec. Brussels: Latomus.

Eco, U. 2004. *Mouse or Rat? Translation As Negotiation*. London: Phoenix.

Edelman, D. 2005. "Excavating the Past: Settlement Patterns and Military Installations in Persian-Era Yehud." In *The Origins of the "Second" Temple: Persian Imperial Policy and the Rebuilding of Jerusalem*, 281–330. Edited by D. Edelman. London: Equinox.

Edelstein, E. J. and L. E. Edelstein. 1945. *Asclepius: Collection and Interpretation of the Testimonies*. Baltimore: Johns Hopkins University.

Edwards, C. M. 1985. "Greek Votive Reliefs to Pan and the Nymphs." Ph.D. diss., New York University.

———. 1990. "Tyche at Corinth." *Hesperia* 59: 529–42.

Egger, E. 1863. *Mémoires d'histoire ancienne et de philologie*. Paris: August Durand.

Eilers, C. 2002. *Roman Patrons of Greek Cities*. Oxford: Oxford University Press.

Elderkin, G. 1939. "The Bee of Artemis." *AJP* 60: 203–13.

———. 1941. "The Natural and Artificial Grotto." *Hesperia* 10: 125–32.

Engberg-Pedersen, T. (ed.). 2001. *Paul Beyond the Judaism/Hellenism Divide*. Louisville: Westminster-John Knox Press.

Engelmann, E. 1993. "Zum Kaiserkult in Ephesos." *ZPE* 97: 279–89.

———. 1995. "Philostrat und Ephesos." *ZPE* 108: 77–87.

Engels, D. 1990. *Roman Corinth: An Alternative Model for the Classical City*. Chicago: University of Chicago Press.

Eriksson, A. 1998. *Traditions as Rhetorical Proof: Pauline Argumentation in 1 Corinthians*. Stockholm: Almqvist & Wiksell International.

Famerie, E. (ed.). 2006. *Jean-Baptiste-Gaspard d'Ansse de Villoison: De l'Hellade à la Grèce. Voyage en Grèce et au Levant (1784–1786)*. Hildesheim: G. Olms.

Faraone, C., and D. Obbink (eds.). 1991. *Magika Hiera: Ancient Greek Magic and Religion*. New York: Oxford University Press.

Faraone, C., and J. L. Rife. 2007. "A Greek Curse against a Thief from the Koutsongila Cemetery at Roman Kenchreai." *ZPE* 160: 141–76.

Farnell, L. R. 1921. *Greek Hero Cults and Ideas of Immortality*. Oxford: Oxford University Press.

Favro, D. 1996. *The Urban Image of Augustan Rome*. Cambridge: Cambridge University Press.

Fedalto, G. 1988. *Hierarchia ecclesiastica orientalis 1*. Padua: Messaggero.

Fee, G. D. 1987. *The First Epistle to the Corinthians*. Grand Rapids: W. B. Eerdmans.

Feeley-Harnick, G. 1994. *The Lord's Table*. Washington: Smithsonian Institution Press.

Fehr, B. 2004. "Aspekte politischer und religiöser Bildsymbolik zur Zeit Hadrians." In *Ikonographie und Ikonologie: interdisziplinäres Kolloquium, Münster 2001: Veröffentlichungen des Sonderforschungsbereichs 493*, 93–123. Edited by W. Hübner and K. Stähler. Münster: Ugarit-Verlag.

Feissel, D. 1981. "Notes d'épigraphie chrétienne, XIV: Dates consulaires à Corinthe." *BCH* 105: 491–98.

———. 1985a. "Inscriptions du IVᵉ au VIᵉ Siècle." *TMByz* 9: 267–98.

———. 1985b. "Bibliographie complémentaire (IVᵉ–VIᵉ)." *TMByz* 9: 358–74.

Fiore, B. 1982. "The Function of Personal Example in the Socratic and Pastoral Epistles." Ph.D. Dissertation, Yale University.

Fiorenza, E. S. 1984. *Bread Not Stone. The Challenge of Feminist Biblical Interpretation*. Boston: Beacon Press.

———. 1992. *But She Said: Feminist Practices of Biblical Interpretation*. Boston: Beacon Press.

Fishwick, D. 1991. *The Imperial Cult in the Latin West*. Leiden: E. J. Brill.

———. 1999. "Coinage and Cult: The Provincial Monuments at Lugdunum, Tarraco and Emerita." In *Roman Coins and Public Life under the Empire*, 95–121. Edited by G. M. Paul and M. Ierardi. Ann Arbor: University of Michigan Press.

———. 2004. *The Imperial Cult in the Latin West: Studies in the Ruler Cult of the Western Provinces of the Roman Empire (III.3: Provincial Cult)*. Leiden: Brill.

Fittà, M. 1997. *Giochi e giocattoli nell'antichità*. Milan: Leonardo Arte.

Fitzmyer, J. A. 1993. *Romans*. New York: Doubleday.

Flower, H. 2006. *The Art of Forgetting: Disgrace and Oblivion in Roman Political Culture*. Chapel Hill: University of North Carolina.

Foerster, G. 1981. "Remains of a Synagogue at Corinth." In *Ancient Synagogue Revealed*, 185. Edited by L. Levine. Jerusalem: Israel Exploration Society.

Foley, H. P. (ed.). 1994. *Homeric Hymn to Demeter: Translation, Commentary, and Interpretive Essays*. Princeton: Princeton University Press.

Forsén, B. 1996. *Griechische Gliederweihungen: Eine Untersuchung zu ihrer Typologie und ihrer religions- und sozialgeschichtlichen Bedeutung.* Helsinki: Papers and Monographs of the Finnish Institute at Athens.

Fossel-Peschl, E. 1982. *Die Basilika am Staatsmarkt in Ephesos.* Graz: E. A. Fossel-Peschl.

Foucault, M. 1980. *Power/Knowledge: Selected Interviews and Other Writings, 1972–1977.* New York: Pantheon.

Frankfurter, D. 1998. *Religion in Roman Egypt: Assimilation and Resistance.* Princeton: Princeton University Press.

——. 2005a. "Beyond Magic and Superstition." In *A People's History of Christianity. Late Antique Christianity,* 255–84. Edited by V. Burrus. Minneapolis: Fortress Press.

Frantz, A. 1965. "From Paganism to Christianity in the Temples of Athens." *DOP* 16: 187–205.

Fraser, P. M., and E. Matthews. 1987. *A Lexicon of Greek Personal Names.* Oxford: Oxford University Press.

Fredrickson, P. 2006. "Mandatory Retirement: Ideas in the Study of Christian Origins Whose Time Has Come to Go." *Studies in Religion/Sciences Religieuses* 35.2: 231–46.

Frier, B. 1999. "Roman Demography." In *Life, Death, and Entertainment in the Roman Empire,* 85–109. Edited by D. S. Potter and D. J. Mattingly. Ann Arbor: University of Michigan Press.

Friesen, S. 1993. *Twice Neokoros: Ephesus, Asia, and the Cult of the Flavian Imperial Family.* Leiden: Brill.

——. 1999. "Ephesian Women and Men in Public Office During the Roman Imperial Period." In *100 Jahre österreichische Forschungen in Ephesos: Akten des Symposions Wien 1995,* 107–13. Edited by H. Friesinger and F. Krinzinger. Vienna: Österreichischen Akademie der Wissenschaften.

——. 2001. *Imperial Cults and the Apocalypse of John: Reading Revelation in the Ruins.* New York: Oxford University Press.

——. 2004. "Poverty in Pauline Studies: Beyond the So-Called New Consensus." *JSNT* 26: 323–61.

——. 2005. "Prospects for a Demography of the Pauline Mission: Corinth among the Churches." In *URRC,* 351–70.

Frothingham, A. 1911. "Medusa, Apollo, and the Great Mother." *AJA* 15: 349–77.

Gagé, J. 1955. *Apollo Romain: Essai sur le culte d'Apollon et le développement du 'ritus Graecus' à Rome des origins à Auguste.* Paris: Bibiotèque des Écoles Françaises d'Athènes et de Rome.

Gager, J. 1992. *Curse Tablets and Binding Spells from the Ancient World.* New York: Oxford University Press.

Gaggiotti, M. 1990. "*Saepinum:* Modi e forme della romanizzazione." In *Basilicata: L'espansionismo romano nel sud-est d'Italia (il quadro archeologico),* 257–61. Edited by M. Salvatore. Venice: Osanna Venosa.

——. 1991. "Nota sulla classe dirigente Sepinate di età Augustea." *Athenaeum* 69: 495–508.

Galinsky, K. 1996. *Augustan Culture: An Interpretive Introduction.* Princeton: Princeton University Press.

Garland, R. 1986. *The Piraeus.* London: Cornell University Press.

Gelzer, M. 1912. *Die Nobilität der römischen Republik.* Leipzig: Teubner.

Garnett, K. S. 1975. "Late Roman Korinthian Lamps from the Fountain of the Lamps." *Hesperia* 44: 173–206.

Garnsey, P. 1999. *Food and Society in Classical Antiquity.* Cambridge: Cambridge University Press.

Geagan, D. 1968. "Notes on the Agonistic Institutions of Roman Corinth." *GRBS* 9: 69–80.

——. 1989. "The Isthmian Dossier of P. Licinius Priscus Iuventianus." *Hesperia* 58: 349–60.

Gebhard, E. R. 1993. "The Isthmian Games and the Sanctuary of Poseidon in the Early Empire." In *The Corinthia in the Roman Period*, 78–94. Edited by T. E. Gregory. Ann Arbor: JRA.

——. 2005. "Rites for Melikertes-Palaimon in the Early Roman Corinthia." In *URRC*, 165–203.

Gebhard, E. R., F. P. Hemans, and J. W. Hayes. 1998. "University of Chicago Excavations at Isthmia, 1989: III." *Hesperia* 67: 405–56.

Gebhard, E. R., and M. W. Dickie. 1995. "Melikertes-Palaimon, Hero of the Isthmian Games." In *Ancient Greek Hero Cult. Proceedings of the Fifth International Seminar on Ancient Greek Cult, Göteborg University (21–23 April 1995)*, 159–65. Edited by Robin Hägg. Stockholm: Swedish Institute in Athens.

——. 2003. "The View from the Isthmus, ca. 200 to 44 B.C." In *Corinth* XX: 261–78.

Georgiades, A. S. 1907. *Les Ports de la Grèce dans l'antiquité qui subsistent encore aujourd'hui*. Athens: N. Tarrousopoulos.

Gianotti, G. F. 1981. "Gli 'anteludia' della processione isiaca in Apuleio." *Civiltà classica e cristiana* 2: 315–31.

Giddens, A. 1979. *Central Problems in Social Theory: Action, Structure, and Contradiction in Social Analysis*. Berkeley: University of California Press.

——. 1984. *The Constitution of Society: Outline of the Theory of Structuration*. Berkeley: University of California Press.

Gill, D. 1989. "Erastus the Aedile." *TynBul* 40: 293–300.

Gilkes, O. 2003. "Luigi Maria Ugolini and the Italian Archaeological Mission to Albania." In *The Theater at Butrint: Luigi Maria Ugolini's Excavations at Butrint (1928–1932)*, 3–23. Edited by O. J. Gilkes. London: British School at Athens.

Gilkes, O. J. (ed.). 2003. *The Theater at Butrint: Luigi Maria Ugolini's Excavations at Butrint (1928–1932)*. London: British School at Athens.

Gilliam, J. F. 1961. "The Plague under Marcus Aurelius." *AJP* 82: 225–51.

Ginouvès, R. 1994. "L'eau dans les sanctuaires médicaux." In *L'eau, la santé et la maladie dans le monde grec*, 237–46. Edited by R. Gionouvès et al. Athens: Bullétin de correspondance hellénique.

Girone, M. 1998. *Ιάματα: Guarigioni miracolose di Asclepio in testi epigrafici*. Bari: Levante.

Giuliani, C. F. and P. Verduchi. 1980. *Foro Romano: L'area centrale*. Florence: Leo S. Olschki.

Glinister, F. 2006. "Reconsidering 'Religious Romanization.'" In *Religion in Republican Italy*, 10–33. Edited by C. E. Schultz and P. B. Harvey, Jr. New Haven: Yale University Press.

Goette, H. R. 1990. "Eine grosse Basis vor dem Dipylon in Athen." *MDAI(A)* 105: 269–78.

Goldhill, S. 2001a. *Being Greek under Rome: Cultural Identity, the Second Sophistic, and the Development of Empire*. Cambridge: Cambridge University Press.

——. 2001b. "Introduction, Setting an Agenda: 'Everything is Greece to the Wise.'" In *Being Greek under Rome: Cultural Identity, the Second Sophistic and the Development of Empire*, 1–25. Edited by S. Goldhill. Cambridge: Cambridge University Press.

Gooch, P. D. 1993. *Dangerous Food: 1 Corinthians 8–10 in Its Context*. Waterloo: Wilfred Laurie University Press.

Gordon, R. 1990. "The Veil of Power." In *Pagan Priests: Religion and Power in the Ancient World*, 201–31. Edited by M. Beard and J. North. Ithaca: Cornell University Press.

Gorissen, P. 1978. "Litterae lunatae." *AncSoc* 9: 149–62.

Gosling, A. 1992. "Political Apollo: From Callimachus to the Augustans." *Mnemosyne* 45: 501–12.

Grace, V. 1934. "Stamped Amphora Handles Found in 1931–1932." *Hesperia* 3: 197–310.

Gradel, I. 2002. *Emperor Worship and Roman Religion.* Oxford: Clarendon Press.

Graf, F. 1992. "Heiligtum und Ritual: das Beispiel der griechisch-römischen Asklepieia." In *Le sanctuaire grec: huit exposés suivis de discussions. Vandœuvres-Genève, 20–25 août 1990 (Entretiens sur l'antiquité classique 37),* 159–203. Edited by A. Schachter. Geneva: Fondation Hardt.

——. 1999. "Ephesische und andere Kureten." In *100 Jahre österreichische Forschungen in Ephesos: Akten des Symposions Wien 1995,* 255–62. Edited by H. Friesinger and F. Krinzinger. Vienna: Österreichischen Akademie der Wissenschaften.

Grandjean, C. 2003. *Les Messéniens de 370/369 au 1er siècle de notre ére.* Paris: Diffusion De Boccard.

Granino Cecere, M. G. 1988. "Trebula Suffenas." In *Supplementum Italica (Nuova seria, vol. 4),* 117–240. Rome: Quasar.

Grant, M. 1950. *Roman Anniversary Issues: An Exploratory Study of the Numismatic and Medallic Commemoration of Anniversary Years.* Cambridge: Cambridge University Press.

Gregory, T. E. 1984. "Diporto: A Byzantine Maritime Settlement in the Gulf of Korinth." *Deltion tes Christianikes Archaiologikes Etaireias* 12: 287–304.

——. 1985. "An Early Byzantine Complex at Akra Sophia near Corinth." *Hesperia* 54: 411–28.

——. 1986a. "Intensive Archaeological Survey and its Place in Byzantine Studies." *ByzSt* 13: 155–75.

——. 1986b. "The Survival of Paganism in Christian Greece: A Critical Essay." *AJP* 107: 229–42.

——. 1993. "*An Early Byzantine (Dark-Age) Settlement at Isthmia: Preliminary Report.*" In *The Corinthia in the Roman Period,* 149–60. Edited by T. E. Gregory. Ann Arbor: JRA.

——. 1995. "The Roman Bath at Isthmia: Preliminary Report 1972–1992." *Hesperia* 64: 279–313.

Gregory, T. E., and P. N. Kardulias. 1990. "Geophysical and Surface Surveys in the Byzantine Fortress at Isthmia." *Hesperia* 59: 467–511.

Gregory, T. E., P. N. Kardulias, and J. Sawmiller. 1995. "Bronze Age and Late Antique Exploitation of an Islet in the Saronic Gulf, Greece." *JFA* 22: 3–21.

Gritsopoulos, T. 1973. Ἐκκλησιαστικὴ Ἱστορία καὶ Χριστιανικὰ Μνημεῖα Κορινθίας 1: Ἱστορία. Athens: Vivliopōleion ho Pan.

Gsell, S., and C. Joly. 1922. *Mdaourouch: Khamissa, Mdaourouch, Announa 2.* Paris: Carbonel.

Guadagno, G. 1983. "*Herculanensium Augustalium Aedes.*" *CronErc* 13: 159–73.

Guarducci, M. 1939. "Intorno ad una iscrizione di Kenchreai." *Epigraphica* 1: 17–20.

——. 1974. *Epigrafia greca III: Epigrafi di carattere privato.* Rome: Istituto poligrafico dello Stato.

Gurval, R. 1995. *Actium and Augustus: The Politics and Emotions of Civil War.* Ann Arbor: University of Michigan.

Gutiérrez, O. 2004. *El teatro romano de Itálica: Estudio arqueoarquitectónico.* Madrid: Servicio de Publicaciones de la Universidad Autónoma de Madrid.

wyn Griffiths, J. 1975. *Apuleius of Madauros: The Isis-Book (Metamorphoses, Book XI).* Leiden: Brill.

alfmann, H. 1982. "Die Senatoren der kleinasiatischen Provinzen." In *Epigrafia e ordine senatorio,* 603–50. Rome: Edizioni di storia e letteratura.

allager, E. 2006. *Videnskab & Kunst.* Athens: The Danish Institute at Athens.

Hallett, C. 2005. *The Roman Nude: Heroic Portrait Statuary 200 B.C.–A.D. 300*. Oxford: Oxford University Press.

Hammond, M. 1957. "Composition of the Senate, A.D. 68–235." *JRS* 47: 74–81.

Hammond, N. 1968. "The Campaign and the Battle of Marathon." *JHS* 88: 13–57.

Hanlein-Schafer, H. 1985. *Veneratio Augusti: eine Studie zu den Tempeln des ersten römischen Kaisers*. Rome: Bretschneider.

Hannestad, N. 1994. *Tradition in Late Antique Sculpture: Conservation, Modernization, Production*. Aarhus: Aarhus University Press.

Hansen, I. L. 2007. "The Trojan Connection: Butrint and Rome." In *Roman Butrint: An Assessment*, 44–61. Edited by I. L. Hansen and R. Hodges. Oxford: Oxbow.

Hansen, I. L., and Richard Hodges (eds.). 2007. *Roman Butrint: An Assessment*. Oxford: Oxbow Books for the Butrint Foundation.

Harland, P. 2003. *Associations Synagogues and Congregations: Claiming a Place in Ancient Mediterranean Society*. Minneapolis: Fortress Press.

Harrison, J. 1899. "Delphica: (A) The Erinyes; (B) The Omphalos." *JHS* 19: 205–51.

Hart, L. 1992. *Time, Religion, and Social Experience in Rural Greece*. Lanham, M.D.: Rowman and Littlefield.

Hartnett, J. 2008. "*Si quis hic sederit*: Streetside Benches and Urban Society in Pompeii." *AJA* 112: 91–119.

Harvey, S. A. 2006. *Scenting Salvation: Ancient Christianity and the Olfactory Imagination*. Berkeley: University of California Press.

Hasenohr, C. 2001. "Les monuments des colleges italiens sur l'"Agora des compétaliastes" à Délos." In *Constructions publiques et programmes édilitaires en Grèce entre le IIe siècle av. J.-C. et le Ier siècle ap. J.-C.*, 329–47. Edited by J.-Y. Marc and J.-C. Moretti. Athens: Ecole française d'Athènes.

Haskell, P. 1980. "Temple E at Corinth: A Re-evaluation." *AJA* 84: 210–11.

Hawthorne, J. 1958. "The Myth of Palaemon." *TAPA* 89: 92–98.

———. 1965. "Cenchreae: Port of Corinth." *Archaeology* 18: 191–299.

Hayes, J. W. 1973. "Roman Pottery from the South Stoa at Corinth." *Hesperia* 42: 416–70.

Head, B. V. 1889. *British Museum Catalog of Greek Coins: Corinth*. London: Longmans and Co.

Hellerman, J. 2005. *Reconstructing Honor in Roman Philippi*: Carmen Christi *as Cursus Pudorum*. Cambridge: Cambridge University Press.

Herbert, S. 1972. "Corinthian Red Figured Pottery." Ph.D. diss., Stanford University.

———. 1986. "The Torch-Race at Corinth." In *Corinthiaca: Studies in Honor of Darrel A. Amyx*, 29–35. Edited by M. Del Chiaro and W. R. Biers. Columbia: University of Missouri Press.

Hill, A. E. 1980. "The Temple of Asclepius: An Alternative Source for Paul's Body Theology?" *JBL* 99: 437–39.

Hill, B. H. 1964. *The Springs. Peirene, Sacred Spring, Glauke*. Princeton, N. J. ASCSA.

Hoare, R. C. 1819. *Classical Tour through Italy and Sicily Tending to Illustrate Some Districts, Which Have Not Been Described by Mr. Eustace, in His Classical Tour*. London: J. Mawman.

Hock, R. 1980. *Tentmaking and Apostleship: The Social Context of Paul's Ministry*. Philadelphia: Fortress Press.

Hoff, M. C. 1996. "The Politics and Architecture of the Athenian Imperial Cult." In *Subject and Ruler: The Cult of the Ruling Power in Classical Antiquity (JRASup 17)*, 185–200. Edited by A. Small. Ann Arbor: JRA.

Hofius, O. 1993. "The Lord's Supper and the Lord's Supper Tradition: Reflections on 1 Corinthians 23b–25." In *One Loaf, One Cup: Ecumenical Studies of 1 Cor and Other Eucharistic Texts*, 75–115. Edited by B. Meyer. Macon, G. A.: Mercer University Press.

Hohlfelder, R. L. 1970. "A Collation of Archaeological and Numismatic Evidence." *Hesperia* 39: 326–31.

——. 1973. "A Sixth Century Hoard from Kenchreai." *Hesperia* 42: 89–101.

——. 1976. "Kenchreai on the Saronic Gulf: Aspects of its Imperial History." *CJ* 71: 217–26.

Højte, J. M. 2005. *Roman Imperial Statue Bases from Augustus to Commodus (Aarhus Studies in Mediterranean Antiquity 7)*. Aarhus: Aarhus University Press.

Holmberg, B. 1980. *Paul and Power: The Structure of Authority in the Primitive Church as Reflected in the Pauline Epistles*. Philadelphia: Fortress Press.

Hood, S. 1970. "Isles of Refuge in the Early Byzantine Period." *ABSA* 65: 37–45.

Hopkins, K. 1983. *Death and Renewal*. Cambridge: Cambridge University Press.

——. 1999. *A World Full of Gods: Pagans, Jews, and Christians in the Roman Empire*. London: Weidenfeld and Nicolson.

Hopkinson, N. 1984. *Callimachus: Hymn to Demeter*. Cambridge: Cambridge University Press.

Hölscher, T. 2003. "Images of War in Greece and Rome: Between Military Practice, Public Memory, and Cultural Symbolism." *JRS* 93: 1–17.

Horrell, D. G. 2004. "Domestic Space and Christian Meetings at Corinth: Imagining New Contexts and the Buildings East of the Theatre." *NTS* 50: 349–69.

——. 2005. *Solidarity and Difference: A Contemporary Reading of Paul's Ethics* London: T & T Clark.

Horsley, G. R. 1981. *New Documents Illustrating Early Christianity*. North Ryde: Macquarie University.

Horsley, R. A. (ed.). 2004. *Hidden Transcripts and the Art of Resistance*. Atlanta: Society of Biblical Literature.

Horsley, R. 2003. "Subverting Disciplines." In *Toward a New Heaven and a New Earth*, 90–105. Edited by F. F. Segovia. Maryknoll: Orbis Books.

——. 2005a. "Unearthing a People's History." In *A People's History of Christianity: Christian Origins*, 1–20. Edited by R. A. Horsley. Minneapolis: Fortress Press.

——. 2005b. "Paul's Assembly in Corinth: An Alternative Society." In *URRC*, 377–81.

Howgego, C. 1989. "After the Colt Has Bolted: A Review of Amandry on Roman Corinth." *NC* 149: 99–208.

Hurd, J. 1965. *The Origin of 1 Corinthians*. London: S. P. C. K.

Hutton, W. 2005a. "The Construction of Religious Space in Pausanias." In *Pilgrimage in Graeco-Roman and Early Christian Antiquity*, 291–317. Edited by J. Elsner and I. Rutherford. Oxford: Oxford University Press.

——. 2005b. *Describing Greece: Landscape and Literature in the* Periegesis *of Pausanias*. Cambridge: Cambridge University Press.

Iaculli, G. 1990. "L'iscrizione pavimentale del foro." In *Iuvanum: Atti del convegno di studi (Chieti, maggio 1983)*, 81–89. Chieti: Solfanelli.

Imhoof-Blumer, F., and P. Gardner. 1885. "Numismatic Commentary on Pausanias I." *JHS* 6: 50–101.

——. 1887. *A Numismatic Commentary on Pausanias*. London: R. Clay.

——. 1923. "Fluß- und Meergötter auf griechischen und römischen Münzen," *RSNum* 23: 173–421.

——. 1964. *Ancient Coins Illustrating Lost Masterpieces of Greek Art: A Numismatic Commentary on Pausanias*. Enlarged edition. Chicago: Argonaut, Inc.

Irmsher, J. 1981. "Paganismus im justinianischen Reich." *Klio* 63: 683–88.

Ivison, E. A. 1996. "Burial and Urbanism at Late Antique and Early Byzantine Corinth (c. AD 400–700)." In *Towns in Transition: Urban Evolution in Late Antiquity and the Early Middle Ages*, 99–125. Edited by N. Christie and S. Loseby. Aldershot: Scholar Press.

Jacob-Felsch, M. 1969. *Die Entwicklung griechischer Statuenbasen und die Aufstellung der Statuen*. Bayern: Stiftland-Verlag.

Janowitz, N. 2001. *Magic in the Roman World: Pagans, Jews and Christians.* New York: Routledge.

Jeffery, L. 1961. *The Local Scripts of Archaic Greece: A Study of the Origin of the Greek Alphabet and Its Development from the Eighth to Fifth Centuries B.C.* Oxford: Clarendon Press.

Jewett, R. 2007. *Romans: A Commentary.* Minneapolis: Fortress.

Jobst, W. 1980. "Zur Lokalisierung des Sebasteion-Augusteum in Ephesos." *IstMitt* 30: 241–60.

Jones, A. H. M. 1964 (= 1986). *The Later Roman Empire, 284–602: A Social, Economic and Administrative Survey.* Two volumes. Oxford: Oxford University Press.

Jones, C. 2005. "Ten Dedications: 'To the Gods and Goddesses' and the Antonine Plague." *JRA* 18: 293–301.

Jones, H. L. 1949. *The Geography of Strabo.* Cambridge: Harvard University Press.

Jongmann, W. M. 2007. "The Early Roman Empire: Consumption." In *The Cambridge Economic History of the Greco-Roman World*, 592–618. Edited by W. Scheidel, I. Morris, and R. Saller. Cambridge: Cambridge University Press.

Jordan, D. 1985. "A Selection of Greek *Defixiones* Not Included in the Special Corpora." *GRBS* 26: 151–97.

———. 1994. "Inscribed Lamps from a Cult at Corinth in Late Antiquity." *HTR* 87: 223–29.

———. 2000. "New Greek Curse Tablets (1985–2000)." *GRBS* 41: 5–46.

Jordan, D., H. Montgomery and E. Thomassen (eds.). 1999. *The World of Ancient Magic: Papers from the first International Samson Eitrem Seminar at the Norwegian Institute at Athens, 4–8 May 1997.* Bergen: The Norwegian Institute at Athens.

Jouanna, J. 1999. *Hippocrates.* Translated by M. B. DeBevoise. Baltimore: Johns Hopkins University Press.

Kajanto, I. 1965. *The Latin Cognomina.* Helsinki: Helsingfors.

Kalinowski, A. 2002. "The Vedii Antonini: Aspects of Patronage and Benefaction in Second-Century Ephesos." *Phoenix* 56: 109–49.

Kanellopoulos, C. 2000. *Το υστερορομαϊκό "τείχος": περίβολος τεμένους και περιμετρική στοά στο Ασκληπιείο της Επιδαύρου.* Athens.

Kajava, M. 2002. "When Did the Isthmian Games Return to the Isthmus? (Rereading Corinth 8.3.153)." *CP* 97: 168–78.

Kardulias, P. N. 1995. "Architecture, Energy, and Social Evolution at Isthmia, Greece: Some Thoughts about Late Antiquity in the Korinthia." *JMA* 8: 33–59.

———. 2005. *From Classical to Byzantine: Social Evolution in Late Antiquity and the Fortress at Isthmia, Greece.* Oxford: Archaeopress.

Karivieri, A. 1996. *The Athenian Lamp Industry in Late Antiquity (Papers and Monographs of the Finnish Institute at Athens 5).* Helsinki: Finnish Institute at Athens.

Kearsley, R. A. 1999. "Women in Public Life in the Roman East: Iunia Theodora, Claudia Metrodora and Phoebe, Benefactress of Paul." *TynBul* 50: 189–211.

Kent, J. H. 1952. "The Victory Monument of Timoleon at Corinth." *Hesperia* 21: 9–18.

Kim, C.-H. 1975. "The Papyrus Invitation." *JBL* 94: 393–94.

Klauck, H.-J. 1993. "Presence in the Lord's Supper: 1 Corinthians 11:23–26 in the Context of Hellenistic Religious History." In *One Loaf, One Cup: Ecumenical Studies of 1 Cor 11 and Other Eucharistic Texts*, 57–74. Edited by B. Meyer. Macon, G. A.: Mercer University Press.

Knibbe, D. 1981. *Der Staatsmarkt: die Inschriften des Prytaneions.* Vienna: Österreichischen Akademie der Wissenschaften.

———. 1999. "Via Sacra Ephesiaka." In *100 Jahre österreichische Forschungen in Ephesos. Akten des Symposions Wien 1995*, 449–54. Edited by H. Friesinger and F. Krinzinger. Vienna: Österreichischen Akademie der Wissenschaften.

Knibbe, D. and G. Langmann (eds.). 1993. *Via Sacra Ephesiaca.* Vienna: Schindler.

Knibbe, D. and H. Thür (eds.). 1995. *Via Sacra Ephesiaca: Grabungen und Forschungen 1992 und 1993*. Vienna: Schindler.

Knoepfler, D., and M. Piérart (eds.). 2001. *Editer, traduire, commenter Pausanias en l'an 2000 (Actes du colloque de Neuchâtel et de Fribourg, 18–22 septembre 1998)*. Geneva: Université de Neuchâtel.

Kockel, V. 1983. *Die Grabbauten vor dem Herkulaner Tor in Pompeji*. Mainz: Philipp von Zabern.

Koester, H. (ed.). 1995. *Ephesos, Metropolis of Asia: An Interdisciplinary Approach to its Archaeology, Religion, and Culture*. HTS 41. Valley Forge, PA: Trinity Press International.

———. (ed.). 1998. *Pergamon, Citadel of the Gods: Archaeological Record, Literary Description, and Religious Development*. HTS 46. Harrisburg, PA: Trinity Press International.

———. 1999. "Melikertes at Isthmia: A Roman Mystery Cult." In *Greeks, Romans, and Christians: Essays in Honor of Abraham J. Malherbe*, 355–66. Edited by D. Balch, E. Ferguson, and W. Meeks. Minneapolis: Fortress.

König, J. 2001. "Favorinus' *Corinthian Oration* in its Corinthian Context." *PCPhS* 47: 141–71.

Kopestonsky, T. 2009. "Kokkinovrysi: A Classical Shrine to the Nymphs at Corinth." Ph.D. diss., The State University of New York at Buffalo.

Kordosis, M. 1981. Συμβολὴ στὴν Ἱστορία καὶ Τοπογραφία τῆς Περιοχῆς Κορίνθου στοὺς Μέσους Χρόνους. Athens.

Kountoura-Galaki, E. 1996. "Η ‘Εἰκονοκλαστική’ *Notitia 3* και το Λατινικό Πρότυπο της." *Σύμμεικτα* 10: 45–73.

Kraft, J. Í., Kayan, H. Brückner and G. Rapp. 2000. "A Geologic Analysis of Ancient Landscapes and the Harbors of Ephesus and the Artemision in Anatolia." *JOAI* 69: 175–210.

Kraynak, L. H. 1992. "The Basilica." In *Nemea I: Excavations at Nemea, Topographical and Architectural Studies*, 99–187. Edited by S. G. Miller. Berkeley: University of California Press.

Kreikenbom, D. 1992. *Griechische und römische Kolossalporträts bis zum späten ersten Jahrhundert nach Christus*. Berlin and New York: Walter de Gruyter.

Kristalli-Votsi, K. 1984. "Ἐφορεία Κλασσικῶν Ἀρχαιοτήτων Ναυπλίου· Νόμος Κορινθίας, Κεγχρεές." *ArchDelt* 31: 64–65.

Lahusen, G. 1982. "Zur Funktion und Bedeutung der Ehrenstatuen für Privatpersonen in Rom." *Jahresinhaltsverzeichnis der wissenschaftlichen Zeitschrift der Humboldt-Universität zu Berlin* 31: 239–41.

Laird, M. 2000. "Reappraising the so-called 'Sede degli Augustali' at Ostia." *MAAR* 45: 41–84.

———. 2002. "Evidence in Context: The Public and Funerary Monuments of the *seviri Augustales* at Ostia." Ph.D. diss, Princeton University.

———. 2006. "Private Memory and Public Interest: Municipal Identity in Imperial Italy." In *The Art of Citizens, Soldiers and Freedmen in the Roman World: An Illustrated Anthology*, 31–43. Edited by E. D'Ambra and G. P. R. Métraux. Oxford: Archeopress.

Lamberton, R. 1986. *Homer the Theologian: Neoplatonist Allegorical Reading and the Growth of the Epic Tradition*. Berkeley: University of California Press.

Lambrinoudakis, V. 2002. "Conservation and Research: New Evidence on a Long-living Cult. The Sanctuary of Apollo Maleatas and Asklepios at Epidauros." In *Excavating Classical Culture: Recent Archaeological Discoveries in Greece*, 213–24. Edited by M. Stamatopoulou and M. Yaroulanou. Oxford: Beazley Archive and Archaeopress.

Lampe, G. 1961. *A Patristic Greek Lexicon*. Oxford: Clarendon Press.

Lampe, P. 2003. *From Paul to Valentinus: Christians at Rome in the First Two Centuries*. Minneapolis: Fortress.

Lampakis, G. 1907. "Χριστιανικαὶ Κεγχρεαί. Τοπογραφία τῶν Κεγχρεῶν." In *Miscellanea di archeologia, storia e filologia dedicata a Professore Antonio Salinas nel XL anniversario del suo insegnamento accademico*, 71–80. Palermo: Virzi.

Lanci, J. 2005. "The Stones Don't Speak and the Texts Tell Lies: Sacred Sex at Corinth." In *URRC*, 205–20.

Landon, M. E. 1994. "Contributions to the Study of the Water Supply of Ancient Corinth." Ph.D. diss., University of California, Berkeley.

——. 2003. "Beyond Peirene: Toward a Broader View of Corinthian Water Supply." In *Corinth XX*, 43–62.

Lang, M. 1977. *Cure and Cult in Ancient Corinth: A Guide to the Askelpieion*. Princeton: ASCSA.

Lapenna, S. 2006. "Il foro." In *Iuvanum: l'area archeologica*, 67–71. Edited by S. Lapenna. Sulmona, Italy: Synapsi.

Larsen, J. 1938. "Roman Greece." In *An Economic Survey of Ancient Rome*, 258–498. Edited by T. Frank. Baltimore: Johns Hopkins Press.

Lattanzi, E. 1998. "L'attività archeologica in Calabria nel 1995." In *Eredità della Magna Grecia: Atti del trentacinquesimo convegno di studi sulla Magna Grecia, Taranto (6–10 ottobre 1995)*, 673–90. Taranto: Istituto per la storia e l'archeologia della Magna Grecia.

Lauer, J., and C. Picard. 1955. *Les Statues ptolémaïques du Serapieion de Memphis*. Paris: Presses universitaires de France.

Laurence, R., and J. Berry. 1998. *Cultural Identity in the Roman Empire*. London: Routledge.

Laurent, J. 1899. "Delphes chrétiennes." *BCH* 23: 206–79.

Lawall, M. L. 2005. "Amphoras and Hellenistic Economies: Addressing the (Over)emphasis on Stamped Amphora Handles." In *Making, Moving and Managing: The New World of Ancient Economies, 323–31 BC*, 188–232. Edited by Z. Archibald, J. K. Davies and V. Gabrielsen. Oxford: Oxbow.

Lawrence, L. 2005. *Reading with Anthropology: Exhibiting Aspects of New Testament Religion*. Waynesboro, GA Paternoster Press.

Leader-Newby, R. 2005. "Personifications and *Paideia* in Late Antique Mosaics from the Greek East." In *Personification in the Greek World: From Antiquity to Byzantium*, 231–46. Edited by E. Stafford and J. Herrin. Aldershot: Ashgate.

Leake, W. M. 1830. *Travels in the Morea*. London: J. Murray.

Lefantzis, M. and J. T. Jensen. 2009. "The Athenian Asklepieion on the South Slope of the Akropolis I: Early Development, ca. 420–360 B.C." In *Aspects of Ancient Greek Cult: Context, Ritual, Iconography*. Edited by J. Jensen, G. Hinge, P. Schultz, and B. Wickkiser. Aarhus: Aarhus University.

Lefebvre, H. 1991. *The Production of Space*. Translated by D. Nicholson-Smith. Oxford: Blackwell.

Lehmann-Hartleben, K. 1923. *Die antike Hafenanlagen des Mittelmeeres*. Leipzig: Dieterich.

Leipoldt, J. and K. Regling. 1925. "Archäologisches zur Isis-Religion." *Angelos* 1, 126–30.

Levick, B. 1967. *Roman Colonies in Southern Asia Minor*. Oxford: Clarendon.

——. 1990. *Claudius*. New Haven: Yale University Press.

LiDonnici, L. R. 1995. *The Epidaurian Miracle Inscriptions: Text, Translation, and Commentary*. Atlanta: Society of Biblical Literature.

Limberis, V. 2002. "Ecclesiastical Ambiguities: Corinth in the Fourth and Fifth Centuries." In *URRC*, 443–57.

Lintott, A. 1990. "Electoral Bribery in the Roman Republic." *JRS* 80: 1–16.

——. 1993. *Imperium Romanum: Politics and Administration*. London: Routledge.

Lisle, R. 1955. "The Cults of Corinth." Ph.D. diss., Johns Hopkins University.

Lloyd Jones, H. 1983. "Artemis and Iphigeneia." *JHS* 103: 87–102.

Lomas, K., and T. Cornell. 2003. *Bread and Circuses: Euergetism and Municipal Patronage in Roman Italy.* London: Routledge.

Lorsch, R. S. 1997. "Augustus' Conception and the Heroic Tradition." *Latomus* 56: 790–99.

Lotman, J., *et al.* 1975. "Theses on the Semiotic Study of Cultures (as Applied to Slavic Texts)." In *The Tell-Tale Sign: A Survey of Semiotics,* 57–84. Edited by T. A. Sebeok. Lisse: Peter de Ridder Press.

Lozano, F. 2004. "*Thea Livia* in Athens: Redating *IG²* II 3242." *ZPE* 148: 177–80.

Luraghi, N. 2002. "Becoming Messenian." *JHS* 122: 45–69.

MacDonald, C. 1976. *Cicero: In Catilinam I–IV, Pro Murena, Pro Sulla, Pro Flacco.* Cambridge: Harvard University Press.

MacDowall, D. 1965. "The Byzantine Coin Hoard Found at Isthmia." *Archaeology* 18: 264–67.

MacMullen, R. 1981. *Paganism in the Roman Empire.* New Haven: Yale University Press.

———. 1982. "The Epigraphic Habit in the Roman Empire." *AJP* 103: 233–46.

Maderna, C. 1988. *Iuppiter Diomedes und Merkur als Vorbilder für römische Bildnisstatuen (Archäologie und Geschicht 1).* Heidelberg: Archäologie und Geschichte.

Magie, D. 1950. *Roman Rule in Asia Minor to the End of the Third Century.* Princeton: Princeton University Press.

Majno, G. 1975. *The Healing Hand: Man and Wound in the Ancient World.* Cambridge: Harvard University Press.

Malherbe, A. 1983. *The Social Aspects of Early Christianity.* Second edition. Philadelphia: Fortress Press.

Mallwitz, A. 1972. *Olympia und seine Bauten.* Munich: Prestel-Verlag.

———. 1988. "Olympia und Rom." *Antike Welt* 19: 21–45.

Mallwitz, A., and W. Schiering. 1964. *Die Werkstatt des Pheidias in Olympia (Olympische Forschungen 5).* Berlin: De Gruyter.

Malina, B. 1986. "'Religion' in the World of Paul." *BTB* 16: 92–101.

Malina, B., and J. Pilch. 2005. *Social-Science Commentary on the Letters of Paul.* Minneapolis: Fortress Press.

Marlowe, E. 2006. "Framing the Sun: The Arch of Constantine and the Roman Cityscape." *ArtB* 88: 223–43.

Marquardt, N. 1995. *Pan in der hellenistischen und kaiserzeitlichen Plastik.* Bonn: Habelt.

Martin, D. 1995. *The Corinthian Body.* New Haven: Yale University Press.

Martin, L. 1994. "The Anti-Individualistic Ideology of Hellenistic Culture." *Numen* 41: 117–40.

Martin, T. 1977. "Inscriptions at Corinth." *Hesperia* 46: 178–98.

Marty, J. 1993. "Three Pottery Deposits and the History of Roman Isthmia." In *The Corinthia in the Roman Period,* 115–29. Edited by T. E. Gregory. Ann Arbor: JRA.

Mason, H. J. 1974. *Greek Terms for Roman Institutions: A Lexicon and Analysis.* Toronto: Hakkert.

Masuzawa, T. 2000. "The Production of 'Religion' and the Task of the Scholar: Russell McCutcheon among the Smiths." *Culture and Religion* 1: 123–30.

Matthews, J. F. 2000. *Laying Down the Law: A Study of the Theodosian Code.* New Haven: Yale University.

McDonald, W. A., and G. R. Rapp (eds.). 1972. *The Minnesota Messenia Expedition.* Minneapolis: University of Minnesota Press.

McDonnell, M. 1986. "*Ambitus* and Plautus' *Amphitruo* 65–81." *AJP* 107: 564–76.

McGowen, A. 1999. *Ascetic Eucharist: Food and Drink in Early Christian Ritual Meals.* Oxford: Clarendon Press.

McLean, B. H. 2002. *An Introduction to Greek Epigraphy of the Hellenistic and Roman Periods from Alexander the Great down to the Reign of Constantine (323 B.C.–A.D. 337)*. Ann Arbor: University of Michigan Press.

McPhee, I. 1981. "Red-Figured Pottery from Corinth: Sacred Spring and Elsewhere." *Hesperia* 50: 264–84.

Meeks, W. 1983. *The First Urban Christians*. New Haven: Yale University Press.

Meeks, W., and J. T. Fitzergald (eds.). 2007. *The Writings of St. Paul: Annotated Texts, Reception and Criticism*. Second edition. New York: W.W. Norton.

Meggitt, J. J. 1996. "The Social Status of Erastus (Rom 16: 23)." *NovT* 38: 218–23.

——. 1998. *Paul, Poverty and Survival*. Edinburgh: T & T Clark.

Melfi, M. 2007a. "The Sanctuary of Asclepius." In *Roman Butrint: An Assessment*, 17–32. Edited by I. L. Hansen and R. Hodges. Oxford: Oxbow.

——. 2007b. *I santuari di Asclepio in Grecia*. Rome: L'Erma di Bretschneider.

Merker, G. 2000. *The Sanctuary of Demeter and Kore: Terracotta Figurines of the Classical, Hellenistic, and Roman Periods*. Princeton: American School of Classical Studies.

——. 2003. "Corinthian Terracotta Figurines: The Development of an Industy." In *Corinth XX*, 233–45. Edited by C. K. Williams and N. Bookidis. Princeton: ASCSA.

Metcalf, D. 1962. "The Slavonic Threat to Greece circa 580: Some Evidence from Athens." *Hesperia* 31: 134–57.

Metzger, M. 1985. *Les Constitutions apostoliques 1 (Sources chrétiennes 320)*. Paris: Editions du Cerf.

Meyer, E. 1990. "Explaining the Epigraphic Habit in the Roman Empire: The Evidence of Epitaphs." *JRS* 80: 74–96.

Meyer, M. *et al.* (eds.). 1994. *Ancient Christian Magic: Coptic Texts of Ritual Power*. San Francisco: Harper San Francisco.

Meyers, C. 2005. *Households and Holiness: The Religious Culture of Israelite Women*. Minneapolis: Fortress Press.

Mikalson, J. D. 2005. *Ancient Greek Religion*. Malden, MA: Blackwell.

Millar, F. 1981. "The World of the *Golden Ass*." *JRS* 71: 63–7.

——. 1984. "The Political Character of the Classical Roman Republic, 200–151 B.C." *JRS* 74: 1–19.

——. 1986. "Politics, Persuasion and the Plebs before the Social War." *JRS* 76: 1–11.

——. 1989. "Political Power in Mid-Republican Rome: Curia or Comitium?" *JRS* 79: 138–50.

——. 1998. *The Crowd in Rome in the Late Republic*. Ann Arbor: University of Michigan Press.

Miller, J. 2004. "Propertian Reception of Virgil's Actian Apollo." *Materiali e discussioni per l'analisi dei testi classici* 52: 73–84.

Miller, S. 1972. "A Mosaic Floor from a Roman Villa at Anaploga." *Hesperia* 41: 332–54.

Milleker, E. 1985. "Three Heads of Sarapis from Corinth." *Hesperia* 54: 121–36.

Millis, B. 2004. "Work on Corinth Guide Progresses." *Akoue: The Newsletter of ASCSA* 51: 4–16.

——. 2006. "'Miserable Huts' in Post-146 B.C. Corinth." *Hesperia* 75: 397–404.

Milne, J. G. 1925. "The *Kline* of Sarapis." *JEA* 11: 6–9.

Miltner, F. 1959. "22. Vorläufiger Bericht." *JOAI* 44: 243–314.

Miniero, P. (ed.). 2000. *The Sacellum of the Augustales at Miseno*. Naples: Electa Napoli.

Mitchell, L. 2001. "Euboean Io." *CQ* 51: 339–52.

Mitchell, M. 1991. *Paul and the Rhetoric of Reconciliation: An Exegetical Investigation of the Language and Composition of 1 Corinthians*. Louisville: Westminster-John Knox Press.

Mitchell, S. and M. Waelkens. 1998. *Pisidian Antioch: The Site and Its Monuments.* London: Duckworth.

Mithen, S. 2001. "Archaeological Theory and Theories of Cognitive Evolution." In *Archaeological Theory Today,* 98–121. Edited I. Hodder. Cambridge: Blackwell.

Mitsopoulos-Leon, V. 1991. *Die Basilika am Staatsmarkt in Ephesos: Kleinfunde.* Vienna: Schindler.

Mitsopoulos-Leon, V. and C. Lang-Auinger. 2007. *Die Basilika am Staatsmarkt in Ephesos: Funde der klassischen bis römischen Zeit.* Vienna: Schindler.

Mitsos, M. 1936. "'Επιγραφαι ἐξ Ἀρκαδίας, Ἐπιδαυρίας και Κορινθίας." *ArchEph:* 136–46.

Mollo, S. 1997. "L'Augustalità a Brescia." *Atti della Accademia Nazionale dei Lincei* 9.8: 267–367.

Monceaux, P. 1884. "Fouilles et récherches archéologiques au sanctuaire des jeux isthmiques." *GazArch* 9: 273–85; 354–63.

———. 1885. "Fouilles et récherches archéologiques au sanctuaire des jeux isthmiques." *GazArch* 10: 205–14; 402–12.

Moo, D. J. 1996. *The Epistle to the Romans.* Grand Rapids: Eerdmans.

Moore, A. 1977. *Iconography of Religions: An Introduction.* Philadelphia: Fortress.

Moorhead, S., S. Gjongecaj, and R. Abdy. 2007. "Coins from the Excavations at Butrint, Diaporit and the Vrina Plain." In *Roman Butrint: An Assessment,* 78–94. Edited by I. L. Hansen and R. Hodges. Oxford: Oxbow.

Morgan, C. H. 1937. "Excavations at Corinth, 1936–37." *AJA* 41: 539–52.

Morricone, L. 1986. "Le iscrizioni del teatro di Butrinto." *La Parola del Passato* 41: 161–425.

Mouritsen, H. 1997. "Mobility and Social Change in Italian Towns during the Principate." In *Roman Urbanism: Beyond the Consumer City,* 59–82. Edited by H. M. Parkins. London and New York: Routledge.

Moutzale, A. 1984. "Ἅγιος Βασίλειος." *ArchDelt* 39: 109–10.

Moyer, I. Forthcoming. "Carnival in Cenchreae: Ritual and Interpretation in Apuleius *Metamorphoses* 11.8–17."

Mueller, J. G. 2004. *L'Ancien Testament dans l'ecclésiologie des pères: Une lecture des Constitutions apostoliques.* Turnhout: Brepols.

Murphy-O'Connor, J. 1997. *Paul: A Critical Life.* Oxford: Oxford University Press.

———. 2002. *St. Paul's Corinth: Text and Archaeology.* Third edition. Collegeville, MN: Liturgical Press.

Musial, D. 1992. *Le développement du culte d'Esculape au monde romain.* Translated by I. Woszczyk. Torun: Nicolaus Copernicus University.

Musti, E., and M. Torelli. 1986. *Pausanias: Guida della Grecia II (La Corinzia e l'Argolide).* Milan: Fondazione Lorenzo Valla.

Nanos, M. 2002. "What Was at Stake in Peter's 'Eating with Gentiles.'" In *The Galatians Debate,* 282–318. Edited by M. Nanos. Peabody, MA: Hendrickson.

Nasrallah, L., C. Bakirtzis, and S. J. Friesen. 2010. *From Roman to Early Christian Thessalonikê: Studies in Religion and Archaeology.* HTS. Cambridge, MA: Harvard University Press.

Newton, D. 1998. *Deity and Diet: The Dilemma of Sacrificed Food at Corinth.* Sheffield: Sheffield Academic Press, 1998.

Nilsson, M. 1940. *Greek Folk Religion.* Philadelphia: University of Pennsylvania Press.

———. 1952. *Dionysos Liknites (Bulletin de la Société royale des lettres de Lund 1951– 1952, 1).* Lund: Gleerup.

———. 1957. *The Dionysiac Mysteries of the Hellenistic and Roman Age.* Lund: Gleerup.

———. 1960. "Roman and Greek Domestic Cult." In *Opuscula Selecta,* 271–85. Edited by M. Nilsson. Lund: Gleerup.

Nixon, P. 1938. *Plautus*. Cambridge: Harvard University Press.

Noy, D. 2000. *Foreigners at Rome: Citizens and Strangers*. London: Duckworth.

Nutton, V. 2005. *Ancient Medicine*. London and New York: Routledge.

Oakes, P. 2004. "Constructing Poverty Scales for Graeco-Roman Society: A Response to Steven Friesen's 'Poverty in Pauline Studies.'" *JSNT* 26: 367–71.

O'Brien, J. V. 1993. *The Transformation of Hera: A Study of Ritual, Hero, and the Goddess in the* Iliad. Lanham: Rowman and Littlefield.

Ogden, D. 2001. *Greek and Roman Necromancy*. Princeton: Princeton University Press.

——. 2002. Magic, *Witchcraft, and Ghosts in the Greek and Roman Worlds*. New York: Oxford University Press.

Oikonomidou, M. K. 1975. *Η Νομισματοκοπία της Νικοπόλεως*. Athens: Bibliotheke tes en Athenais Arkhaiologikes Etaireias.

Økland, J. 2004. *Women in Their Place: Paul and the Corinthian Discourse of Gender and Sanctuary Space*. New York: T & T Clark.

Økland, J., and R. Boer. 2008. "Towards Marxist Feminist Biblical Criticism." In *Marxist Feminist Criticism of the Bible*, 1–25. Edited by R. Boer and J. Økland. Sheffield: Sheffield Phoenix Press.

Oliver, G. J. (ed.). 2000. *The Epigraphy of Death: Studies in the History and Society of Greece and Rome*. Liverpool: Liverpool University Press.

Oliver, J. H. 1970. *Marcus Aurelius: Aspects of Civic and Cultural Policy in the East*. Princeton: Princeton University Press.

——. 1978. "Panachaeans and Panhellenes." *Hesperia* 47: 185–91.

Orlandos, A. K. 1935. "Ἡ 'βασιλικὴ' τῶν Κεγχρεῶν." *Praktika tes Akadimias Athinon* 10: 55–57.

——. 1936. "Délos chrétienne." *BCH* 60: 68–100.

——. 1952. *Η Ξυλόστεγος Παλαιοχριστιανική Βασιλική*. Two volumes. Athens: Athens Archaeological Society.

Orr, W., and J. A. Walther. 1976. *I Corinthians: A New Translation*. Garden City, NY: Doubleday.

Osanna, M. 2001. "Tra monumenti, *agalmata* e *mirabilia*: Organizzazione del percorso urbano di Corinto nella *Periegesi* di Pausania." In *Editer, traduire, commenter Pausanias en l'an 2000 (Actes du colloque de Neuchâtel et de Fribourg, 18–22 septembre 1998)*, 185–202. Edited by D. Knoepfler and M. Pierart. Geneva: Université de Neuchâtel.

Osiek, J., and M. MacDonald. 2006. *A Woman's Place: House Churches in Earliest Christianity*. Minneapolis, MN: Augsburg Fortress.

Ostenfeld, E. N. (ed.). 2002. *Greek Romans and Roman Greeks: Studies in Cultural Interaction*. Aarhus: Aarhus University Press.

Ostrow, S. 1990. "The *Augustales* in the Augustan Scheme." In *Between Republic and Empire: Interpretations of Augustus and His Principate*, 364–79. Edited by K. A. Raaflaub and M. Toher. Berkeley: University of California Press.

Oulton, J. E. 1980. *Eusebius: Ecclesiastical History*. Loeb Classical Library. Cambridge: Harvard University Press.

Page, D. L. 1981. *Further Greek Epigrams*. Cambridge: Cambridge University Press.

Pallas, D. I., S. Charitonides, and J. Venencie. 1959. "Inscriptions lyciennes trouvées a Solômos près de Corinthe." *BCH* 83: 496–508.

Pallas, D. I. and S. Dantis. 1977. "Ἐπιγραφὲς ἀπὸ τὴν Κόρινθο." *ArchEph* 61–85.

Pallas, D. 1955. "Ἀνασκαφὴ Ρωμαϊκῆς επαύλεως παρά την Κόρινθον." *Πρακτικά της εν Αθήναις Αρχαιολογικής Εταιρείας*: 210–16.

——. 1957. "Πρωτοχριστιανικὴ Κόρινθος." *Peloponnesiaki Protochronia* 1957: 52–62.

——. 1959. "Scoperte archeologiche in Grecia negli anni 1956–1958." *RAC* 35: 187–223

——. 1961. "Ἀνασκαφὴ ἐν Λεχαίῳ. Τὸ Βαπτιστήριον τῆς παλαιοχριστιανικῆ βασιλικῆς." *Prakt.* (1956): 37–154.

——. 1967. "Ἀνασκαφικαὶ ἔρευναι ἐν Λεχαίῳ." *Prakt.* (1965) 135–66.

——. 1975. "Investigations sur les monuments chrétiens de Grèce avant Constantin." *Cahiers archéologiques* 24: 1–19.

——. 1977. *Les monuments paléochrétiens de grèce découverts de 1959 à 1973.* Vatican: Pontificio istituto di archeologia cristiana.

——. 1980. "Ἀνασκαφὴ τῆς βασιλικῆς τοῦ Κρανείου ἐκ Κορίνθου." *Prakt.* (1977): 162–183.

——. 1987–89. "Ἡ Βασιλικὴ τῶν Κεγχρεῶν." *EEBS* 47: 295–309.

Papaioannou, S. 2006. "'[O]pus est ... Apolline nato': Liminality and Closure in the Aesculapius Episode in *Metamorphoses* 15.626–744." *CetM* 57: 125–56.

Papathomas, A. 1997. "Das agonistische Motiv 1 Kor 9:24ff. im Spiegel zeitgenossischer dokumentarischer Quellen." *NTS* 43: 223–41.

Papostolou, J. A. 1986. "Aedes Augustalium à Patras." *Dodone* 15: 261–84.

Parker, R. 2005. *Polytheism and Society at Athens.* Oxford: Oxford University Press.

Parrish, D. 2001. "Introduction: The Urban Plan and Its Constituent Parts." In *Urbanism in Western Asia Minor: New Studies on Aphrodisias, Ephesos, Hierapolis, Pergamon, Perge and Xanthos,* 9–41. Edited by D. Parrish. Portsmouth, R.I.: *JRA.*

Patterson, J. R. 2007. "A Dedication to Minerva Augusta from Butrint." In *Roman Butrint: An Assessment,* 40–43. Edited by I. L. Hansen and R. Hodges. Oxford: Oxbow.

Payne, H. 1931. *Necrocorinthia: A Study of Corinthian Art in the Archaic Period.* Oxford: Clarendon Press.

Pease, M. 1937. "A Well of the Late Fifth Century at Corinth." *Hesperia* 6: 257–316.

Peek, W. 1988. *Greek Verse Inscriptions: Epigrams on Funerary Stelae and Monuments.* Chicago: Ares Publications, Inc.

Penn, R. 1994. *Medicine on Ancient Greek and Roman Coins.* London: Seaby.

Peppers, J. M. 1978. "The Nymphs at Poseidon's Sanctuary." In *Hommages à Maarten J. Vermaseren (2),* 931–37. Edited by M. D. De Boer and T. Eldridge. Leiden: Brill.

——. 1979. "Selected Roman Pottery, Isthmia Excavations." PhD diss., University of Pennsylvania.

Perrin, B. 1982–90. *Plutarch's Lives.* Ten volumes. Cambridge: Harvard University Press.

Petersen, L. H. 2006. *The Freedman in Roman Art and Art History.* Cambridge: Cambridge University Press.

Petridis, P. 1997. "Delphes dans l'antiquité tardive: première approche topographique et céramologique." *BCH* 121: 681–95.

Pettegrew, D. K. 2006. "Corinth on the Isthmus: Studies of the End of an Ancient Landscape." Ph.D. diss., Ohio State University.

——. 2007. "The Busy Countryside of Late Roman Corinth: Ceramic Data, Source Analysis, and Regional Settlement Patterns." *Hesperia* 76: 743–84.

Pfaff, C. 2003. "Archaic Corinthian Architecture ca. 600–480 B.C." In *Corinth XX,* 95–140.

Pfitzner, V. C. 1967. *Paul and the Agon Motif: Traditional Athletic Imagery in the Pauline Literature (NovTSup 16).* Leiden: Brill.

Phillips, C., III. 2000. "Ancient Roman Religion in the Late 1990s." *RSR* 26: 140–45.

Phougias, M. G. 1997. *Ἱστορία τῆς Ἀποστολικῆς Ἐκκλησίας Κορίνθου ἀπ Ἀρχῆς μέχρι Σήμερον.* Second edition. Athens: "Nea Synora" Ekdotikos Organismos Livanē.

Pierart, M. 1998. "Panthéon et hellénisation dans la colonie romaine de Corinthe: La redécouverte du culte de Palaimon à l'Isthme." *Kernos* 11: 19–330.

Pipili, M. 1987. *Laconian Iconography of the Sixth Century B.C.* Oxford: Oxbow.

Plekett, H. W. 1985. Review of Meeks 1983. *VC* 39: 192–96.

Pojani, I. 2007. "The Monumental Togate Statue from Butrint." In *Roman Butrint: An Assessment,* 62–77. Edited by I. L. Hansen and R. Hodges. Oxford: Oxbow.

Popović, V. 1975. "Les témoins archéologiques des invasions avaro-slaves dans l'Illyricum byzantin." *MEFRA* 87: 445–504.

Popper, K. 2002. *Conjectures and Refutations: The Growth of Scientific Knowledge*. London: Routledge.

Poulou-Papademetriou, N. 2001. "Βυζαντνή κεραμική από τον ελληνικό νησιωτικό χώρο και από τη Πελοπόννησο (7ος–9ος αι.). Μια πρώτη προσέγγηση." In *The Dark Centuries of Byzantium, 7th–9th c.*, 231–48. Athens: National Hellenic Research Foundation / Institute for Byzantine Research.

Prayon, F. 1982. "Projektierte Bauen auf römischen Munzen." In *Praestant interna: Festschrift für Ulrich Hausmann*, 319–30. Edited by B. von Freytag Loringhoff, D. Mannsperger, and F. Prayon. Tubingen: E. Wasmuth.

Preller, L., and C. Robert. 1894. *Griechische Mythologie I*. Berlin: Weidmann.

Price, M., and Trell, B. 1977. *Coins and Their Cities: Architecture on the Ancient Coins of Greece, Rome and Palestine*. London: V. C. Vecchi and Sons.

Price, S. 1984. *Rituals and Power: The Roman Imperial Cult in Asia Minor*. Cambridge: Cambridge University Press.

Purcell, N. 1995. "On the sacking of Carthage and Corinth." In *Ethics and Rhetoric: Classical Essays for Donald Russell on His Seventy-Fifth Birthday*, 133–48. Edited by D. Innes, H. Hine, and C. Pelling. New York: Oxford University Press.

Reed, J. L. 2007. Review of D. N. Schowalter and S. J. Friesen (eds.), *Urban Religion in Roman Corinth: Interdisciplinary Approaches*, *Review of Biblical Literature*: http://www.bookreviews.org/pdf/4897_5109.pdf. Accessed 3 November 2007.

Reger, G. 1994. *Regionalism and Change in the Economy of Independent Delos, 314–167 B.C.* Berkeley: University of California Press.

Renberg, G. H. 2006. "Was Incubation Practiced in the Latin West?" *Archiv für Religionsgeschichte* 8: 105–47.

——. 2006–07. "Public and Private Places of Worship in the Cult of Asclepius at Rome." *MAAR* 51–52: 87–172.

Renfrew, C., and M. Wagstaff (eds.). 1982. *An Island Polity: The Archaeology of Exploitation in Melos*. Cambridge: Cambridge University Press.

Renfrew, C. 1998. "Mind and Matter: Cognitive Archaeology and External Symbolic Storage." In *Cognition and Material Culture: The Archaeology of Symbolic Storage*, 1–6. Edited by C. Rendrew and C. Scarre. Cambridge: McDonald Institute for Archaeological Research.

——. 2001. "Symbol Before Concept: Material Engagement and the Early Development of Society." In *Archaeological Theory Today*, 122–40. Edited by I. Hodder. Cambridge: Blackwell.

Richardson, R. B. 1891. "Discoveries by the American School at Plateia in 1890: Votive Inscription." *AJA* 7: 406–21.

——. 1895. "A Scarificial Calendar from the Epakria." *AJA* 10: 209–26.

——. 1902. "An Ancient Fountain in the Agora at Corinth." *AJA* 6: 306–20.

Ridgway, B. S. 1984. *Roman Copies of Greek Sculpture: The Problem of the Originals*. Ann Arbor: University of Michigan Press.

Rieche, A. 1984. *Römische Kinder- und Gesellschaftspiel*. Stuttgart: Gesellschaft für Vor- und Frühgeschichte in Württemberg und Hohenzollern mit Unterstützung des Württembergischen Landesmuseums Stuttgart und der Stadt Aalen.

Riethmüller, J. W. 2005. *Asklepios: Heiligtümer und Kulte*. Two volumes. Heidelberg: Verlag Archäologie und Geschichte.

Rife, J. L. 1999. "Death, Ritual and Memory in the Greek World during the Early and Middle Roman Periods." Ph.D diss., University of Michigan.

Rife, J. L. 2007. "Inhumation and Cremation at Early Roman Kenchreai (Corinthia) in Local and Regional Context." In *Körpergräber des 1.–3. Jh. in der römischen Welt. Internationales Kolloquium Frankfurt am Main 19.–20. November 2004* (Schriften des Archäologischen Museums Frankfurt 21), 99–120. Edited by A. Faber P. Fasold, M. Struck, and M. Witteyer. Frankfurt am Main: Archäologisches Museum Frankfurt.

Rife, J. L., M. M. Morison, A. Barbet, R. K. Dunn, D. H. Ubelaker, and F. Monier. 2007. "Life and Death at a Port in Roman Greece: The Kenchreai Cemetery Project 2002–2006." *Hesperia* 76: 143–81.

Rizakis, A. D. 1995. *Achaïe I: Sources textuelles et histoire regionale*. Athens: Centre de recherches de l'antiquité grecque et romain.

———. 1996. "Les Colonies romaines des côtes occidentales grecques: populations et territoires." *Dialogues d'histoire ancienne* 22: 255–324.

———. 1998. *Achaie II, la cité de Patras: Épigraphie et histoire*. Athens: Centre de recherches de l'antiquité grecque et romain.

———. 2001. "La constitution des élites municipales dans les colonies romaines de la province d'Achaïe." In *The Greek East in the Roman Context: Proceedings of a Colloquium Organised by the Finnish Institute at Athens (May 21–22, 1999)*, 37–49. Edited by O. Salomies. Athens: Foundation of the Finnish Institute at Athens.

Robb, J. 2005. "Agency." In *Archaeology: The Key Concepts*, 3–7. Edited by C. Renfrew and P. G. Bahn. London: Routledge.

Robert, J., and L. Robert. 1950. "Bulletin épigraphique." *REG* 63: 157.

———. 1958. "Bulletin épigraphique." *REG* 71: 265–66.

———. 1959. "Bulletin épigraphique." *REG* 72: 186.

———. 1960. "Bulletin épigraphique." *REG* 73: 159–60.

———. 1961. "Bulletin épigraphique." *REG* 74: 165–66.

———. 1964. "Bulletin épigraphique." *REG* 77: 162.

———. 1968. "Bulletin épigraphique." *REG* 81: 463–64.

Robert, L. 1960a. "Inscriptions de Didymes et de Milet, 1re partie." *Hellenica* 11–12: 440–89.

———. 1960b. "Epitaphes et acclamations byzantines à Corinthe." *Hellenica* 11–12: 21–52.

———. 1966. "Inscriptions de l'Antiquité et du Bas-Empire à Corinthe." *REG* 79: 733–70.

Robinson, B. A. 2005. "Fountains and the Formation of Cultural Identity at Roman Corinth." In *URRC*, 111–40.

———. 2001. "Fountains and the Culture of Water at Roman Corinth." Ph.D. diss., University of Pennsylvania.

———. 2006. Review Panel Presentation on *A Woman's Place: House Churches in Earliest Christianity*. Washington, D.C.: Society of Biblical Literature Meeting.

Robinson, H. S. 1962. "Excavations at Corinth." *Hesperia* 31: 95–133.

———. 1965a. "Excavations at Corinth." *ArchDelt* 18: 76–80.

———. 1965b. *The Urban Development of Ancient Corinth*. Athens: American School of Classical Studies.

———. 1966. "A Green-Glazed 'Modiolus' from Kenchreai." In Χαριστήριον εἰς Ἀναστάσιον Κ. Ὀρλάνδον (3), 179–85. Athens: Archeological Society.

———. 1972. "A Green-Glazed 'Modiolus' from Kenchreai." *Hesperia* 41: 355–56.

Rodríguez, O. 2001. "Das Römische Theater von Italica (Santiponce, Sevilla)." *AW* 32: 241–50.

Rogers, G. 1991. *The Sacred Identity of Ephesos: Foundation Myths of a Roman City*. London: Routledge.

———. 1999a. "The Philosebastoi Kuretes of Ephesos." In *Steine und Wege: Festschrift fur Dieter Knibbe zum 65. Geburtstag*, 125–36. Edited by P. Scherrer, H. Taueber and H. Thür. Vienna: Österreichisches Archäologisches Institut.

———. 1999b. "The Mysteries of Artemis at Ephesos." In *100 Jahre österreichische Forschungen in Ephesos: Akten des Symposions Wien 1995*, 241–50. Edited by H. Friesinger and F. Krinzinger. Vienna: Österreichischen Akademie der Wissenschaften.

Romano, D. G. 1993. "Post 146 B.C. Land Use in Corinth, and Planning of the Roman Colony of 44 B.C." In *The Corinthia in the Roman Period (JRASup 8)*, 9–30. Edited by T. E. Gregory. Ann Arbor: JRA.

——. 2000. "A Tale of Two Cities: Roman Colonies at Corinth." In *Romanization and the City: Creation, Transformations, and Failures*, 83–104. Edited by E. Fentress and S. E. Alcock. Portsmouth: JRA.

——. 2003. "City Planning, Centuriation, and Land Division in Roman Corinth: *Colonia Laus Iulia Corinthiensis* and *Colonia Iulia Flavia Augusta Corinthiensis*." In *Corinth* XX, 279–301.

——. 2005a. "Urban and Rural Planning in Roman Corinth." In *URRC*, 25–59.

——. 2005b. "A Roman Circus in Corinth." *Hesperia* 74: 585–611.

Romano, I. B. 1994. "A Hellenistic Deposit from Corinth: Evidence for Interim Period Activity, 146–44 B.C." *Hesperia* 63: 57–104.

Roos, A. G. 1930. "De titulo quodam latino Corinthi nuper reperto." *Mnemosyne* 58: 160–65.

Rose, C. B. 1997. *Dynastic Commemoration and Imperial Portraiture in the Julio-Claudian Period*. Cambridge: Cambridge University Press.

Rose, H. J. 1957. "The Religion of a Greek Household." *Euphrosyne* 1: 115–16.

Rosenzweig, R. 2004. *Worshipping Aphrodite: Art and Cult in Classical Athens*. Ann Arbor: University of Michigan Press.

Ross, L. 1834. *Inscriptiones Graecae ineditae*. Berlin: C.A. Rhallis.

Rosser, J. 1996. "Byzantine 'Isles of Refuge' in the Chronicle of Galaxeidi." In *The Archaeology of Medieval Greece*, 139–46. Edited by P. Lock and G. Sanders. Oxford: Oxbow.

Rothaus, R. M. 2000. *Corinth, the First City of Greece: An Urban History of Late Antique Cult and Religion*. Leiden: Brill.

——. 2002. "The Kenchreai Glass Opus Sectile Panels and the Culture of Late Antique Greece." In *Hyalos, Vitrum, Glass: History, Technology and Conservation of Glass and Vitreous Materials in the Hellenic World*, 205–08. Edited by G. Kordas. Athens: Glasnet Publications.

Rothaus, R. M., and J. L. Rife. 1996. "Kenchreai Excavations 1993–1995." *AJA* 100: 343.

Rouse, W. H. D. 1902. *Greek Votive Offerings: An Essay in the History of Greek Religion*. Hildesheim: Georg Olms.

Roux, G. 1958. *Pausanias en Corinthie (livre II I à 15): Text, traduction, commentaire archéologique et topographique*. Paris: Les Belles Lettres.

——. 1979. *L'Amphictionie, Delphes et le temple d'Apollon au IVᵉ siècle*. Lyon: Maison de l'Orient.

Sakellariou, M. V., and N. Faraklas. 1971. *Corinth-Cleonaea*. Athens: Athens Center of Ektistics.

Said, E. 1978. *Orientalism*. New York: Pantheon.

——. 1993. *Culture and Imperialism*. New York: Knopf.

Salmon, E. 1969. *Roman Colonization under the Republic*. London: Thames and Hudson.

Salza Prina Ricotti, E. 1995. *Giochi e giocattoli*. Rome: Edizione Quasar.

Sanders, G. D. R. 2004. "Problems in Interpreting Rural and Urban settlement in Southern Greece, AD 365–700." In *Landscapes of Change: Rural Evolutions in Late Antiquity and the Early Middle Ages*, 163–93. Edited by N. Christie and S. Scott. Aldershot: Ashgate.

——. 2005. "Archaeological Evidence for Early Christianity and the End of Hellenic Religion in Corinth." In *URRC*, 419–42.

——. (Forthcoming). "Platanistas, the Course and Carneus: Their Place in the Topography of Sparta." *BSA Studies*.

Saradi, H. G. 2006. *The Byzantine City in the Sixth Century: Literary Images and Historical Reality*. Athens: Society of Messenian Archaeological Studies.

Sarris, A., R. K. Dunn, J. L. Rife, N. Papadopoulos, E. Kokkinou, and C. Mundigler 2007. "Geological and Geophysical Investigations in the Roman Cemetery at Kenchreai (Korinthia), Greece." *Archaeological Prospection* 14.1: 1–23.

Sartori, A. 1997. "Le forme della communicazione epigrafica." In *Monumenti sepocrali Romani in Aquileia e nella Cisalpina (Antichità Altoadriatiche 43)*, 39–65. Edited by M. M. Roberti. Trieste: Editreg.

Sasel Kos, M. 1979. *Inscriptiones latinae in Graecia repertae: Additamenta ad CIL III*. Faenza: Fratelli Lega.

Scheid, J. 1986. "Le Thiase du Metropolitan Museum (IGUR I, 160)." In *L'Association dionysiaque dans les sociétés grecques*, 275–90. Rome: Ecole française de Rome.

——. 1995. "*Graeco ritu*: A Typically Roman Way of Honoring the Gods." *HSCP* 97: 15–31.

——. 2003. *An Introduction to Roman Religion*. Bloomington: Indiana University Press.

——. 2005. "Augustus and Roman Religion: Continuity, Conservatism, and Innovation." In *The Cambridge Companion to the Age of Augustus*, 175–95. Edited by K. Galinsky. Cambridge: Cambridge University Press.

Scheidel, W. 2001. "Progress and Problems in Roman Demography." In *Debating Roman Demography*, 1–81. Edited by W. Scheidel. Leiden: Brill.

Scheidel, W. and S. Friesen. 2009. "The Size of the Economy and the Distribution of Income in the Roman Empire." Journal of Roman Studies 99:61–91.

Scherrer, P. 1990. "Augustus, die Mission des Vedius Pollio und die Artemis Ephesia." *Jahreshefte des österreichischen archäologischen Instituts* 60: 87–101.

Scherrer, P. et al. 1995. *Ephesos, der neue Führer: 100 Jahre österreichishn Ausgrabungen 1895–1995*. Vienna: Österreichisches Archäologisches Institut.

Schmidt, I. 1995. *Hellenistiche Statuenbasen (Archäologische Studien 9)*. Frankfurt: Peter Lang.

Schlier, H. 1977. *Der Römerbrief*. Freiburg: Herder.

Scott, J. 1986. *Weapons of the Weak: Everyday Forms of Peasant Resistance*. New Haven: Yale University Press.

——. 1990. *Domination and the Arts of Resistance: Hidden Transcripts*. New Haven: Yale University Press.

Scotton, P. D. 1997. "The Julian Basilica at Corinth: An Architectural Investigation." Ph.D. diss., University of Pennsylvania.

Scranton, R. L. 1951. *Monuments in the Lower Agora and North of the Archaic Temple*. Princeton, N.J.: ASCSA.

——. 1957. *Medieval Architecture in the Central Area of Corinth*. Princeton, N.J.: ASCSA.

Scranton, R., and E. Ramage. 1964. "Investigations at Kenchreai, 1963." *Hesperia* 33: 134–45.

——. 1967. "Investigations at Corinthian Kenchreai." *Hesperia* 36: 124–86.

Scribner, B. 1989. "Is a History of Popular Culture Possible?" *History of European Ideas* 10.2: 175–91.

Seaford, R. 1987. "The Tragic Wedding." *JHS* 107: 106–30.

Sear, F. 2003. "The Theatre at Butrint: Parallels and Function." In *The Theater at Butrint: Luigi Maria Ugolini's Excavations at Butrint (1928–1932)*, 181–94. Edited by O. Gilkes. London: British School at Athens.

Seelinger, R. A. 1998. "The Dionysiac Context of Melikertes/Palaimon at the Isthmian Sanctuary of Poseidon." *Maia* 50: 271–80.

Seltman, C. 1948. "Greek Sculpture and Some Festival Coins." *Hesperia* 17: 71–85.

Semeria, A. 1986. "Per un censimento degli *Asklepieia* della Grecia continentale e delle isole.*" Annali della scuola normale superiore di Pisa: Classe di lettere e filosofia* 3.16: 931–58.

Shackleton Bailey, D. 2002. *Handbook on Electioneering*. Loeb Classical Library. Cambridge: Harvard University Press.

Shapiro, H. 1993. *Personifications in Greek Art*. Zurich: Akanthus.

Shear, T. 1929. "Excavations in the Theatre District and Tombs of Corinth in 1929." *AJA* 32: 515–46.

——. 1981. "Athens: From City-State to Provincial Town." *Hesperia* 50: 356–77.

Sherwin-White, A. 1973. *The Roman Citizenship*. Oxford: Clarendon Press.

Sinn, U. 1978. "Das Heiligtum der Artemis Limnatis bei Kombothekra." *MDAI(A)* 93: 48–82.

——. 1981. "Das Heiligtum der Artemis bei Lombothekra." *MDAI(A)* 96: 25–71.

——. 2002. "Ειδωλολάτρες προσκυνητές, αθλητές και Χριστιανοί. Η εξέλιξη της Ολυμπίας στη ύστερη αρχαιότητα." In *Πρωτοβυζαντινή Μεσσήνη και Ολυμπία*, 189–94. Edited by T. G. Themeles and V. Konte. Athens: Institute of Byzantine Research.

Sinn, U., G. Ladstätter, A. Martin, and T. Völling. 1994. "Bericht über das Forschungsprojekt 'Olympia während der römischen Kaiserzeit und in der Spätantike.' III. Die Arbeiten im Jahr 1994." In *Nikephoros* 7: 239–50.

Skias, A. N. 1907. "Ἀνασκαφὴ ἐν Κορίνθῳ τοῦ ἔτους 1906." *Prakt.* (1906): 145–66.

Skutsch, O. 1987. "Helen, Her Name and Nature." *JHS* 107: 188–93.

Slane, K. W., and G. D. R. Sanders. 2005. "Corinth: Late Roman Horizons." *Hesperia* 74: 243–97.

Slane, K. W. 2008. "The End of the Sanctuary of Demeter and Kore on Acrocorinth." *Hesperia* 77: 465–96.

Smit, J. F. M. 2000. *About the Idol Offerings*. Leuven: Peeters.

Smith, D. 1977. "The Egyptian Cults at Corinth." *HTR* 70: 201–31.

——. 1981. *Meals and Morality in Paul and his World*. Chico, CA: Scholars Press.

——. 2003. *From Symposium to Eucharist*. Minneapolis: Fortress Press.

Smith, H. 2001. *Why Religion Matters*. San Francisco: Harper San Francisco.

Smith, J. Z. 1982. *Imagining Religion: From Babylon to Jonestown*. Chicago: University of Chicago Press.

——. 1987. *To Take Place*. Chicago: University of Chicago Press.

——. 1993. *Map Is Not Territory*. Reprinted edition. Chicago: University of Chicago Press.

——. 2004. *Relating Religion*. Chicago: University of Chicago Press.

Smith, K. 1919. "Greek Inscriptions from Corinth." *AJA* 23: 331–93.

Smith, L. T. 1999. *Decolonizing Methodologies: Research and Indigenous Peoples*. London: Zed Books.

Smith, R. R. R. 1990. "Late Roman Philosopher Portraits from Aphrodisias." *JRS* 80: 127–55.

——. 2006. *Roman Portrait Statuary from Aphrodisias*. Mainz: von Zabern.

Smith, W. C. 1963. *The Meaning and End of Religion*. New York: Harper and Row.

——. 1979. *Faith and Belief*. Princeton: Princeton University Press.

Smith, W. D. 1994. *Hippocrates: Volume VII*. Loeb Classical Library. Cambridge: Harvard University.

Soldan, U. 1999. "Frauen als Funktionsträgerinnen im kaiserzeitlichen Ephesos: die weiblichen Prytaneis." In *100 Jahre österreichische Forschungen in Ephesos: Akten des Symposions Wien 1995*, 115–19. Edited by H. Friesinger and F. Krinzinger. Vienna: Österreichischen Akademie der Wissenschaften.

Sotiriou, G. A. 1929. "Αι Παλιοχριστιανικαί Βασιλικαί της Ελλάδος." *ArchEph* (1929): 161–248.

Sourvinou-Inwood, C. 1991. "Persephone and Aphrodite at Locri: A Model for Personality Divisions in Greek Religion." In *"Reading" Greek Culture: Texts and Images, Rituals and Myths*, 147–88. Edited by C. Sourvinou-Inwood. Oxford: Clarendon.

Spadea, R. (ed.). 2005. *Scolacium: Una città romana in Calabria (il museo e il parco archeologico)*. Milan: ET.

Spaeth, B. S. 1996. *The Roman Goddess Ceres*. Austin: University of Texas Press.

——. 2006. "Cultic Discontinuity in Roman Corinth: The Sanctuary of Demeter and Kore on Acrocorinth." Paper read at the Society of Biblical Literature Annual Meeting, Washington, D.C. 18 November 2006.

——. 2007. "The Epigraphical Evidence for the Prevalence of Roman Cult in Ancient Corinth." Paper read at the Society of Biblical Literature Annual Meeting, San Diego, California. 17 November 2007.

Spawforth, A. J. 1974. "The Appaleni of Corinth." *GRBS* 15: 295–303.

——. 1996. "Roman Corinth: The Formation of a Colonial Elite." In *Roman Onomastics in the Greek East: Social and Political Aspects*, 167–82. Edited by A. D. Rizakis. Athens: Research Center for Greek and Roman Antiquity.

——. 2002. "Italian Elements among Roman Knights and Senators from Old Greece." In *Les Italiens dans le monde grec: IIᵉ siècle av. J.-C.-Iᵉʳ siècle ap. J.-C. (circulation, activités, intégration)*, 101–07. Edited by C. Müller and C. Hasenohr. Paris: De Boccard.

——. 2007. "'*Kapetôleia Olympia*': Roman Emperors and Greek *Agônes*." In *Pindar's Poetry, Patrons, and Festivals: From Archaic Greece to the Roman Empire*, 378–90. Edited by S. Hornblower and C. Morgan. Oxford: Oxford University Press.

Spieser, J.-M. 1976. "La christianisation des sanctuaries païens en grèce." In *Neue Forschungen in griechischen Heiligtümern*, 309–20. Edited by U. Jantzen. Tübingen: Wasmuth.

Spitzl, T. 1984. *Lex Municipii Malacitana (Vestigia 36)*. Munich: C. H. Beck'sche.

Spivak, G. 1988. "Can the Subaltern Speak?" In *Marxism and the Interpretation of Culture*, 279–313. Edited by C. Nelson and L. Grossberg. Urbana: University of Illinois Press.

Spivak, G. (ed.). 1987. *In Other Worlds: Essays in Cultural Politics*. New York: Methuen.

Staïs, E. 1903. "Ἀνασκαφαί εν Ἰσθμία." Πρακτικά της εν Ἀθήναις Αρχαιολογικής Ἑταιρεία 1903: 14–17.

Stamps, D. 1993. "Rethinking the Rhetorical Situation: The Entextualization of the Situation in New Testament Epistles." In *Rhetoric and the New Testament: Essays from the 1992 Heidelberg Conference*, 193–210. Edited by S. Porter and T. Olbricht. Sheffield: Sheffield University Press.

Staples, A. 1997. *From Good Goddess to Vestal Virgins: Sex and Category in Roman Religion*. London: Routledge.

Stavropoulos, S. G. 1996. *Τά Ἀσκληπιεία τῆς Πελοποννήσου*. Patras.

Stegemann, E. W., and W. Stegemann. 1999. *The Jesus Movement: A Social History of its First Century*. Minneapolis: Fortress Press.

Steiner, A. 1992. "Pottery and Cult in Corinth: Oil and Water at the Sacred Spring." *Hesperia* 61: 385–408.

Stephens, S. 1994. "Who Read Ancient Novels?" In *The Search for the Ancient Novel*, 405–18. Edited by J. Tatum. Baltimore: Johns Hopkins University.

Stewart, C. (ed.). 2007. *Creolization: History, Ethnography, Theory*. Walnut Creek: Left Coast Press.

Stewart, P. 2003. *Statues in Roman Society: Representation and Response*. Oxford and New York: Oxford University Press.

Stikas, E. 1964. "Κοιμητηριακὴ Βασιλικὴ Παλαιᾶς Κορίνθου." *Prakt.* (1961): 129–36.

——. 1966. "Ἀνασκαφὴ Κοιμητηριακῆς βασιλικῆς Παλαιᾶς Κορίνθου." *Prakt.* (1962) 51–56.

Stirling, L. 2008. "Pagan Statuettes in Late Antique Corinth: Sculpture from the Panayia Domus." *Hesperia* 77: 89–161.

Storey, I. 1990. "Dating and Re-Dating Eupolis." *Phoenix* 44: 1–30.

——. 1997. "Review of M. Vickers, *Pericles on Stage: Political Comedy in Aristophanes' Early Plays*." No pages. Cited September 15, 1997. Online: http://ccat.sas.upenn.edu/bmcr/1997/97.9.15.html.

——. 2003. *Eupolis: Poet of Old Comedy*. Oxford: Oxford University Press.

Strauss, G. and W. Beik. 1993. "Debate: The Dilemma of Popular History." *P&P* 141: 207–19.

Strauss, G. 1991. "The Dilemma of Popular History." *P&P* 132: 130–49.
Stroud, R. S. 1971a. "An Ancient Fort on Mt. Oneion." *Hesperia* 40: 127–45.
——. 1971b. "Thucydides and the Battle of Solygeia." *California Studies in Classical Antiquity* 4: 227–47.
——. 1993. "The Sanctuary of Demeter on Acrocorinth in the Roman Period." In *The Corinthia in the Roman Period*, 65–74. Edited by T. E. Gregory. Ann Arbor: JRA.
——. Forthcoming. *Magical Tablets from the Sanctuary of Demeter and Kore on Acrocorinth*.
Stucchi, S. 1984. "Una moneta detta 'di Pergamo' ed il monumento augusteo nel santuario di Athena Polias Nikephoros." *ArchCl* 36: 198–215.
Sumney, J. 1990. *Identifying Paul's Opponents: The Question of Method in 2 Corinthians*. Sheffield: Sheffield University Press.
Susini, G. 1988. "Spelling Out along the Road: Anthropology of the Ancient Reader, or Rather, the Roman Reader." *Alma Mater Studiorum* 1: 117–24.
Sutton, D. E. 2001. *Remembrance of Repasts: An Anthropology of Food and Memory*. Oxford: Berg.
Swain, S. 1996. *Hellenism and Empire: Language, Classicism, and Power in the Greek World, AD 50–250*. Oxford: Clarendon Press.
Szemerényi, O. 1994. "Etyma Graeca VII (35)." In *Indogermanica et Caucasica: Festschrift für Karl Horst Schmidt zum 65. Geburtstag, 211–23*. Edited by R. Bielmeier and R. Stempel. Berlin: W. de Gruyter.
Tartaron, T. F. *et al.* 2006. "The Eastern Korinthia Archaeological Survey: Integrated Methods for a Dynamic Landscape." *Hesperia* 75: 453–524.
Taylor, L. R. 1949. *Party Politics in the Age of Caesar*. Berkeley: University of California Press.
Taylor, N. 1995. "The Social Nature of Conversion in the Early Christian World." In *Modelling Early Christianity: Social-Scientific Studies of the New Testament in its Context*, 128–36. Edited by P. F. Esler. New York: Routledge.
Theissen, G. 1982. *The Social Setting of Pauline Christianity: Essays on Corinth*. Philadelphia: Fortress.
Thiselton, A. C. 2000. *The First Epistle to the Corinthians: A Commentary on the Greek Text*. Grand Rapids: Eerdmans.
Thomas, C. M. 1995. "At Home in the City of Artemis: Religion in Ephesos in the Literary Imagination of the Roman Period." In *Ephesos Metropolis of Asia: An Interdisciplinary Approach to its Archaeology, Religion, and Culture*, 81–117. Edited by H. Koester. Cambridge: Harvard University.
——. 1998. "The Sanctuary of Demeter at Pergamon: Cultic Space for Women and Its Eclipse." In *Pergamon, Citadel of the Gods: Archaeological Record, Literary Description, and Religious Development*, 277–98. Edited by H. Koester. Harrisburg: Trinity Press International.
——. 2004. "The 'Mountain Mother': The Other Anatolian Goddess at Ephesos." In *Les cultes locaux dans les mondes grec et romain*, 249–62. Edited by G. Labarre. Paris: Diffusion de Boccard.
Thomas, J. 2001. "Archaeologies of Place and Landscape." In *Archaeological Theory Today*, 165–86. Edited by I. Hodder. Cambridge: Blackwell.
Thür, H. 1999. "Via Sacra Ephesiaka." In *Steine und Wege: Festschrift fur Dieter Knibbe zum 65. Geburtstag*, 163–72. Edited by P. Scherrer, H. Taueber and H. Thür. Vienna: Österreichisches Archäologisches Institut.
Tiussi, C. 1999. *Il culto di Esculapio nell'area nord-Adriatica*. Rome: Quasar.
Tomlinson, R. A. 1969. "Two Buildings in Sanctuaries of Asklepios." *JHS* 89: 106–17.
Torelli, M. 2001. "Pausania à Corinto: Un intellettuale greco del secondo secolo e la propaganda imperiale romana." In *Éditer, traduire, commenter Pausanias en l'an 2000*, 135–84. Edited by D. Knoepfler and M. Piérart. Geneva: Université de Neuchâtel.

Travlos, I. 1971. *Bildlexikon zur Topographie des antiken Athen.* Tübingen: E. Wasmuth.

Treggiari, S. 1969. *Roman Freedmen during the Late Republic.* Oxford: Clarendon.

Trombley, F. R. 1985. "Paganism in the Greek World at the End of Antiquity: The Case of Rural Anatolia and Greece." *HTR* 78: 327–52.

——. 1993. *Hellenic Religion and Christianization, c. 370–529.* Two volumes. Leiden: Brill.

Trümper, M. 2003. "Material and Social Environment of Greco-Roman Households in the East: The Case of Hellenistic Delos." In *Early Christian Families in Context: An Interdisciplinary Dialogue,* 19–43. Edited by D. Balch and C. Osiek. Grand Rapids: Eerdmans.

Tuchelt, K. 1979. *Frühe Denkmäler Roms in Kleinasien: Beiträge zur archäologischen Überlieferung aus Zeit der Republik und des Augustus (IstMitt Beiheft 23).* Tübingen: Ernst Wasmuth.

Turfa, J. M. 2006. "Etruscan Religion at the Watershed: Before and After the Fourth Century B.C.E." In *Religion in Republican Italy,* 62–89. Edited by C. E. Schultz and P. B. Harvey, Jr. New Haven: Yale University.

Tweed, T. A. 2006. *Crossing and Dwelling: A Theory of Religion.* Cambridge: Harvard University Press.

Tzouvara-Souli, C. 2001. "The Cults of Apollo in Northwestern Greece." In *Foundation and Destruction: Nikopolis and Northwestern Greece (The Archaeological Evidence for the City Destructions, the Foundation of Nikopolis, and the Synoecism),* 233–55. Edited by J. Isager. Aarhus: Monographs of the Danish Institute at Athens.

Ubelaker, D. H., and J. L. Rife. 2007. "The Practice of Cremation in the Roman-Era Cemetery at Kenchreai, Greece: The Perspective from Archaeology and Forensic Science." *Bioarchaeology of the Near East* 1: 35–57.

——. 2008. "Approaches to Commingling Issues in Archaeological Samples: A Case Study from Roman-Period Tombs in Greece." In *Recovery, Analysis and Identification of Commingled Human Remains,* 97–122. Edited by B. Adams and J. Byrd. Totowa, NJ: Humana.

Ugolini, L. M. 1942. *L'acropoli di Butrinto.* Rome: Scalia Editore.

Ugolini, L. M., and I. Pojani. 2003. "The Sculpture from the Theatre." In *The Theater at Butrint: Luigi Maria Ugolini's Excavations at Butrint (1928–1932)* 195–252. Edited by O. J. Gilkes. London: British School at Athens.

van den Heever, G. 2005. "Redescribing Graeco-Roman Antiquity: On Religion and History of Religion." *R&T* 12.3/4: 219–21.

van der Toorn, K. 2002. "Israelite Figurines: A View from the Texts." In *Sacred Time, Sacred Place: Archaeology and the Religion of Israel,* 45–62. Edited by B. Gittlen. Winona Lake, In: Eisenbrauns.

van Andel, T. H., and C. N. Runnels. 1984. *Beyond the Acropolis: A Rural Greek Past.* Stanford: Stanford University Press.

van Henten, J. W. (ed.). 1999. *Food and Drink in the Biblical Worlds (Semeia 86).* Atlanta: Society of Biblical Literature.

van Nijf, O. 1997. *The Civic World of Professional Associations in the Roman East.* Amsterdam: J. C. Gieben.

——. 2000. "Inscriptions and Civic Memory in the Roman East." In *The Afterlife of Inscriptions: Reusing, Rediscovering, Reinventing and Revitalizing Ancient Inscriptions,* 21–36. Edited by A. E. Cooley. London: Institute of Classical Studies.

von Petrikovits, H. 1980. *Die Rheinlande in römanischer Zeit.* Düsseldorf: Schwann.

van Straten, F. T. 1981. "Gifts for the Gods," In *Faith, Hope and Worship. Aspects of Religious Mentality in the Ancient World,* 65–151. Edited by H. Versnel. Leiden: Brill.

Vanderpool, E. 1959. "Athens Honors the Emperor Tiberius." *Hesperia* 28: 86–90.

Versluys, M. J. 2002. *Aegyptiaca Romana: Nilotic Scenes and the Roman Views of Egypt.* Leiden: Brill.

Versnel, H. 1991. "Beyond Cursing: The Appeal to Justice in Judicial Prayers." In *Magika Hiera: Ancient Greek Magic and Religion*, 60–106. Edited by C. A. Faraone and D. Obbink. Oxford and London: Oxford University Press.

Veyne, P. 1965. "Apulée à Cenchrées." *RPh* 39: 241–51.

———. 1990. *Bread and Circuses*. Translated by B. Pearce. London: Penguin.

Vickers, M. 1997. *Pericles on Stage: Political Comedy in Aristophanes' Early Plays*. Austin: University of Texas Press.

Vida, T., and T. Völling. 2000. *Das slawische Brandgräberfeld von Olympia*. Rahden: M. Leidorf.

von Harnack, A. 1924. *Die Mission und Ausbreitung des Christentums 2*. Fourth edition. Leipzig: J. C. Hinrichs.

von Hesberg, H. 2002. "Die Basilika von Ephesos: die kulturelle Kompetenz der neuen Stifter." In *Patris und Imperium: Kulturelle und politische Identität in den Städten der römischen Provinzen Kleinasiens in der frühen Kaiserzeit*, 149–58. Edited by H. von Hesberg, C. Berns, L. Vandeput and M. Waelkens. Leuven: Peeters.

Vout, C. 2005. "Antinous: Archaeology and History." *JRS* 95: 80–96.

Waage, F. O. 1935. "Bronze Objects from Old Corinth." *AJA* 39: 79–91.

Wachter, R. 2001. *Non-Attic Greek Vase Inscriptions*. Oxford: Oxford University Press.

Waelkens, M. 1989. "Hellenistic and Roman Influence in the Imperial Architecture of Asia Minor." In *The Greek Renaissance in the Roman Empire: Papers from the Tenth British Museum Classical Colloquium*, 77–88. Edited by S. Walker and Averil Cameron. London: Institute of Classical Studies.

Walbank, Mary E. H. 1989a. "Pausanias, Octavia and Temple E at Corinth." *BSA* 84: 361–94.

———. 1989b. "Marsyas at Corinth." *AJN* 79–87.

———. 1996. "Evidence for the Imperial Cult in Julio-Claudian Corinth." In *Subject and Ruler: The Cult of the Ruling Power in Classical Antiquity*, 201–14. Edited by A. Small. Ann Arbor: JRA.

———. 1997a. "The Foundation and Planning of Early Roman Corinth." *JRA* 10: 95–130.

———. 1997b. "Aspects of the Corinthian Coinage in the Late 1st and Early 2nd Centuries A.C." In *Corinth XX*, 337–49.

———. 2002. "What's in a Name? Corinth under the Flavians." *ZPE* 139: 251–64.

———. 2003. "Corinthian Coinage in the First and Second Centuries A.C." In *Corinth XX*, 337–349.

———. 2005. "Unquiet Graves: Burial Practices of the Roman Corinthians." In *URRC*, 249–80.

Walbank, M. E. H., and M. B. Walbank. 2006. "The Grave of Maria, Wife of Euplous. A Christian Epitaph Reconsidered." *Hesperia* 75: 267–88.

Walde-Psenner, E. 1979. "Der bronzen Poseidon auf der Hafenmole von Kenchreai." In *Bronzes hellénistiques et romains: Traditions et renouveau*, 61–64. Lausanne: Diffusion de Boccard.

Wallace, P. M. 1969. "Strabo on Acrocorinth." *Hesperia* 38: 495–99.

Wallace-Hadrill, A. 1994. *Houses and Society in Pompeii and Herculaneum*. Princeton: Princeton University Press.

———. 2003. "*Domus* and *Insulae* in Rome: Families and Housefuls." In *Early Christian Families in Context: An Interdisciplinary Dialogue*, 3–18. Edited by D. Balch and C. Osiek. Grand Rapids: Eerdmans.

Walters, E. J. 1985. *Attic Grave Reliefs that Represent Women in the Dress of Isis*. Ann Arbor: University of Michigan Press.

Walters, J. 1993. *Ethnic Issues in Paul's Letter to the Romans: Changing Self-Definitions in Earliest Roman Christianity*. Valley Forge: Trinity Press International.

———. 1993. "'Phoebe' and 'Junia(s)'—Rom. 16:1–2, 6." In *Essays on Women in Earliest Christianity* 1, 167–90. Edited by C. D. Osburn. Joplin, MO: College Press Publishing.

——. 2005. "Civic Identity in Roman Corinth and its Impact on Early Christians." In *URRC*, 397–417.

Weaver, P. R. C. 1967. "Social Mobility in the Early Roman Empire: The Evidence of the Imperial Freedmen and Slaves." *P&P* 37: 3–20.

——. 1972. *Familia Caesaris: A Social Study of the Emperor's Freedmen and Slaves.* Cambridge: Cambridge University Press.

Weinstock, S. 1971. *Divus Julius.* Oxford: Oxford University.

Weir, R. 1998. "Roman Delphi and its Pythian Games." PhD diss., Princeton University.

Welborn, L. 1987. "On the Discord in Corinth: 1 Corinthians 1–4 and Ancient Politics." *JBL* 106: 83–113.

West, M. L. 1963. "Three Presocratic Cosmologies." *CQ* 13: 154–76.

White, H. 1899. *The Roman History of Appian of Alexandria.* New York: Macmillan Co.

White, L. M. 2005. "Favorinus's 'Corinthian Oration': A Piqued Panorama of the Hadrianic Forum." In *URRC*, 61–110.

Whitley, J., G. Germanidou, D. Urem-Kotsou, A. Dimoula, I. Nikolakopoulou A. Karnava and E. Hasaki. 2006. "Archaeology in Greece, 2005–06." *Archaeological Reports* 52: 1–112.

Whittaker, C. R. 1993. *Land, City, and Trade in the Roman Empire.* Aldershot: Variorum.

——. 1997. "Imperialism and Culture: The Roman Initiative." In *Dialogues in Roman Imperialism: Power, Discourse, and Discrepant Experience in the Roman Empire,* 143–63. Edited by D. J. Mattingly and S. E. Alcock; Portsmouth: JRA.

Wickens, J. M. 1986. "The Archaeology and History of Cave Use in Attica, Greece from Prehistoric through Late Roman Times." Ph.D. diss., Indiana University.

Wickkiser, B. L. 1999. "Famous Last Words: Putting the Sphragis Back into Ovid's *Metamorphoses.*" *Materiali e discussioni per l'analisi dei testi classici* 42: 113–42.

——. 2005. "Augustus, Apollo, and an Ailing Rome: Images of Augustus as a Healer of State." *Studies in Latin Literature and Roman History* 12: 267–89.

——. 2006. "Chronicles of Chronic Cases and Tools of the Trade at Asklepieia." *Archiv für Religionsgeschichte* 8: 25–40.

——. 2008. *Asklepios, Medicine, and Politics in Fifth Century Greece: Between Craft and Cult.* Baltimore: Johns Hopkins University Press.

Wilkins, J. and S. Hill. 2006. *Food in the Ancient World.* Malden, MA: Blackwell.

Wilkens, U. 1982. *Der Brief an die Römer 3: Röm 12–16.* Zürich: Einsiedeln.

Will, E. 1955. *Korinthiaka.* Paris: E. de Boccard.

Williams, C. K. 1970. "Corinth 1969: Forum Area." *Hesperia* 39: 1–12.

——. 1978a. "Corinth 1977, Forum Southwest." *Hesperia* 47: 1–39.

——. 1978b. "Pre-Roman Cults in the Area of the Forum of Ancient Corinth." Ph.D. diss., University of Pennsylvania.

——. 1981. "The City of Corinth and its Domestic Religion." *Hesperia* 50: 408–21.

——. 1986. "Corinth and the Cult of Aphrodite." In *Corinthiaca: Studies in Honor of Darrell A. Amyx,* 12–24. Edited by M. del Chairo. Columbia: University of Missouri Press.

——. 1987a. "The Refounding of Corinth: Some Roman Religious Attitudes." In *Roman Architecture in the Greek World,* 26–37. Edited by S. Macready and F. H. Thompson. London: Society of Antiquaries of London.

——. 1987b. "Corinth, 1896–1987: A Study of Changing Attitudes." *AJA* 91: 473–74.

——. 1987c. "*Laus Iulia Corinthiensis* et Diana Nemorensis?" *In Φιλία ἔπη εἰς Γ. Ε. Μυλωνάν,* 384–89. Athens.

——. 1989. "A Re-Evaluation of Temple E and the West End of the Forum of Corinth." In *The Greek Renaissance in the Roman Empire: Papers from the Tenth British Museum Classical Colloquium,* 156–62. Edited by S. Walker and Averil Cameron. London: Institute of Classical Studies.

———. 1993. "Roman Corinth as a Commercial Center." In *The Corinthia in the Roman Period (JRASup 8)*, 31–46. Edited by T. E. Gregory. Ann Arbor: JRA.

———. 2005. "Roman Corinth: The Final Years of Pagan Cult Facilities along East Theater Street." In *URRC*, 221–47.

Williams, C. K., and J. Fisher. 1971. "Corinth 1970: Forum Area." *Hesperia* 40: 1–51.

———. 1975. "Corinth 1974: Forum Southwest." *Hesperia* 1975: 1–50.

———. 1976. "Corinth 1975: Forum Southwest." *Hesperia* 45: 127–33.

Williams, C. K., and P. Russell. 1981. "Corinth: Excavations of 1980." *Hesperia* 50: 1–44.

Williams, C. K., and O. H. Zervos. 1969. "Excavations at Corinth, 1968." *Hesperia* 38: 36–63.

———. 1983. "Corinth, 1982: East of the Theater." *Hesperia* 54: 1–47.

———. 1987. "Corinth, 1986: Temple E and East of the Theater." *Hesperia* 56: 1–46.

———. 1988. "Corinth, 1987: South of Temple E and East of the Theater." *Hesperia* 57: 95–146.

———. 1990. "Excavations at Corinth, 1989: The Temenos of Temple E." *Hesperia* 59: 325–69.

———. 1991. "Corinth 1990: Southeast Corner of Temenos E." *Hesperia* 60: 1–58.

Williams, E. R. 1985. "Isis Pelagia and a Roman Marble Matrix from the Athenian Agora." *Hesperia* 54: 109–19.

Williams, H. 2004. "The Ships on the Kenchreai Glass Panels." In *Metamorphic Reflections: Essays Presented to Ben Hijmans at his 75th Birthday*, 297–307. Edited by M. Zimmerman and R. van der Paardt. Leiden: Brill.

Winkler, J. 1991. *The Constraints of Desire: The Anthropology of Sex and Gender in Ancient Greece*. NY: Routledge.

Winter, B. 1994. *Seek the Welfare of the City: Christians as Benefactors and Citizens*. Grand Rapids: Eerdmans.

———. 2001. *After Paul Left Corinth: The Influence of Secular Ethics and Social Change*. Grand Rapids: Eerdmans.

Winter, F. 1963. "Ancient Corinth and the History of Greek Architecture and Town Planning: A Review Article." *Phoenix* 17: 275–92.

Wire, A. 2006. Response to Jorunn Økland's book *Women in Their Place*. Paper read at the Society of Biblical Literature Annual Meeting, Washington, D.C.

Wiseman, J. 1967a. "Excavations at Corinth. The Gymnasium Area, 1965." *Hesperia* 36: 13–41.

———. 1967b. "Excavations at Corinth. The Gymnasium Area, 1966." *Hesperia* 36: 402–28.

———. 1969. "Excavations in Corinth. The Gymnasium Area, 1967–1968." *Hesperia* 38: 64–106.

———. 1978. *The Land of the Ancient Corinthians*. Göteborg: P. Åström.

———. 1979. "Corinth and Rome I: 228 B.C.–A.D. 267." *ANRW* 2.17.1: 438–548.

———. 1970. "The Fountain of the Lamps." *Archaeology* 23: 130–37.

———. 1972. "The Gymnasium Area at Corinth, 1969–1970." *Hesperia* 41: 1–42.

Wohl, B. Lindros. 1981. "A Deposit of Lamps from the Roman Bath at Isthmia." *Hesperia* 50: 112–40.

———. 1993. "Lamps from the Excavations at Isthmia by UCLA." In *The Corinthia in the Roman Period*, 130–38. Edited by T. E. Gregory. Ann Arbor: JRA.

———. 2005. "Darkness and Light: Lamps from a Tunnel at Isthmia, Greece." In *Lychnological Acts (Actes du 1er Congrès international d'études sur le luminaire antique)*, 211–16. Edited by L. Chrzanovski. Mentangac: Monogr. Instrumentum.

———. Forthcoming. *Lamps from the UCLA/Ohio State University Excavations, 1967–2002*. Princeton: ASCSA.

Woolf, G. 1994. "Becoming Roman, Staying Greek: Culture, Identity, and the Civilizing Process in the Roman East." *PCPhS* 40: 116–43.

——. 1996. "Monumental Writing and the Expansion of Roman Society in the Early Empire." *JRS* 86: 22–39.

——. 1998. *Becoming Roman: The Origins of Provincial Civilization in Gaul*. Cambridge: Cambridge University Press.

——. 2001. "Inventing Empire in Ancient Rome." In *Empires: Perspectives from Archaeology and History*, 311–22. Edited by S. Alcock *et al.* Cambridge: Cambridge University Press.

Wortmann, D. 1968. "Die Sandale der Hekate-Persephone-Selene," *ZPE* 2: 155–60.

Yakobson, A. 1999. *Elections and Electioneering in Rome: A Study in the Political System of the Late Republic*. Stuttgart: Franz Steiner.

Yalouris, N. 1950. "Athena als Herrin der Pferde." *Museum Helveticum* 6: 19–101.

Yannopoulos, P. A. 1980. "Le pénétration slave en Argolide." In *Études argiennes: Bulletin de correspondance hellénique (Supplement 6)*, 323–27. Athens and Paris: Diffusion de Boccard.

Yegül, F. 2000. "Memory, Metaphor, and Meaning in the Cities of Asia Minor." In *Romanization and the City: Creation, Transformations, and Failures*, 133–53. Edited by E. Fentress and S. E. Alcock. Portsmouth: JRA.

Young, R. 2001. *Postcolonialism: An Historical Introduction*. Oxford: Blackwell Publishers.

Youtie, H. 1948. "The *Kline* of Sarapis." *HTR* 41.1: 9–29.

Zanker, P. 1990. *The Power of Images in the Age of Augustus*. Ann Arbor: University of Michigan Press.

——. 1998. *Pompeii: Public and Private Life*. Cambridge: Harvard University Press.

Zovatto, P. L. 1971. *Portogruaro museo Nazionale concordiese: Concordia scavi, battistero. Summaga abbazia. Sesto al Réghena abbazia. Caorle*. Bologna: Calderini.

Züchner, W. 1942. Griechische Klappspiegel (JDAI Ergänzungsheft 14). Berlin: W. de Gruyter.

INDEX

MAPS

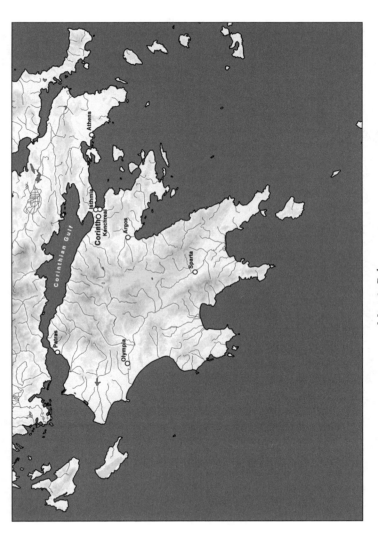

Map 1. Peloponnese.

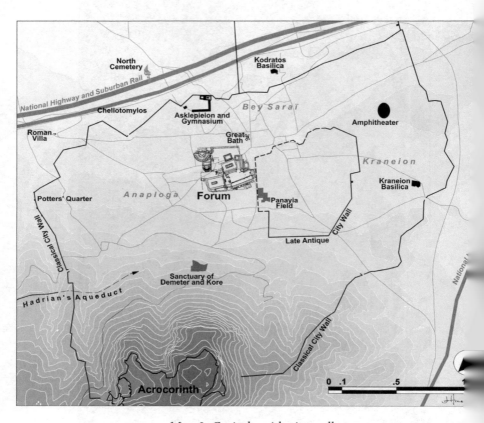

Map 2. Corinth, with city walls.

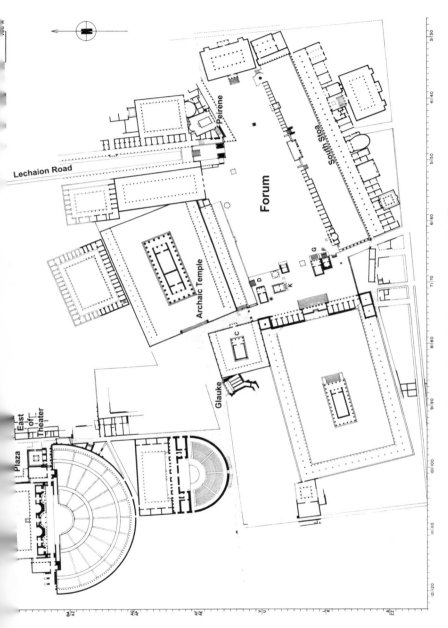

Map 3. Corinth: city center ca. 200 CE.